IN THEIR HONOR

★★★

THE MEN BEHIND THE
NAMES OF OUR
MILITARY INSTALLATIONS

IN THEIR HONOR
★★★
THE MEN BEHIND THE NAMES OF OUR MILITARY INSTALLATIONS

by

Linda D. Swink

Foreword by

Edward J. Mechenbier
Major General, USAF (Ret.)

LITTLE MIAMI PUBLISHING CO.
Milford, Ohio
2009

Little Miami Publishing Co.
P.O. Box 588
Milford, Ohio 45150-0588
www.littlemiamibooks.com

Copies of this book can be obtained by contacting the publisher.

Copyright ©2009 by Linda D. Swink. All rights reserved. No part of this book may be reproduced or transmitted in any form or by any means, electronic or mechanical, including photocopying, recording or by any information storage and retrieval system without written permission from the author, except for the inclusion of brief quotations in a review.

Printed in the United States of America on acid-free paper.

ISBN-13: 978-1-932250-51-0
ISBN-10: 1-932250-51-4

Library of Congress Control Number: 2006935757

Dedication

In memory of my Father, John B. Smith, who served with the 1st Marine Division and fought in the Battle of Peleliu during World War II. You will never be forgotten.

Semper fi

Contents

Dedication **v**
Foreword **ix**
Preface **xi**
Acknowledgments **xv**
★

Chapter One
UNITED STATES AIR FORCE **1**

Chapter Two
AIR NATIONAL GUARD **109**

Chapter Three
UNITED STATES ARMY **131**

Chapter Four
UNITED STATES ARMY AIRFIELDS, STAGEFIELDS, AND HELIPORTS **189**

Chapter Five
ARMY NATIONAL GUARD **229**

Chapter Six
ARMY BARRACKS AND KASERNES GERMANY **267**

Chapter Seven
ARMY CAMPS SOUTH KOREA **343**

Chapter Eight
UNITED STATES MARINE CORPS **361**

Chapter Nine
UNITED STATES NAVY **397**
★
Appendix A **443**
Appendix B **449**
Bibliography **459**
Index **467**
About the Author **519**

Foreword

When asked to write a foreword for a book I hadn't read, my first reaction was "Why me?" Is it an honor? What is expected? Should it be complementary or complimentary or both to the text itself? How long should it be and how witty should I try to be?

Why would I undertake Linda's out of the blue request for me to take time to write a foreword? Obviously I have decided to accept the challenge, but for a reason not really related to any clinical examination of the material which follows as I have had access to only a few pages of the manuscript. *In Their Honor* really sums up my reason for sitting here this afternoon typing these words.

We live in a world no longer measured in days, weeks, or months. Hours and minutes have been parsed into seconds and nanoseconds. Change is no longer an evolutionary thing or even physical; we live in a revolutionary world where change is electronic. Cell phones, wireless laptops, and Personal Digital Assistants make us instantly accessible and in touch with the world around us. "I'll get back to you" no longer means tomorrow or the next day. We can literally get the data and "close the loop" without moving ten feet. Teenagers spend more time with all these electronic gadgets than my generation ever spent in front of the television that was going to fry our brain.

Now, lest you think I am setting you up for some grand rejection of all these slavish conveniences or espouse a techno-theocracy on their behalf, let me say neither is the case. Therein, however, I do find my motivation for writing this foreword on the assumption the author and the publisher deem it worthy of its insertion. For better or worse, we do live in a world of techno-wonder where every day we see magic beyond the wildest ideas of even a few years ago. It's hard to startle us anymore. We are accustomed to learning of some fantastic capability being available when we have barely begun to understand and use the new, now old, gizmo we just purchased last month. Yes Dorothy, we aren't in Kansas anymore.

No matter what silicone-based computer capability you buy in the store, some carbon-based computer, a human being, had the idea, and created and produced that item. The human being is the engine that drives all this change. So this book is about ordinary men who, as you will read, did great things. It is important in this high-powered, fast-paced world to recognize those who have created the environment in which today's creative genius reigns seemingly supreme. This book is about people whose achievements were so astounding they were memorialized by a military installation that bears their name. It's not about the machines they used in some extraordinary way. Things don't work; people do. This book is about people who, by their individual commitment, integrity, and performance, made a difference. A difference we would be well served to remember when it seems the answer to every question can be found in the electronics stuffed in a small case on a desk or in the palm of your hand. Every generation can learn from the example of these 524 biographies.

So, why am I writing this? Simply put, to toast again, *In Their Honor: The Men Behind the Names of Our Military Installations.*

Edward J. Mechenbier
Major General, USAF (Ret.)
POW, Vietnam

Preface

"I'M PROUD TO BE AN AMERICAN where I know that I am free . . . ," wrote lyricist Lee Greenwood in his song "God Bless the USA," he adds, "and I won't forget the men who died who gave that right to me."

Unfortunately, most of us have forgotten.

While driving past the gates of Fort Benjamin Harrison in Indianapolis, Indiana, the thought struck me, who was the post named for? Was it President Benjamin Harrison or another man with the same name? After asking the local historian, I was told that yes, the post was named for the twenty-third president of the United States.

From that first question began a four-year search to find the story behind every man who ever had a military installation named in his honor. Starting with names of air force bases at which I had been stationed, I expanded my search to include the army posts that my husband had been assigned to during his twenty-year military career. Once I began, I couldn't stop. I had to know what made each man so special that the military would choose his name to grace the gate of an installation. What I thought would be an easy task turned into a enormous undertaking.

I discovered that many names had faded into obscurity after a military installation closed. Once no longer needed, many airfields were abandoned and much of its history lost. Little or no biographical information about the man for whom the installation was named survived. According to Bruce H. Siemon, Chief of the Military History Office at the headquarters of U.S. Army, Europe, and Seventh Army (USAREUR/7A) in Germany: "When a memorialized installation or facility is closed, regulations call for the memorial plaque to be offered to the next of kin. When USAREUR/7A began planning for a major reduction in 1990–91, we established a link with the Army Personnel Command (as it was then known). From the spring of 1992 on, they assumed full responsibility for identifying and locating next of kin on our behalf, because they preferred to have only one single agency deal with the issue so as to minimize the effect upon next of kin. Even with their much broader assets, locating next of kin was a long, drawn-out process, and often unsuccessful."

Unable to find any information about the man for whom an installation was named, sadly, I had to give up. I offer my sincerest apology to those men and their families. I will not forget them as I continue the search and perhaps include them in a second edition in the future.

Many installations have changed ownership over time and their names were often changed. Installations such as Moffett Field, which I remember as Moffett Air Force Base, has changed ownership several times. "Moffett Federal Airfield (MFA), formerly Naval Air Station (NAS) Moffett Field, is currently operated by the National Aeronautics and Space Administration (NASA)." (*GlobalSecurity*) Another example is Biggs Army Airfield in El Paso, Texas. Biggs Army Airfield was established in 1915 and was referred to as Fort Bliss Aviation Field. On January 5, 1925, the field was officially named Biggs Field. On February 1, 1948, Biggs Field became Biggs Air Force Base. In 1966 when Biggs AFB closed, the airfield reverted to the U.S. Army where it once again became Biggs Army Airfield. Walter Reed Army Medical Center has also changed its name many times over the years. For simplicity, I have used the current name even though the name may have been different at the time a man mentioned in this book was there. I have noted, as much as possible, the former name of an installation.

Large installations such as Fort Rucker and Fort Bragg have several gates and make no claim to being in any one city. Therefore, I have used the closest or largest city as the installation's location.

Information in this book comes from many sources: the Internet, obituaries, military documents, and personal interviews and letters from family members. Other sources include the offices of the Department of the Air Force History Support Office; Department of the Air Force Historical Research Agency; the 82nd Airborne Division Museum at Fort Bragg; the USA Armor School Research Library at Fort Knox; the McClellan Aviation Museum; the Massachusetts National Guard Military Museum & Archives; the Museum Division at Fort Riley; the Fort Bliss Museum; the History office at Hanscom Air Force Base; Military Historical Society of Minnesota; Public Affairs Office at Fort Leavenworth; Special Collections Orange County Library System, Florida; Austin History Center; Selma-Dallas County Public Library; Public Affairs Office at Lackland Air Force Base; and the Department of the Navy, Naval Historical Center to name just a few.

Although I have tried to use the most reliable sources for information, there may still be discrepancies in birth and death dates. For example, most sources say General Ent was born in 1900, however, according to his nephew, his uncle was born in 1901. He fibbed about his age so he could enlist. I used dates from Arlington National Cemetery as the official source for those buried there. Caution must be used when using information found on the World Wide

Web. I discovered some Web sites cite text with one date and a photo of the tombstone gives another date. For example, the text for Lieutenant Barksdale indicates he was born in 1897, another site says, 1895, while his tombstone reads 1896.

I have taken the liberty of changing military dates to the more common civilian dating system. For example: 2 Jun 47 is changed to June 2, 1947, and numerals within award citations were changed into letters, such as the number 3 is changed to three. I also spelled out the individual's rank instead of using the abbreviation. This is strictly a style preference.

When no information was found for the date and place of birth or date and place of death, I indicated that with "No Data Found," and I omitted the Decorations and Honors entirely when no awards were found. I have omitted military installations that are now part of the National Parks System and are considered historic sites.

It is not my purpose to write a complete biographical history on each man. In many cases I could find only a sentence or two. The biographies of well-known, high-ranking officers and political figures fill volumes on library bookshelves. My purpose is to highlight the main accomplishments of these 524 men who proudly and bravely served our country in such a manner that the military deemed them important enough to name an installation in their honor. These men left their marks on history and changed the course of military history forever. My intention is to honor them and keep their memories alive in the hearts of today's generation, as well as those in the future. We must not forget them; their sacrifice was too great. Therefore, I am please to share with you, *In Their Honor: The Men Behind the Names of Our Military Installations*.

Linda D. Swink

Acknowledgments

SO MANY PEOPLE have given of their time, knowledge, and willingness to help make this book possible. To all the following I am most grateful.

To the many librarians: Lorraine Allen, Armor School Research Library; Louisa Berger, Youngstown and Mahoning County Public Library; Sandra E. Cortez, San Marcos Public Library; Michael Elliott, Akron Public Library; Judy Fabry, Georgetown Public Library; Virginia Kniesner, Austin Public Library; Kathleen M. Lloyd, Navy Operational Archives Branch; Elizabeth A. Locher, Clifton Forge Public Library; Irene Mann, Bradford Public Library; Latasha McCoy, Thomas County Public Library; Joe Moreno, Laredo Public Library; Nancy Mulhern, Wisconsin Historical Society Library; Carol Passmore, Durham County Library; Willard Rocker, Washington Memorial Library; Pamela Sage, Montgomery Public Library; Sarah Samson, Georgetown Public Library; Earl Santos, Jackson Barracks Military Library; Cathy K. Silbert, Longmont Public Library; Susan Smith, Bangor Public Library; Carrie Sullivan, European Regional Library; Gillian Wiseman, Waco-McLennan County Library; Shawna Woodard, Dayton Genealogy. To the staff members at: Alpena County George N. Fletcher Public Library; Brown County Public Library; El Reno Carnegie Library; Elizabeth Jones Library; Hillsborough County Public Library; Kearny County Library; Leavenworth Public Library; Mesa Public Library; Orange County Library; Pulaski County Public Library; Selma-Dallas County Public Library; Smyrna Public Library; Warren Trumbull County Library; Yakima Valley Regional Library.

My heartfelt thanks to the following historians for not only their help but enthusiasm for this book: Stephen Allie, Museum Director, Fort Leavenworth; Colonel Warren Aney, Oregon National Guard; Alan Archambault, Fort Lewis Museum; Bruce Ashcroft, Randolph AFB; Robert V. Aquilina, Quantico, VA; Lane Bourgeois, Randolph AFB; LTC Pete Conlin, North Dakota National Guard; Dr. John R. Dabrowski, Fort Rucker; Margaret C. DePalma, Whiteman

AFB; Archie DiFante, Maxwell AFB; TSgt Tracy L. English, Lackland AFB; Sherman Fleek, Army LTC (Ret.); MSgt James R. Frank, Elmendorf AFB.; Daniel A. Frederick, USAREUR; SMSgt Keith R. Fulton, Forbes Field; TSgt John B. Gazaway, Alaska Air National Guard; Tom Graham, New Hampshire National Guard; TSgt Richard S. Guinan, Altus AFB; Beth Hoad, Palmyra, NY; TSgt Brian E. Hoppe, Tyndall AFB; Jim Kitchens, Maxwell AFB; Dr. Roger D. Launius, chief historian, National Aeronautics and Space Administration; TSgt Peter A. Law, Randolph AFB; Charles Machon, Missouri National Guard; R. Steven Maxham, US Army Aviation Museum; MSgt Jeffrey S. Michalke, Hurlburt Field; Jim Neville, Fort Drum; MSgt Neil A. Nichols, Seymour Johnson AFB; Greg Parsons, Camp Blanding; Gustav Person, Fort Belvoir; Raymond L. Puffer, History Office, Air Force Flight Test Center; Lauren Y. Pursley, Mississippi Armed Forces Museum; Dr. Roberts, Fort Leonard Wood; Ronald L. Roussel, Maine Army National Guard; Mary L. Scalla, Fort Hunter Liggett; John C. L. Scribner, Austin, TX; Bruce H. Siemon, Chief, Military History Office (USAREUR/7A) Germany; Frederick Smith, Scott AFB; John Q. Smith, Eglin AFB; Towana D. Spivey, Fort Sill; Dr. Jim Williams, Fort Rucker; TSgt Craig P. Wolfe, Buckley AFB.

And to the following: Albert E. Anderson, Moses Lake, Washington; Casey J. Behrend, The Citadel Archives and Museum; Russell V. Bierl, Iowa Gold Star Military Museum; Debbie Bingham, White Sands Missile Range; Cpl Brian Buckwalter, Henderson Hall; John D. Campbell, Lawson Army Airfield; Linda J. Card, Bolling AFB; Eileen Carlton, Caterpillar Club; Bradley K. Castleberry, Fort Benning; Denise J. Clark, U.S. Naval Academy Alumni Association; Tom Clinard, AMMS Alum; Francis J DeMaro Jr., US Military Academy; Duane Denfeld, Fort Bragg; Sandy Erickson, Minnesota Military Museum; Georgia Historical Society; Amy Grissom, Levelland, Texas, Chamber of Commerce; Vicki Hester, Fort Stewart; Vicki O. Kirby, Louisiana National Guard; Major Debbie Kelley, Maine National Guard; SFC James A. Loffler, Rhode Island National Guard; Linda A. Jeleniewski, Fort Devens; Vic Johnston, Langley AFB; LC Ron Kinsley, Camp Rilea; Sgt Leon Le, Portland, Oregon; SFC Linda Lindsay, Nevada National Guard; Colonel Lopez, West Virginia Adjutant Generals Office; Michele Michael, Fort Bragg; Stacey Nelson, *Air Age Media;* Charles B. Oellig, Pennsylvania National Guard Military Museum; Alan Renga, San Diego Aerospace Museum; Mary Elizabeth Ruwell, Peterson Air & Space Museum; Rosemary Shultz, Camp Roberts; SFC Erick Studenicka, Nevada National Guard; Jill Swiatowicz, *Model Airplane News;* John Tipton, Maryland Aviation Museum; Janet Wray, Laughlin AFB.

Thanks to: Fred Alexander; Warren Aney; Ralph S. Cooper; Menzo W. Driskell; Charles H. Dyess; Captain Kone C. Faulkner; TSgt Rick Johnson; Navy Captain Paul Klote, (Ret.); Allen Mackall, Mackall family member; Simine Short; Floyd Jensen Skoubo; Chester Steele; Alex White; and to BG Uzal W. Ent, Ent family member; Mrs. F. L. Hafer, Stewart family member; Karen McLarty, Reese family member; the Press-Enterprise in Southern California; and Mariangela Venturini, Spinelli family member.

I give a special thanks and hugs to my mother for her support and encouragement, and to my husband for answering my many questions about military terminology and for not complaining when dinner was late.

Lastly, but certainly not least, I say thank you to my publisher, Barbara Gargiulo, for seeing the importance of this book and believing in my ability to write it. Thank You.

United States Air Force

High Flight

Oh, I have slipped the surly bonds of earth,
And danced the skies on laughter-silvered wings;
Sunward, I've climbed and joined the tumbling mirth
Of sun-split clouds—and done a hundred things
You have not dreamed of—wheeled and soared and swung
High in the sunlit silence. Hov'ring there,
I've chased the shouting wind along and flung
My eager craft through footless halls of air.
Up, up the long, delirious, burning blue
I've topped the wind-swept heights with easy grace,
Where never lark, or even eagle, flew;
And, while with silent, lifting mind I've trod
The high untrespassed sanctity of space,
Put out my hand, and touched the face of God.

—John Gillespie Magee, Jr.

CHAPTER 1

United States Air Force

Albrook Air Base (formerly, Balboa Field)

Location: Panama City, Panama
Status: Closed
Named for: First Lieutenant Frank P. Albrook
Date of Birth: July 6, 1892
Place of Birth: Delhi, Iowa
Date of Death: September 17, 1924
Place of Death: Walter Reed Army Medical Center in Washington, D.C.
Place of Burial: Evergreen Cemetery in Delhi, Iowa

First Lieutenant Frank P. Albrook was assigned to the 7th Observation Squadron on March 16, 1921, and served under the command of Captain Henry "Hap" Arnold at France Field in the Panama Canal Zone.

Albrook graduated from Iowa State College in Ames, Iowa, in 1917 with a bachelor of science degree. In 1922, he assumed command of the 8th Air Park at the Balboa Field in Panama, which was later renamed in his honor. He flew the open cockpit British de Havilland DH-4, sometimes called "the flaming coffin."

Considered a daredevil, he was photographed flying over a volcano in Nicaragua. Another photograph shows his aircraft upside down in tall grass in a jungle. On the photo he had written, "You cannot land in tall grass!"

Albrook was also the post engineering officer until he was reassigned to Chanute Field in Illinois on May 13, 1924, where he became a member of the Fairfield Air Intermediate Depot.

He was injured in a plane crash on August 12, 1924, at Chanute Field when the engine of his plane failed and the plane spun out of control and crashed. He died a little more than one month later from the injuries he received in that crash.

Andersen Air Force Base

Location: Yigo, Guam
Status: Active
Named for: Brigadier General James Roy Andersen
Date of Birth: May 10, 1904
Place of Birth: Racine, Wisconsin
Date of Death: February 26, 1945 (declared dead on February 25, 1946)
Place of Death: Lost at sea near the Marshall Islands
Decorations and Honors: Legion of Merit
Place of Burial: Memorialized at Arlington National Cemetery, Section K, Site 7

Brigadier General James Roy Andersen is credited with forming the first flight training class at West Point.

Andersen graduated from West Point in 1926 and was assigned to the infantry and ordnance departments of the U.S. Army Air Corps. He earned his pilot wings in 1936 and later became the director of Training at the Army Air Force Basic Advanced Flying School from March 1942 to June 1943. He also served as a staff officer in Strategic Planning during World War II, with assignments in Washington, D.C. and the Pacific.

In 1944, as a colonel, he was assigned to Hawaii as the chief of staff, Headquarters Army Air Forces, Pacific Ocean Area (AAF/POA), where he was instrumental in moving the headquarters to Guam in January 1945. He was promoted to brigadier general in January 1945.

Andersen, along with Lieutenant General Millard F. Harmon, commanding general of the Army Air Forces–Pacific Ocean Areas, was lost at sea while flying a Consolidated B-24 Liberator bomber en route to Hawaii. An eighteen-day search of the ocean failed to locate the downed plane and his body was never found.

Andrews Air Force Base

Location: Spring Hill, Maryland
Status: Active
Named for: Lieutenant General Frank Maxwell Andrews
Date of Birth: February 3, 1884
Place of Birth: Nashville, Tennessee
Date of Death: May 3, 1942
Place of Death: Near Iceland
Decorations and Honors: Distinguished Service Medal; Distinguished Flying
  Cross with oak leaf cluster; Air Medal with nine oak leaf clusters; Purple
  Heart; Commander of the Crown of Italy; Cruz Peruna de Aviacion of Peru;

Order of the Sun of Peru; Army of Occupation Medal (Germany); Order of Boyaca of Columbia (Grand Officer); Presidential Medal of Merit of Nicaragua; Order of Vasco Nunez de Balboa of Panama; El Sol del Peru (Grand Officer); the Emblem of the Ejercito Argentino; inducted into the National Aviation Hall of Fame (1986)

Place of Burial: Arlington National Cemetery, Section 5, Site 1885

Lieutenant General Frank Maxwell Andrews helped establish an air force equal to the other U.S. military branches.

Andrews graduated from West Point on June 12, 1906, and served with the cavalry. He transferred to the Signal Corps and earned his pilot wings in 1918. He graduated from the Air Corps Tactical School in 1928, the Army Command and General Staff College in 1929, and the Army War College in 1933. In the fall of 1934, Andrews was placed in command of the 1st Pursuit Group at Selfridge Field in Michigan.

His many assignments included commanding general, General Headquarters (GHQ) Air Force, Langley Field in Virginia from 1935 to 1939; air officer, VIII Corps Area from March to August 1939; assistant chief of staff for Operations and Training, War Department General Staff from 1939 to 1940; commander, Panama Canal Air Force from 1940 to 1941; commander, Caribbean Defense Command and Panama Canal Department from 1941 to 1942; commander, United States Army Air Forces in the Middle East from 1942 to 1943; commanding general, United States Army Air Forces in the European Theater of Operations in 1943.

Andrews supported the use of air power, especially that of the four-engine, Boeing B-17 Flying Fortress as a weapon during wartime. He proved the B-17's capabilities on February 27, 1938, when it made a 5,225-mile Pan-American Goodwill Flight from Miami, Florida, to Buenos Aires, Argentina.

On August 24, 1935, he helped demonstrate the usefulness of the Martin B-12 bomber when he piloted it to a new 1,000 kilometer closed-course record.

On June 29, 1936, he, along with Major John Whitely, established an international distance record by flying a Douglas YOA-5 amphibian, powered by two Wright Cyclone 800 horsepower engines, from San Juan, Puerto Rico, to Langley Field in Virginia, a distance of 1,430 miles.

He was killed when his Consolidated B-24 Liberator bomber crashed in a dense fog while trying to find its way to Reykjavik, Iceland. All fourteen people on board were killed. His last message, "Continuing," became a slogan sent in time of danger and distress and set a new tradition for the U.S. Air Force. He was married to Jeanette Allen.

His Distinguished Service Medal citation reads as follows:

For exceptionally meritorious service to the Government in a position of great responsibility. As Commanding General of the European Theater of Operations, General Andrews successfully met and solved many complex problems. His calm judgment, courage, resourcefulness and superior leadership have been an inspiration to the Armed Forces and of great value to his country.

Arnold Air Force Base

Location: Manchester, Tennessee
Status: Now, Engineering Development Center
Named for: General Henry Harley "Hap" Arnold
Date of Birth: June 25, 1886
Place of Birth: Gladwyne, Pennsylvania
Date of Death: January 15, 1950
Place of Death: Sonoma, California
Decorations and Honors: Distinguished Service Cross with two oak leaf clusters; Distinguished Flying Cross; Air Medal; Decorations from Morocco, Brazil, Yugoslavia, France, Mexico, and Great Britain; inducted into the National Aviation Hall of Fame (1963); inducted into the International Aerospace Hall of Fame (1972); Mackay Trophy (1912 and 1934)
Date of Retirement: June 30, 1946
Place of Burial: Arlington National Cemetery, Section 34

General Henry Harley Arnold was appointed a five-star General of the Army (1944) and the Air Force (1949) and was one of the founders of the United States Air Force.

Arnold graduated from West Point in 1907, received a commission in the infantry, and, in 1911, having been taught to fly by the Wright brothers, earned a pilot rating and received aviator's certificate number 29.

On June 1, 1912, Arnold established a new altitude record, piloting a Burgess-Wright airplane to a height of 6,540 feet. He was the first military aviator to use a radio to report maneuver observations and the first army officer to have his name inscribed on the Mackay Trophy.

During his long military career, he organized and activated the first Army Aerial Forest Fire Patrol in Washington, Oregon, and California; transformed March Field in California into an operational base for bombers and pursuit units; and commanded a record round-trip flight of ten Martin B-10 bombers from Washington, D.C., to Fairbanks, Alaska.

He wrote a prophetic article for *The Infantry Journal*, in which he outlined the benefits of the airplane in warfare. In the article he wrote of the planes usefulness in reconnaissance, messenger services, artillery operations, supply distribution, and its offensive and defensive capabilities in air battles against hostile aircraft.

Arnold was instrumental in the production of the Boeing B-29 Superfortress bomber that became the Strategic Air Command's (SAC) first bomber used against the Japanese during World War II. He testified on behalf of General Billy Mitchell during Mitchell's famed court-martial trial in 1925. In March 1942, Arnold became Commanding General of the U.S. Army Air Force where he directed air activities against Germany and Japan.

He received his fourth star in March 1943. On April 1944, he took command of the Twentieth Air Force. He was married to Eleanor Poole.

Bakalar Air Force Base (formerly, Atterbury Army Airfield)

Location: Columbus, Indiana
Status: Closed (now, Columbus Municipal Airport)
Named for: First Lieutenant John Edmond "Buck" Bakalar
Date of Birth: August 29, 1920
Place of Birth: Hammond, Indiana
Date of Death: September 1, 1944
Place of Death: Gael, France
Decorations and Honors: Distinguished Service Cross; Air Medal with three oak leaf clusters; Purple Heart
Place of Burial: Brittany American Cemetery in St. James, France, Plot P, Row 4, Grave 3

First Lieutenant John Edmond Bakalar was a member of the famous Pioneer Mustang Group.

Bakalar attended the University of Idaho and was employed as an electrician at the E. I. Du Pont de Nemours Company before enlisting in the Army Air Corps on January 26, 1942, at Fort Benjamin Harrison in Indiana. He was commissioned and received his pilot wings in October 1942 at Luke Field in Arizona where he later became a flight instructor. He was assigned to the Ninth Air Force, 353rd Fighter Squadron, 354th Fighter Group, flying the North American P-51 Mustang aircraft.

In May 1944, he was sent to England where he participated in dive bombing and strafing missions in support of Allied ground troops in France. Bakalar was credited with three aerial victories on his first low-flying combat mission on August 16, 1944, and later went on to successfully complete forty-five combat missions during the war.

Bakalar was killed when the engine of his aircraft failed just after takeoff. The plane cleared the end of the runway, then crashed into a grove of trees. He was survived by his wife, Dorothea, his mother, and two children.

Barksdale Air Force Base

Location: Shreveport, Louisiana
Status: Active
Named for: Second Lieutenant Eugene Hoy Barksdale
Date of Birth: November 5, 1896
Place of Birth: Goshen Springs, Mississippi
Date of Death: August 11, 1926
Place of Death: McCook Field in Dayton, Ohio
Place of Burial: Arlington National Cemetery, Section 3, Grave 4184SS

Second Lieutenant Eugene Hoy Barksdale was an aviator during World War I.

Barksdale attended Mississippi State College before volunteering for the aviation section of the U.S. Army Signal Corps. He was assigned to the 41st Squadron, Royal Flying Corps, as a pilot in England where he participated in the Somme and Amiens offensives in France in August 1918.

Barksdale was credited with destroying three enemy aircraft during aerial combat and for the destruction of five additional enemy aircraft on the ground. He was wounded on September 2, 1918, during the Cambrai offensive.

After the war, he became a test pilot and was later assigned to the 25th Aero Squadron.

Barksdale was killed while flight testing a Douglas O-2 airplane when it went into a tail spin. He attempted to bail out, but his parachute became entangled in the brace wires and he fell to his death. He was married to Lura Lee Dunn.

Beale Air Force Base

Location: Marysville, California
Status: Active
Named for: General Edward Fitzgerald "Ned" Beale
Date of Birth: February 4, 1822
Place of Birth: Washington, D.C.
Date of Death: April 22, 1893
Place of Death: Washington, D.C.

General Edward Fitzgerald Beale was a nineteenth-century pioneer, an Indian agent, and founder of the United States Army Camel Corps.

Beale graduated from the United States Naval Academy at Annapolis, Maryland, in 1842 and served under Commodore Robert Stockton on the frigate USS *Congress*. In July 1846, when hostilities with Mexico began, he was assigned to land forces and served with the army.

Beale, along with his friend "Kit" Carson, fought a battle in southern California, when they became surrounded by the Mexican army. With courage and cunning, they made their way past the enemy to San Diego and secured reinforcements that saved the Americans.

He served as superintendent of Indian Affairs for California and Nevada from 1852 to 1856. California governor John Bigler appointed Beale brigadier general of the state militia, with the assignment to negotiate a peace treaty between the Indians and the American army. While surveying a wagon road from Fort Defiance in Arizona to the Colorado River, Beale used camels for transportation and to move heavy equipment, but because of the stubborn nature of the animals, the experiment failed.

In 1861, he was appointed surveyor general of California. While in that position, he acquired almost 270,000 acres of prime ranch land in the southern San Joaquin Valley, making him one of California's largest landholders. In 1876, President Ulysses S. Grant appointed Beale as minister to Austria-Hungary.

Beale died at home. He was married to Mary Edwards.

Bellows Air Force Base

Location: Waimanalo, Hawaii
Status: Now, Hawaii Army National Guard Military Academy
Named for: Second Lieutenant Franklin Barney Bellows
Date of Birth: July 9, 1896
Place of Birth: Evanston, Illinois
Date of Death: September 13, 1918
Place of Death: Saint Mihiel, France
Decorations and Honors: Distinguished Service Cross, posthumously
Place of Burial: Saint Mihiel American Cemetery and Memorial in Thiaucourt, France

Second Lieutenant Franklin Barney Bellows was a World War I pilot.

Bellows volunteered for service and entered the First Officers Training Camp at Fort Serican in Illinois on May 13, 1917, just one month short of graduating from Northwestern University. He was the only member of his class to receive his diploma in uniform. He reported to the School of Military Aeronautics at the University of Texas at Austin, and on February 12, 1918, was commissioned a second lieutenant in the aviation section of the Signal Corps.

Bellows was sent to France on March 29, 1918, where he was put in charge of the 19th Engineers. There, he took advanced aerial observer training and, on August 15, he was assigned to the 50th Aero Squadron.

He was killed when his plane was hit by machine-gun fire while flying on a reconnaissance mission over enemy lines at an altitude of less than 300 meters. His pilot, Second Lieutenant David C. Beebe, brought the plane safely back behind allied lines.

His Distinguished Service Cross citation reads as follows:

The Distinguished Service Cross is presented to Franklin B. Bellows, Second Lieutenant (Air Service), U.S. Army, for extraordinary heroism in action near Saint Mihiel, France, September 13, 1918. Second Lieutenant Bellows, with Second Lieutenant David C. Beebe, pilot, executed a reconnaissance mission early in the morning of the second day of the Saint Mihiel offensive in spite of low clouds, high winds, and mist, flying at an altitude of only 300 meters, and without protection of accompanying battle planes. Although subjected to severe fire from ground batteries, they penetrated eight kilometers beyond the German lines. Lieutenant Beebe's motor was badly damaged, and Lieutenant Bellows was mortally wounded and died just after the disabled machine landed safely in friendly territory.

Bergstrom Air Force Base

Location: Austin, Texas
Status: Now, Austin-Bergstrom International Airport
Named for: Captain John August Earl Bergstrom
Date of Birth: August 25, 1907
Place of Birth: Austin, Texas
Date of Death: December 10, 1941
Place of Death: Clark Field in the Philippine Islands
Decorations and Honors: Purple Heart
Place of Burial: Memorialized at the Manila American Cemetery and Memorial in Manila, Philippines

Captain John August Earl Bergstrom was the first World War II casualty from Austin, Texas.

Bergstrom graduated from Texas A&M University in September 1929. He was a reservist and worked for the Austin National Bank until July 1, 1941, when he was called to active duty. He was killed while serving as an administrative officer with the 19th Bombardment Group in the Philippines when the Japanese bombed the field.

His Purple Heart was presented to the Austin-Bergstrom International Airport by members of the Bergstrom family on December 7, 2002, and is on display there.

Biggs Air Force Base (see Biggs Army Airfield)

Bolling Air Force Base

Location: Washington, D.C.
Status: Active
Named for: Colonel Raynal Cawthorne Bolling
Date of Birth: September 1, 1877
Place of Birth: Hot Springs, Arkansas

Date of Death: March 26, 1918
Place of Death: Amiens-Saint-Quentin, France
Decorations and Honors: Distinguished Service Medal, posthumously; Cross of the Legion of Honor
Place of Burial: Somme American Cemetery and Memorial in Bony, France

Colonel Raynal Cawthorne Bolling, an aviation pioneer, was the first high-ranking American officer killed in combat during World War I.

Bolling grew up in Greenwich, Connecticut, and graduated from Penn Charter School in Philadelphia in 1896, from Harvard University in 1900, and from Harvard Law in 1902. He left his position as general solicitor of U.S. Steel to join the military where he helped establish the U.S. Military Aviation Service. In 1917, he rose to the rank of colonel with the U.S. Army Signal Corps and was made assistant chief of the U.S. Air Service. That same year, representing the secretary of war and the Air Service Production Board, he headed the Bolling Mission in Europe to report on aircraft production of the British de Havilland DH-4. He was also commander of the 102nd Rescue Squadron.

Bolling was ambushed and killed in an exchange of gunfire with German soldiers while driving near the front lines in France. He was married to Anna Tucker Phillips. They had five children.

"Let's look inside and remember that it's our ideals, our endeavors, our affections and love that are the realities in life." —*Colonel Raynal C. Bolling*

Brookley Air Force Base (formerly, Bates Field)

Location: Mobile, Alabama
Status: Closed
Named for: Captain Wendell Holsworth Brookley
Date of Birth: ca. 1896
Place of Birth: No Data Found
Date of Death: February 28, 1934
Place of Death: en route between Middletown, Pennsylvania, and Washington, D.C.
Place of Burial: Arlington National Cemetery, Section 7, Grave 10070

Captain Wendell Holsworth Brookley served in World War I.

Brookley attended one year of college in Nebraska before enlisting in the Signal Corps in 1917. He completed flight training at Fort Logan in Denver, Colorado, received his pilot wings, and was commissioned in April 1918. He placed second in the Pulitzer Trophy Race at the National Air Races in Dayton, Ohio, in 1924, achieving a speed of 114 miles per hour in a Curtiss R-6 racer and, in 1929, he flew in the Ford Air Tour as part of the Commercial Airplane Reliability Tour for the Edsel B. Ford Trophy.

He served in the Philippines and at Fort Sill in Oklahoma. In 1922, he was transferred to McCook Field in Dayton, Ohio, as a test pilot, flying newly designed aircraft where he conducted experimental night flying. He also helped in the development of navigation lights, parachute flares, boundary lights, and wind indicators.

Brookley was killed while flying a Douglas BT2-B biplane when the plane's propeller broke apart and the engine ripped from its mounting, causing the airplane to spin out of control. Brookley's observer, Captain Merritt G. Esterbrook, parachuted to safety, but Brookley's parachute failed to open in time.

Brooks Air Force Base

Location: San Antonio, Texas
Status: Now, Brooks City Base
Named for: Cadet Sidney Johnston Brooks, Jr.
Date of Birth: May 21, 1895
Place of Birth: San Antonio, Texas
Date of Death: November 13, 1917
Place of Death: San Antonio, Texas
Decorations and Honors: Aviator's wings and commission, posthumously
Place of Burial: Sidney Johnston Brooks Jr. Memorial Park in San Antonio, Texas

Cadet Sidney Johnston Brooks, Jr., was killed while making his first solo flight to earn his pilot wings and commission, making him the first San Antonian to lose his life in World War I.

Brooks enrolled in the University of Texas at Austin but left school to enlist in the army when the United States entered World War I. After ground school at Camp Funston in Alabama and aviation school in Austin, Texas, he reported to Kelly Field in Texas for flight training.

Brooks was killed while returning from Hondo Airfield en route to Kelly Field (now, Kelly Air Force Base) when his Curtiss JN-4 Jenny biplane nosed downward and crashed. Just before the crash, witnesses said they saw Brooks slumped over in the cockpit, his body pressing upon the stick. Speculation was that the rigorous physical examination and immunizations he received earlier that morning may have caused him to pass out.

At his relative's request, Brooks's remains were exhumed from the Alamo Masonic Cemetery and reinterred at the Brooks Memorial on Brooks Air Force Base. The base performed the reinterment ceremony on Veterans Day, November 11, 1993.

Placing his remains on the base makes Brooks Air Force Base the only air force base with its namesake buried on the premises.

Buckley Air Force Base

Location: Denver, Colorado
Status: Now, Air National Guard Base
Named for: First Lieutenant John Harold Buckley
Date of Birth: ca. 1895
Place of Birth: Longmont, Colorado
Date of Death: September 27, 1918
Place of Death: Argonne, France
Place of Burial: Meuse-Argonne American Cemetery and Memorial in Romagne, France, Plot B, Grave 15

First Lieutenant John Harold Buckley was the first Longmont native killed in World War I.

Buckley graduated from Longmont High School and entered the service in April 1917. After attending Officers Training School at Fort Riley in Kansas, Buckley was commissioned a second lieutenant and assigned to the 28th Aero Squadron in France.

Buckley was killed when his plane was shot down while on a strafing mission behind enemy German lines in France.

In a letter sent to Buckley's mother, Lieutenant J. G. Fater wrote,

Buck flew on all patrols during his career at the front. He did his share in all bombing expeditions. Our squadron was the only personnel bombing and strafing outfit in the American and French armies during the Saint Mihiel drive. He was greatly admired by his fellow officers, and the entire personnel of the squadron always spoke highly of him. He was always anxious to do his duty; in fact, more than his duty, as several times he volunteered for special patrols.

Cannon Air Force Base

Location: Clovis, New Mexico
Status: Active
Named for: General John Kenneth Cannon
Date of Birth: March 2, 1892
Place of Birth: Salt Lake City, Utah
Date of Death: January 12, 1955
Place of Death: Arcadia, California
Decorations and Honors: Distinguished Service Medal; Legion of Merit; Bronze Star; Air Medal; Decorations from Great Britain, France, Italy, Poland, Yugoslavia, and Morocco
Date of Retirement: March 31, 1954
Place of Burial: Arlington National Cemetery, Section 34, Site 725

General John Kenneth Cannon was a World War II combat commander who was recognized as one of the nation's outstanding leaders in the development of airpower.

Cannon graduated from Utah Agricultural College in 1914 with a bachelor of science degree and joined the Infantry Reserve in November 1917 as a second lieutenant.

Among Cannon's many assignments were operations officer of the 5th Composite Group with the 6th Pursuit Squadron at Luke Field in Hawaii in January 1925; commanding officer of the 94th Pursuit Squadron at Selfridge Field in Michigan in 1927; director of Pursuit Training in 1929; director of Training at Randolph Field in Texas in August 1931; chief of the U.S. Military Mission in Buenos Aires, Argentina, in June 1938; chief of staff of the First Air Force, taking command of the 1st Interceptor Command at Mitchel Field in New York in January 1941; commanding general of the 12th Air Support Command for the Western Task Force during the invasion of French Morocco in 1942; commanding general of the 12th Bomber Command; deputy commanding general of the Allied Tactical Air Force for the Sicilian campaign and the invasion of Italy in 1943; commanding general of the Twelfth Air Force and the Mediterranean Allied Tactical Air Force, where he was responsible for all air operations for the invasion of southern Europe in August 1944; air commander in chief of all Allied air forces in the Mediterranean Theater of Operations; commanding general of Air Training Command at Barksdale Field in Louisiana in 1946; commanding general of U.S. air forces in Europe in 1950; and commanding general of Tactical Air Command at Langley Air Force Base in Virginia.

General William W. Momyer, who served under Cannon in North Africa and Italy, said of him:

General Cannon was not only a great airman in every sense of the word, but he was also a man of great moral courage, a humanitarian, a scholar of air power, and perhaps most of all, a developer of men in the finest tradition of our country. His contributions to the development of air power during the North African campaign in the years 1942 and 1943 are the most important historical milestones in the emergence of airpower as a coequal military force with ground and sea forces.

Cannon died of a heart attack at his home.

Carswell Air Force Base

Location: Fort Worth, Texas
Status: Now, Naval Air Station Joint Reserve Base
Named for: Major Horace Seaver "Stump" Carswell, Jr.
Date of Birth: July 18, 1916
Place of Birth: Fort Worth, Texas

Date of Death: October 26, 1944
Place of Death: South China Sea
Decorations and Honors: Medal of Honor; Distinguished Flying Cross; Distinguished Service Cross; Air Medal; Purple Heart, posthumously
Place of Burial: Oakwood Cemetery in Fort Worth, Texas

Major Horace Seaver Carswell, Jr., was the only officer of the Fourteenth Air Force to receive the Medal of Honor.

Carswell graduated from Texas Christian University in August 1939 with a degree in business administration. He enlisted as a flying cadet on March 26, 1940, and was commissioned a second lieutenant and received his pilot wings after completing flight training in November 1940.

He attended the Army Air Force Combat Crew School at Hendricks Field in Florida. Later, Carswell became an instructor and flight commander with bomb squadrons at Davis-Monthan Field in Arizona and Biggs Field in Texas. He served in the Pacific Theater of Operations in April 1944, and was a pilot and operations officer of the 374th Bomb Squadron, 308th Bombardment Group, Fourteenth Air Force. He was also assigned to the 356th Bomb Squadron and Headquarters, 302nd Bomb Group, at Clovis Air Force Base in New Mexico. He was married to Virginia Ede.

His Medal of Honor citation for action during World War II reads as follows:

He piloted a B-24 bomber in a one-plane strike against a Japanese convoy in the South China Sea on the night of October 26, 1944. Taking the enemy force of twelve ships escorted by at least two destroyers by surprise, he made one bombing run at 600 feet, scoring a near-miss on one warship and escaping without drawing fire. He circled and fully realizing that the convoy was thoroughly alerted and would meet his next attack with a barrage of antiaircraft fire, began a second low-level run that culminated in two direct hits on a large tanker. A hail of steel from Japanese guns riddled the bomber, knocking out two engines, damaging a third, crippling the hydraulic system, puncturing one gasoline tank, ripping uncounted holes in the aircraft, and wounding the copilot; but by magnificent display of flying skill, Major Carswell controlled the plane's plunge toward the sea and carefully forced it into a halting climb in the direction of the China shore. On reaching land, where it would have been possible to abandon the staggering bomber, one of the crew discovered that his parachute had been ripped by flak and rendered useless; the pilot, hoping to cross mountainous terrain and reach a base, continued onward until the third engine failed. He ordered the crew to bail out while he struggled to maintain altitude and, refusing to save himself, chose to remain with his comrade and attempt a crash landing. He died when the airplane struck a mountainside and burned. With consummate gallantry and intrepidity, Major Carswell gave his life in a supreme effort to save all members of his crew. His sacrifice, far beyond that required of him, was in keeping with the traditional bravery of America's war heroes.

Castle Air Force Base

Location: Merced, California
Status: Closed
Named for: Brigadier General Frederick Walker Castle
Date of Birth: October 14, 1908
Place of Birth: Fort McKinley in Manila, Philippines
Date of Death: December 24, 1944
Place of Death: Liege, Belgium
Decorations and Honors: Medal of Honor, posthumously; Distinguished Service Cross; Silver Star; Legion of Merit; Distinguished Flying Cross with three oak leaf clusters; Purple Heart; Air Medal with four oak leaf clusters; Croix de Guerre with palm (Belgium); French Legion of Honor; Order of Kutuzov, 2nd and 3rd Degree (USSR); Virtuti Militari Silver Cross Class V (Poland)
Place of Burial: Henri-Chapelle American Cemetery and Memorial in Henri-Chapelle, Belgium, Plot D, Grave 53

Brigadier General Frederick Walker Castle was a bomber pilot during World War II and commander of the 4th Combat Bomb Wing.

Castle graduated from West Point in June 1930, seventh in a class of 241 cadets. He received his pilot wings in October 1931 and served as a pilot and assistant operations officer with the 17th Pursuit Squadron at Selfridge Field in Michigan.

He was one of several officers selected to accompany Major General Ira Eaker to England to form the Eighth Air Force where he was given command of the 94th Bomb Group at Rougham. There, he led a bombing strike on July 28, 1943, against the Focke-Wulf aircraft factory at Oschersleben, Germany. The attack was made into a movie titled *Twelve O'clock High*. Castle was promoted to brigadier general on November 20, 1944.

His Medal of Honor citation for action during World War II reads as follows:

He was air commander and leader of more than 2,000 heavy bombers in a strike against German airfields on December 24, 1944. En route to the target, the failure of one engine forced him to relinquish his place at the head of the formation. In order not to endanger friendly troops on the ground below, he refused to jettison his bombs to gain speed maneuverability. His lagging, unescorted aircraft became the target of numerous enemy fighters which ripped the left wing with cannon shells, set the oxygen system afire, and wounded two members of the crew. Repeated attacks started fires in two engines, leaving the Flying Fortress in imminent danger of exploding. Realizing the hopelessness of the situation, the bailout order was given. Without regard for his personal safety he gallantly remained alone at the controls to afford all other crew members an opportunity to escape. Still another attack exploded gasoline tanks in the right wing, and the bomber plunged earthward carrying General Castle to his death. His intrepidity and willing sacrifice of his life to save members of the crew were in keeping with the highest traditions of the military service.

Chanute Air Force Base

Location: Rantoul, Illinois
Status: Closed
Named for: Octave Chanute, civilian
Date of Birth: February 18, 1832
Place of Birth: Paris, France
Date of Death: November 23, 1910
Place of Death: Chicago, Illinois
Decorations and Honors: Inducted into the National Aviation Hall of Fame
    (1963); inducted into the International Aerospace Hall of Fame (1974)
Place of Burial: Springdale Cemetery in Peoria, Illinois

Octave Chanute (born Octave Alexandre Chanut) was a scientist.
    Chanute came to the United States at a young age. He became a railroad engineer and played an important role in the construction of many railroads throughout the United States. He also was responsible for the first railroad bridge over the Missouri River and for railroads supporting the Union stockyards in Kansas City and Chicago.
    In 1894, Chanute published *Progress in Flying Machines* in New York in which he described the accomplishments of the world's early aviators. The book became a guide for many aviators, including the Wright brothers, with whom he corresponded for many years, helping them develop their aircraft.
    His "Recent Progress in Aviation" was read to the Western Society of Engineers on October 20, 1909, thirteen months before his death. An excerpt from the conclusion of this publication reads as follows:

Let us hope that the advent of a successful flying machine, now only dimly foreseen and nevertheless thought to be possible, will bring nothing but good into the world; that it shall abridge distance, make all parts of the globe accessible, bring men into closer relation with each other, advance civilization, and hasten the promised era in which there shall be nothing but peace and goodwill among all men.

Chennault Air Force Base

Location: Lake Charles, Louisiana
Status: Closed
Named for: Lieutenant General Claire Lee Chennault
Date of Birth: September 6, 1893
Place of Birth: Commerce, Texas
Date of Death: July 27, 1958
Place of Death: New Orleans, Louisiana
Decorations and Honors: Distinguished Service Medal with oak leaf cluster; Distinguished Flying Cross with oak leaf cluster; inducted into the National Aviation Hall of Fame (1972)
Place of Burial: Arlington National Cemetery, Section 2, Lot 872

Lieutenant General Claire Lee Chennault was the commander of Allied air forces in the Far East and founder of the "Flying Tigers" American Volunteer Group.

Chennault graduated from Louisiana State Normal School at Natchitoches and became a teacher. He enlisted in the army at the beginning of World War I and was commissioned in the Infantry Reserve. After World War I, he transferred to the Signal Corps' aviation section and received his pilot wings in 1919.

His career assignments included aviation engineer officer of the 12th Aero Squadron at Fort Bliss in Texas from 1922 to 1924; senior instructor of Pursuit Aviation; chief of Pursuit Section, Air Corps Tactical School; stations operations officer, Maxwell Field in Alabama in 1936; and executive officer, 10th Fighter Group, from 1936 to 1937.

In April 1937, Chennault accepted an offer from Madame Chiang Kai-shek to study the capabilities of the Chinese air force. While there, he worked to improve the Chinese air force and train their pilots. He was responsible for the United States sending one hundred planes and one hundred volunteer pilots to China who became known as the American Volunteer Group, and who flew combat missions against the Japanese during the early days of World War II.

After the American Volunteer Group was disbanded on July 4, 1942, the China Air Task Force of the United States Army Air Forces, commanded by Chennault, officially took over air operations in China. In March 1943, Chennault took command of the Fourteenth Air Force that replaced the China Air Task Force. He remained in that position until the end of July 1945. He was married twice. His first wife was Nell Thompson, and his second wife was Ann Chen.

He was the author of *The Role of Defensive Pursuit*, 1935, and *Way of a Fighter: The Memoirs of Claire Lee Chennault*, (New York, G. P. Putnam, 1949).

Clark Air Base

Location: Philippine Islands
Status: Closed
Named for: Major Harold Melville Clark
Date of Birth: October 4, 1890
Place of Birth: St. Paul, Minnesota
Date of Death: May 2, 1919
Place of Death: Miraflores Locks, Panama
Place of Burial: Arlington National Cemetery, Section S DIV, Site 4222

Major Harold Melville Clark was the first aviator to fly regularly in the Hawaiian islands.

Clark's military career began in 1913 when he was assigned to the 1st Cavalry Division. In 1916, Clark requested a transfer to the Signal Corps' aviation section and was sent to the North Island Flying School in San Diego, California. On May 3, 1917, Clark received his rating as a junior military aviator and was assigned to the 1st Aero Squadron where he flew missions from bases in New Mexico, Texas, and Oklahoma. On November 17, 1917, he was transferred to Fort Kamehameha in Hawaii as the commander of the 6th Aero Squadron and as the Hawaii Department's aviation officer where he learned to fly in the Hawaiian Islands' challenging environment by focusing on the islands' prevailing winds and making short local flights over Oahu.

On March 15, 1918, he flew from Fort Kamehameha to Molokai and back, making the first inter-island flight ever made in the Hawaiian Islands. He was also the first to deliver letters to the residences of the Hawaiian Islands by airmail.

While returning from Balboa Field en route to France Field in an army seaplane, Clark and two other aviators experienced engine problems. The pilot, Lieutenant Tonkin, tried to make it to safety, but the plane crashed into the Miraflores Locks.

The best account of the crash is taken from the May 3, 1919, issue of the *Panama Star & Herald*. It states,

The machine crumpled up like a house of cards, and the three men were thrown into the water of the lock. Lieutenant Tonkin was undoubtedly killed instantly by the twisting timbers of the machine . . . Major Clark sank to the bottom of the lock, and it's not known whether he was killed in the crash or whether he drowned.

The article went on to report that a diver was sent to retrieve Clark's body.

According to the Defense Department, the army ruled his death an accident due to internal injuries caused by "aeroplane traumatism" and awarded his mother ten thousand dollars.

Connally Air Force Base

Location: Waco, Texas
Status: Closed
Named for: Colonel James Thomas Connally
Date of Birth: June 12, 1910
Place of Birth: McGregor, Texas
Date of Death: May 29, 1945
Place of Death: Yokohama, Japan
Decorations and Honors: Legion of Merit; Distinguished Flying Cross; Purple Heart; Air Medal; the British Air Force Cross

Colonel James Thomas Connally was a World War II pilot.
    Connally graduated from Texas A&M University in 1932. He completed pilot training and received a commission at Randolph Field in Texas in 1933.
    He flew airmail as an army pilot in 1934 and, in 1941, accompanied the first Boeing B-17 Flying Fortress bomber sent to England. Connally was sent to Clark Field in the Philippines in 1942 where he was assigned to the 19th Bombardment Group. After attending the School of Applied Tactics in Orlando, Florida, he returned to the Philippines in December 1944.
    He was aboard the Boeing B-29 Superfortress named *Thumper* as an observer during a five-hundred-plane bombing mission when his plane exploded after being hit by antiaircraft fire.
    The Distinguished Flying Cross was awarded to Connally for his participation in a mission while at Clark Field that destroyed a Japanese tanker ship and for helping rescue twenty-three stranded American pilots.

Cooke Air Force Base (see Camp Cooke and Vandenberg Air Force Base)

Craig Air Force Base

Location: Selma, Alabama
Status: Closed
Named for: Second Lieutenant Bruce Kilpatrick Craig, Jr.
Date of Birth: April 8, 1914
Place of Birth: Selma, Alabama
Date of Death: June 3, 1941
Place of Death: San Diego Bay, California
Decorations and Honors: Posthumously awarded a commission
Place of Burial: Old Live Oak Cemetery in Selma, Alabama, Plot 126

Second Lieutenant Bruce Kilpatrick Craig, Jr., soloed at age sixteen to become the youngest pilot in the state of Alabama.

Craig showed an interest in aviation at a young age when he formed a glider club while a student at Dinkins Military Academy. After graduating from the academy, he enrolled in the Georgia School of Technology and earned a bachelor of science degree in aeronautical engineering. He worked for American Airlines where he helped develop engineering changes for their aircraft.

In 1938, he went to work for the Consolidated Aircraft Corporation in Buffalo, New York, in the manufacturer of the B-24 Liberator bomber, as a flight test engineer and aerodynamicist. He was killed while flight testing the B-24.

Davis-Monthan Air Force Base

Location: Tucson, Arizona
Status: Active
Named for: Lieutenant Samuel Howard Davis and Second Lieutenant Oscar Monthan
Date of Birth: Davis, November 20, 1896; Monthan, 1885
Place of Birth: Davis, Dyer County, Tennessee; Monthan, Dewsbury, England
Date of Death: Davis, December 28, 1921; Monthan, March 27, 1924
Place of Death: Davis, Carlstrom Field in Arcadia, Florida; Monthan, Luke Field in Hawaii

Lieutenant Samuel Howard Davis served during World War I.

Davis graduated from Tucson High School in 1913, attended Texas A&M University for one year, and then returned to Tucson to attend the University of Arizona.

In 1917, Davis enlisted in the army and served at Fort Huachuca in Arizona and Kelly Field in San Antonio, Texas, as a flight instructor. He was discharged in 1919, but later, he was recalled to serve in the reserves. In 1920, he was assigned to Carlstrom Field in Arcadia, Florida. After he left the service, Davis managed a commercial airport in the Tucson area. He married Marjorie Cameron in 1918. Davis was killed in an aircraft crash.

Second Lieutenant Oscar Monthan enlisted in the U.S. Army Air Corps in 1917 as a private. He received a commission in 1918, became a pilot after the armistice, and worked with General Billy Mitchell in the development of military bombers.

In 1920, Monthan became the chief engineer at Rockwell Field in San Diego and, in 1921, he worked with advanced aeronautics at Dayton, Ohio. In 1923, he was assigned to Luke Field in Hawaii where he worked as an aeronautical engineer.

Monthan was killed along with four other men in a crash of a Martin B-2 bomber. He married Mae Poquette in 1922.

Dobbins Air Force Base

Location: Marietta, Georgia
Status: Now, Joint Air Reserve Base
Named for: Captain Charles M. Dobbins
Date of Birth: 1916
Place of Birth: Marietta, Georgia
Date of Death: July 11, 1943
Place of Death: Mediterranean Sea, off the coast of Sicily
Decorations and Honors: Air Medal; Purple Heart
Place of Burial: Memorialized at the Sicily-Rome American Cemetery and Memorial in Nettuno, Italy

Captain Charles M. Dobbins was a World War II pilot and served with the 45th Squadron, 316th Troop Carrier Group.

Dobbins was reported missing in action on his eighty-eighth combat mission. He was the copilot of the Douglas C-47 serving with the 316th Troop Carrier Group when his plane was hit by friendly fire and failed to return from transporting paratroopers of the 376th Parachute Field Artillery Battalion, 82nd Airborne Division, during Operation Husky II that took place in southern Sicily. There was no trace of the crew and the two observers.

Donaldson Air Force Base

Location: Greenville, South Carolina
Status: Closed
Named for: Captain John Owen Donaldson
Date of Birth: May 14, 1897
Place of Birth: Fort Yates, North Dakota
Date of Death: September 7, 1930
Place of Death: Near Philadelphia, Pennsylvania
Decorations and Honors: Distinguished Flying Cross; Distinguished Service Cross; Mackay Trophy for winning the U.S. Army's Transcontinental Air Race in October 1919
Place of Burial: Westville Cemetery, Atlanta, Georgia

Captain John Owen Donaldson was a World War I ace pilot assigned to the British Royal Air Force (RAF).

Donaldson attended Furman University in South Carolina and Cornell University in New York. He volunteered for service at the beginning of the war and trained in England. He was shot down and captured on September 1, 1918. He, along with another prisoner, escaped and managed to flee to the Netherlands.

After resigning his commission in 1920, he became president of Newark Air Service in New Jersey and continued to participate in air races. Donaldson was killed when his plane crashed during an exhibition flight while performing aerial stunts at an American Legion air meet.

His Distinguished Service Cross citation reads as follows:

The Distinguished Service Cross is presented to John Owen Donaldson, Second Lieutenant (Air Service), U.S. Army, for extraordinary heroism in action near Mont-Notre-Dame, France, July 22, 1918, when, on patrol, he attacked a formation of twenty Fokker enemy biplanes. Singling out one of the hostile machines Lieutenant Donaldson engaged it from behind, firing a short burst at close range, the plane bursting into flames and crashing to the ground. On August 8, 1918, he engaged five enemy scout planes over Licourt, France; singling out one and diving on it, he opened fire at close range, causing it to crash to the ground. On August 9, 1918, over Licourt, France, observing a British plane being attacked by three enemy scout planes, he immediately engaged one of the enemy, firing a long burst at very close range, the enemy plane bursting into flames and crashing to the ground. On August 25, 1918, over Hancourt, France, he attacked four Fokker enemy planes, diving into their midst and firing a short burst at one of them from a short range, destroying the plane, the pilot of which descended to safety in a parachute. On July 25, 1918, over Fismes, France, he drove down out of control an enemy Fokker plane; on August 10, over Perrone, France, one Fokker biplane; and on August 29 over Cambrai, France, one Fokker biplane. In all these engagements Lieutenant Donaldson displayed the greatest devotion to duty and gallantry in the face of the enemy.

Dow Air Force Base

Location: Bangor, Maine
Status: Now, Air National Guard Base
Named for: Second Lieutenant James Frederick Dow
Date of Birth: November 20, 1913
Place of Birth: Oakfield, Maine
Date of Death: June 17, 1940
Place of Death: Queensborough, New York

Second Lieutenant James Frederick Dow was commissioned through the Reserve Officers' Training Corps (ROTC) program at the University of Maine and graduated from there in 1938. He was a varsity halfback on the football team, a member of Phi Gamma Delta fraternity, and president of the Scabbard and Blade.

After graduation, Dow entered flight school at Randolph Field in San Antonio, Texas, where he was commissioned and earned his pilot wings in

March 1940. Dow was killed three months later when his twin engine Douglas aircraft collided in midair with another aircraft.

Duke Field

Location: Valparaiso, Florida
Status: Auxiliary field number three at Eglin Air Force Base in Florida
Named for: First Lieutenant Robert Lewis Duke
Date of Birth: 1919
Place of Birth: No Data Found
Date of Death: December 29, 1943
Place of Death: Tullahoma, Tennessee

First Lieutenant Robert Lewis Duke joined the Army Air Corps in 1941 at the age of twenty-two.

Duke attended flight training schools in Texas, Oklahoma, and Kansas, and received his pilot wings and commission on June 26, 1943. In July of 1943, he was assigned to the Army Air Forces Proving Ground Command at Eglin Air Force Base in Florida. There, he flew missions testing guns, cameras, radios, bombs, bullets, and aircraft equipment used by the Air Corps. While testing a system on an Douglas A-3 Skywarrior "Whale" aircraft, he lost control of the aircraft, crashed and died.

Dyess Air Force Base

Location: Abilene, Texas
Status: Active
Named for: Lieutenant Colonel William Edwin Dyess
Date of Birth: August 9, 1916
Place of Birth: Albany, Texas
Date of Death: December 22, 1943
Place of Death: Burbank, California
Decorations and Honors: Distinguished Service Cross with oak leaf cluster;
    Silver Star; Legion of Merit; Soldier's Medal

Lieutenant Colonel William Edwin Dyess was a combat pilot, infantry commander, prisoner of war, guerrilla fighter in the Philippines, and a survivor of the Bataan Death March.

Dyess attended John Tarleton College at Stephenville, Texas, before entering the service. He completed flight training in 1937 and was transferred to the Philippine Islands in 1941 where he participated in the aerial defense of the islands after the attack by the Japanese. Dyess was later transferred to Bataan, and when Bataan fell on April 8, 1942, he was captured and tortured along with with many of his squadron members during what became known as the Bataan Death March.

Dyess survived the brutal torture inflicted by the enemy while held in a concentration camp at O'Donnell and Cabanatuan but managed to escape along with ten other men, and spent six months in the jungle with guerilla fighters evading the Japanese. He and his comrades were rescued and taken back to Australia by submarine.

Dyess was killed while attempting to land a disabled Lockheed P-38 Lightning in a vacant lot rather than allowing it to crash into an urban area. He was recommended for the Congressional Medal of Honor, but it was never approved.

He authored *The Dyess Story* (G. P. Putnam's Sons, 1944) which tells about his escape from the Japanese. He was married to Marajen Stevick.

Eaker Air Force Base

Location: Blytheville, Arkansas
Status: Closed
Named for: Lieutenant General Ira Clarence Eaker
Date of Birth: April 13, 1896
Place of Birth: Field Creek, Texas
Date of Death: August 6, 1987
Place of Death: Malcolm Grow Medical Center at Andrews Air Force Base in Maryland
Decorations and Honors: Air Force Distinguished Service Medal; Army Distinguished Service Medal with two oak leaf clusters; Navy Distinguished Service Medal; Silver Star; Legion of Merit; Distinguished Flying Cross with oak leaf cluster; Air Medal; World War I and II Victory Medals; American Defense Service Medal; American Campaign Medal; European-African-Middle Eastern Campaign Medal with bronze service star; inducted into the International Aerospace Hall of Fame (1981); Mackay Trophy (1926)
Date of Retirement: August 31, 1947
Place of Burial: Arlington National Cemetery, Section 30, Grave 490-2

Lieutenant General Ira Clarence Eaker was an early aviator who supported the idea of an independent air force.

Eaker graduated from Southeastern Oklahoma State University at Durant in 1917. When World War I began, he enlisted as an army private and was assigned to active duty with the 64th Infantry at El Paso, Texas. He later transferred to the Signal Corps' aviation section where he trained as a pilot at Kelly

Field in San Antonio, Texas, earning his Army Air Service wings in 1918.

After an assignment in the Philippines, with duties on the staff of the Chief of Air Service, Eaker participated in the Pan-American Goodwill Flight of 1926–27. In 1929, flying a Douglas C-1 while refueling a modified Atlantic-Fokker C-2A monoplane called the *Question Mark*, he set an endurance air refueling record when he logged eleven thousand miles, flying back and forth between San Diego and Los Angles in 150 hours, 40 minutes and 15 seconds. He also took part in the Pacific naval maneuvers in 1935 aboard the aircraft carrier USS *Lexington* in Hawaii and Guam.

In October 1934, Eaker was assigned to March Field in California where he commanded the 34th Pursuit Squadron, and later the 17th Pursuit Squadron. In 1940, he commanded the 20th Pursuit Group at Hamilton Field in California.

In January 1942, Eaker organized the Eighth Air Force Bomber Command, and on August of that year, he personally led the first strike on continental Europe. He served with the Eighth until January 1944 when he was assigned to command all Allied air forces in the Mediterranean area. There, he led the invasion of Italy and southern France. He became deputy commanding general and chief of Air Staff from 1945 to 1947. He achieved twelve thousand flying hours during his thirty years of flying.

After he retired, Eaker became vice president of the Hughes Tool Company, the executive of the Douglas Aircraft Company, and a consultant for the Hughes Aircraft Company. In 1964, Eaker became a syndicated columnist for the Copley News Service and the *Los Angeles Times*. He was the founding president of the United States Strategic Institute in 1973.

Along with General Henry Arnold, Eaker coauthored *This Flying Game* (New York: Funk & Wagnalls, 1936), *Winged Warfare* (New York: Harper & Brothers, 1941), and *Army Flyer* (New York: Harper & Brothers, 1942).

Eareckson Air Force Base

Location: Shemya, Alaska
Status: Active (now, Eareckson Air Station)
Named for: Colonel William "Eric" Olmstead Eareckson
Date of Birth: May 30, 1900
Place of Birth: No Data Found
Date of Death: October 25, 1966
Place of Death: No Data Found
Decorations and Honors: Navy Cross; Silver Star; Distinguished Service Cross; Purple Heart; Paul W. Litchfield Trophy
Date of Retirement: 1954
Place of Burial: Arlington National Cemetery, Section 37, Site 692

Colonel William Olmstead Eareckson was one of the air force's top combat commanders during the Aleutians bombing campaign, in which he personally led unprecedented low-level attacks against the Japanese on Kiska in the Aleutian Islands of Alaska.

Eareckson enlisted in the army in 1917 at the age of seventeen and was sent to France where he was wounded. He entered West Point in 1920 and graduated in 1924. He wanted to be an airplane pilot but was unable to qualify so he went to balloon school instead and became an army balloon pilot.

After winning the National Balloon Race, he earned his pilot wings, and in 1939, he went on to command the 36th Bombardment Squadron. Later, he became commander of the Eleventh Air Force Bomber Command.

On June 3, 1942, when Japanese planes hit the Dutch Harbor on Unalaska Island, Eareckson led a flight of Martin B-26 Marauders to find and attack the Japanese fleet. Following the Aleutian campaign, Eareckson served on the staff of Admiral Chester W. Nimitz.

Edwards Air Force Base

Location: Rosamond, California
Status: Active
Named for: Captain Glen Walter Edwards
Date of Birth: March 5, 1918
Place of Birth: Medicine Hat, Alberta, Canada
Date of Death: June 5, 1948
Place of Death: Muroc Dry Lake, California
Decorations and Honors: Distinguished Flying Cross with three oak leaf clusters; Air Medal with five oak leaf clusters

Captain Glen Walter Edwards was a test pilot.

Edwards grew up in Lincoln, California, and graduated from Placer College in Auburn, the University of California at Berkeley, and Princeton University in New Jersey.

He joined the U.S. Army in 1941 as an aviation cadet. He completed flight training at Luke Field in Arizona in February 1942 and was commissioned a second lieutenant. He was assigned to the 86th Light Bombardment Squadron, 47th Bombardment Group, and was sent to North Africa where he made fifty combat missions flying the Douglas A-20 Havoc bomber, sometimes making five missions in one day.

In 1943, he was assigned to the Pilot Standardization Board, and in 1944, to the Flight Test Division at Wright Field in Dayton, Ohio. After attending Flight Performance School, he was assigned to the Bomber Test Operations Section where he helped set a transcontinental speed record in the experimental Douglas XB-42 Mixmaster in December 1945.

Edwards was killed while testing a Northrop YB-49 Flying Wing. Other members of the crew that were also killed included the pilot, Major Daniel H. Forbes, Jr.; flight engineer, Lieutenant Edward Lee Swindell; Air Force civilian engineers, Clare C. Lesser and Charles H. LaFountain.

Eglin Air Force Base

Location: Valparaiso, Florida
Status: Active
Named for: Lieutenant Colonel Frederick Irving Eglin
Date of Birth: 1891
Place of Birth: New York City, New York
Date of Death: January 1, 1937
Place of Death: Anniston, Alabama

Lieutenant Colonel Frederick Irving Eglin served in World War I.

Eglin entered military service with the Indiana Infantry and fought on the Mexican border. In 1917, after earning a rating as a military aviator, he became a flight instructor. In 1920, Eglin served in the Philippines before becoming the director of Bombardment at the Advanced Flying School in Texas. He was also assigned to Kelly Field in Texas where he flew the British de Havilland DH-4 and Douglas aircrafts between the West Coast and Texas.

He attended the Air Corps Tactical School at Langley Field in Virginia and, after attending the Army Command and General Staff College at Fort Leavenworth in Kansas, he was assigned as an instructor there.

Eglin was killed when his Northrop A-17 pursuit aircraft crashed during a flight from Langley Field in Virginia en route to Maxwell Field in Alabama.

Eielson Air Force Base

Location: Near Fairbanks, Alaska
Status: Active
Named for: Colonel Carl Benjamin Eielson
Date of Birth: July 20, 1897
Place of Birth: Hatton, North Dakota
Date of Death: November 9, 1929
Place of Death: Northern Coast of Siberia
Decorations and Honors: Distinguished Flying Cross; Harmon International Trophy; Rough Rider Award, posthumously; inducted into the National Aviation Hall of Fame (1985)
Place of Burial: Saint Johns Cemetery in Hatton, North Dakota

Colonel Carl Benjamin Eielson was an Arctic explorer and pioneer aviator known as the "Father of Aviation" in Alaska.

Eielson attended the University of North Dakota and the University of Wisconsin. He enlisted in the aviation section of the Signal Corps in 1918, but the war ended before he finished flight training. He took a job in Fairbanks, Alaska, as a teacher, but seeing an opportunity to fly, he secured financial backing and formed the Farthest North Aviation Company in 1922, and in 1924, he began flying the first airmail route in Alaska.

In 1926, Eielson became the first aviator to fly across the Arctic Ocean and land a plane on the Arctic Slope. On April 15, 1928, Eielson, along with Australian explorer Sir Hubert Wilkins, flew twenty-two hundred miles over the polar ice cap from the North Slope of Alaska to Spitzbergen Island, Greenland, making him the first aviator to fly from North America over the North Pole. In September 1928, Wilkins and Eielson completed a twelve hundred mile flight over the Antarctic where they discovered six new islands. In April 1929, Eielson joined the National Guard in Grand Forks, North Dakota, and was promoted to colonel.

Eielson was killed, along with Earl Borland, his mechanic, while attempting to rescue stranded passengers and recover furs aboard the icebound freighter, *Nanuk,* in the Bering Strait off the Siberian coast. Seventy-nine days later, a multinational air and ground effort discovered the wreckage of Eielson's airplane on a small island. It wasn't until February 1930 that both bodies were recovered and returned to the United States for burial.

In 1948, the U.S. Air Force renamed its Mile 26 Airfield, located twenty-six miles southeast of Fairbanks, Alaska, in his honor. A mountain peak near Mount McKinley was also named for Eielson.

Ellington Air Force Base

Location: Houston, Texas
Status: Now, Air National Guard Base
Named for: Lieutenant Eric Lamar Ellington
Date of Birth: 1889
Place of Birth: Olney, Illinois
Date of Death: November 24, 1913
Place of Death: San Diego, California
Place of Burial: Clayton City Cemetery in North Carolina

Lieutenant Eric Lamar Ellington was an ace pilot.

Ellington was appointed to the United States Naval Academy at Annapolis, Maryland, at the age of sixteen and graduated in 1909 seventh in the class. He was assigned to midshipman training duty aboard the battleship USS *California* and was recommended for promotion to ensign but left the navy to accept a commission in the U.S. Army where he was assigned to the 3rd Cavalry at Fort Sam Houston in Texas. Later, he requested a transfer to the aeronautical service and was sent to aviation school at College Park in Maryland. After flight training, he was assigned to the 1st Aero Squadron at Rockwell Field in San Diego, California.

During a training flight in the Wright C Flyer, Ellington and Lieutenant Hugh Kelly lost control of the airplane when the engine broke loose from its mountings. The plane lost altitude and crashed, killing both men. The cause of the crash was never confirmed. The plane was ordered to be burned.*

* In 1913, it was customary to destroy an aircraft when a pilot was killed in a crash. The concern was that if the wreckage were stored at the field, it would have a negative psychological impact on the other pilots.

Ellsworth Air Force Base (formerly, Weaver Air Force Base)

Location: Rapid City, South Dakota
Status: Active
Named for: Brigadier General Richard Elmer Ellsworth
Date of Birth: July 18, 1911
Place of Birth: Erie, Pennsylvania
Date of Death: March 18, 1953
Place of Death: Nut Cove, Newfoundland
Decorations and Honors: Legion of Merit; Distinguished Flying Cross with oak leaf cluster; Air Medal with two oak leaf clusters; Chinese Air Force Wings
Place of Burial: Black Hills National Cemetery in Sturgis, South Dakota

Brigadier General Richard Elmer Ellsworth served in the China-Burma-India theater, flying four hundred combat missions with the Tenth and Fourteenth Air Forces.

Ellsworth graduated from West Point in 1935 and became a pilot after flight training at Randolph and Kelly fields in Texas. In 1942, he became a transport pilot in Alaska.

Among his many assignments were chief of Operations and Training for the Air Weather Service in Washington, D.C.; commander of the 308th Reconnaissance Group at Morrison Field in Florida and Fairfield-Suisun Air Force Base in California; chief of Plans for the Second Air Force at Barksdale Air Force Base in Louisiana; and wing commander of the 28th Strategic Reconnaissance Wing at Rapid City Air Force Base in South Dakota.

Ellsworth lost his life in one of the worst peacetime tragedies when his Convair B-36 Peacemaker and its entire crew of twenty-three crashed in Newfoundland while returning from a routine exercise in Europe. On June 13, 1953, President Dwight D. Eisenhower made a personal visit to dedicate the base in his memory.

Elmendorf Air Force Base

Location: Anchorage, Alaska
Status: Active
Named for: Captain Hugh Merle Elmendorf
Date of Birth: January 3, 1895
Place of Birth: Ithaca, New York
Date of Death: January 13, 1933
Place of Death: Wright Field in Dayton, Ohio
Place of Burial: Arlington National Cemetery, Section 7, Site 10022

Captain Hugh Merle Elmendorf pioneered high altitude formation flying tactics during the 1920s and early 1930s.

Elmendorf graduated from Cornell University in New York in May 1917 with a degree in mechanical engineering. He served as an infantry instructor throughout World War I until he transferred to the Army Air Service where he received flight training at Carlstrom Field in Arcadia, Florida, and earned the rating of Pursuit Pilot on December 7, 1921.

His many duty stations included Ellington Field in Texas; Selfridge Field in Michigan; Wheeler Field and Ford Island in Hawaii; Patterson Field in Ohio; and Bolling Field in Washington, D.C.

He commanded the 19th Pursuit Squadron from 1922 to 1924. In 1927, Elmendorf won the Army Air Corps gunnery competition at Langley Field in Virginia with the highest score recorded at that time. On July 14, 1927, Elmendorf broke his back in a ground collision at Selfridge Field and was hospitalized for months at Walter Reed Army Medical Center in Washington, D.C.

On April 12, 1930, he led nineteen Boeing P-12 pilots of the 95th Pursuit Squadron to set an unofficial world record for altitude formation flying over Mather Field in California. The pilots reached thirty thousand feet, surpassing the previous record of seventeen thousand feet.

Elmendorf was killed while testing a Consolidated Y1P-25. It was believed that high G-forces aggravated his old spinal injury, causing Elmendorf to lose consciousness. He was observed slumped forward and unresponsive in the cockpit. His rear seat observer managed to bail out one hundred feet above the ground, but Elmendorf died in the crash.

He was survived by his wife, Irene, and daughter, Virginia.

England Air Force Base

Location: Alexandria, Louisiana
Status: Closed
Named for: Lieutenant Colonel John B. England
Date of Birth: January 15, 1923
Place of Birth: Caruthersville, Missouri
Date of Death: November 17, 1954
Place of Death: Toul-Rosières Air Base in France
Decorations and Honors: Silver Star; Distinguished Flying Cross with three oak leaf clusters; French Croix de Guerre
Place of Burial: Arlington National Cemetery, Section 6, Site 5810-B

Lieutenant Colonel John B. England was a World War I ace pilot who flew the North American P-51 Mustang in 108 combat missions for a total of 460 combat hours, destroying seventeen German aircraft in the air and four enemy planes on the ground.

England enlisted in the military as a private in April 1942. After attending aviation cadet training, he received a commission and was assigned as a fighter pilot. In November 1943, he served with the 362nd Fighter Squadron, 357th Fighter Group, Eighth Air Force, in Great Britain.

England was killed while attempting to land at the air base after returning from a training flight in his North American F-86 Sabre. Rather than risk hitting the barracks and killing those inside, he turned the plane away and crashed.

Ent Air Force Base

Location: Colorado Springs, Colorado
Status: Closed
Named for: Major General Uzal Girard Ent
Date of Birth: April 3, 1901
Place of Birth: Northumberland, Pennsylvania
Date of Death: March 5, 1948
Place of Death: Denver, Colorado
Decorations and Honors: Distinguished Service Cross; Distinguished Service Medal with oak leaf cluster; Distinguished Flying Cross with oak leaf cluster; Air Medal with oak leaf cluster; Legion of Merit; Commander of the Order of the British Empire (Honorary); Cheney Award; Aviation Cross (Peru); Condor of the Andes (Bolivia)
Date of Retirement: October 31, 1946

Major General Uzal Girard Ent directed and executed the low-level Consolidated B-24 Liberator bombing attack during Operation Tidalwave on the Ploesti oil field complex in Romania in August 1, 1943.

Ent graduated from West Point in June 1924, was commissioned a second lieutenant in the Air Service, and was assigned to Brooks Field in Texas.

Ent's military schooling included Chemical Warfare School, May 1925; Balloon and Airship School, June 1925; Air Corps Advanced Flying School, June 1928 and 1936; School of Navigation, 1929; Air Corps Tactical School, 1937; and Command and General Staff College, 1938.

Among his many assignments were 19th Airship Company in August 1927, returned there as engineer officer in 1929; post inspector at Crissy Field in California in 1930; 2nd Observation Squadron at Nichols Field in Rizal, Philippines; post adjutant at Langley Field in Virginia in 1933; engineer officer of the 18th Reconnaissance Squadron at Mitchel Field in New York; military attaché and air attaché in Lima Peru; chief of staff, U.S. Air Force in 1942; commander, Second Air Force at Peterson Air Force Base in Colorado; and commanding general of the Ninth Air Force. During his career, he flew in more than thirteen air raids.

He received the Cheney Award for his courageous actions during the National Elimination Balloon Race in 1928 in Pennsylvania when he rode the balloon to the ground instead of parachuting from it, staying with the balloon's pilot, Lieutenant Paul Evert, who, unknown to Ent, had been killed by lightning that had struck the balloon.

Ent was awarded the Aviation Cross (1st Class) from Peru, the Condor of the Andes (Officer Grade) from Bolivia, and the Distinguished Service Medal from the United States for his part in peacefully settling a border dispute between Peru and Ecuador when he flew representatives of Peru and Ecuador over the disputed area, asking them what there was below worth going to war over. The two representatives saw the wisdom in Ent's question, and war was averted. He personally selected Colonel Paul Tibbets to lead the Boeing B-29 Superfortress unit that dropped the atomic bomb on Hiroshima.

Ent was paralyzed from the waist down when his North American B-25 Mitchell bomber crashed in October 1944. Afterward, he designed braces for paraplegics that were put into production by General Omar N. Bradley, head of the Veteran's Administration.

Ent died from a leg infection at the age of forty-seven. His ashes were scattered over Northumberland, Pennsylvania, by a North American B-25 Mitchell bomber as his family watched. He was married to Eleanor Marwitz. They had a son, Girard.

Epler Field

Location: Valparaiso, Florida
Status: Auxiliary field number seven at Eglin Air Force Base in Florida
Named for: Colonel Robin Bruce Epler
Date of Birth: June 9, 1908
Place of Birth: Brooklyn, Iowa
Date of Death: January 28, 1944
Place of Death: Eglin Field in Florida
Place of Burial: Arlington National Cemetery, Section 3, Site 1783-A

Colonel Robin Bruce Epler attended Cotner College in Lincoln, Nebraska, from 1926 to 1929 where he earned letters in football, basketball, track, and tennis. He graduated from West Point in 1933 and received pilot training at Randolph and Kelly fields in San Antonio, Texas.

From December 1934 to May 1937, Epler was stationed at France Field in the Panama Canal Zone where he served as squadron officer and pilot. He became an observation aviation instructor at Kelly Field in 1939 and later was transferred to Edgewood Arsenal as chief of the Munitions Development in the Technical Division until September 1942.

After Pearl Harbor, Epler requested transfer to the air force where he was assigned as commander of the Second Army Air Forces Ground Command Detachment. He served there until September 1943. Later, at Eglin Field he was promoted to colonel and became deputy commander of the Technical Army Air Force Proving Ground Command in charge of all flying activities. He died in an airplane crash.

Fairchild Air Force Base

Location: Spokane, Washington
Status: Active
Named for: Major General Muir Stephen Fairchild
Date of Birth: September 2, 1894
Place of Birth: Bellingham, Washington
Date of Death: March 17, 1950
Place of Death: Fort Myer in Virginia
Decorations and Honors: Distinguished Flying Cross; Honorary Doctor of Military Science conferred by Georgetown University; Mackay Trophy (1926)
Place of Burial: Arlington National Cemetery, Section 34, Site 48

Major General Muir Stephen Fairchild was a test pilot and the first director of the Air University at Maxwell Field in Alabama.

Fairchild entered military service with the Washington National Guard as a private in 1916. In January 1918, he was commissioned a second lieutenant in the aviation section of the Signal Officer Reserve Corps. He attended flight school at Berkeley, California, and completed his flight training in France and Italy where he flew night bombing missions over the Rhine River with the French forces in World War I.

After the war, he attended Air Service Engineering School in 1923; Air Corps Engineering School in 1929; Air Corps Tactical School in 1935; Army Industrial College in 1936; and the Army War College in 1937.

A few of his many career assignments included chief, Engines and Plane Maintenance Branch at McCook Field in Ohio from 1923 to 1925; assistant to the Chief of Air Corps from 1941 to 1942; member of the Joint Strategic Survey Committee, Joint Chiefs of Staff from 1942 to 1946; commander of the Air University from 1946 to 1948; and vice chief of staff, USAF, from 1948 to 1950.

In 1926 and 1927, Fairchild flew in the Pan-American Goodwill Flight with Captain Ira Eaker. He became one of the first airmen to receive the Distinguished Flying Cross. He also made the Explorer I balloon flight into the stratosphere in 1933.

Believing that military leaders needed an educational system that would prepare them for future wars, Fairchild proposed the idea of an advanced school for military air officers and worked to establish the Air University. In December 1945, he was selected as the director of the newly formed school that set the standards for Air Force officers' education.

Fairchild authored "Thinking and Planning for the Future," and *The Pegasus*, (June 1948). The main academic building at the United States Air Force Academy is also named in his honor.

Forbes Air Force Base

Location: Topeka, Kansas
Status: Now, Air National Guard Base
Named for: Major Daniel Hugh Forbes, Jr.
Date of Birth: June 6, 1920
Place of Birth: Carbondale, Kansas
Date of Death: June 5, 1948
Place of Death: Muroc Dry Lake, California
Decorations and Honors: Distinguished Flying Cross, posthumously; Air Medal with oak leaf cluster
Place of Burial: Overbrook Cemetery in Overbrook, Kansas

Major Daniel Hugh Forbes, Jr., was a veteran World War II photo reconnaissance pilot and test pilot.

Forbes attended Wichita University and received a degree in business administration from Kansas State College. He enlisted in the military as an army aviation cadet in Wichita on June 5, 1941, and earned his pilot wings and a commission as a second lieutenant.

He began his flying career in January 1942, piloting the Lockheed P-38 Lightning, the Boeing B-17 Flying Fortress, and the Consolidated B-24 Liberator bomber on combat missions from bases in Tunisia, Algiers, India, and Egypt. Returning to the United States, he was assigned to Smokey Hill Air Force Base in Kansas where he trained to fly the Boeing B-29 Superfortress. He was later sent to the Pacific theater and was stationed at Guam and Okinawa as part of the a B-29 Superfortress photo squadron. Following the war, he was assigned to the 509th Bomb Group where he photographed the Bikini Atoll atomic bomb tests.

Forbes received test pilot training at Wright Field in Dayton, Ohio, and was assigned to Muroc Air Force Base in California as a project test pilot for the Northrop YB-49 Flying Wing bomber prototype. He was killed, along with Captain Glen Walter Edwards, Lieutenant Edward Lee Swindell, Clare C. Lesser, and Charles H. LaFountain while flight testing the YB-49. He was married to Hazel Moog of Defiance, Ohio.

Foster Air Force Base

Location: Victoria, Texas
Status: Closed
Named for: Lieutenant Arthur Lee Foster
Date of Birth: November 25, 1887
Place of Birth: Weir, Texas
Date of Death: February 10, 1925
Place of Death: Brooks Field in San Antonio, Texas
Place of Burial: Odd Fellows Cemetery in Georgetown, Texas

Lieutenant Arthur Lee Foster was an Army Air Corps instructor killed in an airplane crash during a training mission.

Before joining the service in 1917, Foster was a Mason and member of the Blue Lodge in San Antonio. He was also a member of the Shrines of Colon in Panama and the Knights Templar in Riverside, California. He belonged to the Methodist church and attended the University of Texas at Austin. He was married to Ruth Young.

★★★

Francis E. Warren Air Force Base (formerly, Fort Francis E. Warren)

Location: Cheyenne, Wyoming
Status: Active
Named for: Captain and Senator Francis Emory Warren
Date of Birth: June 20, 1844
Place of Birth: Hinsdale, Massachusetts
Date of Death: November 24, 1929
Place of Death: Washington, D.C.
Decorations and Honors: Medal of Honor
Place of Burial: Lakeview Cemetery in Cheyenne, Wyoming

Senator Francis Emory Warren was a veteran of the Civil War. He was also a landowner, banker, rancher, the last Territorial governor of Wyoming, first Statehood governor, and first United States senator of Wyoming.

Warren served with Company C, 49th Massachusetts Volunteer Infantry, during the Civil War and later was a captain in the Massachusetts militia. He traveled to Wyoming after the war and helped found the city of Cheyenne in 1873.

During his long career he served as president of the Territorial Senate from 1873 to 1874; treasurer of Wyoming in 1876, 1879, 1882, and 1884; member of the Territorial Senate from 1884 to 1885; mayor of Cheyenne 1885; elected as the first governor of Wyoming in September 1890, but resigned in November 1890 after being elected senator; elected as a Republican to the U.S. Senate on November 18, 1890, serving until March 4, 1893; re-elected to the U.S. Senate in 1895, 1901, 1907, 1913, 1918, and 1924, serving until his death. As chairman of the Senate Appropriations Committee for twelve years, he helped supervise the expenditure of some forty billion dollars of public funds.

He served in the Senate for thirty-seven years and one month before succumbing to bronchial pneumonia. His son-in-law, General John J. Pershing, was at his bedside. His funeral services were held in the Chamber of the U.S. Senate. At age eighty-five, he was the Senate's oldest member and its last Civil War veteran.

His Medal of Honor citation for action at the siege of Port Hudson during the Civil War at the age of nineteen reads as follows:

Volunteered in response to a call, and took part in the movement that was made upon the enemy's works under a heavy fire there from in advance of the general assault.

Gary Air Force Base (formerly, Camp Gary)

Located: San Marcos, Texas
Status: Now, San Marcos Airport
Named for: Second Lieutenant Arthur Edward "Tex" Gary
Date of Birth: January 24, 1918
Place of Birth: San Marcos, Texas
Date of Death: December 7, 1941
Place of Death: Clark Field in the Philippines
Place of Burial: San Marcos City Cemetery in San Marcos, Texas

Second Lieutenant Arthur Edward Gary was the first San Marcos resident and "Aggie" killed in World War II when the Japanese attacked Clark Field.

Gary attended Southwest Texas State College and then transferred to Texas A&M University where he received a bachelor of science degree. He joined the Air Corps in February 1940 and earned his pilot wings at Kelly Field in Texas where he trained as a copilot on the Boeing B-17 Flying Fortress bomber.

According to accounts made by Frank Kurtz, Gary's pilot, Gary was preparing for a mission to Formosa when the first bombs hit Clark Field. Gary was attempting to lead his crew to safety when a bomb exploded, killing him and the crew. A street in San Marcos is also named in his honor.

Geiger Air Force Base

Location: Spokane, Washington
Status: Now, Spokane International Airport
Named for: Major Harold C. Geiger
Date of Birth: October 7, 1884
Place of Birth: East Orange, New Jersey
Date of Death: May 17, 1927
Place of Death: Olmsted Field in Middletown, Pennsylvania
Place of Burial: Arlington National Cemetery, Section 4, Site 3181

Major Harold C. Geiger was a pioneer in army aviation and ballooning.

Geiger was a 1908 graduate of West Point and was assigned to the Coast Artillery Corps after graduation. He served in France and was attached to the ambassador's staff in Berlin.

He was a strong supporter of the dirigible and, while in Germany, he urged the chief of the Army Air Service to purchase the dirigible, *Los Angeles*, then the ZR-3, for the army. Later, he was aboard the ZR-3 on its transatlantic flight.

On May 10, 1926, he collided in midair with Horace M. Hickam, a fellow student, and had to parachute to safety, making him a member of the "Caterpillar Club," a fraternal order of pilots who survived an emergency parachute jump.

Geiger was killed when his British de Havilland DH-4 plunged to the ground and burst into flames. He was survived by his wife, the former Frances Bridges, and two small children.

George Air Force Base

Location: Victorville, California
Status: Closed
Named for: Brigadier General Harold Huston George
Date of Birth: July 19, 1893
Place of Birth: Lockport, New York
Date of Death: April 29, 1942
Place of Death: Darwin, Australia
Decorations and Honors: Distinguished Service Cross; Distinguished Service Medal
Place of Burial: Arlington National Cemetery, Section 9, Site 5952

Brigadier General Harold Huston George was a World War I ace pilot.

George enlisted in the New York National Guard's 3rd Infantry in 1916, completed flight training, and was commissioned a first lieutenant in the Signal Corps' aviation section.

In October 1917, after additional training at Kelly Field in Texas, he was sent to Tours, France, where he served as commanding officer of the 201st Aero Squadron. In August 1918, he saw combat with the 185th Aero Squadron where he shot down five German planes to become an ace pilot. George later served with the 139th Aero squadron, 4th Pursuit Group, in Europe, and from November 1919 to March 1922, he served as flight commander and commanding officer of the 19th Pursuit Squadron at March Field in California.

His other duty assignments included air officer of the 104th Division at Fort Douglas in Utah, commanding officer of the 43rd School Squadron at Kelly Field in Texas, operations officer and commanding officer of the 24th and 7th Squadrons in Panama, commanding officer of the 8th Pursuit Group, and intelligence and operations officer of the 33rd Squadron at Langley Field in Virginia.

In 1937, he graduated from the Air Corps Tactical School at Maxwell Field in Alabama and from the Command and General Staff College at Fort Leavenworth in Kansas in 1938. In May 1941, he was assigned to the Philippines as commander of all air units and was a member of General Douglas MacArthur's staff where he directed air operations.

George lost his life when a pursuit plane crashed into the plane he was boarding. He was married to Vera Cline. An airfield in Lawrenceville, Illinois, was also named in his honor.

His Distinguished Service Cross citation for action near Bantheville, France, on October 27, 1918, reads as follows:

Lieutenant George displayed great courage in attacking a formation of four enemy planes (Fokker type), destroying two of them in a terrific fight and driving the other two back to their own territory.

George Wright Air Force Base (see Fort George Wright)

Goodfellow Air Force Base

Location: San Angelo, Texas
Status: Active
Named for: Lieutenant John James Goodfellow, Jr.
Date of Birth: May 17, 1895
Place of Birth: Fort Worth, Texas
Date of Death: September 17, 1918
Place of Death: Thiaucourt, France
Place of Burial: Saint Mihiel American Military Cemetery and Memorial in Thiaucourt, France

Lieutenant John James Goodfellow, Jr., served during World War I.

Goodfellow graduated from San Angelo High School in 1913 and attended the University of Texas to study civil engineering. He left school when World War I began and joined the military, and became an infantry officer. With an interest in aviation, he requested reassignment to the Air Corps. After graduating from ground and flight school, Goodfellow was commissioned a second lieutenant in February 1918 and was sent to England where he was an observation pilot with the 24th Aero Squadron. He was transferred to France and, in August 1918, he was attached to the First Army Observation Group at Gondreville.

Goodfellow and his observer, First Lieutenant Elliot M. Durant, Jr., were killed when their Salmson 2A-2 aircraft was shot down during a dogfight. Goodfellow's remains were recovered from the plane three days later.

Gray Air Force Base (see Gray Army Airfield)

Grenier Air Force Base

Location: Manchester, New Hampshire
Status: Closed
Named for: Second Lieutenant Jean Donat Grenier
Date of Birth: 1909
Place of Birth: Manchester, New Hampshire
Date of Death: February 16, 1934
Place of Death: Utah

Second Lieutenant Jean Donat Grenier was an Army Air Corps aviator with the Air Corps Mail Service.
    Grenier graduated from the University of New Hampshire in 1930. When President Franklin D. Roosevelt cancelled airmail contracts with the commercial airlines, inexperienced military pilots were assigned the task of delivering mail often in hazardous weather conditions. Flights and maintenance were often done in subzero weather, causing many in-flight emergencies and accidents. It was during one of these route-familiarization flights over the Rocky Mountains that Grenier lost his life when his Curtiss A-12 Shrike plane crashed during a storm.

Griffiss Air Force Base

Location: Rome, New York
Status: Closed
Named for: Lieutenant Colonel Townsend E. Griffiss
Date of Birth: April 4, 1900
Place of Birth: Buffalo, New York
Date of Death: February 15, 1942
Place of Death: Off the southwest coast of England
Decorations and Honors: Distinguished Service Medal; French Legion of Honor
Place of Burial: Memorialized at the Cambridge American Cemetery and Memorial in Cambridge, England

Lieutenant Colonel Townsend E. Griffiss was the first American airman to die in the line of duty in Europe during World War II.
    Griffiss graduated from West Point in June 1922. After flight training at Brooks and Kelly fields in Texas, he received his pilot wings and, in May 1925, he was transferred to Hawaii where he served with the 19th Pursuit Squadron. In June 1928, he was assigned to March Field in California as an instructor and commandant of cadets.

In September 1933, he was transferred to Bolling Field in Washington, D.C., as commanding officer of the Air Corps Detachment there. In August 1935, he was assigned as the assistant military attaché in France and Spain and was later assigned to Germany. After returning to the United States in May 1939, he attended the Air Corps Tactical School at Maxwell Field in Alabama.

In March 1940, Griffiss was assigned to the War Department and was promoted to major. As a member of a special Army Observers Group, Griffiss left for London in May 1941 to investigate the efficiency of foreign aircraft used on ferry routes for the shipment of aircraft from England to Russia. While returning from Russia, the aircraft in which he was flying was mistaken for an enemy aircraft and shot down by two Royal Air Force pilots.

Busy Park military installation in England was also named Camp Griffiss in his honor.

Grissom Air Force Base (formerly, Bunker Hill Air Force Base)

Location: Kokomo, Indiana
Status: Now, Air Reserve Base
Named for: Lieutenant Colonel Virgil "Gus" Ivan Grissom
Date of Birth: April 3, 1926
Place of Birth: Mitchell, Indiana
Date of Death: January 27, 1967
Place of Death: Kennedy Space Center in Florida
Decorations and Honors: Congressional Space Medal of Honor, posthumously; Distinguished Flying Cross; Air Medal with oak leaf cluster for Korean service; two NASA Distinguished Service Medals; NASA Exceptional Service Medal; inducted into the National Aviation Hall of Fame (1987); Honorary Doctorate, Florida Institute of Technology
Place of Burial: Arlington National Cemetery, Section 3, Lot 2503-E

Lieutenant Colonel Virgil Ivan Grissom was the second American in space.

Grissom graduated from Purdue University with a bachelor of science degree in mechanical engineering. He received his pilot wings in March 1951 and served with the 75th Fighter Squadron at Presque Isle Air Force Base in Maine as a fighter pilot. He completed one hundred combat missions in Korea, flying a North American F-86 Sabre with the 334th Fighter Interceptor Squadron.

In 1952, he became a flight instructor at Bryan, Texas, and in August 1955, he attended the Air Force Institute of Technology at Wright-Patterson Air Force Base in Ohio to study aeronautical engineering. In October 1956, he attended the Test Pilot School at Edwards Air Force Base in California, and in May

1957, he became a test pilot assigned to the 56th Fighter Interceptor Squadron at Wright-Patterson Air Force Base.

On April 9, 1959, the National Aeronautics and Space Administration (NASA) selected Grissom as an astronaut, assigned to the manual and automatic control systems. His first mission was aboard Mercury/Redstone-4, named the *Liberty Bell 7* in which he achieved an altitude of 126 miles into space. After supporting the Gemini 6 mission, he was assigned as command pilot aboard the first manned Apollo mission, *Apollo 1*.

He was killed, along with senior pilot, Lieutenant Colonel Edward White, and pilot, Lieutenant Commander Roger Chaffee, while conducting a test on the launch pad when a fire swept through their *Apollo 1* command module.

He was married to Betty Moore and had two children.

Hamilton Air Force Base

Location: San Rafael, California
Status: Closed
Named for: First Lieutenant Lloyd Andrews Hamilton
Date of Birth: June 13, 1894
Place of Birth: Troy, New York
Date of Death: August 24, 1918
Place of Death: Lagnicourt, France
Decorations and Honors: Distinguished Service Cross; Distinguished Flying Cross

First Lieutenant Lloyd Andrews Hamilton flew with the Royal Flying Corps and was an ace pilot.

Hamilton received a bachelor of arts degree from Syracuse University in 1916. He also attended Harvard University before entering military service. He served with the U.S. Air Service, 17th Aero Squadron, where he achieved ten aerial victories, earning him the status of an air ace. He was killed when his Sopwith Camel was shot down while leading a low-level bombing attack against German observation balloons.

His Distinguished Flying Cross citation reads as follows:

On August 13, 1918, Lieutenant Hamilton led his flight on a special mission against Varssenaere [now Varsenare] aerodrome. He dropped four bombs from 200 feet on some aeroplane hangars, making two direct hits and causing a large amount of damage. He then machine gunned the German officers' billets and made four circuits of the aerodrome, shooting up various targets. On the first circuit, he destroyed one EA on the ground, which burst into flames when he shot it up. On the third circuit, he repeated this performance, setting afire another Fokker biplane. His dash and skill very materially helped in the success of the operation. In addition, this officer destroyed a Fokker biplane over Armentieres on August 7, 1918. On July 12, he brought down two EA in flames, and on two other occasions has driven down out of control enemy machines. He is an excellent patrol leader.

His Distinguished Service Cross citation reads as follows:

For extraordinary heroism in action at Varssenaere, Belgium, August 13, 1918. Leading a low-bombing attack on a German aerodrome 30 miles behind the lines, Lieutenant Hamilton destroyed the hangars on the north side of the aerodrome and then attacked a row of enemy machines, flying as low as twenty feet from the ground, despite intense machine gun fire, and setting fire to three of the German planes. He then turned and fired bursts through the windows of the chateau in which the German pilots were quartered, twenty-six of whom were afterwards reported killed.

Hancock Air Force Base

Location: Syracuse, New York
Status: Closed
Named for: Captain and Congressman Clarence Eugene Hancock
Date of Birth: February 13, 1885
Place of Birth: Syracuse, New York
Date of Death: January 3, 1948
Place of Death: Washington, D.C.
Place of Burial: Woodlawn Cemetery in Syracuse, New York

Clarence Eugene Hancock served in the U.S. Army during World War I.

Hancock graduated from Wesleyan University in Middletown, Connecticut, in 1906 and from New York Law School in 1908. He was admitted to the bar that same year and began law practice in Syracuse, New York.

During World War I, he was a sergeant in the 1st New York Cavalry and served on the Mexican border. He also served overseas as a captain with the 104th Machine Gun Battalion, 27th Division.

Hancock became the corporation counsel of Syracuse from 1926 to 1927, was a trustee of Wesleyan University and was elected as a Republican to the Seventieth Congress on November 8, 1927, to fill the vacancy caused by the death of Walter W. Magee.

Hancock was an alternate delegate to the Republican National Convention from New York in 1928. He was reelected to the Seventy-first Congress and to the eight succeeding Congresses, serving until January 3, 1947.

★★★

Hanscom Air Force Base

Location: Bedford, Massachusetts
Status: Active
Named for: Laurence Gerard Hanscom, civilian
Date of Birth: August 20, 1906
Place of Birth: No Data Found
Date of Death: February 9, 1941
Place of Death: Saugus, Massachusetts
Place of Burial: Wildwood Cemetery in Wilmington, Massachusetts

Laurence Gerard Hanscom was the Massachusetts State House reporter for the *Worcester Telegram-Gazette* and the *Evening Gazette*, and the founder of the Massachusetts Wing of the Civil Air Reserve.

Hanscom received his pilot license in 1929, achieved more than three thousand hours flying time, and acquired the reputation of being a tireless supporter of aviation. He photographed and reported on the 1938 floods resulting from a hurricane that swept the East Coast.

Unable to join the Air Corps because of his age, Hanscom applied for service with the Royal Canadian Air Force. He was accepted, but never got to serve. He was killed when his Fleet biplane crashed while giving private flying lessons. Hanscom had been flying acrobatic maneuvers at an altitude above fifteen hundred feet over a sparsely populated area when the plane crashed following a series of loops. It was reported that at the top of its final loop, the plane fell into a tailspin. The plane appeared to level out, but instead of straightening out, it went into a power dive and crashed. Hanscom was lobbying for the establishment of the airport at Bedford at the time of this death.

One month before his accident, Hanscom had been inducted into "The Quiet Birdmen," an organization for those who flew many hours, contributing to aviation without bragging about it.

Harmon Air Force Base

Located: Guam
Status: Closed
Named for: Lieutenant General Millard Fillmore Harmon
Date of Birth: January 19, 1888
Place of Birth: Fort Mason, California
Date of Death: February 26, 1945 (declared dead February 25, 1946)
Place of Death: Lost at sea near the Marshall Islands
Decorations and Honors: French Croix de Guerre

Lieutenant General Millard Fillmore Harmon was the commanding general of the South Pacific during World War II.

Harmon graduated from West Point in 1912, was commissioned in the infantry, and later served with the 28th and 9th Infantry Regiments. While serving in the Philippines, he was assigned to the aviation section on the Signal Corps. Prior to the United States entering World War I, Harmon was sent to France where he attended aviation school in Paris. He served at the Allied and American headquarters, and later was assigned to the French 13th Group de Combat as a pilot and fought in the Somme defensive.

After the war, Harmon graduated from the Command and General Staff College and the Army War College, and taught military science and tactics at the University of Washington in Seattle.

In April 1921, he served as a member of the Advisory Board of the Air Service. In August 1927, Harmon became base commander and commandant of the flying school at March Field in California and served there until 1930. He also was the commander of Barksdale Field (now, Air Force Base) in Shreveport, Louisiana, and the 20th Pursuit Group for four years.

In 1936, he was assigned to Hawaii to command Luke Field and the 5th Bombardment Group. In 1938, he became assistant commandant of the Air Corps Tactical School at Maxwell Field in Alabama. From January to April 1941, Harmon served as a member of the Harriman Mission in England. He also served as commanding general of the Interceptor Command of the Fourth Air Force; commander of the Second Air Force; acting commanding general of the Air Force Combat Command; and chief of the Air Staff, Army Air Forces.

From July 1942 until his death, he served as commanding general of U.S. Army Forces in the South Pacific; commander of the Army Air Forces in the Pacific Ocean areas; and deputy commander of the Twentieth Air Force where, under his command, Boeing B-29 Superfortress bombers bombed Japan. Harmon, along with Brigadier General James Andersen, chief of staff of the U.S. Air Force, died when his Consolidated B-24 Liberator fell into the ocean while en route to Hawaii. An eighteen-day search of the ocean failed to locate the downed plane and his body was never found.

Harmon Air Force Base

Location: Stephenville, Newfoundland
Status: Closed
Named for: Captain Ernest Emery Harmon
Date of Birth: February 8, 1893
Place of Birth: Dallas, Texas
Date of Death: August 27, 1933
Place of Death: Near Stamford, Connecticut

Decorations and Honors: Detroit News Trophy
Place of Burial: Arlington National Cemetery, Section 4, Site 2788

Captain Ernest Emery Harmon flew the Martin B-10 Bomber "Round-the-Rim"* flight.

Harmon attended Bethany College in West Virginia and George Washington University in Washington, D.C.

Harmon enlisted in the aviation section of the Signal Corps Reserve in 1917. From there he was sent to Austin, Texas, for flight training and was commissioned a second lieutenant in the regular army on April 5, 1918.

Harmon received the Detroit News Trophy at the International Air Races for flying the Huff-Daland light bomber at an average speed of 119.19 miles per hour. He was killed when his Douglas 0-25C observation plane ran out of fuel and crashed while making a test flight from Washington, D.C., en route to Mitchel Field in New York.

* The Round the Rim flight began at Bolling Field in Washington, D.C., on July 24, 1919, and returned to Bolling Field on November 9, 1919, during which time the army bomber flew over every border and coastal state starting westward across the northern states, down the Pacific Coast, and eastward along the Mexican border and across the southern states, for a total distance of approximately ten thousand miles in 114 hours, 45 minutes.

Hickam Air Force Base

Location: Honolulu, Hawaii
Status: Active
Named for: Lieutenant Colonel Horace Meek Hickam
Date of Birth: August 14, 1885
Place of Birth: Spencer, Indiana
Date of Death: November 5, 1934
Place of Death: Fort Crockett in Galveston, Texas
Decorations and Honors: Silver Star
Place of Burial: Arlington National Cemetery, Section 6, Site 5003

Lieutenant Colonel Horace Meek Hickam was a pioneer Air Service aviator and advocate of air power.

Hickam graduated from West Point in 1908. His early assignments included serving with the 11th Cavalry in Vermont; 8th Cavalry in the Philippines; and with General John J. Pershing in the 7th Cavalry. He saw combat on April 22, 1916, in a fight with Cervantes, one of Pancho Villa's famous bandits, and his band of Villistas at Tomochic, Mexico.

Hickam was a professor of military science and tactics at the University of Maine from 1916 to 1917. He qualified as a Junior Military Aviator in 1918 after receiving flight training at Rockwell Field in San Diego, California. He was assigned to Dorr Field in Florida for gunnery training and pursuit flight training. He later became the commander there. In January 1919, he was appointed chief of the Information Division, Office of the Director of Air Service, in Washington, D.C., where he established the Air Corps Newsletter, writing about the history of the Air Corps. In 1923, he was assigned as the assistant commandant of the Advanced Flying School at Kelly Field in Texas.

As a strong proponent of air power, Hickam testified before the Morrow Board in 1925 to investigate the formation of an independent Air Service. On May 10, 1926, while attending the Air Corps Tactical School at Langley Field in Virginia, he collided in midair with Harold C. Geiger, a fellow student, and had to parachute to safety, making him a member of the Caterpillar Club, a fraternal order of pilots who survived an emergency parachute jump.

In 1928, he graduated from the Air Command and Staff College, the Army War College, and the Air Corps Tactical School. He was assigned to the War Plans Division, War Department General Staff, and later became commander of the 3rd Attack Group at Fort Crockett in Galveston, Texas.

Hickam was killed while practicing night landings on an unlighted runway when his Curtiss A-12 Shrike hit an embankment and flipped over. He was survived by his wife, Helen, and two children.

Hill Air Force Base

Location: Ogden, Utah
Status: Active
Named for: Major Ployer Peter Hill
Date of Birth: October 24, 1894
Place of Birth: Newburyport, Massachusetts
Date of Death: October 30, 1935
Place of Death: Wright Field in Dayton, Ohio
Place of Burial: Newburyport, Massachusetts

Major Ployer Peter Hill was a test pilot.

Hill graduated from Brown University in 1916 with a bachelor of science degree in civil engineering. He enlisted in the aviation section of the U.S. Army Signal Enlisted Reserve Corps in 1917, received his pilot wings in 1918, and was commissioned a second lieutenant in the regular army where he served as a flight instructor.

During his career that spanned seventeen years, from 1918 to 1935, Hill served in the office of the chief of the Air Corps in Washington, D.C.; was assigned to the engineer office of the Air Service Flying Station in Weissenthurm, Germany; served with the 12th Aero Squadron at Fort Bliss in El Paso, Texas; worked in the Training and War Plans Division under the chief of the Air Service in Washington, D.C.; was appointed commanding officer of the 14th Photo Section at Mitchel Field in New York; was the commanding officer of the 6th Photo Section at Nichols Field in Manila; and was assigned as the chief of the Flying Branch of the Materiel Division at Wright Field in Dayton, Ohio, where he flight tested and evaluated new military aircraft designs of the Consolidated P-30, the Martin B-10 and B-12 bombers. He piloted nearly sixty of the Army Air Corps' aircraft, testing and evaluating their capabilities for service.

Hill died from injuries received in the crash of the Boeing experimental aircraft Model 299, the prototype of what would later become the famous Boeing B-17 Flying Fortress.

Holloman Air Force Base

Location: Alamogordo, New Mexico
Status: Active
Named for: Colonel George Vernon Holloman
Date of Birth: September 17, 1902
Place of Birth: Rich Square, Virginia
Date of Death: March 19, 1946
Place of Death: Northern Formosa (now, Taiwan)
Decorations and Honors: Distinguished Flying Cross; Mackay Trophy (1937)
Place of Burial: Arlington National Cemetery, Section 12, Site 5399

Colonel George Vernon Holloman was a guided missile pioneer and an expert in aircraft navigational equipment.

Holloman graduated from North Carolina State University, earning a bachelor of science degree in electrical engineering. He entered the service as a second lieutenant in the infantry, then transferred to the Army Air Force in 1927 where he developed the automatic landing gear for aircraft.

In 1944, he successfully duplicated the German buzz-bomb. He also developed the air position indicator, the McDonnell-Douglas F-4 Phantom II airspeed indicator, and the high intensity runway markers for the Boeing B-29 Superfortress.

He was the chief of the equipment laboratory in the Air Technical Service Command at Wright Field in Ohio. Holloman was killed in the crash of a Boeing B-17 Flying Fortress bomber while en route from Shanghai to Nichols Field in Formosa where he was serving as deputy chief of staff of the Twentieth Air Force of Guam at the time.

His gravestone is engraved with a special saying he frequently used, "Life Jest Caint Be Simple Ennymore, They's Too Many Gadgets!"

He was married to Dorothy Darling of Kenilworth, Illinois.

Hunter Air Force Base (see Hunter Army Airfield)

Hurlburt Field

Location: Valparaiso, Florida
Status: Auxiliary field number nine at Eglin Air Force Base in Florida
Named for: First Lieutenant Donald Wilson Hurlburt
Date of Birth: June 16, 1919
Place of Birth: Harmony in Chautauqua County, New York
Date of Death: October 1, 1943
Place of Death: Eglin Air Force Base
Decorations and Honors: Distinguished Flying Cross; Air Medal with three oak leaf clusters; World War II Victory Medal; American Defense Service Medal; European-African-Middle Eastern Campaign Medal with bronze star for participation in Air Offensive Europe Campaign

First Lieutenant Donald Wilson Hurlburt enlisted in the U.S. Army in August 1941 and, after basic training, he was assigned as an aviation cadet in the Preflight Training School at Maxwell Field in Alabama.

In 1942, he attended Advanced Flying School at Moody Field in Georgia. That same year he was commissioned a second lieutenant and assigned as a pilot with the 358th Bomb Group at Alamogordo Army Air Base in New Mexico. In October, he was transferred to the 258th Bomb Squadron, 303rd Bomb Group, in Europe. Additional duties took him to Headquarters, First Air Force, at Mitchel Field in New York and to the 1st Proving Ground Electronics Unit at Eglin Field in Valparaiso, Florida.

Hurlburt died from injuries sustained when the aircraft he was piloting crashed upon takeoff during a local training mission.

Johnson Air Base

Location: Iruma, Japan
Status: Closed
Named for: Colonel Gerald Richard Johnson (not to be confused with Gerald W. Johnson)

Date of Birth: June 1920
Place of Birth: Kenmore, Ohio
Date of Death: October 7, 1945
Place of Death: Tokyo Bay, Japan
Decorations and Honors: Distinguished Service Cross with oak leaf cluster; Silver Star; Legion of Merit; Distinguished Flying Cross with five oak leaf clusters; Air Medal

Colonel Gerald Richard Johnson was an ace pilot who, at the age of twenty-five, was the youngest full colonel in the Army Air Force.

Johnson joined the service in 1941 and completed flight training in May of 1942. His first assignment was with the 54th Fighter Group in Alaska where he piloted the Bell P-39 Airacobra and the Curtiss P-40 Warhawk. During his career, he flew 265 combat missions and was credited with shooting down twenty-two enemy planes while flying a Lockheed P-38 Lightning. In July 1943, he was transferred to the 49th Fighter Group in the Pacific, and in August, he was placed in command of the 9th Fighter Squadron, the "Flying Knights," with the additional duties of deputy group commander of the 49th Fighter Group.

Johnson was killed while piloting a North American B-25 Mitchell bomber when he flew into a typhoon, lost radio control, and became lost. With fuel running low, he ordered everyone to bail out, but one person neglected to bring a parachute. Johnson gave his parachute to the passenger and tried to fly the B-25 back to safety. Johnson's copilot also elected to stay behind to help Johnson. Tragically, both were lost and disappeared without a trace.

Johnson Air Base was the only active U.S. air base in Japan named after an American military hero.

K. I. Sawyer Air Force Base

Location: Marquette, Michigan
Status: Closed
Named for: Kenneth Ingalls Sawyer, civilian
Date of Birth: November 30, 1884
Place of Birth: Menominee, Michigan
Date of Death: January 12, 1944
Place of Death: Ishpeming, Michigan
Place of Burial: Ishpeming Cemetery in Michigan

Kenneth Ingalls Sawyer served as mayor of Ishpeming, Michigan, and was a county road commissioner.

Sawyer graduated from the University of Michigan with a bachelor of science degree in civil engineering in 1907. In 1916, he became the engineer and superintendent of the county highway department in Marquette County where he drafted Michigan's first state gas and weight tax laws.

In 1917, he placed what is believed to be the first highway centerline on a stretch of rural road on old U.S. Highway 41 in Marquette County known as "Dead Man's Curve." He also was credited for introducing bituminous surface treatments to the roads and for setting picnic tables on roadsides, creating the first roadside parks.

Sawyer was a founder and secretary treasurer for the County Road Association of Michigan. He served for eight years as president of the Upper Peninsula Road Builders Association.

Keesler Air Force Base

Location: Biloxi, Mississippi
Status: Active
Named for: Second Lieutenant Samuel Reeves Keesler, Jr.
Date of Birth: April 11, 1896
Place of Birth: Greenwood, Mississippi
Date of Death: October 10, 1918
Place of Death: Verdun, France
Decorations and Honors: Distinguished Service Cross, posthumously
Place of Burial: Saint Mihiel American Military Cemetery and Memorial in
    Thiaucourt, France, Plot C, Row 13

Second Lieutenant Samuel Reeves Keesler, Jr., was a World War I aerial observer.

Keesler attended Davidson College in North Carolina. He joined the U.S. Army on May 13, 1917, and was commissioned in August. He received training as an aerial observer at Fort Sill in Oklahoma and was transferred to France in March 1918. He received additional training in aerial gunnery and artillery fire control before being assigned to the 24th Aero Squadron in the Verdun sector of the Western Front on August 26, 1918.

Keesler, along with his pilot, First Lieutenant Harold W. Riley, was killed while flying on a reconnaissance mission when his British Sopwith Camel was attacked and shot down by four German Fokkers. Keesler was shot six times before the plane crashed. He was shot several more times when the enemy fighters strafed them on the ground. Captured by German ground troops, the two airmen were unable to receive immediate medical attention.

★★★

Kelly Air Force Base

Location: San Antonio, Texas
Status: Now, privatized
Named for: Lieutenant George Edward Maurice Kelly
Date of Birth: December 14, 1878
Place of Birth: London, England
Date of Death: May 10, 1911
Place of Death: Fort Sam Houston in San Antonio, Texas
Place of Burial: San Antonio National Cemetery in San Antonio, Texas, Section A, Grave 117

Lieutenant George Edward Maurice Kelly holds the unfortunate title of being the first American military aviator to die in the crash of a military aircraft.

Kelly's family immigrated to America and settled in Great Falls, Montana, in 1886. Kelly became an American citizen, joined the U.S. Army as an officer, and was assigned to the 30th Infantry. He was sent to the Philippines in July 1907 where he worked making a topographical survey of Luzon.

While attached to an aviation battalion at Selfridge Field in Michigan, he took aerial photographs from a balloon during an aviation meet. In February 1911, Kelly received pilot training at the Glenn Curtiss Flying School in San Diego, California. In April of that year, he was assigned to Fort Sam Houston.

Kelly was killed while attempting to land his Curtiss Type-4 Pusher (term used when the engines on a propeller aircraft sit behind the wing or on the tail of the fuselage) when a front wing strut collapsed. Apparently realizing that his plane would crash into the tents of the 11th Infantry encampment, he turned his disabled plane away and hit the ground.

Kincheloe Air Force Base

Location: Sault Ste. Marie, Michigan
Status: Closed
Named for: Captain Iven Carl Kincheloe, Jr.
Date of Birth: July 2, 1928
Place of Birth: Detroit, Michigan
Date of Death: July 26, 1958
Place of Death: Mojave Desert near Edwards Air Force Base in California
Decorations and Honors: Silver Star; Distinguished Flying Cross with oak leaf cluster; Air Medal with two oak leaf clusters; Mackay Trophy (1956); inducted into the Michigan Aviation Hall of Fame in Kalamazoo, Michigan; Schelling Award, posthumously
Place of Burial: Arlington National Cemetery, Section 2, Lot 4872

Captain Iven Carl Kincheloe, Jr., was a Korean War ace pilot and a test pilot of the Bell X-2.

Kincheloe graduated from Purdue University in Lafayette, Indiana, in 1949 with a bachelor of science degree in aeronautical engineering. He received his commission through the Reserve Officers' Training Corps program and earned his pilot wings at Perrin Air Force Base in Texas in 1950.

His first overseas assignment was in Korea with the 25th Fighter-Interceptor Squadron where he completed 101 missions in a North American F-86 Sabre and thirty missions in the Lockheed F-80 Shooting Star, and, where he became a jet ace pilot after downing more than ten enemy planes. From 1952 to 1953, he served as an instructor in the gunnery school at Nellis Air Force Base in Nevada; and in 1954, he completed the course in the School of Aeronautics, Empire Test Pilot School in Farnborough, England.

Kincheloe entered the Air Force Fight Test Center at Edwards Air Force Base in California in 1955 and participated in testing the North American F-100 Super Sabre, the McDonnell F-101 Voodoo, the Convair F-102 Delta Dagger, the Lockheed F-104 Starfighter, the Republic F-105 Thunderchief, and the Convair F-106 Delta Dart.

On September 7, 1956, Kincheloe flew the Bell X-2 rocket-powered research craft at more than fifteen hundred miles per hour and attained a world's altitude record of 126,000 feet on September 7, 1956, and was hailed as "The first of the spacemen."

The Society of Experimental Test Pilots established the Kincheloe Trophy in his honor. Neil Armstrong and his fellow *Apollo 11* astronauts, Colonel Edwin "Buzz" Aldrin and Major General Michael Collins, are among the recipients of the award.

Kincheloe died after ejecting from of a F-104 Starfighter at a low altitude when the plane's engine quit. His parachute failed to open and he plunged to his death.

Kindley Air Force Base

Located: Bermuda
Status: Now, Bermuda International Airport
Named for: Captain Field Eugene Kindley
Date of Birth: March 13, 1896
Place of Birth: Pea Ridge, Arkansas
Date of Death: February 1, 1920
Place of Death: Kelly Field, in San Antonio, Texas
Decorations and Honors: Distinguished Service Cross with oak leaf cluster; Distinguished Flying Cross; British Distinguished Flying Cross with oak leaf cluster

Place of Burial: Hillcrest Cemetery in Gravette, Arkansas

Captain Field Eugene Kindley was a World War I ace pilot with twelve air victories.

Prior to joining the Kansas National Guard in May 1917, Kindley worked as a motion picture operator in Coffeyville, Kansas. After transferring to the U.S. Army's Signal Corps, he attended the School of Military Aeronautics at the University of Illinois and was sent to England for advanced flight training at Oxford. There, he was assigned to the 65th Squadron of the Royal Air Force on May 22, 1918, where he scored his first victory on June 26, 1918. In January 1920, he was assigned to the 148th Pursuit Squadron as a flight commander and took command of the 94th Pursuit Squadron at Kelly Field in Texas.

Kindley was killed while rehearsing for a simulated bombing run for the visiting General John J. Pershing. Seeing a group of men on the flight line, he attempted to avoid hitting them by pulling up the nose of the plane. In the process, the engine of his British SE-5 stalled, the wing wires broke, and the plane crashed.

In additional to the air base in Bermuda, the high school in Coffeyville, Kansas, the Memorial Park in Gravette, Arkansas, and an airfield at Fort Mills on Corregidor Island in the Philippines were all named in his honor.

His Distinguished Flying Cross citation reads as follows:

On September 24, 1918, Lieutenant Kindley led his flight down on seven Fokkers north of Bourlon Wood, one of which he followed down and saw crash and burst into flames. On September 26, 1918, while working in conjunction with another of our flights, Lieutenant Kindley's flight accounted for two EA crashed, one of which he got. On September 27, 1918, this officer on low flying duty dropped bombs on railways near Marcoing, then attacked a balloon near Noyelles-sur-l'Escaut, driving same down and compelling the two observers to jump. He then, at an altitude of 600 feet, attacked and silenced an enemy machine gun and shot up troops. Being then attacked by a Halberstadt, he engaged it and brought it down in flames. Lieutenant Kindley's ammunition then being used up, he started for the lines but on the way back, he saw two EA which he dived on. They turned and went east. This officer has been on active service in France since May 23, 1918. His work in this squadron has been consistently good and since July 30, 1918, he has been leading 'A' Flight with marked success. He has accounted for a total of seven and one half EA destroyed and has driven down out of control, three.

His first Distinguished Service Cross citation reads as follows:

The Distinguished Service Cross is presented to Field E. Kindley, First Lieutenant (Air Service), U.S. Army, for extraordinary heroism in action near Bourlon Wood, France, September 24, 1918. Lieutenant Kindley attacked a formation of seven hostile planes (type Fokker) and sent one crashing to the ground.

His second Distinguished Service Cross citation reads as follows:

The Distinguished Service Cross is presented to Field E. Kindley, First Lieutenant (Air Service), U.S. Army, for extraordinary heroism in action near Marcoing, France, September 27, 1918: Flying at a low altitude, First Lieutenant Kindley bombed the railway at Marcoing and drove down an enemy balloon. He then attacked German troops at a low altitude and silenced a hostile machine gun, after which he shot down in flames an enemy plane (type Halberstadt) which had attacked him. Lieutenant Kindley has so far destroyed seven enemy aircraft and driven down three out of control.

Kirtland Air Force Base

Location: Albuquerque, New Mexico
Status: Active
Named for: Colonel Roy Carrington Kirtland
Date of Birth: May 14, 1874
Place of Birth: Fort Benton, Montana
Date of Death: May 2, 1941
Place of Death: Moffett Field in Sunnyvale, California
Date of Retirement: 1938

Colonel Roy Carrington Kirtland was one of the U.S. Army's oldest aviation pioneers and one of the first students to fly with the Wright brothers, and the first certified army pilot.

Kirtland was commissioned a second lieutenant in the infantry on August 29, 1901. In 1911, he transferred to the Air Service and was assigned to the U.S. Aviation School at College Park in Maryland where he supervised the construction of hangars for the school, and where he learned to fly. While at the school, Kirtland made one the first nighttime landings, made aerial maps taken from aerial photographs, took aerial motion pictures, and attempted ground-to-air communications by means of smoke signals.

Kirtland commanded the 1st Aero Squadron in 1913, but returned to the Signal Corps in 1915. In 1917, while in France, he organized a motor mechanic regiment, then assumed command of the 3rd Regiment. In England, he served as inspector of aviation activities and of Air Service rest camps throughout Europe.

After World War I, Kirtland became a flight instructor and commander of aviation supply depots. He graduated from the Army War College in 1926 and was appointed as commandant of Langley Field in Virginia, and later became acting commandant of the Air Corps Tactical School.

After retiring, Kirtland returned to active duty in 1941 and served at the West Coast Army Air Forces Training Center where he died. He was the third oldest military pilot in the U.S. Army at the time of his death. He was married to Helen Kansas Parker.

Lackland Air Force Base

Location: San Antonio, Texas
Status: Active
Named for: Brigadier General Frank Dorwin Lackland
Date of Birth: September 13, 1884
Place of Birth: Fauquier County, Virginia
Date of Death: April 27, 1943
Place of Death: Walter Reed Army Medical Center in Washington, D.C.
Decorations and Honors: American Defense Service Medal; World War I Victory Medal; American Theater Medal
Date of Retirement: June 30, 1942
Place of Burial: Arlington National Cemetery, Section 4, Site 3322A

Brigadier General Frank Dorwin Lackland proposed the idea of establishing an aviation cadet reception and training center in Texas.
 Lackland joined the infantry in 1911 as a second lieutenant and transferred to the Air Corps in 1917. He was the commanding officer of Kelly Field Advanced Flying School from 1938 to 1940. He served six tours of duty in San Antonio, Texas, where he commanded Duncan Field and Brooks Field and was the air officer of the 8th Corps at Fort Sam Houston in Texas.
 Lackland was a command pilot and served tours at Selfridge Field in Michigan; Langley Field in Virginia; and Davis-Monthan Air Force Base in Arizona, with the 19th Bombardment Group. He was the commander of the 1st Wing of the Air Force at March Field when he died.

Langley Air Force Base

Location: Hampton, Virginia
Status: Active
Named for: Professor Samuel Pierpont Langley, civilian
Date of Birth: August 22, 1834
Place of Birth: Roxbury, Massachusetts
Date of Death: February 27, 1906
Place of Death: Aiken, South Carolina
Decorations and Honors: Rumsford Medal (1886); Henry Draper Medal from the National Academy of Sciences; inducted into the National Aviation Hall of Fame (1963)

Place of Burial: Forest Hills Cemetery in Jamaica Plain, Massachusetts

Professor Samuel Pierpont Langley was an aviation pioneer and one of America's most accomplished astronomers and physicists.

Langley began his career as a civil engineer before accepting an assistantship at the Harvard Observatory. He taught mathematics at the United States Naval Academy at Annapolis, Maryland, and, in 1867, he served as professor of physics and astronomy at the University of Pittsburgh in 1867, in addition to being director of the Allegheny Observatory at the Western University of Pennsylvania. In 1887, he was appointed secretary of the Smithsonian Institution in Washington, D.C., serving until 1906.

Among his many inventions was the bolometer, a radiant-heat detector that is sensitive to differences in temperature to one hundred-thousandth of a degree Celsius.

He built the failed "aerodrome," an unmanned heavier-than-air flying machine. He was a correspondent of the French Academy, a foreign member of the Royal Society at Edinburgh and the National Academy of Science, and a Fellow of the Royal Astronomical Society. He authored "Story of Experiments in Mechanical Flight," *The Annual Aeronautical*, no. 3 (Boston: n.p., 1897) 11–25; Smithsonian Report, Washington, D.C., 1897. He also wrote *The New Astronomy* (Boston: Ticknor, 1888) and *Experiments in Aerodynamics* (1891).

Larson Air Force Base

Location: Moses Lake, Washington
Status: Now, Grant County International Airport
Named for: Major Donald A. Larson
Date of Birth: April 2, 1915
Place of Birth: Yakima, Washington
Date of Death: August 4, 1944
Place of Death: Near Uelzen, Germany
Decorations and Honors: Silver Star; Distinguished Flying Cross with oak leaf cluster; Bronze Star with oak leaf cluster; Purple Heart; Air Medal with three oak leaf clusters; American Defense Service Medal; European Theater Ribbon; American Theater Medal; World War II Victory Medal
Place of Burial: Ardennes American Cemetery and Memorial in Neupre, Belgium, Plot D, Grave 9

Major Donald A. Larson was a World War II ace pilot.

Larson attended the University of Washington before working as a reporter with the *Yakima Morning Herald*. He enlisted as a flying cadet at McChord Field in Tacoma, Washington, in April 1941. After completing flight training in

California, he became a flight instructor in Florida, and in January 1944, he was sent overseas.

Larson flew with the 505th Fighter Squadron, 339th Fighter Group, where he was credited with downing six enemy aircraft in the air and three on the ground. He had flown fifty-seven combat missions when his Republic P-47 Thunderbolt he called *Mary Queen of Scots* was shot down.

Laughlin Air Force Base

Location: Del Rio, Texas
Status: Active
Named for: First Lieutenant Jack Thomas Laughlin
Date of Birth: September 17, 1914
Place of Birth: Del Rio, Texas
Date of Death: January 29, 1942
Place of Death: Java, Indonesia

First Lieutenant Jack Thomas Laughlin became the first combat casualty in World War II when his Boeing B-17 Flying Fortress was shot down by enemy ground fire.

Laughlin graduated from Del Rio High School in 1932 and worked with archaeological excavation crews from the University of Texas and the Smithsonian Institution. He later enrolled at the University of Texas and received a degree in business administration in 1938. He became the supervisor of an archaeological laboratory in San Antonio where he restored, classified, and cataloged archaeological items for the university's museum.

He joined the Army Air Corps Aviation Cadet Program in September 1940. While at Stockton, California, in 1941, he received his pilot wings and was assigned to a B-17 heavy bombardment unit at Fort Douglas in Utah.

Laughlin received orders for Java in December 1941. While en route to Africa on his first combat mission, his plane was lost over the Makassar Straits.

Lawson Air Force Base

Located: Columbus, Georgia
Status: Now, Lawson Army Airfield
Named for: Second Lieutenant Ted W. Lawson, and also for Walter Rolls Lawson (see Army Airfields, Stagefields and Heliports)
Date of Birth: March 7, 1917
Place of Birth: Fresno, California

Date of Death: January 19, 1992
Place of Death: Chico, California
Decorations and Honors: Distinguished Flying Cross; Purple Heart; Chinese Army, Navy, and Air Corps Medal, Class A, 1st Grade
Date of Retirement: February 2, 1945
Place of Burial: Chico Cemetery in Chico, California

Second Lieutenant Ted W. Lawson is best known for his participation in the Doolittle Raid on Tokyo in 1942 as pilot of crew number 7.

Lawson attended Los Angeles City College and had worked for the Douglas Aircraft Company before joining the Army Air Corps in March 1940.

He received his pilot wings in November 1940 and, on April 18, 1942, he piloted the North American B-25B Mitchell bomber, known as the *Ruptured Duck*, on the highly secret mission led by Lieutenant Colonel Jimmy Doolittle to bomb Tokyo. The raid was carried out by sixteen bombers that took off from the deck of the aircraft carrier (CV-8) USS *Hornet*. All the planes completed their bombing missions over Japan, but because of the earlier-than-planned launch, they ran low on fuel and were unable to land in China. His plane was forced down off the coast of China and Lawson injured his leg during the crash. He was marooned on the island of Nan Tien before the Chinese underground smuggled him and his crew out of Japanese Occupied China. When infection set in, his badly injured leg had to be amputated in the field. He later wrote his memoir of the Doolittle Raid which was made into a Hollywood movie titled *Thirty Seconds Over Tokyo*.

From 1943 to 1944, Lawson served as liaison officer to the U.S. Air Mission in Santiago, Chile. After the war, Lawson operated a machine shop and was a representative for Reynolds Metals with the military. He died of natural causes.

Loring Air Force Base

Location: Limestone, Maine
Status: Closed
Named for: Major Charles Joseph Loring, Jr.
Date of Birth: October 2, 1918
Place of Birth: Portland, Maine
Date of Death: November 22, 1952
Place of Death: Near Sniper Ridge in North Korea
Decorations and Honors: Medal of Honor, posthumously; Distinguished Flying Cross; Air Medal with eleven oak leaf clusters; Purple Heart; and Korean Service Medal
Place of Burial: Arlington National Cemetery, Section MK, Site 89

Major Charles Joseph Loring, Jr., was a Korean War hero who deliberately crashed his damaged Lockheed F-80 Shooting Star into enemy gun emplacements near Sniper Ridge.

After completing flight training in February 1943, Loring served with the 36th Fighter Squadron patrolling the Caribbean Sea in Bell P-39 Airacobras and Curtiss P-40 Warhawks. In 1944, he was sent to Kingsnorth, England, with the Ninth Air Force to prepare for the allied landings in Normandy. During the invasion, he was wounded while flying a close support mission.

On December 24, 1944, while on his fifty-fifth mission during the Battle of the Bulge, Loring was hit by ground fire, causing him to crash land in Belgium. He spent the next four months as a prisoner of war.

Following the war, he became an instructor before going to Korea in June 1952. There, he was assigned to the 8th Fighter-Bomber Wing, flying F-80s. Later, he became a squadron operations officer.

His Medal of Honor citation for action during the Korean War reads as follows:

Major Loring distinguished himself by conspicuous gallantry and intrepidity at the risk of his life above and beyond the call of duty. While leading a flight of four F-80 type aircraft on a close support mission, Major Loring was briefed by a controller to dive-bomb enemy gun positions which were harassing friendly ground troops. After verifying the location of the target, Major Loring rolled into his dive bomb run. Throughout the run, extremely accurate ground fire was directed on his aircraft. Disregarding the accuracy and intensity of the ground fire, Major Loring aggressively continued to press the attack until his aircraft was hit. At approximately 4,000 feet, he deliberately altered his course and aimed his diving aircraft at active gun emplacements concentrated on a ridge northwest of the briefed target, turned his aircraft 45 degrees to the left, pulled up in a deliberate, controlled maneuver, and elected to sacrifice his life by diving his aircraft directly into the midst of the enemy emplacements. His selfless and heroic action completely destroyed the enemy gun emplacement and eliminated a dangerous threat to United Nations ground forces. Major Loring's noble spirit, superlative courage, and conspicuous self-sacrifice in inflicting maximum damage on the enemy exemplified valor of the highest degree and his actions were in keeping with the finest traditions of the U.S. Air Force.

Lowry Air Force Base

Location: Denver, Colorado
Status: Closed
Named for: First Lieutenant Francis Brown Lowry
Date of Birth: December 1, 1894
Place of Birth: Denver, Colorado

Date of Death: September 26, 1918
Place of Death: Crepion, France
Decorations and Honors: Distinguished Service Cross, posthumously
Place of Burial: Fairmount Cemetery in Denver, Colorado

First Lieutenant Francis Brown Lowry was the only airman from Colorado killed in World War I.

Lowry graduated from the University of Michigan in 1917 and enlisted in the army where he was assigned to the 91st Aero Squadron, American Expeditionary Force.

Lowry was shot down and killed while on his thirty-third photographic mission when German antiaircraft fire destroyed the Salmson 2A-2 aircraft in which he was an observer. He was originally buried in Meuse-Argonne Cemetery in Romagne, France, but in 1921, his remains were returned to the United States and placed adjacent to the land that later became Lowry Field.

His Distinguished Service Cross citation reads as follows:

Distinguished Service Cross is presented to Francis B. Lowry, Second Lieutenant (Field Artillery), U.S. Army, for extraordinary heroism in action near Crepion, France, September 26, 1918. On September 26, while on a very important photographic mission, Lieutenant Lowry, with Lieutenant [Asher] Kelty, pilot, realized the importance of the mission and chose to continue their course through a harassing antiaircraft barrage. A shell made a direct hit on the plane, brought it down in fragments and instantly killed Lieutenant Lowry.

Luke Air Force Base

Location: Glendale, Arizona
Status: Active
Named for: First Lieutenant Frank Luke, Jr.
Date of Birth: May 19, 1897
Place of Birth: Phoenix, Arizona
Date of Death: September 29, 1918
Place of Death: Murvaux, France
Decorations and Honors: Medal of Honor; Distinguished Service Cross with oak leaf cluster, posthumously; Croix de Guerre (Italy); inducted into the National Aviation Hall of Fame (1975)
Place of Burial: Meuse-Argonne American Cemetery and Memorial in Romagne, France, Plot A, Grave 13

First Lieutenant Frank Luke, Jr., known as the "Arizona Balloon Buster," was an ace pilot and the first American aviator to receive the Medal of Honor.

Luke enlisted in the Signal Corps' aviation section on September 25, 1917. He soloed on December 12 at Rockwell Field in California, was commissioned in January 1918, and sent to France where he was assigned to the 27th Aero Squadron of the 1st Pursuit Group.

Luke was recognized as the most spectacular air fighter of World War I for shooting down eighteen airplanes and balloons, making him an ace pilot. Later, he went on to surpass Eddie Rickenbacker's record. Thirteen of his victories were obtained in a single week. He was only twenty-one years old when he was killed.

His Medal of Honor citation for action during World War I reads as follows:

After having previously destroyed a number of enemy aircraft within seventeen days he voluntarily started on a patrol after German observation balloons. Though pursued by eight German planes which were protecting the enemy balloon line, he unhesitatingly attacked and shot down in flames three German balloons, being himself under heavy fire from ground batteries and the hostile planes. Severely wounded, he descended to within fifty meters of the ground, and flying at this low altitude near the town of Murvaux opened fire upon enemy troops, killing six and wounding as many more. Forced to make a landing and surrounded on all sides by the enemy, who called upon him to surrender, he drew his automatic pistol and defended himself gallantly until he fell dead from a wound in the chest.

His first Distinguished Service Cross award reads as follows:

The Distinguished Service Cross is presented to Frank Luke, Jr., Second Lieutenant (Air Service), U.S. Army, for extraordinary heroism in action near Saint Mihiel, France, September 12 to 15, 1918. Lieutenant Luke, by skill, determination, and bravery, and in the face of heavy enemy fire, successfully destroyed eight enemy observation balloons in four days.

His second Distinguished Service Cross award reads as follows:

The Distinguished Service Cross is presented to Frank Luke, Jr., Second Lieutenant (Air Service), U.S. Army, for extraordinary heroism in action near Etain, France, September 18, 1918. Immediately after destroying two enemy observation balloons, Lieutenant Luke was attacked by a large formation of German planes, Fokker type. He turned to attack two, which were directly behind him, and shot them down. Sighting an enemy biplane, although his gasoline was nearly gone, he attacked and destroyed this machine also.

---

* Luke Field (now, closed) on Ford Island in Hawaii, also was named in honor of Lieutenant Frank Luke, Jr.

MacDill Air Force Base

Location: Tampa, Florida
Status: Active
Named for: Colonel Leslie MacDill
Date of Birth: February 18, 1889
Place of Birth: Monmouth, Illinois
Date of Death: November 9, 1938
Place of Death: Anacostia, Washington, D.C.
Place of Burial: Arlington National Cemetery, Section 5, Site 5708

Colonel Leslie MacDill was an aviation pioneer.

MacDill graduated from Hanover College in Indiana in 1909 with a bachelor of arts degree, and from the University of Indiana in 1911 with a master of arts degree. After receiving a commission as a second lieutenant, he was assigned to the 6th Company, Coast Artillery Corps, in 1912. He then transferred to the aviation section of the Signal Corps in 1914 and was rated as a Junior Military Aviator on July 2, 1915. MacDill served with the 1st Aero Squadron from July to November 1915 and with the 2nd Aero Squadron in the Philippines until May 1917. He was promoted to captain on May 15, 1917; to major July 1, 1920; to lieutenant colonel August 1, 1935; and to colonel on August 26, 1936.

MacDill was killed after taking off from Bolling Field in Washington, D.C., in a North American BC-1 aircraft. When the engine of the aircraft failed, he was unable to return to Bolling Field. MacDill attempted to guide the plane away from homes in his path, but the plane clipped a tree and hit telephone and power wires before plunging to the ground and bursting into flames. Private Joseph G. Gloxner, a passenger, was also killed. At the time of his death, MacDill was serving as a member of the General Staff in Washington, D.C.

Malmstrom Air Force Base

Location: Great Falls, Montana
Status: Active
Named for: Colonel Einar Axel Malmstrom
Date of Birth: July 14, 1907
Place of Birth: Chicago, Illinois
Date of Death: August 21, 1954
Place of Death: Great Falls Air Force Base in Montana
Decorations and Honors: Bronze Star
Place of Burial: Arlington National Cemetery, Section 6, Site 9685-A

Colonel Einar Axel Malmstrom enlisted in the Washington State National Guard on May 12, 1929, and was commissioned a second lieutenant on May 25, 1931. On September 16, 1940, he was called to active duty as a first lieutenant.

Malmstrom was sent to Europe in May 1943 and became commander of the 356th Fighter Group in November of that year. On April 24, 1944, while flying his fifty-eighth combat mission, he was shot down over France and taken prisoner of war. While held captive, he was made American commander of the south compound, POW Camp Stalag Luft 1, Barth, Germany.

He returned to the United States in May 1945 and was assigned as air inspector for the 312nd Base Unit at Barksdale Air Force Base in Louisiana. He also served with the 19th Tactical Air Command at Biggs Field in El Paso, Texas.

Malmstrom served as deputy for Reserve Forces with the Ninth Air Force at Langley Field in Virginia until August 1949. He attended the Air War College and, after graduating, was assigned as senior air force instructor there for three years.

He became the division director of Personnel at Lockbourne Air Force Base in Ohio, and on February 1, 1945, he was assigned to the 407th Strategic Fighter Wing at Great Falls Air Force Base in Montana. Malmstrom was killed when his Lockheed T-33 Shooting Star crashed near the base.

March Air Force Base

Location: Riverside, California
Status: Now, Air Reserve Base
Named for: Second Lieutenant Peyton Conway March, Jr.
Date of Birth: December 31, 1896
Place of Birth: Fort Monroe in Virginia
Date of Death: February 13, 1918
Place of Death: Fort Worth, Texas
Place of Burial: Arlington National Cemetery, Section C.L., Grave 1476

Second Lieutenant Peyton Conway March, Jr., was a pioneer aviator and the son of General Peyton C. March, the World War I Army Chief of Staff.

March enlisted in the United States Army on August 6, 1917, and was assigned to the Signal Corps' aviation section. He trained as a pilot in Toronto, Canada, and Austin, Texas, graduating in November 1917. After completing flight and gunnery training, he was commissioned a second lieutenant in the Air Corps on January 28, 1918.

He was seriously injured on February 11 in an accident while flying a Curtiss JN-4 Jenny biplane when his plane fell one thousand feet onto Hicks Field. He died two days later.

Mather Air Force Base (formerly, Mills Field)

Location: Sacramento, California
Status: Now, Mather Airport
Named for: Second Lieutenant Carl Spencer Mather
Date of Birth: 1894
Place of Birth: Paw Paw, Michigan
Date of Death: January 25, 1918
Place of Death: Ellington Field in Texas

Second Lieutenant Carl Spencer Mather was an early aviator and test pilot.
 Mather earned his pilot license at the age of sixteen and was commissioned a second lieutenant in the U.S. Army Signal Corps on January 20, 1918. He became one of the first World War I pilots to train at Mills Field in California.
 He was killed when his plane collided midair with another plane while on a training flight. His classmates stationed at Mills Field requested that the facility be renamed in Mather's honor, and on May 2, 1918, the name was changed to Mather Field.

Maxwell-Gunter Air Force Base

Location: Montgomery, Alabama
Status: Active
Named for: Second Lieutenant William C. Maxwell and William A. Gunter, civilian
Date of Birth: Maxwell, November 1892; Gunter, October 9, 1872
Place of Birth: Maxwell, Natchez, Mississippi; Gunter, Marengo County, Alabama
Date of Death: Maxwell, August 12, 1920; Gunter, December 4, 1940
Place of Death: Maxwell, Luzon, Philippines; Gunter, Montgomery, Alabama

Second Lieutenant William C. Maxwell joined the army at Fort McPherson in Georgia and was assigned to the 5th Company, 7th Provisional Training Regiment. He was later assigned to the School of Military Aeronautics, but transferred to San Antonio to take the flying cadet course at Kelly Field. After completing the course in April 1918, he was commissioned a second lieutenant.
 He was killed when his British de Havilland DH-4 developed engine trouble after takeoff, forcing him to attempt an emergency landing on a sugar plantation. As Maxwell tried to land the plane, he saw a group of children directly in his path. He swerved to avoid hitting them and struck a flagpole hidden by a stand of sugar cane. He died instantly.

William A. Gunter was the mayor of Montgomery, Alabama, for twenty-seven years and an advocate of air power. He was instrumental in the development of Maxwell Field for Air Corps training and the establishment of the municipal airport that bears his name.

His first political job was as a clerk to the Alabama secretary of state. He served as senator from the Twenty-eighth District and president of the City Commission. He was elected mayor in 1911 and served until 1915. He was re-elected in 1919 and remained mayor until his death.

McChord Air Force Base

Location: Tacoma, Washington
Status: Active
Named for: Colonel William Caldwell McChord
Date of Birth: December 29, 1881
Place of Birth: Lebanon, Kentucky
Date of Death: August 18, 1937
Place of Death: Near Maidens, Virginia
Place of Burial: Ryder Cemetery in Lebanon, Kentucky

Colonel William Caldwell McChord was a pioneer aviator and a proponent of aviation in the military.

McChord graduated from West Point on June 14, 1907, and was commissioned a second lieutenant in the cavalry. He received flight training at Rockwell Field in San Diego, California, and was rated a junior military aviator in 1918. In March 1919, after training in Bombardment Aviation at Ellington Field in Houston, Texas, he was transferred to the Office of the Director of Air Service in Washington, D.C.

Among his many assignments were duty in the Finance Section of the Supply Group; a member of the Air Service Claims Board; assistant to the chief of the Materials Disposal and Salvage Division of the Supply Group; assistant to the chief of the Property Division of the Supply Group; and air officer of the Central Department.

He was commander of Chanute Field in Illinois and commandant of the Air Corps Technical School until early 1928. He was transferred to the Advanced Flying School at Kelly Field in Texas where he completed the Special Observer's course and received the rating of airplane observer on June 25, 1928. He graduated from the Army War College in Washington, D.C., and was assigned as an instructor at the Command and General Staff College for four years. He was later transferred to the Panama Canal Department for duty as commanding officer of the 19th Composite Wing. In October 1935, he was assigned to duty in the Plans Division, Office of the Chief of the Air Corps,

Washington, D.C., and later as chief of the Training and Operations Division.

McChord was killed when his Northrop A-17 single engine attack bomber malfunctioned while flying from Bolling Field in Washington, D.C., en route to Randolph Field in Texas.

McClellan Air Force Base

Location: Sacramento, California
Status: Closed
Named for: Major Hezekiah McClellan
Date of Birth: May 1, 1894
Place of Birth: Hall, Illinois
Date of Death: May 25, 1936
Place of Death: Centerville, Ohio
Decorations and Honors: Distinguished Flying Cross, posthumously

Major Hezekiah McClellan was an aeronautical pioneer and explorer who helped chart Alaskan air routes.

McClellan enlisted in the aviation section of the U.S. Army Signal Corps in 1917 and attended the University of California at Berkeley to study military aeronautics. After flight training at Kelly Field in Texas, he was commissioned a reserve second lieutenant.

Considered one of the Air Corps' top pilots, Lieutenant Colonel Henry Arnold chose McClellan to fly with an elite group of pilots on the historic flight of ten Martin B-10 bombers from Washington, D.C., to Alaska and back, the first such flight by that type of aircraft.

In the summer of 1935, flying over land and water, McClellan and two enlisted men flew a Douglas C-29 Dolphin, an amphibian aircraft from Washington, D.C., to Nome and Point Barrow, Alaska, and back to test the aircraft's capabilities. In mid-July, McClellan made the first landing of a military aircraft above the Arctic Circle in the C-29. During the flight, McClellan took aerial photos and gathered information about the area. Later, those photographs were used to compile charts and records of the Arctic that helped pilots who later flew there.

He was promoted to major in September 1935, and later was appointed chief of the Material Division's flying branch at Wright Field in Ohio.

McClellan died when the Consolidated P-30 aircraft he was flight-testing went into a spin and crashed.

★★★

McConnell Air Force Base

Location: Wichita, Kansas
Status: Active
Named for: Captain Fred J. McConnell; Lieutenant Colonel Edwin M. McConnell; Second Lieutenant Thomas Laverne McConnell
Date of Birth: Fred, 1918; Edwin, 1921; Thomas, 1923
Place of Birth: Wichita, Kansas
Date of Death: Fred, October 25, 1945; Edwin, August 1997; Thomas, July 10, 1943
Place of Death: Fred, Garden Plain Airport in Kansas; Edwin, no data found; Thomas, Bougainville Island in the Pacific
Decorations and Honors: Thomas, Air Medal, Purple Heart
Place of Burial: Fred, No Data Found; Edwin, Fort Logan National Cemetery, Denver, Colorado; Thomas, National Memorial Cemetery of the Pacific in Honolulu, Hawaii, Section B, Grave 1195

Fred, Edwin, and Thomas McConnell, known as the "Flying McConnell Brothers," attended North High School in Wichita, joined the Army Air Force at Fort Riley, and earned their pilot wings at Luke Field in Arizona.

They trained together at air bases in New Mexico, Kansas, California, and Guadalcanal. All three were copilots on the Consolidated B-24 Liberator bomber, and flew combat missions in the South Pacific.

Fred flew more than sixty combat missions without an accident, but died when his private plane hit a high-tension wire and crashed. He was a military flight instructor stationed in Garden City at the time of his death.

Edwin resigned from the air force in 1945 and worked as a commercial airline pilot in Colorado. He died of natural causes at age seventy-six.

Thomas flew with the 424th Bomber Squadron, 307th Bomber Group, and, at the age of twenty, was killed when his B-24 bomber crashed into a fog-covered mountain en route to his home base in Guadalcanal after a bombing mission on a Japanese airfield.

McCoy Air Force Base (formerly, Pinecastle Army Airfield)

Location: Pinecastle, Florida
Status: Closed
Named for: Colonel Michael Norman Wright McCoy
Date of Birth: October 9, 1905
Place of Birth: Orleans, Indiana

Date of Death: November 1957
Place of Death: Pinecastle, Florida
Decorations and Honors: Legion of Merit; Distinguished Flying Cross; Bronze Star; Air Medal

Colonel Michael Norman Wright McCoy flew the first nonstop forty-two-hour flight from the United States to Hawaii and back to prove the capability of the Boeing B-50 Superfortress (formerly the B-29) in an around-the-world flight of a bomber, using the air refueling system he helped develop.

In November 1951, McCoy piloted the first operational Boeing B-47 Stratojet from the aircraft factory in Wichita, Kansas, to MacDill Air Force Base in Florida. In April 1953, as commander of the 306th Bombardment Wing, McCoy trained the unit to combat readiness and led it through the first successful rotation of a Strategic Air Command (SAC) jet bomber force from MacDill Air Force Base to Fairford, England, a 3,120-mile trip in 5 hours, 38 minutes. In May 1954, he became commander of the 321st Bomb Wing at Pinecastle Army Airfield, which would later honor his name.

McCoy was killed when his B-47 exploded while preparing for the annual Strategic Air Command Bombing Navigation and Reconnaissance Competition.

McEntire Air Force Base

Location: Columbia, South Carolina
Status: Now, Air National Guard Base
Named for: Brigadier General Barnie B. McEntire, Jr.
Date of Birth: 1919
Place of Birth: Columbia, South Carolina
Date of Death: May 25, 1961
Place of Death: Harrisburg, Pennsylvania
Decorations and Honors: Certificate of Valor, posthumously from the governor of Pennsylvania; inducted into the South Carolina Aviation Association Hall of Fame (1992)

Brigadier General Barnie B. McEntire, Jr., was the first commander of the South Carolina Air Guard, its first general officer, and the first Air National Guard pilot to fly at the speed of Mach 3 in a Lockheed F-104 Starfighter.

McEntire graduated from the University of South Carolina. In 1939, he entered pilot training, earned his pilot wings in 1940, and was assigned to the Army Air Corps. He was chief pilot for Air Transport Command's North Atlantic Division, logging more than six thousand flying hours in a Consolidated B-24 Liberator bomber during World War II. In 1946, he organized the first South

Carolina Air National Guard units, and on February 18, 1959, he earned the rank of brigadier general.

He was killed when his F-104 plunged into the Susquehanna River while attempting to avoid crashing in the populated area of the city. According to witnesses, the plane was about eight hundred feet and bearing down on the city of Harrisburg, a city of about fifteen thousand, surrounded by a heavy concentration of industry and homes.

At the time of his death, at the age of forty-two, he was the youngest Air Guard general in the United States.

His Certificate of Valor reads as follows:

General McEntire was at sufficient altitude and flying at such air speed that would have permitted him to eject safely from his aircraft. However, the use of this particular runway at Olmsted Air Force Base leads directly into the heavily populated areas of Harrisburg and the West Shore communities. An aircraft abandoned after takeoff on this runway would almost surely land in these built up areas and result in casualties among the inhabitants in the area where it struck the ground. He never attempted to utilize his escape system, but from eyewitness reports, brought his aircraft in for a water landing in the river, which is the only possible place he could land his aircraft without causing injury or death of others. General McEntire, in performing this act of self-sacrifice, saved the nearby community and its inhabitants from possible death and destruction. His thoughts were concerned with the welfare of others not himself.

McGhee Tyson Air Force Base

Location: Alcoa, Tennessee
Status: Now, Air National Guard Base
Named for: Lieutenant Charles McGhee Tyson, USN
Date of Birth: 1889
Place of Birth: Knoxville, Tennessee
Date of Death: October 10, 1918
Place of Death: North Sea off the coast of England
Place of Burial: Old Gray Cemetery in Knoxville, Tennessee

Lieutenant Charles McGhee Tyson was an early naval aviator and the son of General Lawrence Davis Tyson.

Tyson graduated from Princeton University in 1912. He enlisted in the Naval Reserve Flying Corps in July 1917, took a course in naval aviation in Boston, and an advanced air training course at Naval Air Station, Pensacola, Florida. In August 1918, he was sent to England where he was assigned to an aerial unit that dropped mines into the North Sea to deter U-boats.

He was killed after takeoff when his plane, carrying four crew members, fell into the ocean. The pilot survived. Rescuers recovered the bodies of two crew members, and Tyson was listed as missing in action. Soon after Armistice Day, a month after the crash, they found Tyson's body which his father had to identify.

McGuire Air Force Base

Location: Trenton, New Jersey
Status: Active
Named for: Major Thomas Buchanan "Tommy" McGuire, Jr.
Date of Birth: August 1, 1920
Place of Birth: Ridgewood, New Jersey
Date of Death: January 7, 1945
Place of Death: Negros Island in the Philippines
Decorations and Honors: Medal of Honor, posthumously; Distinguished Service Cross with three silver oak leaves; Distinguished Flying Cross with five oak leaf clusters; Purple Heart with two oak leaf clusters; Air Medal with fourteen oak leaf clusters; inducted in the National Aviation Hall of Fame (2000)
Place of Burial: Arlington National Cemetery, Section 11, Grave 426

Major Thomas Buchanan McGuire, Jr., was an ace pilot during World War II.

McGuire studied aeronautical engineering at Georgia Institute of Technology before entering the service in July 1941. He received flight training at Randolph Field and Kelly Field in Texas, and earned his pilot wings and commission in February 1942.

During his first assignment, he flew patrols over the Aleutian Islands and Alaska. In March 1943, he flew a Lockheed P-38 Lightning with the 49th Fighter Group in the South Pacific. He was assigned to the 431st Fighter Squadron, 475th Fighter Group, flying cover for bombers from Australia to New Guinea. In October 1943, he was shot down over Oro Bay and wounded. He managed to bail out of his plane and land in the water only to discover that his life raft had been damaged by bullet holes. He stayed afloat long enough to be rescued by a PT boat. In May 1944, he became commander of the 431st Squadron and made thirty-eight confirmed aerial victories, two short of Major Richard Bong's record. He was married to Marilynn Giesler.

His Medal of Honor citation for action during World War II reads as follows:

He fought with conspicuous gallantry and intrepidity over Luzon, Philippine Islands. Voluntarily, he led a squadron of fifteen P-38s as top cover for heavy bombers striking Mabalacat Airdrome, where his formation was attacked by twenty aggressive Japanese fighters. In the ensuing action he repeatedly flew to the aid of embattled comrades, driving off enemy assaults while himself under attack and at times outnumbered three to one, and even after his guns jammed, continuing the fight by forcing a hostile plane into his wingman's line of fire. Before he started back to his base he had shot down three Zeros. The next day he again volunteered to lead escort fighters on a mission to strongly defended Clark Field. During the resultant engagement he again exposed himself to attacks so that he might rescue a crippled bomber. In rapid succession he shot down one aircraft, parried the attack of four enemy fighters, one of which he shot down, single-handedly engaged three more Japanese, destroying one, and then shot down still another, his 38th victory in aerial combat. On January 7, 1945, while leading a voluntary fighter sweep over Los Negros Island, he risked an extremely hazardous maneuver at low altitude in an attempt to save a fellow flyer from attack, crashed, and was reported missing in action. With gallant initiative, deep and unselfish concern for the safety of others, and heroic determination to destroy the enemy at all costs, Major McGuire set an inspiring example in keeping with the highest traditions of the military service.

"Go in close, and when you think you are too close, go in closer."
—*Major Thomas B. "Tommy" McGuire, USAAF*

Moody Air Force Base

Location: Valdosta, Georgia
Status: Active
Named for: Major George Putnam Moody
Date of Birth: May 13, 1908
Place of Birth: Manila, Philippines
Date of Death: May 5, 1941
Place of Death: Wichita, Kansas
Place of Burial: West Point Cemetery in New York, Section 6J, Site 45

Major George Putnam Moody flew for the U.S. Airmail Service in 1934.

Moody was a 1929 West Point graduate and an aviation pioneer who was killed while attempting to takeoff in an experimental Beechcraft AT-10. He was about one hundred feet into the air when the plane suddenly climbed sharply, the motors sputtered, the plane fell, and then crashed and burned.

He was on temporary assignment from Maxwell Field in Alabama at the time of the accident and was serving with the Beech Aircraft Company in Wichita, Kansas, where he worked on the inspection board for the AT-10 that was flown at Moody Air Force Base.

Nellis Air Force Base

Location: Las Vegas, Nevada
Status: Active
Named for: First Lieutenant William Harrell Nellis
Date of Birth: March 8, 1916
Place of Birth: Santa Rita, New Mexico
Date of Death: December 27, 1944
Place of Death: Bagstone, Belgium
Decorations and Honors: Air Medal with six oak leaf clusters; Purple Heart
Place of Burial: Henri-Chapelle American Cemetery and Memorial in Henri-Chapelle, Belgium, Plot G, Grave 34

First Lieutenant William Harrell Nellis was killed in the Battle of the Bulge.

Nellis enlisted in the Enlisted Reserve Corps on December 9, 1942, and reported for active duty as an aviation cadet on March 2, 1943. After completing primary pilot training in Albany, Georgia, on August 27, 1943, he became a flight officer with the 495th Replacement Group. Later, he was assigned to the 513th Fighter Squadron, 406th Fighter Group, where he flew seventy aerial combat missions in a Republic P-47 Thunderbolt.

He was flying aerial support for the 101st Airborne Division when his plane was hit by ground fire from a German convoy. The plane burst into flames and crashed. He was married to Shirley R. Fletcher. They had two children.

Norton Air Force Base

Location: San Bernardino, California
Status: Closed
Named for: Captain Leland F. Norton
Date of Birth: 1920
Place of Birth: San Bernardino, California
Date of Death: May 27, 1944
Place of Death: Amiens, France
Decorations and Honors: Distinguished Flying Cross, posthumously

Captain Leland F. Norton was a World War II bomber pilot.

Wanting to fly, Norton left San Bernardino Valley College to enlist in the Royal Canadian Air Force in 1941. When the United States entered the war, he returned to the United States and joined the U.S. Army Air Corps in 1942. He flew rescue missions out of Labrador and Greenland for two years before applying for combat duty.

Norton was shot down on his sixteenth bombing mission while piloting a Douglas A-20 light Havoc bomber as he attacked railroad marshaling yards in France. He gave orders for his crew to bail out, but he and another crew member stayed with the plane and perished.

The propeller of his plane, brought back from France by his parents, hung for many years in Haywood's Ice Cream Parlor on Highland Avenue, in San Bernardino, California, where Norton had worked as a teenager.

Offutt Air Force Base

Location: Omaha, Nebraska
Status: Active
Named for: First Lieutenant Jarvis Jennes Offutt
Date of Birth: October 26, 1894
Place of Birth: Omaha, Nebraska
Date of Death: August 13, 1918
Place of Death: Valheureux, France
Place of Burial: Forest Lawn Cemetery in Omaha, Nebraska

First Lieutenant Jarvis Jennes Offutt was Omaha's first World War I air casualty.

Offutt graduated from Yale University where he was a member of the varsity, glee, and banjo clubs. He also was a member of the Alpha Delta Phi fraternity and Phi Beta Kappa society.

He joined the service in 1916 and served as a supply sergeant in Company B, Yale Field Artillery. He attended officer's training at Fort Snelling in Minnesota, but wanting to fly, he asked for a transfer to aviation. On November 8, 1917, he was assigned to the 56th Squadron of the Royal Canadian Air Force aviation section, and was sent to Canada to train with the Royal Canadian Flying Corps where he earned his pilot wings and was commissioned a lieutenant. He was sent to England in 1918 as a ferry pilot, delivering combat aircraft from factories in England to camps at the front in Europe.

He died of injuries sustained when the British SE-5 he was ferrying crashed after being hit by enemy fire.

Olmsted Air Force Base

Location: Middletown, Pennsylvania
Status: Now, Harrisburg International Airport
Named for: First Lieutenant Robert Sanford Olmsted
Date of Birth: July 28, 1886

Place of Birth: Sheldon, Vermont
Date of Death: September 23, 1923
Place of Death: Nistelrode, Holland
Place of Burial: Sheldon Village Cemetery in Franklin County, Vermont

First Lieutenant Robert Sanford Olmsted was an aviation pioneer who served in the engineering section, Balloon and Airship Division, of the U.S. Army Air Service.

Olmsted was killed when his hot-air balloon was struck by lightning while competing in the Gordon-Bennett International Balloon Race in Brussels, Belgium.

Onizuka Air Station

Location: Sunnyvale, California
Status: Closed
Named for: Lieutenant Colonel Ellison Shoji Onizuka
Date of Birth: June 24, 1946
Place of Birth: Kealakekua, Kona, Hawaii
Date of Death: January 28, 1986
Place of Death: Over Florida coast
Decorations and Honors: Air Force Commendation Medal; Air Force Meritorious Service Medal; National Defense Service Medal
Place of Burial: National Memorial Cemetery of the Pacific in Honolulu, Hawaii, Section D, Grave 1

Lieutenant Colonel Ellison Shoji Onizuka was a mission specialist on STS-51-C Discovery orbiter and the ill-fated Challenger flight.

Onizuka graduated from the University of Colorado in 1969 with a bachelor's and master of science degree in aerospace engineering. He was commissioned a second lieutenant in January 1970 and was assigned as an aerospace flight test engineer with the Sacramento Air Logistics Center at McClellan Air Force Base in California. Later, he became chief of the engineering support section.

In January 1978, he was selected for the Astronaut Corps, completed a one-year training program, and then became a mission specialist. He worked on orbiter tests and checkout teams and launch support crews at the Kennedy Space Center for the first two shuttle missions. His first mission into space was on the Discovery in 1985. During his career he logged more than seventeen hundred hours flight time, with seventy-four hours in space.

Onizuka died in the explosion during the launch of the Challenger spacecraft from the Kennedy Space Center. The Challenger flight was his second shuttle mission. He was married to Lorna Leido Yoshida.

Otis Air Force Base

Location: Falmouth, Massachusetts
Status: Now, Air National Guard Base
Named for: First Lieutenant Frank J. Otis
Date of Birth: 1905
Place of Birth: Chicago, Illinois
Date of Death: January 11, 1937
Place of Death: Near Peoria, Illinois

First Lieutenant Frank J. Otis was a pilot, a Massachusetts Air National Guard flight surgeon, and a resident surgeon at Boston City Hospital.

Otis graduated from Moline High School in 1923. He attended Harvard University where he received a bachelor of science degree in 1927 and a doctor of medicine degree in 1931.

Otis was killed while en route from Chicago to Moline, Illinois, when the engine of his Douglas O-46A aircraft failed and the plane crashed.

Paine Air Force Base

Location: Everett, Washington
Status: Closed
Named for: Second Lieutenant Topliff Olin Paine
Date of Birth: April 26, 1893
Place of Birth: Orwell, Ohio
Date of Death: April 30, 1922
Place of Death: Utah

Second Lieutenant Topliff Olin Paine was a World War I Army Air Corps pilot and flew with the experimental U.S. Air Mail Service.

Paine graduated from the University of Washington in 1914, majoring in civil engineering. After graduation, he worked for the U.S. Forest Service as a forest ranger before enlisting in the army in 1915. In May 1918, he received flight training at March Field in California and was commissioned a second lieutenant.

He left the Army Air Corps in 1919 to become a commercial pilot, flying between California and Mexico. In 1920, he became a pilot with the then experimental Western Division of the U.S. Air Mail Service, flying airmail routes from Rock Springs, Wyoming, to Salt Lake City, Utah, sometimes in treacherous weather. On one such flight his goggles frosted over and for a while he was flying blind. On another occasion he found the landing field only because the ground crew had built a smoke fire to guide him in. Paine died of a gunshot wound that was first thought to be self-inflicted but was later ruled an accident.

Patrick Air Force Base

Location: Cocoa Beach, Florida
Status: Active
Named for: Major General Mason Matthew Patrick
Date of Birth: December 13, 1863
Place of Birth: Lewisburg, West Virginia
Date of Death: January 29, 1942
Place of Death: Walter Reed Army Medical Center in Washington, D.C.
Date of Retirement: December 12, 1927
Place of Burial: Arlington National Cemetery, Section 6, Site 5692

Major General Mason Matthew Patrick was the chief of Air Service in the Army Expeditionary Corps during World War I.

Patrick graduated second in his class from West Point in 1886. One of his classmates was General John J. Pershing.

He played a key role in helping the citizens of Johnstown, Pennsylvania, during the flood of 1889. He supervised river and harbor work in North and South Carolina, instructed at West Point, commanded the 2nd Battalion of engineers in Cuba, and organized the 1st Regiment of engineers in San Antonio, Texas.

As chief of the Air Service during World War I, Patrick recommended legislation that changed the Air Service to the Air Corps, which later became today's Air Force. As chief of the Air Service in 1924, he approved the first flight around the world by army pilots. He also approved the Pan-American Goodwill Flight of 1926–27 that flew to every capital in Central and South America. Patrick earned his pilot wings in 1923 at the age of sixty. He authored *The United States in the Air* (Garden City, N.Y.: Doubleday, Doran, and Co., 1928). He was married to Grace W. Cooley of Plainfield, New Jersey.

Pease Air Force Base

Location: Portsmouth, New Hampshire
Status: Closed (now, Air National Guard Base)
Named for: Captain Harl Pease, Jr.
Date of Birth: April 10, 1917
Place of Birth: Plymouth, New Hampshire
Date of Death: August 7, 1942 (believed to have been seen alive as late as September 1942)*
Place of Death: Near Rabaul, New Britain
Decorations and Honors: Medal of Honor, posthumously; Distinguished Flying Cross with oak leaf cluster; Purple Heart; Air Medal

Place of Burial: Memorialized at Manila American Cemetery and Memorial in Manila, Philippines

Captain Harl Pease, Jr., flew a Boeing B-17 Flying Fortress in the first mass formation flight from Hamilton Field in California to Hawaii.

Pease was commissioned and received his pilot wings in June 1940 and served with the 93rd Bomber Squadron of the 19th Bombardment Group.

His Medal of Honor citation for action during World War II reads as follows:

For conspicuous gallantry and intrepidity above and beyond the call of duty in action with the enemy on August 6–7, 1942. When one engine of the bombardment airplane of which he was pilot failed during a bombing mission over New Guinea, Captain Pease was forced to return to a base in Australia. Knowing that all available airplanes of his group were to participate the next day in an attack on an enemy-held airdrome near Rabaul, New Britain, although he was not scheduled to take part in this mission, Captain Pease selected the most serviceable airplane at this base and prepared it for combat, knowing that it had been found and declared unserviceable for combat missions. With the members of his combat crew, who volunteered to accompany him, he rejoined his squadron at Port Moresby, New Guinea, at 1 a.m. on August 7th, after having flown almost continuously since early the preceding morning. With only three hours rest, he took off with his squadron for the attack. Throughout the long flight to Rabaul, New Britain, he managed by skillful flying of his unserviceable airplane to maintain his position in the group. When the formation was intercepted by about thirty enemy fighter airplanes before reaching the target, Captain Pease, on the wing which bore the brunt of the hostile attack, by gallant action and the accurate shooting by his crew, succeeded in destroying several Zeros before dropping his bombs on the hostile base as planned, this in spite of continuous enemy attacks. The fight with the enemy pursuit lasted twenty-five minutes until the group dived into cloud cover. After leaving the target, Captain Pease's aircraft fell behind the balance of the group due to unknown difficulties as a result of the combat, and was unable to reach this cover before the enemy pursuit succeeded in igniting one of his bomb bay tanks. He was seen to drop the flaming tank. It is believed that Captain Pease's airplane and crew were subsequently shot down in flames, as they did not return to their base. In voluntarily performing this mission Captain Pease contributed materially to the success of the group, and displayed high devotion to duty, valor, and complete contempt for personal danger. His undaunted bravery has been a great inspiration to the officers and men of his unit.

---

* In September 1942, Father George Lepping, a Catholic missionary in the South Pacific, was taken to a prison camp on Rabaul. There he found five American airmen, one of whom was Captain Harl Pease. Father Lepping later wrote how on the morning of October 8, 1942, two survivors of the B-17 Flying Fortress, tail number 41-2617, were taken into the jungle and made to dig shallow graves where they were buried after their execution by sword.

Perrin Air Force Base

Location: Sherman, Texas
Status: Closed
Named for: Lieutenant Colonel Elmer Daniel Perrin
Date of Birth: April 7, 1896
Place of Birth: Boerne, Texas
Date of Death: June 21, 1941
Place of Death: Baltimore, Maryland
Place of Burial: Arlington National Cemetery, Section 8, Site 5296

Lieutenant Colonel Elmer Daniel Perrin was a test pilot.

Perrin enlisted in the army in October 1917 and was assigned to the 165th Depot Brigade in the Signal Enlisted Reserve Corps. He was later transferred to the 49th Company, 13th Training Battalion, where he served until July 4, 1918.

On July 5, 1918, Perrin was commissioned a second lieutenant in the Army Air Service and rated as a command pilot and combat observer. He served in the Philippines and was a flight instructor and commanding officer of the 41st School Squadron at Kelly Field in San Antonio, Texas. In 1939, he became an Air Corps representative at the Glenn L. Martin Aircraft Company for the Eastern Air Corps procurement district.

Perrin was killed while flight testing the Martin B-26 Marauder twin-engine medium bomber when the plane went into a nose dive after takeoff. The plane crashed one mile from the Martin Airport, killing Perrin and A. J. Bowman, a civilian inspector. Sabotage was suspected. Perrin was promoted to colonel, posthumously. He was married to Bessie King.

Peterson Air Force Base

Location: Colorado Springs, Colorado
Status: Active
Named for: First Lieutenant Edward Joseph Peterson
Date of Birth: November 16, 1917
Place of Birth: Orleans, Nebraska
Date of Death: August 8, 1942
Place of Death: Colorado Springs, Colorado

First Lieutenant Edward Joseph Peterson was the first Coloradan killed in a flying accident at Lowry Field.

Peterson graduated from Denver University with a bachelor's and master's of arts degree. After graduating from flight school in October 1941, he was commissioned a second lieutenant in the Army Air Force. He was promoted to first lieutenant in February 1942 and was assigned to Colorado Springs Army Air Base on July 26, 1942, where he was the operations officer for the 14th Photo Reconnaissance Squadron.

Peterson died in a plane crash when the left engine of his Lockheed F-4 Lightning (a reconnaissance version of the Lockheed P-38 Lightning) failed. The plane hit the runway and burst into flames. A base fire department crew rescued Peterson from the burning wreckage, but he died later that afternoon at a local hospital. He was married to Ruth Wallrich.

Piccolo Field

Location: Valparaiso, Florida
Status: Auxiliary field number five at Eglin Air Force Base in Florida
Named for: Captain Anthony D. Piccolo
Date of Birth: June 18, 1918
Place of Birth: Italy
Date of Death: October 6, 1942
Place of Death: Eglin Field in Valparaiso, Florida

Captain Anthony D. Piccolo was the commanding officer of the 386th Single Engine Gunnery Training Squadron at Eglin Field in Florida.

Piccolo arrived in the United States from Italy in 1929 and graduated from Memorial High School in Campbell, Ohio, before attending Youngstown College in Ohio where he majored in chemical engineering. He learned to fly at Bernard Airport while at Youngstown College and enlisted in the military in January 1941 as a second lieutenant. Piccolo died from injuries received in an airplane accident while flying a target-towing plane.

Pope Air Force Base

Location: Fayetteville, North Carolina
Status: Active
Named for: First Lieutenant Harley Halbert Pope
Date of Birth: May 26, 1879
Place of Birth: Mitchell, Indiana
Date of Death: January 7, 1919
Place of Death: Near Fayetteville, North Carolina
Place of Burial: Green Hill Cemetery in Bedford, Indiana, Section 4, Lot 23

First Lieutenant Harley Halbert Pope was a World War I pilot.

Pope left high school before graduating to work for Commonwealth Edison where he trained as an electrical engineer. At age thirty-eight, Pope wrote letters to the War Department requesting to join the aviation section of the Signal Corps, but was rejected because of his age. After pleading his case, he was accepted and given orders to report to the U.S. Army Aviation School at North Island, San Diego, California. He completed the Reserve Military Aviator (RMA) test on September 10, 1917, and was sent to Aerial Observers School at Fort Sill in Oklahoma where he was commissioned a first lieutenant on December 2. Later he became a flight instructor and received the rating of Expert Army Corps Pilot.

On July 2, 1918, Pope was sent to Camp Jackson in South Carolina where his duty was to locate landing fields for an airmail route between Virginia and South Carolina. While mapping the coastline in a two-seater Curtiss JN-4 Jenny, Pope and Sergeant Walter Flemming were killed when their plane slammed into a stanchion of the Clarendon Bridge. It took several months to recover the missing bodies from the Cape Fear River.

Ramey Air Force Base

Location: Aguadilla, Puerto Rico
Status: Closed
Named for: Brigadier General Howard Knox Ramey
Date of Birth: October 14, 1896
Place of Birth: Waynesboro, Mississippi
Date of Death: Missing on March 26, 1943 (declared dead November 19, 1945)
Place of Death: In the Torres Strait, South Pacific
Decorations and Honors: Distinguished Service Cross; Distinguished Service Medal; Legion of Merit; Purple Heart; Order of Daedalians*

Brigadier General Howard Knox Ramey was commanding general of the 6th Bomber Command in 1942 and commanding general of the 5th Bomber Command in 1943.

Ramey entered the service as a private first class and was commissioned a second lieutenant in the aviation section of the Signal Officer Reserve Corps in April 1918. Ramey's schooling included Air Service Photography School (1921), Air Corps Tactical School (1934), and Command and General Staff College (1936).

He served as a company and field grade officer from 1918 to 1942 and as deputy commander of the Hawaiian Air Force from 1942 to 1943.

Ramey was a passenger on a Boeing B-17 Flying Fortress that was on a routine administrative flight from Port Moresby to Horn Island en route to Brisbane in the South Pacific when it disappeared. His plane, named *Pluto*, was assigned to the 63rd Bombardment Squadron at the time and was never found. Ramey's disappearance caused great concern at the time because General Douglas MacArthur worried that Ramey might been taken prisoner by the Japanese.

* Commissioned officers who, before the Armistice of 1918, held a military pilot rating in a heavier-than-air powered aircraft.

Randolph Air Force Base

Location: San Antonio, Texas
Status: Active
Named for: Captain William Millican Randolph
Date of Birth: September 19, 1893
Place of Birth: Austin, Texas
Date of Death: February 17, 1928
Place of Death: Gorman Field in Texas
Place of Burial: Fort Sam Houston National Cemetery in San Antonio, Texas, Section Q, Grave 133

Captain William Millican Randolph was commander of the 25th Bombardment Squadron at France Field in Panama.

Randolph attended Texas A&M University in 1910. He enlisted in the army as a sergeant in the 2nd Texas Infantry in May 1916 and served on the Mexican border. He entered officer's training in Texas in August 1917, and received a commission. He served at Camp Travis in Texas, and later he was assigned to the 345th Machine Gun Battalion.

In 1918, he received flight training at Kelly Field in Texas, earned his pilot wings in 1919, and was assigned to Rockwell Field in San Diego, California. In 1927, he returned to Kelly Field as adjutant to the Air Corps Advanced Flying School. While at Kelly, he served on a committee to rename the field.

Randolph was killed while returning to Kelly Field from Gorman Field when his Curtiss AT-4 crashed on takeoff. According to the accident report, Randolph took off into a strong wind, climbed, and banked, then the nose of the plane fell. The plane rolled over and struck the ground from an altitude of about three hundred feet.

Reese Air Force Base

Location: Lubbock, Texas
Status: Closed
Named for: First Lieutenant Augustus Franklin Reese, Jr.
Date of Birth: November 8, 1917
Place of Birth: Shallowater, Texas
Date of Death: May 14, 1943
Place of Death: Sardinia, Italy
Place of Burial: Fort Sam Houston National Cemetery in San Antonio, Texas

First Lieutenant Augustus Franklin Reese, Jr., joined the army in 1940 and attended flight school in Los Angeles before being sent to London and North Africa with his squadron.

Reese was killed while flying a Lockheed P-38 Lightning on a voluntary strafing mission to destroy a railroad supply train during World War II.

Richard Bong Air Force Base

Location: Superior, Wisconsin
Status: Closed
Named for: Major Richard Ira Bong
Date of Birth: September 24, 1920
Place of Birth: Poplar, Wisconsin
Date of Death: August 6, 1945
Place of Death: Van Nuys, California
Decorations and Honors: Medal of Honor; Distinguished Service Cross; Silver Star with oak leaf cluster; Distinguished Flying Cross with six oak leaf clusters; Air Medal with thirteen oak leaf clusters; inducted into the National Aviation Hall of Fame (1986); inducted into the Wisconsin Aviation Hall of Fame
Place of Burial: Poplar Cemetery in Poplar, Wisconsin

Major Richard Ira Bong was an American ace pilot during World War II.

Bong enlisted in the Army Air Corps Aviation Cadet Program in 1941 and earned a commission and his pilot wings in January of 1942. He was assigned to the "Flying Knights" of the 9th Fighter Squadron, 49th Fighter Group. On December 27, 1942, while flying with the 35th Fighter Group, Bong scored his first aerial victories, a Zero and an Oscar. During his career, with more than five hundred combat hours, he shot down forty Japanese planes in two hundred combat missions to surpass Eddie Rickenbacker's record.

After a public relations tour across the United States, he worked at Wright Field in Ohio as a test pilot, testing the Lockheed P-80 Shooting Star.

After surviving two years of combat flying, Bong died while on a routine flight when his P-80 malfunctioned just after takeoff, and although he bailed out, he was too close to the ground. The plane crashed and burned.

His Medal of Honor citation for action during World War II reads as follows:

For conspicuous gallantry and intrepidity in action above and beyond the call of duty in the Southwest Pacific area from October 10 to November 15, 1944. Though assigned to duty as gunnery instructor and neither required nor expected to perform combat duty, Major Bong voluntarily and at his own urgent request engaged in repeated combat missions, including unusually hazardous sorties over Balikpapan, Borneo, and in the Leyte area of the Philippines. His aggressiveness and daring resulted in his shooting down eight enemy airplanes during this period.

Richards-Gebaur Air Force Base

Location: Grandview, Missouri
Status: Closed
Named for: First Lieutenant John Francisco Richards and Lieutenant Colonel Arthur William Gebaur, Jr.
Date of Birth: Richards, July 31, 1894; Gebaur, February 22, 1919
Place of Birth: Both, Kansas City, Missouri
Date of Death: Richards, September 26, 1918; Gebaur, August 29, 1952 (presumed dead December 31, 1953)
Place of Death: Richards, France; Gebaur, Korea
Decorations and Honors: Gebaur, Distinguished Service Cross, posthumously; Distinguished Flying Cross; Air Medal with four oak leaf clusters; Purple Heart; Korean War Medal
Place of Burial: Richards, Meuse-Argonne American Cemetery and Memorial in Romagne, France, Plot D, Grave 19; Gebaur, Memorialized at the National Memorial Cemetery of the Pacific in Honolulu, Hawaii

First Lieutenant John Francisco Richards served with the 1st Aero Squadron and was killed on the first day of the Meuse-Argonne offensive while on an artillery spotting mission during World War I.

Lieutenant Colonel Arthur William Gebaur, Jr., of the 7th Fighter-Bomber Squadron, 49th Fighter-Bomber Group, was killed on his ninety-ninth mission while flying a Republic F-84 Thunderjet during a low-level bombing run. Gebaur is still listed as Missing In Action.

Gebaur's Distinguished Service Cross citation reads as follows:

Lieutenant Colonel Arthur W. Gebaur, Jr., United States Air Force. Colonel Gebaur distinguished himself by extraordinary heroism in connection with military operations against an armed enemy of the United Nations as Group Leader of thirty-five F-84 aircraft, 49th Fighter-Bomber Wing, Fifth Air Force, on August 29, 1952. Realizing that the successful accomplishment of three quick turnaround missions required the utmost in careful planning and execution, Colonel Gebaur determined it his duty to lead his squadron in all three attacks. Immediately after returning from the first mission, Colonel Gebaur carefully briefed the Group on the flak positions and evasive tactics to be employed on the next attack, then led the Group back to the target. After turning in on his bomb run, Colonel Gebaur received a damaging, glancing hit from an 85 mm explosive shell but continued his attack, accurately scoring hits on the assigned target. Coming off his bomb run, Colonel Gebaur spotted eight quadruple .50 caliber gun positions firing at the Group. Completely disregarding the damage to his aircraft and with concern only for the safety of those he led, Colonel Gebaur attacked the blazing gun positions through intense smoke. Through Colonel Gebaur's superior airmanship, and high personal courage, the gun positions were silenced and the remainder of the Group successfully completed their attacks on the assigned target. Through his keen flying skill, outstanding gallantry in the face of a determined enemy and exemplary devotion to duty, Colonel Gebaur reflected great credit upon himself, the Far East Air Forces, and the United States Air Force.

Rickenbacker Air Force Base

Location: Columbus, Ohio
Status: Now, Air National Guard Base
Named for: Captain Edward "Eddie" Vernon Rickenbacker (born Rickenbacher)
Date of Birth: October 8, 1890
Place of Birth: Columbus, Ohio
Date of Death: July 23, 1973
Place of Death: Zurich, Switzerland
Decorations and Honors: Medal of Honor; Distinguished Service Cross with seven oak leaf clusters; French Legion of Honor (chevalier); French Croix de Guerre with palm; Mackay Trophy (1918); inducted into the International Aerospace Hall of Fame (1966); inducted into the National Aviation Hall of Fame (1965)
Date of Retirement: 1963
Place of Burial: Greenlawn Cemetery in Columbus, Ohio

Captain Edward Vernon Rickenbacker was a race car driver, owner of the Indianapolis Speedway, fighter pilot, president of Eastern Airlines, author of *Fighting the Flying Circus* (New York: Frederick A. Stokes, 1919), and the nation's leading ace pilot during World War I with twenty-six confirmed victories (including four observation balloons).

Rickenbacker first gained fame as a race car driver from 1912 to 1916, racing three times in the Indianapolis 500 and setting a speed record of 134 mph in a Blitzen Benz at Daytona Beach, Florida. He enlisted in the U.S. Army Signal Enlisted Reserve Corps on May 25, 1917, and was sent to France in June, assigned to the Aviation Headquarters American Expeditionary Force.

In 1918, he served with the 1st Pursuit Group's 94th Aero Pursuit Squadron, the famed "Hat in the Ring" Squadron. Later, he was made commander of that squadron. In October 1942, while on a tour of the Pacific theater from Hawaii to Australia, his Boeing B-17 Flying Fortress bomber ran out of fuel while flying to Port Moresby, New Guinea, and landed in the ocean. He and six crew members survived twenty-four days afloat on life rafts. Navy pilots rescued the crew in the Ellice Island chain on Friday, November 13, 1942, more than five hundred miles beyond Canton Island.

After the war, Rickenbacker left the air service and began his own automotive company, and became general manager of Eastern Airlines (later American Airlines). He died of pneumonia while visiting Switzerland. He was married to Adelaide Frost.

His Medal of Honor citation for action during World War I reads as follows:

For conspicuous gallantry and intrepidity above and beyond the call of duty in action against the enemy near Billy, France, September 25, 1918. While on a voluntary patrol over the lines, First Lieutenant Rickenbacker attacked seven enemy planes (five type Fokker, protecting two type Halberstadt). Disregarding the odds against him, he dived on them and shot down one of the Fokkers out of control. He then attacked one of the Halberstadts and sent it down also.

His Distinguished Service Cross reads as follows:

The Distinguished Service Cross is presented to Edward Vernon Rickenbacker, Captain (Air Service), U.S. Army, for extraordinary heroism in action near Montsec, France, April 29, 1918. Captain Rickenbacker attacked an enemy Albatross monoplane, and after a vigorous fight in which he followed his foe into German territory, he succeeded in shooting it down near Vigneulles-les-Hatton Chatel.

"Fighting in the air is not sport. It is scientific murder."
— *Captain Edward V. "Eddie" Rickenbacker, USAS,*
Fighting the Flying Circus

Robins Air Force Base

Location: Macon, Georgia
Status: Active
Named for: Brigadier General Augustine Warner Robins
Date of Birth: September 29, 1882
Place of Birth: Gloucester County, Virginia
Date of Death: June 16, 1940
Place of Death: Randolph Field in San Antonio, Texas
Place of Burial: Arlington National Cemetery, Section 6, Site 5738

Brigadier General Augustine Warner Robins was chief of Materiel Division of the Army Air Corps.

Robins was the son of a Confederate Civil War hero and was indirectly related to President George Washington and General Robert E. Lee.

Robins graduated from West Point in 1907 and spent a decade in the cavalry. He fought Pancho Villa in the Punitive Expedition with General John Pershing in 1916.

He was seriously injured in a plane crash while flying from Bolling Field on January 3, 1921. Robins was a logistician and helped establish the Air Service and the Air Corps, created a supply accountability system, and began a logistics school for nonflying officers. In 1939, he became commander of the Air Corps Training Center in Texas. Robins died from a heart attack at his home. He was married to Dorothy Gretchen Hyde.

Sampson Air Force Base

Location: Geneva, New York
Status: Now, Sampson State Park
Named for: Rear Admiral William Thomas Sampson, USN
Date of Birth: February 9, 1840
Place of Birth: Palmyra, New York
Date of Death: May 6, 1902
Place of Death: Washington, D.C.
Place of Burial: Arlington National Cemetery, Section 21, Grave S-9

Rear Admiral William Thomas Sampson was the commander of the battleship USS *Maine* that was sunk in Havana Harbor on February 15, 1898, setting off the Spanish-American War.

Sampson graduated head of his class from the United States Naval Academy at Annapolis, Maryland, in 1861 and served on the frigate USS *Potomac*.

In 1864, Sampson was executive officer on the ironclad USS *Patapsco*, that blocked ports in the south and destroyed mines that filled the waters. From 1865 to 1884, Sampson served aboard the battleship USS *Colorado*; the frigate USS *Congress*; and the sloop USS *Swatara*. He headed the department of physics at the Naval Academy at Annapolis, Maryland; was assistant superintendent of the Naval Observatory in Washington, D.C.; commanded the Naval Torpedo Station at Newport, Virginia; was a delegate to the International Prime Meridian Conference; and was Superintendent of the Naval Academy.

In 1892, he worked at the Washington Navy Yard, and the following year, he became chief of the Ordinance Bureau. He lectured at the War College on torpedoes and, in 1897, took command of the battleship USS *Iowa*. After the start of the Spanish-American War, he was promoted to acting rear admiral and became commander of the North Atlantic Squadron.

Sampson was promoted to commodore in 1898 and to rear admiral in 1899. He married his first wife, Margaret Sexton Aldrich, in 1863, and his second wife, Elizabeth Susan Buring, in 1882.

Schilling Air Force Base

Location: Salina, Kansas
Status: Closed
Named for: Colonel David Carl Schilling
Date of Birth: December 15, 1919
Place of Birth: Leavenworth, Kansas
Date of Death: August 14, 1956
Place of Death: Eriswell, Suffolk, England
Decorations and Honors: Distinguished Service Cross with oak leaf cluster; Silver Star with two oak leaf clusters; Distinguished Flying Cross with eight oak leaf clusters; Air Medal; British Distinguished Flying Cross; French Croix de Guerre; Harmon International Trophy
Place of Burial: Arlington National Cemetery, Section 8, Site 459

Colonel David Carl Schilling was an ace pilot during World War II.

Schilling graduated from Dartmouth College in 1939, joined the army as an aviation cadet, and was accepted for pilot training that same year. He was commissioned a second lieutenant in the Air Reserves in 1940 and served with the 8th Pursuit Group at Langley Field in Virginia. He served at Mitchel Field in New York and, in June 1941, with the 56th Fighter Group at Charlotte Air Base in North Carolina.

In 1943, Schilling participated in the first preoperational "circus" over Pas-de-Calais, France. Although his plane was hit, knocking out his radio, he returned to base, and later went on to lead a mission over Ypres, Belgium, and a "rodeo" of four fighter groups. From August 1944 to January 1945, Schilling was commander of the 56th Fighter Group.

Schilling returned to the United States and, as commander, took the 56th Fighter Group to the United Kingdom on the first USAF transatlantic jet flight in July 1948, and was the leader of the first nonstop transatlantic flight of a jet aircraft from Great Britain to the United States on September 22, 1950.

During his career, flying 132 low-flying missions, he was credited with twenty-two air victories and ten ground destroys. He was killed in an automobile accident.

Schriever Air Force Base

Location: Colorado Springs, Colorado
Status: Active
Named for: General Bernard Adolph Schriever
Date of Birth: September 14, 1910
Place of Birth: Bremen, Germany
Date of Death: June 20, 2005
Place of Death: Washington, D.C.
Decorations and Honors: Arnold Trophy; inducted into the National Aviation Hall of Fame (1980)
Date of Retirement: August 1, 1966
Place of Burial: Arlington National Cemetery, Section 34, Grave 16

General Bernard Adolph Schriever, considered the father of the U.S. Air Force missile program, pioneered and developed the Atlas, Thor, Jupiter, Titan, and Minuteman.

Schriever and his family immigrated to the United States in 1917 and became naturalized citizens in 1923. He grew up in San Antonio and graduated from Texas A&M University in 1931 with a bachelor of science degree in engineering. He joined the army in 1931 and was commissioned in field artillery but transferred to the Army Air Corps Flying School for flight training at Kelly Field in Texas where he graduated and received his pilot wings in 1933.

His early assignments took him to March and Hamilton fields in California where he flew the Martin B-4 and B-10 bombers, and to Panama, with duty at Albrook Field, flying the Boeing P-12. He served with the 7th Bomb Group before becoming a test pilot at Wright Field in Ohio where he also attended the Air Corps Engineering School, graduating in July 1941. He served with the 19th Bomb Group in the Pacific, taking part in the Bismarck Archipelago, Leyte, Luzon, Papua, North Solomon, South Philippine, and Ryukyu campaigns.

In June 1942, he earned a master of science degree in aeronautical engineering from Stanford University, and by the end of World War II, he was commander of the Advanced Headquarters, Far East Air Service Command. In January 1946, Schriever was assigned to the Army Air Forces Headquarters at the Pentagon as chief of the Scientific Liaison Branch in the Office of the Deputy Chief of Staff for Materiel. In July 1950, he served as the deputy assistant for Evaluation in the Office of the Deputy Chief of Staff for Development. In 1955, he served as the first commander of the Western Development Division and was responsible for the Weapon System 117L, the initial U.S. Air Force space program. In February 1958, he left the Ballistic Missile Division, formerly the Western Development Division, and became deputy commander for Ballistic Missiles at the Air Research and Development Command. In April 1961, he assumed command of Air Force Systems Command where he remained until he retired. Schriever retired as a four-star general after thirty-three years of U.S. Air Force service.

Following retirement, Schriever began a second career serving as chairman of the president's Foreign Intelligence Advisory Board, the Defense Science Board, and the Ballistic Missile Defense Organization Advisory Committee.

Scott Air Force Base

Location: Belleville, Illinois
Status: Active
Named for: Corporal Frank S. Scott
Date of Birth: December 2, 1883
Place of Birth: Braddock, Pennsylvania
Date of Death: September 28, 1912
Place of Death: College Park, Maryland
Place of Burial: Arlington National Cemetery, Grave No. 5331S

Corporal Frank S. Scott was the first enlisted fatality in the Signal Corps.

Scott enlisted in the Field Artillery in 1908 but transferred to the Signal Corps in 1911 where he was assigned to the army's airfield at College Park in Maryland. There, he worked with balloons and soon became the chief mechanic on the Wright biplanes.

Scott was a passenger, flying with Second Lieutenant Lewis G. Rockwell, who was testing for his military aviator ratings when their Wright Military Flyer crashed. With more than three hundred people watching, the two men took off in the open biplane. After reaching an altitude of 150 feet, the biplane leveled off and flew for about ten minutes. While coming in for a landing, the plane developed engine trouble, nosed downward, and crashed. Scott was dead when soldiers reached the splintered wood remains of the aircraft. Rockwell died a few hours later.

Selfridge Air Force Base

Location: Mount Clemens, Michigan
Status: Active (now, Joint Air Reserve Base)
Named for: Lieutenant Thomas Etholen Selfridge
Date of Birth: February 8, 1882
Place of Birth: San Francisco, California
Date of Death: September 17, 1908
Place of Death: Fort Myer in Arlington, Virginia
Decorations and Honors: inducted into the National Aviation Hall of Fame (1965); Scientific American Trophy (1908)
Place of Burial: Arlington National Cemetery, Section 3, Lot 2158

Lieutenant Thomas Etholen Selfridge was the first army officer to die in an airplane accident.

Selfridge graduated from West Point with the class of 1903 and flew with Orville Wright. In 1907, Selfridge was appointed secretary of the Aerial Experiment Association, an organization that built some of the first airplanes. In 1908, he designed and flew the Aerodrome number 1, called the Red Wing, and flew the associations second plane, the Aerodrome number 2, or White Wing. He also designed a propeller for the Baldwin airship. In August 1908, Selfridge tested the Army Signal Corps' first dirigible at Fort Myer in Virginia.

Selfridge was killed while flying in an army performance test in a Wright Flyer, piloted by Orville Wright. During the test, the wing flexed, and the propeller blade snapped off, cutting into the fabric of the plane, causing it to crash. Orville Wright received serious injuries but survived the crash.

Sewart Air Force Base

Located: Smyrna, Tennessee
Status: Closed
Named for: Major Allan Jackson Sewart, Jr.
Date of Birth: No Data Found
Place of Birth: Nashville, Tennessee
Date of Death: November 18, 1942
Place of Death: Solomon Islands
Decorations and Honors: Distinguished Service Cross; Distinguished Flying Cross with oak leaf cluster; Air Medal with two oak leaf clusters; Silver Star, posthumously
Place of Burial: Memorialized at Manila American Cemetery and Memorial in Manila, Philippines

Major Allan Jackson Sewart, Jr., was a native of Tennessee who died while flying in an aerial bombing mission against the Japanese.

In 1936, Sewart was attached to the 27th Pursuit Squadron with the Air Reserve. In 1942, he became the commander of the 26th Space Aggressor Squadron (redesignated, 26th Bombardment Squadron).

Seymour Johnson Air Force Base

Location: Goldsboro, North Carolina
Status: Active
Named for: Lieutenant Seymour Anderson Johnson, USN
Date of Birth: February 15, 1904
Place of Birth: Goldsboro, North Carolina
Date of Death: March 5, 1941
Place of Death: Norbeck, Maryland
Place of Burial: Arlington National Cemetery, Section 7, Site 8153

Lieutenant Seymour Anderson Johnson was a test pilot.

Johnson attended the University of North Carolina at Chapel Hill before entering and graduating from the United States Naval Academy at Annapolis, Maryland, in 1927. He was commissioned an ensign and received flight training at Naval Air Station, Pensacola, Florida. He earned his pilot wings in 1929 and served as a pilot aboard aircraft carriers. In 1937, he volunteered for duty as a test pilot and, in 1938, was assigned to Anacostia Naval Air Station, Washington, D.C.

Johnson had recorded more than four thousand flying hours before being killed while piloting a Grumman F4F-3 Wildcat fighter. His plane crashed soon after he reported getting low on oxygen. He holds the distinction of being the only naval officer to have an air force base named in his honor. He was married to Alice Kelly.

Shaw Air Force Base

Location: Sumter, South Carolina
Status: Active
Named for: First Lieutenant Ervin David Shaw
Date of Birth: September 30, 1894
Place of Birth: Alcolu, South Carolina
Date of Death: July 9, 1918
Place of Death: Germany
Place of Burial: British Military Cemetery in Grandcourt, France

First Lieutenant Ervin David Shaw was among the first American pilots to see air action in World War I.

Shaw attended the University of Georgia and Davidson College in North Carolina. He left school when World War I began and joined the U.S. Army in Savannah. He later accepted a commission in the Royal Canadian Signal Corps and was sent to England in the spring of 1918 as a member of the Royal Air Force's 48th Squadron, flying reconnaissance and combat missions, where he shot down two German aircraft.

Shaw, along with his British observer, Sergeant Tom Smith, was killed after taking off in a British Bristol F.2 Brisfit fighter. While flying over German territory, they were attacked by enemy airplanes. No details of the dogfight are known, but it is believed that Shaw's plane broke up in midair and crashed. Their bodies were later recovered. He was nicknamed, "Molly," from using his favorite exclamation of "Hot Tamale."

Sheppard Air Force Base

Location: Wichita Fall, Texas
Status: Active
Named for: Senator Morris Sheppard, civilian
Date of Birth: May 28, 1875
Place of Birth: Wheatville, Texas
Date of Death: April 9, 1941
Place of Death: Washington, D.C.
Place of Burial: Hillcrest Cemetery in Texarkana, Texas

Senator Morris Sheppard was chairman of the Senate Military Affairs Committee, a U.S. senator, and champion of the Eighteenth Amendment.

Sheppard graduated from the University of Texas in 1895 with a bachelor of arts degree and from Yale University in 1898 where he earned a master of laws degree.

In 1902, Sheppard ran for Congress, won, and served for ten years in the House of Representatives. Sheppard supported policies on tariff reductions, solutions to border conflicts with Mexico, and the League of Nations. He promoted rural credit programs, child labor laws, antitrust laws, and women's rights. As a supporter of Prohibition, he authored an act that abolished the sale of liquor in the District of Columbia in March 1917.

In 1921, Sheppard introduced the Sheppard-Towner Act that provided for maternal and pediatric clinics and for an investigation of infant and maternal mortality. He added the Federal Credit Union Act to the New Deal. As chairman of the Military Affairs Committee, he worked to increase military spending, especially for the Air Corps. He also supported bills to aid veterans and to increase the number of cadets at West Point and for the passage of the Selective Service Act. He was married to Lucile Sanderson.

"A nation that can not preserve itself ought to die, and it will die—die in the grasp of the evils it is too feeble to overthrow." —*Morris Sheppard*

Sherman Air Force Base (see Sherman Army Airfield)

Slocum Air Force Base (formerly, Fort Slocum)

Located: Davids Island, New York
Status: Closed
Named for: Major General Henry Warner Slocum
Date of Birth: September 24, 1827
Place of Birth: Delphi, Onondaga County, New York
Date of Death: April 14, 1894
Place of Death: Brooklyn, New York
Place of Burial: Green-Wood Cemetery in Brooklyn, New York

Major General Henry Warner Slocum was a commander with the Union army during the Civil War.

Slocum graduated from West Point with the class of 1852 and was commissioned a second lieutenant in artillery. He served in the Seminole War in Florida and at Fort Moultrie in Charleston Harbor, and fought in battles in the Eastern theater of Georgia and the Carolinas.

Slocum left the army to practice law in Syracuse, and served in the U.S. House of Representatives from New York. When the Civil War began, he joined the military as a colonel of the 27th New York Volunteers.

He fought in the first and second battles of Bull Run, Peninsula campaign, Seven Days' battles, battle of Gaines's Mill, and in the battle of South Mountain. He also participated in the battle of Averasborough and the battle of Bentonville. He commanded XII Corps and led the corps in the battle of Fredericksburg and the battle of Chancellorsville.

Slocum had the dubious honor of being given the nickname "Slow Come" for his slow action of getting his men to Gettysburg. During the summer of 1864, Slocum commanded the District of Vicksburg and XVII Corps in the Department of the Tennessee. He was put in command of XX Corps, a combination of the XI and XII Corps. Later he commanded the Army of Georgia. Slocum also commanded the Department of the Mississippi, and was present with General William Tecumseh Sherman when General Joseph E. Johnston's surrendered after Appomattox.

After the war, Slocum took an interest in politics and ran for secretary of state of New York, but was defeated. Later, he was elected to the Forty-first and Forty-second Congresses and served from March 4, 1869, to March 3, 1873.

After national service, he returned to his law practice in Syracuse and became the president of the Board of Trustees of the New York State Soldiers' and Sailors' Home. He was a member of the Board of Gettysburg Monuments Commissioners. He was married to Clara Rice.

Stead Air Force Base

Location: Reno, Nevada
Status: Active
Named for: Second Lieutenant Croston K. Stead
Date of Birth: No Data Found
Place of Birth: Sparks, Nevada
Date of Death: December 11, 1949
Place of Death: Reno, Nevada

Second Lieutenant Croston K. Stead was a member of the 192nd Fighter Squadron, Nevada Air National Guard, and a veteran of World War II.

Stead attended the University of Nevada and joined the Nevada Air National Guard in 1946. He was the brother of Bill Stead, a Nevada rancher, hydroplane racer, and World War II ace pilot.

Stead died from injuries received when his North American P-51 Mustang developed engine trouble and crashed, bursting into flames.

Thornbrough Air Force Base

Located: Cold Bay, Alaska
Status: Closed
Named for: Captain George Wayne Thornbrough
Date of Birth: July 7, 1914
Place of Birth: Kearny County, Kansas
Date of Death: June 4, 1942
Place of Death: Bering Sea
Decorations and Honors: Distinguished Service Cross
Place of Burial: Hartland Cemetery in Kearny County, Kansas

Captain George Wayne Thornbrough was a member of the 73rd Bombardment Squadron killed while flying a Martin B-26 Marauder in an attempt to bomb a Japanese carrier.

After dropping his bombs on the first run over the Japanese carrier *Ryujo,* he went back to base to reload and refuel. Returning for another attack, he became lost in the fog. Five Martin B-26 Marauders were sent to look for his plane. It was several weeks before his plane was found east of Fort Randall near Cold Bay, Alaska.

Tinker Air Force Base

Location: Oklahoma City, Oklahoma
Status: Active
Named for: Major General Clarence Leonard Tinker
Date of Birth: November 21, 1887
Place of Birth: Osage County, Oklahoma
Date of Death: June 7, 1942
Place of Death: At sea in the Pacific
Decorations and Honors: Distinguished Service Medal; Distinguished Flying
    Cross, posthumously; Soldier's Medal
Place of Burial: Memorialized at the National Memorial Cemetery of the Pacific
    in Honolulu, Hawaii

Major General Clarence Leonard Tinker was the first American general to die in action during World War II.

Tinker grew up near Pawhuska in the Osage Nation in Oklahoma. During his youth he worked in the print shop of the *Wah-Sha-She News*, the newspaper that his father founded and published. Tinker attended an Osage Nation boarding school in Pawhuska, and later the Haskell Institute in Lawrence, Kansas. He graduated from the Wentworth Military Academy in Lexington, Missouri, in 1908.

Tinker served in the Hawaiian Islands after receiving a commission as lieutenant in the U.S. Army Infantry in March 1912. During World War I, he served along the United States–Mexican border. After the war, Tinker transferred to the Army Air Corps and became a pilot. Assignments took him to posts in Oklahoma, Texas, California, Louisiana, Virginia, and England.

In 1927, he was named commandant of the Air Corps Advanced Flying School at Kelly Field in Texas. Tinker was commander of various pursuit and bombardment units during the 1930s. He was promoted to brigadier general in May 1940. Following the Japanese attack on Pearl Harbor on December 7, 1941, Tinker became commander of the Seventh Air Force at Hickam Field in Hawaii and led Consolidated B-24 Liberator bombers against Japan.

Tinker and his crew of eleven were lost during a predawn bombing raid on Wake Island when their plane fell out of formation and crashed into the sea. His body was never recovered. He was married to Madeline Doyle of Halifax, Nova Scotia.

Travis Air Force Base (formerly, Fairfield-Suisun Air Force Base)

Location: Fairfield, California
Status: Active
Named for: Brigadier General Robert Falligant Travis
Date of Birth: December 26, 1905
Place of Birth: Savannah, Georgia
Date of Death: August 5, 1950
Place of Death: Fairfield, California
Decorations and Honors: Distinguished Flying Cross with three oak leaf clusters; Purple Heart; Air Medal with three oak leaf clusters; French Croix de Guerre with palm; Legion of Honor
Place of Burial: Arlington National Cemetery, Section 2, Site E-325 RH

Brigadier General Robert Falligant Travis led thirty-five combat missions over Nazi-occupied Europe during World War II.

Travis was a 1928 West Point graduate. In June 1939, Travis was appointed commander of a bombardment squadron at Hickam Field in Hawaii. As a brigadier general in 1944, he became the commander of the 41st Combat Wing in England, and later he returned to Hickam as commanding general of the Pacific Air Command (PAC).

He supervised the Strategic Air Command's (SAC) development of Fairfield-Suisun Air Force Base in California in 1949. At the time of his death, Travis was commander of the 9th Heavy Bombardment Wing, Fifteenth Air Force, and was the base's commanding general.

Travis, along with pilot, Captain Eugene Q. Steffes, was killed when their Boeing B-29 Superfortress crashed and exploded five minutes after takeoff from Fairfield-Suisun Air Force Base en route to the eastern Pacific. The plane was carrying a Mark IV nuclear bomb. The crash killed ten people in the rear compartment and one passenger in the forward compartment. All other crew members and passengers escaped with only minor injuries.

Tyndall Air Force Base

Location: Panama City, Florida
Status: Active
Named for: Lieutenant Frank B. Tyndall
Date of Birth: September 24, 1894
Place of Birth: Sewall's Point, Florida
Date of Death: July 16, 1930
Place of Death: Mooresville, North Carolina

Decorations and Honors: Silver Star
Place of Burial: Arlington National Cemetery, Section 7, Site 9040

Lieutenant Frank B. Tyndall was the test pilot of the Keystone XB-1B, an army five-ton heavy bomber.

Tyndall was a Reserve Officers' Training Corps instructor at Georgia Tech University. In 1917, he was sent to France where he took part in the Saint Mihiel and Meuse-Argonne offensives with the American Expeditionary Force's Air Corps. In October 1919, as flight commander of the 22nd Aero Squadron, he was credited with four aerial victories.

In 1920, Tyndall was assigned to the 147th Aero Squadron, and later he became the squadron's commander. On June 2, 1923, Tyndall flew the Boeing Model 15 prototype fighter on its first successful test flight from Camp Lewis in Washington to McCook Field in Ohio. Tyndall was killed while conducting aerial inspections of airfields when his Curtiss P-1 Hawk crashed.

Vance Air Force Base

Location: Enid, Oklahoma
Status: Active
Named for: Lieutenant Colonel Leon Robert Vance, Jr.
Date of Birth: August 11, 1916
Place of Birth: Enid, Oklahoma
Date of Death: July 26, 1944
Place of Death: Between Iceland and Newfoundland
Decorations and Honors: Medal of Honor; Purple Heart, posthumously
Place of Burial: Memorialized at the Cambridge American Cemetery and
    Memorial in Cambridge, England

Lieutenant Colonel Leon Robert Vance, Jr., graduated from West Point in June 1939 and took flight training at Tulsa, Oklahoma, and at Randolph and Kelly fields in Texas, receiving his pilot wings in June 1940.

In September 1940, Vance was assigned at Randolph Field as a flight instructor. In February 1941, he became a squadron commander at Goodfellow Field at San Angelo, Texas. In 1942, he was assigned to Strother Field in Kansas as director of flying and, in 1943, he was assigned to Wendover Field in Utah as deputy commander of the 489th Bomb Group, which he helped train and take to Europe in April 1944.

While leading his bomb group, and flying a Consolidated B-24 Liberator bomber against the enemy on June 5, 1944, Vance was severely wounded by enemy aircraft fire over Wimereux, resulting in the amputation of the right foot.

Vance died while being transported on a Douglas C-54 Skymaster back to the United State when the plane fell into the Atlantic. No trace of the plane was ever found.

His Medal of Honor citation for action during World War II reads as follows:

For conspicuous gallantry and intrepidity above and beyond the call of duty on June 5, 1944, when he led a Heavy Bombardment Group, in an attack against defended enemy coastal positions in the vicinity of Wimereaux, France. Approaching the target, his aircraft was hit repeatedly by antiaircraft fire which seriously crippled the ship, killed the pilot, and wounded several members of the crew, including Lieutenant Colonel Vance, whose right foot was practically severed. In spite of his injury, and with three engines lost to the flak, he led his formation over the target, bombing it successfully. After applying a tourniquet to his leg with the aid of the radar operator, Lieutenant Colonel Vance, realizing that the ship was approaching a stall altitude with the one remaining engine failing, struggled to a semi-upright position beside the copilot and took over control of the ship. Cutting the power and feathering the last engine he put the aircraft in glide sufficiently steep to maintain his airspeed. Gradually losing altitude, he at last reached the English coast, whereupon he ordered all members of the crew to bail out as he knew they would all safely make land. But he received a message over the interphone system which led him to believe one of the crew members was unable to jump due to injuries; so he made the decision to ditch the ship in the channel, thereby giving this man a chance for life. To add further to the danger of ditching the ship in his crippled condition, there was a 500-pound bomb hung up in the bomb bay. Unable to climb into the seat vacated by the copilot, since his foot, hanging on to his leg by a few tendons, had become lodged behind the copilot's seat, he nevertheless made a successful ditching while lying on the floor using only aileron and elevators for control and the side window of the cockpit for visual reference. On coming to rest in the water the aircraft commenced to sink rapidly with Lieutenant Colonel Vance pinned in the cockpit by the upper turret which had crashed in during the landing. As it was settling beneath the waves an explosion occurred which threw Lieutenant Colonel Vance clear of the wreckage. After clinging to a piece of floating wreckage until he could muster enough strength to inflate his life vest he began searching for the crewmember whom he believed to be aboard. Failing to find anyone he began swimming and was found approximately 50 minutes later by an Air-Sea Rescue craft. By his extraordinary flying skill and gallant leadership, despite his grave injury, Lieutenant Colonel Vance led his formation to a successful bombing of the assigned target and returned the crew to a point, where they could bail out with safety. His gallant and valorous decision to ditch the aircraft in order to give the crewmember he believed to be aboard a chance for life exemplifies the highest traditions of the U.S. Armed Forces.

★★★

Vandenberg Air Force Base (formerly, Camp Cooke)

Location: Santa Maria, California
Status: Active
Named for: General Hoyt Sanford Vandenberg
Date of Birth: January 24, 1899
Place of Birth: Milwaukee, Wisconsin
Date of Death: April 2, 1954
Place of Death: Walter Reed Army Medical Center in Washington, D.C.
Decorations and Honors: Distinguished Service Medal with oak leaf cluster; Silver Star; Legion of Merit; Distinguished Flying Cross; Bronze Star; Air Medal with four oak leaf clusters; World War II Victory Medal; American Campaign Medal; American Defense Service Medal; European-African-Middle Eastern Campaign Medal; inducted into the National Aviation Hall of Fame (1991)
Place of Burial: Arlington National Cemetery, Section 30, Lot 719

General Hoyt Sanford Vandenberg was director of the Central Intelligence Agency, U.S. Chief of Military Intelligence during World War II, and commanding general of the Ninth Air Force.

Vandenberg graduated from West Point in 1923 and served as a fighter pilot for the first decade of he career.

His schooling included Air Service Flying School, Brooks Field in Texas, February 1924; Air Service Advanced Flying School, Kelly Field in Texas, September 1924; Air Corps Tactical School, Maxwell Field in Alabama, June 1934; Command and General Staff College, Fort Leavenworth in Kansas, June 1936; and Army War College, 1939.

His many assignments included commander, 90th Attack Squadron, Kelly Field in Texas; instructor, Air Corps Primary Flying School, March Field in California, 1927; commander, 6th Pursuit Squadron, Schofield Barracks in Hawaii, November 1929; flight instructor, Randolph Field in Texas, September 1931; flight commander and deputy stage commander, Randolph Field in Texas, March 1933; instructor, Air Corps Tactical School, Maxwell Field in Alabama from 1933 to 1936; chief of staff, Twelfth Air Force, 1943; deputy chief of air staff, Air Corps Headquarters, August 1943; deputy air commander in chief of the Allied Expeditionary Forces and commander of its American Air Component, April 1944; commander, Ninth Air Force; assistant chief of air staff, Air Corps Headquarters; director of Central Intelligence; vice chief of staff of the Air Force, October 1, 1947; and chief of staff of the Air Force from April 30, 1948, to 1953.

As chief of staff, Vandenberg played an important role in the formation of the Strategic Air Command (SAC); unification of the armed services; formation of an independent air force; the Berlin Airlift; the Convair B-36 Peacemaker super carrier controversy with the navy; the development of the hydrogen bomb; and in the Korean War.

At his burial ceremony at Arlington National Cemetery, six Boeing B-47 Stratojets flew over in V-formation with the second position on the right empty as a salute to a fallen comrade. The bombers were followed by sixteen Republic F-84 Thunderjets and sixteen North American F-86 Sabrejets.

Walker Air Force Base (formerly, Roswell Army Airfield)

Location: Roswell, New Mexico
Status: Closed
Named for: Brigadier General Kenneth Newton Walker
Date of Birth: July 18, 1898
Place of Birth: Cerrillos, New Mexico
Date of Death: January 5, 1943
Place of Death: Rabaul, New Britain, New Guinea
Decorations and Honors: Medal of Honor, posthumously; Silver Star; Purple Heart
Place of Burial: Memorialized at Arlington National Cemetery, Section C, Site 36-M

Brigadier General Kenneth Newton Walker was the commander of V Bomber Command. He was reported missing in action after flying a Boeing B-17 Flying Fortress over Japanese territory. His body was never found.

His Medal of Honor citation for action during World War II reads as follows:

For conspicuous leadership above and beyond the call of duty involving personal valor and intrepidity at an extreme hazard to life. As commander of the 5th Bomber Command during the period from September 5, 1942, to January 5, 1943, Brigadier General Walker repeatedly accompanied his units on bombing missions deep into enemy-held territory. From the lessons personally gained under combat conditions, he developed a highly efficient technique for bombing when opposed by enemy fighter airplanes and by antiaircraft fire. On January 5, 1943, in the face of extremely heavy antiaircraft fire and determined opposition by enemy fighters, he led an effective daylight bombing attack against shipping in the harbor at Rabaul, New Britain, which resulted in direct hits on nine enemy vessels. During this action his airplane was disabled and forced down by the attack of an overwhelming number of enemy fighters.

★★★

Walseth Air Force Base

Located: McGrath, Alaska
Status: Closed
Named for: Major Marvin E. Walseth
Date of Birth: No Data Found
Place of Birth: Seattle, Washington
Date of Death: July 18, 1942
Place of Death: Cape Udak, Aleutian Islands, Alaska
Place of Burial: Nikolski Village, Aleutian Island, Alaska

Major Marvin E. Walseth graduated from the University of Minnesota. He was assigned to the 36th Bombardment Squadron at Ladd Field in Alaska on April 1940 and helped form the Cold Weather Test Detachment there.

Walseth was killed when his Boeing B-17 Flying Fortress crashed in heavy fog while on a photo reconnaissance mission to Kiska. All aboard the plane were also killed.

Weaver Air Force Base

Located: Rapid City, South Dakota
Status: Now, Ellsworth Air Force Base
Named for: Major General Walter Reed Weaver
Date of Birth: February 23, 1885
Place of Birth: Charleston, South Carolina
Date of Death: October 27, 1944
Place of Death: Walter Reed Army Medical Center in Washington, D.C.
Place of Burial: Arlington National Cemetery, Section South, Site 1908

Major General Walter Reed Weaver was commander of the Army Air Forces Technical Training Command.

Weaver attended Virginia Military Institute, graduated from West Point in 1908, and was assigned to the infantry. He commanded the Signal Corps' flying cadets at Wright Field in Ohio and earned his pilot wings at March Field in California following World War I.

Weaver was instrumental in staging relief efforts during the Great Flood of 1929 in southeast Alabama, flying in supplies and food to residents stranded by the high water.

Among his many assignments were commanding officer of Maxwell Field in Alabama from 1927 to 1931, commandant of the Air Corps Tactical School from 1939 to 1940, and commander of the Southeast Air Corps Training Center headquartered at Maxwell Field from 1940 to 1941.

As commander of the Army Air Forces Technical Training Command, from 1942 to 1943, Weaver organized and commanded more than a hundred training stations where airman were trained to become technicians. He died of heart disease.

Westover Air Force Base

Location: Springfield, Massachusetts
Status: Now, Joint Air Reserve Base
Named for: Major General Oscar M. Westover
Date of Birth: July 23, 1883
Place of Birth: Bay City, Michigan
Date of Death: September 21, 1938
Place of Death: Burbank, California
Decorations and Honors: Distinguished Service Medal; World War I Victory Medal
Place of Burial: Arlington National Cemetery, Section 6, Site 5697

Major General Oscar M. Westover was a pioneer of modern military aviation and a proponent of a modern and well-equipped air force.

Westover enlisted in the U.S. Army in 1901, graduated from West Point in 1906, and was commissioned a second lieutenant in the infantry. In 1919, Westover was assigned to the aviation section of the Signal Corps, and later was transferred to the Air Service in 1920. In 1922, he won the Milwaukee Balloon Race by covering a distance of 850 miles.

His schooling included Air Service Balloon School, 1921; Air Service Airship School, 1922; Air Service Primary Flying and Advanced Flying School, 1923; Air Corps Tactical School, 1927; and Command and General Staff College, January 1932, both as a student and as an instructor. He was awarded aeronautical ratings as a balloon observer, airship pilot, airplane pilot, and airplane observer.

Westover served as executive in the Office of Chief of the Air Service from November 1918 to November 1920; director of aircraft production in the Office of Chief of the Air Corps from April 1921 to December 1922; commandant of the Air Service Tactical School at Langley Field in Virginia from 1924 to 1926; commander, Langley Field; and assistant to the chief of the Air Corps, December 22, 1931.

He was named chief of the Air Corps and promoted to major general on December 22, 1935. From 1935 to 1937, he flew to bases around the country promoting the importance of aviation. Westover was killed when his Northrop A-17 crashed and burst into flames. He was married to Adelaide Bainbridge.

Wheeler Air Force Base

Location: Wahiawa, Oahu, Hawaii
Status: Now, Wheeler Army Airfield
Named for: Major Sheldon Harley Wheeler
Date of Birth: 1889
Place of Birth: New York City, New York
Date of Death: July 13, 1921
Place of Death: Luke Field in Hawaii
Place of Burial: Lakeview Cemetery in Burlington, Vermont

Major Sheldon Harley Wheeler was a World War I pilot and former commander of Luke Field on Ford Island, Hawaii.
 Wheeler graduated from West Point in 1914 and was assigned to the infantry. Later, he transferred to the Signal Corps where he flew reconnaissance and scouting flights supporting General John J. Pershing's operations near the Mexican border.
 Wheeler was killed when his army observation biplane went into a nosedive and crashed during a demonstration.

Whiteman Air Force Base

Location: Knob Noster, Missouri
Status: Active
Named for: Second Lieutenant George Allison Whiteman
Date of Birth: October 12, 1919
Place of Birth: Longwood, Missouri
Date of Death: December 7, 1941
Place of Death: Pearl Harbor, Hawaii
Decorations and Honors: Silver Star; Purple Heart; American Defense Service Medal with a foreign service clasp; American Campaign Medal; Asiatic-Pacific Campaign Medal with bronze star; and World War II Victory Medal, all posthumously
Place of Burial: Memorial Park Cemetery in Sedalia, Missouri

Second Lieutenant George Allison Whiteman was one of the first American airmen killed at Pearl Harbor.
 Whiteman attended Rolla School of Mines in Rolla, Missouri, before enlisting in the army on October 20, 1939. He was assigned to Fort Leavenworth in Kansas and then to Fort Winfield in California. He received flight training at Randolph Field in Texas and applied for officers training. He was commissioned a second lieutenant on November 15, 1940, and was sent to

Hawaii where he was assigned to the 44th Fighter Squadron, 18th Pursuit Group, at Wheeler Field.

On the day the Japanese attacked Pearl Harbor, Whiteman raced from his quarters on Bellows Field to Wheeler Field. He jumped into a Curtiss P-40 Warhawk with its engine still cold and attempted to takeoff. Reaching only fifty feet into the air, his plane was hit by enemy fire. He tried to land, but the plane crashed and burned.

Williams Air Force Base

Location: Chandler, Arizona
Status: Closed
Named for: First Lieutenant Charles Linton Williams
Date of Birth: January 3, 1898
Place of Birth: Fort Huachuca in Sierra Vista, Arizona
Date of Death: July 6, 1927
Place of Death: Near Fort DeRussy in Hawaii

First Lieutenant Charles Linton Williams was an aerial photographer.

Williams graduated from West Point on November 1, 1918, and was assigned to the infantry in 1919. He served with the 30th Infantry at Camp Pike in Arkansas before being assigned to the Air Service at Carlstrom Field in Florida for flight training at the Air Service Primary Flying School. After graduating on June 30, 1922, he attended the Advanced Flying School at Kelly Field in Texas, graduating in December 1922. He served with the 13th Attack Group and was assigned to Chanute Field in Illinois to attend the Air Service Technical School, graduating in September 1923. He was sent to Langley Field in Virginia and served there from October 20, 1923, to April 22, 1926, and was then assigned to Luke Field in Hawaii.

Williams died while flying a Boeing PW-9A pursuit aircraft in formation when it stalled and fell into the sea. Fragments of his aircraft were found floating in the water several months later.

The fact that he was held in high esteem by those he served with is evident in the following letter from Major General Charles P. Summerall, chief of staff:

Lieutenant Williams had displayed a keen interest in the activities of the Air Corps and had efficiently performed all duties assigned him without thought of the hazard involved. Capable, conscientious and loyal, he won the admiration and respect of those under whom he served. The regrettable accident, which caused his untimely death, is deeply deplored throughout the service.

★★★

Wolters Air Force Base (see Fort Wolters)

Wright-Patterson Air Force Base

Location: Dayton, Ohio
Status: Active
Named for: Wilbur and Orville Wright and First Lieutenant Frank Stuart Patterson
Date of Birth: Wilbur, April 16, 1867; Orville, August 19, 1871; Patterson, November 6, 1897
Place of Birth: Wilbur, Blountville, Indiana; Orville, Dayton, Ohio; Patterson, Dayton, Ohio
Date of Death: Wilbur, May 20, 1912; Orville, January 20, 1948; Patterson, June 19, 1918
Place of Death: Orville and Wilbur, Dayton, Ohio; Patterson, near Fairfield Aviation General Supply Depot in Ohio
Place of Burial: All, Woodland Cemetery in Dayton, Ohio
Decorations and Honors: Wilbur and Orville inducted into the International Aerospace Hall of Fame (1965) and inducted into the National Aviation Hall of Fame (1962)

Wilbur and Orville Wright are best known for their famous flight on December 17, 1903, at Kitty Hawk, North Carolina, when they made the first powered air flight. Orville flew approximately one hundred feet in twelve seconds and, at noon, Wilbur made the fourth and longest flight of the day, covering 852 feet.

Wilbur died from typhoid fever. Orville died of a heart failure.

First Lieutenant Frank Stuart Patterson attended Yale University and graduated with a bachelor of arts degree. He enlisted as a private in the aviation section of the Enlisted Reserve Corps in May 1917. After completing ground, primary, and advanced flight training, he was assigned to Fort Sill in Oklahoma for training in aerial observation. He was then commissioned and assigned to the U.S. Army Officers Reserve Corps. In May 1918, he was assigned to the 137th Aero Squadron at Wright Field in Dayton, Ohio, where he flight tested the British de Havilland DH-4 and British Bristol fighter airplane.

Patterson and his aerial observer, Lieutenant LeRoy Amos Swan, died while testing newly installed machine guns on the de Havilland DH-4. Climbing to fifteen thousand feet, Patterson put the airplane into a dive. The wings of the airplane collapsed and separated from the fuselage, causing the plane to crash. An investigation determined that the tie rods sheared under the strain.

Wurtsmith Air Force Base

Location: Oscoda, Michigan
Status: Closed
Named for: Major General Paul Bernard Wurtsmith
Date of Birth: August 9, 1906
Place of Birth: Detroit, Michigan
Date of Death: September 13, 1946
Place of Death: Cold Mountain, near Asheville, North Carolina
Decorations and Honors: Distinguished Service Medal; Silver Star; Distinguished Flying Cross; Air Medal; Commander of the Order of the British Empire
Place of Burial: Arlington National Cemetery, Section 3, Site 4022

Major General Paul Bernard Wurtsmith was commander of the Thirteenth Air Force during World War II.

Wurtsmith graduated from the University of Detroit with a degree in aeronautical engineering. He enlisted in the Army Air Corps in August 1927. He earned his pilot wings and received a commission at Kelly Field in Texas in 1928 and was assigned to the 94th Pursuit Squadron, known as the "Hat in the Ring" Squadron. From September 1939 until July 1940, he commanded the 17th and 41st Pursuit Squadron and the 50th Pursuit Group at Selfridge Field in Michigan. In 1941, he became commander of the 49th Pursuit Group and was sent to Australia where the group was responsible for shooting down thirty-eight enemy bombers and forty enemy fighters. In 1943, he became commander of the 5th Fighter Group.

After the war, Wurtsmith assumed command of the advanced headquarters of the Far Eastern Air Forces, which included the Fifth Fighter Command in Japan and Korea and the Seventh Air Force in the Ryukyu Islands.

Wurtsmith was killed during a routine flight from Detroit, Michigan, to Tampa, Florida, while flying in a North American B-25 Mitchell bomber. The pilot reported his position as ten miles west of the Johnson City Airport, flying at about 230 miles per hour and descending to lower altitude because of bad weather. The plane crashed into a fog-covered mountain. Four others died in the crash. He was married to Irene Gillispie.

Air National Guard

Muster

What shall we say of each man in turn
when the travail of each is done?
These men of the bold fraternity,
who held they could touch the sun?
This breed which lifted its face aloft, this clan of the high frontier.
Oh, what shall we say at the end of the day, when we muster the pioneer?

—Author Unknown

CHAPTER 2

Air National Guard

Bluethenthal Field

Location: Wilmington International Airport in North Carolina
Status: Active
Named for: Sergeant Arthur "Bluey" Bluethenthal
Date of Birth: November 1, 1891
Place of Birth: Wilmington, North Carolina
Date of Death: June 5, 1918
Place of Death: France
Decorations and Honors: French Croix de Guerre with star and with palm; Medaille Militaire
Place of Burial: Esquennoy, Oise, France, reinterred Wilmington, North Carolina

Sergeant Arthur Bluethenthal was a center on Princeton's varsity team and an All-American, taking his team to an undefeated year in 1912. He also was a line coach at Princeton University and the University of North Carolina.

Following graduation, Bluethenthal first worked in his father's dry goods business and then joined the service in May 1916 where he was assigned to the American Field (ambulance) Service and fought in the Battle of Verdun with the French 129th Infantry Division.

In 1917, Bluethenthal joined the French Foreign Legion where he attended flight training. In March 1918, he was assigned to the French Lafayette Flying Corps, which consisted of a group of Americans in French service as pilots. He reported to Escadrille 227 by mistake and became the only American in the squadron.

He was killed on an artillery observation mission when his plane crashed after being hit by enemy fire.

★★★

Bradley Field

Location: Bradley International Airport in Windsor Locks, Connecticut
Status: Active
Named for: Lieutenant Eugene Morris Bradley
Date of Birth: July 15, 1917
Place of Birth: Antler, Oklahoma
Date of Death: August 21, 1941
Place of Death: Windsor Locks in Connecticut
Place of Burial: Fort Sam Houston National Cemetery in San Antonio, Texas

Lieutenant Eugene Morris Bradley was the first fatality at the Windsor Locks Airfield.

Bradley attended Murray Junior College at Stillwater, Oklahoma, and worked briefly in the Civilian Conservation Corps before enlisting in the military. He entered active duty on September 16, 1940, and after basic training was sent to Kelly Field in San Antonio, Texas, for flight training where he graduated, received his pilot wings, and was commissioned on May 29, 1941. He was then assigned to the 64th Pursuit Squadron, 57th Pursuit Group, Army Air Corps Reserve, at Mitchel Field in Long Island, New York.

On August 19, 1941, he moved with his squadron to Windsor Locks where he flew the Curtiss P-40 Warhawk. Bradley was killed during a practice dogfight when his plane crashed into a wooded section of the base, embedding the nose, engine, and cockpit of the plane six feet into the ground. He was married to Ann M. Blackerwick of San Antonio, Texas.

Byrd Field

Location: Richmond International Airport in Virginia
Status: Active
Named for: Rear Admiral Richard Evelyn Byrd, USN
Date of Birth: October 25, 1888
Place of Birth: Winchester, Virginia
Date of Death: March 11, 1957
Place of Death: Boston, Massachusetts
Decorations and Honors: Medal of Honor; Navy Cross; Distinguished Service Medal; Legion of Merit with gold star; Distinguished Flying Cross; inducted into the International Aerospace Hall of Fame (1968); inducted into the National Aviation Hall of Fame (1968)
Place of Burial: Arlington National Cemetery, Section 2, Site 4969-1

Rear Admiral Richard Evelyn Byrd, known for his exploration of Antarctica, was referred to as the "Mayor of Antarctica."

Byrd entered the United States Naval Academy at Annapolis, Maryland, was commissioned in 1912, and later earned his pilot wings at Naval Air Station Pensacola, Florida. He experimented with a number of scientific instruments ranging from drift indicators to bubble sextants. Because of his experience with these instruments, the navy assigned him to plan the flight navigation for the 1919 transatlantic flight of the U.S. Navy seaplanes, NC-1, NC-3, and NC-4.

In 1926, Byrd flew over the North Pole, which was followed by a transatlantic flight in 1927. He also led eleven expeditions to Antarctica from 1928 to 1955.

He was the author of *Skyward* (New York: G. P. Putnam's Sons, 1928); *Little American* (New York, Putnam, 1930); *Discovery, the Story of the Second Byrd Antarctic Expedition* (New York: G. P. Putnam's Sons, 1935); and *Alone* (New York: G. P. Putnam's Sons, 1938). He was married to Marie Donaldson.

His Medal of Honor citation reads as follows:

For distinguishing himself conspicuously by courage and intrepidity at the risk of his life, in demonstrating that it is possible for aircraft to travel in continuous flight from a now inhabited portion of the earth over the North Pole and return.

Dannelly Field

Location: Montgomery Regional Airport in Alabama
Status: Now, joint facility with Army National Guard Base
Named for: Ensign Clarence Moore Dannelly, Jr., USN
Date of Birth: February 3, 1916
Place of Birth: Enterprise, Alabama
Date of Death: December 17, 1940
Place of Death: Pensacola, Florida

Ensign Clarence Moore Dannelly, Jr., was a navy pilot.

Dannelly was a graduate of the University of Alabama.

He was killed while serving as a flight instructor at Naval Air Station Pensacola, Florida, where he had earned his pilot wings in 1938.

Francis S. Gabreski Field

Location: Westhampton Beach, New York
Status: Active
Named for: Lieutenant Colonel Francis "Gabby" S. Gabreski

Date of Birth: January 28, 1919
Place of Birth: Oil City, Pennsylvania
Date of Death: January 31, 2002
Place of Death: Long Island, New York
Decorations and Honors: Distinguished Service Cross; Silver Star; Distinguished Flying Cross; Bronze Star; Air Medal; French Legion of Honor; French Croix de Guerre; Polish Croix des Vaillants; inducted into the National Aviation Hall of Fame (1978)
Date of Retirement: 1967
Place of Burial: Calverton National Cemetery in Calverton, New York, Section 14, Site 724

Lieutenant Colonel Francis S. Gabreski was the top American ace pilot in Europe.

Gabreski attended Notre Dame University but enlisted in the U.S. Army Air Corps before graduating. He was commissioned a second lieutenant in the Air Reserves where he flew sorties (low-flying missions) with the 45th Fighter Squadron against the Japanese at Pearl Harbor. He was a flight leader with the 56th Fighter Group, and being fluent in the Polish language, he was attached to the 315th (Polish) Squadron, RAF.

In July 1944, Gabreski surpassed Captain Eddie Rickenbacker's World War I ace record with twenty-eight enemy fighters destroyed in aerial combat, plus three on the ground. After attacking an airfield in Germany, his plane crashed. He was taken prisoner and held captive at Stalag Luft I for ten months until the Russian army liberated him in April 1945. In April 1947, Gabreski was assigned as commanding officer of the 55th Fighter Squadron, 20th Fighter Group, at Shaw Air Force Base in South Carolina. In August 1949, he became commander of the 56th Fighter Group at Selfridge Air Force Base in Michigan.

In June 1951, he was assigned to the 4th Fighter Interceptor Wing in Korea where he achieved another record as an ace pilot with six enemy fighters shot down in aerial combat. During his career, he accumulated more than five thousand flying hours, with four thousand hours of that time in a jet aircraft.

Gabreski became commander of the 51st Fighter Interceptor Wing, and in 1954, he attended the Air War College at Maxwell Air Force Base in Montgomery, Alabama, graduating in 1955. He ended a distinguished air force career as commander of several tactical and air defense wings, and retired to become the presidential assistant for Grumman Aerospace Corporation. He lived in retirement on Long Island for many years as "America's greatest living ace." He was married to Kay Cochran.

He authored *Gabby: A Fighter Pilot's Life,* as told to Carl Molesworth (Atglen, Pa.: Schiffer Pub., 1998).

★★★

General Billy Mitchell Field

Location: General Billy Mitchell International Airport in Milwaukee, Wisconsin
Status: Now, Air Reserve Base
Named for: Major General William Lendrum "Billy" Mitchell
Date of Birth: December 29, 1879
Place of Birth: Nice, France
Date of Death: February 19, 1936
Place of Death: New York City, New York
Decorations and Honors: Special Medal of Honor, posthumously; Distinguished Service Cross; Distinguished Service Medal; inducted into the International Aerospace Hall of Fame (1970); inducted into the National Aviation Hall of Fame (1966)
Place of Burial: Forest Home Cemetery in Milwaukee Country, Wisconsin

Major General William Lendrum Mitchell, a proponent of air power is best remembered for his famous court-martial.

Mitchell supported the idea of a separate branch of service, independent of the army and navy. When several aircraft were lost, Mitchell published an article on September 5, 1925, in which he blamed these aviation accidents, and others, on the naval and war departments. He was court-martialed and sentenced to a five-year suspension from duty without pay. Mitchell resigned from the Army on February 1, 1926, but continued to support his idea of air power. Ten years later his ideas proved correct when the Boeing B-17 Flying Fortress, the world's first long-range, high-altitude strategic bomber, made a significant impact in helping win the war.

In 1946, Congress posthumously awarded him a special Congressional Medal of Honor, and posthumously restored him to the rank of major general. The North American B-25 Mitchell bomber was named in his honor, the only U.S. airplane ever named after a person.

His Distinguished Service Cross citation reads as follows:

William "Billy" Mitchell, Brigadier General (Signal Corps), U.S. Army, for repeated acts of extraordinary heroism in action at Noyon, France, March 26, 1918; near the Marne River, France, during July, 1918; and in the Saint Mihiel salient, France, September 12 to 16, 1918. For displaying bravery far beyond that required by his position as chief of Air Service, 1st Army, American Expeditionary Forces, setting a personal example to the United States aviation by piloting his airplane over the battle lines since the entry of the United States into the war, some instances being a flight in a monoplane over the Battle of Noyon on March 26, 1918, and the back areas, seeing and reporting upon the action of both air and ground troops, which led to a change in our aviation's tactical methods; a flight in a monoplane over the bridges which the Germans had laid across the Marne during July 1918, which led to the first definite reports of the location of these bridges and the subsequent attack upon the German troops by our air forces; daily reconnaissance over the lines during the battle of Saint Mihiel salient, September 12 to 16, securing valuable information of the enemy troops in the air and on the ground, which led to the excellent combined action by the allied air services and ground troops particularly this battle.

His Medal of Honor was ordered by Congress with his citations:

An Act Authorizing the President of the United States to award posthumously in the name of Congress a Medal of Honor to William Mitchell.

Be it enacted by the Senate and House of Representatives of the United States of America in Congress assembled, That the President of the United States is requested to cause a gold medal to be struck, with suitable emblems, devices and inscriptions, to be presented to the late William Mitchell, formerly a Colonel, United States Army, in recognition of his outstanding pioneer service and foresight in the field of American military aviation.

SEC. 2. When the medal provided for in section I of this Act shall have been struck, the President shall transmit the same to William Mitchell, Junior, son of the said William Mitchell, to be presented to him in the name of the people of the United States.

SEC. 3. A sufficient sum of money to carry this Act into effect is hereby authorized to be appropriated, out of money in the Treasury not otherwise appropriated. Approved August 8, 1946. Private Law 884.

Gowen Field

Location: Boise, Idaho
Status: Active
Named for: First Lieutenant Paul R. Gowen
Date of Birth: February 1, 1909
Place of Birth: Caldwell, Idaho
Date of Death: July 11, 1938
Place of Death: Panama
Place of Burial: Canyon Hill Cemetery in Caldwell, Idaho

First Lieutenant Paul R. Gowen graduated ninth in his class at West Point on June 13, 1933, and was a candidate for a Rhodes Scholarship.

Gowen attended the Army Air Corps Flying School at Randolph Field in Texas, graduated from the Primary Flying School on June 30, 1934, and then attended the Advanced Flying School at Kelly Field in Texas, and received his pilot wings in October of that year.

His first duty assignment was with the 77th Pursuit Squadron, 20th Pursuit Group, at Barksdale Field in Louisiana. Later, he became a flight instructor there. While instructing a student in a Fleetwings BT-12 plane, he encountered a dust storm and had to bailout of the plane which resulted in his induction into the Caterpillar Club, a fraternal order of pilots who survived an emergency parachute jump. He was later assigned to Albrook Field in Panama.

On July 2, 1938, he submitted a request for a patent for four designs of a mileage meter and an aircraft fuel consumption indicator.

Gowen was killed after taking off from Albrook Field in Panama City, Panama, when one engine of his Martin B-10 bomber failed. Unable to keep the plane in the air, he glided toward the water of Paitilla Point less than two miles away. The plane, with its engine on fire, plunged into the heavy jungle. Private Gareth H. Bundy, the radioman, and First Lieutenant Kenneth R. Crosher, the navigator, crawled out of the wreckage, but Gowen was killed instantly.

On June 15, 1942, his wife, the former Betty Wilson of Twin Falls, Idaho, was notified that her husband's patent had been approved and that Serial No. 309,847 had been allowed by the patent office under the date of June 12, 1942.

Joe Foss Field

Location: Sioux Falls, South Dakota
Status: Active
Named for: Brigadier General Joseph Jacob Foss, USMC
Date of Birth: April 17, 1915
Place of Birth: Sioux Falls, South Dakota
Date of Death: January 1, 2003
Place of Death: Scottsdale, Arizona
Decorations and Honors: Medal of Honor; Distinguished Flying Cross; National Veteran Award; Audie Murphy Award; inducted into the American Combat Airman Hall of Fame, Arizona Aviation Hall of Fame, Arizona Veterans Hall of Fame, National Aviation Hall of Fame (1984), Oklahoma Aviation and Space Hall of Fame, South Dakota Aviation Hall of Fame, and the South Dakota Sports Hall of Fame
Place of Burial: Arlington National Cemetery, Section 7A, Lot 162

Brigadier General Joseph Jacob Foss was a World War II Marine Corps ace pilot, governor of South Dakota, commissioner of the American Football League, and a television actor.

Foss graduated from the University of South Dakota in 1940 with a degree in business administration and joined the Marine Corps Reserve right after graduation. He was called to active duty and sent to Pensacola, Florida, where he received flight training, earned his pilot wings, and was commissioned a second lieutenant.

He was sent to the Pacific where he became the first pilot to match Captain Eddie Rickenbacker's World War I record of twenty-six confirmed aerial victories.

After the war, Foss was elected to the South Dakota State House of Representatives, and in 1954, he became South Dakota's youngest governor, serving two terms. In 1960, he was appointed founding commissioner of the American Football League. He also hosted the television program, *The American Sportsman,* and starred in the TV series *The Outdoorsman—Joe Foss.* He was married to Donna Wild Hall. They had five children.

His Medal of Honor citation for action during World War II reads as follows:

For outstanding heroism and courage above and beyond the call of duty as executive officer of Marine Fighting Squadron 121, 1st Marine Aircraft Wing, at Guadalcanal. Engaging in almost daily combat with the enemy from October 9 to November 19, 1942, Captain Foss personally shot down twenty-three Japanese planes and damaged others so severely that their destruction was extremely probable. In addition, during this period, he successfully led a large number of escort missions, skillfully covering reconnaissance, bombing, and photographic planes as well as surface craft. On January 15, 1943, he added three more enemy planes to his already brilliant successes for a record of aerial combat achievement unsurpassed in this war. Boldly searching out an approaching enemy force on January 25, Captain Foss led his eight [Grumman] F-4F Marine planes and four Army [Lockheed] P-38s into action and, undaunted by tremendously superior numbers, intercepted and struck with such force that four Japanese fighters were shot down and the bombers were turned back without releasing a single bomb. His remarkable flying skill, inspiring leadership, and indomitable fighting spirit were distinctive factors in the defense of strategic American positions on Guadalcanal.

"There's nothing I wouldn't do for this country."—*Joe Foss*

Kegelman Air Force Auxiliary Field

Location: Cherokee, Oklahoma
Status: Auxiliary field for Vance Air Force Base in Enid, Oklahoma
Named for: Colonel Charles Clark "Sonny" Kegelman
Date of Birth: ca. 1916
Place of Birth: El Reno, Oklahoma
Date of Death: March 10, 1945
Place of Death: Mindanao, Philippines
Decorations and Honors: Distinguished Service Cross; British Distinguished Service Order

Colonel Charles Clark Kegelman, commander of the 15th Bomb Squadron, was the first bomber pilot to bomb a target in Europe.

Kegelman graduated from the University of Oklahoma where he studied medicine. Instead of a medical career, he joined the service and attended flight training at Randolph Field in Texas. He received his pilot wings and commission in 1936, graduated from bomber pilot training in Nevada in May 1942, and was sent to England.

On July 4, 1942, Kegelman and his crew were among a twelve-plane formation of the Royal Air Force's 226 Squadron that flew a low-level attack on four German airfields in Holland, one of which was De Kooy Airfield.

On that mission, the right engine of Kegelman's Douglas A-20 Havoc bomber was hit, the propeller sheared off, causing the engine to catch on fire. He fought to control the bomber, but the plane's right wingtip struck the ground, and then the tail hit the ground, ripping off part of the lower fuselage. Kegelman managed to pull the plane into the air and brought it back safely to home base. Afterward, he continued to lead aerial assaults on channel ports and Nazi airfields for nine months until he was ordered to Tunisia where he supported the North African campaign.

After returning to the United States in 1943, he trained new pilots until September 1944 when he was recalled to combat. He was sent to the South Pacific where he carried out attacks against the Japanese on Guadalcanal, Rabaul, Borneo, Noemfoor, Morotai, Mapia, Ceram, and the Philippines, flying North American P-51s. Kegelman was killed when his plane collided with another and plunged into the jungle.

Key Field

Location: Meridian, Mississippi
Status: Active
Named for: Colonels Algene and Frederick Key
Date of Birth: Algene, February 8, 1905; Frederick, April 28, 1909
Place of Birth: Both, Kemper County, Mississippi
Date of Death: Algene, July 17, 1976; Frederick, September 15, 1971
Place of Death: Both, Mississippi
Decorations and Honors: Algene, Distinguished Service Cross; Distinguished
 Flying Cross; Bronze Star with six oak leaf clusters; Air Medal; British
 Distinguished Service Cross: Fredrick, Distinguished Flying Cross
Place of Burial: Both, Magnolia Cemetery in Meridian, Mississippi

The Key brothers, Algene and Frederick, were pioneers in air-to-air refueling and holders of flight endurance records.

On June 4, 1935, the Key brothers began an air-to-air refueling flight that lasted for twenty-seven days, totaling 653 hours and 34 minutes in the air. The flight set a record of 52,320 miles, twice the distance around the earth, at an average speed of about eighty miles per hour. The brothers stayed in the air, maintaining the plane's engine by walking outside on a catwalk that went around the sides of the engine.

Both brothers served in the Pacific as bomber pilots during World War II and contributed to the design of the Boeing B-17 Flying Fortress bomber.

Algene remained in the air force until his retirement in 1960 holding the rank of colonel. He died in a car accident.

Frederick ran the Key Brothers Flying Service at Key Field until his death resulting from emphysema.

Kingsley Field

Location: Klamath Falls, Oregon
Status: Active
Named for: Second Lieutenant David Richard Kingsley
Date of Birth: June 27, 1918
Place of Birth: Portland, Oregon
Date of Death: June 23, 1944
Place of Death: Ploesti, Rumania
Decorations and Honors: Medal of Honor; Purple Heart, posthumously; Air Medal
Place of Burial: Arlington National Cemetery, Section 34, Grave 4786

Second Lieutenant David Richard Kingsley was a bombardier.

Kingsley served as an altar boy at St. Michael's Catholic Church in Portland before enlisting in the army in 1942. After completing bomber school at Kirtland Field in Albuquerque, New Mexico, he was commissioned a second lieutenant. He then attended navigation school, graduated in 1943, and was assigned to the 53rd Bomb Squadron, 46th Bomb Group, at Will Rogers Field in Oklahoma City, Oklahoma. He was later transferred to the 59th Bomb Squadron, 396th Bomb Group, at Drew Field in Tampa, Florida. In April 1944, he was assigned to the 341st Bomb Squadron, 97th Bomb Group, while serving in Europe.

His Medal of Honor citation for action during World War II reads as follows:

For conspicuous gallantry and intrepidity in action at the risk of life above and beyond the call of duty, June 23, 1944 near Ploesti, Rumania, while flying as bombardier of a B17 type aircraft. On the bomb run Second Lieutenant Kingsley's aircraft was severely damaged by intense flak and forced to drop out of formation but the pilot proceeded over the target and Second Lieutenant Kingsley successfully dropped his bombs, causing severe damage to vital installations. The damaged aircraft, forced to lose altitude and to lag behind the formation, was aggressively attacked by three ME-109 aircraft, causing more damage to the aircraft and severely wounding the tail gunner in the upper arm. The radio operator and engineer notified Second Lieutenant Kingsley that the tail gunner had been wounded and that assistance was needed to check the bleeding. Second Lieutenant Kingsley made his way back to the radio room, skillfully applied first aid to the wound, and succeeded in checking the bleeding. The tail gunner's parachute harness and heavy clothes were removed and he was covered with blankets, making him as comfortable as possible. Eight ME-109 aircraft again aggressively attacked Second Lieutenant Kingsley's aircraft and the ball turret gunner was wounded by 20 mm shell fragments. He went forward to the radio room to have Second Lieutenant Kingsley administer first aid. A few minutes later when the pilot gave the order to prepare to bail out, Second Lieutenant Kingsley immediately began to assist the wounded gunners in putting on their parachute harness. In the confusion the tail gunner's harness, believed to have been damaged, could not be located in the bundle of blankets and flying clothes which had been removed from the wounded men. With utter disregard for his own means of escape, Second Lieutenant Kingsley unhesitatingly removed his parachute harness and adjusted it to the wounded tail gunner. Due to the extensive damage caused by the accurate and concentrated 20 mm fire by the enemy aircraft the pilot gave the order to bail out, as it appeared that the aircraft would disintegrate at any moment. Second Lieutenant Kingsley aided the wounded men in bailing out and when last seen by the crewmembers he was standing on the bomb bay catwalk. The aircraft continued to fly on automatic pilot for a short distance, then crashed and burned. His body was later found in the wreckage. Second Lieutenant Kingsley by his gallant heroic action was directly responsible for saving the life of the wounded gunner.

Kulis Field

Location: Anchorage, Alaska
Status: Active
Named for: First Lieutenant Albert Kulis
Date of Birth: August 27, 1922
Place of Birth: Brooklyn, New York
Date of Death: November 16, 1954
Place of Death: Anchorage, Alaska

First Lieutenant Albert Kulis was assigned to the 144th Fighter Bomber Squadron, Alaska Air National Guard.

Kulis began his military career as a pilot during World War II. After the war in 1946, he went to Alaska, and in 1952, he enlisted in the Alaska Air

National Guard shortly after its formation, and worked as a civilian pilot. He was killed while working for Cordova Airlines based in Cordova, Alaska, when his Lockheed F-80 Shooting Star crashed during a nighttime training mission.

Lambert Field

Location: Lambert–St. Louis International Airport in Bridgeton, Missouri
Status: Active
Named for: Major Albert Bond Lambert
Date of Birth: December 6, 1875
Place of Birth: St. Louis, Missouri
Date of Death: November 12, 1946
Place of Death: St. Louis, Missouri
Place of Burial: Bellefontaine Cemetery in St. Louis, Missouri, Block 23, Lot 3736

Major Albert Bond Lambert was the first person in St. Louis to receive a private pilot license.

Lambert attended Smith Academy and graduated from Page's School in Virginia. He was president of Lambert Pharmacal Company and the Paint, Oil & Drug Company, a director of the Mechanics American Bank, president of the Board of Police Commissioners, and active in civic organizations.

Using his own funds, he turned a hayfield into a 170-acre airfield that later became the Lambert–St. Louis International Airport and the site from which Charles Lindbergh made his famous solo flight across the Atlantic. Lambert became a balloon pilot in 1908 and an airplane pilot in 1911, after taking his first flight in an airplane with Orville Wright. In 1917, he joined the aviation section of the Signal Corps where he was commissioned a first lieutenant on active duty and given flying status.

His military career ended with his discharge, at his own request, in February 1919. He died of heart failure at his home. He was married to Myrtle McGrew.

Mansfield-Lahm Field

Location: Mansfield-Lahm Municipal Airport in Mansfield, Ohio
Status: Active
Named for: Brigadier General Frank Purdy Lahm
Date of Birth: November 17, 1877
Place of Birth: Mansfield, Ohio
Date of Death: July 7, 1965
Place of Death: Sandusky, Ohio

Decorations and Honors: Distinguished Service Medal; Legion of Merit; French Legion of Honor; Portuguese Order of Avis; inducted into the National Aviation Hall of Fame (1963)
Date of Retirement: November 1941

Brigadier General Frank Purdy Lahm was an aviation pioneer and the first qualified dirigible pilot.

Lahm, a February 18, 1901, graduate of West Point, won the first Gordon-Bennett International Balloon Race in an army balloon on September 30, 1906. Defeating fifteen other contestants from six other nations, he took off from Paris, France, and landed at Searborough, England, after traveling 402.40 miles.

Lahm also flew with Orville Wright on September 9, 1908, to become the first officer to fly as a passenger in an airplane and the second person to solo in an airplane. He made a two-man flight endurance record of one hour, twelve minutes, forty seconds, during an army acceptance test for the Wright plane. He won the National Balloon Race at Kansas City, Missouri, by traveling a distance of 577 miles to La Paz, Indiana, on July 10, 1911.

During his long military career, Lahm organized the Army Signal Corps Aviation School in the Philippines in 1912, was the secretary of the Aviation School at San Diego in 1916, commanded a balloon school in Omaha, Nebraska, in 1917, and served with the American Expeditionary Force in 1917 and 1918. He also organized the Lighter-Than-Air Service and was the first Army Air Service chief of staff and commander. In 1930, he organized the Second Army Air Service and activated Duncan Field in San Antonio, Texas, in 1926 and Randolph Field in Texas in 1930. He was air attaché to France in 1931 and II Corps area air officer in 1935. He became Army Chief of Aviation as a brigadier general, a position he held until he retired.

His National Aviation Hall of Fame award reads as follows:

To Frank Purdy Lahm, for outstanding contribution to aviation by his vision of the potential of aircraft for military purposes and his dedication to the task of organizing proper training facilities for the Army Air Corps, which earned for him the unofficial title "Father of the West Point of the Air," this award is most solemnly and respectively dedicated.

Morris Field

Location: Charlotte, North Carolina
Status: Closed
Named for: Major William Colb Morris
Date of Birth: August 4, 1891
Place of Birth: Harrisburg, North Carolina

Date of Death: September 4, 1939
Place of Death: Dayton, Ohio
Decorations and Honors: Order of Daedalians*
Place of Burial: Arlington National Cemetery, Section 9, Site 5977

Major William Colb Morris was a World War I pilot and flight instructor.

Morris attended Davidson College in North Carolina and was a cadet at West Point for six months. He first served in the Royal Canadian Air Force before transferring to the U.S. Air Corps as a private in the aviation section of the Signal Officers Reserve Corps when World War I began. After basic flight training at Rockwell Field in San Diego, California, and Gerstner Field in Lake Charles, Louisiana, and advanced pursuit training in Issoudun, France, he received his Reserve Military Aviator's rating on March 7, 1918; airplane pilot rating in October 1920; air observer rating in 1936; and military airplane pilot rating in December 1937.

He became a flight instructor at March Field in Riverside, California, and a test pilot and engineering officer with the 95th Squadron, 14th Air Service. As one of the first pilots to fly an airplane in wartime, he became illegible as a member of the Order of Daedalians on February 27, 1935.

Morris authored a training book for officers. He was a member of the staff of the Chief of Air Corps at the time of his death from complications after surgery. He was married to Maurine Garrett of Texas. An airfield in Charlotte, North Carolina, was also named in his honor.

* Commissioned officers who, before the Armistice of 1918, held a military pilot rating in a heavier-than-air powered aircraft.

Phelps Collins Field

Location: Alpena County Regional Airport in Alpena, Michigan
Status: Active
Named for: Captain Phelps Collins
Date of Birth: 1893
Place of Birth: Alpena, Michigan
Date of Death: March 12, 1918
Place of Death: Paris, France
Place of Burial: Mount French Cemetery in France

Captain Phelps Collins was an ace pilot and the first member of the U.S. Air Service to lose his life on a combat mission during World War I.

Collins enlisted in 1917 and was sent to Avord, France, for training. There, he joined French and American pilots in the Lafayette Escadrille, a French flying corps. He became the first of his class to enter combat as a scout pilot and was credited with shooting down three enemy planes. When the American Flying Corps was formed, he transferred to it and was assigned to the aviation section and was promoted to captain.

He was killed while piloting a French-built SPAD VII plane with the 103rd Aero Pursuit Squadron when the plane crashed on a combat patrol mission to intercept enemy airplanes.

It is unclear how Collins died, but Major Thaw, his commander, wrote, "It will never be known whether he was shot down in a combat, fought at so great an altitude that it could neither be seen nor heard, whether some vital part of his machine gave way or whether he fainted as a result of the terrible strain he had placed upon himself."

In a letter to Collins's father, the unit chaplain wrote, "He lies among heroes in the sunlit soil of France, but his spirit has gone forth as an inspiration to others. . . . May the thoughts of his bravery and the deep regard in which he was held by his comrades be a source of strength to you in this time of sorrow."

Rosecrans Field

Location: St. Joseph, Missouri
Status: Active
Named for: Sergeant Guy Wallace Rosecrans
Date of Birth: July 28, 1896
Place of Birth: Omaha, Nebraska
Date of Death: October 16, 1918
Place of Death: Saint Jean de Monts, France
Place of Burial: Mount Auburn Cemetery in St. Joseph, Missouri

Sergeant Guy Wallace Rosecrans was the only enlisted airman from St. Joseph killed during World War I.

Rosecrans was employed by Swift and Company in St. Joseph, Missouri, before enlisting in the army. He trained at Fort Logan in Denver, Colorado; San Antonio, Texas; and Rantoul, Illinois. In February 1918, he transferred to the 153rd Air Squadron of the Royal Air Force in England.

Rosecrans died after being struck by an airplane propeller while helping a fellow aviator start his airplane engine. He was first buried at Saint Jeans, France, but was later returned to St. Joseph, Missouri, on October 17, 1920, for reinterment there.

Stewart Field

Location: Stewart International Airport in Newburgh, New York
Status: Active
Named for: Lachlan Stewart, sea captain
Date of Birth: November 19, 1830
Place of Birth: Greenock, Scotland
Date of Death: June 22, 1899
Place of Death: Newburgh, New York

Captain Lachlan Stewart was a Scottish-born sea captain who skippered schooners, packets, and other sailing vessels from 1850 to 1870.
 At the age of eleven, Stewart sailed to the West Indies on a merchant vessel. In 1842, he settled in Newburgh, New York, where he assisted in the building of the old cotton factory there, helped lay the cornerstone, and built ships. He purchased a schooner and sailed the East Coast. In 1862, he disposed of his schooner and became the foreman of the dockyard for Homer Ramsdell & Company. He purchased Brookside Dairy farm and settled down for the remainder of his days. He died in his home after a brief illness.

Stratton Air National Guard Base

Location: Schenectady, New York
Status: Active
Named for: Captain and U.S. Representative Samuel Studdiford Stratton, USN
Date of Birth: September 27, 1916
Place of Birth: Yonkers, Westchester County, New York
Date of Death: September 13, 1990
Place of Death: Rockville, Maryland
Decorations and Honors: Bronze Star with V device
Place of Burial: Arlington National Cemetery, Section 5, Lot 40-2

Captain Samuel Studdiford Stratton was a conservative Democratic who represented Albany, New York.
 Stratton graduated from the University of Rochester in 1937, Haverford College in Pennsylvania in 1938, and Harvard University in 1940. He joined the Naval Reserve on June 26, 1942, and was commissioned an ensign. He served in the Southwest Pacific Theater of Operations as a naval combat intelligence officer on the staff of General Douglas MacArthur. After the war, he interrogated the Japanese supreme commander, General Tomoyuki Yamashita, who was later hanged as a war criminal.
 He left the service as a lieutenant in 1946 but was recalled to active duty

during the Korean Conflict as a lieutenant commander and served as an instructor at the Naval Intelligence School in Washington, D.C., from 1951 to 1953.

After the war, Stratton served on the Schenectady City Council from 1945 to 1956 when he became mayor of Schenectady, serving from 1956 to 1959. He served as U.S. Representative from New York from 1959 to 1989 (32nd District, 1959–63; 35th District, 1963–71; 29th District, 1971–73; 28th District, 1973–83; 23rd District, 1983–89).

Stratton was a Presbyterian and member of the American Legion, Amvets, Veterans of Foreign Wars, Freemasons, and Eagles.

Truax Field

Location: Madison, Wisconsin
Status: Active
Named for: First Lieutenant Thomas Leroy Truax
Date of Birth: June 1, 1917
Place of Birth: Ames, Iowa
Date of Death: November 2, 1941
Place of Death: San Francisco, California

First Lieutenant Thomas Leroy Truax was a 1939 graduate of Wisconsin-Madison High School. He joined the Army Air Corps after graduating from college and was assigned to the 57th Pursuit Group at Windsor Locks, Connecticut.

Truax, along with Lieutenant R. E. Stockman, was killed when their Curtiss P-40 Warhawk encountered heavy fog and struck Bald Hill, about twenty miles north of San Francisco. Truax died the day following his promotion to first lieutenant.

Volk Field Air National Guard Base

Location: Adjacent to Fort McCoy in Sparta, Wisconsin
Status: Active
Named for: First Lieutenant Jerome A. Volk
Date of Birth: March 17, 1925
Place of Birth: Harvey, North Dakota
Date of Death: November 7, 1951
Place of Death: Korea

First Lieutenant Jerome A. Volk was the first Wisconsin Air National Guard pilot killed during the Korean War.

After graduating from Rufus King High School in Milwaukee, Volk joined the Enlisted Reserve Corps on June 15, 1943, and graduated from the Air Cadet Training program. He was commissioned a second lieutenant in the Army Air Corps on December 22, 1943, and later flew North American P-51 Mustangs.

On January 12, 1949, he joined the Officers' Reserve Corps with the Wisconsin Air National Guard, was assigned to the 126th Fighter Squadron in Milwaukee, and promoted to first lieutenant on August 24, 1949.

Volk was called to active duty on February 28, 1951, and was sent to Korea where he was killed while flying a mission in a Lockheed F-80 Shooting Star. His remains were never recovered.

While in the reserves, he had attended Marquette University in Milwaukee and was awarded his degree posthumously in June 1956 in recognition of his service and sacrifice.

Yeager Field

Location: Charleston, West Virginia
Status: Active
Named for: Brigadier General Charles Elwood "Chuck" Yeager
Date of Birth: February 13, 1923
Place of Birth: Myra, West Virginia
Decorations and Honors: Congressional Gold Medal; Presidential Medal of Freedom; Silver Star with oak leaf cluster; Distinguished Service Medal; Air Force Commendation Medal; Legion of Merit with oak leaf cluster; Distinguished Flying Cross with two oak leaf clusters; Bronze Star with V device; Purple Heart; Air Medal with ten oak leaf clusters; Mackay Trophy (1947); Collier Trophy; Harmon International Trophy; Honorary Doctor of Science degree from West Virginia University; Honorary Doctor of Science degree from Marshall University; inducted into the National Aviation Hall of Fame (1973)
Date of Retirement: March 1, 1975

Brigadier General Charles Elwood Yeager was the first man to fly faster than the speed of sound, breaking the sound barrier on October 14, 1947.

Yeager enlisted in the Army Air Corps in September 1941, received his pilot wings, and was appointed as a flight officer in March 1943 at Luke Field in Arizona. In November 1943, he was assigned to the 363rd Fighter Squadron, 357th Fighter Group, where he flew the North American P-51 Mustang. Between 1943 and 1945, he flew sixty-four combat missions over France and Germany and shot down thirteen enemy aircraft, five in a single day, making him an ace pilot.

On March 5, 1944, he was shot down over German-occupied France. He bailed out and escaped capture with the help of the French Maquis, who led him to the safety of the Spanish border. In August 1947, he was selected as a pilot for the nation's first research rocket aircraft, the rocket-powered Bell X-1, at Edwards Air Force Base in California. In addition to being the first man to fly faster than the speed of sound, he also became the first man to fly more than twice the speed of sound at 1,650 mph, flying the Bell X-1A on December 12, 1953.

In 1954, he was transferred to Germany where he commanded the 417th Fighter Squadron. The following year, he was assigned to the 1st Tactical Fighter Squadron at Moron Air Base in Spain where he remained until November 1958.

He was seriously injured in December 1963 while testing a Lockheed F-104 Starfighter at more than twice the speed of sound when the engine failed and he was forced to bail out. As he ejected, the seat hit his helmet, ripping off his visor. Flames from the ejector rocket set his flight suit on fire, resulting in burns that required many skin grafts. Yeager returned to military combat in July 1966 and took command of the 405th Fighter Wing at Clark Air Base in the Philippines. During the Vietnam War, he flew a total of 127 combat missions.

His later assignments included commander of the 4th Tactical Fighter Wing at Seymour Johnson Air Force Base in North Carolina, vice commander of the 17th Air Force at Ramstein Air Base in Germany, U.S. Defense Representative to Pakistan, and director of the Air Force Inspection and Safety Center at Norton Air Force Base in California.

Fifty years after his first Mach One flight, at age seventy-four, he broke the sound barrier again, flying a McDonnell-Douglas F-15 on October 14, 1997. At the time of his retirement, he had flown more than ten thousand hours in more than 115 different types and models of aircraft. He married Glennis Faye Dickhouse, deceased, and is currently married to Victoria Scott D'Angelo. He has two sons and two daughters.

His Congressional Medal citation reads as follows:

For conspicuous gallantry and total disregard for his personal safety on October 14, 1947, as pilot of the XS-1 research aircraft. On this date, Brigadier General (then Captain) Yeager advanced aerospace science a quantum step by proving that an aircraft could be flown at supersonic speeds. He dispelled for all time the mythical "sound barrier" and set the stage for unprecedented aviation advancement. Through his selfless dedication to duty and his heroic challenge of the unknown, General Yeager performed inestimable service to the Nation far above and beyond the call of duty and brought great credit upon himself and the United States of America.

"The first time I ever saw a jet, I shot it down."—*General Chuck Yeager, USAF, describing his first confrontation with an Me262*

United States Army

Better than Honor and Glory . . .

Glory and Honor and Fame; the pomp that a soldier prizes;
The league-long waving line as the marching falls and rises;
Rumbling of Caissons and guns;
the clatter of horses feet,
And a million awestruck faces far down the waiting street.
But better than martial woe,
and the pageant of civic sorrow;
Better than praise of today,
or the statue we build tomorrow;
Better than honor and glory,
and history's iron pen,
Was the thought of duty done
and the love of his fellowmen.

—Richard Watson Gildner, during the Civil War

CHAPTER 3

United States Army

Brann Barracks

Location: Vienna, Austria
Status: Closed
Named for: Major General Donald Weldon Brann
Date of Birth: September 26, 1895
Place of Birth: Rushville, Indiana
Date of Death: December 29, 1945
Place of Death: Europe
Place of Burial: Arlington National Cemetery, Section 11, Site 836

Major General Donald Weldon Brann helped plan the invasion of Anzio during World War II.

Brann was a 1917 graduate of Purdue University and was commissioned in the Infantry Officer Reserve Corps. He served with the 15th Infantry Regiment in China from 1923 to 1927, and also with the 10th Infantry Regiment from 1926 to 1931.

After an assignment as an instructor in the Weapons Department of the Infantry School at Fort Benning in Georgia from 1931 to 1933, he was assigned to the University of Hawaii at Honolulu as professor of Military Science and Tactics. He graduated from the Command and General Staff College on June 21, 1935, and from the Army War College in 1938.

From March 1942 to May 1943, he served as chief of staff of the 95th Infantry Division, and later became assistant chief of staff for Operations with the Fifth Army. In December 1944, he was assigned as G-3 of the Fifteenth Army as deputy chief of staff for Operations where he directed the planning of the invasion of North Africa. He was promoted to major general in June 1945. In October of that year he was appointed deputy commander, U.S. forces, in Austria where he served until his death. He was married to Dorothy Teel.

Camp Barkeley

Location: Abilene, Texas
Status: Closed
Named for: Private David Bennes Barkeley (Misspelled, born Barkley)
Date of Birth: 1899
Place of Birth: Laredo, Texas
Date of Death: November 9, 1918
Place of Death: France
Decorations and Honors: Medal of Honor; French Croix de Guerre; Croce Merito (Italy)
Place of Burial: San Antonio National Cemetery in San Antonio, Texas, Section G, Site 1302

Private David Bennes Barkeley was assigned to Company A, 356th Infantry, 89th Division.

Barkeley didn't want to be known as a Mexican for fear he would not be allowed on the front lines of battle. In 1921, an elementary school in San Antonio was named for him. He was the second person to lay in state at the Alamo in San Antonio, Texas.

His Medal of Honor citation for action during World War I reads as follows:

When information was desired as to the enemy's position on the opposite side of the Meuse River, Private Barkeley, with another soldier, volunteered without hesitation and swam the river to reconnoiter the exact location. He succeeded in reaching the opposite bank, despite the evident determination of the enemy to prevent a crossing. Having obtained his information, he again entered the water for his return, but before his goal was reached, he was seized with cramps and drowned.

Camp Bondsteel

Location: Kosovo
Status: Active
Named for: Staff Sergeant James Leroy Bondsteel
Date of Birth: July 18, 1947
Place of Birth: Jackson, Michigan
Date of Death: April 9, 1987
Place of Death: Anchorage, Alaska
Decorations and Honors: Medal of Honor
Place of Burial: Fort Richardson National Cemetery in Alaska, Plot H-19

Staff Sergeant James Leroy Bondsteel served with Company A, 2nd Battalion, 2nd Infantry, 1st Infantry Division, in Vietnam, and with the U.S. Task Force Falcon, in Kosovo.

His Medal of Honor citation for action during Vietnam reads as follows:

For conspicuous gallantry and intrepidity in action at the risk of his life above and beyond the call of duty. Staff Sergeant Bondsteel distinguished himself while serving as a platoon sergeant with Company A, near the village of Lang Sau. Company A was directed to assist a friendly unit which was endangered by intense fire from a North Vietnamese Battalion located in a heavily fortified base camp. Staff Sergeant Bondsteel quickly organized the men of his platoon into effective combat teams and spearheaded the attack by destroying four enemy occupied bunkers. He then raced some 200 meters under heavy enemy fire to reach an adjoining platoon, which had begun to falter. After rallying this unit and assisting their wounded, Staff Sergeant Bondsteel returned to his own sector with critically needed munitions. Without pausing he moved to the forefront and destroyed four enemy occupied bunkers and a machine gun, which had threatened his advancing platoon. Although painfully wounded by an enemy grenade, Staff Sergeant Bondsteel refused medical attention and continued his assault by neutralizing two more enemy bunkers nearby. While searching one of these emplacements Staff Sergeant Bondsteel narrowly escaped death when an enemy soldier detonated a grenade at close range. Shortly thereafter, he ran to the aid of a severely wounded officer and struck down an enemy soldier who was threatening the officer's life. Staff Sergeant Bondsteel then continued to rally his men and led them through the entrenched enemy until his company was relieved. His exemplary leadership and great personal courage throughout the four-hour battle ensured the success of his own and nearby units, and resulted in the saving of numerous lives of his fellow soldiers. By individual acts of bravery he destroyed ten enemy bunkers and accounted for a large toll of the enemy, including two key enemy commanders. His extraordinary heroism at the risk of his life was in the highest traditions of the military service and reflect great credit on him, his unit, and the U.S. Army.

Camp Claiborne

Located: Alexandria, Louisiana
Status: Closed
Named for: Governor William Charles Cole Claiborne, civilian
Date of Birth: 1775
Place of Birth: Sussex County, Virginia
Date of Death: November 23, 1817
Place of Death: New Orleans, Louisiana
Place of Burial: Metairie Cemetery in New Orleans, Louisiana

William Charles Cole Claiborne was Louisiana's first governor after the state's admission into the Union in 1812, serving until 1816.

Claiborne studied law in Richmond, Virginia, was admitted to the bar, and practiced law in Sullivan County, Tennessee. He was a delegate to the State constitutional convention from Sullivan County in 1796 and was appointed judge of the superior court in 1796. He was elected as a Republican from Tennessee to the Fifth and Sixth Congresses, serving from November 23, 1797, to March 3, 1801, although he was not yet twenty-five years old, the required constitutional age for that position.

Among his many other political positions were: appointed governor of the Territory of Mississippi in 1801; appointed in October 1803 as one of the commissioners to take possession of Louisiana when it was purchased from France; and served as governor of the Territory of Orleans from 1804 to 1812. He was elected as a Democrat from Louisiana to the U.S. Senate and served from March 4, 1817, until his death. He was an Episcopalian and member of the Freemasons.

Claiborne died of a liver ailment. Counties in Louisiana, Mississippi, and Tennessee are also named in his honor.

Camp Cooke (formerly, Cooke AFB. Now, Vandenberg Air Force Base)

Location: Santa Maria, California
Status: Active
Named for: Major General Philip St. George Cooke
Date of Birth: June 13, 1809
Place of Birth: Leesburg, Virginia
Date of Death: March 20, 1895
Place of Death: Detroit, Michigan
Date of Retirement: 1873
Place of Burial: Elmwood Cemetery in Detroit, Michigan, Section H, Lot 94

Major General Philip St. George Cooke was an Indian fighter, explorer, and cavalry officer.

Cooke graduated from West Point in 1827 and was assigned to the 16th Infantry Regiment at Jefferson Barracks in Missouri. His first combat assignment was fighting the Comanche Indians along the upper Arkansas River with the First Dragoon Regiment. He was the commander of the famous Mormon Battalion, which left Santa Fe, New Mexico, in October 1846, pulling wagons over uncharted wilderness to San Diego, California. He was also a U.S. observer in the Crimean War in 1850.

During the American Civil War, he fought in the battles at Williamsburg,

Gaines's Mill, and White Oak Swamp. He took part in General George B. McClellan's Peninsula campaign and led a cavalry division at Yorktown.

As a native Virginian, Cooke's loyalty to the Union came under suspicion during the Civil War when most of his family sided with the South. His son, John R. Cooke, became a Confederate army general. Two of his daughters joined the Confederate cause, one marrying Confederate cavalry commander J.E.B. Stuart. Cooke and one of his daughters remained loyal to the Union.

The rest of his war service was administrative, serving on courts-martial until August 1863, when he was placed in command of the district of Baton Rouge, serving there until May 1864. Later, he headed the Union's recruiting service until the Confederate surrender.

Camp Croft

Location: Greenville, South Carolina
Status: Closed
Named for: Major General Edward Croft
Date of Birth: July 11, 1875
Place of Birth: Greenville, South Carolina
Date of Death: January 28, 1938
Place of Death: Greenville, South Carolina
Decorations and Honors: Silver Star; Purple Heart
Date of Retirement: 1937
Place of Burial: Arlington National Cemetery, Section 2, Site 4941

Major General Edward Croft served in the Spanish-American War, the Philippine Insurrection, and World War I.

Croft graduated from the Citadel in Charleston, South Carolina, in 1896 and was assigned to the 19th Infantry. Croft served in Puerto Rico from 1898 to 1899 and in the Philippines from 1899 to 1901 where he was wounded at Labangon Barrio. While serving on the Mexican border, Croft commanded a company-battalion in fighting the Mexican marauders.

He served in France during World War I, commanding the 2nd Battalion, 26th Infantry, 1st Division. Later, he served with the 76th Division where he was in charge of the Division School and Officers' Training Corps at Camp Devens near Boston, Massachusetts.

During his career, he also served with the 380th Infantry; was the executive officer at Camp Custer in Michigan; executive officer at Camp Meade in Baltimore, Maryland; student officer to the School of the Line at Fort Leavenworth in Kansas; commander, Fort Hamilton in New York; commander, 16th Infantry at Fort Jay in New York; and assistant chief of staff, G-3, Training and Operations Division. After the war, Croft was placed in charge of exploring and mapping the Philippine Islands and Puerto Rico.

His Silver Star citation for action during the Philippine Insurrection reads as follows:

For gallantry in action against Insurgents near Cuba, Philippine Islands, on July 27, 1901. During this engagement Lieutenant Croft was seriously wounded, but in spite of his wound he retained command and coolly directed the action of his troops until a senior officer arrived with reinforcements.

Camp Funston

Located: Adjacent to Fort Riley in Junction City, Kansas
Status: Closed
Named for: Brigadier General Frederick N. Funston
Date of Birth: September 11, 1865
Place of Birth: New Carlisle, Ohio
Date of Death: February 19, 1917
Place of Death: Fort Sam Houston, San Antonio, Texas
Decorations and Honors: Medal of Honor
Place of Burial: San Francisco National Cemetery, Presidio of San Francisco, California

Brigadier General Frederick N. Funston served during the Spanish-American War and in the Philippine Insurrection.

Before entering the military, Funston worked for several newspapers as a reporter and then with the Department of Agriculture as part of an expedition to the Dakota Territory and Death Valley in California where he studied plant life.

He joined the Cuban army in 1986 as a captain and served under Maximo Gomez and Calixto Garcia. He fought in twenty-two battles and was wounded several times. Later, he was assigned to the 20th Kansas Regiment of the Kansas National Guard on May 13, 1898, and was sent to the Philippines. There, in 1899, he led nineteen battles, one of which was at Calumpit where he earned the Medal of Honor. He also participated in the capture of Philippine president, Emilio Aquinaldo.

After returning to the United States, he was assigned second-in-command of the army's Department of California and helped restore order to San Francisco following the earthquake of 1906. He served as commandant of the Army Service School at Fort Leavenworth in Kansas from 1908 to 1910.

In 1914, he became commander of the Department of Luzon in the Philippines and occupied the port of Veracruz, Mexico. In 1916, he served during the Punitive Expedition and fought Pancho Villa. He authored *Memories of Two Wars* (University of Nebraska Press, 1911). He was the first person to lie in state at the Alamo. He was married to Edna Blankart. They had three children.

His Medal of Honor for action on April 27, 1899, during the Philippine Insurrection reads as follows:

Crossed the river on a raft and by his skill and daring enabled the general commanding to carry the enemy's entrenched position on the north bank of the river and to drive him with great loss from the important strategic position of Calumpit.

Camp Gordon Johnston

Location: Carrabelle, Florida
Status: Closed
Named for: Colonel Gordon Johnston
Date of Birth: May 25, 1874
Place of Birth: Charlotte, North Carolina
Date of Death: March 8, 1934
Place of Death: No Data Found
Decorations and Honors: Medal of Honor; Distinguished Service Cross; Distinguished Service Medal with two oak leaf clusters; Silver Star with two oak leaf clusters; Purple Heart; French Legion of Honor
Place of Burial: Arlington National Cemetery, Section 7, Site 10092

Colonel Gordon Johnston was a cavalryman who served during the Philippine Insurrection; Cuban Occupation; on the Mexican border; and with the American Expeditionary Force in France during World War I.

Johnston graduated from Princeton University in 1896. He first served in Company M, 2nd Mississippi Volunteer Infantry Regiment, and beginning July 1, 1898, he served with Troop M, 1st U.S. Volunteer Cavalry, known as the Rough Riders. He later transferred to the cavalry where he remained throughout his military career.

In October 1902, Johnston attended the army's infantry and cavalry schools, graduating with honors in 1903. He attended the German Riding Academy in 1907. His other military schooling included the General Command and Staff College in June 1918, the Cavalry Advanced Course in 1925, and the Army War College in 1926.

In October 1918, as a colonel, Johnston became chief of staff for the 82nd Infantry Division where he helped direct the unit's Argonne-area operations. He died as a result of a polo accident.

His Medal of Honor citation for action during the Philippine Insurrection reads as follows:

Voluntarily took part in and was dangerously wounded during an assault on the enemy's works.

His Distinguished Service Cross citation for service during the Philippine Insurrection reads as follows:

While in command of a small detachment of scouts, he displayed remarkable gallantry and leadership in charging a greatly superior force of entrenched insurgents in the face of cannon and rifle fire, driving the enemy from their position and capturing the town of Palo.

He earned the Purple Heart for wounds received at Bud Dajo in the Philippines.

Camp Grant

Location: Rockford, Illinois
Status: Closed
Named for: President and General Ulysses Simpson Grant
Date of Birth: April 27, 1822
Place of Birth: Point Pleasant, Ohio
Date of Death: July 23, 1885
Place of Death: Mount McGregor, New York
Decorations and Honors: Congressional Gold Medal
Place of Burial: Riverside Park in New York City, New York

Ulysses Simpson Grant was the eighteenth president of the United States from 1869 to 1877.

Grant graduated from West Point in 1843 and saw his first military action in 1846 as a second lieutenant in the Mexican-American War under General Zachary Taylor. In March 1864, Grant became general-in-chief of the army and commanded General William Tecumseh Sherman during his drive through the South, while he himself directed the Army of the Potomac and surrounded General Robert E. Lee's Army of Northern Virginia, which helped end the war.

At Appomattox Court House on April 9, 1865, when the Confederate commander asked for terms, Grant made the famous reply, "No terms except an unconditional and immediate surrender can be accepted."

During his presidency, Grant filled many White House positions with his old army staff. His presidency was riddled with scandal and his honesty was questioned when he was seen with two gold speculators, Jay Gould and James Fisk. Realizing their scheme, Grant authorized the secretary of the treasury to sell enough gold to flood the market; unfortunately, the damage had already been done.

After his presidency, Grant became a partner in a financial firm that went bankrupt. When he learned that he had cancer of the throat, he began writing his memoirs to pay off his debts. He died soon after completing the last page.

Camp Livingston

Location: Louisiana
Status: Now, part of the Kisatchie National Forest
Named for: Chancellor Robert R. Livingston, Jr., civilian
Date of Birth: November 27, 1746
Place of Birth: New York City, New York
Date of Death: February 26, 1813
Place of Death: Clermont, New York
Place of Burial: Saint Paul's Episcopal Church in Tivoli, New York

Chancellor Robert R. Livingston, Jr., was the negotiator of the Louisiana Purchase.

Livingston studied law, was admitted to the bar in 1773, and practiced law in New York City. He was recorder for the City of New York but had to relinquish the position in 1775 because of his patriotic views.

Livingston was secretary of foreign affairs for the United States from 1781 to 1783. In 1788, he was appointed chairman of the state convention at Poughkeepsie to consider the adoption of the U.S. Constitution. Although he was a member of the Committee of Five, comprised of John Adams of Massachusetts, Thomas Jefferson of Virginia, Benjamin Franklin of Pennsylvania, and Robert Sherman of Connecticut, who were appointed to draw up the Declaration of Independence, he never signed the document.

In 1792, he received an honorary Doctor of Laws degree from regents of the University of the State of New York. He was also a founder of the American Academy of Fine Arts in New York in 1801. While in France, he became friends with Napoleon Bonaparte. That friendship later resulted in the purchase of Louisiana in 1803.

Livingston retired from public life and engaged in agriculture and raising livestock. He was the first to introduce powdered gypsum in agriculture, and merino sheep west of the Hudson River.

Congress placed a statue of him in the Capitol in Washington. He was married to Mary Stevens of New Jersey. They had two children.

Camp Mackall

Location: Adjacent to Fort Bragg in Fayetteville, North Carolina
Status: Active
Named for: Private John Thomas "Tommy" Mackall
Date of Birth: May 17, 1920
Place of Birth: Negley, Ohio
Date of Death: November 12, 1942

Place of Death: Gibraltar
Place of Burial: Glenview Cemetery in East Palestine, Ohio

Private John Thomas Mackall was a U.S. paratrooper killed in Operation Torch.

Mackall grew up in Wellsville, Ohio, entered the army on January 7, 1942, and was sent to Camp Wolters in Mineral Wells, Texas, for training. He graduated from Parachute School at Fort Benning in Georgia in May and was assigned to Fort Bragg in North Carolina where he served in Company E, 503rd Parachute Infantry Battalion.

Mackall was wounded near Oron, Algeria, during the Allied invasion of North Africa on November 8, 1942, when the plane he was flying in was attacked. He was taken by air to a British hospital at Gibraltar where he died four days later. He was assigned to the 2nd Battalion, 503rd Parachute Infantry Regiment, at the time of his death.

Camp Monteith

Location: Kosovo
Status: Closed
Named for: First Lieutenant Jimmie W. Monteith, Jr.
Date of Birth: July 1, 1917
Place of Birth: Low Moor, Virginia
Date of Death: June 6, 1944
Place of Death: Colleville-sur-Mer, France
Decorations and Honors: Medal of Honor, posthumously; Purple Heart
Place of Burial: Normandy American Cemetery and Memorial in Colleville-sur-Mer, France

First Lieutenant Jimmie W. Monteith, Jr., served with the 16th Infantry, 1st Infantry Division, and took part in the Normandy landings on D-Day.

His Medal of Honor citation for action during World War II reads as follows:

For conspicuous gallantry and intrepidity above and beyond the call of duty on June 6, 1944, near Colleville-sur-Mer, France. First Lieutenant Monteith landed with the initial assault waves on the coast of France under heavy enemy fire. Without regard to his own personal safety he continually moved up and down the beach reorganizing men for further assault. He then led the assault over a narrow protective ledge and across the flat, exposed terrain to the comparative safety of a cliff. Retracing his steps across the field to the beach, he moved over to where two tanks were buttoned up and blind under violent enemy artillery and machine-gun fire. Completely exposed to the intense fire, First Lieutenant Monteith led the tanks on foot through a minefield and into firing positions. Under his direction several enemy positions were destroyed. He then rejoined his company and under his leadership his men captured an advantageous position on the hill. Supervising the defense of his newly won position against repeated vicious counterattacks, he continued to ignore his own personal safety, repeatedly crossing the 200 or 300 yards of open terrain under heavy fire to strengthen links in his defensive chain. When the enemy succeeded in completely surrounding First Lieutenant Monteith and his unit and while leading the fight out of the situation, First Lieutenant Monteith was killed by enemy fire. The courage, gallantry, and intrepid leadership displayed by First Lieutenant Monteith are worthy of emulation.

Camp Sherman

Location: Chillicothe, Ohio
Status: Now, site of VA Medical Center
Named for: General William Tecumseh Sherman
Date of Birth: February 8, 1820
Place of Birth: Lancaster, Ohio
Date of Death: February 14, 1891
Place of Death: New York City, New York
Date of Retirement: 1884
Place of Burial: Calvary Cemetery in St. Louis, Missouri

General William Tecumseh Sherman is best remembered for his march to the sea during the Civil War, when he directed troops through the South and burned the city of Atlanta.

Sherman graduated sixth in his class from West Point in 1840 and was assigned to artillery. During the Civil War, he served in more than thirteen different divisions and departments. He was honored twice by Congress, first for his service at Chattanooga, and second for his leadership in Atlanta and Savannah.

After the war, he remained in the service and was promoted to general, replacing General Ulysses Grant as commander in chief. As commander of the Missouri district, which stretched from the Rocky Mountains to the Mississippi River, he helped protect transcontinental railroad workers from Indian attack.

Sherman was outspoken in his belief that the army should set Indian policy and that tribes should be placed on reservations. He once declared that all Indians not on reservations "are hostile and will remain so until killed off."

Sherman helped establish the Louisiana State University, and became its first superintendent. He also helped establish the School of Application for Cavalry and Infantry that later became the Command and General Staff College at Fort Leavenworth in Kansas City, Kansas.

"It is only those who have neither fired a shot nor heard the shrieks and groans of the wounded who cry aloud for blood. . . . War is hell."—*General William Tecumseh Sherman*

Camp Taliaferro

Located: Fort Worth, Texas
Status: Closed
Named for: Second Lieutenant Walter R. Taliaferro
Date of Birth: September 9, 1880
Place of Birth: Campbell County, Kentucky
Date of Death: October 11, 1915
Place of Death: San Diego, California
Place of Burial: Mount Hope Cemetery in San Diego, California

Second Lieutenant Walter R. Taliaferro was a junior military aviator and holder of the American record for a sustained solo flight.

Taliaferro entered the military as a private and was promoted to sergeant in the 110th Coast Artillery before being commissioned a second lieutenant in the 21st Infantry on August 2, 1908.

After serving in the Philippines, where he surveyed Luzon and made maps of the islands, his assignments took him to Fort Sam Houston in Texas and to North Island in San Diego. In December 1913, along with Lieutenant Joseph E. Carberry, Taliaferro set an altitude record of seven thousand feet. In January 1914, he flew from San Diego to Elsinore, California, a distance of 260 miles in 225 minutes. He set another aviation record on September 17, 1914, when he remained in the air for 9 hours and 48 minutes, to become one of the army's top flyers.

Taliaferro died when his Curtiss Tractor #30 plunged into the bay after making loop maneuvers. He was married to Leicester Sehon.

Camp Truscott

Located: Salzburg, Austria
Status: Closed
Named for: Captain Al Truscott
Date of Birth: No Data Found
Place of Birth: No Data Found
Date of Death: April 22, 1945
Place of Death: Furth, Germany

Captain Al Truscott was the commanding officer of Company H, 222nd Infantry Regiment, 42nd Infantry Division.

Truscott suffered wounds to his shoulder on January 6, 1945, at La Wantzenau, France. Despite his injury he refused to leave his troops. After having his wound dressed at the battalion aid station, he returned to his company to assist and encourage his men who were experiencing their first contact with the enemy. Although the pain of his shoulder was severe, Truscott remained with his men for six more hours before having his wound properly dressed.

He was killed three months later while leading an attack on Furth, Germany.

Camp Wallace Air Station

Located: Luzon, Philippines
Status: Closed
Named for: Second Lieutenant George W. Wallace
Date of Birth: No Data Found
Place of Birth: Fort Riley in Kansas
Date of Death: March 4, 1900
Place of Death: Philippine Islands
Decorations and Honors: Medal of Honor

Second Lieutenant George W. Wallace served with the 9th U.S. Infantry.

His Medal of Honor citation for action during the Philippine Insurrection reads as follows:

With another officer and a native Filipino, was shot at from an ambush, the other officer falling severely wounded. Second Lieutenant Wallace fired in the direction of the enemy, put them to rout, removed the wounded officer from the path, returned to the town, a mile distant, and summoned assistance from his command.

Fort A. P. Hill

Location: Caroline County, Virginia
Status: Active
Named for: Lieutenant General Ambrose Powell Hill
Date of Birth: November 9, 1825
Place of Birth: Culpeper, Virginia
Date of Death: April 2, 1865

Place of Death: Petersburg, Virginia
Place of Burial: A.P. Hill Monument in Richmond, Virginia

Lieutenant General Ambrose Powell Hill fought in the Mexican-American War, Seminole Wars, and the American Civil War.

Hill, a 1847 West Point graduate, ranked fifteenth in his class of thirty-eight graduates and was nicknamed "Little Powell." In March 1861, Powell resigned his U.S. Army commission and joined the Confederacy where he served with the 13th Virginia Infantry Regiment and fought at the battle of First Bull Run in 1861.

Hill commanded troops in the battle of Williamsburg during the Peninsula campaign in the summer of 1862. He also fought in the battles at Seven Days' in May 1862, Cedar Mountain in August 1862, Second Bull Run in August 1862, Antietam in September 1862, and Fredericksburg in December 1862.

As a major general, he was considered one of the most prominent and successful division commanders of General Robert E. Lee's Army of Northern Virginia. As a lieutenant general, Hill was placed in command of III Corps of General Lee's army, which he led at Gettysburg in 1863. Because of an undisclosed illness, he gave a poor performance and was responsible for the disaster at Bristoe Station in October 1863. He fought in the Overland campaign during June 1864. He was shot during an encounter with a group of Federal soldiers and died a week before the surrender at Appomattox. He was married to Kitty Morgan McClung.

Fort Benjamin Harrison

Location: Indianapolis, Indiana
Status: Closed
Named for: President and General Benjamin Harrison
Date of Birth: August 20, 1833
Place of Birth: North Bend, Ohio
Date of Death: March 13, 1901
Place of Death: Indianapolis, Indiana
Place of Burial: Crown Hill Cemetery in Indianapolis, Indiana

Benjamin Harrison, nicknamed "Little Ben," was the twenty-third president of the United States from 1889 to 1893.

A graduate of Miami University in Ohio, Harrison began practicing law in Indiana in March 1854 and became active in Republican politics. During the Civil War, he assisted in forming the 70th Indiana Regiment, was promoted to the rank of colonel, and served mainly in the West guarding railroads. He was placed in command of his brigade and increased the size of the 1st Division of

XI Corps. He fought in campaigns from Chattanooga to Atlanta and rose to the rank of brigadier general. He was made brevet brigadier general of volunteers in January 1865.

He was elected as a Republican senator from Indiana in 1880. As senator, he favored a judicious tariff reform, advocated the rights of the working class, opposed President Cleveland's veto of pension bills, advised the restoration of the American Navy, voted for civil service reform, and helped create the Interstate Commerce Commission. He also signed the Sherman Antitrust Act and the McKinley Tariff Act.

In 1888, he received the Republican nomination for president on the eighth ballot. Though behind in the popular vote, he defeated Grover Cleveland in the Electoral College by 233 to 168. Harrison was nominated again in 1892 but lost the election. After his presidency, he resumed his law practice.

Fort Benning

Location: Columbus, Georgia
Status: Active
Named for: General Henry Lewis "Old Rock" Benning
Date of Birth: April 2, 1814
Place of Birth: Columbia County, Georgia
Date of Death: July 10, 1875
Place of Death: Columbus, Georgia
Place of Burial: Linwood Cemetery in Columbus, Georgia

General Henry Lewis Benning was a Confederate soldier, attorney, politician, and justice of the Georgia Supreme Court.

Benning practiced law in Columbus, Georgia, in 1835 and was elected associate justice of the Georgia Supreme Court in 1853. At the beginning of the war, he recruited men and formed the 17th Regiment of Georgia Volunteers. He fought in the battle of Second Bull Run in August 1862, and his brigade played a crucial role in guarding Burnside's brigade at the battle of Antietam in September 1862. He commanded General John Hood's division at Gettysburg on July 2, 1863, where he led his brigade in an assault at Devil's Den. At the battle of Chickamauga, Georgia, in September 1863 his horse was shot out from under him, and in the Overland campaign in 1864, he fought against General Ulysses S. Grant.

He led Major General Charles W. Field's division in the battle of the Wilderness where he was severely wounded in the left shoulder on May 5, 1864. Benning was present at the surrendering ceremony at Appomattox Court House on April 9, 1865.

After the war, he returned to his law practice in Columbus, Georgia. He was married to Mary Howard Jones.

Fort Bliss

Location: El Paso, Texas
Status: Active
Named for: Lieutenant Colonel William Wallace Smith Bliss
Date of Birth: August 17, 1815
Place of Birth: Whitehall, New York
Date of Death: August 5, 1853
Place of Death: East Pascagoula, Mississippi
Decorations and Honors: Gold Medal for his bravery in Mexico
Place of Burial: Fort Bliss Post Cemetery in El Paso, Texas

Lieutenant Colonel William Wallace Smith Bliss was General Zachary Taylor's chief of staff during the Mexican-American War, and later he was President Taylor's private secretary.

Bliss graduated from West Point in 1833, ninth in a class of forty-three graduates. While at the academy, he got the nickname "Perfect Bliss." He mastered six languages and had a reading knowledge of thirteen. From 1834 to 1840, he was an assistant professor of mathematics at West Point.

He was commissioned a second lieutenant and assigned to the 4th Infantry Regiment. In 1845, he took part in the military occupation of Texas and fought the Cherokee Indians. On May 8, 1846, during the Mexican-American War, he fought in the battle of Palo Alto and also in the battle of Buena Vista where he was promoted to lieutenant colonel in 1847.

In 1848, he received a master of arts degree from Dartmouth College in New Hampshire. He was also a member of the Royal Society of Northern Antiquaries of Copenhagen, Denmark, and an honorary member of the American Ethnological Society.

Bliss died from yellow fever and was first buried in a Protestant cemetery in Pascagoula, Mississippi, but was later reinterred at Fort Bliss. He was married to Mary Elizabeth Taylor.

Fort Bragg

Location: Fayetteville, North Carolina
Status: Active
Named for: General Braxton Bragg
Date of Birth: March 22, 1817
Place of Birth: Warrenton, North Carolina
Date of Death: September 27, 1876
Place of Death: Galveston, Texas
Place of Burial: Mobile, Alabama

General Braxton Bragg was a writer, plantation owner and commander in chief of the Confederate army in 1864.

Bragg graduated from West Point in 1837 and was commissioned a second lieutenant in artillery. He fought in the Seminole Wars and served under General Zachary Taylor during the Mexican-American War.

Among his assignments during the Civil War were: commander, Department of Louisiana; commander, Department of Alabama and West Florida; commander, Army of Pensacola; commander, Army of the Mississippi; commander, II Corps, Army of the Mississippi; commander, Army of Tennessee; commander, Department of Tennessee; commander, Department of North Carolina; and supervisor of Hoke's division, Hardee's corps, Army of Tennessee.

He fought in the battles of Shiloh (April 1862); Perryville (October 1862); Murfreesboro (Stone's River), from December to January 1863; Chickamauga, Georgia (September 1863); and at Chattanooga (November 1863). In November 1864, he was placed in command of the Department of North Carolina.

Bragg lost his plantation during the war, and for a short time afterward, he served as Alabama's chief engineer. The remaining years of his life were spent as an inspector for a large railroad in Galveston, Texas, where he died while walking down the street with a friend.

Fort Buchanan

Location: San Juan, Puerto Rico
Status: Active
Named for: President James Buchanan
Date of Birth: April 23, 1791
Place of Birth: Mercersburg, Pennsylvania
Date of Death: June 1, 1868
Place of Death: Lancaster, Pennsylvania
Place of Burial: Wheatland, Pennsylvania

James Buchanan was the fifteenth president of the United States from 1857 to 1861 and the only president to remain a bachelor throughout his term of office.

Buchanan was an 1809 graduate of Dickinson College in Carlisle, Pennsylvania. He was a lawyer and Federalist, and after the Federalist Party disbanded, he became a Jacksonian Democrat. He served in the House of Representatives from 1821 to 1831; was a minister to St. Petersburg from 1832 to 1833; and served in the U.S. Senate from 1834 to 1845. That same year he became President James Polk's secretary of state. In 1853, he became minister to Britain where he helped draft the expansionist Ostend Manifesto that suggested that the United States should take Cuba by force if Spain refused to sell. As president, Buchanan believed the question of slavery should be handled by the Supreme Court and took a policy of inactivity on the matter.

Fort Buckner

Location: Okinawa
Status: Active
Named for: Lieutenant General Simon Bolivar Buckner, Jr.
Date of Birth: July 18, 1886
Place of Birth: Munfordville, Kentucky
Date of Death: June 18, 1945
Place of Death: Okinawa
Place of Burial: Frankfort Cemetery in Frankfort, Kentucky

Lieutenant General Simon Bolivar Buckner, Jr., was the highest-ranking field commander to lose his life in the Pacific Theater of Operations during World War II.

Buckner graduated from West Point in 1908 and was commissioned a second lieutenant in the infantry. He graduated from the Command and General Staff College in 1925 and later taught there. He was also an instructor at Fort Benning in Georgia. In 1933, Buckner returned to West Point as an instructor, and later became commander of cadets.

In October 1939, Buckner was assigned to the 6th Division as chief of staff, and in July 1940, he was sent to Fort Richardson in Anchorage, Alaska, in charge of the Alaskan Defense Command. While there, he established Elmendorf Field in Anchorage; Ladd Field in Fairbanks; Fort Randall in Cold Bay; and Fort Glenn on Umnak Island.

Buckner was promoted to lieutenant general in May 1943 and transferred to Hawaii in August 1944, assigned to the Tenth Army, which he commanded during the battle of Okinawa. He was killed by enemy artillery fire while visiting the 8th Marine Regiment on the front lines.

A small memorial was erected in his honor at the location where he died. He was first buried in the Tenth Army Cemetery on Okinawa, but later his body was retuned to Kentucky to lie beside his father, who was a Civil War Confederate lieutenant general and governor of Kentucky. Congress posthumously promoted him to the rank of general in 1954.

Fort Campbell

Location: Hopkinsville, Kentucky
Status: Active
Named for: Brigadier General William Bowen Campbell
Date of Birth: February 1, 1807
Place of Birth: Hendersonville, Sumner County, Tennessee
Date of Death: August 19, 1867

Place of Death: Lebanon, Tennessee
Place of Burial: Cedar Grove Cemetery in Lebanon, Tennessee

Brigadier General William Bowen Campbell was the last Whig governor of Tennessee, serving from 1851 to 1853.

Campbell studied law in Abingdon and Winchester, Virginia, and practiced law in Carthage, Tennessee. He was elected district attorney for the 4th District in 1831, and he was captain of a cavalry company in General William Trousdale's regiment of the Tennessee Mounted Volunteers during the Florida Wars of 1836. During his political career, he served in the 6th District of Tennessee from 1837 to 1843 and became a state court judge in 1847.

In 1846, he served in the Mexican-American War where he distinguished himself while commanding a brigade in the battles of Monterey and Cerro Gordo. He is also remembered for leading his men with the battle cry, "Boys, follow me!"

Campbell traveled throughout Tennessee expressing his opposition to secession. On June 30, 1862, President Abraham Lincoln appointed him brigadier general in the Union army, but Campbell resigned on January 26, 1863, because of failing health. He was later elected to Congress for the 5th District, serving until March 3, 1867. He was married to Frances Owen.

Fort Carson

Location: Colorado Springs, Colorado
Status: Active
Named for: Brigadier General Christopher Houston "Kit" Carson
Date of Birth: December 24, 1809
Place of Birth: Madison County, Kentucky
Date of Death: May 23, 1868
Place of Death: Fort Lyons, Colorado
Place of Burial: Taos, New Mexico

Brigadier General Christopher Houston Carson was a trapper, military scout and guide, Indian agent, soldier, rancher, and authentic legend of the West.

Carson lived and worked among the Indians. His first two wives were Arapahoe and Cheyenne women. As a trapper, in the early part of the nineteenth century, he traveled throughout the West working for the Rocky Mountain Fur Company.

In 1842, he met John C. Frémont who hired Carson as a guide for his first expedition to map and describe the Western trails to the Pacific Ocean. In 1843, Carson married his third wife, fifteen-year-old Maria Josefa Jaramillo.

In 1853, Carson was appointed Federal Indian agent for Northern New

Mexico. He held that post until he became an officer in the Civil War. During the war, he helped organize and lead the New Mexico Volunteer Infantry, fighting the Confederate army. Much of his military career was spent attempting to eliminate the Navajo, Utes, Pueblos, Hopis, and Zunis Indians. He was responsible for placing four hundred Apache on a reservation and forced eight thousand Navajo to march three hundred miles on what became known as the "Long Walk" from Arizona to New Mexico. After the Civil War, he became a rancher in Colorado.

Fort Chaffee

Location: Fort Smith, Arkansas
Status: Now, Army National Guard Base
Named for: Major General Adna Romanza Chaffee, Jr.
Date of Birth: September 23, 1884
Place of Birth: Junction City, Kansas
Date of Death: August 22, 1941
Place of Death: Boston, Massachusetts
Place of Burial: Arlington National Cemetery, Section 3, Lot 1944 (next to his father)

Major General Adna Romanza Chaffee, Jr., was considered the "Father of the Armor Branch."

Chaffee graduated from West Point in 1906, thirty-first in his class of seventy-eight cadets, and was commissioned a lieutenant with the 15th Cavalry. He attended the Mounted Service School at Fort Riley in Kansas from 1907 to 1911, served with the 7th Cavalry in the Philippines from 1914 to 1915, and became the senior cavalry instructor in the Tactical Department at West Point from 1916 to 1917.

During World War I, Chaffee served with IV Corps in the Saint Mihiel and Meuse-Argonne offensives. After completing duty with the occupation in 1919, he became an instructor at the Command and General Staff College at Fort Leavenworth in Kansas City, Kansas. In 1921, he became head of operations for the 1st Cavalry Division at Fort Bliss in El Paso, Texas, until 1924. After attending the Army War College, he assumed command of a squadron of the 3rd Cavalry from 1925 to 1927.

As an advocate of mechanized warfare, Chaffee believed that mechanized armies would become the fighting machine of the future, and helped in the development of the army's tanks. He left the General Staff in 1931 to serve as the executive officer of the newly formed 1st Cavalry (Mechanized) at Fort Knox in Radcliff, Kentucky. In 1938, he became commander of the 7th Cavalry Brigade (Mechanized), the army's only armored force and fought for suitable equipment and for the establishment of tank divisions.

In June 1940, Chaffee took command of the Armored Force where he was responsible for combining all branches of the army into a single mechanized unit. He died after a long illness.

Fort Detrick

Location: Frederick, Maryland
Status: Active
Named for: Captain Frederick Louis Detrick
Date of Birth: April 21, 1889
Place of Birth: New Market, Frederick County, Virginia
Date of Death: June 3, 1931
Place of Death: Baltimore, Maryland

Captain Frederick Louis Detrick was a medical doctor.

Detrick entered the military on March 12, 1918, as a lieutenant in the Medical Reserve Corps. His first assignment was at the hospital at Camp Wadsworth in South Carolina on April 21, 1918, and later with the 28th Aero Squadron, 3rd Pursuit Group, in France where he was a battlefield medic during the major American offensives, including the battles of Meuse-Argonne and Saint Mihiel.

He returned to Baltimore after serving in Europe, began a private medical practice, and in 1923, joined the Maryland National Guard. There, he was appointed as a captain in the Medical Reserve Corps, assigned to the Medical Department Detachment, 29th Division Air Service. Later, he was named to the staff and faculty of Johns Hopkins University Hospital where he earned the reputation as a competent surgeon and teacher.

Detrick was at home when he suffered three heart attacks and died. He was promoted to major, posthumously. He was married to Marian Amelia Douglas.

Fort Devens (formerly, Camp Devens)

Location: Near Boston, Massachusetts
Status: Now, Devens Reserve Forces Training Area
Named for: Major General Charles Devens, Jr.
Date of Birth: April 4, 1820
Place of Birth: Charlestown, Massachusetts
Date of Death: January 7, 1891
Place of Death: Boston, Massachusetts

Place of Burial: Mount Auburn Cemetery in Cambridge, Massachusetts, Plot Tulip Path, Lot 1594

Major General Charles Devens, Jr., served in the Union army during the Civil War.

Devens graduated from Harvard University in 1838 and from Harvard Law in 1840. He practiced law in Northfield and Greenfield, Massachusetts. He was a Massachusetts State Senator from 1848 to 1849 and U.S. Marshal from 1849 to 1853. He left that position to resume his law practice in Worcester, Massachusetts, in 1854.

When the Civil War began, he enlisted in the Union army and served with the 3rd Battalion Rifles, and later with the 15th Massachusetts Volunteers. He was severely wounded during the battle of Seven Pines at Fair Oaks, and during the battle of Antietam in September 1862 when his horse was shot from under him.

In 1864, he commanded the 3rd Division, XXIV Corps, where his troops were the first to occupy Richmond after its evacuation. From 1865 to 1866, he commanded the military district of Charleston, South Carolina.

He left the service in June 1866, and returned to his law practice, and later he served as a judge of the superior court of Massachusetts from 1866 to 1873 and as a judge of the supreme judicial court of Massachusetts in 1873. He resigned that position in March 1877 to become attorney general of the United States in the cabinet of President Rutherford B. Hayes. In 1881, he was reappointed as Massachusetts Supreme Court Justice.

Fort Dix

Location: Lewistown, New Jersey
Status: Active
Named for: Major General John Adams Dix
Date of Birth: July 24, 1798
Place of Birth: Boscawen, New Hampshire
Date of Death: April 21, 1879
Place of Death: New York City, New York
Place of Burial: Trinity Cemetery in New York City, New York

Major General John Adams Dix served in the War of 1812 and the Civil War.

His long and distinguished career began when he was admitted to the bar in Washington, D.C., in 1824. He became adjutant general of New York in 1830, and was elected to the United States Senate, serving from January 27, 1845, until March 3, 1849, where he served on the Pensions Committee and Commerce Committee. He became assistant treasurer of the United States in

1853 and was appointed postmaster of New York City where he served for one year. In 1861, he became secretary of the treasury, but when the Civil War began, he left his post to serve with the Union army where he commanded the Department of Maryland, the Department of Pennsylvania, the Department of Virginia, and the Department of the East until the end of the war. After the war, he served as minister to France from 1866 until 1869. He was elected governor of New York and served from 1873 until 1875.

During his fifty-two days as secretary of the treasury, Dix made the famous remark, which graces the frame of his statehouse portrait: "If anyone attempts to haul down the American flag, shoot him on the spot."

He authored *Sketch of the Resources of the City of New York* . . . (New York: G. & C. Carville, 1827); *Decisions of the Superintendent of Common School of the State of New York* (Albany: Print by Croswell, Van Benthuysen & burt, 1837); *A Winter in Madeira, and a Summer in Spain and Florence* (New York: William Holdredge, 1850). Dix was married to Catherine Morgan.

Fort Drum (formerly, Pine Camp; formerly, Camp Drum)

Location: Watertown, New York
Status: Active
Named for: Lieutenant General Hugh Aloysius Drum
Date of Birth: September 19, 1879
Place of Birth: Fort Brady in Sault Ste. Marie, Michigan
Date of Death: October 3, 1951
Place of Death: His office in the State Building in New York City, New York
Decorations and Honors: Silver Star; Distinguished Service Medal; French
     Croix de Guerre
Date of Retirement: 1943
Place of Burial: Arlington National Cemetery, Section 2, Site 1447 RH

Lieutenant General Hugh Aloysius Drum fought in the Spanish-American War, the Philippine Insurrection, and World Wars I and II.

Drum graduated from Boston College in 1898. After joining the military, he was commissioned a second lieutenant in the 12th Infantry, and served in the Philippine Islands where he fought the Moros in Mindanao.

In 1914, he traveled to Veracruz as aide-de-camp and assistant chief of staff to General Frederick Funston. In 1917, he accompanied General John J. Pershing to France as assistant chief of staff and, in 1918, he became the first chief of staff of the First Army of the American Expeditionary Force where he coordinated the planning that resulted in victory in the Saint Mihiel and Meuse-Argonne offensive.

After World War I, Drum was assigned as director of the School of the Line at Fort Leavenworth in Kansas City, Kansas, and as commandant of the General Service School. From 1923 to 1926, he was assistant chief of Operations and Training in Washington, D.C. In 1930, he became inspector general of the army. Between 1931 and 1933, he commanded the V Corps Area and also became deputy chief of staff of the army under General Douglas MacArthur in Washington.

In October 1933, as head of the War Department board, Drum opposed Billy Mitchell's idea of the air force becoming a separate branch of the service and was successful, at that time, in lobbying Congress to stop the Air Corps from being made into a separate branch of service.

In 1935, Drum commanded the U.S. Army, Pacific (Hawaiian Department), and in 1939, he commanded the First Army. In 1940, he was appointed lieutenant general of the New York State Guard. In 1944, he became the president of the Empire State Incorporation, serving there until his death. He was married to Mary Reaume.

Fort Eustis

Location: Newport News, Virginia
Status: Active
Named for: Brigadier General Abraham Eustis
Date of Birth: March 28, 1786
Place of Birth: Petersburg, Virginia
Date of Death: June 27, 1843
Place of Death: Portland, Maine
Place of Burial: Mount Auburn Cemetery in Boston, Massachusetts

Brigadier General Abraham Eustis was prominent in fighting the Creek Indians in the Second Seminole War and was the founder and first commandant of the Artillery School at Fort Monroe in Hampton, Virginia.

Eustis graduated from Harvard University in 1804 where he studied law. He practiced law in Boston before entering the army as captain of artillery in 1808. During the War of 1812, he commanded a regiment in the capture of York, Upper Canada. He was brevetted lieutenant colonel for meritorious services in 1813, and he was promoted to lieutenant colonel of the 4th Artillery in 1822, and to brigadier general in 1834.

Fort George Wright

Location: Spokane, Washington
Status: Closed
Named for: General George Wright
Date of Birth: October 21, 1803
Place of Birth: Norwich, Vermont
Date of Death: July 30, 1865
Place of Death: at sea

General George Wright fought Chief Kamiakin in the Yakima Indian War of 1850 near present day Spokane, Washington.

Wright graduated from West Point on July 1, 1822, twenty-fourth in a class of forty cadets and was assigned to the 3rd Infantry. He first served at Fort Howard in Wisconsin and at Fort Leavenworth in Kansas. In 1838, he was transferred to the 8th Infantry where he served during the Canadian border disputes and at Sackett's Harbor, New York, until 1840.

He received a brevet promotion to major "for meritorious conduct in zeal, energy, and perseverance" for fighting the Seminole Indians in Florida. Wright also fought in the Mexican-American War at Veracruz and Molino del Rey where he was wounded and received a brevet promotion of colonel. In 1855, he served with the 4th Infantry, and later with the 9th Infantry. While in command of the northern district of the Department of the Pacific, he led battles against the Indians throughout Oregon. On December 19, 1864, Wright was brevetted brigadier general "for long, faithful, and meritorious services."

Wright drowned in the wreck of the *Brother Jonathan* while on his way to assume command of the Department of the Columbia.

Fort Gillem

Location: Forest Park, Georgia
Status: Active satellite installation for Fort McPherson in Atlanta, Georgia
Named for: Lieutenant General Alvan Cullom Gillem, Jr.
Date of Birth: August 8, 1888
Place of Birth: Nashville, Tennessee
Date of Death: February 13, 1973
Place of Death: Atlanta, Georgia
Date of Retirement: August 31, 1950
Place of Burial: Arlington National Cemetery, Section 6, Site 9547 A-1

Lieutenant General Alvan Cullom Gillem, Jr., was the first commanding general of the 3rd Armored Division during World War II.

Gillem enlisted as a private with the 17th Infantry in 1910 at Fort McPherson in Georgia. He served in the Philippines with General John J. Pershing on the Mexican border. He later served with XIII Corps in the European Theater of Operations.

After retiring, Gillem lived in Atlanta and became active in civic organizations. From 1959 to 1963, he worked for the State of Georgia. He also served as executive director of the National Foundation for the March of Dimes. He was married to Virginia L. Harrison.

Fort Gordon

Location: Augusta, Georgia
Status: Active
Named for: Lieutenant General John Brown Gordon
Date of Birth: February 6, 1832
Place of Birth: Upton City, Georgia
Date of Death: January 9, 1904
Place of Death: Miami, Florida
Place of Burial: Oakland Cemetery in Atlanta, Georgia

Lieutenant General John Brown Gordon was a Confederate officer during the Civil War, governor of Georgia, and a U.S. senator.

Gordon graduated from the University of Georgia and studied law before entering the military. His military assignments included: captain, Company I, 6th Alabama; major, 6th Alabama; colonel, 6th Alabama; commander, Rodes's brigade, D. H. Hill's division, Department of the Virginia; commander, Lawton's (old) brigade, Early's division, II Corps, Army of Northern Virginia; commander, Edward Johnson's (old) division; commander, Valley District, Department of Northern Virginia; and commander, II Corps, Army of Northern Virginia.

Gordon distinguished himself at the battle of Seven Pines during the Peninsula campaign in Virginia when he assumed command of the brigade. He was wounded while leading the regiment at Antietam in September 1862. He was given command of a Georgia brigade, fought at Chancellorsville in May 1863, at Gettysburg in July 1863, and during the Wilderness campaign in May 1864.

He earned a promotion to major general at Spotsylvania in May 1864, and saw action in Washington at Monocacy, Winchester, Fisher's Hill, and at Cedar Creek. Along with General Robert E. Lee at Petersburg, he planned and directed the attack on Fort Stedman in Virginia. His unit made the last charge of the Army of Northern Virginia at Appomattox. He was married to Mary Sarah Chapman.

Fort Greely

Location: Delta Junction, Alaska
Status: Active
Named for: Major General Adolphus Washington Greely
Date of Birth: March 27, 1844
Place of Birth: Newburyport, Massachusetts
Date of Death: October 20, 1935
Place of Death: Washington, D.C.
Decorations and Honors: Medal of Honor at age ninety-one
Place of Burial: Arlington National Cemetery, Section 1, Site 129

Major General Adolphus Washington Greely was an arctic explorer and one of the founders of the National Geographic Society.

Greely entered the military as a private with the 19th Massachusetts Volunteer Infantry. During the Civil War, he fought at Fredericksburg, and after being commissioned, he was placed in charge of the 81st Colored Troops. He spent twenty years serving with the Army Signal Corps, heading the U.S. Weather Service, and overseeing the relief efforts after the San Francisco earthquake of 1906.

In the summer of 1881, Greely led a scientific expedition to the Arctic to establish a polar colony. There, he collected data and carried out extensive meteorological and geophysical research and observations. The expedition explored the interior regions where they discovered Lake Hazen and Greely Fjord. When supplies and relief ships failed to reach the expedition, Greely and the expedition party left camp and headed south by boat to Cape Sabine where they became stranded. By the time relief arrived in June 1884, only seven of the original twenty-five were still alive. Another man died while returning home.

Greely authored *Three Years of Arctic Service* (New York: Charles Scribner's Sons, 1886), about his adventures and went on to write several more books and hundreds of magazine articles.

From 1887 to 1906, Greely served as chief signal officer, overseeing the installation and operations of telegraph communication in Puerto Rico, Cuba, and the Philippine Islands during the Spanish-American War. In 1892, Greely helped establish the Balloon Corps for the purpose of collecting and transmitting information.

His Medal of Honor citation reads as follows:

For his life of splendid public service, begun on March 27, 1844, having enlisted as a private in the U.S. Army on July 26, 1861, and by successive promotions was commissioned a major general February 10, 1906, and retired by operation of law on his 64th birthday.

Fort Holabird

Location: Baltimore, Maryland
Status: Closed
Named for: Brigadier General Samuel Beckley Holabird
Date of Birth: June 16, 1826
Place of Birth: Canaan, Litchfield County, Connecticut
Date of Death: February 3, 1907
Place of Death: Washington, D.C.
Date of Retirement: June 16, 1890
Place of Burial: U.S. Soldiers' and Airmen's Home National Cemetery in Washington D.C., Officers' Section, Lot 9

Brigadier General Samuel Beckley Holabird was quartermaster general of the army and was noted for designing fatigue uniforms, which were issued to enlisted men for free.

Holabird graduated from West Point in 1849, and was assigned to the 1st Infantry where he served on frontier duty in Texas as a scout and as regimental quartermaster from 1852 to 1858. In 1859, he was appointed as adjutant at West Point, and in 1861, he was made assistant quartermaster.

During the Civil War, he fought in the Northern Virginia campaign, served with the Army of the Potomac in the Maryland campaign, and at the battle of Antietam. From 1862 to 1865, he was assigned to New Orleans where he became chief quartermaster of the Department of the Gulf. He was brevetted brigadier general on March 13, 1865, for his faithful and meritorious services during the war.

After the war, Holabird was appointed deputy quartermaster general in the Quartermaster's Department, serving in Dakota, Texas, Missouri, and California. He later served with the 17th Quartermaster General until he retired.

Fort Hood

Location: Killeen, Texas
Status: Active
Named for: General John Bell Hood
Date of Birth: June 29, 1831
Place of Birth: Owingsville, Kentucky
Date of Death: August 30, 1879
Place of Death: New Orleans, Louisiana
Place of Burial: Metairie Cemetery in New Orleans, Louisiana

General John Bell Hood was an 1853 graduate of West Point. Three days after the beginning of the Civil War, Hood resigned his lieutenant's commission and enlisted in the Confederate army.

During his career, Hood served with the 4th Texas Volunteers in 1861; commanded a Texas Brigade in William Henry Whiting's division, Department of Northern Virginia, in 1862; commanded a division in I Corps, Army of Northern Virginia; commanded a division in the Department of Virginia and North Carolina in 1863; commanded the Department of Southern Virginia in 1863; commanded II Corps, Army of Tennessee, in 1864; and commanded the Department of Tennessee and Georgia from August 15, 1864, to January 25, 1865. Hood suffered a crippling wound to his hand at Gettysburg and, while commanding the corps at Chickamauga, Georgia, he was wounded in the leg.

After the war, Hood entered the cotton brokerage and insurance business in New Orleans. He married and fathered eleven children. He lost all of his money during the winter of 1878/79 because of a yellow fever epidemic that closed the New Orleans Cotton Exchange and wiped out almost every city insurance company.

He died of yellow fever within days of his wife, the former Anna Marie Hennen, and oldest child. His ten remaining children, all under the age of ten, were left orphaned and penniless. Eventually, seven different families in Louisiana, New York, Mississippi, Georgia, and Kentucky adopted them.

Fort Hunter Liggett

Location: Monterey, California
Status: Active
Named for: Lieutenant General Hunter Liggett
Date of Birth: March 21, 1857
Place of Birth: Reading, Pennsylvania
Date of Death: December 30, 1934
Place of Death: San Francisco, California
Decorations and Honors: Distinguished Service Medal; French Legion of Honor; Belgium Order of Leopold; Italian Order of Saints Maurice and Lazarus
Date of Retirement: March 1921
Place of Burial: San Francisco National Cemetery in San Francisco, California

Lieutenant General Hunter Liggett served as General John Pershing's chief of staff and was commanding general of the U.S. First Army and U.S. Third Army during World War I.

Liggett graduated from West Point in 1879 and was assigned to the 5th Infantry. He first served in the Montana and Dakota territories, and then in

Texas and Florida. He served as the post adjutant at Fort McPherson in Georgia from 1894 to 1896 and later became commander of Company D, 5th Infantry.

In June 1897, he fought in Cuba during the Spanish-American War. In June 1899, he was sent to the Philippine Islands with the 31st Infantry Volunteers, and in 1907, he became commander of a battalion in the 13th Infantry Regiment at Fort Leavenworth in Kansas.

Liggett was a student, then faculty member, and finally, president of the Army War College. In 1911, he was appointed commander of the 4th Brigade, 2nd Division, at Texas City, Texas, and in 1916, he returned to the Philippine Islands to command the Provisional Infantry Brigade and Fort William McKinley. He served from April 1916 until April 1917 as commander of the Department of the Philippines, until he was assigned as commander of the Western Department in San Francisco.

In August 1917, he commanded the 41st Division at Camp Fremont in California and in January 1918, Liggett became commander of the 1st American Army Corps in France where he participated in the battles of Cantigny and Belleau Woods, and where he held offensive operations during the second Marne campaign. In April 1919, he commanded the Third Army during the occupation of France. Upon his return to the United States, he commanded the IX Corps Area headquartered in San Francisco.

His Distinguished Service Medal citation reads as follows:

For exceptionally meritorious and distinguished services as commander of the First Army of the American Expeditionary Force. He commanded the 1st Corps and perfected its organization under difficult conditions of early service in France, engaged in active operations in reduction of the Marne salient and of the St. Mihiel salient, and participated in the actions of the forest of Argonne. He was in command of the 1st Army when the German resistance was shattered west of the Meuse.

General Liggett was conspicuous for his ability to rise to any occasion requiring the exercise of the functions of higher command, and his assignment to the command of an army and advancement to a grade second only to that of Commander of the AEF [American Expeditionary Force] was a recognition of this ability. In peace or war the country felt confident of the accomplishment of any object entrusted to him and he will be remembered as one upon whom, in large measure, the dependability of the American Army rested in its most gigantic struggle.—*General John Pershing, G.O. 12.*

The USS *Hunter Liggett*, an attack transport, was also named in his honor.

Fort Irwin

Location: Barstow, California
Status: Active
Named for: Major General George LeRoy Irwin
Date of Birth: April 26, 1868
Place of Birth: Michigan
Date of Death: February 19, 1931
Place of Death: At sea
Decorations and Honors: Distinguished Service Medal; French Legion of Honor; French Croix de Guerre
Place of Burial: Memorialized at West Point Cemetery in New York, Section D, Site 23

Major General George LeRoy Irwin served in the Spanish-American War, the Philippine Insurrection, and the Cuban Pacification.

Irwin graduated from West Point in 1889 and was assigned to artillery where he served the majority of his career. During World War I, he fought in the second battle of the Marne, participated in the attack on Kriemhilde Stellung in Germany

Irwin was the commander of the Artillery School in Saumur, France; inspector general of the army; and commander of the 16th Infantry Brigade and 57th Field Artillery Brigade during World War I. He was also commander of the Artillery School at Fort Sill in Lawton, Oklahoma; commander of the Panama Canal Division, and commander of V Corps from November 1946 to October 1948. He died aboard the steamer *Virgil* en route to Fort Hamilton to take command of the 1st Division.

Fort Jackson (formerly, Camp Jackson)

Location: Columbia, South Carolina
Status: Active
Named for: President and Major General Andrew Jackson
Date of Birth: March 15, 1767
Place of Birth: Waxhaw, South Carolina
Date of Death: June 8, 1845
Place of Death: Hermitage near Nashville, Tennessee
Decorations and Honors: Congressional Gold Medal
Place of Burial: Hermitage in Nashville, Tennessee

Andrew Jackson was the seventh president of the United States from 1829 to 1837.

Jackson joined the militia at the age of thirteen. He was captured by the British in 1781; became the first congressman from Tennessee in 1796; a Tennessee senator from 1797 to 1798; and a superior court judge in Nashville from 1798 to 1804.

He became a national hero during the War of 1812 for his actions at the battle of New Orleans as commander of the Tennessee Militia. At the battle of Horseshoe Bend in Alabama in 1814, he confiscated twenty-three million acres of land from the Creek Indians, opening up most of the south for settlement.

Jackson bought slaves and built a mansion he called the Hermitage near Nashville. As president, he created the Spoils System when he attempted to root out corruption within the bureaucracy by dismissing more than two thousand government employees and appointing his political supporters in their place.

In 1832, he denounced the Second Bank of the United States as an unconstitutional monopoly and vetoed a bill to recharter the bank of the United States. He was married to Rachel Donelson.

Fort Knox

Location: Radcliff, Kentucky
Status: Active
Named for: Major General Henry Knox
Date of Birth: July 25, 1750
Place of Birth: Boston, Massachusetts
Date of Death: October 25, 1806
Place of Death: Thomaston, Maine
Date of Retirement: December 31, 1794
Place of Burial: Thomaston, Maine

Major General Henry Knox was the first secretary of war, the chief artillery officer of the Continental army, and a brigadier general at the age of twenty-five.

Knox left school at the age of twelve to support his mother after his father died. He later opened his own bookstore, the London Book Store, in Boston.

He was present at the Boston Massacre on March 5, 1770. He joined the military at age eighteen, and in 1772, he became second in command of the newly formed Boston Grenadier Corps and served under General Artemas Ward at the battle of Bunker Hill in 1775. Later, he was promoted to colonel in the Continental Regiment of Artillery.

Knox saw action at Princeton, Brandywine, Germantown, Monmouth, and Yorktown during the American Revolutionary War. Knox served with George Washington during the winter of 1777 at Valley Forge and established the Springfield Arsenal. After the battle of Yorktown, Knox was promoted to major general.

He was appointed secretary of war under the Articles of Confederation on March 8, 1785, and served until September 1789 during which time he participated in the creation of a regular navy, was responsible for Indian policy, created a plan for a national militia, and established a series of coastal fortifications.

Knox settled his family on an estate near Thomaston, Maine, called Montpelier, and spent the rest of his life engaged in cattle farming, ship building, and brick making. Although retired, he remained active in the Massachusetts General Assembly.

He died of peritonitis after swallowing a chicken bone that punctured his intestines. He was married to Lucy Flucker.

Fort Kobbe

Location: Panama City, Panama
Status: Closed
Named for: Major General William August Kobbe
Date of Birth: 1841
Place of Birth: No Data Found
Date of Death: November 18, 1931
Place of Death: No Data Found
Place of Burial: San Francisco National Cemetery in San Francisco, California

Major General William August Kobbe was an artillery officer who served with the 3rd Artillery during the Spanish-American War.

Kobbe began his military career as a drummer boy during the Civil War. When the Spanish-American War began in 1898, Kobbe served in Virac in the Philippine Islands and helped the American forces occupy Sorsogon by setting up a provisional military government there, and on March 20, 1900, Kobbe took command of the military district of Mindanao, Jolo, and Palawan and held that position until August 31, 1901.

Fort Leavenworth

Location: Kansas City, Kansas
Status: Active
Named for: Brigadier General Henry Leavenworth
Date of Birth: December 10, 1783
Place of Birth: New Haven, Connecticut

Date of Death: July 21, 1834
Place of Death: Cross Timbers, Indian territory (present-day Oklahoma)
Place of Burial: Fort Leavenworth National Cemetery in Kansas

Brigadier General Henry Leavenworth served under George Washington in the Continental army, was a veteran of the War of 1812, and founded the military post that now bears his name.

Leavenworth grew up in Delhi, New York, and practiced law before joining the army. During the War of 1812, he was appointed captain of the 25th Infantry from Delaware County, and commanded his regiment in the invasion of Canada at Niagara where he was wounded on July 25, 1814.

At the end of the war, he took a leave of absence to serve in the New York State legislature.

In 1818, Leavenworth reentered the military as an Indian agent, with the rank of lieutenant colonel of the 5th Infantry and led an expedition against the Arikara Indians. As a colonel with the 3rd Infantry in 1827, he established a school for the practice of infantry, which later became Fort Leavenworth. In 1832, he was placed in command of the entire southwestern frontier and led an expedition against the Pawnee and Comanche Indians.

He died of a fever resulting from a fall from his horse shortly after being promoted to brigadier general. He was married three times, first to Elizabeth Eunice Morrison, then to Electa Knapp, and finally to Harriet Lovejoy.

Fort Lee

Location: Prince George, Virginia
Status: Active
Named for: General Robert Edward Lee
Date of Birth: January 19, 1807
Place of Birth: Stratford Hall, Westmoreland County, Virginia
Date of Death: October 12, 1870
Place of Death: Lexington, Virginia
Place of Burial: University Chapel in Lexington, Virginia

General Robert Edward Lee was the most famous of the Confederate Civil War commanders and the son of the Revolutionary general Henry Lee, known as "Light-Horse Harry."

Lee graduated from West Point in 1829, ranking second in a class of forty-six, and later became the commander there. In 1855, he saw duty on the Texas border. In 1859, he fought at Harper's Ferry.

Although asked to command the Union army at the beginning of the Civil War, he declined because of his loyalty to his state of Virginia and became an adviser to Jefferson Davis. He commanded the Army of Northern Virginia and fought in the battles of Seven Days, Second Bull Run, Fredericksburg, Chancellorsville, Antietam, and Gettysburg where he was defeated.

Lee was brevetted three times during the Civil War. On April 20, 1861, Lee resigned his commission. His feelings about the war were expressed in a letter to his sister, the wife of an officer in the Federal army, written at the time of his resignation. It reads:

We are now in a state of war which will yield to nothing. The whole south is in a state of revolution, into which Virginia, after a long struggle, has been drawn; and though I recognize no necessity for this state of things, and would have forborne and pleaded to the end for redress of grievances, real or supposed, yet in my own person I had to meet the question whether I should take part against my native state. With all my devotion to the Union, and the feeling of loyalty and duty of an American citizen, I have not been able to make up my mind to raise my hand against my relatives, my children, my home. I have therefore resigned my commission in the army and, save in defense of my native state—with the sincere hope that my poor services may never be needed—I hope I may never be called upon to draw my sword.

Lee went on to lead the south to the conclusion of the Civil War. He died from pneumonia after suffering a stroke. He was married to Mary Anna Randolph Custis.

"What a cruel thing is war . . . to fill our hearts with hatred instead of love for our neighbors, and to devastate the fair face of this beautiful world."
—*Robert E. Lee*

Fort Leonard Wood

Location: Waynesville, Missouri
Status: Active
Named for: Major General Leonard Wood
Date of Birth: October 9, 1860
Place of Birth: Winchester, New Hampshire
Date of Death: August 7, 1927
Place of Death: Boston, Massachusetts
Decorations and Honors: Medal of Honor
Date of Retirement: 1921
Place of Burial: Arlington National Cemetery, Section 21, Grave S-10

Major General Leonard Wood was the chief of staff of the U.S. Army, a physician, and the governor general of the Philippine Islands.

Wood graduated from Harvard Medical School in 1884, and earned a Doctor of Laws degree from Harvard Law School in 1899. He also graduated from the University of Pennsylvania in 1903. He entered the army in 1885 and was assigned to Fort Huachuca in Sierra Vista, Arizona, as a physician. While there, he participated in a battle against Geronimo in 1886. When war with Spain began, he joined with his friend Theodore Roosevelt and fought in the attack on Santiago, Cuba. Given command of the 1st Volunteer Cavalry, known as the Rough Riders, Wood led his men at Las Guasimas and San Juan Hill.

After the end of the conflict, Wood stayed in Cuba and became its military governor where he instituted a number of political, social, and educational reforms. As a medical man, he also worked to improve the medical and sanitary conditions there.

In 1902, he went to the Philippine Islands where he became commander of the Philippines Division, and later he was assigned as commander of the Department of the East. In 1903, he was appointed governor of Moro Province, and in 1906 the governor of the Philippines. There, he fought in several campaigns, including the Moro Crater massacre, against Moslem rebels.

As chief of staff, Wood established the position of senior officer of the army, reduced the influence of the old bureau system, and was instrumental in developing the Maneuver Division and the mobile army concept which led to the formation of the combined arms divisions. He returned to the Philippine Islands in 1921 and served as governor general, serving there until 1927. He died following unsuccessful surgery for a brain tumor. He was married to Laura Condit Smith.

His Medal of Honor citation for action during the Indian War campaigns reads as follows:

Voluntarily carried dispatches through a region infested with hostile Indians, making a journey of seventy miles in one night and walking thirty miles the next day. Also for several weeks, while in close pursuit of Geronimo's band and constantly expecting an encounter, commanded a detachment of infantry, which was then without an officer, and to the command of which he was assigned upon his own request.

Fort Lewis (formerly, Camp Lewis)

Location: Parkland, Washington
Status: Active
Named for: Captain Meriwether Lewis
Date of Birth: August 18, 1774
Place of Birth: Albemarle County, Virginia
Date of Death: October 8, 1809
Place of Death: Near Nashville, Tennessee
Place of Burial: Meriwether Lewis Park in Hohenwald, Tennessee

Captain Meriwether Lewis is best known for the Lewis and Clark Expedition to explore and search for a northwest passage to the Pacific Ocean.

In the summer of 1804, accompanied by his associate, Captain William Clark, fourteen soldiers, two Canadian boatmen, an interpreter, a hunter, and a Negro servant, Lewis began the expedition up the Missouri River. The party succeeded in reaching the Pacific Ocean and returned along nearly the same route by which they had traveled, reaching St. Louis in September of 1806, after traveling more than two years and covering a total distance of eight thousand miles. As a reward for his service, President Thomas Jefferson named Lewis governor of the Louisiana Territory in 1809, but Lewis died under questionable circumstances before assuming office. It was speculated that personal and professional problems may have driven him to suicide, but some people believed he was murdered.

In his *Voyage of Discovery* journal, Lewis wrote: "This immense river waters one of the fairest portions of the globe. Nor do I believe that there is in the universe a similar extent of country. As we passed on, it seemed as if those scenes of visionary enchantment would never have an end."

Fort McClellan

Location: Anniston, Alabama
Status: Active (now, Army National Guard Base)
Named for: Major General George Brinton McClellan
Date of Birth: December 3, 1826
Place of Birth: Philadelphia, Pennsylvania
Date of Death: October 29, 1885
Place of Death: Orange, New Jersey
Place of Burial: Riverview Cemetery in Trenton, New Jersey

Major General George Brinton McClellan was general-in-chief of the U.S. Army from 1861 to 1862 and the governor of New Jersey from 1878 to 1881.

McClellan graduated second in his class at West Point in 1846 and was assigned as an engineer. He earned two brevets under General Winfield Scott during the Mexican-American War, but resigned his commission to become chief engineer for the Illinois Central Railroad. He later became vice president and a division president for the Ohio & Mississippi Railroad.

During the Civil War his assignments included Ohio Volunteers April 23, 1861; commander, Ohio Militia from April 23 to May 13, 1861; commander, Department of the Ohio from May 13 to July 23, 1861; commander, Military Division of the Potomac from July 25 to August 15, 1861; commander, Department of the Potomac from August 15, 1861 to November 9, 1862; and commander-in-chief, USA, from November 5, 1861 to March 11, 1862.

Because of his constant demand for more troops and his lackluster performance during battle, McClellan was considered by many to be totally incapable of commanding an army.

After the war, McClellan became chief engineer of the New York Department of Docks, serving from 1870 to 1872, and in 1872, he became president of the Atlantic and Great Western Railroad. He was married to Mary Ellen Marcy.

Fort McCoy (formerly, Camp McCoy)

Location: Sparta, Wisconsin
Status: Active
Named for: Major General Robert Bruce McCoy
Date of Birth: September 5, 1867
Place of Birth: Kenosha, Wisconsin
Date of Death: January 5, 1926
Place of Death: Sparta, Wisconsin
Decorations and Honors: Distinguished Service Medal; French Croix de Guerre
Place of Burial: Woodlawn Cemetery in Sparta, Wisconsin

Major General Robert Bruce McCoy was a lawyer, district attorney, county judge, and mayor of Sparta, Wisconsin. His thirty-one years of military service included the Spanish-American War, the Punitive War, and World War I.

McCoy graduated from the University of Wisconsin Law School in 1891 where he was captain of the varsity baseball team. In 1893, he became publisher of the *Monroe County Democrat*. In 1894, he practiced law in Sparta, and with an interested in politics, he accepted the Democratic nomination for district attorney. He was nominated again in 1896. In 1897, he was elected Monroe County judge and served in that office for sixteen years.

McCoy believed that in order to wage battle in future wars, armies would need larger and more powerful guns, troops would need specialized training, and larger training areas would need to be developed. By 1905, he had acquired approximately four thousand acres of land in the Sparta area for this purpose.

As mayor of Sparta, he helped form the 32nd Division Association. On December 20, 1920, he was appointed brigadier general and placed in command of the 64th Infantry Brigade of the Wisconsin National Guard, and in 1924, he was promoted to major general where he commanded the 32nd Infantry Division (the Red Arrow Division) of the Wisconsin and Michigan National Guard. McCoy died from pernicious anemia. He was married to Lillian Riege of Platteville, Wisconsin. He was later married to Mae B. Oswald of Minneapolis, Minnesota.

Fort McDowell

Location: Angel Island, San Francisco Bay, California
Status: Closed
Named for: Major General Irwin McDowell
Date of Birth: October 15, 1818
Place of Birth: Ohio
Date of Death: May 4, 1885
Place of Death: California
Date of Retirement: 1882
Place of Burial: San Francisco National Cemetery in San Francisco, California

Major General Irwin McDowell served in the Mexican-American War, led the Union army in the battle of First Bull Run, and was the commanding officer of the Department of the Pacific.

McDowell graduated from West Point in 1838 and was assigned to artillery.

His Civil War assignments included: assistant adjutant general, March 31, 1856; commander, Department of Northeastern Virginia from May 27 to July 25, 1861; commander, Department of Northeastern Virginia, Division of the Potomac, from July 25 to August 17, 1861; commander, Division of the Potomac from October 3, 1861, to March 13, 1862; commander, I Corps, Army of the Potomac, from March 13 to April 4, 1862; commander, Department of the Rappahannock from April 4 to June 26, 1862; commander, III Corps, Army of Virginia, from June 26 to September 5, 1862; and commander, Department of the Pacific from July 1, 1864 to June 27, 1865.

His actions at Cedar Mountain in Virginia earned him the brevet of major general in 1865.

Fort McNair

Location: Washington, D.C.
Status: Active
Named for: Lieutenant General Lesley James McNair
Date of Birth: May 25, 1883
Place of Birth: Verndale, Minnesota
Date of Death: July 25, 1944
Place of Death: Normandy, France
Decorations and Honors: Distinguished Service Medal with three oak leak clusters; French Legion of Honor
Place of Burial: Normandy American Cemetery and Memorial in Colleville-sur-Mer, France, Plot F, Row 28, Grave 42

Lieutenant General Lesley James McNair, known as "Educator of the Army," was the highest-ranking American officer killed at Normandy.

McNair graduated from West Point in 1904 and was commissioned in field artillery. He served in the Veracruz Expedition in 1914 and the Punitive Expedition in 1916. By 1917, when World War I began, McNair was the youngest brigadier general in the army. During the war, he served in France with the 1st Division, and later became an artillery officer with the American Expeditionary Force.

His postwar assignments included: teaching at the General Service School from 1919 to 1921, staff officer in Hawaii from 1921 to 1924, and professor of military science at Purdue University from 1924 to 1928. He graduated from the Army War College in 1929, and served as assistant commandant of the Field Artillery School at Fort Sill in Lawton, Oklahoma, from 1929 to 1933. In April 1939, he became the commandant of the Command and General Staff College at Fort Leavenworth in Kansas City, Kansas.

On July 26, 1940, he was appointed as chief of staff at General Headquarters, with the responsibility of training, organizing, and mobilizing the army for war. On March 9, 1942, McNair became commander of Army Ground Forces where he improved the training and organization of the army. Under his command, the Army Ground Forces reached the strength of twenty-two million men.

In June 1944, McNair was assigned to England where he was placed in command of the "phantom" First Army Group. He was killed during Operation Cobra when bad weather caused American bombers to drop their loads "blind." Congress posthumously promoted him to the rank of general in 1954.

Fort McPherson

Location: Atlanta, Georgia
Status: Active
Named for: General James Birdseye McPherson
Date of Birth: November 14, 1828
Place of Birth: Clyde, Ohio
Date of Death: July 22, 1864
Place of Death: Atlanta, Georgia
Place of Burial: Loup Cemetery in Logan County, Nebraska

General James Birdseye McPherson was the commander of the Union army of Tennessee and the highest-ranking Union commander killed in action during the Civil War.

McPherson graduated first in his class from West Point in 1853 and taught engineering there following graduation. He was the chief engineer to General

Ulysses Grant and fought in the campaigns of Fort Henry and Fort Donelson, the battle of Shiloh, and the Union occupation of West Tennessee.

Following the battle of Shiloh, he was appointed brigadier general of volunteers, and then major general of volunteers on October 8, 1862. He fought in battles at Ports Gibson (May 1, 1863) and Raymond (May 12, 1863); Vicksburg (May to July 1863); Champion's Hill (May 16, 1863); and the Meridian campaign in Mississippi (February 1864). He was also commander of the Army of the Tennessee (March 12, 1864).

In 1864, he took part in the Union's advance on Atlanta with General William T. Sherman where he was mortally wounded. He was married to Emily Hoffman.

Fort Meade (formerly, Camp Meade)

Location: Baltimore, Maryland
Status: Active
Named for: Major General George Gordon Meade
Date of Birth: December 31, 1815
Place of Birth: Cadiz, Spain
Date of Death: November 6, 1872
Place of Death: Philadelphia, Pennsylvania
Place of Burial: Laurel Hill Cemetery in Philadelphia, Pennsylvania

Major General George Gordon Meade was a surveyor and commander during the Civil War.

Meade graduated from West Point in 1835, ranking nineteenth in his class of fifty-six cadets. He was assigned to the 3rd Artillery and served in Florida where he fought the Seminole Indians. He resigned from the military in October 1836, and became a civil engineer where, in 1840, he was employed as a surveyor in the astronomical branch to survey the boundary line between the United States and Texas. In August of that year, he surveyed the northeastern boundary between the United States and British North America.

In 1842, he rejoined the army and was appointed a second lieutenant in the Corps of Topographical Engineers. In September 1845, he joined the staff of General Zachary Taylor at Corpus Christi, Texas, and fought during the Mexican-American War in the battles of Pale Alto, Resaca de la Palma, and Monterey. He also served during the occupation of Matamoras. From 1851 to 1855, he worked constructing lighthouses at Carysfort Reef, Sand Key, Cedar Key, and in the Florida Keys.

During the Peninsula campaign of the Civil War, Meade fought in the Seven Days' battles at Mechanicsville, Gaines's Mill, and Glendale where he was severely wounded. After recovering, he took part in the battle of Second

Bull Run (August 29–30, 1862), and South Mountain (September 14, 1862). At Fredericksburg, he commanded the 3rd Division, and later he was appointed to command V Corps, which he led at Chancellorsville. He commanded the Department of the East, the military district of Georgia and Alabama, the Department of the South, and the military division of the Atlantic. He was known for his defensive strategy during the battle of Gettysburg that played a major role in winning the war for the North.

After the war, he received a Doctor of Laws degree from Harvard Law School and was a member of the American Philosophical Society, the Pennsylvania Historical Society, and the Philadelphia Academy of Natural Sciences. He was also one of the commissioners of Fairmount Park in Philadelphia.

Meade died from pneumonia cause by an old gunshot wound that he had received during the battle at New Market Cross Roads, Virginia, in June 1862.

Fort Monroe

Location: Hampton, Virginia
Status: Active
Named for: President James Monroe
Date of Birth: April 28, 1758
Place of Birth: Westmoreland County, Virginia
Date of Death: July 4, 1831
Place of Death: New York City, New York
Place of Burial: Hollywood Cemetery in Richmond, Virginia

James Monroe was the fifth president of the United States from 1817 to 1825 and author of the Monroe Doctrine, one of the most fundamental statements of foreign policy in the history of American diplomacy.

Monroe attended the College of William and Mary, fought in the Continental army, and practiced law in Fredericksburg, Virginia. He enlisted in the 3rd Virginia Regiment in the spring of 1776 and fought in battles in New York, Trenton, Valley Forge, and Monmouth.

Monroe was elected to the Virginia House of Delegates in 1782, beginning a career of public service that lasted more than forty years. He served in the Congress of the Confederation from 1783 to 1786 and joined the anti-Federalists in the Virginia Convention where he helped shape the Constitution. In 1790, as an advocate of Jeffersonian policies, he was elected United States senator. During his presidency, Florida was purchased from Spain in 1819 and Missouri was admitted to the Union in 1821 under the Missouri Compromise.

He died on the fifty-fifth anniversary of the signing of the Declaration of Independence. He was married to Elizabeth Kortright.

Fort Myer

Location: Arlington, Virginia
Status: Active
Named for: Brigadier General Albert James Myer
Date of Birth: September 20, 1828
Place of Birth: Newburgh, New York
Date of Death: August 24, 1880
Place of Death: Buffalo, New York
Place of Burial: Walden-Myer Mausoleum in Forest Lawn Cemetery in Buffalo, New York

Brigadier General Albert James Myer was the U.S. Army's first chief signal officer.

Myer graduated from Hobart College in New York in 1847 and Buffalo Medical College in 1851. He joined the army as an assistant surgeon and was assigned to duty in Texas. He developed a system of signals using flags and torches for sending messages, both by day or night, and introduced the study of military signals at West Point.

In December 1863, he was assigned duty on the Mississippi River, and in 1870, he instituted the first systematized simultaneous meteorological observations at twenty-four stations around the country, which were placed on telegraphic wires for transmission. He also established a system of cautionary day and night signals used for lake and ocean commerce and navigation. He created a system of reliable river reports for the benefit of interior commerce, and a special series of weather reports for farmers and planters. He was married to Catherine Walden of Buffalo.

After leaving the army, he returned to Buffalo, New York, where he wrote the *Manual of Signals for the United States Army and Navy*, U.S. military education pamphlets (New York, 1868).

Fort Ord

Location: Monterey Bay Peninsula, California
Status: Closed
Named for: Major General Edward Ortho Cresap Ord
Date of Birth: October 18, 1818
Place of Birth: Cumberland, Maryland
Date of Death: July 22, 1883
Place of Death: Havana, Cuba
Date of Retirement: 1881
Place of Burial: Arlington National Cemetery, Section 2, Site 982

Major General Edward Ortho Cresap Ord was a Union soldier.

After graduation from West Point in 1839, Ord was assigned to the 3rd Artillery. He fought the Seminole Indians in 1839. In 1847, he served on garrison duty on the East Coast, and later he was sent to California where he helped keep law and order in Monterey during the latter part of the Mexican-American War.

From 1852 to 1855, he served on coast survey duty. In 1856, he fought in the campaigns against the Rogue River Indians in Oregon, and in 1858, he fought the Spokane Indians in Washington Territory.

During the Civil War, Ord served as a field commander on the Western Frontier at the Presidio in San Francisco, and commanded the Army of the Potomac in September 1861. In November 1861, he was assigned to the 3rd Brigade of the Pennsylvania Reserves and fought at the battles of First Bull Run on July 21, 1861; Ball's Bluff on October 21, 1861; and Dranesville on December 20, 1861, where he defeated the Confederates.

On May 2, 1862, he was transferred to a command in the Department of the Mississippi. He was severely wounded in 1862. In June 1863, he became commander of XIII Corps in the Army of the Tennessee, and after the surrender of Vicksburg on July 4, 1863, he served with General William T. Sherman's army in the capture of Jackson, Mississippi.

In July 1864, Ord commanded VIII and XVIII Corps in the vicinity of Petersburg, Virginia. During his attack on Fort Harrison in Richmond, Virginia, in September 1864, he was wounded again and did not resume command until January 1865, when he took command of the Army of the James and the Department of North Carolina. His actions there resulted in the evacuation of Richmond and the surrender of General Robert E. Lee. His final assignment was with the Department of the Ohio where he remained until he left the army.

After the war, he commanded various military departments and was made a brigadier general in the regular army on July 26, 1866. He later accepted an appointment as engineer on the construction of a Mexican railroad, but died of yellow fever en route to Veracruz from New York.

Fort Pickett

Location: Blackstone, Virginia
Status: Now, Army National Guard Base
Named for: General George Edward Pickett
Date of Birth: January 28, 1825*
Place of Birth: Richmond, Virginia
Date of Death: July 30, 1875
Place of Death: Norfolk, Virginia
Place of Burial: Hollywood Cemetery in Richmond, Virginia

General George Edward Pickett was a Confederate officer best remembered for the military maneuver known as "Pickett's Charge."

Pickett graduated from West Point in 1846. During the Mexican-American War, Pickett served in the Siege of Veracruz and in the advance on Mexico City. He also served in Texas, Virginia, and in the Washington Territory. He resigned his commission to join the Confederacy when the Civil War began.

In January 1862, as a commander of a brigade in General James Longstreet's 2nd Division, he fought during the Peninsula campaign at Williamsburg (May 5, 1862), Seven Pines (May 31–June 1, 1862), and Gaines's Mill (June 27, 1862), where he was wounded in the left shoulder. He was promoted to major general on October 10, 1862, and given command of a division of Virginians attached to Longstreet's corps.

In late June 1863, Pickett was ordered to Gettysburg where he made his famous and ill-fated charge that cost the lives of almost all of his field officers. Approximately half of the twelve thousand men that weren't captured were either wounded or killed in the assault.

After Gettysburg, he fought in battles at Petersburg (April 2, 1865) and at Five Forks (April 1, 1865). General Robert E. Lee relieved Pickett of his command after Sayler's Creek (April 6, 1865) only days before the final surrender at Appomattox. Following the war, Pickett became an insurance salesman in Richmond.

---

* One document lists Pickett's birth date as January 25, another as January 28. His baptismal record shows his parents listing his birthday as January 16.

Fort Polk

Location: Alexandria, Louisiana
Status: Active
Named for: The Right Reverend Leonidas Polk
Date of Birth: April 10, 1806
Place of Birth: Raleigh, North Carolina
Date of Death: June 14, 1864
Place of Death: Pine Mountain, Georgia
Place of Burial: Christ Church Cathedral in New Orleans, Louisiana

The Right Reverend Leonidas Polk was known as the "Fighting Bishop" during the Civil War.

Polk graduated from West Point in 1827, but resigned his commission to do missionary work in Mississippi and Louisiana. In 1841, he became the first bishop of Louisiana.

At the beginning of the Civil War, Polk joined the Confederate army as a major general with command of Department Number 2 at Columbus, Kentucky. Polk served under General Braxton Bragg where he saw action at the battle of Shiloh at Pittsburgh Landing on the Tennessee River (April 6–7, 1862); Perryville in Kentucky; and at Stone's River at Murfreesboro, Tennessee (December 31, 1862– January 2, 1863). He fought at Chickamauga, Georgia, in the Tullahoma campaign (September 1863). He helped defeat Ulysses S. Grant at Belmont, Missouri, and he fought with the Army of Tennessee during the Atlanta campaign.

Polk died from a gunshot wound during battle. The Polk Monument was erected on the spot where he fell.

Fort Richardson

Location: Anchorage, Alaska
Status: Active
Named for: Brigadier General Wilds Preston "Dick" Richardson
Date of Birth: March 20, 1861
Place of Birth: Hunt County, Texas
Date of Death: May 20, 1929
Place of Death: Walter Reed Army Medical Center in Washington, D.C.
Decorations and Honors: Distinguished Service Medal
Place of Burial: West Point Cemetery in New York

Brigadier General Wilds Preston Richardson was a military pioneer explorer in Alaska.

Richardson graduated from West Point in 1884. He was first assigned infantry duty in the western United States followed by six years as an instructor at West Point.

In 1898, he was sent to Alaska where he designed and led the construction of highways along the rugged Alaska territory and Yukon River. He served there for the next twenty years supervising the construction of Fort Egbert (formerly, the Yukon River U.S. Army Post) near Fort William H. Seward, (formerly, Chilkoot Barracks), which is now a historic site.

In 1905, Richardson became the first president of the War Department's Alaska Road Commission where he was responsible for surveying and building railroads, roads, and bridges. By 1907, the Valdez-Fairbanks Trail was developed into a wagon route, now named the Richardson Highway in his honor.

In 1918, he was appointed commander of the 78th Infantry Brigade, 39th Division, at Camp Beauregard in Pineville, Louisiana, which saw action at Brest, France, on September 3, 1918. Promoted to general, Richardson commanded forces in the attempt to stop the Russian Revolution. He retired to Washington, D.C., in 1920 after thirty-six years of active service.

Fort Riley

Location: Junction City, Kansas
Status: Active
Named for: Major General Bennett C. Riley
Date of Birth: November 27, 1787
Place of Birth: St. Mary's County, Maryland
Date of Death: June 10, 1853
Place of Death: Buffalo, New York
Place of Burial: Forest Lawn Cemetery in Buffalo, New York

Major General Bennett C. Riley led the first military escort along the Santa Fe Trail and was considered a hero in the Mexican-American War.

Riley entered the army and was appointed an ensign of rifles on January 19, 1813. He served in the War of 1812, and in 1823, he fought the Arikara Indians. He was brevetted colonel for his services in the battle of Chokachotta, Florida, on June 2, 1840.

During the Mexican-American War, Riley led the 2nd Infantry in the siege of Veracruz and at the battle of Cerro Gordo in Mexico. He was placed in command of the 2nd Brigade where he fought in the battles of Contreras and Churubusco. He was appointed brevet brigadier general on April 18, 1847, for gallantry at Cerro Gordo, and major general in August 20, 1847, for his actions in Contreras.

After the war, Riley was given command of the Pacific Department at Monterey, and later was appointed military governor of California from April 12 to December 20, 1849, where he served as the first chief magistrate of the territory until the state was admitted into the Union.

His brevet citation reads as follows:

The charge of his noble brigade down the slope, in full view of friend and foe, unchecked even for a moment until he had planted all his colors upon the farthest works, was a spectacle that animated the Army 'to the boldest deeds.'

Fort Rucker

Location: Near Ozark, Alabama
Status: Active
Named for: General Edmund Winchester Rucker
Date of Birth: July 22, 1835
Place of Birth: Murfreesboro, Tennessee
Date of Death: April 13, 1924
Place of Death: Birmingham, Alabama
Place of Burial: Oak Hill Cemetery in Birmingham, Alabama

General Edmund Winchester Rucker was a Confederate officer who held the honorary title of general.

Rucker worked as a civil engineer in Memphis, Tennessee, before the war. He enlisted and was sent to Columbus, Kentucky, and then was assigned to the Tennessee Artillery. In 1863, he fought in the battle of Chickamauga, Georgia (September 18–20, 1863), and on June 10, 1864, he fought at Brice's Crossroad, also known as Tishomingo Creek in Mississippi.

Rucker served with the 7th Alabama Cavalry and with the 5th Mississippi Cavalry; 7th, 12th, 14th, 15th Tennessee cavalries; Forrest's Tennessee Cavalry Regiment; and Colonel Jacob B. Biffle's 10th Tennessee Cavalry. He was wounded in the arm and taken prisoner on December 16, 1864, near Nashville where a Union surgeon amputated his arm.

After the war, Rucker worked with General Nathan Forrest engaged in a railroad-building partnership in Alabama. In 1869, he settled in Birmingham, Alabama, and became an industrial leader there. He was married twice, first to Mary A. Woodfin, and second to Mary T. Bentley.

Fort Sam Houston

Location: San Antonio, Texas
Status: Active
Named for: General Samuel Houston
Date of Birth: March 2, 1793
Place of Birth: Rockbridge County, Virginia
Date of Death: July 26, 1863
Place of Death: Huntsville, Walker County, Texas
Place of Burial: Oakwood Cemetery in Huntsville, Texas

General Samuel Houston, known as "The Raven," is best remembered for his victory at the battle of the Alamo.

Houston was raised and adopted by Cherokee Indians after his father died. He enlisted in the 7th Infantry and was made a sergeant during the War of 1812 where he was wounded at the battle of Horseshoe Bend. He resigned from the army in 1818 to study law, was admitted to the bar, and practiced law in Lebanon, Tennessee. He served in the U.S. Congress in 1823 and again in 1825. He was elected governor of Tennessee in 1827, and later he became the district attorney of the Davidson District in Nashville, adjutant general of Tennessee, and commander in chief of the Army of Texas.

On April 21, 1836, Houston retaliated for the killing of James Bowie, David Crockett, and Colonel William B. Travis in the battle at the Alamo where 185 men died. With 750 men, he met the division of one thousand Mexicans under the command of General Antonio Lopez de Santa Anna on the banks of the San Jacinto River near the mouth of Buffalo Bayou, and with his famous battle cry of "Remember the Alamo!" he defeated Santa Anna and secured Texas's independence.

On October 22, 1836, Houston became the president of the Republic of Texas. In 1838, he took the first step toward securing the annexation of Texas to the United States. After Texas was admitted into the Union on December 29, 1845, Houston entered the U.S. Senate in March 1846. He served there until 1859 when he was elected as governor of the state of Texas, and served until March 1861. He was opposed to Abraham Lincoln as president, but when the south seceded from the Union, he refused to take an oath of allegiance to the Confederacy.

Fort Shafter

Location: Oahu, Hawaii
Status: Active
Named for: Major General William Rufus Shafter
Date of Birth: October 16, 1835
Place of Birth: Kalamazoo, Michigan
Date of Death: November 12, 1906
Place of Death: Bakersfield, California
Decorations and Honors: Medal of Honor
Place of Burial: San Francisco National Cemetery in San Francisco, California

Major General William Rufus Shafter was commander of V Corps, which included Theodore Roosevelt's Rough Riders, and led the United States expedition to Cuba during the Spanish-American War in 1898.

Shafter was a teacher before accepting a commission with the 7th Michigan Volunteers during the Civil War. He served at Ball's Bluff (October 21, 1861), in the Seven Days' battles (June 25–July 1, 1862), and Fair Oaks (October 27–28, 1864).

Toward the end of the war, he served with the 19th Michigan and was given command of the 17th U.S. Colored Infantry. In 1867, he was assigned to the 24th Infantry. After the war, he commanded the 1st Infantry where he served until 1887.

His Medal of Honor citation for action during the Civil War reads as follows:

Lieutenant Shafter was engaged in bridge construction and not being needed there returned with his men to engage the enemy participating in a charge across an open field that resulted in casualties to eighteen of the twenty-two men. At the close of the battle his horse was shot from under him and he was severely flesh wounded. He remained on the field that day and stayed to fight the next day only by concealing his wounds. In order not to be sent home with the wounded he kept his wounds concealed for another three days until other wounded had left the area.

Fort Sheridan

Location: Chicago, Illinois
Status: Closed
Named for: General Philip Henry Sheridan
Date of Birth: March 6, 1831
Place of Birth: Undetermined; possibly Albany, N.Y. or Boston, Massachusetts
Date of Death: August 5, 1888
Place of Death: Nonquitt, Massachusetts
Place of Burial: Arlington National Cemetery, Section 2, Site S-1

General Philip Henry Sheridan was a Union general during the Civil War.

Sheridan graduated from West Point in July 1853 and spent most of his military career in the cavalry. Among the many battles he fought in were Perryville, Stones River, Chickamauga, Chattanooga, Wilderness, Todd's Tavern, Yellow Tavern, Trevilian Station, and the Overland Campaign. He commanded the Army of the Potomac and the Army of the Shenandoah before becoming General of the Army. He was present at the signing of the Confederate surrender at Appomattox on April 9, 1865.

President Ulysses S. Grant promoted Sheridan to major general with the following citation:

For personal gallantry, military skill, and just confidence in the courage and patriotism of his troops, displayed by Philip H. Sheridan on the 19th of October at Cedar Run, where, under the blessing of Providence, his routed army was reorganized, a great national disaster averted, and a brilliant victory achieved over the rebels for the third time in pitched battle within thirty days, Philip H. Sheridan is appointed major general in the United States army, to rank as such from the 8th day of November, 1864.

After the war, Sheridan was sent to Texas to maintain order with Mexico when the French attempted to put Archduke Maximilian in control of that country. In 1867, he was appointed military governor of Texas and Louisiana where he dismissed both state governors for "political dishonesty," but was dismissed himself by President Andrew Johnson who considered his tactics absolute tyranny.

During the Indian Wars, Sheridan fought the Cheyenne, Kiowa, and Comanche. He helped maintain martial law during the Great Chicago Fire in 1871 and was appointed Commanding General of the Army in 1883. Sheridan died from a heart attack.

In addition to the fort in Illinois, the M551 tank and a mountain in Yellowstone National Park were named in his honor. His likeness appears on a ten dollar U.S. Treasury note, issued in 1890 and 1891, and on the five dollar silver certificate, issued in 1896. Several counties in the United States bear his name, and the liberty ship, USS *Philip H. Sheridan,* was named in his honor. He was married to Irene Rucker.

"Always make your opponent think you know more than you really know."—*General Philip Henry Sheridan*

Fort Sill

Location: Lawton, Oklahoma
Status: Active
Named for: General Joshua Woodrow Sill
Date of Birth: December 6, 1831
Place of Birth: Chillicothe, Ohio
Date of Death: December 31, 1862
Place of Death: Stone's River, Tennessee
Place of Burial: Grandview Cemetery in Chillicothe, Ohio

General Joshua Woodrow Sill graduated from West Point in 1853 and was assigned to ordnance. After duty at the Watervliet Arsenal in New York, he returned to West Point as an instructor, teaching geography, history, and ethics from September 23, 1854, to August 29, 1857.

Sill resigned from the army in 1861 to accept the professorship of mathematics and civil engineering in the Brooklyn Collegiate and Polytechnic Institute. At the beginning of the Civil War, he was appointed assistant adjutant general of Ohio, and on August 27, he was commissioned a colonel in the 33rd Ohio Volunteers. From September 1861 to September 1862, he had duty in Kentucky, Tennessee, and Alabama. In late 1863, he fought in the battle of Perryville and in the Tennessee campaign. Sill was shot in the face with a musket ball and died while trying to rally his men.

Fort Stewart

Location: Savannah, Georgia
Status: Active
Named for: Brigadier General Daniel Stewart
Date of Birth: December 20, 1761
Place of Birth: Saint Johns Parish, (now, Liberty County, Georgia)

Date of Death: May 27, 1829
Place of Death: Cedar Hill, Georgia
Place of Burial: Midway Cemetery in Liberty County, Georgia, Section C-19

Brigadier General Daniel Stewart was a hero in the American Revolutionary War and the War of 1812. He was also the great-grandfather of Theodore Roosevelt.

Stewart joined the army at the age of fifteen. When the British invaded Georgia, he fled to South Carolina and joined the military. He was wounded by a saber in 1778 and taken prisoner aboard a prison ship in Charleston Harbor but escaped and swam to shore.

After the war, he established Cedar Hill plantation in Liberty County in Georgia, and was involved in resolving the Creek Indian Wars. He served as state representative from 1785 to 1787, Liberty County sheriff from 1795 to 1797, and state senator for three terms between 1802 and 1811. During the War of 1812, Stewart commanded a cavalry brigade in the Georgia Militia.

He was married three times. His first wife, Martha Pender, died during childbirth. His second wife was Sarah Susannah Oswald and his third wife was Sarah Hines.

Fort Story

Location: Virginia Beach, Virginia
Status: Active subinstallation of Fort Eustis in Newport News, Virginia
Named for: Major General John Patton Story
Date of Birth: 1843
Place of Birth: Waukesha, Wisconsin
Date of Death: March 25, 1915
Place of Death: Pasadena, California
Date of Retirement: 1905
Place of Burial: Arlington National Cemetery, Section SD, Site 1881

Major General John Patton Story was a coast artillery officer during the Reconstruction of the South following the Civil War. He fought in the Indian Wars and took part in the pioneer migration west.

Story graduated from West Point on July 1, 1865, twentieth in his class of sixty-eight cadets and was assigned to artillery in 1870. He was promoted to colonel in 1902. He served as commander of Fort Monroe in Virginia from March 1902 to January 1904. He was promoted to brigadier general in 1904, and served as a member of the general staff as chief of artillery in 1905. He contributed to the science of gunnery and the development of range-finding equipment. Later in his career, he was a member of the Coast Defense Board where he was sent to the Far East to survey forts in Honolulu, Manila, Subic Bay, and Guam.

Fort Wainwright

Location: Fairbanks, Alaska
Status: Active
Named for: General Jonathan Mayhew Wainwright
Date of Birth: August 23, 1883
Place of Birth: Walla Walla, Washington
Date of Death: September 2, 1953
Place of Death: San Antonio, Texas
Decorations and Honors: Medal of Honor; Distinguished Service Medal
Date of Retirement: 1947
Place of Burial: Arlington National Cemetery, Section 1, Grave 358-B

General Jonathan Mayhew Wainwright earned distinction as the hero of Bataan and Corregidor in the defense of the Philippine Islands against the Japanese during World War II.

After graduating from West Point in 1906, Wainwright joined the cavalry and saw action in Europe during World War I, serving on the general staff of the 82nd Division at Toul, Saint Mihiel, and Meuse-Argonne.

During World War II, leading his forces through some of the most horrendous combat in world military history, known as the Bataan Death March, on the Bataan Peninsula and Corregidor Island, Wainwright survived by eating cavalry horses. With few supplies, outdated weapons, no air or sea support, and facing overwhelming odds, he fought the enemy for almost five months, surrendering only when he believed that no relief would come. During his captivity of three-and-a-half years, he feared he would be labeled a coward for surrendering. However, upon his return to the United States, President Harry S. Truman took him into the Rose Garden at the White House, and in front of reporters and photographers, presented him with the Medal of Honor.

Wainwright received his fourth star in commemoration of his release as a prisoner of war. After the war, he became chief engineer for the State of Alabama and supervised the improvements in Mobile Bay. He was married to Adele Holley.

His Medal of Honor citation for action during World War II reads as follows:

Distinguished himself by intrepid and determined leadership against greatly superior enemy forces. At the repeated risk of life above and beyond the call of duty in his position, he frequented the firing line of his troops where his presence provided the example and incentive that helped make the gallant efforts of these men possible. The final stand on beleaguered Corregidor, for which he was in an important measure personally responsible, commanded the admiration of the Nation's allies. It reflected the high morale of American arms in the face of overwhelming odds. His courage and resolution were a vitally needed inspiration to the then sorely pressed freedom-loving peoples of the world.

Fort Wint

Location: Grand Island, Subic Bay, Philippines
Status: Closed
Named for: Brigadier General Theodore Jonathan Wint
Date of Birth: March 6, 1845
Place of Birth: Scranton, Pennsylvania
Date of Death: March 21, 1907
Place of Death: Philadelphia, Pennsylvania
Decorations and Honors: Civil War Campaign Medal; Philippine Campaign Medal; China Relief Expedition Medal
Place of Burial: Arlington National Cemetery, Section 2, Site 847

Brigadier General Theodore Jonathan Wint was a veteran of the Civil War, the Indian Wars, the Spanish-American War, and the Philippine Insurrection.

Wint served as a private in the General Mounted Service in 1865 before being appointed to the regular army as a second lieutenant in the 4th U.S. Cavalry on November 24, 1865. He was promoted to first lieutenant on May 9, 1866; to captain on April 21, 1872; to major with the 10th U.S. Cavalry on May 6, 1892; to lieutenant colonel of 6th U.S. Cavalry on April 8, 1899; to colonel on February 23, 1901; and to brigadier general, U.S. Army, on June 9, 1902.

Wint's assignments included: Indian Frontier from 1866 to 1888, Cuba in 1898, China from 1900 to 1901, the Philippines from 1901 to 1904, and the Army of Cuban Pacification from 1906 to 1907. He died of heart failure while in the field. He was married to Lydia Porter Bullis.

Fort Wolters (formerly, Camp Wolters and Wolters Air Force Base)

Location: Mineral Wells, Texas
Status: Closed
Named for: Brigadier General Jacob Franklin Wolters
Date of Birth: September 2, 1871
Place of Birth: New Ulm, Texas

Date of Death: October 8, 1935
Place of Death: No Data Found
Decorations and Honors: Gold Medal from the Texas Legislature; Texas Cavalry Service Medal
Date of Retirement: November 1, 1934
Place of Burial: Forest Lawn Cemetery in Houston, Texas

Brigadier General Jacob Franklin Wolters served during the Spanish-American War and World War I.

Wolters joined the Texas National Guard on May 31, 1891, as a private in Company D, 1st Texas Infantry. He was admitted to the Texas Bar in 1892, and later served as county attorney for Fayetteville County. He was commissioned a first lieutenant in January 1898 and served during the Spanish-American War with Troop H, 1st Texas Cavalry. He was promoted to lieutenant colonel in 1911, brigadier general in April 1918, and to brevet major general in November 1934. He served as presidential executive from 1900 to 1904, and in 1912, he ran for the U.S. Senate.

At the beginning of World War I, Wolters made a speaking campaign throughout Texas promoting enlistment of volunteer soldiers.

In 1921, he organized the 56th Cavalry Brigade, Texas National Guard, and served as its commander until November 1934.

Later, he was instrumental in obtaining a grant to construct a field training camp in Texas. Fifty acres of land east of Mineral Wells was allocated for the headquarters site that was later named in his honor. He was married to Sally Drane of Columbus, Texas.

Schofield Barracks

Location: Honolulu, Hawaii
Status: Active
Named for: Lieutenant General John McAllister Schofield
Date of Birth: September 29, 1831
Place of Birth: Gerry, Chautauqua County, New York
Date of Death: March 4, 1906
Place of Death: Saint Augustine, Florida
Decorations and Honors: Medal of Honor
Date of Retirement: 1895
Place of Burial: Arlington National Cemetery, Section 2, Lot 1108

Lieutenant General John McAllister Schofield was a Union officer in the Civil War and secretary of war from 1868 to 1869.

Schofield graduated seventh in his class from West Point in 1853 in the same class with Philip H. Sheridan, James B. McPherson, and John B. Hood.

He served throughout the Civil War in command positions, becoming one of forty-three fully commissioned brigadier generals. In April 17, 1863, he took command of a division in the XIV Corps of the Army of the Cumberland. In 1864, as commander of the Army of the Ohio, he took part in the Atlanta campaign under Major General William T. Sherman. Schofield's troops captured Wilmington, North Carolina, and defended Franklin, Tennessee, in 1864. In June 1865, he went to Europe as an envoy from the state department to oversee the French intervention in Mexico. In August 1866, he became commander of the Department of the Potomac, and was placed in charge of the 1st Military District in Virginia from March 1867 to May 1868.

Schofield recommended that Pearl Harbor, Hawaii, be established as a U.S. military base. He commanded the Division of the Pacific from 1870 to 1876 and again in 1882 and 1883; was superintendent at West Point from 1876 to 1881; commanded the Division of the Missouri from 1883 to 1886; and later, commanded the Division of the Atlantic. He became commanding general of the U.S. Army from 1888 until his retirement.

His Medal of Honor citation for action during the Civil War reads as follows:

Was conspicuously gallant in leading a regiment in a successful charge against the enemy.

His legacy still lives on at West Point and the Air Force Academy by all cadets who must memorize the following:

The discipline which makes the soldiers of a free country reliable in battle is not to be gained by harsh or tyrannical treatment. On the contrary, such treatment is far more likely to destroy than to make an army. It is possible to impart instruction and give commands in such a manner and such a tone of voice as to inspire in the soldier no feeling, but an intense desire to obey, while the opposite manner and tone of voice cannot fail to excite strong resentment and a desire to disobey. The one mode or the other of dealing with subordinates springs from a corresponding spirit in the breast of the commander. He who feels the respect which is due to others cannot fail to inspire in them respect for himself. While he who feels, and hence manifests, disrespect towards others, especially his subordinates, cannot fail to inspire hatred against himself.—*John M. Schofield*

Army Airfields, Stagefields, and Heliports

Those who have long enjoyed such
privileges as we enjoy forget in time
that men have died to win them.

—*Franklin D. Roosevelt*

CHAPTER 4

Army Airfields, Stagefields, and Heliports

Allen Army Airfield

Location: Adjacent to Fort Greely in Delta Junction, Alaska
Status: Active
Named for: Lieutenant Colonel Robert Lloyd Allen
Date of Birth: November 17, 1923
Place of Birth: Missouri
Date of Death: August 10, 1964
Place of Death: Brooke Army Medical Center in San Antonio, Texas
Decorations and Honors: Air Medal with two gold stars; Presidential Unit Citation; American Campaign Medal; Asiatic-Pacific Campaign Medal; World War II Victory Medal; Navy Occupation Service Medal; National Defense Service Medal; Korean Service Medal; United Nations Service Medal
Place of Burial: Arlington National Cemetery, Section 35, Site 5073

Lieutenant Colonel Robert Lloyd Allen was an army aviator.

Allen first joined the Naval Reserve in October 1942 before accepting a commission as a second lieutenant in the U.S. Marine Corps Reserve. He served with the 2nd Marine Aircraft Wing during the Okinawa and Ryukyu campaigns during World War II.

After serving in Korea, he was commissioned in the regular army and became a pilot in October 1960. He served at Fort Rucker near Ozark, Alabama, until June 1963, when he was assigned to the U.S. Army Arctic Test Center in Alaska. He suffered from burns received in a plane crash and died seven days later.

★★★

Biggs Army Airfield (formerly, Biggs Air Force Base)

Location: Adjacent to Fort Bliss in El Paso, Texas
Status: Active
Named for: Lieutenant James Berther "Buster" Biggs
Date of Birth: 1898
Place of Birth: Sabinal, Texas
Date of Death: October 27, 1918
Place of Death: Beltran, France

Lieutenant James Berther Biggs was an aviator.

Biggs won many athletic honors as a member of the track and field teams at Lamar School in El Paso, Texas, and was one of the founders of the Calumos Club. Biggs worked at a bank prior to enlisting in the U.S. Army in May 1917 at Leon Springs, Texas.

He was commissioned and sent to France where he served with the 22nd Pursuit Squadron. While serving with the U.S. Aviation Service, he was killed testing a new type of plane. As he took off, the engine stalled. He tried to return to the field but lost control of the plane and crashed.

Brown Stagefield

Location: Adjacent to Fort Rucker near Ozark, Alabama
Status: Active
Named for: Chief Warrant Officer 3 Jerry L. Brown
Date of Birth: July 10, 1955
Place of Birth: No Data found
Date of Death: March 11, 1986
Place of Death: Elba, Alabama
Decorations and Honors: Meritorious Service Medal with oak leaf cluster; Army Commendation Medal with oak leaf cluster; Army Achievement Medal

Chief Warrant Officer 3 Jerry L. Brown joined the service in 1973 as a Bell UH-1 Huey helicopter mechanic. He was accepted into the Aviation Warrant Officer Course at Fort Rucker in Alabama and received his pilot license. He was an instructor pilot in Korea, and later served with the 101st Aviation Battalion at Fort Campbell in Kentucky.

He returned to Fort Rucker as a standardization instructor pilot where he developed flight standardization procedures. He died in the crash of a Bell UH-60 Blackhawk helicopter.

Butts Army Airfield

Location: Adjacent to Fort Carson in Colorado Springs, Colorado
Status: Active
Named for: Second Lieutenant John Edward Butts
Date of Birth: 1922
Place of Birth: Medina, New York
Date of Death: June 23, 1944
Place of Death: Normandy, France
Decorations and Honors: Medal of Honor, posthumously
Place of Burial: Saint Mary's Cemetery in Medina, New York

Second Lieutenant John Edward Butts served with Company E, 60th Infantry, 9th Infantry Division.

His Medal of Honor citation for action during World War II reads as follows:

Heroically led his platoon against the enemy in Normandy, France, on June 14, 16, and 23, 1944. Although painfully wounded on the fourteenth near Orglandes and again on the 16th while spearheading an attack to establish a bridgehead across the Douve River, he refused medical aid and remained with his platoon. A week later, near Flottemanville Hague, he led an assault on a tactically important and stubbornly defended hill studded with tanks, antitank guns, pillboxes, and machine-gun emplacements, and protected by concentrated artillery and mortar fire. As the attack was launched, Second Lieutenant Butts, at the head of his platoon, was critically wounded by German machine-gun fire. Although weakened by his injuries, he rallied his men and directed one squad to make a flanking movement while he alone made a frontal assault to draw the hostile fire upon himself. Once more he was struck, but by grim determination and sheer courage continued to crawl ahead. When within ten yards of his objective, he was killed by direct fire. By his superb courage, unflinching valor and inspiring actions, Second Lieutenant Butts enabled his platoon to take a formidable strong point and contributed greatly to the success of his battalion's mission.

Cairns Army Airfield

Location: Adjacent to Fort Rucker near Ozark, Alabama
Status: Active
Named for: Major General Bogardus Snowden Cairns
Date of Birth: February 14, 1910
Place of Birth: New York City, New York
Date of Death: December 9, 1958

Place of Death: Fort Rucker in Alabama
Decorations and Honors: Legion of Merit; Bronze Star with two oak leaf clusters and V device; Purple Heart; French Croix de Guerre; Most Excellent Order of the British Empire

Major General Bogardus Snowden Cairns was instrumental in the development of the armed helicopter.

Cairns graduated from West Point in 1932 and was assigned to the cavalry. He instructed horsemanship at the Cavalry School at Fort Riley in Kansas and was a member of the Olympic Pentathlon team. In 1939, Cairns was assigned to the 1st Armored Division, 13th Armored Regiment, where he served in Africa and Italy, and saw action in the campaigns at Oran, Algeria, Tunisia, Naples-Foggia, Rome-Arno, and Anzio.

In 1944, Cairns was assigned to the operations division of the War Department General Staff, and later to the staff and faculty of the Armored School.

During his career, he attended the Combined Arms Course at the Command and General Staff College and the Armed Forces Staff College. Later, he became an instructor in the Command and General Staff College, and attended the National War College in 1951–52.

In Europe, he became commander of Combat Command "R" of the 2nd Armored Division; assistant chief of staff, G-3, at V Corps Headquarters in Frankfurt, Germany; and commanding general of the base section of the U.S. Army, Europe, Communications Zone, in France.

He was deputy to the assistant chief of staff, G-3, Headquarters, Continental Army Command (CONARC), before being assigned to the Aviation School where he took flight training and earned the rating of army aviator in May 1957. Later, as commander of the Aviation Center, he became commandant of the Aviation School and was promoted to major general on September 1, 1958.

Cairns was killed when his Bell H-13 Sioux helicopter crashed in dense woods minutes after takeoff while en route to Matteson Range to observe a firepower rehearsal in preparation for a full-scale armed helicopter display.

Carlstrom Field

Located: Arcadia, Florida
Status: Closed
Named for: First Lieutenant Victor Carlstrom
Date of Birth: April 13, 1890
Place of Birth: Sweden
Date of Death: May 9, 1917
Place of Death: Newport News, Virginia

First Lieutenant Victor Carlstrom was a pioneer aviator, exhibition flyer, and chief instructor at the Glenn Curtiss Flying School in Newport News, Virginia.

Carlstrom came to the United States in 1904 and settled in Colorado with his family. He learned to fly in California, and his first flying job was giving rides at county fairs.

When World War I began, Carlstrom joined the army and was commissioned a lieutenant and assigned to the Aviation Reserve Corps. Later, he became an instructor at the Atlantic Coast Aeronautical Station in Newport News, Virginia.

In 1916, Carlstrom set an altitude record of 11,180 feet in a Curtiss R-2 airplane at Newport News, Virginia. That same year, he won a twenty-eight-mile airplane race at Sheepshead Bay, New York, with a time of 14 minutes, 21 seconds. He went on to the set a world's speed and distance record in 1917, flying a modified Curtiss JN-4 Jenny.

Carlstrom, along with a student pilot, Carey Epes, was killed when the plane's wings struts broke causing the plane to plunge to the ground.

Charles L. Kelly Army Heliport

Location: Fort Sam Houston in San Antonio, Texas
Status: Active
Named for: Major Charles L. Kelly
Date of Birth: April 11, 1925
Place of Birth: Warm Springs, Georgia
Date of Death: July 1, 1964
Place of Death: South Vietnam
Decorations and Honors: Distinguished Service Cross, posthumously; Silver Star; Distinguished Flying Cross with two oak leaf clusters; Bronze Star; Air Medal with 18 oak leaf clusters; Purple Heart with oak leaf cluster; Army Commendation Medal; Good Conduct Medal; Military Order Medal of Vietnam; Cross of Gallantry with palm; inducted into the Dustoff Hall of Fame, February 17, 2001

Major Charles L. Kelly served in World War II, Korea, and Vietnam.

Kelly was the commanding officer of the 57th Medical Detachment (Helicopter Ambulance) in Vietnam in 1964. His call sign, "Dustoff," could be heard throughout the Delta as he called to distant outposts, saying, "This is Dustoff. Just checking in to see if everything is okay." Kelly's Dustoff became the call sign for all aeromedical missions in Vietnam.

Concerned that medical helicopters would be converted and used for assault and general-purpose missions, Kelly increased operations to prove the helicopter's worth. He flew almost every night checking for casualties and personally evacuated one-fourth of all evacuees, preventing many wounded from having to wait overnight for ground transportation.

It was on such a mission aboard the Bell UH-1B Huey helicopter (tail number 63-08591) that Kelly went to pick up wounded soldiers, only to find the enemy waiting. Advised repeatedly to withdraw, he replied to the ground element's advisor, "When I have your wounded." Shortly afterward, a round went through the door's window and pierced his heart. His last words were, "My God." His ship pitched up, nosed to the right, rolled over, and crashed.

His saying, "When I have your wounded" became the personal and collective credo of the many gallant medevac pilots who followed him.

Cochran Army Airfield

Location: Macon, Georgia
Status: Closed
Named for: First Lieutenant Robert James Cochran
Date of Birth: August 22, 1895
Place of Birth: Camilla, Georgia
Date of Death: No Data Found
Place of Death: Toul, France

First Lieutenant Robert James Cochran attended the University of Georgia and entered the U.S. Army on May 11, 1917. He attended officers training at Fort McPherson in Atlanta, Georgia, where he was commissioned a first lieutenant in the infantry. He later applied for flight training at Austin, Texas, and received his pilot wings. He was sent overseas on March 12, 1918, where he was attached to the 8th Aero Squadron, 82nd Division, in France.

He and his pilot were killed when German planes attacked them in an air battle. Cochran was reportedly killed instantly, but his pilot jumped from the burning plane, only to have the falling plane strike him and carry him to his death.

Condron Army Airfield

Location: White Sands, New Mexico
Status: Active
Named for: Second Lieutenant Max Henderson Condron
Date of Birth: May 30, 1921
Place of Birth: Valley, Nebraska
Date of Death: December 3, 1942

Place of Death: El Paso, Texas
Place of Burial: Prospect Hill Cemetery in Elkhorn, Nebraska

Second Lieutenant Max Henderson Condron went to Wentworth Military Academy in Lexington, Missouri, where he completed two years of college and began his primary civilian pilot training. He completed his secondary training at the University of Nebraska.

Condron enlisted in the military on October 30, 1941, and received his pilot wings and commission on April 16, 1942. After flight training at Garner, Perrin, and Brooks fields in Texas, he served at Fort Sill in Lawton, Oklahoma, and Fort Riley in Junction City, Kansas, and was later transferred to the 6th Tow Target Squadron at Biggs Field in El Paso, Texas. He was killed when his aircraft crashed while towing targets on an antiaircraft training mission.

Davison Army Airfield

Location: Adjacent to Fort Belvoir in Alexandria, Virginia
Status: Active
Named for: Brigadier General Donald Angus Davison
Date of Birth: October 26, 1892
Place of Birth: San Carlos, Arizona
Date of Death: May 6, 1944
Place of Death: Bangalore, India
Decorations and Honors: Legion of Merit with oak leaf cluster; promoted to major general, posthumously
Place of Burial: Arlington National Cemetery, Section 3, Site 3893 WS

Brigadier General Donald Angus Davison was an aviation engineer during World War II, serving in the North African campaign.

Davison graduated from West Point in 1915 with the class that became known as "the class the stars fell on," which included Dwight D. Eisenhower and Omar Bradley. He attended the Engineer School at Fort Humphreys (now, Fort Belvoir) in Virginia and was commissioned a second lieutenant in the Corps of Engineers. Later, he became a senior instructor at the school. He was also a professor of military science and tactics for two years at Yale University in New Haven, Connecticut.

In July 1924, he was assigned to the 11th Engineers at Corozal in the Panama Canal Zone. In August 1927, he attended the Command and General Staff College and, after graduation, was transferred to Washington, D.C., for duty in the Office of the Engineer Commissioner. In 1932, he became an instructor at the Command and General Staff College at Fort Leavenworth in Kansas, and, in 1936, he attended the Army War College. He assumed command of the 21st

Engineers at Fort Benning in Georgia in 1939. Later, he was assigned as engineer officer at General Headquarters, Air Force, at Langley Field in Virginia.

Davison served in England in May 1941 with the Aviation Engineers as an observer with the Twelfth Air Force, and later he took command of the Twelfth Air Force Engineer Command (Provisional). He became the engineer officer for Allied Force Headquarters in the North African Theater of Operations in 1942. He served there until 1943, when he was designated aviation engineer for Northwest African air forces. He was assigned to the Asiatic area at the time of his death.

Dodd Field

Location: Adjacent to Fort Sam Houston in San Antonio, Texas
Status: Closed
Named for: Colonel Townsend Foster Dodd
Date of Birth: March 6, 1886
Place of Birth: Anna, Illinois
Date of Death: October 5, 1919
Place of Death: Bustleton Field in Philadelphia, Pennsylvania
Decorations and Honors: Mackay Trophy (1914)
Place of Burial: Arlington National Cemetery, Section S, Site 4062

Colonel Townsend Foster Dodd was a World War I aviation pioneer and the fifth commander of Langley Field in Virginia.

Dodd graduated from the University of Illinois in 1907 with a bachelor of science degree in engineering. He joined the service and was appointed second lieutenant in the Coast Artillery Corps on September 25, 1909. In 1912, he transferred to the aviation section of the Signal Corps. On February 1913, he set a record by flying nonstop 244.18 miles in 4 hours, 43 minutes in a U.S. Signal Corps (SC 26) Burgess H Model tractor biplane.

Dodd was assigned to the 1st Aero Squadron at Texas City, Texas, on March 9, 1913. In June of that year, he transferred to the San Diego Signal Corps Aviation School with the 1st Aero Squadron, and in December, he qualified as a military aviator.

In 1914, he was sent to Galveston, Texas, to protect U.S. citizens during the political unrest in Veracruz, Mexico. Another assignment took him to Fort Sam Houston as commander of the Aviation Post where he participated, along with Captain Benjamin D. Foulois, in the first tactical reconnaissance mission over hostile territory in General John Pershing's Punitive Expedition into Mexico on March 15, 1916.

Pershing selected Dodd as aviation officer of the American Expeditionary Force in 1917. Later Dodd was assigned to the Signal Corps. He also served as chief of Materiel and assistant chief of Supply for the Air Service, then as G-2, Air Service, First Army.

Dodd was killed in an air crash while participating in the New York to Los Angeles Transcontinental Air Race. He was commander of Langley Field at the time.

Dorr Army Airfield

Location: Arcadia, Florida
Status: Closed
Named for: Cadet Stephen Higginson Dorr, Jr.
Date of Birth: 1893
Place of Birth: Nutley, New Jersey
Date of Death: August 18, 1917
Place of Death: Toronto, Canada
Place of Burial: Rosedale Cemetery in Orange, New Jersey, Lot 433

Cadet Stephen Higginson Dorr, Jr., was killed in an airplane collision on his first solo flight.

Dorr graduated from the Princeton Training School. He joined the Officers' Reserve Corps at Fort Myer in Virginia and became one of ten men selected for flight training with the Royal Flying Corps in Toronto, Canada.

He was killed when his plane collided with another in the air, burst into flames, and fell to the ground. Bystanders extricated him from the plane but not before he had been severely burned. He died a few minutes later.

Felker Army Airfield

Location: Adjacent to Fort Eustis in Newport News, Virginia
Status: Active
Named for: Warrant Officer Junior Grade Alfred Clinton Felker
Date of Birth: August 7, 1929
Place of Birth: Spokane, Washington
Date of Death: February 10, 1953
Place of Death: Winterville, Georgia
Place of Burial: Arlington National Cemetery, Section 3, Site 4081-A

Warrant Officer Junior Grade Alfred Clinton Felker entered the U.S. Army in April 1951 and was enrolled in an army helicopter pilot course at Fort Sill in Oklahoma. He graduated in November 1952 and was assigned to the 506th Transportation Helicopter Company at Fort Benning in Georgia. He died in a helicopter accident while on an extended cross-country flight.

Forney Army Airfield

Location: Adjacent to Fort Leonard Wood in Waynesville, Missouri
Status: Active
Named for: Colonel Frank Hartman Forney
Date of Birth: 1906
Place of Birth: South Dakota
Date of Death: November 29, 1950
Place of Death: North Korea
Decorations and Honors: Silver Star; Air Medal with oak leaf cluster; World War II Victory Medal; Korean Service Medal; Purple Heart
Place of Burial: Memorialized at the National Memorial Cemetery of the Pacific in Honolulu, Hawaii

Colonel Frank Hartman Forney was commander of the 19th Engineer Group, serving in Korea. He entered West Point in 1925, graduating in 1929. He was killed in action.

Fort MacArthur Army Airfield

Location: San Pedro, California
Status: Closed
Named for: Lieutenant General Arthur MacArthur, Jr.
Date of Birth: June 2, 1845
Place of Birth: Springfield, Massachusetts
Date of Death: September 5, 1912
Place of Death: Milwaukee, Wisconsin
Decorations and Honors: Medal of Honor; Civil War Campaign Medal; Indian Campaign Medal; Spanish Campaign Medal; Philippine Campaign Medal
Date of Retirement: June 2, 1909
Place of Burial: Arlington National Cemetery, Section 2

Lieutenant General Arthur MacArthur, Jr., the father of General Douglas MacArthur, fought in the Civil War, Spanish-American War, and the Philippine Insurrection.
  At the beginning of the Civil War, MacArthur joined the 24th Wisconsin Volunteer Infantry, and saw action at Chickamauga, Stone's River, and in the Atlanta and Franklin campaigns. After the war, he studied law for a short time but returned to the army and received a commission as a second lieutenant.
  MacArthur took part in the campaign against Geronimo in 1885 and was stationed in the Dakota Territory at the beginning of the Spanish-American War

in 1898. As a brigadier general, he participated in the capture of Manila, and afterward, he was made military governor of the Philippines.

After an assignment in Manchuria in 1905, he served as military attaché to the U.S. Embassy in Tokyo. In 1906, he was placed in command of the Pacific Division, and later he became the army chief of staff. He died while addressing a reunion of his Civil War unit, when he suffered a massive heart attack on the dais.

His Medal of Honor citation for action during the Civil War reads as follows:

Seized the colors of his regiment at a critical moment and planted them on the captured works on the crest of Missionary Ridge.

Freeman Army Airfield

Location: Seymour, Indiana
Status: Closed
Named for: Captain Richard Shafle Freeman
Date of Birth: June 22, 1907
Place of Birth: Winamac, Indiana
Date of Death: February 19, 1941
Place of Death: Lovelock, Nevada
Decorations and Honors: Distinguished Flying Cross; Mackay Trophy (1939)
Place of Burial: Crown Hill Cemetery in Winamac, Indiana

Captain Richard Shafle Freeman was a pioneer in the Army Air Mail Service.

Freeman graduated from Winamac High School and attended Notre Dame University for one year before entering and graduating from West Point in 1930. He was assigned to the Army Air Corps and completed flight training at Brooks and Kelly fields in San Antonio, Texas. Flying the Boeing B-17 Flying Fortress, he participated in the Pan-American Goodwill Flight to Buenos Aires, Argentina, in February 1938. He flew mercy flights carrying Red Cross supplies to relieve earthquake victims in Chile in 1939, and later he led a mercy mission to a leper colony near Molokai in the Pacific. He served at Ladd Field in Alaska from September 1940 to January 1941, and later became its first commander. He also served at Langley Field in Hampton, Virginia.

Freeman was killed, along with the eight-member crew, while en route to Wright Field in Dayton, Ohio, from McClellan Field in Sacramento, California, when the B-17 he was piloting caught fire and crashed. Sabotage was suspected but never proven. The aircraft was equipped with the secret Norden bombsight and had extensive equipment for cold weather flying experiments. At the time of his death, he had accumulated six thousand flying hours.

Godman Army Airfield

Location: Adjacent to Fort Knox in Radcliff, Kentucky
Status: Active
Named for: Lieutenant Louis K. Godman
Date of Birth: ca. 1893
Place of Birth: Oregon
Date of Death: September 29, 1918
Place of Death: Columbia, South Carolina
Decorations and Honors: Resolution by the Executive Committee of the Fourth Liberty Loan
Place of Burial: Los Angeles, California

Lieutenant Louis K. Godman was killed in a plane crash while distributing Liberty Loan pamphlets over Columbia, South Carolina. Godman lost control of the plane but managed to guide it away from parade watchers, narrowly missing the crowd below and crashing several hundred feet away into a vacant lot.

Ironically, the pamphlets he was distributing read: "We are giving our lives for our country. It's up to you to offer your dollars. Buy More Liberty Bonds."

The resolution reads as follows:

Be it resolved by the executive committee of the Fourth Liberty Loan campaign in Columbia and Richland County.

That we have learned with inexpressible sorrow of the death of Louis Godman, aviator and lieutenant in the army of our country

That we realize that his death was as freely an offering to his country as if he had been called upon the field of battle: That we appreciate that through his coolness and gallantry the lives of citizens have been spared

That we consider it a sad but glorious circumstance of coincidence that at the time of the accident, which took him away, he was engaged in circulating an appeal for help for his country, to wit, 'We are giving our lives for our country.'

That, on behalf of this entire city and for those who have gathered here, we wish to express to those who have been bereft, our tenderest sympathy, and to indulge the firm conviction that in this city the memory of Louis Godman ever will be kept alive in the most kindly Sentiment.

Goldberg Stagefield

Location: Adjacent to Fort Rucker near Ozark, Alabama
Status: Active
Named for: Chief Warrant Officer Joseph A. Goldberg
Date of Birth: September 27, 1930

Place of Birth: Linwood, New Jersey
Date of Death: July 15, 1962
Place of Death: South Vietnam

Chief Warrant Officer Joseph A. Goldberg was the first cargo helicopter pilot killed in action while flying a combat support mission. Also aboard the helicopter was Specialist Fifth Class Harold Lee Guthrie (see Guthrie Stagefield).

Gray Army Airfield

Location: Adjacent to Fort Lewis in Parkland, Washington
Status: Active
Named for: Captain Hawthorne C. Gray
Date of Birth: February 16, 1889
Place of Birth: Pasco, Washington
Date of Death: November 4, 1927
Place of Death: Scott Field in Belleville, Illinois
Decorations and Honors: Distinguished Flying Cross, posthumously

Captain Hawthorne C. Gray set a world's record for reaching an altitude of 42,470 feet in a hot air balloon on May 4, 1927.
Gray enlisted in the U.S. Army and was assigned to the 1st Battalion, 2nd Infantry, in the Hospital Corps at Coeur d'Alene, Idaho. On June 18, 1917, he was promoted to second lieutenant, assigned to the 32nd Infantry. He graduated from the Balloon School in 1921, the Air Service Flying School in 1923, and the Air Service Balloon and Airship School in 1924.
On April 29, 1926, he won second place in the National Elimination Balloon Race, which began at Little Rock, Arkansas, and ended at Mt. Holly, North Carolina. In May of that same year, he took second place in the Gordon-Bennett International Balloon Race that ran from Antwerp, Belgium, to Germany.
His Distinguished Flying Cross citation reads as follows:

For heroism while participating in aerial flights. On March 9, 1927, he attempted to establish the world's altitude record for aircraft, but due to faulty oxygen apparatus he fainted at an altitude of 27,000 feet, recovering consciousness after 52 minutes, when his balloon, having overshot its equilibrium point, descended to an atmosphere low enough to sustain life. Undaunted by this experience, Captain Gray, on March 4, 1927, made a record attempt when he attained an altitude of 42,470 feet, higher than any other earth creature has ever gone. On his descent, however, his balloon failed to parachute, and it was necessary for him to descend from 8,000 feet in a parachute. With faith still unshaken, and displaying great courage and self-reliance, Captain Gray, on November 4, 1927, made the third attempt, which resulted in his making the supreme sacrifice. Having attained an altitude of 42,000 feet he waited for 10 minutes, testing his reactions, before making a last rapid climb to his ceiling and a more rapid descent to safe atmosphere. Undoubtedly his courage was greater than his supply of oxygen, which gave out at about 37,000 feet.

Guthrie Stagefield

Location: Adjacent to Fort Rucker near Ozark, Alabama
Status: Inactive
Named for: Specialist Fifth Class Harold Lee Guthrie
Date of Birth: April 3, 1929
Place of Birth: Burlington, North Carolina
Date of Death: July 15, 1962
Place of Death: South Vietnam

Specialist Fifth Class Harold Lee Guthrie was a crew chief on a Bell CH-21 Shawnee helicopter assigned to the 8th Transportation Company.
 Guthrie had served in the military for fourteen years before he was killed when his helicopter was shot down while flying a combat support mission. Also aboard the helicopter was Warrant Officer Joseph A. Goldberg (see Goldberg Stagefield).
 Guthrie's name is on panel 01E, line 011 of the Vietnam Memorial Wall in Washington, D.C.

Hagler Army Airfield

Location: Adjacent to Camp Shelby in Hattiesburg, Mississippi
Status: Active
Named for: Chief Warrant Officer 2 Bill "Jimmie" Hagler
Date of Birth: October 26, 1925
Place of Birth: Johnson City, Tennessee
Date of Death: July 2, 1966
Place of Death: Gulfport, Mississippi

Chief Warrant Officer 2 Bill Hagler was assigned to the 123rd Medical Company (Air Ambulance) of the National Guard at Camp Shelby in Mississippi.
 Hagler attended Greenville High School in South Carolina and graduated from Air Force Base High School in 1947. Afterward, he attended the Infantry School at Camp Blanding in Georgia and the Jacksonville School of Technology in Florida.

Hagler was a machine gunner and served with the 71st Division, 14th Infantry, in Europe from February to December 1945; with the 9th Air Force in Germany from September 1948 to August 1949; and with the 126th Bomb Wing in Bordeaux, France, from November 1951 to March 1952. In 1962, he attended a junior college at Camp Wolters in Mineral Wells, Texas, and the United States Army Aviation School at Fort Rucker in Alabama where he studied to become a Rotary Wing Aviator.

At the time of his death, Hagler was returning from taking soldiers to Keesler Field in Biloxi, Mississippi, when he encountered severe weather. Because of poor visibility, the aircraft hit power lines, crashed, and burned. Hagler managed to escape from the burning helicopter but went back twice to rescue other crew members. All four were hospitalized, but only the copilot survived. Hagler died three days later from burns and smoke inhalation.

Hanchey Army Heliport

Location: Adjacent to Fort Rucker near Ozark, Alabama
Status: Active
Named for: Lieutenant Colonel Charles Wesley Hanchey
Date of Birth: April 15, 1918
Place of Birth: Birmingham, Alabama
Date of Death: May 31, 1957
Place of Death: Fort Leavenworth in Kansas City, Kansas
Date of Retirement: March 31, 1946

Lieutenant Colonel Charles Wesley Hanchey was an artillery observation pilot in Europe during World War II.

Hanchey enlisted in the U.S. Army and graduated from Army Officer Candidate School in November 1942. In 1948, he attended the Helicopter Pilot's Course at San Marcos, Texas, and, from 1949 to 1952, he was assigned to the Department of Air Training at Fort Sill in Lawton, Oklahoma.

He helped develop the helicopter design that is used today. He died while attending the Command and General Staff College at Fort Leavenworth in Kansas City, Kansas, when he suffered a heart attack.

Hancock Army Airfield

Location: Santa Maria, California
Status: Closed
Named for: Captain George Allan Hancock
Date of Birth: July 26, 1875

Place of Birth: No Data Found
Date of Death: 1965
Place of Death: California
Place of Burial: Calvary Cemetery in Los Angeles, California

Captain George Allan Hancock was a Marine Corps scientist and explorer, railroad engineer, pilot, oilman, banker, philanthropist, and musician.

Hancock was the captain and director of the oceanographic research vessel *Velero III*, a ship that was involved in expeditions to both the Pacific and Atlantic tropics.

In October 1928, he established the Hancock School of Aeronautics that grew into a major primary pilot training school during World War II. Hancock also helped start the Santa Maria Junior College in 1954, now G. Allan Hancock Community College, by purchasing forty acres of land at the airport site.

He donated much of the land, buildings, and his library to the University of Southern California. He also donated twenty-three acres of Hancock Park to the County of Los Angeles in 1924, which became the La Brea Tar Pits, to preserve and exhibit fossils exhumed from Rancho La Brea. He was the founder of the California Bank, predecessor to the United California Bank.

Hatch Stagefield

Location: Adjacent to Fort Rucker near Ozark, Alabama
Status: Active
Named for: Major Steve Eldredge Hatch
Date of Birth: July 2, 1918
Place of Birth: Woods Cross, Utah
Date of Death: October 16, 1944
Place of Death: Urbach, Germany
Place of Burial: Bountiful Memorial Park in Bountiful, Utah

Major Steve Eldredge Hatch was the first army aviator killed during World War II. He was a member of Flight B detachment of the Class Before One. He was killed when a ME-109 Messerschmitt attacked his aircraft.

Henry J. Reilly Army Airfield

Location: Adjacent to Fort McClellan in Anniston, Alabama
Status: Closed
Named for: Captain Henry Joseph Reilly
Date of Birth: September 24, 1845

Place of Birth: Ireland
Date of Death: August 15, 1900
Place of Death: Peking, China
Place of Burial: Arlington National Cemetery, Section E, Site 844

Captain Henry Joseph Reilly was killed by enemy fire while commanding a battery of the 5th U.S. Artillery during the Boxer Rebellion in China in 1900.

The inscribed on his tombstone reads: "I have fought the good fight. I have finished my course. I have kept the faith."

Henry Post Army Airfield

Location: Adjacent to Fort Sill in Lawton, Oklahoma
Status: Active
Named for: Second Lieutenant Henry Burnet "Roy" Post
Date of Birth: June 15, 1885
Place of Birth: New York
Date of Death: February 9, 1914
Place of Death: San Diego Bay, California
Place of Burial: Arlington National Cemetery, Section 3

Second Lieutenant Henry Burnet Post was a pioneer military pilot.

Post joined the U.S. Army in 1911 and was assigned to the 25th Infantry, 1st Aero Squadron. On May 26, 1913, he was assigned for training at the Signal Corps Aviation School in San Diego, California, and on December 18, 1913, he set an altitude record of 10,500 feet.

Post was killed while attempting to exceed his previous altitude records by reaching 12,140 feet when the right wing of his hydro-aeroplane fell apart during the descent.

Hunt Army Heliport

Location: Adjacent to Fort Rucker near Ozark, Alabama
Status: Active
Named for: Major William Patrick Hunt, Jr.
Date of Birth: May 9, 1921
Place of Birth: Panama, Canal Zone
Date of Death: June 21, 1952
Place of Death: Korea
Decorations and Honors: Distinguished Flying Cross; Purple Heart; Air Medal

with oak leaf cluster; Army Commendation Medal; American Defense Service Medal
Place of Burial: Memorialized at the National Memorial Cemetery of the Pacific in Honolulu, Hawaii

Major William Patrick Hunt, Jr., joined the U.S. Army on July 1, 1939, and was assigned to a field artillery battery at Fort Monroe in Hampton, Virginia. He graduated from West Point in 1943 and was commissioned a second lieutenant in the regular army. He first served in the Coastal Artillery Corps until 1946, before being transferred to the infantry with assignments in the Philippines and Korea, serving there from July 1945 to 1947. From 1947 to 1950, he served as an assistant professor of Military Science at the Citadel in Charleston, South Carolina, and at the Infantry School at Fort Benning in Georgia.

In 1951, he attended the Air Force Liaison Pilot School at San Marcos, Texas, which was followed by training at Fort Sill in Lawton, Oklahoma. In February 1952, he was once again sent to Korea and served with the 7th Infantry Division where he was killed in a plane crash.

Hunter Army Airfield

Location: Adjacent to Fort Stewart in Savannah, Georgia
Status: Active
Named for: Major General Frank "Monk" O'Driscoll Hunter
Date of Birth: December 8, 1894
Place of Birth: Savannah, Georgia
Date of Death: June 25, 1982
Place of Death: Savannah, Georgia
Decorations and Honors: Distinguished Service Cross with four oak leaf clusters; Distinguished Service Medal; Silver Star; Legion of Merit
Date of Retirement: March 31, 1946
Place of Burial: Savannah, Georgia

Major General Frank O'Driscoll Hunter, a Savannah native, was a World War I ace pilot.

Hunter was a stockbroker before joining the aviation section of the Signal Enlisted Reserve Corps in 1917. He was later commissioned in the Signal Officer Reserved Corps.

Flying a French-built SPAD XIII in 1918, he downed seven Fokker D.VII fighters and one Halberstadt C reconnaissance plane, making him the second highest scoring pilot of his squadron and one of only 109 American pilots credited with downing five or more planes in one day.

During World War II, Hunter was the first commanding general of the 8th

Fighter Command in Europe where he delivered five fighter groups, each with approximately eighty-five Lockheed P-38 Lightning aircraft, to Britain in what was called Operation Bolero.

In 1943, Hunter became the head the First Air Force where he was responsible for planning and executing the movement of air echelons of the Twelfth Air Force from Great Britain to North Africa. He carried the nicknamed, "Monk," because of his youthful antics and colorful personality, and was one of the few individuals to ever have a base named after a living person.

His first Distinguished Service Cross citation reads as follows:

For extraordinary heroism in action in the region of Ypres, Belgium, June 2, 1918. Lieutenant Hunter, while on patrol, attacked two enemy by-place planes, destroyed one and forced the other to retire. In the course of the combat, Lieutenant Hunter was wounded in the forehead. Despite his injuries, he succeeded in returning his damaged plane to his own airdrome.

His second Distinguished Service Cross citation reads as follows:

For extraordinary heroism in action in the region of Champeny, France, September 13, 1918. Lieutenant Hunter, accompanied by one other plane, attacked an enemy patrol of six planes. Despite the numerical superiority and in a decisive combat he destroyed one enemy plane and with the aid of his companion forced the others within their own lines.

His third Distinguished Service Cross citation reads as follows:

For extraordinary heroism in action near Verneville, France, September 17, 1918. Lieutenant Hunter, leading a patrol of three planes, attacked an enemy formation of eight planes. Although outnumbered, they succeeded in bringing down four of the enemy. Lieutenant Hunter accounted for two of these.

His forth Distinguished Service Cross citation reads as follows:

For extraordinary heroism in action in the region of Ligny devant Dun, France, October 4, 1918. Lieutenant Hunter, while separated from his patrol, observed an Allied patrol of seven planes (Bréguets) hard pressed by an enemy formation of ten planes (Fokker type). He attacked two of the enemy that were harassing a single Bréguet and in a decisive fight destroyed one of them; meanwhile, five enemy planes approached and concentrated their fire upon him. Undaunted by their superiority, he attacked and brought down a second plane.

His fifth Distinguished Service Cross citation reads as follows:

For extraordinary heroism in action in the region of Bantheville, France, October 6, 1918. Lieutenant Hunter, while on patrol, encountered an enemy formation of six monoplace planes. He immediately attacked and destroyed one enemy plane and forced the others to disperse in confusion.

Joseph G. LaPointe Heliport

Location: Adjacent to Fort Benning in Columbus, Georgia
Status: Active
Named for: Specialist Fourth Class Joseph Guy LaPointe, Jr.
Date of Birth: July 2, 1948
Place of Birth: North Dayton, Ohio
Date of Death: June 2, 1969
Place of Death: Hill 376, Quang Tin Province, Republic of Vietnam
Decorations and Honors: Medal of Honor, posthumously; Silver Star; Bronze
    Star; Purple Heart; inducted into the Army Aviation Hall of Fame 1998
Place of Burial: Riverside Cemetery in West Milton, Ohio

Specialist Fourth Class Joseph Guy LaPointe, Jr., served with the 2nd Air Cavalry Squadron, 17th Cavalry, 101st Airborne Division.

LaPointe graduated from Northridge High School in Dayton, Ohio, in 1966 and worked as a mail carrier before being drafted in May 1968. At the time he was drafted, he had just applied for college. He wanted to study biology in hopes of working for the National Park System, the National Audubon Society, or the Ohio Department of Natural Resources. He was classified as a conscientious objector and was assigned as a medic. He received training at Fort Sam Houston in San Antonio, Texas, before being assigned to the 2nd Battalion, 27th Cavalry. He was married to Cindy Failor.

His Medal of Honor citation for action during Vietnam reads as follows:

For conspicuous gallantry and intrepidity in action at the risk of his life above and beyond the call of duty. Specialist Fourth Class LaPointe, Headquarters and Headquarters Troop, 2nd Squadron, distinguished himself while serving as a medical aidman during a combat helicopter assault mission. Specialist Fourth Class LaPointe's patrol was advancing from the landing zone through an adjoining valley when it suddenly encountered heavy automatic weapons fire from a large enemy force entrenched in well fortified bunker positions. In the initial hail of fire, two soldiers in the formation vanguard were seriously wounded. Hearing a call for aid from one of the wounded, Specialist Fourth Class LaPointe ran forward through heavy fire to assist his fallen comrades. To reach the wounded men, he was forced to crawl directly in view of an enemy bunker. As members of his unit attempted to provide covering fire, he administered first aid to one man, shielding the other with his body. He was hit by a burst of fire from the bunker while attending the wounded soldier. In spite of his painful wounds, Specialist Fourth Class LaPointe continued his lifesaving duties until he was again wounded and knocked to the ground. Making strenuous efforts, he moved back again into a shielding position to continue administering first aid. An exploding enemy grenade mortally wounded all three men Specialist Fourth Class LaPointe's courageous actions at the cost of his life were an inspiration to his comrades. His gallantry and selflessness are in the highest traditions of the military service and reflect great credit on him, his unit, and the U.S. Army.

His Silver Star citation for action in Vietnam reads as follows:

For gallantry in action while engaged in military operations involving conflict with an armed hostile force in the Republic of Vietnam on April 12, 1969. Specialist LaPointe distinguished himself while serving as a medical aidman on a combat operation in the A Shau Valley, Republic of Vietnam. As Specialist LaPointe's platoon was moving up a hill to set up a night defensive position, the third squad fell behind because of several heat casualties, but before he reached their position, an artillery round impacted near the position of the main body of the platoon. Realizing that there were probably casualties due to the artillery, he rushed to the aid of his fallen comrades. While moving up the hill, three more rounds impacted between him and the platoon. Never pausing to take cover, he ran headlong through the bursting artillery to the aid of the wounded. He treated seventeen casualties, several of which were severe. He was directly instrumental in saving the life of one man and his quick thinking and expert treatment prevented the possible loss of more lives. Specialist LaPointe's personal bravery and devotion to duty were in keeping with the highest traditions of the military service and reflect great credit upon himself, his unit, and the United States Army.

Ladd Field

Location: Fairbanks, Alaska
Status: Active (now, Fort Wainwright)
Named for: Major Arthur K. Ladd
Date of Birth: 1890
Place of Birth: Texas
Date of Death: December 13, 1935
Place of Death: South Carolina
Place of Burial: Arlington National Cemetery, Section 6, Site 9245

Major Arthur K. Ladd was a World War I pilot killed in an airplane crash in which he was a passenger. The flight originated in Virginia where Ladd was stationed at the time and was en route to Florida. The cause of the crash was classified as engine failure.

Lawson Army Airfield

Location: Adjacent to Fort Benning in Columbus, Georgia
Status: Active*
Named for: Captain Walter Rolls Lawson
Date of Birth: October 25, 1893
Place of Birth: Glen Alta, Georgia
Date of Death: April 21, 1923
Place of Death: McCook Field in Dayton, Ohio
Decorations and Honors: Distinguished Service Cross with oak leaf cluster; Mexican Border Service Medal; World War I Victory Medal; French Patriot Medallion

Captain Walter Rolls Lawson first served with Company K, 4th Infantry Regiment, and in May 1918, he was assigned to the 91st Aero Squadron as operations officer and aerial observer. He participated in the Meuse-Argonne and Saint Mihiel offensives in 1918. In 1919, he was transferred to Washington, D.C., where he was assigned to the office of the Director of Military Aeronautics to assist in the reorganization of the Army Air Service. He graduated from the Air Service Field Officers School in 1921.

Lawson was killed when the Martin bomber he was piloting crashed into a nearby river on takeoff during a sudden, severe rain and windstorm

His Distinguished Service Cross citation reads as follows:

The Distinguished Service Cross is presented to Walter Rolls Lawson, Captain (Air Service), U.S. Army, for repeated acts of extraordinary heroism in action near St. Mihiel, France, July 30 and September 13, 1918. Captain Lawson showed rare courage on a reconnaissance far over the enemy lines when he continued on his mission after being seriously wounded by antiaircraft fire. On September 13, although he was still convalescing from his wound, he volunteered for a particularly dangerous mission requiring a flight of seventy-five kilometers within the enemy lines. Because of weather conditions he was forced to fly at a dangerously low altitude and was repeatedly fired on by antiaircraft and machine guns. He successfully accomplished his mission and returned with important information.

---

* Lawson Army Airfield was also named for Ted W. Lawson (see Air Force chapter).

★★★

Libby Army Airfield (also, Camp Libby)

Location: Adjacent to Fort Huachuca in Sierra Vista, Arizona (also, Pohang, Republic of Korea)
Status: Active/Closed
Named for: Sergeant George Dalton Libby
Date of Birth: December 4, 1919
Place of Birth: Bridgeton, Maine
Date of Death: July 20, 1950
Place of Death: Near Taejon, Korea
Decorations and Honors: Medal of Honor; Purple Heart, posthumously
Place of Burial: Arlington National Cemetery, Section 34

Sergeant George Dalton Libby served with Company C, 3rd Engineer Combat Battalion, 24th Infantry Division.
 His Medal of Honor citation for action during the Korean War reads as follows:

Sergeant Libby distinguished himself by conspicuous gallantry and intrepidity above and beyond the call of duty in action. While breaking through an enemy encirclement, the vehicle in which he was riding approached an enemy roadblock and encountered devastating fire which disabled the truck, killing or wounding all the passengers except Sergeant Libby. Taking cover in a ditch Sergeant Libby engaged the enemy and despite the heavy fire crossed the road twice to administer aid to his wounded comrades. He then hailed a passing M-5 artillery tractor and helped the wounded aboard. The enemy directed intense small-arms fire at the driver, and Sergeant Libby, realizing that no one else could operate the vehicle, placed himself between the driver and the enemy thereby shielding him while he returned the fire. During this action he received several wounds in the arms and body. Continuing through the town the tractor made frequent stops and Sergeant Libby helped more wounded aboard. Refusing first aid, he continued to shield the driver and return the fire of the enemy when another roadblock was encountered. Sergeant Libby received additional wounds but held his position until he lost consciousness. Sergeant Libby's sustained, heroic actions enabled his comrades to reach friendly lines. His dauntless courage and gallant self-sacrifice reflect the highest credit upon himself and uphold the esteemed traditions of the U.S. Army.

Lowe Army Airfield

Location: Adjacent to Fort Rucker near Ozark, Alabama
Status: Active
Named for: Thaddeus S. C. Lowe, civilian

Date of Birth: August 20, 1832
Place of Birth: Jefferson Hills, New Hampshire
Date of Death: January 16, 1913
Place of Death: Pasadena, California
Place of Burial: Mountain View Cemetery in Altadena, California

Thaddeus S. C. Lowe established a hot air balloon corps and became the chief aeronaut to the Army of the Potomac during the Civil War.

Lowe made his first balloon flight in 1858 during the celebrations of the laying of the first transatlantic cable. In April 1861, Lowe made a nine-hundred-mile, nine-hour trip from Cincinnati, Ohio, to Pea Ridge, South Carolina.

To prove that balloons could be useful in wartime, Lowe sent a telegraph message from a balloon to Washington revealing troop movements during the battle of Bull Run. Because of his efforts, balloons were used for artillery spotting and were credited with saving the Union army from destruction at the battles of Fair Oaks and Gaines's Mills during the Peninsula campaign of 1862. Working closely with Matthew Brady, Lowe also made photographs from the air balloon.

After the Civil War, Lowe built a device to record longitude and latitude without the benefit of a horizon, the first commercial ice-making machine in the United States, a refrigerated steamer, and a regenerative metallurgical furnace. Lowe also built a series of hotels and connecting inclined railroads in the mountains near Pasadena, California. Unfortunately, because of fires and natural disasters, all that remains today are foundations and walls.

Lucas Army Airfield

Location: Adjacent to Fort Rucker near Ozark, Alabama
Status: Active
Named for: Lieutenant Colonel Andre Cavaro Lucas
Date of Birth: October 2, 1930
Place of Birth: Washington, D.C.
Date of Death: July 23, 1970
Place of Death: Thua Thien-Hue Province, South Vietnam
Decorations and Honors: Medal of Honor, posthumously
Place of Burial: West Point Cemetery in New York

Lieutenant Colonel Andre Cavaro Lucas served with the 2nd Battalion, 506th Infantry, 101st Airborne Division. He was a 1954 graduate of West Point.

His Medal of Honor citation for action in Vietnam reads as follows:

Lieutenant Colonel Lucas distinguished himself by extraordinary heroism while serving as the commanding officer of the 2nd Battalion. Although the fire base was constantly subjected to heavy attacks by a numerically superior enemy force throughout this period, Lieutenant Colonel Lucas, forsaking his own safety, performed numerous acts of extraordinary valor in directing the defense of the allied position. On one occasion, he flew in a helicopter at treetop level above an entrenched enemy directing the fire of one of his companies for over three hours. Even though his helicopter was heavily damaged by enemy fire, he remained in an exposed position until the company expended its supply of grenades. He then transferred to another helicopter, dropped critically needed grenades to the troops, and resumed his perilous mission of directing fire on the enemy. These courageous actions by Lieutenant Colonel Lucas prevented the company from being encircled and destroyed by a larger enemy force. On another occasion, Lieutenant Colonel Lucas attempted to rescue a crewman trapped in a burning helicopter. As the flames in the aircraft spread, and enemy fire became intense, Lieutenant Colonel Lucas ordered all members of the rescue party to safety. Then, at great personal risk, he continued the rescue effort amid concentrated enemy mortar fire, intense heat, and exploding ammunition until the aircraft was completely engulfed in flames. Lieutenant Colonel Lucas was mortally wounded while directing the successful withdrawal of his battalion from the fire base. His actions throughout this extended period inspired his men to heroic efforts, and were instrumental in saving the lives of many of his fellow soldiers while inflicting heavy casualties on the enemy. Lieutenant Colonel Lucas' conspicuous gallantry and intrepidity in action, at the cost of his own life, were in keeping with the highest traditions of the military service and reflect great credit on him, his unit and the U.S. Army.

Marshall Army Airfield

Location: Adjacent to Fort Riley in Junction City, Kansas
Status: Active
Named for: Brigadier General Francis Cutler Marshall
Date of Birth: March 26, 1867
Place of Birth: Galena, Illinois
Date of Death: December 7, 1922
Place of Death: Cuyamaca Mountains near San Diego, California
Decorations and Honors: Distinguished Service Medal; French Croix de Guerre with palm
Place of Burial: West Point Cemetery in New York, Section 8, Site 41

Brigadier General Francis Cutler Marshall graduated from West Point in 1880 and was assigned to the 8th Cavalry.
Marshall served in the China Relief Expedition during the Boxer Rebellion and was an instructor with the New England National Guard from 1911 to

1914. He served three tours in the Philippines from 1902 to 1917.

Marshall became commander of the 165th Field Artillery Brigade, serving in France in June 1918. In October of that year, he was assigned to the 1st Division and commanded the 2nd Brigade in the Meuse-Argonne offensive, and later he commanded the 1st and 4th Divisions of the Third Army in the occupation of Germany.

Marshall was killed in a plane crash while flying from Rockwell Field in San Diego, California, en route to Fort Huachuca in Sierra Vista, Arizona. An extensive search for the lost plane took five months before wreckage of the plane was found.

His Distinguished Service Medal citation reads as follows:

For exceptionally meritorious and distinguished services in command of the 2nd Brigade, 1st Division, during the Meuse-Argonne offensive from October 20 to November 11, 1918, when by his energy, professional skill, and his pronounced qualities of leadership, especially in the attack of the 1st Division on the line of the Meuse, November 6, 1918, and the subsequent operations against Sedan, November 6–7, 1918, he contributed in large measure to the success of his division.

McCook Field

Location: Dayton, Ohio
Status: Incorporated into Wright Field (now, Wright-Patterson Air Force Base)
Named for: Major General Alexander McDowell McCook
Date of Birth: April 22, 1831
Place of Birth: Columbiana County, Ohio
Date of Death: June 12, 1903
Place of Death: Dayton, Ohio
Date of Retirement: 1895
Place of Burial: Spring Grove Cemetery in Cincinnati, Ohio

Major General Alexander McDowell McCook was a Civil War general.

McCook was one of seven brothers and five cousins, known as "The Fighting McCooks," who served in the military. He graduated from West Point in 1852 and fought the Apaches and Utes in New Mexico from 1853 to 1857. He returned to West Point as an assistant instructor of infantry tactics from 1858 to 1861.

During the Civil War, McCook served with the 1st Ohio Infantry and fought in battles of Stone's River and First Bull Run. He commanded a brigade in Kentucky and a division in Tennessee and Mississippi; commanded I Corps in Kentucky; and saw combat in the battle of Perryville. He also commanded a corps in the battles of Stone's River and Chickamauga.

After the war, McCook resigned from the volunteer service and was commissioned in the regular army, serving with the 26th Infantry. From 1875 to 1880, he served as the aide-de-camp to General William T. Sherman. From 1886 to 1890, he was placed in command of the Infantry and Cavalry School at Fort Leavenworth in Kansas.

Moore Army Airfield

Location: Adjacent to Fort Devens near Boston, Massachusetts
Status: Closed
Named for: Warrant Officer 1 Douglas Fillebrown Moore
Date of Birth: July 5, 1948
Place of Birth: Ayer, Massachusetts
Date of Death: May 22, 1969
Place of Death: Kontum, South Vietnam
Decorations and Honors: Distinguished Flying Cross; Bronze Star; Purple Heart; Air Medal with eight oak leaf clusters; Vietnam Military Merit Medal; Vietnam Cross of Gallantry with palm

Warrant Officer 1 Douglas Fillebrown Moore was an observation helicopter pilot killed in action.

Moore graduated from Ayer High School in 1966 first in his class where he was a member of the National Honor Society, and was on the school's cross-country tract team. He was also a Boy Scout in Troop 2, earning Life Scout rank.

Moore attended the University of Minnesota, but left to enlist in the army flight program. He graduated from the helicopter school at Fort Rucker in Alabama as a warrant officer in December 1968.

He was sent to Vietnam on January 14, 1969, assigned to the 189th Aviation Company, 52nd Aviation Battalion, where he supported the Army of the Republic of Vietnam. His call sign was "Ghostriders." He was killed by a sniper's bullet while unloading troops in a landing zone.

Muir Army Airfield

Location: Fort Indiantown Gap, Pennsylvania
Status: Now, Army National Guard Base
Named for: Major General Charles Henry Muir
Date of Birth: July 18, 1860

Place of Birth: Erie, Michigan
Date of Death: December 8, 1933
Place of Death: Baltimore, Maryland
Decorations and Honors: Distinguished Service Cross; Distinguished Service Medal; Silver Star; Purple Heart; French Legion of Honor; British Knight Commander of the Order of St. Michael and St. George; French Croix de Guerre with palm
Date of Retirement: July 18, 1924
Place of Burial: Arlington National Cemetery, Section 3, Site 1999 DH

Major General Charles Henry Muir was known as "Uncle Charley" by the Iron Division doughboys during World War I.

Muir graduated eighth in his class at West Point in 1885. He served in the Spanish-American War and the Philippine Insurrection. He was commanding general of IV Corps of the Army of Occupation in Germany; commanding general of the 28th Division (Pennsylvania National Guard at Camp Hancock in Georgia) during World War I from 1917 to 1918; and commandant of the U.S. Army Command and General Staff College from July 1919 to August 1920. He also served as an observer in China during the Boxer Rebellion.

He fought in the battles of the Marne, Aisne, and Aire, in the storming of Apremont and Chatel-Chehery, and at Le Chene Tondu. After the war, he became commander of Camp Merritt in Hoboken, New Jersey, and, prior to his retirement in 1924, he commanded the III Corps Area in Baltimore.

He died from apoplexy while on a hunting trip at the age of seventy-three. He was married to May Bennet.

His Distinguished Service Cross citation reads as follows:

At the risk of his life, Lieutenant Muir voluntarily exposed himself to a heavy hostile artillery and infantry fire in a successful attempt as a sharpshooter to silence a piece of Spanish artillery at the Battle of Santiago.

Phillips Army Airfield

Location: Adjacent to Aberdeen Proving Ground in Maryland
Status: Active
Named for: First Lieutenant Wendell Kingsley Phillips
Date of Birth: April 30, 1900
Place of Birth: New Jersey
Date of Death: June 5, 1923
Place of Death: Aberdeen Proving Grounds in Maryland
Place of Burial: Arlington National Cemetery, Section 3

First Lieutenant Wendell Kingsley Phillips enlisted as a private in the Signal Corps Reserve on February 9, 1918. On October 6, 1918, he was commissioned a second lieutenant, and on July 1, 1920, he was promoted to first lieutenant. At the time of his death in an aircraft accident, Phillips was assigned to the 49th Bomb Squadron.

Ray S. Miller Army Airfield

Location: Adjacent to Camp Ripley in Little Falls, Minnesota
Status: Active
Named for: General Ray Simeon Miller
Date of Birth: August 14, 1891
Place of Birth: Van Wert, Ohio
Date of Death: May 31, 1961
Place of Death: No Data Found
Decorations and Honors: Bronze Star; Minnesota Distinguished Service Medal; Minnesota Medal for Merit; Minnesota Service Ribbon with thirty-year bar; World War I Campaign Medal; World War II Campaign Medal; Dupont Trophy
Date of Retirement: May 31, 1952
Place of Burial: Acacia Park Cemetery in St. Paul, Minnesota

General Ray Simeon Miller was instrumental in getting the War Department to include aviation units in the National Guard.
    Miller was a flight instructor for the Curtiss Aviation Company, but left that position to join the Minnesota National Guard in 1919. There, he promoted the acceptance of an aviation unit in the National Guard, and flew to Washington to convince General Billy Mitchell of the idea. With the establishment of 109th Observation Squadron in Minnesota, Miller secured land and built aircraft hangers. He was the commander of the unit for twenty years. He was also a special deputy where he promoted the use of aircraft in law enforcement.
    Because of his reputation as a leader, Miller was selected to command all the National Guard aviation units involved in an aerial exhibition at Wright Field in Dayton, Ohio, in 1931. In 1934, he was appointed chairman of the Minnesota Aeronautics Commission, a position he held until War World II, when he was called to active duty.
    He was assigned to the Inspector General's office at Wright Field, and later he was given command of Griffiss Air Force Base in Rome, New York. He was in commanded there until 1945 when he was reassigned to the Ninth Air Force in Europe as Air Inspector. At the end of the war, he was named chief of staff and was promoted to general.

Robert Gray Army Airfield

Location: Adjacent to Fort Hood in Killeen, Texas
Status: Active
Named for: Captain Robert Manning Gray
Date of Birth: May 24, 1919
Place of Birth: Killeen, Texas
Date of Death: October 18, 1942
Place of Death: near Assam, India
Decorations and Honors: Distinguished Flying Cross; Chinese Army, Navy, and Air Corps Medal
Place of Burial: Killeen City Cemetery in Killeen, Texas

Captain Robert Manning Gray was the pilot of crew number 3 on the famous Doolittle Raid on Tokyo in April 1942.

Gray attended Tarleton College in Stephenville, Texas, where he took flying lessons and earned a private pilot license. He also attended Texas A&M University before enlisting in the Army Air Corps on June 29, 1940. He received a pilot rating and commission at Randolph Field in San Antonio, Texas, and was first assigned to the 34th Bomb Squadron, and then to the 95th Bomb Squadron of the 17th Bomb Group at McChord Field in Washington.

Gray described his experience during the raid on Tokyo in the following report:

Giving orders thirty (30) minutes before time to bail out all personnel were in chutes. Gave an order fifteen (15) minutes before time again to make sure. When all personnel were gone, I switched on AFCE and jumped (6200 ft). I landed on summit of a mountain and remained there the remainder of the night. The next morning I looked for other personnel but could not find them. Walked all day and came to village where I stayed that night. Was directed in wrong direction for six miles and ended up where I started from that morning. Sergeant Aden Jones joined me there that night and we rode in chairs the next day to river side. Stayed there all night and until 16:30 o'clock the next day waiting on Lieutenant Jack Manch. On Lieutenant Manch's arrival we loaded a small boat and traveled until night. Traveled by boat all the next day and part of the night arriving in Chuchow [China]. Stayed two days in Chuchow. Went by train and bus to Hangyen [Hang Yen] that took four days. Took plane from Hangyen to Chunking.—*Robert M. Gray, 1st Lt., A.C.*

Gray was portrayed by Robert Mitchum in the movie *Thirty Seconds Over Tokyo*. Gray was killed in the crash of a North American B-25 Mitchell bomber.

★★★

Robinson Army Airfield (formerly, Camp Robinson)

Location: North Little Rock, Arkansas
Status: Active
Named for: Joseph Taylor Robinson, civilian
Date of Birth: August 26, 1872
Place of Birth: Lonoke, Arkansas
Date of Death: July 14, 1937
Place of Death: Washington, D.C.
Place of Burial: Roselawn Memorial Park in Little Rock, Arkansas

Joseph Taylor Robinson was a representative and Democratic senator from Arkansas who played an important role in the enactment of the New Deal legislation.

Robinson studied law at the University of Arkansas at Fayetteville, North Carolina, and the University of Virginia at Charlottesville. He was admitted to the bar in 1895 and became a member of the state general assembly that same year. He was elected as a Democrat to the Fifty-eighth Congress in 1902, as well as the four succeeding Congresses. During his term in the Sixty-second Congress from 1911 to 1913, Robinson was chairman of the Committee on Public Lands. At the end of his term, he became United States senator after serving as governor of Arkansas for three months.

Robinson also served as the minority leader from 1923 to 1933, and was the first Democrat to serve as U.S. Senate majority leader from 1933 to 1937. He was chairman of the committee on expenditures in the Treasury Department and served on the Committee on Claims. He was reelected in 1918, 1924, 1930, and 1936, serving until his death. His funeral service was held in the Chamber of the United States Senate.

Runkle Tactical Site

Location: Adjacent to Fort Rucker near Ozark, Alabama
Status: Active
Named for: Lieutenant Colonel Robert Leslie Runkle
Date of Birth: March 20, 1926
Place of Birth: No Data Found
Date of Death: April 4, 1968
Place of Death: South Vietnam
Decorations and Honors: Silver Star; Distinguished Flying Cross with oak leaf cluster; Bronze Star with oak leaf cluster; Purple Heart with two oak leaf clusters; Air Medal; Army Commendation Medal with two oak leaf clus-

ters; World War II Victory Medal; Army of Occupation Medal; Korean Service Medal
Place of Burial: Fort Snelling National Cemetery in Minneapolis, Minnesota, Plot A2, 376

Lieutenant Colonel Robert Leslie Runkle was commander of the 1st Battalion, 5th Cavalry, in Vietnam.

Runkle served on active duty in the U.S. Navy from 1944 to 1946 and with the Navy and Army Reserve before transferring to the U.S. Army in 1949.

Runkle served as platoon leader and company commander of the 5th Cavalry in Korea, serving there until 1951. Later, he served at Fort Jackson in South Carolina and Fort Bragg in North Carolina. In 1953, he was assigned to troop and staff duties in Germany. In 1956, he attended the Infantry Officer Advanced Course, and received flight training at Camp Gary in San Marcos, Texas. He earned his pilot wings and was designated an army aviator in 1958. He attended the Army Aviation School in 1961, and then was assigned to Vietnam to serve with the Army Utility Tactical Helicopter Company where he pioneered the use of machine guns and rockets mounted on helicopters.

While serving with the 1st Cavalry Division, Runkle was killed when his helicopter was hit by enemy ground fire while leading his battalion in an air assault as part of Operation Pegasus.

Shell Army Heliport

Location: Adjacent to Fort Rucker near Ozark, Alabama
Status: Inactive
Named for: Lieutenant John R. Shell
Date of Birth: December 17, 1917
Place of Birth: Franklin, Arkansas
Date of Death: May 6, 1943
Place of Death: Mateur, Tunisia
Decorations and Honors: Silver Star, posthumously; Purple Heart, posthumously; European-African-Middle Eastern Campaign Medal with bronze star for Tunisia Campaign; World War II Victory Medal
Place of Burial: North African American Cemetery and Memorial in Carthage, Tunisia

Lieutenant John R. Shell was an aviation officer with the 1st Armored Division.

Shell enlisted as a private on December 2, 1937, and served with Battery C, 206th Coast Artillery (antiaircraft), in the Arkansas National Guard. He was commissioned a second lieutenant in the Field Artillery Reserve on May 12,

1941, and graduated as a pilot in 1942 after completing flight training at Fort Sill in Lawton, Oklahoma.

In 1942, along with two groups of pilots, he flew to Bermuda and joined the aircraft carrier USS *Ranger*. He was one of three aviators to fly the Piper L-4 Grasshopper ashore in the North African invasion. He was killed by a German 88 mm gun shell.

Sherman Army Airfield

Location: Adjacent to Fort Leavenworth in Kansas City, Kansas
Status: Active
Named for: Lieutenant Colonel William Carrington Sherman
Date of Birth: May 5, 1888
Place of Birth: Augusta, Georgia
Date of Death: November 22, 1927
Place of Death: Fort Leavenworth in Kansas
Place of Burial: National Cemetery at Fort Leavenworth in Kansas City, Kansas

Lieutenant Colonel William Carrington Sherman was an aviation pioneer.

Sherman graduated from West Point in 1910, third in his class of eighty-three cadets, and was assigned to the Corps of Engineers. He served as an apprentice with civil engineers at Rock Island, Illinois; Memphis, Tennessee; Pittsburgh, Pennsylvania; and in Panama. After his tour in Panama, Sherman attended the Engineer Corps Special Service School at College Park, Maryland.

During the conflict with Mexico, Sherman was sent to Texas City, Texas, in March 1913 with the 2nd Division where the 1st Aero Squadron was formed. While there, he, along with Lieutenant Thomas Milling, set a new American endurance record for flying four hours and twenty-two minutes. During the flight, Sherman sketched the first aerial map of essential military features such as railroads, bridges, roads, towns, and other topographical points of interest.

After returning to the Corps of Engineers, Sherman served as a company commander of the Independent Engineer Battalion in Texas and Mexico. In July 1916, he became commander of Company A, 1st Battalion of Mounted Engineers, and acted as the division engineer of the Cavalry Division. He attended the Command and General Staff College of the American Expeditionary Force while in Europe in 1917. He also served in the Meuse-Argonne offensive, and later he was assigned to aviation duty as the chief of staff of the First Army Service. In 1920, Sherman was transferred to the Air Service and was sent to Langley Field in Hampton, Virginia, where he became chief of staff, 1st Provisional Air Brigade. From November 1922 to February 1923, he served as military aviation advisor on the Rules of War Commission of Jurist at The Hague, Netherlands.

After the war, he returned to the United States and served in Washington, D.C., as chief of training in the Office of the Chief of the Air Service. Sherman died of a sudden illness.

Sherman wrote *Air Warfare* (New York: The Ronald Press, 1926), and the *Tentative Manual for the Employment of the Air Service*, revised as *Notes on Recent Operations*. He also was the editor of *Tactical History*.

Simmons Army Airfield

Location: Adjunct to Fort Bragg in Fayetteville, North Carolina
Status: Active
Named for: Warrant Officer (JG) Herbert W. Simmons, Jr.
Date of Birth: ca. 1928
Place of Birth: Cedartown, Georgia
Date of Death: November 3, 1953
Place of Death: Fort Bragg in North Carolina

Warrant Officer (JG) Herbert W. Simmons, Jr., was one of the first pilots assigned to the 509th Transportation Company (Helicopter).

Simmons was killed when his Bell H-29B helicopter collided with another helicopter and crashed into the Boonie Doone area two hundred yards east of Bragg Boulevard. Simmons had served five years in the military at the time of his death.

Skelly Stagefield

Location: Adjacent to Fort Rucker near Ozark, Alabama
Status: Active
Named for: Major Thomas McFarland Skelly
Date of Birth: No Date Found
Place of Birth: New Castle County, Delaware
Date of Death: March 11, 1945
Place of Death: Linkfert, Germany
Decorations and Honors: Purple Heart
Place of Burial: Netherlands American Cemetery and Memorial in Margraten, Netherlands, Plot 0, Grave 2

Major Thomas McFarland Skelly was a liaison pilot and member of the 252nd Field Artillery Group, Field Artillery. He died from wounds received when his plane was shot down in combat during World War II.

Strother Army Airfield

Location: Winfield, Kansas
Status: Now, Strother Field Industrial Park
Named for: Captain Donald Root Strother
Date of Birth: No Data Found
Place of Birth: Winfield, Kansas
Date of Death: February 13, 1942
Place of Death: Java
Decorations and Honors: Distinguished Service Cross; Purple Heart, posthumously
Place of Burial: Manila American Cemetery and Memorial in Manila, Philippines

Captain Donald Root Strother was attached to the 27th Pursuit Squadron, and was the first Army Air Force pilot from Winfield to lose his life in World War I.

He was a graduate of Winfield High School and Southwestern College and the youngest of four Strother brothers, who all served in the war.

Toth Stagefield

Location: Adjacent to Fort Rucker near Ozark, Alabama
Status: Active
Named for: Captain Donald Bonney Toth
Date of Birth: May 23, 1921
Place of Birth: Pen Argyl, Pennsylvania
Date of Death: January 11, 1963
Place of Death: Ben Tre, Vietnam
Decorations and Honors: Distinguished Flying Cross; Air Medal

Captain Donald Bonney Toth died in a Bell CH-21 Shawnee helicopter crash.

Medical reports from the scene of the accident indicated that all seven members aboard the aircraft died instantly.

His Distinguished Flying Cross citation reads as follows:

For heroism while participating in aerial fights.

Tusi Army Heliport

Location: Adjacent to Fort Hunter Liggett in Monterey, California
Status: Active
Named for: Chief Warrant Officer 2 Ronald L. Tusi
Date of Birth: No Data Found
Place of Birth: No Data Found
Date of Death: August 6, 1974
Place of Death: Hunter–Liggett Military Reservation in California
Decorations and Honors: Distinguished Service Cross with four silver stars; Distinguished Flying Cross with seven oak leaf clusters; Bronze Stars with two oak leaf clusters and one V device; sixty-seven Air Medals; Vietnam Cross of Gallantry with gold star; American Legion Aviation Award for Valor in 1972; inducted into the Army Aviation Hall of Fame (1983)

Chief Warrant Officer 2 Ronald L. Tusi was an attack helicopter pilot, and was considered to be the Army Aviation's leading tank killer.

Tusi served five tours in Vietnam. Until 1983, his record of destroying ten tanks from a helicopter had never been equaled. He was killed in a Cobra helicopter accident while participating in the Night Owl experiments, which became a basis for today's night fighting techniques.

His skill as a helicopter pilot was described in the following citation:

On April 15, 1972, at An Loc, Vietnam, when enemy tanks penetrated within a few meters of the 5th Division Headquarters of the Republic of Vietnam Army, U.S. advisors to the Division Headquarters requested AH-1 Cobra helicopter support. Tusi responded immediately and while under intense antiaircraft fire, single-handedly attacked the enemy, destroying four tanks, damaging a fifth, and forcing the others to withdraw.

Wheeler Army Airfield (see Wheeler Air Force Base)

Wheeler-Sack Army Airfield

Location: Adjacent to Fort Drum in Watertown, New York
Status: Active
Named for: Captain Curtis Wheeler and Lieutenant Carl J. Sack
Date of Birth: Wheeler, ca. 1895; Sack, ca. 1904
Place of Birth: Both, New York
Date of Death: Both, July 1927
Place of Death: Both, Pine Camp in Watertown, New York (now, Fort Drum)

Captain Curtis Wheeler and Lieutenant Carl J. Sack were aviators assigned to the New York National Guard's 27th Brigade.

The two were flying in a two-seater Curtiss JN-4 Jenny biplane on a liaison mission, practicing dropping messages to soldiers on the ground, when Wheeler suddenly slumped forward onto the control stick. Sack lost control of the aircraft and the plane fell from an estimated height of one hundred meters and crashed, killing them both.

Wright Army Airfield

Location: Adjacent to Fort Stewart in Savannah, Georgia
Status: Active
Named for: Colonel Lyle Henry Wright
Date of Birth: September 17, 1921
Place of Birth: Princeton, Illinois
Date of Death: 1968
Place of Death: No Data Found
Decorations and Honors: Silver Star; Distinguished Flying Cross with oak leaf cluster; Bronze Star with oak leaf cluster; Air Medal with eleven oak leaf clusters; Army Commendation Medal with oak leaf cluster; Korean Service Medal
Place of Burial: Lorena Cemetery in Lorena, Texas

Colonel Lyle Henry Wright was an army aviator.

Wright entered the military in 1941 and attended Officer Training School at Fort Sill in Oklahoma, graduating and receiving a commission in 1942. He served as company commander with the 631st Tank Destroyer Battalion at Camp Claiborne in Louisiana, Camp Shelby in Mississippi, and during World War II with the 37th Engineer Group.

In 1948, he was sent to the Far Eastern Command as liaison pilot with the 11th Airborne Division, and then, in 1950, he was assigned as an aviation officer with the 7th Infantry Division during the Korean War. Between 1953 and 1963, Wright served as group aviation officer of the 37th Engineer Group and then as division aviation officer of the 2nd Armored Division. He served a second tour in Korea in 1963 as battalion commander of the 2nd Tank Battalion, 15th Armored, 1st Cavalry Division. He also served with the Second Army at Fort Meade and the Office of Army Aviation in Washington, D.C. Wright was the assistant deputy commandant of the U.S. Aviation School Element at Fort Stewart/Hunter Army Airfield in Savannah, Georgia, from 1966 to 1968.

He held a dual rating for both rotary and fixed-wing aircraft, with more than five thousand hours flying time. Wright died from a heart attack.

Army National Guard

But fame is theirs—and future days
On pillar's brass shall tell their praise;
Shall tell—when cold neglect is dead—
"These for their country fought and bled."

—Philip Freneau

CHAPTER 5

Army National Guard

Camp Abbot

Location: Bend, Oregon
Status: Closed
Named for: Major General Henry Larcom Abbot
Date of Birth: August 13, 1831
Place of Birth: Beverly, Massachusetts
Date of Death: October 1, 1927
Place of Death: Cambridge, Massachusetts
Date of Retirement: 1906
Place of Burial: Mount Auburn Cemetery in Cambridge, Massachusetts, Plot Fuschia Path, Lot 3705

Major General Henry Larcom Abbot was an officer in the Union army who developed a system of submarine mines for coastal and river defense.

Abbot graduated second in his class from West Point in 1855. He was a topographical engineer during the Civil War with the Office of the Pacific Railroad Surveys in Washington. In 1855, he was assigned to survey the route between California and Oregon. Afterward, he served on the hydrographic survey of the Mississippi River Delta.

Abbot was wounded during the battle of First Bull Run (1861) while serving on the staff of Major General Irwin McDowell. He served as the Army of the Potomac's chief engineer throughout the Peninsular campaign of 1862, and commanded the 1st Connecticut Heavy Artillery Regiment in January 1863, and later he was assigned to command the defenses of Washington, D.C. He commanded the Union forces during the Siege of Petersburg in the summer of 1864 and was brevetted brigadier general, U.S. Volunteers, for "gallant and distinguished services in the operations before Richmond, and especially in the lines before Petersburg, Virginia."

On March 13, 1865, Abbot was brevetted brigadier general in the regular army and major general, U.S. Volunteers, for "gallant and meritorious services during the war." After the war, he was instrumental in establishing the Army Engineer School at Fort Totten in New York City. He was married to Mary Susan Everett.

Camp Adair

Location: Corvallis, Oregon
Status: Closed
Named for: Lieutenant Henry Rodney Adair
Date of Birth: 1882
Place of Birth: Astoria, Oregon
Date of Death: June 21, 1916
Place of Death: Carrizal, Mexico

Lieutenant Henry Rodney Adair was the first cavalry officer killed while serving in the Punitive Expedition in Mexico.

Adair, a descendant of Oregon pioneers and a 1904 graduate of West Point, served as an officer in the 10th Cavalry under General John J. Pershing during the search for the bandit, Pancho Villa.

During the battle of Carrizal, he wiped out two machine-gun nests. After the death of his commander, Adair took command of Troop C and ordered it to storm the town of Carrizal. When Troop K, on his right flank, came under heavy fire, it fell back, leaving Troop C exposed to the hostile fire. When Adair discovered that his men were short of ammunition, he went back to get the belts from wounded soldiers. He died after being shot just above the heart while crossing an irrigation ditch.

Camp Atterbury

Location: Edinburgh, Indiana
Status: Now, Joint Forces Maneuver Training Center
Named for: Brigadier General William Wallace Atterbury
Date of Birth: January 31, 1866
Place of Birth: New Albany, Indiana
Date of Death: September 20, 1935
Place of Death: Bryn Mawr Hospital in Pennsylvania
Decorations and Honors: Commander of the Legion of Honor; Companion of

the Order of the Bath; Commander of the Belgian Order of the Crown; Grand Officer of the Order of the Crown of Rumania; Order of the White Eagle of Serbia; Honorary Masters of Arts degree from Yale University; Honorary Doctor of Laws degree from University of Pennsylvania, Yale, Villanova University, and Temple University
Place of Burial: Old St. David's Church Cemetery in Radnor, Pennsylvania

Brigadier General William Wallace Atterbury was a World War I military transportation expert, who later became president of the Pennsylvania Railroad.

Atterbury graduated from Yale University in 1886 and went to work for the Pennsylvania Railroad. During the American Railway Union strike of 1894, he kept the Western Division running by climbing out of the cab and throwing the switches as he rode through troubled areas.

During World War I, Atterbury was appointed Director General of Transportation for the U.S. armed forces in France where he was in charge of construction, operation, and reorganization of the European Railroad network and port facilities.

After the war, Atterbury returned to the Pennsylvania Railroad as its chief operating officer, and was a Pennsylvania delegate to the 1920 Republican National Convention. In 1925, he became president of the Pennsylvania Railroad, a position he held until just before his death. The Pennsylvania Railroad named a passenger train the *General* to honor his memory. He was married to Arminia Rosengarten MacLeod.

Camp Beauregard

Location: Pineville, Rapides Parish, Louisiana
Status: Active
Named for: General Pierre Gustave Toutant Beauregard
Date of Birth: May 28, 1818
Place of Birth: St. Bernard Parish, Louisiana
Date of Death: February 20, 1893
Place of Death: New Orleans, Louisiana
Place of Burial: Metairie Cemetery in New Orleans, Louisiana

General Pierre Gustave Toutant Beauregard was a Confederate officer, known as "The Hero of Fort Sumter."

Beauregard graduated from West Point in 1838 second in his class where he was given the nickname "The Little Napoleon." He was first assigned to artillery, but later, he transferred to engineering.

Beauregard won two brevets and was wounded during the battles of Churubusco and Chapultepec in Mexico in August 1847. He became the superintendent at West Point on January 1861, but because of his support for the South, he was removed from that office, serving the shortest term of any superintendent, from January 23 to January 28.

His Confederate assignments included: commander of Charleston Harbor from March 3 to May 27, 1861; commander of the Alexandria Line from June 2 to June 20, 1861; commander of the Army of the Potomac from June 20 to October 22, 1861; commander of the Potomac District, Department of Northern Virginia, from October 22, 1861, to January 29, 1862; commander of the Army of the Mississippi from March 17 to 29 and, again, from April 6 to May 7, 1862. He also commanded the Department of South Carolina, Georgia, and Florida from August 1862 to April 1865.

He authored, *A Commentary on the Campaign and Battle of Manassas* (New York: G. P. Putnam's Sons, 1891).

Camp Blanding

Location: Starke, Florida
Status: Active
Named for: Lieutenant General Albert Hazen Blanding
Date of Birth: November 9, 1876
Place of Birth: Lyon, Iowa
Date of Death: December 26, 1970
Place of Death: Barrow, Florida
Decorations and Honors: Distinguished Service Medal; Florida Cross
Date of Retirement: 1940

Lieutenant General Albert Hazen Blanding was one of Florida's most distinguished soldiers.

Blanding graduated first in his class from the East Florida Seminary (now, the University of Florida) in 1894 and enlisted in the Gainesville Guard, Florida State Troops, in 1895.

In 1899, Blanding was commissioned a captain in the Florida National Guard, and, in 1909, with the rank of colonel, he commanded the 2nd Florida Infantry Regiment during the Mexican border dispute until 1917. He was transferred into the Federal Service in 1917, and was promoted to brigadier general by President Woodrow Wilson.

During World War I, he saw action in France, was promoted to major general in 1924, and was placed in command of the 53rd Brigade of the 27th Infantry Division. In 1936, President Franklin D. Roosevelt appointed Blanding chief of the National Guard Bureau.

Following World War I, Blanding helped organize the American Legion, Department of Florida, and was promoted to lieutenant general in 1940.

After retirement, he served as military advisor to the governor of Florida and was the coordinating director for the State Defense Council. He was also a member of the Everglades National Park Commission.

Camp Bowie

Location: Brownwood, Texas
Status: Active
Named for: James Bowie, civilian
Date of Birth: April 10, 1796
Place of Birth: Terrapin Creek (now, Spring Creek), Kentucky
Date of Death: March 6, 1836
Place of Death: San Antonio, Texas
Place of Burial: San Fernando Cathedral in San Antonio, Texas

James Bowie, a folk hero of early Texas history, was a slave trader, gambler, brawler, adventurer, gold prospector, and land speculator, but he was best known as the defender of the Alamo and for his famous Bowie knife.

During the War of 1812, Bowie joined the 2nd Division Consolidated that consisted of the 17th, 18th, and 19th Regiments, created with men from Avoyelles, Rapides, Natchitoches, Catahoula, and Ouachita parishes in Louisiana.

After the war, he bought and sold slaves from pirate Jean Laffite. He was proclaimed the South's most formidable knife fighter after stabbing a man during a fight. Along with his brother, Rezin, he established the eighteen-hundred-acre Arcadia sugar plantation near the town of Thibodaux, Louisiana, where they set up the first steam-powered sugar mill.

During the Texas revolution, from October 2, 1835, to April 21, 1836, Bowie fought at the battle of Concepción and in the Grass Fight near San Antonio.

Bowie died at the battle of the Alamo. He was confined to his cot with pneumonia when the Mexicans attacked before dawn, killing all 188 defenders of the Alamo. When General Antonio Lopez de Santa Anna asked to see his corpse, Bowie was found with a bullet hole in his head. He was married to Ursula de Veramendi.

Camp Bullis

Location: San Antonio, Texas
Status: Active
Named for: Brigadier General John Lapham Bullis

Date of Birth: April 17, 1841
Place of Birth: Macedon, New York
Date of Death: May 26, 1911
Place of Death: San Antonio, Texas
Decorations and Honors: Presented two ceremonial swords, one silver and one gold, by the people of Kinney County, Texas
Date of Retirement: 1904
Place of Burial: San Antonio National Cemetery in San Antonio, Texas

Brigadier General John Lapham Bullis was a Civil War Union officer who fought in the Spanish-American War and the Philippine Insurrection.

Bullis enlisted as a corporal in August 1862 with the 126th New York Volunteer Infantry. The following month, he fought in the battle of Harper's Ferry where he was wounded and captured. He was commissioned in 1864 and served with the 41st Infantry during the Civil War. He was wounded and captured again at Gettysburg and held at the Libby Prison in Virginia. After being exchanged for a Confederate prisoner and released, he joined the 118th U.S. Infantry.

After the Civil War, Bullis reenlisted in the army as a second lieutenant and was assigned to border duty along the Rio Grande. In 1873, while stationed at Fort Clark in Texas, he took command of Black Seminole scouts who fought against the Kickapoo Indians at Remolino in the Red River War.

For his actions there, he received a brevet citation for his "gallant service." Between the years 1875 and 1881, he also received citations for his actions on the Pecos River near Saragosa, Mexico, and in fighting the Lipan Apaches at Burro Mountains in Coahuila, Mexico.

In 1897, he was appointed paymaster of the Department of Texas Headquarters at Fort Sam Houston. In 1904, President Theodore Roosevelt promoted Bullis to the rank of brigadier general. After the war, he invested in silver mines and became wealthy. He was married to Josephine Withers.

Camp Clark

Location: Nevada, Missouri
Status: Active
Named for: Brigadier General Harvey C. Clark
Date of Birth: September 17, 1869
Place of Birth: Cooper County, Missouri
Date of Death: 1921
Place of Death: No Data Found
Place of Burial: Oak Hill Cemetery in Butler, Missouri

Brigadier General Harvey C. Clark was adjutant general of Missouri and commander of the Missouri National Guard in 1899.

In 1888, Clark organized Company B, 2nd Regiment, Missouri National Guard, in Butler, Missouri. He graduated from Wentworth Male Academy at Lexington, Missouri, in 1889, and was elected prosecuting attorney of Bates County in 1896.

In June 1897, he resigned his captaincy to accept an appointment as major and quartermaster on the staff of Brigadier General Milton Moore. During the Spanish-American War in 1898, he helped organize the 6th Missouri Volunteer Infantry Regiment, the only Missouri regiment to fight in Cuba. In 1916, Clark commanded the Missouri troops along 145 miles of the Mexican border in the Laredo District. During World War I, as brigadier general, he served from August 5, 1917, to December 22, 1917, with the 1st Missouri Brigade, 25th Division.

Camp Cook

Location: Ball, Louisiana
Status: Active
Named for: Command Sergeant Major Harold Bobby Cook
Date of Birth: December 3, 1934
Place of Birth: Marthaville, Louisiana
Date of Death: May 1999
Place of Death: Alexandria, Louisiana
Decorations and Honors: Distinguished Service Medal; Meritorious Service Medal; Army Commendation Medal; Louisiana Distinguished Service Medal; Louisiana Commendation Medal; Louisiana Longevity Ribbon with one silver and two bronze fleur de lis; the forty-year Louisiana Longevity Medal
Date of Retirement: December 3, 1994

Command Sergeant Major Harold Bobby Cook was the first command sergeant major to be inducted into the Forces Command's Sergeant Audie Murphy Program.*

Cook enlisted in the Louisiana Army National Guard on May 8, 1953, and was assigned to Headquarters Company, 2nd Battalion, 199th Infantry. He also served in he 256th Infantry Brigade and the 225th Engineer Group. From July 1960 to May 1972, he worked through the ranks from private to first sergeant, serving with Company A, 156th Infantry; Company B, 4th Battalion; and Company B, 1st Battalion. From May 1972 to August 1973, he served as battalion operations sergeant, and later as battalion sergeant major with the 1st Battalion, 156th Infantry.

He was promoted to the rank of command sergeant major on August 1973 with the 527th Engineer Battalion and served with that unit until December 1980 when he was promoted to state command sergeant major, the highest enlisted rank in the Louisiana Army National Guard. During his assignment as state command sergeant major from December 1980 to December 1994, he was instrumental in establishing the NCO Academy located at Camp Beauregard in Pineville, Louisiana. He died of cancer after forty-one years of military service.

* Induction and membership in the Forces Command's Sergeant Audie Murphy Program (FORSCOMSAMC) is a reward for noncommissioned officers (NCOs) whose leadership achievements and performance merit special recognition.

Camp Crowder (formerly, Fort Crowder)

Location: Neosho, Missouri
Status: Active
Named for: Major General Enoch Herbert Crowder
Date of Birth: April 11, 1859
Place of Birth: Edinburgh, Missouri
Date of Death: May 7, 1932
Place of Death: Washington, D.C.
Place of Burial: Arlington National Cemetery, Section 2, Site 18

Major General Enoch Herbert Crowder served as United States Ambassador to Cuba from 1923 to 1927.

Crowder graduated from West Point in 1881 and served with the 8th U.S. Cavalry. He was professor of military tactics at the University of Missouri from 1885 to 1889. While an instructor at the university, he studied law and graduated from the law school in 1886. From 1889 to 1891, he saw duty on the frontier in the Dakotas. In 1891, he was appointed acting judge advocate general of the Department of the Platte at Omaha, Nebraska. In 1898, he served as judge advocate on the staff of General Wesley Merritt in the Philippines and as military secretary to the governors there.

In April 1903, Crowder became chief of the 1st Division of the army's first General Staff. He was an observer in the Russo-Japanese War from 1904 to 1905, and in Cuba from 1906 to 1909 where he served on the staff of the provisional governor. He supervised the election of 1908, and helped draft a body of organic law. In 1910, he was a delegate to the Fourth Pan-American Conference in Buenos Aires, and in February 1911, he was appointed Judge Advocate General of the Army. As provost marshal general, he was responsible for administering the Selective Service Program during World War I. He was promoted to major general in October 1917, and in 1921, he was assigned to Cuba as President Woodrow Wilson's personal representative to settle a dispute over elections there.

After his retirement, he returned to his law practice in Chicago. He was the author of *The Spirit of the Selective Service* (New York: The Century Co., 1920), which described the method used in mobilizing troops in World War I.

Camp Curtis Guild

Location: Wakefield, Massachusetts
Status: Active
Named for: Lieutenant General Curtis Guild, Jr.
Date of Birth: February 2, 1860
Place of Birth: Boston, Massachusetts
Date of Death: April 6, 1915
Place of Death: Boston, Massachusetts
Place of Burial: Forest Hills Cemetery in Boston, Massachusetts

Lieutenant General Curtis Guild, Jr., was governor of Massachusetts from 1906 to 1909.

Guild graduated from Harvard University and worked on the staff of his father's newspaper, becoming a partner in 1884. He became owner of the newspaper in 1902, which was later published as the *Wool Market Review*.

He served as a member of the Massachusetts House of Representatives in 1881 and served in the Massachusetts Volunteer Militia in 1891 with the rank of brigadier general. He became inspector general of Havana during the Spanish-American War in 1898 with the rank of lieutenant general.

After the war, Guild returned to Massachusetts and became active in the Republican Party where he was elected as lieutenant governor and later governor. He supported laws for improving working conditions for women and children and for improving factory sanitation. Following an assassination attempt in 1907 at the state house, Guild declined to run for a fourth term, choosing instead to accept a post as Special Ambassador to Russia where he served from 1911 to 1913.

Camp Dawson

Location: Kingwood, West Virginia
Status: Active
Named for: William Mercer Owens Dawson, civilian
Date of Birth: May 21, 1853

Place of Birth: Bloomington, Maryland
Date of Death: March 12, 1916
Place of Death: Charleston, West Virginia

William Mercer Owens Dawson was governor of West Virginia from 1905 to 1908.

Dawson was educated in Preston County, West Virginia, where he earned an apprenticeship in making barrels as a cooper. He entered politics as a state senator in 1881, serving until 1887, during which time he was also the owner and editor of the *Preston County Journal*.

He served as chair of the Republican State Executive Committee where he was instrumental in writing the party's tax reform plan. In 1895, he served as clerk of the House of Delegates, and in 1897, became secretary of state.

During his time in office, he passed legislation to increase the powers and duties of the state tax commissioner; reorganized the state's educational, charitable, penal, and correctional institutions; and passed the election reform bill. However, he lost his proposals for the environment, a pure food drug act, workers' compensation, and the creation of a public service commission. After his term as governor, Dawson served on the Virginia Debt Commission, the Board of Control, and the Public Service Commission.

Camp Dodge

Location: Johnston, Iowa
Status: Active
Named for: Major General Grenville Mullen Dodge
Date of Birth: April 12, 1831
Place of Birth: Danvers, Massachusetts
Date of Death: January 3, 1916
Place of Death: Council Bluffs, Iowa
Decorations and Honors: Inducted into the Hall of Great Westerners Section of
    the National Cowboy Hall of Fame in Oklahoma City, Oklahoma (1963)
Place of Burial: Walnut Hill Cemetery in Council Bluffs, Iowa

Major General Grenville Mullen Dodge was a railroad engineer for the Union Pacific.

Dodge graduated from Norwich University in Vermont with a degree in civil engineering. During the Civil War, he served with the 4th Iowa Volunteer Infantry Regiment where he helped rebuild many of the southern railroads. He directed counter intelligence operation for the Union army, Western Division, under General Ulysses S. Grant. He commanded the 1st Tennessee Cavalry and distinguished himself at the battle of Pea Ridge in Arkansas in March of 1862 where he was wounded. He also commanded a corps in General William T. Sherman's Atlanta campaign where he was again wounded.

After the war, from 1865 to 1866, Dodge led campaigns against Native Americans. He was elected as a Republican to the Fortieth Congress on March 4, 1867. As chief engineer for the Union Pacific railroad from 1866 to 1870, he helped build the railway west from Omaha, Nebraska, to connect with the Central Pacific at Promontory Point, Utah, completing the Transcontinental Railroad on May 25, 1869.

Camp Edsall

Location: Las Vegas, Nevada
Status: Now, Floyd Edsall Training Center
Named for: Major General Floyd L. Edsall
Date of Birth: September 14, 1921
Place of Birth: Covelo, California
Decorations and Honors: Distinguished Service Medal; Silver Star; Legion of Merit; Bronze Star with two oak leak clusters and V device; American Campaign Medal; World War II Victory Medal; Army Commendation Medal; Distinguished Service Medal (Army National Guard); French Croix de Guerre; inducted into the Hall of Fame at Fort Benning Infantry Officers School

Major General Floyd L. Edsall was appointed adjutant general of Nevada in 1967 and served in that position until 1979.

Edsall graduated from the University of Nevada in October 26, 1942, where he received a master of arts degree in education. He enlisted in the U.S. Army in June 1943, was assigned to Officers' Candidate School at Fort Benning in Columbus, Georgia, and received a commission in July 1944.

He served with the 254th Infantry and 398th Infantry from July 1944 to March 1946, both in the United States and in Europe. He later enlisted in the Air National Guard where he served in the Korean War as a company, battalion, and group commander.

He was a member of the Organized Reserve Corps until November 1949, when he became a member of the Nevada National Guard. He was selected to attend the Army War College in 1967 at Carlisle Barracks in Pennsylvania, but declined when he was appointed as adjutant general. He also served as a member of the Joint Army-Air National Guard Bureau Advisory Council. He is married to the former Laverne Stout.

Camp Edwards

Location: Bourne, Massachusetts
Status: Active
Named for: Major General Clarence Ransom Edwards
Date of Birth: January 1, 1860
Place of Birth: Cleveland, Ohio
Date of Death: February 14, 1931
Place of Death: Massachusetts General Hospital in Boston, Massachusetts
Decorations and Honors: Distinguished Service Medal; Silver Star; French Croix de Guerre with palm; Grand Cross of the Order of Leopold (Belgium); commander of the Legion of Honor (France); Polonia Restituta (Poland); Honorary Doctor of Laws degree from Syracuse University
Date of Retirement: November 1, 1922
Place of Burial: Arlington National Cemetery, Site 4073

Major General Clarence Ransom Edwards was commander of the 26th (Yankee) Division during World War I.

Edwards graduated from West Point in 1883 and was assigned to the 23rd Infantry as post adjutant at Fort Porter in Buffalo, New York, and Fort Davis in Texas before being assigned to the Adjutant General's Office in Washington, D.C. He was appointed as regimental quartermaster in 1896.

During the Spanish-American War, Edwards organized a regiment at New Orleans. He was adjutant of the Provisional Brigade and also adjutant general of IV Corps. In 1902, Edwards was appointed chief of the Bureau of Insular Affairs. After commanding brigades in Texas and Hawaii, he was given command of the Panama Canal Zone in 1915. Later, he commanded the newly formed Department of the Northeast in Boston. He was given command of the 26th Division in 1917 and, in 1920, Edwards was assigned to the 1st Division and took command of the I Corps Area.

After retiring from the army, he was elected commander of the Massachusetts Department of the American Legion. Thousands of mourners filed past his bier in the Hall of Flags at the Massachusetts State House to show their respect.

Camp G. C. Grafton

Location: Fargo, North Dakota
Status: Active
Named for: Lieutenant Colonel Gilbert Collins Grafton
Date of Birth: October 6, 1860
Place of Birth: Bowden, England
Date of Death: February 5, 1919

Place of Death: Camp Hospital number 24 in France
Place of Burial: Saint Mihiel American Cemetery and Memorial in Thiaucourt, France, Grave 6, Row 9

Lieutenant Colonel Gilbert Collins Grafton served in the Spanish-American War and World War I.

Grafton enlisted in Company B, 1st Infantry, North Dakota National Guard, in June 1885. He was sent to Mobilization Camp in San Antonio, Texas, in 1911 and was attached to the 28th U.S. Infantry. He was called into federal service on June 19, 1916, as a lieutenant colonel to serve on the Mexican border, serving there until his discharge at Fort Snelling in St. Paul, Minnesota, in 1917. He was called to active duty again on July 15, 1917, as a lieutenant colonel to serve during World War I where he was assigned to field and staff duty with the 164th Infantry.

Camp George West

Location: Golden, Colorado
Status: Active
Named for: General George West
Date of Birth: November 6, 1826
Place of Birth: Claremont, New Hampshire
Date of Death: November 15, 1907
Place of Death: No Data Found

General George West was the founder of the *Golden Transcript* newspaper in Golden, Colorado. He began his newspaper career as a printer's devil, washing presses. At the age of seventeen, he went to Boston and worked on the editorial staff for the *Boston Transcript*.

When gold was discovered in Pike's Peak, West recruited a group of men who formed the Mechanics Trading Company of Boston, better known as the Boston Company, and headed west. There, he published the *Western Mountaineer* for one year.

West served in the Civil War from 1862 to 1865, and was commissioned a captain and commanded Company H, 1st Massachusetts Volunteer Militia. He later served with the 2nd Regiment of Colorado Volunteer Infantry where he played an important part in the recapture of Fort Smith, Arkansas. West was placed in command of F Troop, 2nd Colorado Cavalry, in 1863.

In 1866, West became city editor of the *Rocky Mountain News,* and later he established the *Colorado Transcript*. The *Transcript* is now the second-oldest newspaper in Colorado, with only the *Rocky Mountain News* predating it.

West was appointed adjutant general of Colorado in 1887 and served for two years, during which time he helped stop the uprising of the Ute Indians. In 1897, West became one of the original members of the Grand Army of the Republic and helped establish the Soldiers and Sailors Home at Homelake in Colorado.

Camp Greene

Location: Narragansett, Rhode Island
Status: Active
Named for: General Nathanael Greene
Date of Birth: July 27, 1742
Place of Birth: Potowomut, Rhode Island
Date of Death: June 19, 1786
Place of Death: "Mulberry Grove" in Bamberg County, Georgia

General Nathanael Greene was appointed brigadier general in command of the Rhode Island Troops in Boston in 1771.

Greene was elected to the Rhode Island General Assembly in 1770. He was reelected in 1771, 1772, and again in 1775. In August 1774, Greene helped organize, and was a member of, the Kentish Guards. On May 8, 1775, he was promoted from private to brigadier general for his action during the siege of Boston, and in June of that year, the Continental Congress placed him in charge of the Continental army on Long Island where he fought in battles at Harlem Heights, Trenton, Princeton, Brandywine, Germantown, and Monmouth. He became quartermaster general in 1778, and, in 1780, he was placed in command of the Army of the South where he lost the battle of Guilford Court House, Hobkirk's Hill, Ninety-Six, and Eutaw Springs in South Carolina. After the war, he settled in Georgia. He died from sunstroke. He was married to Catharine Littlefield.

Camp Gruber

Location: Braggs, Oklahoma
Status: Active
Named for: Brigadier General Edmund Louis "Snitz" Gruber
Date of Birth: November 11, 1879
Place of Birth: Cincinnati, Ohio
Date of Death: May 30, 1941
Place of Death: Fort Leavenworth in Kansas City, Kansas
Decorations and Honors: Distinguished Service Medal

Brigadier General Edmund Louis Gruber is best remembered as the author of the 5th Artillery Regimental song titled "The Caissons Go Rolling Along," which was adopted by all regiments of the artillery, first becoming the field artillery song, and later the U.S. Army's official song.

Gruber graduated from West Point in 1904 and was commissioned a second lieutenant in the Artillery Corps. He first served from 1904 to 1906 with various field artillery units until he was assigned to the Mounted Service School at Fort Riley in Kansas. He was sent to the Imperial Military Riding School at Hanover, Germany, as a student officer, and served there until August 1912, and later he was assigned as an equestrian instructor at the Mounted Service School. Later, he became an army polo team champion.

He served at West Point as an instructor in the Department of Tactics until August 1917 when World War I began. During the war, he commanded the 332nd Field Artillery at Camp Grant in Illinois; commanded the 116th Field Artillery at Camp Wheeler in Georgia; was assistant to the Chief of Field Artillery in Washington, D.C.; commanded the Field Artillery Brigade Firing Center at Fort Sill in Oklahoma; and served in the Office of the Chief of Field Artillery and with the War Plans Division of the War Department General Staff in Washington, D.C.

After the war, he became president and superintendent of the Kentucky Military Institute at Lyndon, Kentucky. He rejoined the military and was once again commissioned in the army on July 1, 1920.

From 1922 to 1939, Gruber was a student officer at the Command and General Staff College at Fort Leavenworth in Kansas; an instructor at the Cavalry School at Fort Riley in Kansas; a student officer at the Army War College; an instructor at the Command and General Staff College; served in the Panama Canal Zone; served on the War Department General Staff; and was chief of the artillery section of the 1st Division. In October 1940, he became commandant of the Command and General Staff College and commanding general of the VII Corps Area at Fort Leavenworth. Gruber died from natural causes.

His Distinguished Service Medal citation reads as follows:

He displayed exceptional ability in planning the organization of Field Artillery Brigade Firing Centers; in April 1918, established such a center at Fort Sill and during the remainder of the war displayed rare judgment and high professional attainments in the administration of this center.

Camp Hartell

Location: Windsor Locks, Connecticut
Status: Active
Named for: First Lieutenant Lee Ross Hartell
Date of Birth: August 23, 1923

Place of Birth: Philadelphia, Pennsylvania
Date of Death: August 27, 1951
Place of Death: Near Kobangsan-ni, Korea
Decorations and Honors: Medal of Honor, posthumously
Place of Burial: New Saint Peters Cemetery in Danbury, Connecticut

First Lieutenant Lee Ross Hartell served with the 15th Field Artillery Battalion, 2nd Infantry Division.

His Medal of Honor citation for action during the Korean War reads as follows:

First Lieutenant Hartell, a member of Battery A, distinguished himself by conspicuous gallantry and intrepidity at the risk of his life above and beyond the call of duty in action against an armed enemy of the United Nations. During the darkness of early morning, the enemy launched a ruthless attack against friendly positions on a rugged mountainous ridge. First Lieutenant Hartell, attached to Company B, 9th Infantry Regiment, as forward observer, quickly moved his radio to an exposed vantage on the ridge line to adjust defensive fires. Realizing the tactical advantage of illuminating the area of approach, he called for flares and then directed crippling fire into the onrushing assailants. At this juncture a large force of hostile troops swarmed up the slope in banzai charge and came within ten yards of First Lieutenant Hartell's position. First Lieutenant Hartell sustained a severe hand wound in the ensuing encounter but grasped the microphone with his other hand and maintained his magnificent stand until the front and left flank of the company were protected by a close-in wall of withering fire, causing the fanatical foe to disperse and fall back momentarily. After the numerically superior enemy overran an outpost and was closing on his position, First Lieutenant Hartell, in a final radio call, urged the friendly elements to fire both batteries continuously. Although mortally wounded, First Lieutenant Hartell's intrepid actions contributed significantly to stemming the onslaught and enabled his company to maintain the strategic strongpoint. His consummate valor and unwavering devotion to duty reflect lasting glory on himself and uphold the noble traditions of the military service.

Camp Johnson

Location: Colchester, Vermont
Status: Active
Named for: Major General Herbert Thomas Johnson
Date of Birth: January 27, 1872
Place of Birth: Bradford, Vermont
Date of Death: November 4, 1942

Place of Death: No Data Found
Date of Retirement: December 16, 1941
Place of Burial: Bradford Town Cemetery in Bradford, Vermont

Major General Herbert Thomas Johnson fought in the Spanish-American War.

Johnson joined the service on May 18, 1898, and was elected adjutant general for Vermont in 1910, serving until 1941. He served as the chairman of the legislative committee of the Vermont National Guard Association and presided over the National Guard's intervention in violent labor strikes in Wilder and Bellows Falls, Vermont, in 1921.

Johnson played an active role in maintaining order during the flood of November 1927 by supervising the local troops, maintaining boats, manning the only gas station in the area still in service, and regulating the flow of supplies from local stores.

While on the legislative committee of the National Guard Association, Johnson obtained money for the National Guard during the depression year of 1932.

Camp Keyes

Location: Augusta, Maine
Status: Active
Named for: Major General Erasmus Darwin Keyes
Date of Birth: May 29, 1810
Place of Birth: Brimfield, Massachusetts
Date of Death: October 14, 1895
Place of Death: Nice, France
Place of Burial: West Point Cemetery in New York, Section 26, Row C, Grave 31

Major General Erasmus Darwin Keyes was a Civil War Union commander.

Keyes graduated from West Point in 1832 and served with the 3rd Artillery, fighting Native Americans on the frontier. He was General Winfield Scott's aide and military secretary and taught artillery and cavalry skills at West Point from 1844 to 1848.

When the Civil War began, Keyes served with the 11th U.S. Infantry, and later he commanded the 1st Brigade, 1st Division, at the battle of First Bull Run in 1861. President Abraham Lincoln appointed him commander of the newly formed IV Corps in March 1862 and promoted him to major general on May 5, 1862, after which time he led the corps in General McClellan's Peninsula campaign until August 1862. He saw action at Lee's Mill, Yorktown, Bottom's Bridge, Savage's Station, Charles City Cross Roads, Malvern Hill, and Harrison's Landing. He was brevetted a brigadier general for gallantry at the battle of Fair Oaks.

He resigned from the army on May 6, 1864, and moved to San Francisco where he became a prosperous gold miner, banker, and winemaker. He died while on vacation in Europe.

Keyes was the author of "The Rear Guard at Malvern Hill" as part of The Century Company's *Battles and Leaders of the Civil War* series. He also wrote, *Fifty Years' Observation of Men and Events*, (New York: C. Scribner's sons, 1884).

Camp Labonte

Location: Concord, New Hampshire
Status: Closed
Named for: Captain Roland Charles Labonte
Date of Birth: July 28, 1935
Place of Birth: Nashua, New Hampshire
Date of Death: April 19, 1969
Place of Death: South Vietnam

Captain Roland Charles Labonte was the first New Hampshire National Guardsman killed in Vietnam.

Labonte was commissioned in August 1960 and served with B Battery, 2nd Battalion, 172nd Artillery, at Fort Bragg in North Carolina when the unit was activated in 1961 during the Berlin Crisis.

He assumed command of B Battery, 3rd Battalion, 197th Artillery Regiment, known as "Jungle Battery," in September of 1967, and again in 1968, when the battalion was activated during Vietnam. In March of 1969, Labonte was assigned as battalion liaison officer, working with Delta Battery, where he directed fire support for a Special Forces operation. Labonte died of wounds sustained from exploding 82mm mortar rounds that were targeted at Delta Battery's base camp's briefing tent. Labonte was riding nearby in his jeep at the time.

Camp Mabry

Location: Austin, Texas
Status: Active
Named for: Major General Woodford Haywood Mabry
Date of Birth: September 3, 1856
Place of Birth: Jefferson, Texas
Date of Death: January 4, 1899

Place of Death: Havana, Cuba
Place of Burial: Jefferson, Texas

Major General Woodford Haywood Mabry became the adjutant general of Texas on January 22, 1891, serving until May 5, 1898.

Mabry attended Virginia Military Institute and later joined the Confederacy. Acting on orders from Governor Charles Allen Culberson in February 1896, Mabry prevented the prizefight between Peter Maher and Robert Fitzsimmons from being held in Texas. In January 1897, he prevented mob violence in the case of George Harrison, who was being tried for murder at Woodville, Texas. During the Mexican border dispute of 1898, Mabry led two companies of Texas Rangers against Mexican rebel, Catarino E. Garza, who directed a battle from the Texas side of the Rio Grande.

At the beginning of the Spanish-American War in 1898, Mabry resigned his office as adjutant general to become a colonel in the 1st Texas Volunteer Infantry. He helped establish a permanent Texas Volunteer Summer Encampment location by collecting donations throughout the state to purchase a two-hundred-acre site in Austin, Texas. He died while taking the 1st Texas Volunteer Infantry to Cuba after he developed pneumonia and meningitis.

Camp Maxey

Location: Paris, Texas
Status: Closed
Named for: General Samuel Bell Maxey
Date of Birth: March 30, 1825
Place of Birth: Tompkinsville, Kentucky
Date of Death: August 16, 1895
Place of Death: Eureka Springs, Arkansas
Place of Burial: Evergreen Cemetery in Paris, Texas

General Samuel Bell Maxey was a Texas senator and superintendent of Indian affairs during the Civil War.

Maxey was an 1846 graduate of West Point. He was brevetted second lieutenant and served in the 7th Infantry Regiment. He fought in the battle for Contreras and participated in the battles of Churubusco and Molino del Rey in Mexico. He also commanded a company of city police guard in Mexico City.

He resigned from the army in September 1849 and returned to Albany, Kentucky, to study law. In April 1851, he joined his father's law firm and was elected clerk of the circuit and county courts of Clinton County.

At the beginning of the Civil War, Maxey joined the Confederacy and organized a group of Paris, Texas, men called the "Lamar Rifles," and took control of the abandoned Federal forts in Indian Territory, preventing the Union invasion of north Texas.

Maxey was taken prisoner of war in 1865, and received a presidential pardon on July 20, 1867, through a recommendation from his old West Point classmate, Ulysses S. Grant, which allowed him to practice law again and participate in Texas politics. He was elected as a Democrat to the United States Senate in 1875. He was reelected in 1881, serving from March 4, 1875, to March 3, 1887. He was married to Marilda Cass Denton.

Camp McCain

Location: Grenada, Mississippi
Status: Active
Named for: Major General Henry Pinckney McCain
Date of Birth: January 23, 1861
Place of Birth: Teoc Creek, Carroll County, Mississippi
Date of Death: July 25, 1941
Place of Death: Washington, D.C.
Decorations and Honors: Distinguished Service Medal; British Order of St. Michael and St. George
Place of Burial: Arlington National Cemetery, Section 9, Site 5831

Major General Henry Pinckney McCain served during the Spanish-American War.

McCain graduated from West Point in 1885. He served as an infantry officer with the 3rd, 14th, and 21st Infantry in Alaska and the Philippine Islands, before becoming a professor of military science at Louisiana State University at Baton Rouge from March 1889 to August 1891.

McCain served as acting judge advocate and acting adjutant general for the Department of Columbia at Vancouver, Canada. He was also on general staff duty in the Department of Mindanao at Zamboanga, Philippine Islands, from August 1903 to April 1904; was an assistant to the adjutant general, Philippine Division, in Manila from December 1912 to July 1914; and the adjutant general of the U.S. Army in Washington, D.C., from August 1914 to August 1918.

McCain commanded Camp Devens near Boston, Massachusetts, from August 1918 to July 1920 and served as department and corps area adjutant, Central Department, VI Corps Area, at Chicago and Fort Sheridan in Chicago, Illinois, from July 1920 to July 1921. He served as governor of the United States Soldiers' Home in Washington, D.C., until April 30, 1936.

His Distinguished Service Medal citation reads as follows:

For exceptionally meritorious and distinguished services. In administering the

Adjutant General's Department during the early period of the war. Through his efficient management this Department was able to meet excessive burdens placed upon it.

Camp Pendleton

Location: Virginia Beach, Virginia
Status: Active (now, Army National Guard Base)
Named for: Brigadier General William Nelson Pendleton
Date of Birth: December 26, 1809
Place of Birth: Richmond, Virginia
Date of Death: January 15, 1883
Place of Death: Lexington, Virginia
Place of Burial: Stonewall Jackson Memorial Cemetery in Lexington, Virginia

Brigadier General William Nelson Pendleton was a teacher, minister, and chief of artillery of the Army of Northern Virginia during the Civil War.

Pendleton graduated from West Point in 1830 and was assigned to artillery. He served briefly as assistant professor of mathematics at West Point, and in 1833, he became a professor of mathematics in Bristol College in Pennsylvania. Later, he received a Doctor of Divinity degree and became a clergyman in the Episcopal Church.

During the Civil War, with the nickname "Parson," he served with the Army of Northern Virginia carrying guns he named Matthew, Mark, Luke, and John. He fought in the battle of First Manassas and at Gettysburg, and he commanded the Rockbridge Artillery. It was said that he would pause before battle to say with a prayer for those he was about to kill. After the war he returned to his position as rector of Grace Church in Virginia.

Camp Perry

Location: Port Clinton, Ohio
Status: Active
Named for: Commodore Oliver Hazard Perry, USN
Date of Birth: August 23, 1785
Place of Birth: South Kingston, Rhode Island
Date of Death: August 23, 1819
Place of Death: At sea near Trinidad
Decorations and Honors: Congressional Gold Medal
Place of Burial: Island Cemetery in Newport, Rhode Island

Commodore Oliver Hazard Perry was the hero of the battle of Lake Erie.

At the age of thirteen, Perry entered the navy as a midshipman and was sent to the Caribbean. Later assignments took him to Europe and Africa during the first Barbary Wars in 1801.

In 1811, as commander of the USS *Revenge*, a fourteen-gun vessel, Perry was sent to survey harbors in Rhode Island where his ship became shrouded in fog and was wrecked on a reef near Watch Hill Point.

During the War of 1812, as commander of the destroyer USS *Lawrence* at the battle of Lake Erie on September 10, 1813, Perry faced severe storms that wrecked his ship and killed or wounded more than 80 percent of the crew. To continue the battle, Perry transferred from the USS *Lawrence* to the smaller and less damaged USS *Niagara* with his battle flag that read "Don't Give Up The Ship." Following the victory, Perry made the famous statement, "We have met the enemy and they are ours" in his report to General William Henry Harrison.

In 1814, Perry was given command of the USS *Java*, a new forty-four-gun frigate, in which he participated in the defense of both Washington and Baltimore during the British invasion of the Chesapeake Bay region and where, later, he sailed the USS *Java* to the Mediterranean to help stop pirate raids along the north African coast.

Perry received a court-martial for slapping an officer while commander of the USS *Java,* and because of another dueling incident, President James Monroe sent Perry on a diplomatic mission to South America aboard the frigate USS *John Adams,* in June 1819.

While aboard the armed schooner, USS *Nonsuch*, he contracted yellow fever and died. He was first buried at Port of Spain, Trinidad. In 1826, his remains were moved from Trinidad to Newport, Rhode Island, where the state erected a monument in his honor. He was married to Elizabeth Champlin Mason.

Camp Pike

Location: North Little Rock, Arkansas
Status: Now, Robinson Army Airfield
Named for: Brigadier General Zebulon Montgomery Pike
Date of Birth: January 5, 1779
Place of Birth: Lamington, New Jersey
Date of Death: March 27, 1813
Place of Death: York, Ontario
Place of Burial: Sackett's Harbour on Lake Ontario, Canada

Brigadier General Zebulon Montgomery Pike was an explorer and is best known for discovering the mountain peak in Colorado that bears his name.

In 1805, Pike set out with a twenty-man exploring party with orders to discover the headwaters of the Mississippi River, to negotiate a peace treaty with the Sioux Indians, set claim to their land, and to build a fort there. Pike traveled two thousand miles from St. Louis to northern Minnesota but mistook Leech Lake in Minnesota for the source of the Mississippi.

In 1806, Pike led another expedition to the southwestern borders of the Louisiana Purchase with orders to explore the Arkansas and Red Rivers and to obtain information about nearby Spanish territory. Unfortunately, when he entered what is now northern New Mexico, he was charged with illegal entry into Spanish-held territory and the Spanish seized all his maps, notes, and papers. Pike died at the Battle of York when a British power magazine exploded.

Camp Rilea

Location: Warrenton, Oregon
Status: Active
Named for: Brigadier General Thomas E. Rilea
Date of Birth: May 5, 1895
Place of Birth: Chicago, Illinois
Date of Death: February 3, 1959
Place of Death: No Data Found
Decorations and Honors: Distinguished Service Medal; Legion of Merit; Bronze Star; Commendation Ribbon with metal pendant; Purple Heart; Presidential Unit Citation; Mexican Border Service Medal; Army of Occupation Medal (Germany); World War I Victory Medal; Mexican Service Medal; World War II Victory Medal; Armed Forces Reserve Medal; National Guard Association Distinguished Service Medal
Place of Burial: Riverview Abby Mausoleum in Portland, Oregon

Brigadier General Thomas E. Rilea served as Oregon's adjutant general in 1941.

Rilea entered military service on December 8, 1914, and was assigned to Company B, 3rd Oregon Infantry, as a bugler on the Mexican border. He served with that unit until June 26, 1916. He served in France during World War I and was commissioned a second lieutenant in February 1918. He also served on General John Pershing's staff as a captain.

During his career, he served in the infantry as intelligence officer with Headquarters, 186th Infantry, in 1923, and with Headquarters Company, 82nd Infantry Brigade, in August 1924. He also served as executive office of the same brigade in November 1924. With a promotion to lieutenant colonel, he was assigned to Headquarters, 41st Division, as adjutant general. He commanded the 82nd Infantry Brigade again in 1931.

He attended the Army War College in 1929 and the IX Corps Area Command and Staff School for National Guard Officers in 1939. Rilea took time out from his job as adjutant general to serve as the assistant division commander with the 41st Division in World War II. Sent to New Guinea, he participated in the Papuan, Sanananda, and Buna campaigns. He was assigned duties as base commander at a supply base in Sydney, Australia, where he organized and coordinated the logistics of combat supplies and material.

In 1945, Rilea became commanding general of the Infantry Replacement Center at Fort McClellan in Alabama where he served until retirement from active duty. He served on Oregon's State Police organizational committee, and later returned as Oregon's adjutant general, a position he held until his death.

Camp Ripley

Location: Little Falls, Minnesota
Status: Active
Named for: General Eleazar Wheelock Ripley
Date of Birth: April 15, 1782
Place of Birth: Hanover, New Hampshire
Date of Death: March 2, 1839
Place of Death: West Feliciana, Louisiana
Decorations and Honors: Congressional Gold Medal
Place of Burial: Locust Grove Cemetery in Saint Feliciana, Louisiana

General Eleazar Wheelock Ripley was a lawyer and a member of the Massachusetts legislature.

Ripley served from 1810 to 1812 as the state's speaker and senator until he volunteered for duty in the War of 1812. He was commissioned a lieutenant in the 21st Infantry and fought on the frontier until April 14, 1814, when he was appointed brigadier general and put in command of the 2nd Brigade of General Jacob Brown's army. He fought in the battles at Chippewa and Niagara where he was wounded.

Ripley resigned from the military in 1820 and moved to Louisiana where he practiced law and became a member of the state senate. He was elected to Congress as a Jackson Democrat in 1834, and served until his death. He died from the result of his old war wounds.

His Gold Medal was awarded for gallantry while fighting in defense of Fort Erie where he was wounded in 1814. The inscription simply reads: "Niagara, Chippewa, Erie," and is on display in the Minnesota Military Museum.

★★★

Camp Roberts

Location: Paso Robles, California
Status: Active
Named for: Corporal Harold W. Roberts
Date of Birth: October 14, 1899
Place of Birth: San Francisco, California
Date of Death: October 4, 1918
Place of Death: Montrebeau Forest, France
Decorations and Honors: Medal of Honor; French Croix de Guerre with palm; French Military Medal; Italian War Cross, posthumously
Place of Burial: Meuse-Argonne American Cemetery and Memorial in Romagne, France

Corporal Harold W. Roberts was a tank driver in World War I.

Roberts enlisted in the U.S. Army in San Francisco and, after basic training at Fort McDowell on Angel Island in San Francisco Bay, he was sent to the Philippines. After additional training, he was transferred to France where he was assigned to Company A, 344th Light Tank Brigade, 1st Division, under the command of Lieutenant Colonel George S. Patton, Jr., and fought in the Saint Mihiel and Meuse-Argonne offensives. A photo of his dog, Frisky, was found on him when he died.

His Medal of Honor citation for action during World War I reads as follows:

Corporal Roberts, a tank driver, was moving his tank into a clump of bushes to afford protection to another tank which had become disabled. The tank slid into a shell hole, ten feet deep, filled with water, and was immediately submerged. Knowing that only one of the two men in the tank could escape, Corporal Roberts said to the gunner, 'Well, only one of us can get out, and out you go,' where upon he pushed his companion through the back door of the tank and was himself drowned.

Camp Shelby

Location: Hattiesburg, Mississippi
Status: Active
Named for: Colonel Isaac Shelby
Date of Birth: December 11, 1750
Place of Birth: Hagerstown, Maryland
Date of Death: July 18, 1826
Place of Death: At his home, Traveller's Rest, Kentucky

Decorations and Honors: Congressional Gold Medal
Place of Burial: Private family graveyard in Lincoln County, Kentucky

Colonel Isaac Shelby was a farmer, surveyor, Indian fighter, Revolutionary War hero, and first governor of Kentucky.

Shelby fought in battles against the Chickamauga Indians. During the American Revolution, he commanded an army that defeated the British at the battle of King's Mountain, North Carolina, on October 7, 1780. He retired after the war and became a member of the Virginia state legislature, a member of the North Carolina state legislature, and a delegate to the Kentucky state constitutional convention. He was elected governor of Kentucky in 1792, serving until 1796. He was elected again in 1812 and served until 1816. As governor, he implemented Kentucky's first constitution, sought federal help in fighting the Indians, and secured use of the Mississippi River.

At the age of sixty-three, during the War of 1812, Shelby organized and personally led four thousand Kentucky volunteers in an attack against a British army at the battle of the Thames, also known as the battle of Moraviantown, on October 5, 1813, at Chatham, Ontario, in Upper Canada. He died at home at age seventy-six. He was married to Susannah Hart.

Camp Stanley

Located: San Antonio, Texas
Status: Closed
Named for: Major General David Sloane Stanley
Date of Birth: June 1, 1828
Place of Birth: Cedar Valley, Ohio
Date of Death: March 13, 1902
Place of Death: Washington, D.C.
Decorations and Honors: Medal of Honor
Date of Retirement: 1892
Place of Burial: Soldiers Home National Cemetery in Washington, D.C.

Major General David Sloane Stanley was chief of cavalry in the Army of the Cumberland.

Stanley graduated from West Point in 1852. He commanded the 1st Division, IV Corps, in the Atlanta campaign and at Spring Hill during the Franklin campaign during the Civil War.

Stanley was appointed brigadier general of volunteers in September 1861, brevetted brigadier general in March 1865, and was promoted to major general on March 13, 1865. Following the war he served on the frontier and commanded the Yellowstone Expedition.

His Medal of Honor citation for action in the battle of Franklin during the Civil War reads as follows:

At a critical moment rode to the front of one of his brigades, reestablished its lines, and gallantly led it in a successful assault.

Camp Swift

Location: Bastrop, Texas
Status: Active
Named for: Major General Eben Swift
Date of Birth: May 11, 1854
Place of Birth: Fort Chadbourne, Texas
Date of Death: April 25, 1938
Place of Death: Washington, D.C.
Date of Retirement: May 11, 1918
Place of Burial: Arlington National Cemetery, Section South, Site 38899

Major General Eben Swift fought in the Indian Wars and World War I.

Swift graduated from West Point in 1876, following schooling at Racine College in Wisconsin, Washington University, and Dickinson College in Pennsylvania.

His first assignment was on the frontiers of Wyoming, Montana, Nebraska, Idaho, and Colorado, fighting the Sioux, Cheyenne, Barrock, and Ute Indians. He served in the 14th Infantry; 5th Cavalry; and the 4th, 7th, and 9th Illinois Infantries.

During the Spanish-American War, he was placed in charge of establishing a civil government in Humacao, Puerto Rico. He also served in the campaign against the Moros in the Philippines; commanded the 2nd Cavalry in the Punitive Expedition in Mexico in 1916; commanded the 82nd Division at Camp Gordon in Georgia, in 1917; was chief of the American Military Mission; and commanded the United States forces in Italy.

Swift also author a number military history books. He was married to Susan Bonaparte Palmer.

Camp Varnum

Location: Narragansett, Rhode Island
Status: Active
Named for: General James Mitchell Varnum

Date of Birth: December 17, 1748
Place of Birth: Dracut, Massachusetts
Date of Death: January 10, 1789
Place of Death: Marietta, Ohio
Place of Burial: Mound Cemetery in Marietta, Ohio

General James Mitchell Varnum was a direct descendant of *Mayflower* passenger Francis Cooke. He was a brigadier general in the Continental army and commander of volunteers during the American Revolution.

Varnum graduated from Rhode Island College (now, Brown University) in 1769 and was admitted to the bar in 1771. His military career began as the first commander of the Kentish Guards in October 16, 1774. In 1775, he was commissioned a colonel of the First Regiment of Infantry and commanded the 12th and 9th Continental Regiment. During the Revolutionary War, he fought in the siege of Boston and in battles at Long Island, White Plains, Red Bank, Valley Forge, and Rhode Island.

Varnum supported the establishment of a battalion of black soldiers in Rhode Island, and urged Congress to pass an act giving freedom to all slaves who enlisted in the army. He was elected twice to the Continental Congress, first from 1780 to 1782 and again, from 1786 to 1787.

In June 1788, he was sent to Marietta, Ohio, as a judge of the Northwest Territory. In December 1788, Varnum became ill and soon died of consumption. He was married to Martha Child.

Camp Villere

Location: Slidell, Louisiana
Status: Active
Named for: Governor Jacques Philippe Roi de Villere
Date of Birth: August 28, 1761*
Place of Birth: Kenner, Louisiana
Date of Death: March 7, 1830
Place of Death: St. Bernard Parish, Louisiana

Governor Jacques Philippe Roi de Villere was elected the first native governor of the state of Louisiana.

Villere joined the French army in 1774 at the age of thirteen and was educated in France. In 1778, he was detained for several years by the Spanish government of Louisiana. Six years later, he took the oath of allegiance to Spain.

Villere served on the municipal council of New Orleans in 1803, and was appointed a major general in the territorial militia in 1804, a police juror in Orleans Parish, and a justice of the peace for St. Bernard Parish. He was a delegate to Louisiana's first constitutional convention in 1812.

In January 1815, he was placed in command of the 1st Division of the Louisiana Militia when the British army invaded New Orleans. During the battle of New Orleans, the British army overran the Villere Plantation, his home was destroyed, and fifty-two slaves were taken prisoner. He served as governor of Louisiana from July 1, 1816 to December 17, 1820. In 1830, he was chosen to be a presidential elector from Louisiana for John Quincy Adams.

* There are two dates for Villere's birth. One is April 1761, the other August 1761. Records show he was baptized on September 15.

Camp W. G. Williams

Location: Riverton, Utah
Status: Active
Named for: Brigadier General William Gray Williams
Date of Birth: July 17, 1872
Place of Birth: Tredegar, Wales
Date of Death: 1948
Place of Death: No Data Found
Date of Retirement: 1946

Brigadier General William Gray Williams was Utah's longest serving adjutant general, serving from November 1, 1920 to May 31, 1946.

Williams came to the United States when he was eleven years old and enlisted in the National Guard in 1900 as a private. Later, as an officer, he graduated from the Army War College at Carlisle Barracks in Pennsylvania. He commanded a cavalry unit during an expedition into Mexico, and served in France during World War I and in England as commander of a military rest camp there.

Governor Henry H. Blood said of him, "Your unfailing devotion to duty has been an outstanding feature of your administration. You have never faltered in difficult situations but in a masterful way have handled them."

Colonel Fred A. Prince said of him, "In General Williams you have one of the most capable and outstanding Adjutant Generals with who [sic] I have ever come into contact."

"Those who dealt with Williams remembered how professional, sincere and dedicated he was," said retired Colonel Richard Roberts.

Camp White

Location: White City, Oregon
Status: Closed
Named for: Major General George Ared White
Date of Birth: July 18, 1880
Place of Birth: Long Branch, Illinois
Date of Death: November 23, 1941
Place of Death: Clackamas, Oregon
Decorations and Honors: Distinguished Service Medal, posthumously; French Cross of the Black Star; French Legion of Honor
Place of Burial: Riverview Cemetery in Portland, Oregon

Major General George Ared White was a newspaperman and Oregon's longest serving adjutant general, serving for twenty-two years.

White was the associate editor of the *Oregonian* in Portland and used the pseudonym Ared White for his magazine articles and novels. He enlisted in the Utah National Guard in August 1895 as a private in the infantry and served during the Spanish-American War. He was commissioned a first lieutenant in the 3rd Infantry on August 4, 1907, and to captain in 1911. In 1915, White was appointed to the post of adjutant general of Oregon. He commanded Troop A, Oregon Cavalry, while serving on the Mexican border from June 1916 to February 1917.

During World War I, he served on General John J. Pershing's staff and resumed his duties as Oregon's adjutant general in 1920. He graduated from the Command and General Staff College at Fort Leavenworth in Kansas in 1926 and the Army War College in 1928. In 1930, he was placed in command of the 41st Division. When the division was federalized in 1940, White brought the division to full strength and readiness. White was also credited with establishing the American Legion in France and became its first national vice president. He founded the *American Legion Magazine* and was its first editor.

Camp Williams

Location: Adjacent to Volk Field in Sparta, Wisconsin
Status: Active
Named for: Lieutenant Colonel Charles R. Williams
Date of Birth: September 19, 1870
Place of Birth: Rio, Wisconsin
Date of Death: September 15, 1926
Place of Death: France

Place of Burial: Near the main gate of Fort McCoy in Sparta, Wisconsin, next to his son

Lieutenant Colonel Charles R. Williams served as chief quartermaster for thirty years at Camp McCoy.

Williams enlisted in Company E, 4th Infantry, Wisconsin National Guard, on October 24, 1888, and was commissioned a second lieutenant in the infantry five days later. At the beginning of World War I, he was called to active duty as a lieutenant colonel and served with the 32nd "Red Arrow" Division as its quartermaster. He was appointed U.S. Property and Disbursing Officer for Wisconsin on September 16, 1919.

Camp Withycombe

Location: Clackamas, Oregon
Status: Active
Named for: Governor James Withycombe, civilian
Date of Birth: March 21, 1843
Place of Birth: Devonshire, England
Date of Death: March 3, 1919
Place of Death: Oregon
Place of Burial: Mount Crest Abbey Mausoleum in Salem, Oregon

Governor James Withycombe was state veterinarian, state agriculturist, and director of the Agricultural Experiment Station.

Withycombe came to Oregon in 1871, and attended Oregon Agricultural College at Corvallis in 1898 where he earned a master's degree in agriculture. He was a charter member of the Farmington Grange, and later he became a leader in the state Grange movement. His farming methods became a model for farmers across the Pacific Northwest.

He was elected Republican governor in 1915, and as governor, he promoted agricultural development, the building of better roads and highways. He also supported the war efforts during World War I by encouraging volunteer military service. He opposed labor unions, saying they crippled industry. He died of a heart attack shortly after being elected to his second term.

Charles E. Kelly Support Facility

Location: Oakdale, Pennsylvania
Status: Active
Named for: Corporal Charles E. Kelly
Date of Birth: September 25, 1920
Place of Birth: Pittsburgh, Pennsylvania
Date of Death: January 11, 1985
Place of Death: Pittsburgh, Pennsylvania
Decorations and Honors: Medal of Honor; Silver Star with oak leaf cluster; Medals of Valor (Italy and Britain)
Place of Burial: Highwood Cemetery in Pittsburgh, Pennsylvania

Corporal Charles E. Kelly served with Company L, 143rd Infantry, 36th Infantry Division, and was the first soldier in the European Theater of Operations to receive the nation's highest military award for valor.

Kelly carried the nickname "Commando Kelly" after his exploits during the assault on San Pietro and the bloody three-day crossing of the Rapido River in Italy.

His Medal of Honor citation for action during World War II reads as follows:

For conspicuous gallantry and intrepidity at risk of life above and beyond the call of duty. On September 13, 1943, near Altavilla, Italy, Corporal Kelly voluntarily joined a patrol, which located and neutralized enemy machine-gun positions. After this hazardous duty he volunteered to establish contact with a battalion of U.S. infantry, which was believed to be located on Hill 315, a mile distant. He traveled over a route commanded by enemy observation and under sniper, mortar, and artillery fire; and later he returned with the correct information that the enemy occupied Hill 315 in organized positions. Immediately thereafter Corporal Kelly, again a volunteer patrol member, assisted materially in the destruction of two enemy machine-gun nests under conditions requiring great skill and courage. Having effectively fired his weapon until all the ammunition was exhausted, he secured permission to obtain more at an ammunition dump. Arriving at the dump, which was located near a storehouse on the extreme flank of his regiment's position, Corporal Kelly found that the Germans were attacking ferociously at this point. He obtained his ammunition and was given the mission of protecting the rear of the storehouse. He held his position throughout the night. The following morning the enemy attack was resumed. Corporal Kelly took a position at an open window of the storehouse. One machine gunner had been killed at this position and several other soldiers wounded. Corporal Kelly delivered continuous aimed and effective fire upon the enemy with his automatic rifle until the weapon locked from overheating. Finding another automatic rifle, he again directed effective fire upon the enemy until this weapon also locked. At this critical point, with the enemy threatening to overrun the position, Corporal Kelly picked up 60 mm mortar shells, pulled the safety pins, and used the shells as grenades, killing at least five of the enemy. When it became imperative that the house be evacuated, Corporal Kelly, despite his sergeant's injunctions, volunteered to hold the position until the remainder of the detachment could withdraw. As the detachment moved out, Corporal Kelly was observed deliberately loading and firing a rocket launcher from the window. He was successful in covering the withdrawal of the unit, and later in joining his own organization. Corporal Kelly's fighting determination and intrepidity in battle exemplify the highest traditions of the U.S. Armed Forces.

Fort Custer Training Center

Location: Augusta, Michigan
Status: Active
Named for: General George Armstrong Custer
Date of Birth: December 5, 1839
Place of Birth: New Rumley, Ohio
Date of Death: June 25, 1876
Place of Death: Montana in what is now Crow Agency
Place of Burial: West Point Cemetery in New York

General George Armstrong Custer is most remembered for the famous battle at Little Big Horn, known as Custer's Last Stand, at which every member of his unit was killed.

Custer graduated from West Point in 1861 and participated in the first battle of Manassas that same year. On June 26, 1863, he was brevetted a brigadier general of volunteers and placed in command of the 2nd Brigade, 3rd Cavalry Division, at Gettysburg and Yellow Tavern. He commanded the 3rd Cavalry Division in the Shenandoah Valley campaign from May to June 1862. In April 1865, he was promoted to major general of volunteers.

At the battle of Little Big Horn in June 1876, with twelve hundred men of the 7th Cavalry, and seventeen hundred horses and mules, Custer split his command into three battalions and made a decision to attack the Indians. Within a short period of time, Custer and his troops were annihilated by an estimated five thousand Sioux Indians led by Chief Sitting Bull and Chief Crazy Horse. In the search for survivors of Custer's forces, not one of Custer's men was found alive. Only one horse, named Comanche, survived.

Custer was responsible for the song "Garry Owen" being adopted as the official marching song of the 1st Cavalry Division.

Fort William Henry Harrison

Location: Montana
Status: Active
Named for: President and Major General William Henry Harrison
Date of Birth: February 9, 1773
Place of Birth: Charles City County, Virginia
Date of Death: April 4, 1841
Place of Death: Washington, D.C.
Decorations and Honors: Congressional Gold Medal
Place of Burial: William Henry Harrison Memorial State Park in North Bend, Ohio

William Henry Harrison was the ninth president of the United States and has the unfortunate distinction of serving the shortest term in office after contracting pneumonia one month after his inauguration.

Harrison served as a soldier, territorial governor, congressman, senator, and diplomat. After joining the army in 1791, he became active in fighting Indians in the northwest. In 1792, General Anthony Wayne, commander of the American forces, promoted Harrison to second lieutenant and made him his aide-de-camp. In 1794, Harrison was cited for bravery in defeating the Indians at the battle of Fallen Timbers, Ohio, which resulted in the Treaty of Greenville, signed in 1795.

While in Congress, Harrison helped establish the territories of Ohio and Indiana in the Northwest Territory. In 1800, he was appointed governor of the Indiana Territory, which included all or parts of the present-day states of Indiana, Illinois, Wisconsin, Michigan, and Minnesota. During the War of 1812, as a major general, Harrison defeated the British at the battle of the Thames in southern Ontario on October 5, 1813.

After resigning from the army in 1814, Harrison became county recorder in Ohio, and in 1840, he ran for president, defeating President Martin Van Buren. He was married to Anna Symmes.

Fraine Barracks

Location: Bismarck, North Dakota
Status: Active
Named for: Brigadier General John Henry Fraine
Date of Birth: 1861
Place of Birth: England
Date of Death: May 15, 1943

Place of Death: Minneapolis, Minnesota
Decorations and Honors: Silver Star
Date of Retirement: April 2, 1925

Brigadier General John Henry Fraine introduced a bill that proposed the adoption of the flag of the 1st North Dakota Infantry Volunteers as the official state flag of North Dakota.

Fraine entered military service in August 1885 as a private in Company 3, 1st North Dakota Infantry, North Dakota National Guard. In 1898, he became battalion commander of the 1st Infantry volunteers.

While serving in the Philippines from 1898 to 1899, Fraine was appointed to major and was recognized for his service at Paete, Luzon, Philippines. Between 1905 and 1915, Fraine was a state representative and served as the Speaker of the House. In 1915, he served as North Dakota's lieutenant governor. From 1916 to 1917, he served on the Mexican border as a colonel and was a regiment commander. In 1917, during World War I, he was promoted to brigadier general, and in 1923 he became the North Dakota National Guard Paymaster General.

Greenlief Training Site

Location: Hastings, Nebraska
Status: Active
Named for: Lieutenant General Francis Stevens Greenlief
Date of Birth: July 27, 1921
Place of Birth: Hastings, Nebraska
Date of Death: December 18, 1999
Place of Death: Fairfax Hospital in Virginia
Date of Retirement: 1974
Place of Burial: Arlington National Cemetery, Section 30, Grave 950-B

Lieutenant General Francis Stevens Greenlief was a National Guard bureau chief and served in World War II.

Greenlief was an advocate of the National Guard, believing the Guard to be a formable combat force. During Pentagon assignments, first as Army National Guard director, and later as National Guard bureau chief from 1971 to 1974, he instituted important reforms, such as racial integration of the National Guard.

After retiring from active duty, Greenlief continued his service as executive director of the National Guard Association until 1984 to become the association's longest serving chief executive officer. He died of a heart attack after a long fight with cancer.

Nickell Hall

Location: Salina, Kansas
Status: Active
Named for: Lieutenant General Joe Nickell
Date of Birth: May 8, 1896
Place of Birth: Parsons, Kansas
Date of Death: May 13, 1974
Place of Death: Topeka, Kansas
Decorations and Honors: Distinguished Service Medal of the National Guard Association
Date of Retirement: December 1972

Lieutenant General Joe Nickell was a newspaper reporter and editor of the *Daily Capital* (Topeka, Kansas); a radio broadcaster, known as "Big Nick" at WIBW in Topeka; a Kansas state legislator; and the 28th adjutant general of Kansas who served in World Wars I and II.

After attending the University of Omaha, Creighton University Law School, and Washburn Law School, Nickell was admitted to the Nebraska bar in 1923. He graduated from a special course of instruction for National Guard and Reserve officers and was a captain and executive officer of the 1st Battalion, 161st Field Artillery.

During World War I, he was assigned to the Rainbow Division, Field Artillery, and served in the Champaigne-Marne, Chateau-Thierry, Saint Mihiel, and the Meuse-Argonne offensive. He also served as superintendent of the Army Transportation Service and as commander of the Harbor Craft Detachment, Alaska Defense Command.

He was the Kansas adjutant general from April 21, 1951, to December 31, 1972. He also served as a state representative, senator, and state director of the Selective Service.

Nickell was promoted to lieutenant general in July 1970, the only adjutant general of Kansas to attain that rank. While adjutant general, he was responsible for the construction of fifty-eight new Army National Guard armories throughout Kansas. He was married to Ruth Ransom.

Army
Barracks and Kasernes
Germany

And when the wind in the tree-tops roared
The soldier asked from the deep dark grave:
"Did the banner flutter then?"
"Not so, my hero," the wind replied
"The fight is done, but the banner won,
Thy comrades of old have borne it hence,
Have borne it in triumph hence."
Then the soldier spake from the deep dark grave:
"I am content."

—Oliver Wendell Holmes, Jr.

CHAPTER 6

Army Barracks and Kasernes Germany

Adams Barracks

Location: Zirndorf, Germany
Status: Unknown
Named for: Private First Class John W. Adams
Date of Birth: No Data Found
Place of Birth: No Data Found
Date of Death: November 18, 1944
Place of Death: Germany
Decorations and Honors: Distinguished Service Cross

Private First Class John W. Adams served with the 16th Infantry, 1st Infantry Division.
    His Distinguished Service Cross citation reads as follows:

When a strong enemy force assaulted his position, Private First Class Adams poured machine-gun fire into the advancing foe, halting the attack. A second wave of Germans charged his position and alone and greatly outnumbered, Private Adams held his ground against this second attack, continuing to fire until his position was overrun. He was killed by enemy grenades exploding in his emplacement. By his superb heroism and unflinching valor, Private Adams successfully delayed the enemy penetration until reinforcements were brought forward.

★★★

Anderson Barracks

Location: Oppenheim, Germany
Status: Closed
Named for: Technician Fourth Grade Ameth Anderson
Date of Birth: No Data Found
Place of Birth: No Data Found
Date of Death: March 2, 1945
Place of Death: Vockrath, Germany
Decorations and Honors: Distinguished Service Cross, posthumously

Technician Fourth Grade Ameth Anderson served with Company G, 67th Armored Regiment.
 His Distinguished Service Cross citation reads as follows:

When Anderson's tank was knocked out by enemy fire, he continued to fire his 75 mm tank gun at the enemy throughout the day. The next morning, upon learning that enemy tanks were still in the area, he went forward alone and manned a 76 mm gun on another disabled tank. When the Air Corps came over, he marked the enemy positions with smoke. His skill and courage resulted in the destruction of three enemy tanks and one pillbox.

Armstrong Barracks

Location: Büdingen, Germany
Status: Closed
Named for: First Lieutenant Eugene M. Armstrong
Date of Birth: May 19, 1919
Place of Birth: Jefferson, Iowa
Date of Death: March 26, 1944
Place of Death: Anzio Beachhead, Italy
Decorations and Honors: Air Medal, posthumously

First Lieutenant Eugene M. Armstrong was an air observer with the 68th Field Artillery Battalion.
 Armstrong first served at Fort Knox in Kentucky. While serving overseas with the 68th Field Artillery Battalion, 1st Armored Division, he saw action in the North African campaign where he participated in the retreat from Sidi Bon Zid in Algeria and Faid and Kasserine passes in Tunisia. He also participated in all the battles of the Tunisian campaign. Armstrong was killed in action.
 His Air Medal was awarded for meritorious achievement while participating in aerial flights by performing thirty-five field artillery low flying missions against the enemy in Italy during the period of January 3 to March 21, 1944.

Azbill Barracks

Location: Rüsselsheim, Germany
Status: Unknown
Named for: Warrant Officer 1 Roy Gordon Azbill
Date of Birth: January 1, 1940
Place of Birth: Weaverville, California
Date of Death: December 30, 1964
Place of Death: Binh Gia, Vietnam
Decorations and Honors: Silver Star; Distinguished Flying Cross; Purple Heart with oak leaf cluster; Air Medal with twenty oak leaf clusters and one V device; Army Commendation Medal with V device, posthumously
Place of Burial: Golden Gate National Cemetery in San Bruno, California, Section Y, Site 59-A

Warrant Officer 1 Roy Gordon Azbill was a U.S. Army aviator who served as commander of a Bell UH-1B Huey helicopter in Vietnam.

Azbill enlisted in 1960 and completed warrant officer training and the Rotary Wing Aviator Course in 1963. In January 1964, he was sent to Vietnam, assigned to the 68th Aviation Company. His call sign was "Dragon 31." Azbill was killed when his helicopter was shot down by .50 caliber machine-gun fire and crashed inside enemy territory.

Baker Barracks

Location: Bad Tolz, Germany
Status: Unknown
Named for: Colonel A. J. "Bo" Baker
Date of Birth: July 22, 1930
Place of Birth: Searcy, Arkansas
Date of Death: March 24, 1980
Place of Death: Bad Tolz, Germany
Decorations and Honors: Distinguished Service Medal, posthumously; Silver Star; Bronze Star with oak leaf cluster; Meritorious Service Medal; Air Medal with oak leaf cluster; Army Commendation Medal with two oak leaf clusters

Colonel A. J. Baker was a pathfinder, ranger, green beret, and master paratrooper.

Baker enlisted in the U.S. Air Force in 1950 and served until 1953. He left the air force and enrolled at the University of Arkansas, graduating in 1956 with a degree in physical education. Following graduation, he joined the U.S. Army and was commissioned a second lieutenant.

During his career, he served as a platoon leader with 9th Division at Fort Carson in Colorado. He also served with the 22nd Infantry, 4th Infantry Division, at Fort Lewis in Washington and with the 7th Infantry Division in Korea. He was company commander of the 325th Infantry, 82d Airborne Division, at Fort Bragg in North Carolina and an instructor in the Airborne Department at Fort Benning in Georgia.

In August 1964, Baker applied for the Special Forces Officer's Course, graduated in October, and was assigned to the 6th Special Forces Group at Fort Bragg. He served three tours in Vietnam, one of which was with the 5th Special Forces Group (Green Berets). During another tour there, he served on Project Delta during the siege at Plei Me from October 1965 to October 1966. He was also commander of the Jungle Operations Training Center at Fort Sherman in the Panama Canal Zone.

In October 1974, he was assigned to recruit, train, and command the 2nd Airborne Ranger Battalion at Fort Lewis. In July 1977, Baker commanded the 2nd Battalion, Special Forces, in Bad Tolz, Germany. He was commander of the 110th Special Forces Group at the time of his death.

Baker was a member of First Baptist Church of Searcy, a Mason, a Shriner, and a charter member of the Searcy Chapter of the Order of DeMolay.

Barton Barracks

Location: Ansbach, Germany
Status: Active
Named for: Lieutenant Colonel David B. Barton
Date of Birth: No Data Found
Place of Birth: No Data Found
Date of Death: June 3, 1944
Place of Death: Velletri, Italy
Decorations and Honors: Silver Star
Place of Burial: Sicily-Rome American Cemetery and Memorial in Nettuno, Italy

Lieutenant Colonel David B. Barton was a signal officer with the 36th Infantry Division. He served as the assistant director of Training Literature at Fort Monmouth in New Jersey in 1943.

His Silver Star citation reads as follows:

Colonel Barton pressed forward to personally supervise the laying of wire in the forward areas as the break through to Tome was beginning. Fully realizing the urgency of constant communications, Colonel Barton drove reconnaissance missions in front of the lines and was killed by enemy artillery and small arms fire. His gallant actions reflect great credit upon himself and the Armed Forces of the United States.

Camp Bloomquist

Location: Ziegenberg, Germany
Status: Unknown
Named for: Lieutenant Colonel Paul A. Bloomquist
Date of Birth: October 30, 1932
Place of Birth: Salt Lake City, Utah
Date of Death: May 11, 1972
Place of Death: Frankfurt, Germany
Decorations and Honors: Distinguished Flying Cross with three oak leaf clusters; Purple Heart with two oak leaf clusters; Air Medal with thirty-six oak leaf clusters; Army Aviator of the Year, 1965; Selected Outstanding Young American by the U.S. Chamber of Commerce; inducted, posthumously, into the Dustoff Hall of Fame on February 22, 2003

Lieutenant Colonel Paul A. Bloomquist served with the 498th Air Ambulance Company in Vietnam, and spent nearly thirty-five months evacuating wounded troops from the front lines and flying them back to the safety of aid stations.

He was killed when a terrorist group exploded three bombs at the IG Farben building, V Corps Headquarters in Frankfurt, Germany. Bloomquist had just parked his car when a bomb exploded. Although a total of thirteen other people were injured, Bloomquist was the only fatality of the attack.

His Distinguished Flying Cross citation says that even though he was wounded while flying a medevac helicopter, he continued flying for nearly thirteen hours, during which time he rescued many casualties under heavy enemy fire.

Camp Clarke

Location: Hammelburg, Germany
Status: Unknown
Named for: Private Denny T. Clarke
Date of Birth: No Data Found
Place of Birth: No Data Found
Date of Death: November 11, 1944
Place of Death: Viviers, France

Decorations and Honors: Silver Star; Bronze Star; Purple Heart, posthumously
Place of Burial: Lorraine American Cemetery and Memorial in Saint Avold, France

Private Denny T. Clarke joined the U.S. Army on February 4, 1942, and was assigned to the 22nd Armored Field Artillery Battalion. He was sent to Europe as a member of the Medical Detachment and served a short time in England and Wales. He was among those who landed on Utah Beach in France on July 14, 1944.

His Silver Star was awarded to him for his action during an encounter with the enemy near Chateau Salins, France, on September 24, 1944. When he learned that a wounded member of his battery had been left on a fire-swept hill when they were forced to withdraw, he inched his way, under enemy artillery and small arms fire, to the side of his fallen comrade, dragged him into a nearby bomb crater, and administered first aid. Then, under the same intense enemy fire, he crawled back to safety with his wounded comrade, shielding him with his own body. When an M-7 tank from his unit received a direct hit from a German 88 mm gun, Clarke saw one of the runners who had been blown from the tank lying on the ground. Without hesitation he jumped from his foxhole and, under a hail of enemy tank and machine-gun fire, ran to the wounded man to give him first aid. Rolling him under a tank, Clarke bandaged his wounds and started back with him. As they neared safety, Clarke suffered severe head and shoulder wounds. Struggling desperately and weakened by his mortal wounds, he continued laboriously to drag the unconscious man to the security of the aid station. Clarke was taken to a rear area where he died.

Camp Gates

Location: Brand, Germany
Status: Unknown
Named for: Sergeant Beecher J. Gates
Date of Birth: No Data Found
Place of Birth: Massachusetts
Date of Death: January 19, 1945
Place of Death: Europe
Decorations and Honors: Silver Star; Purple Heart; British Military Medal
Place of Burial: Luxembourg American Cemetery and Memorial in Luxembourg City, Luxembourg, Plot F, Row 9

Sergeant Beecher J. Gates served with the 2nd Cavalry Reconnaissance Squadron. He enlisted in the U.S. Army in January 20, 1943.

His Silver Star citation for action during World War II reads as follows:

While serving with the Army of the United States [Gates] distinguished himself by gallantry in action on January 11, 1945, in Luxembourg. Troop "C" was given the mission of capturing Machtum, Luxembourg, and Sergeant Gates led an assault team of the 1st platoon. Immediately following an artillery concentration on the town at 0330, he moved his men toward the town. His team encountered a machine gun nest and was halted, but Sergeant Gates crawled forward trying to pick off the enemy with his rifle. This proved unsuccessful, so he reorganized his team and moved toward the flank of the gun. Seeing it would be too dangerous to move his whole team forward, he instructed a corporal to cover him with fire and he crawled toward the machine gun nest. He killed one enemy with his rifle but his gun jammed. When the man covering him succeeded in killing another enemy, he crawled forward and disposed of the remaining enemy with a hand grenade. By his courage and quick action, Sergeant Gates opened the way for his team to enter the town. He kept his team in contact with the enemy until the town was cleared fifteen hours later. His ability as a leader was evidenced in the fact that his team suffered no casualties. Sergeant Gates, an outstanding noncommissioned officer in his organization, demonstrated by his courage and daring, the importance of personal leadership to the success of the Army of the United States.

Camp Lindsey

Location: Wiesbaden, Germany
Status: Unknown
Named for: Captain Darrell Robins Lindsey
Date of Birth: December 30, 1919
Place of Birth: Jefferson, Iowa
Date of Death: August 9, 1944
Place of Death: France
Decorations and Honors: Medal of Honor; Air Medal with eight oak leaf clusters, posthumously
Place of Burial: Memorialized at the Ardennes American Cemetery and Memorial in Neupre, Belgium

Captain Darrell Robins Lindsey was a pilot and flight commander with the 585th Squadron, 394th Bomb Group.

Lindsey enlisted as an aviation cadet at Fort Des Moines, Iowa, on January 16, 1942, and received his pilot wings and commission in August 1942. After bombardier training at Kirtland Field in Albuquerque, New Mexico, he was assigned to the 314th Bomb Squadron at MacDill Field in Tampa, Florida, with the rank of first lieutenant.

Lindsey accumulated 143 hours of combat time and was flying his forty-sixth mission as group leader, when he was killed. His body was never recovered. A monument stands in his honor in Jefferson, Iowa.

His Medal of Honor citation for action during World War II reads as follows:

On August 9, 1944, Captain Lindsey led a formation of thirty B-26 medium bombers in a hazardous mission to destroy the strategic enemy held L'Isle Adam railroad bridge over the Seine in occupied France. With most of the bridges over the Seine destroyed, the heavily fortified L'Isle Adam bridge was of inestimable value to the enemy in moving troops, supplies, and equipment to Paris. Captain Lindsey was fully aware of the fierce resistance that would be encountered. Shortly after reaching enemy territory the formation was buffeted with heavy and accurate antiaircraft fire. By skillful evasive action, Captain Lindsey was able to elude much of the enemy flak, but just before entering the bombing run his B-26 was peppered with holes. During the bombing run the enemy fire was even more intense, and Captain Lindsey's right engine received a direct hit and burst into flames. Despite the fact that his ship was hurled out of formation by the violence of the concussion, Captain Lindsey brilliantly maneuvered back into the lead position without disrupting the flight. Fully aware that the gasoline tanks might explode at any moment, Captain Lindsey gallantly elected to continue the perilous bombing run. With fire streaming from his right engine and his right wing half enveloped in flames, he led his formation over the target upon which the bombs were dropped with telling effect. Immediately after the objective was attacked, Captain Lindsey gave the order for the crew to parachute from the doomed aircraft. With magnificent coolness and superb pilotage, and without regard for his own life, he held the swiftly descending airplane in a steady glide until the members of the crew could jump to safety. With the right wing completely enveloped in flames and an explosion of the gasoline tank imminent, Captain Lindsey still remained unperturbed. The last man to leave the stricken plane was the bombardier, who offered to lower the wheels so that Captain Lindsey might escape from the nose. Realizing that this might throw the aircraft into an uncontrollable spin and jeopardize the bombardier's chances to escape, Captain Lindsey refused the offer. Immediately after the bombardier had bailed out, and before Captain Lindsey was able to follow, the right gasoline tank exploded. The aircraft sheathed in fire, went into a steep dive and was seen to explode as it crashed. All who are living today from this plane owe their lives to the fact that Captain Lindsey remained cool and showed supreme courage in this emergency.

Camp Pieri

Location: Wiesbaden-Dotzheim, Germany
Status: Unknown
Named for: Captain Francis W. Pieri
Date of Birth: April 29, 1918

Place of Birth: No Data Found
Date of Death: August 22, 1944
Place of Death: Montargis, France
Decorations and Honors: Distinguished Service Cross
Place of Burial: Gettysburg National Cemetery in Gettysburg, Pennsylvania

Captain Francis W. Pieri was commanding officer of Company B, 24th Armored Engineer Battalion. He also served as engineer liaison officer of Combat Command B.

Pieri was killed while accompanying the leading elements of the 51st Armored Infantry Battalion task force in an attack. He was riding toward the front of the column when enemy machine guns and small arms fired upon his troops. The troops immediately took cover while Pieri opened fire with a 30 mm machine gun mounted on his vehicle. He fired two belts of ammunition and killed approximately thirty of the enemy but lost his life in the action.

Camp Whalen

Location: Röhrnbach, Germany
Status: Unknown
Named for: Captain Dennis D. Whalen
Date of Birth: April 12, 1931
Place of Birth: Nevada
Date of Death: July 2, 1962
Place of Death: German-Czechoslovakian border

Captain Dennis D. Whalen commanded Troop F, 2nd Reconnaissance Squadron, 11th Armored Cavalry.

Whalen graduated from West Point in June 1953 and was commissioned a second lieutenant in the infantry. He served with distinction in Korea from 1954 to 1955. He was killed in a vehicle accident while on a surveillance mission.

Campbell Barracks

Location: Heidelberg, Germany
Status: Active
Named for: Staff Sergeant Charles L. Campbell
Date of Birth: No Data Found
Place of Birth: No Data Found

Date of Death: March 28, 1945
Place of Death: Mannheim, Germany
Decorations and Honors: Distinguished Service Cross; Purple Heart, posthumously
Place of Burial: Lorraine American Cemetery and Memorial in Saint Avold, France

Staff Sergeant Charles L. Campbell served with the 14th Infantry Regiment, 71st Infantry Division.

His Distinguished Service Cross was awarded for his action two days before the surrender of Heidelberg when he led a patrol across the Rhine River near Mannheim.

His Distinguished Service Cross citation for action during World War II reads in part as follows:

He and his patrol were subjected to intense enemy fire as they attempted to land on the east bank of the Rhine River. While rushing toward the bank in the face of intense fire, one of the three members of this patrol was seriously wounded. With complete disregard for his personal safety, Campbell courageously rescued and evacuated the wounded soldier and waded into deep water to free the boat that had become entangled in the underwater defenses of the enemy. While covering the patrol's withdrawal to the other shore with vital information, he was killed in a hail of enemy fire, but his mission was successfully completed.

Cawley Kaserne

Location: Seckenheim, Germany
Status: Unknown
Named for: Corporal Arthur Nelson Cawley
Date of Birth: December 4, 1916
Place of Birth: Hazleton, Pennsylvania
Date of Death: August 15, 1944
Place of Death: France
Decorations and Honors: Silver Star, posthumously
Place of Burial: Mountain View Cemetery in West Hazleton, Pennsylvania

Corporal Arthur Nelson Cawley served with 15th Cavalry Reconnaissance Squadron, 15th Cavalry Group.

Cawley had assignments at Camp Maxey in Texas and at Barksdale Field in Shreveport, Louisiana, and underwent desert maneuver training in California. He was a member of the Christ Lutheran Church and the Bunton Bock Gun and Rod Club. Prior to entering the service he was employed at the Hauto Plant of the P. P. & L. Co.

His Silver Star was awarded for his action on August 15, 1944, and reads in part as follows:

While his troop was making an aggressive reconnaissance operation, it was stalled by an enemy road block covered by fire from high ground. As a member of a combat patrol, Cawley got out to gather information and details on the position of the enemy. His unit encircled the position but was pinned down by enemy machine-gun fire. With disregard for his personal safety, Corporal Cawley voluntarily worked his way to a grove of trees and put the enemy machine gun out of action with hand grenades. In this gallant action, he captured two prisoners and obtained vital information. Upon returning to his patrol, he was seriously wounded by sniper fire. Corporal Cawley carried on despite his wounds and delivered the prisoners and information he had obtained to the other members of his patrol. His information made possible the elimination of the road block and its defenders. Corporal Cawley died two days later of wounds he received in action.

Christensen Barracks

Location: Grafenwöhr, Germany
Status: Closed
Named for: Second Lieutenant Dale Eldon Christensen
Date of Birth: May 31, 1920
Place of Birth: Cameron Township, Iowa
Date of Death: August 4, 1944
Place of Death: Afua, Dutch New Guinea
Decorations and Honors: Medal of Honor, posthumously
Place of Burial: Manila American Cemetery and Memorial, Manila, Philippines

Second Lieutenant Dale Eldon Christensen served with Troop E, 112th Cavalry Regiment.

His Medal of Honor citation for action during World War II reads as follows:

For conspicuous gallantry and intrepidity at the risk of his life above and beyond the call of duty along the Driniumor River, New Guinea, from July 16–19, 1944. Second Lieutenant Christensen repeatedly distinguished himself by conspicuous gallantry above and beyond the call of duty in the continuous heavy fighting, which occurred in this area from July 16–19. On July 16, his platoon engaged in a savage firefight in which much damage was caused by one enemy machine gun effectively placed. Second Lieutenant Christensen ordered his men to remain under cover, crept forward under fire, and at a range of fifteen yards put the gun out of action with hand grenades. Again, on July 19, while attacking an enemy position strong in mortars and machine guns, his platoon was pinned to the ground by intense fire. Ordering his men to remain under cover, he crept forward alone to locate definitely the enemy automatic weapons and the best direction from which to attack. Although his rifle was struck by enemy fire and knocked from his hands he continued his reconnaissance, located five enemy machine guns, destroyed one with hand grenades, and rejoined his platoon. He then led his men to the point selected for launching the attack and, calling encouragement, led the charge. This assault was successful and the enemy was driven from the positions with a loss of four mortars and ten machine guns and leaving many dead on the field. On August 4, 1944, near Afua, Dutch New Guinea, Second Lieutenant Christensen was killed in action about two yards from his objective while leading his platoon in an attack on an enemy machine-gun position. Second Lieutenant Christensen's leadership, intrepidity, and repeatedly demonstrated gallantry in action at the risk of his life, above and beyond the call of duty, exemplify the highest traditions of the U.S. Armed Forces.

Coffey Barracks

Location: Stuttgart, Germany
Status: Unknown
Named for: Brigadier General John W. Coffey
Date of Birth: January 12, 1897
Place of Birth: New York City, New York
Date of Death: March 8, 1951
Place of Death: Koblenz, Germany
Decorations and Honors: Distinguished Service Medal; Legion of Merit

Brigadier General John W. Coffey graduated from West Point in 1917 and served in Europe during World War II.

Coffey was recognized for his efforts in establishing Headquarters Command in England and for his outstanding performance as the chief ordnance officer of the Mediterranean Theater of Operations from 1943 to 1945.

He served as commanding officer of the Letterkenny Ordnance Depot in Pennsylvania until his appointment as professor of ordnance at West Point in 1947. Coffey died as the result of injuries suffered in an airplane crash.

Coleman Barracks

Location: Gelnhausen, Germany
Status: Closed
Named for: Second Lieutenant Kenneth W. Coleman

Date of Birth: No Data Found
Place of Birth: No Data Found
Date of Death: November 9, 1944
Place of Death: France
Decorations and Honors: Silver Star; Purple Heart, posthumously
Place of Burial: Lorraine American Cemetery and Memorial in Saint Avold, France

Second Lieutenant Kenneth W. Coleman served with Company C, 761st Tank Battalion.

His Silver Star was awarded for his action while a tank platoon leader when he led an attack until his tank was disabled by enemy antitank fire that halted the advance.

His Silver Star citation reads in part as follows:

He immediately dismounted and courageously led his crew on foot under heavy artillery and small arms fire against a much larger enemy force, driving them from their positions, thus enabling his platoon to proceed on its mission. Coleman was killed by enemy small arms fire during the attack.

Coleman Barracks

Location: Mannheim, Germany
Status: Active
Named for: Lieutenant Colonel Wilson Dudley Coleman
Date of Birth: March 7, 1911
Place of Birth: Fort Logan H. Roots, Arkansas
Date of Death: July 30, 1944
Place of Death: Saint-Denis-le-Gast, France
Decorations and Honors: Distinguished Service Cross; Purple Heart, posthumously
Place of Burial: Arlington National Cemetery, Section 7

Lieutenant Colonel Wilson Dudley Coleman served with the 41st Armored Infantry Regiment.

His Distinguished Service Cross citation was awarded for his action, when shortly after midnight, while checking his defensive, he came upon an enemy armored column approaching his bivouac area. Quickly selecting a protective spot, he fired four antitank rockets at the leading tank and scored three direct hits, destroying the tank and temporarily halting the column. Realizing that a major enemy attack was being directed against his sector, he returned to his command post, driving his small, unarmored vehicle through enemy fire over a tortuous route jammed with stalled vehicles. Upon arrival, he issued the necessary orders for breaking up the attack and proceeded to direct the fire of his machine guns against the enemy. He was killed in action.

Cooke Barracks

Location: Göppingen, Germany
Status: Closed
Named for: Captain Charles H. Cooke
Date of Birth: No Data Found
Place of Birth: Massachusetts
Date of Death: July 11, 1943
Place of Death: Gela, Sicily
Decorations and Honors: Silver Star; Soldier's Medal; Purple Heart, posthumously
Place of Burial: Sicily-Rome American Cemetery and Memorial in Nettuno, Italy

Captain Charles H. Cooke served with the 32nd Field Artillery Battalion, 1st Infantry Division, in Italy.
His Silver Star citation reads as follows:

Captain Cooke's battalion was to accomplish a combat landing on the beaches, bringing equipment and personnel ashore under extreme conditions of high winds and heavy surf. Incessant enemy small arms, artillery, and defensive mine action caused this particular landing to be one that demanded the utmost in courage, devotion, and tenacity on the part of all participating personnel. Ceaseless counter attacks by tanks and other enemy armor concern during the day as to whether or not the beaches could be held. During the initial stages of the landing of Battery "B," 32nd Field Artillery Battalion, Captain Cooke's landing craft became separated from its immediate group resulting in Captain Cooke not being able to locate his assigned beach area. In order to avail himself of the area that his craft had approached, he swam through the raging surf carrying a lifeline, which he established on the shore. Having secured this line he returned through the surf to the craft in order to direct the unloading of his troops. This unloading would have produced disastrous results in the loss of lives and equipment without the lifeline. After Cooke succeeded in landing the bulk of his men and gear, he proceeded forward under heavy small arms fire to locate a position for his battery. It had become evident that a major counter attack by enemy tanks was in progress and the need for his battery to participate in the defense of the beachhead apparently spurred him to such extreme reconnaissance. It was during this constant exposure while performing so vital a mission that Captain Cooke received injuries from enemy small arms fire which resulted in his death a few hours later.

Daley Barracks

Location: Bad Kissingen, Germany
Status: Closed
Named for: Technician Fifth Grade William T. Daley
Date of Birth: No Data Found
Place of Birth: No Data Found
Date of Death: April 15, 1945
Place of Death: Greussen, Germany
Decorations and Honors: Distinguished Service Cross, posthumously

Technician Fifth Grade William T. Daley served with Headquarters and Service Troop, 94th Reconnaissance Squadron (Mechanized), U.S. Army.

Daley was cited for extraordinary heroism in connection with military operations against the enemy near Greussen, Germany.

His Distinguished Service Cross citation reads as follows:

When hostile tanks and supporting infantry ambushed a supply column which Daley's truck was leading, he dismounted beside his vehicle, and firing his carbine from this exposed position, successfully diverted enemy fire away from his comrades seeking cover. Leaving this position for one offering a better field of fire, he ran to the doorstep of a nearby house and resumed firing, even as an enemy 75 mm shell demolished a truck close by. While the enemy maneuvered for better positions, he continued to hold them off until all of his comrades had secured cover. Unfortunately, Daley was killed in the action.

Darby Barracks

Location: Furth, Germany
Status: Closed
Named for: Colonel William Orlando Darby
Date of Birth: February 8, 1911
Place of Birth: Fort Smith, Arkansas
Date of Death: April 30, 1945
Place of Death: Torbole, Italy
Decorations and Honors: Distinguished Service Cross; Silver Star; Purple Heart; British Distinguished Service Order
Place of Burial: Fort Smith National Cemetery in Arkansas

Colonel William Orlando Darby was the leader of the famed World War II "Darby's Rangers" who distinguished themselves in combat in North Africa and Italy.

Darby graduated from West Point on June 13, 1933, and was commissioned a second lieutenant in field artillery. He first served with the 82nd, 3rd, and 80th Field Artillery Divisions and later with the 1st Cavalry. After serving in Europe, he returned to the United States in April 1944 for duty with the Army Ground Forces, and later with the Operations Division, War Department General Staff.

While serving in Europe again in March 1945, he was assigned as assistant commander of the 10th Mountain Division. The following month he was killed in action by an exploding shell. He was posthumously promoted to brigadier general, in addition, the army transport ship T-AP-127 was also named in his honor.

Downs Barracks

Location: Fulda, Germany
Status: Closed
Named for: Second Lieutenant Robert C. Downs
Date of Birth: No Data Found
Place of Birth: Pennsylvania
Date of Death: October 20, 1944
Place of Death: Uckange, France
Decorations and Honors: Distinguished Service Cross; Silver Star; Purple Heart, posthumously
Place of Burial: Lorraine American Cemetery and Memorial in Saint Avold, France, Plot C

Second Lieutenant Robert C. Downs served with Troop C, 43rd Cavalry Reconnaissance Squadron (Mechanized).

His Distinguished Service Cross citation reads as follows:

On October 14, shortly after Lieutenant Downs' unit occupied positions along the Moselle River, plans were made to send night patrols across the river in order to determine the enemy's strength and dispositions. Lieutenant Downs organized and led a volunteer daylight patrol across the river. The patrol encountered a German force of undetermined strength firing from prepared positions. After calling to his organization to protect his crossing, Downs delivered his report by swimming the river in full equipment. His report gave valuable information on enemy disposition, fortification, strength, and the method of defense employed by the enemy during daylight hours. This voluntary daylight crossing of the river in the face of strong enemy force and what seemed like certain death or captivity is in keeping with the highest tradition of the military service.

★★★

Eastman Barracks

Location: Dachau, Germany
Status: Unknown
Named for: Lieutenant Colonel Tobias C. Eastman
Date of Birth: February 25, 1902
Place of Birth: Fryeburg, Maine
Date of Death: April 26, 1945
Place of Death: Germany
Decorations and Honors: Silver Star; Bronze Star with oak leaf cluster; Purple Heart; American Defense Service Medal; American Campaign Medal; European-African-Middle Eastern Campaign Medal with silver service star for participation in the Normandy, Ardennes-Alsace, Central Europe, Northern France, and Rhineland Campaigns; World War II Victory Medal; Belgian Fourragere; Armed Forces Reserve Medal (Reserve)
Place of Burial: Arlington National Cemetery, Section 34, Site 3591

Lieutenant Colonel Tobias C. Eastman entered the service in 1941 and served as battery commander and communications officer with the 37th Field Artillery Battalion and the 2nd Division Artillery at Fort Sam Houston in Texas until April 1942. Later, he was assigned as its battalion commander. He also commanded the same unit in Europe. He died from wounds received in battle.

Emery Barracks

Location: Würzburg, Germany
Status: Unknown
Named for: First Lieutenant Robert M. Emery
Date of Birth: No Data Found
Place of Birth: New Jersey
Date of Death: November 8, 1942
Place of Death: Algeria
Decorations and Honors: Distinguished Service Cross; Purple Heart, posthumously
Place of Burial: North African American Cemetery and Memorial in Carthage, Tunisia

First Lieutenant Robert M. Emery served with the Corps of Engineers, Headquarters 1st Infantry Division.
His Distinguished Service Cross citation reads as follows:

When an enemy machine gun, occupying a commanding position, delayed the advance of a battalion of American troops, Lieutenant Emery left cover and attacked the emplacement single handedly. Armed only with a submachine gun, he advanced over terrain continually swept by automatic weapons fire. He was killed about twenty yards from the hostile position, but his courageous action distracted the enemy long enough for the assault team to outflank and eliminate the machine-gun nest.

Ferris Barracks

Location: Erlangen, Germany
Status: Closed
Named for: Second Lieutenant Geoffrey C. Ferris
Date of Birth: April 6, 1918
Place of Birth: No Data Found
Date of Death: May 7, 1943
Place of Death: Tunisia
Decorations and Honors: Distinguished Service Cross, posthumously
Place of Burial: Long Island National Cemetery in Farmingdale, New York

Second Lieutenant Geoffrey C. Ferris served with the 33rd Field Artillery Battalion, 1st Infantry Division.
   His Distinguished Service Cross citation reads as follows:

As an artillery forward observer with Company E, 26th Infantry Regiment, Lieutenant Ferris crawled forward of his own lines across open terrain swept by intense enemy machine-gun fire. Realizing the danger of his task, he ordered his men to remain behind while he advanced alone. While carrying out his mission Lieutenant Ferris was killed by enemy fire. The courage and personal bravery of Lieutenant Ferris was an inspiration to the men with whom he served.

Fiori Barracks

Location: Aschaffenburg, Germany
Status: Unknown
Named for: Private First Class Nanti J. Fiori
Date of Birth: No Data Found
Place of Birth: No Data Found
Date of Death: September 12, 1944
Place of Death: Belgium
Decorations and Honors: Distinguished Service Cross, posthumously

Private First Class Nanti J. Fiori served with the 18th Infantry Regiment.
His Distinguished Service Cross citation reads as follows:

When his company's advance was halted by fire from two machines guns, Fiori leaped to his feet and charged upon the enemy positions. Firing his automatic rifle, he killed the enemy in the first emplacement. As he continued his heroic attack, he was severely wounded and knocked to the ground by pointblank fire from the second German position. With a courageous effort, again rose directly into the line of fire and, although hit again and fatally wounded, he hurled a hand grenade which destroyed the enemy machine gun. His personal bravery and self-sacrifice reflected the highest credit upon Private First Class Fiori and the Armed Forces of the United States.

Ford Barracks

Location: Ulm, Germany
Status: Unknown
Named for: Major James C. Ford
Date of Birth: No Data Found
Place of Birth: No Data Found
Date of Death: November 8, 1944
Place of Death: Hürtgen Forest, Germany
Decorations and Honors: Silver Star with oak leaf cluster

Major James C. Ford served with the 110th Infantry Regiment, 28th Infantry Division.
His Silver Star citation reads as follows:

For gallantry in action against the enemy. On August 15, 1944, during an attack launched by the battalion in which Major Ford was the S-3, he observed that enemy small arms and artillery fire were inflicting heavy casualties and hampering the progress of the attack. Advancing to the forward positions under heavy enemy fire and reorganizing the surviving elements in the vicinity, he led them in an attack, which contributed largely to the breaking up of enemy resistance and to the success of the operation. He was later killed during subsequent action. Major Ford's gallantry and intrepidity exemplified and are in keeping with the highest traditions of the military service.

Funari Barracks

Location: Käfertal, Germany
Status: Active
Named for: Private First Class Robert Funari, Jr.
Date of Birth: No Data Found
Place of Birth: No Data Found
Date of Death: April 5, 1945
Place of Death: Heilbronn, Germany
Decorations and Honors: Silver Star, posthumously

Private First Class Robert Funari, Jr., served with the 398th Infantry Regiment, 100th Infantry Division.
    His Silver Star citation reads as follows:

Private Funari, a mortarman, was advancing with a rifle platoon along the east bank of the Neckar River when they drew enemy fire on their right flank. The platoon withdrew to reorganize, but Private Funari, who had been wounded, was forced to remain where he was. Noticing the enemy moving up additional men and weapons, he began crawling back to warn his platoon. Despite the seriousness of his wound, Private Funari attained a position within sight of the platoon just as they were moving toward the enemy. While signaling them to hold their attack he was killed by small arms fire. By his gallantry, many lives of his comrades were saved.

George C. Marshall Kaserne

Location: Bad Kreuznach, Germany
Status: Unknown
Named for: Brigadier General George Catlett Marshall
Date of Birth: December 31, 1880
Place of Birth: Uniontown, Pennsylvania
Date of Death: October 16, 1959
Place of Death: Walter Reed Army Medical Center in Washington D.C.
Decorations and Honors: Congressional Gold Medal; Distinguished Service Medal; Silver Star; Knight Grand Cross
Date of Retirement: November 1945
Place of Burial: Arlington National Cemetery, Section 7, Grave 8198

Brigadier General George Catlett Marshall is best remembered for winning the Nobel Peace Prize in December 1953 for his role in the Marshall Plan, which created the plan for rebuilding the allied countries of Europe after World War II.

Marshall graduated first in his class from the Virginia Military Institute in 1901 and joined the U.S. Army in February 1902.

He was assigned to France in the summer of 1917 as the Director of Training and Planning with the 1st Infantry Division. In 1918, he was assigned to the American Expeditionary Force Headquarters where he helped plan American operations. He was also aide-de-camp to General John J. Pershing; taught at the Army War College; instructed at the Infantry School at Fort Benning in Georgia; commanded posts at Fort Stewart in Savannah, Georgia, and Fort Moultrie in Charleston, South Carolina; and was a senior instructor to the Illinois National Guard. He was promoted to brigadier general in October 1936 and was given command of Vancouver Barracks in Washington.

Marshall returned to Washington, D.C., to become head of the War Department's War Plans Division, and later deputy chief of staff from 1938 to 1939. President Franklin D. Roosevelt appointed him as U.S. Army chief of staff from 1939 to 1945. He was named secretary of state in January 1947.

Gerszewski Barracks

Location: Karlsruhe, Germany
Status: Closed
Named for: Sergeant Adolph C. Gerszewski
Date of Birth: April 5, 1912
Place of Birth: No Data Found
Date of Death: April 9, 1945
Place of Death: Heilbronn, Germany
Decorations and Honors: Silver Star, posthumously
Place of Burial: Calvary Cemetery in Grand Forks, North Dakota

Sergeant Adolph C. Gerszewski served with Company D, 397th Infantry Regiment.

His Silver Star citation reads as follows:

Leading his squad, which had been split and surrounded by the enemy who had infiltrated their position prior to launching an attack, Sergeant Gerszewski displayed unusual leadership, aggressiveness and capability in reorganizing his men under cover of darkness. Realizing the great danger to his men, he personally made a reconnaissance, discovering the enemy's position and engaging them in a fire fight, succeeded in killing five Germans, wounding three and driving the remainder from their entrenchment. He was mortally wounded a short time later while attempting to aid a casualty lying in the open. The gallantry and initiative displayed by Sergeant Gerszewski was an inspiration to those who served with him.

Graves Barracks

Location: Aschaffenburg, Germany
Status: Unknown
Named for: Staff Sergeant William E. Graves
Date of Birth: No Data Found
Place of Birth: No Data Found
Date of Death: January 24, 1945
Place of Death: Belgium
Decorations and Honors: Distinguished Service Cross, posthumously

Staff Sergeant William E. Graves served with Company B, 18th Infantry Regiment.
    His Distinguished Service Cross citation reads as follows:

During a vicious assault upon a strongly held enemy position, Staff Sergeant Graves stormed and captured a hostile outpost protecting the strong point. When machine-gun fire pinned down an adjacent platoon, he rushed forward in the face of hostile gunners, silencing the weapon. He wounded two German riflemen in a nearby foxhole with a grenade and captured them. A second enemy machine gun opened fire upon him and, calling to his men to follow, he again rushed forward until he was struck and killed by hostile fire. The gallantry and devotion to duty displayed by Staff Sergeant Graves were in keeping with the finest tradition of the Armed Forces of the United States.

Hammonds Barracks

Location: Seckenheim, Germany
Status: Active
Named for: Private First Class Robert M. Hammonds
Date of Birth: January 19, 1926
Place of Birth: Wickliffe, Kentucky
Date of Death: April 11, 1945
Place of Death: Heilbronn, Germany
Decorations and Honors: Silver Star, posthumously
Place of Burial: Wickliffe, Kentucky

Private First Class Robert M. Hammonds was a wireman with Company G, 297th Infantry Regiment, 100th Division. A bronze plaque explaining Hammond's actions was mounted on a pedestal adjacent to the flagpole on the parade field where he served.
    His Silver Star citation reads as follows:

After a week of hazardous and almost unremitting effort to maintain wire communications during bitter house-to-house fighting for the city of Heilbronn, Private Hammond courageously volunteered to complete installation of a wire line within full view of the enemy. Well aware of the great danger involved, he unhesitatingly exposed himself to hostile fire and had just completed his task when he was mortally wounded by a sniper's bullet. The personal courage and great devotion to duty he thus displayed exemplify the finest ideals of the U.S. Army.

Major General Withers A. Burress, commanding general of the 100th Infantry Division, sent a letter to Hammonds's mother expressing his sympathies for her loss. In his letter, General Burress promised Mrs. Hammonds that her son's "devotion to duty and his courage will not be forgotten, and will serve to inspire us to better efforts."

Harris Barracks

Location: Coburg, Germany
Status: Unknown
Named for: Second Lieutenant James L. Harris
Date of Birth: No Data Found
Place of Birth: Hillsboro, Texas
Date of Death: October 4, 1944
Place of Death: Vagney, France
Decorations and Honors: Medal of Honor, posthumously

Second Lieutenant James L. Harris served with the 756th Tank Battalion.

His Medal of Honor citation for action during World War II reads as follows:

For conspicuous gallantry and intrepidity at risk of life above and beyond the call of duty on October 7, 1944, in Vagney, France. At 9 p.m. an enemy raiding party, comprising a tank and two platoons of infantry, infiltrated through the lines under cover of mist and darkness and attacked an infantry battalion command post with hand grenades, retiring a short distance to an ambush position on hearing the approach of the M-4 tank commanded by Second Lieutenant Harris. Realizing the need for bold aggressive action, Second Lieutenant Harris ordered his tank to halt while he proceeded on foot, fully ten yards ahead of his six-man patrol and armed only with a service pistol, to probe the darkness for the enemy. Although struck down and mortally wounded by machine gun bullets which penetrated his solar plexus, he crawled back to his tank, leaving a trail of blood behind him, and, too weak to climb inside it, issued fire orders while lying on the road between the two contending armored vehicles. Although the tank, which he commanded, was destroyed in the course of the fire fight, he stood the enemy off until friendly tanks, preparing to come to his aid, caused the enemy to withdraw and thereby lose an opportunity to kill or capture the entire battalion command personnel. Suffering a second wound, which severed his leg at the hip, in the course of this tank duel, Second Lieutenant Harris refused aid until after a wounded member of his crew had been carried to safety. He died before he could be given medical attention.

Harvey Barracks

Location: Kitzingen, Germany
Status: Closed
Named for: Captain James R. Harvey
Date of Birth: No Data Found
Place of Birth: No Data Found
Date of Death: June 6, 1945
Place of Death: Normandy, France
Decorations and Honors: Distinguished Service Cross, posthumously

Captain James R. Harvey served with Company E, 359th Infantry.
    His Distinguished Service Cross citation reads as follows:

In the vicinity of Pont L'Abbe, France, from June 12 to 15, 1944, Captain Harvey repeatedly distinguished himself by braving enemy fire to assist a wounded officer to safety, searched out and killed an enemy sniper who was harassing his men, and reorganized his company after it suffered heavy casualties, talking constantly to his men to minimize the danger of the situation. He led a night patrol through enemy territory with skill and daring, and the next day after little rest, led his company under fire to join other elements of his regiment. With utter contempt for strong enemy fire he walked boldly upright across an orchard to encourage his men in an attack against an enemy position. The fearless courage and supreme devotion to duty which he displayed exemplified the highest traditions of the Armed Forces of the United States.

Henry Kaserne

Location: Munich, Germany
Status: Closed
Named for: Private Robert T. Henry
Date of Birth: November 27, 1923
Place of Birth: Greenville, Mississippi

Date of Death: December 3, 1944
Place of Death: Luchem, Germany
Decorations and Honors: Medal of Honor, posthumously
Place of Burial: Greenville Cemetery in Greenville, Mississippi

Private Robert T. Henry served with Company B, 16th Infantry Regiment.

His Medal of Honor citation for action during World War II reads as follows:

Near Luchem, Germany, he volunteered to attempt the destruction of a nest of five enemy machine guns located in a bunker 150 yards to the flank which had stopped the advance of his platoon. Stripping off his pack, overshoes, helmet, and overcoat, he sprinted alone with his rifle and hand grenades across the open terrain toward the enemy emplacement. Before he had gone half the distance he was hit by a burst of machine-gun fire. Dropping his rifle, he continued to stagger forward until he fell mortally wounded only ten yards from the enemy emplacement. His single-handed attack forced the enemy to leave the machine guns. During this break in hostile fire the platoon moved forward and overran the position. Private Henry, by his gallantry and intrepidity and utter disregard for his own life, enabled his company to reach its objective, capturing this key defense and seventy German prisoners.

Jenson Barracks

Location: Munich, Germany
Status: Unknown
Named for: Major Richard N. Jenson
Date of Birth: March 23, 1916
Place of Birth: Washington
Date of Death: April 1, 1943
Place of Death: Tunisia
Place of Burial: Fort Rosecrans National Cemetery in San Diego, California

Major Richard N. Jenson was aide-de-camp to General George S. Patton, Jr.

Jenson attended the Command and General Staff College in 1942 at Fort Leavenworth in Kansas. He landed at Fedala, French Morocco, on November 8, 1942, and was later killed in action there.

Johnson Barracks

Location: Furth, Germany
Status: Closed
Named for: Private Elden Harvey Johnson
Date of Birth: February 13, 1921
Place of Birth: Bivalue, New Jersey
Date of Death: June 3, 1944
Place of Death: Valmontone, Italy
Decorations and Honors: Medal of Honor, posthumously
Place of Burial: Union Cemetery in Scituate, Massachusetts

Private Elden Harvey Johnson served with the 15th Infantry Regiment, 3rd Infantry Division.
    His Medal of Honor citation for action during World War II reads as follows:

For conspicuous gallantry and intrepidity at risk of life above and beyond the call of duty. Private Johnson elected to sacrifice his life in order that his comrades might extricate themselves from an ambush. Braving the massed fire of about sixty riflemen, three machine guns, and three tanks from positions only twenty-five yards distant, he stood erect and signaled his patrol leader to withdraw. The whole area was brightly illuminated by enemy flares. Then, despite 20 mm machine guns, machine pistol, and rifle fire directed at him, Private Johnson advanced beyond the enemy in a slow deliberate walk. Firing his automatic rifle from the hip, he succeeded in distracting the enemy and enabled his twelve comrades to escape. Advancing to within five yards of a machine gun, emptying his weapon, Private Johnson killed its crew. Standing in full view of the enemy he reloaded and turned on the riflemen to the left, firing directly into their positions. He either killed or wounded four of them. A burst of machine-gun fire tore into Private Johnson and he dropped to his knees. Fighting to the very last, he steadied himself on his knees and sent a final burst of fire crashing into another German. With that he slumped forward dead. Private Johnson had willingly given his life in order that his comrades might live. These acts on the part of Private Johnson were an inspiration to the entire command and are in keeping with the highest traditions of the armed forces.

Kapaun Barracks

Location: Kaiserslautern, Germany
Status: Unknown
Named for: Captain Emil Joseph Kapaun, Chaplain

Date of Birth: 1916
Place of Birth: Wichita, Kansas
Date of Death: May 23, 1951
Place of Death: Pyoktong, North Korea
Decorations and Honors: Distinguished Service Cross; Legion of Merit; Bronze Star with V device; Purple Heart; Korean Service Medal; National Defense Service Medal; World War II Victory Medal
Place of Burial: Memorialized at National Memorial Cemetery of the Pacific in Honolulu, Hawaii

Captain Emil Joseph Kapaun served with the 8th Cavalry, 1st Cavalry Division. His Distinguished Service Cross citation reads as follows:

On August 2, 1950, near Kumchon, Korea, Chaplain Emil J. Kapaun received information that there was a wounded soldier in an exposed position on the left flank of the first battalion of his regiment, who could not be removed because there were no litter bearers available. Chaplain Kapaun, together with another officer, immediately proceeded to the front lines and, with total disregard for personal safety, and in the face of intense enemy machine-gun and small-arms fire, reached the wounded soldier, and saved his life.

His Bronze Star citation reads as follows:

Chaplain Kapaun distinguished himself on November 1 and 2, 1950, near Unsan, Korea, for a period of thirty-six hours, the 8th Cavalry was subjected to a relentless attack by hostile troops attempting to break through the perimeter defense. In the early morning hours, the enemy succeeded in breaking through, and hand-to-hand combat ensued in the immediate vicinity of the command post where the aid station had been set up. With disregard for his personal safely, Kapaun calmly moved among the wounded men, gave them medical aid, and eased their fears. His courageous manner inspired all those present and encouraged many men, who might otherwise have fled, to remain and fight. As the battle progressed, the number of the wounded increased and it became apparent that many would be unable to escape. At dusk the remaining able-bodied men were ordered to attempt to break through the enemy forces. Kapaun voluntarily remained behind and when last seen by the departing troops was administering medical treatment and rendering religious rites wherever needed. Taken prisoner, he further distinguished himself by exceptionally meritorious service during his internment from November 4, 1950, until his death.

His body was never recovered.

Kelley Barracks

Location: Möhringen-Stuttgart, Germany
Status: Active
Named for: Staff Sergeant Jonah Edward Kelley
Date of Birth: April 13, 1923
Place of Birth: Roda, West Virginia
Date of Death: January 31, 1945
Place of Death: Kesternich, Germany
Decorations and Honors: Medal of Honor, posthumously
Place of Burial: Queens Meadow Point Cemetery in Keyser, West Virginia

Staff Sergeant Jonah Edward Kelley served with the 311th Infantry, 78th Infantry Division.

His Medal of Honor citation for action during World War II reads as follows:

In charge of the leading squad of Company E, he heroically spearheaded the attack in furious house-to-house fighting. Early on January 30, he led his men through intense mortar and small arms fire in repeated assaults on barricaded houses. Although twice wounded, once when struck in the back, the second time when a mortar shell fragment passed through his left hand and rendered it practically useless, he refused to withdraw and continued to lead his squad after hasty dressings had been applied. His serious wounds forced him to fire his rifle with one hand, resting it on rubble or over his left forearm. To blast his way forward with hand grenades, he set aside his rifle to pull the pins with his teeth while grasping the missiles with his good hand. Despite these handicaps, he created tremendous havoc in the enemy ranks. He rushed one house, killing three of the enemy and clearing the way for his squad to advance. On approaching the next house, he was fired upon from an upstairs window. He killed the sniper with a single shot and similarly accounted for another enemy soldier who ran from the cellar of the house. As darkness came, he assigned his men to defensive positions, never leaving them to seek medical attention. At dawn the next day, the squad resumed the attack, advancing to a point where heavy automatic and small arms fire stalled them. Despite his wounds, Staff Sergeant Kelley moved out alone, located an enemy gunner dug in under a haystack and killed him with rifle fire. He returned to his men and found that a German machine gun, from a well-protected position in a neighboring house, still held up the advance. Ordering the squad to remain in comparatively safe positions, he valiantly dashed into the open and attacked the position single-handedly through a hail of bullets. He was hit several times and fell to his knees when within twenty-five yards of his objective; but he summoned his waning strength and emptied his rifle into the machine-gun nest, silencing the weapon before he died. The superb courage, aggressiveness, and utter disregard for his own safety displayed by Staff Sergeant

Kelley inspired the men he led and enabled them to penetrate the last line of defense held by the enemy in the village of Kesternich.

Kilbourne Barracks

Location: Schwetzingen, Germany
Status: Active
Named for: Major General Charles Evans Kilbourne, Jr.
Date of Birth: December 23, 1872
Place of Birth: Fort Myer, Virginia
Date of Death: November 12, 1963
Place of Death: Walter Reed Army Medical Center in Washington, D.C.
Decorations and Honors: Medal of Honor; Distinguished Service Cross; Distinguished Service Medal; French Croix de Guerre; French Legion of Honor; Philippine and Victory Medals
Date of Retirement: 1945
Place of Burial: Arlington National Cemetery, Section 3, Site 1705

Major General Charles Evans Kilbourne, Jr., at the age of ninety, was the oldest living Medal of Honor recipient, and the only signal officer to receive the Medal of Honor in the performance of a combat communications mission. He served in the Spanish-American War; the Philippine Insurrection; the Boxer Rebellion; and World War I.

Kilbourne graduated from Virginia Military Institute in 1894 with a degree in civil engineering. He was an observer with the U.S. Weather Bureau when the war with Spain began in 1898. He joined the Volunteer Signal Corps where he was assigned to provide tactical communications to the regular army.

He was sent to the Philippine Islands with the 1st Company, Volunteer Signal Corps, and later he served as an infantry officer with the 14th Infantry Regiment. In late 1899, he led his platoon in the assault that captured the Imperial City Gates during the Boxer Rebellion in China.

In 1902, he transferred to the Artillery Corps and attended artillery school at Fort Monroe in Virginia where he graduated with honors. He was later assigned as the post district adjutant there. While commanding the 35th Company, Coast Artillery Corps, Kilbourne helped defend Manila Bay by constructing a defensive fortifications system on Corregidor Island that helped save Australia from Japanese advances.

In 1911, he was assigned to the War Department General Staff where he helped develop plans for the defense of Guantanamo Bay, Cuba. While serving as chief of staff, Southeastern Department, he helped establish Fort Jackson in South Carolina as an army post.

He was wounded by a mortar round while on a fact-finding mission in

France, but despite his injuries, he continued to lead the 89th Infantry Division into combat. In October 1918, he was given command of the 36th Artillery Brigade, and later the 3rd Infantry Brigade, 2nd Division. He was married to Elizabeth Gordon Egbert.

His Medal of Honor citation for action during the Philippine Insurrection on February 5, 1899, reads as follows:

Within a range of 250 yards of the enemy and in the face of a rapid fire climbed a telegraph pole at the east end of the bridge and in full view of the enemy coolly and carefully repaired a broken telegraph wire, thereby reestablishing telegraphic communication to the front.

The Distinguished Service Cross was awarded for his extraordinary heroism in action near Thiacourt, France, September 12, 1918.

The Distinguished Service Medal was awarded for his services in 89th Division and 36th Artillery Brigade. The French Croix de Guerre was awarded for his reconnaissance preparation to assault the Saint Mihiel Salient.

Kimbro Kaserne

Location: Murnau, Germany
Status: Unknown
Named for: Technician Fourth Grade Truman Carol Kimbro
Date of Birth: May 27, 1919
Place of Birth: Madisonville, Texas
Date of Death: December 19, 1944
Place of Death: Rocherath, Belgium
Decorations and Honors: Medal of Honor, posthumously; Purple Heart
Place of Burial: Henri-Chapelle American Cemetery and Memorial in Henri-
    Chapelle, Belgium, Plot R, Row 6, Grave 28

Technician Fourth Grade Truman Carol Kimbro served with Company C, 2nd Engineer Combat Battalion, 2nd Infantry Division.

His Medal of Honor citation for action during World War II reads as follows:

On December 19, 1944, as scout, he led a squad assigned to the mission of mining a vital crossroads near Rocherath, Belgium. At the first attempt to reach the objective, he discovered it was occupied by an enemy tank and at least twenty infantrymen. Driven back by withering fire, Technician 4th Grade Kimbro made two more attempts to lead his squad to the crossroads but all approaches were covered by intense enemy fire. Although warned by our own infantrymen of the great danger involved, he left his squad in a protected place and, laden with mines, crawled alone toward the crossroads. When nearing his objective he was severely wounded, but he continued to drag himself forward and laid his mines across the road. As he tried to crawl from the objective his body was riddled with rifle and machine-gun fire. The mines laid by his act of indomitable courage delayed the advance of enemy armor and prevented the rear of our withdrawing columns from being attacked by the enemy.

Knight Barracks

Location: Regensburg, Germany
Status: Unknown
Named for: First Lieutenant Jimmie S. Knight
Date of Birth: No Data Found
Place of Birth: No Data Found
Date of Death: February 27, 1945
Place of Death: Golkrath, Germany
Decorations and Honors: Bronze Star, posthumously
Place of Burial: Netherlands American Cemetery and Memorial in Margraten, Netherlands

First Lieutenant Jimmie S. Knight was a platoon leader of Troop B, 44th Cavalry Reconnaissance Squadron (Mechanized), 11th Cavalry Group.

His Bronze Star citation reads as follows:

Lieutenant Knight's squadron was assigned the mission of screening the left flank of the XIII Corps. Encountering an enemy road block covered by small arms and antitank fire, Knight gallantly led his platoon into the fight and, though mortally wounded, continued to direct his men until he lost consciousness.

Larson Barracks

Location: Kitzingen, Germany
Status: Closed
Named for: Captain Stanley L. Larson
Date of Birth: January 9, 1920
Place of Birth: Idaho
Date of Death: May 23, 1944
Place of Death: Anzio Beachhead, Italy
Decorations and Honors: Distinguished Service Cross, posthumously

Captain Stanley L. Larson served with Company C, 10th Engineer Combat Battalion, during World War II.

Larson graduated from the University of California at Berkeley and entered the U.S. Army as a second lieutenant. He was killed during the landing on the Anzio beachhead. In an effort to save the lives of his men, and while under intense artillery and machine-gun fire, he cleared mines from the pathway in advance of an armored attack.

Ledward Barracks

Location: Schweinfurt, Germany
Status: Active
Named for: Lieutenant Colonel William J. Ledward
Date of Birth: No Data Found
Place of Birth: No Data Found
Date of Death: June 4, 1944
Place of Death: Albana, Italy

Lieutenant Colonel William J. Ledward was commanding officer of the 27th Armored Field Artillery Battalion. He was killed in action by an exploding land mine.

Lee Barracks

Location: Gonsenheim-Mainz, Germany
Status: Closed
Named for: Captain Robert E. Lee
Date of Birth: No Data Found
Place of Birth: No Data Found
Date of Death: November 17, 1944
Place of Death: Puffendort, Germany

Captain Robert E. Lee served with the 67th Armored Regiment, 2nd Armored Division.

After suffering a heavy loss of tanks, Lee's unit was ordered to withdraw from its position. Acting without orders, Lee chose to keep his three remaining tanks in place to cover the withdrawal of the infantry troops. He then ordered two tanks to withdraw while he remained upon the exposed slope until the last infantry troops had left, making himself the sole target of enemy guns.

Leighton Barracks

Location: Würzburg, Germany
Status: Closed
Named for: Captain John A. Leighton
Date of Birth: No Data Found
Place of Birth: No Data Found
Date of Death: July 18, 1944
Place of Death: Raids, France
Decorations and Honors: Silver Star, posthumously

Captain John A. Leighton was commanding officer of Company G, 10th Armored Infantry Battalion, 4th Armored Division.

His Silver Star citation reads as follows:

On July 16, 1944, Captain Leighton suffered stomach wounds while directing his company in an attack on Raids, France. Despite his wounds he continued to direct the operation until his position became untenable. To alleviate this situation, he directed his company to withdraw to a more suitable position and insisted upon being left behind so as not to endanger the lives of the members of his unit. The company made a withdrawal only after he had assured them that he would be picked up by the medical corps. That was the last that was seen or heard of Captain Leighton until July 28, 1944, when his body was recovered by a search party.

Lloyd Barracks

Location: Wetzlar, Germany
Status: Unknown
Named for: First Lieutenant Edgar Harold Lloyd
Date of Birth: February 28, 1922
Place of Birth: Blytheville, Arkansas
Date of Death: November 16, 1944
Place of Death: Near Pompey, France
Decorations and Honors: Medal of Honor, posthumously
Place of Burial: Courthouse Lawn in Blytheville, Mississippi

First Lieutenant Edgar Harold Lloyd served with Company E, 319th Infantry, 80th Infantry Division.

His Medal of Honor citation for action during World War II reads as follows:

For conspicuous gallantry and intrepidity at the risk of his life above and beyond the call of duty. On September 14, 1944, Company E, 319th Infantry, with which

First Lieutenant Lloyd was serving as a rifle platoon leader, was assigned the mission of expelling an estimated enemy force of 200 men from a heavily fortified position near Pompey, France. As the attack progressed, First Lieutenant Lloyd's platoon advanced to within fifty yards of the enemy position where they were caught in a withering machine-gun and rifle crossfire, which inflicted heavy casualties and momentarily disorganized the platoon. With complete disregard for his own safety, First Lieutenant Lloyd leaped to his feet and led his men on a run into the raking fire, shouting encouragement to them. He jumped into the first enemy machine-gun position, knocked out the gunner with his fist, dropped a grenade, and jumped out before it exploded. Still shouting encouragement he went from one machine-gun nest to another, pinning the enemy down with submachine-gun fire until he was within throwing distance, and then destroyed them with hand grenades. He personally destroyed five machine guns and many of the enemy, and by his daring leadership and conspicuous bravery inspired his men to overrun the enemy positions and accomplish the objective in the face of seemingly insurmountable odds. His audacious determination and courageous devotion to duty exemplify the highest traditions of the military forces of the United States.

Lucius D. Clay Kaserne

Location: Bremerhaven and Berlin, Germany
Status: Closed
Named for: General Lucius DuBignon Clay
Date of Birth: April 23, 1897
Place of Birth: Marietta, Georgia
Date of Death: April 16, 1978
Place of Death: Chatham, Massachusetts
Decorations and Honors: Distinguished Service Medal with oak leaf cluster; Legion of Merit; Bronze Star; American Defense Service Medal; American Campaign Medal; European-African-Middle Eastern Campaign Medal; World War II Victory Medal; Army of Occupation Medal (Germany)
Date of Retirement: May 26, 1949
Place of Burial: West Point Cemetery in New York, Section 18, Row G, Grave 79

General Lucius DuBignon Clay organized the logistics and transportation of the eleven-month-long Berlin Airlift of 1948–49 to become known as "The Father of the Berlin Airlift."

Clay graduated from West Point in 1918 and was commissioned a second lieutenant. In 1940, he was appointed to the Airport Approval Board where he was responsible for the construction and improvement of almost five hundred airports in North America and worldwide.

He was appointed the first military governor of the American section of occupied Germany in Berlin where, in 1948, he airlifted supplies into the city at a rate of more than 140,000 tons a month. On June 25, Douglas C-47 Skytrain transport planes and other Allied aircraft began flying around the clock, taking off or landing approximately every three minutes at Tempelhof Airfield in West Berlin, delivering food, clothing, and medical supplies.

After retiring from the military, Clay became the chief executive officer of the Continental Can Company. He encouraged General Dwight D. Eisenhower to run for president in 1952. After the election, Clay advised Eisenhower on issues regarding Germany. He also was a political advisor to John F. Kennedy.

A memorial from the people of Berlin stands at his grave site at West Point that reads as follows: *"Wir danken dem Bewahrer unserer Freiheit"* (We thank the defender of our freedom).

Mansfield Kaserne

Location: Straubing, Germany
Status: Active
Named for: Colonel Clayton J. Mansfield
Date of Birth: No Data Found
Place of Birth: No Data Found
Date of Death: January 9, 1945
Place of Death: Devantave, Belgium
Decorations and Honors: Silver Star; Purple Heart, posthumously
Place of Burial: Henri-Chapelle American Cemetery and Memorial in Henri-
    Chapelle, Belgium, Plot C

Colonel Clayton J. Mansfield served with the 2nd Armored Division.

His Silver Star citation for action during World War II reads as follows:

Colonel Mansfield was commander of a task force of tanks and infantry, with the mission of attacking and occupying the town of Devantave, Belgium. Throughout the assault, he remained constantly with his most forward elements, inspiring men and officers alike with complete disregard for his own safety and maintaining their confidence through his comprehension of the situation and ability to issue quick, concise, and coherent orders. His courage and professional skill exemplified a superior leadership which reflected great credit upon himself and was in keeping with the highest traditions of the service.

McCully Barracks

Location: Wachenheim, Germany
Status: Active
Named for: First Lieutenant William C. McCully
Date of Birth: No Data Found
Place of Birth: No Data Found
Date of Death: October 20, 1944
Place of Death: Germany
Decorations and Honors: Distinguished Service Cross, posthumously; Purple Heart with oak leaf cluster
Place of Burial: Netherlands American Cemetery and Memorial in Margraten, Netherlands, Plot P

First Lieutenant William C. McCully served with the 66th Armored Regiment, 2nd Armored Division.

His Distinguished Service Cross citation for action during World War II reads as follows:

McCully led his tank platoon to a position well in advance of friendly infantry, mounting an attack on an enemy-held town. For more than three hours, he acted as forward observer for artillery fire, which prevented enemy elements from counterattacking in force. He remained in this position exposed to a hail of fire from German artillery and antitank guns knowing his vehicle could be hit and destroyed. He did not withdraw until ordered to do so, and while this order was being given, his tank was hit and he was killed. The extraordinary heroism and courageous actions of Lieutenant McCully reflect great credit upon himself and are in keeping with the highest traditions of the military service.

McGee Barracks

Location: Bad Cannstatt, Germany
Status: Unknown
Named for: Private William D. McGee
Date of Birth: No Data Found
Place of Birth: Indianapolis, Indiana
Date of Death: March 19, 1945
Place of Death: Near Mülheim an der Ruhe, Germany
Decorations and Honors: Medal of Honor, posthumously
Place of Burial: Luxembourg American Cemetery and Memorial in Luxembourg City, Luxembourg, Plot C

Private William D. McGee served with the Medical Detachment, 304th Infantry, 76th Infantry Division.

His Medal of Honor citation for action during World War II reads as follows:

A medical aid man, he made a night crossing of the Moselle River with troops endeavoring to capture the town of Mülheim. The enemy had retreated in the sector where the assault boats landed, but had left the shore heavily strewn with antipersonnel mines. Two men of the first wave attempting to work their way forward detonated mines which wounded them seriously, leaving them bleeding and in great pain beyond the reach of their comrades. Entirely on his own initiative, Private McGee entered the minefield, brought out one of the injured to comparative safety, and had returned to rescue the second victim when he stepped on a mine and was severely wounded in the resulting explosion. Although suffering intensely and bleeding profusely, he shouted orders that none of his comrades was to risk his life by entering the death-sown field to render first aid that might have saved his life. In making the supreme sacrifice, Private McGee demonstrated a concern for the well-being of his fellow soldiers that transcended all considerations for his own safety and a gallantry in keeping with the highest traditions of the military service.

McGraw Kaserne

Location: Munich, Germany
Status: Closed
Named for: Private First Class Francis X. McGraw
Date of Birth: April 29, 1918
Place of Birth: Philadelphia, Pennsylvania
Date of Death: November 19, 1944
Place of Death: Near Schevenhutte, Germany
Decorations and Honors: Medal of Honor, posthumously; Bronze Star; Purple Heart
Place of Burial: Henri-Chapelle American Cemetery and Memorial in Henri-Chapelle, Belgium, Plot A, Row 18, Grave 25

Private First Class Francis X. McGraw served with Company H, 26th Infantry Regiment, 1st Infantry Division.

His Medal of Honor citation for action during World War II reads as follows:

He manned a heavy machine-gun emplaced in a foxhole near Schevenhutte, Germany, on November 19, 1944, when the enemy launched a fierce counterattack. Braving an intense hour-long preparatory barrage, he maintained his stand and poured deadly accurate fire into the advancing foot troops until they faltered and came to a halt. The hostile forces brought up a machine gun in an effort to dislodge him but were frustrated when he lifted his gun to an exposed but advantageous position atop a log, courageously stood up in his foxhole and knocked out the enemy weapon. A rocket blasted his gun from position, but he retrieved it and continued firing. He silenced a second machine gun and then made repeated trips over fire-swept terrain to replenish his ammunition supply. Wounded painfully in this dangerous task, he disregarded his injury and hurried back to his post, where his weapon was showered with mud when another rocket barely missed him. In the midst of the battle, with enemy troops taking advantage of his predicament to press forward, he calmly cleaned his gun, put it back into action and drove off the attackers. He continued to fire until his ammunition was expended, when, with a fierce desire to close with the enemy, he picked up a carbine, killed one enemy soldier, wounded another and engaged in a desperate firefight with a third until he was mortally wounded by a burst from a machine pistol. The extraordinary heroism and intrepidity displayed by Private McGraw inspired his comrades to great efforts and was a major factor in repulsing the enemy attack.

McKee Barracks

Location: Crailsheim, Germany
Status: Closed
Named for: Major John Lloyd McKee, Jr.
Date of Birth: 1917
Place of Birth: No Data Found
Date of Death: April 12, 1945
Place of Death: Trebnitz, Germany
Decorations and Honors: Silver Star; Legion of Merit; Bronze Star

Major John Lloyd McKee, Jr., served with the 901st Field Artillery Battalion.

McKee was killed while engaged in a reconnaissance mission. The report of McKee's death was recorded in a letter to his father on April 16, 1945, it read:

The armored elements in front of the regiment which Major McKee's battalion was supporting had made rapid advances and, due to lack of communications, there was considerable doubt as to the location of no-fire lines. Major McKee, on his own initiative, went on reconnaissance to determine the disposition of elements on the front. He flew beyond our own armored units to the vicinity of an enemy armored train, which was well camouflaged. The plane was flying at an altitude of 300 to 500 feet and, at about 1600 hours, was fired upon by enemy machine guns. As the plane dove to avoid the fire, enemy AAA fire pierced the right wing, weakening it to such an extent that it folded. The plane never came out of its dive, plunging to earth. It did not burn, so accurate identification of the pilot and Major McKee was possible. Indications were that both officers died instantly as a result of the crash. Enemy fire directed at the plane disclosed the position of the camouflaged enemy train and it was destroyed soon there after.

McPheeters Barracks

Location: Fulda, Germany
Status: Closed
Named for: Lieutenant Colonel John "Jon" W. McPheeters
Date of Birth: 1908
Place of Birth: Indianapolis, Indiana
Date of Death: March 1944
Place of Death: Anzio Beachhead, Italy

Lieutenant Colonel John W. McPheeters was commanding officer of the 91st Field Artillery Battalion and served in the 27th Field Artillery as executive officer of the 1st Armored Division.

McPheeters graduated from Arsenal Technical High School in 1924, attended Butler University in Indianapolis, Indiana, for one year, and then graduated from Purdue University in Indianapolis in 1928 with a degree in electrical engineering. After graduation, he worked for the Pennsylvania Railroad, helped establish the Mid West Soap Company in 1934, and founded the Knoxall Corporation and Griffey Industries in Indianapolis.

McPheeters graduated from the Field Artillery School at Fort Sill in Oklahoma in 1935 as a Reserve Officers' Training Corps cadet and was called to active duty in 1940. From 1942 to 1944, he served in Tunisia and then in Italy as an artillery expert. He died of wounds received while leading a company of tank destroyers attached to his command.

Merrell Barracks

Location: Nürnberg, Germany
Status: Closed
Named for: Private Joseph Frederick Merrell
Date of Birth: August 21, 1926
Place of Birth: Staten Island, New York
Date of Death: April 18, 1945
Place of Death: Lohne, Germany

Decorations and Honors: Medal of Honor, posthumously
Place of Burial: Saint Peters Cemetery in West New Brighton, New York

Private Joseph Frederick Merrell served with Company I, 15th Infantry, 3rd Infantry Division.

His Medal of Honor citation for action during World War II reads as follows:

He made a gallant, one-man attack against vastly superior enemy forces near Lohe, Germany. His unit, attempting a quick conquest of hostile hill positions that would open the route to Nuremberg before the enemy could organize his defense of that city, was pinned down by brutal fire from rifles, machine pistols, and two heavy machine guns. Entirely on his own initiative, Private Merrell began a single-handed assault. He ran 100 yards through concentrated fire, barely escaping death at each stride, and at pointblank range engaged four German machine pistolmen with his rifle, killing all of them while their bullets ripped his uniform. As he started forward again, his rifle was smashed by a sniper's bullet, leaving him armed only with three grenades. But he did not hesitate. He zigzagged 200 yards through a hail of bullets to within ten yards of the first machine gun, where he hurled two grenades and then rushed the position ready to fight with his bare hands if necessary. In the emplacement he seized a Luger pistol and killed what Germans had survived the grenade blast. Rearmed, he crawled toward the second machine gun located thirty yards away, killing four Germans in camouflaged foxholes on the way, but himself receiving a critical wound in the abdomen. And yet he went on, staggering, bleeding, disregarding bullets, which tore through the folds of his clothing and glanced off his helmet. He threw his last grenade into the machine-gun nest and stumbled on to wipe out the crew. He had completed this self-appointed task when a machine pistol burst killed him instantly. In his spectacular one-man attack, Private Merrell killed six Germans in the first machine-gun emplacement, seven in the next, and an additional ten infantrymen who were astride his path to the weapons which would have decimated his unit had he not assumed the burden of the assault and stormed the enemy positions with utter fearlessness, intrepidity of the highest order, and a willingness to sacrifice his own life so that his comrades could go on to victory.

Miller Barracks

Location: Marburg an der Lahn, Germany
Status: Unknown
Named for: Staff Sergeant Andrew Miller
Date of Birth: No Data Found
Place of Birth: Manitowoc, Wisconsin

Date of Death: November 29, 1944
Place of Death: Kerprich Hemmersdorf, Germany
Decorations and Honors: Medal of Honor; Purple Heart, posthumously
Place of Burial: Lorraine American Cemetery and Memorial in Saint Avold, France

Staff Sergeant Andrew Miller served with Company G, 377th Infantry Regiment.

His Medal of Honor citation for action during World War II reads as follows:

For performing a series of heroic deeds from November 16–29, 1944, during his company's relentless drive from Woippy, France, through Metz to Kerprich Hemmersdorf, Germany. As he led a rifle squad on November 16 at Woippy, a crossfire from enemy machine guns pinned down his unit. Ordering his men to remain under cover, he went forward alone, entered a building housing one of the guns and forced five Germans to surrender at bayonet point. He then took the second gun single-handedly by hurling grenades into the enemy position, killing two, wounding three more, and taking two additional prisoners. At the outskirts of Metz the next day, when his platoon, confused by heavy explosions and the withdrawal of friendly tanks, retired, he fearlessly remained behind armed with an automatic rifle and exchanged bursts with a German machine gun until he silenced the enemy weapon. His quick action in covering his comrades gave the platoon time to regroup and carry on the fight. On November 19, Staff Sergeant Miller led an attack on large enemy barracks. Covered by his squad, he crawled to a barracks window, climbed in and captured six riflemen occupying the room. His men, and then the entire company, followed through the window, scoured the building, and took seventy-five prisoners. Staff Sergeant Miller volunteered, with three comrades, to capture Gestapo officers who were preventing the surrender of German troops in another building. He ran a gauntlet of machine-gun fire and was lifted through a window. Inside, he found himself covered by a machine pistol, but he persuaded the four Gestapo agents confronting him to surrender. Early the next morning, when strong hostile forces punished his company with heavy fire, Staff Sergeant Miller assumed the task of destroying a well-placed machine gun. He was knocked down by a rifle grenade as he climbed an open stairway in a house, but pressed on with a bazooka to find an advantageous spot from which to launch his rocket. He discovered that he could fire only from the roof, a position where he would draw tremendous enemy fire. Facing the risk, he moved into the open, coolly took aim and scored a direct hit on the hostile emplacement, wreaking such havoc that the enemy troops became completely demoralized and began surrendering by the score. The following day, in Metz, he captured twelve more prisoners and silenced an enemy machine gun after volunteering for a hazardous mission in advance of his company's position. On November 29, as Company G climbed a hill overlooking Kerprich Hemmersdorf, enemy fire pinned the unit to the ground. Staff Sergeant Miller, on his own initiative, pressed ahead with his squad past the company's leading element to meet the surprise resistance. His men stood up and advanced deliberately, firing as they went. Inspired by Staff Sergeant Miller's leadership, the platoon followed, and then another platoon arose and grimly closed with the Germans. The enemy action was smothered, but at the cost of Staff Sergeant Miller's life. His tenacious devotion to the attack, his gallant choice to expose himself to enemy action rather than endanger his men, his limitless bravery, assured the success of Company G.

Minick Kaserne

Location: Bad Kreuznach, Germany
Status: Closed
Named for: Staff Sergeant John W. Minick
Date of Birth: June 4, 1908
Place of Birth: Wall, Pennsylvania
Date of Death: November 21, 1944
Place of Death: Hürtgenwald, Germany
Decorations and Honors: Medal of Honor, posthumously
Place of Burial: Westminster Cemetery in Carlisle, Pennsylvania

Staff Sergeant John W. Minick served with Company I, 121st Infantry, 8th Infantry Division.
 His Medal of Honor citation for action during World War II reads as follows:

He displayed conspicuous gallantry and intrepidity at the risk of his own life, above and beyond the call of duty, in action involving actual conflict with the enemy on November 21, 1944, near Hurtgen, Germany. Staff Sergeant Minick's battalion was halted in its advance by extensive minefields, exposing troops to heavy concentrations of enemy artillery and mortar fire. Further delay in the advance would result in numerous casualties and a movement through the minefield was essential. Voluntarily, Staff Sergeant Minick led four men through hazardous barbed wire and debris, finally making his way through the minefield for a distance of 300 yards. When an enemy machine gun opened fire, he signaled his men to take covered positions, edged his way alone toward the flank of the weapon and opened fire, killing two members of the guncrew and capturing three others. Moving forward again, he encountered and engaged single-handedly an entire company killing twenty Germans and capturing twenty, and enabling his platoon to capture the remainder of the hostile group. Again moving ahead and spearheading his battalion's advance, he again encountered machine-gun fire. Crawling forward toward the weapon, he reached a point from which he knocked the weapon out of action. Still another minefield had to be crossed. Undeterred, Staff Sergeant Minick advanced forward alone through constant enemy fire and while thus moving, detonated a mine and was instantly killed.

Murphy Barracks

Location: Ludwigsburg, Germany
Status: Unknown
Named for: Private First Class Frederick C. Murphy
Date of Birth: No Data Found
Place of Birth: Boston, Massachusetts
Date of Death: March 18, 1945
Place of Death: Siegfried Line at Saarlautern, Germany
Decorations and Honors: Medal of Honor, posthumously
Place of Burial: Lorraine American Cemetery and Memorial in Saint Avold, France, Plot F, Row 11, Grave 19

Private First Class Frederick C. Murphy served with the Medical Detachment, 259th Infantry, 65th Infantry Division.

His Medal of Honor citation for action during World War II reads as follows:

An aid man, he was wounded in the right shoulder soon after his comrades had jumped off in a dawn attack March 18, 1945, against the Siegfried Line at Saarlautern, Germany. He refused to withdraw for treatment and continued forward, administering first aid under heavy machine gun, mortar, and artillery fire. When the company ran into a thickly sown antipersonnel minefield and began to suffer more and more casualties, he continued to disregard his own wound and unhesitatingly braved the danger of exploding mines, moving about through heavy fire and helping the injured until he stepped on a mine which severed one of his feet. In spite of his grievous wounds, he struggled on with his work, refusing to be evacuated and crawling from man to man administering to them while in great pain and bleeding profusely. He was killed by the blast of another mine which he had dragged himself across in an effort to reach still another casualty. With indomitable courage, and unquenchable spirit of self-sacrifice and supreme devotion to duty which made it possible for him to continue performing his tasks while barely able to move, Private First Class Murphy saved many of his fellow soldiers at the cost of his own life.

Nelson Barracks

Location: Neu-Ulm, Germany
Status: Closed
Named for: Sergeant William Lloyd Nelson
Date of Birth: February 22, 1918
Place of Birth: Dover, Delaware

Date of Death: April 25, 1943
Place of Death: Djebel Dardys, Northwest of Sedjenane, Tunisia
Decorations and Honors: Medal of Honor, posthumously
Place of Burial: Silverbrook Cemetery in Wilmington, Delaware

Sergeant William Lloyd Nelson served with Company H, 60th Infantry Regiment, 9th Infantry Division.

His Medal of Honor citation for action during World War II reads as follows:

For conspicuous gallantry and intrepidity at risk of life, above and beyond the call of duty in action involving actual conflict. On the morning of April 24, 1943, Sergeant Nelson led his section of heavy mortars to a forward position where he placed his guns and men. Under intense enemy artillery, mortar, and small-arms fire, he advanced alone to a chosen observation position from which he directed the laying of a concentrated mortar barrage, which successfully halted an initial enemy counterattack. Although mortally wounded in the accomplishment of his mission, and with his duty clearly completed, Sergeant Nelson crawled to a still more advanced observation point and continued to direct the fire of his section. Dying of hand grenade wounds and only fifty yards from the enemy, Sergeant Nelson encouraged his section to continue their fire and by doing so they took a heavy toll of enemy lives. The skill which Sergeant Nelson displayed in this engagement, his courage, and self-sacrificing devotion to duty and heroism resulting in the loss of his life, was a priceless inspiration to our Armed Forces and were in keeping with the highest tradition of the U.S. Army.

O'Brien Barracks

Location: Schwabach, Germany
Status: Closed
Named for: Captain Thomas F. O'Brien
Date of Birth: No Data Found
Place of Birth: No Data Found
Date of Death: November 16, 1944
Place of Death: Aachen, Germany
Decorations and Honors: Distinguished Service Cross with two oak leaf clusters

Captain Thomas F. O'Brien served with the 7th Field Artillery Battalion, 1st Infantry Division, and distinguished himself during the Tunisian, Sicilian, and Normandy campaigns.

His Distinguished Service Cross citation reads as follows:

Captain O'Brien's gallantry in combat will live on as an example of the highest traditions of the military service.

His two oak leaf clusters were awarded for heroism in action in the Sicilian and Normandy campaigns. He was killed in action.

Oliver Barracks

Location: Berlin, Germany
Status: Unknown
Named for: Lieutenant Colonel Francis M. Oliver
Date of Birth: February 14, 1914
Place of Birth: Georgia
Date of Death: August 9, 1944
Place of Death: Sille-le-Guillaume, France

Lieutenant Colonel Francis M. Oliver was commanding officer of the 106th Cavalry Reconnaissance Squadron (Mechanized), 106th Cavalry Group.

Oliver graduated from West Point with the class of 1936 and served with several cavalry regiments prior to World War II. In 1944, he was assigned to Europe.

He was sent to France with his unit soon after D-Day and saw action on the west flank of the beachhead line while serving with VII Corps. He served as commander throughout the initial engagements and was fatally wounded by an exploding mine while leading a group of engineers forward to clear a path through a minefield. Enemy fire prevented his evacuation and he died while en route to an aid station.

Orsbon Barracks

Location: Weiden, Germany
Status: Unknown
Named for: Staff Sergeant Herman L. Orsbon
Date of Birth: No Data Found
Place of Birth: No Data Found
Date of Death: December 30, 1944
Place of Death: Bastogne, Belgium
Decorations and Honors: Silver Star

Staff Sergeant Herman L. Orsbon enlisted in the U.S. Army on July 18, 1940, and served with the 1st Armored Division until he was transferred to the 4th Armored Division in March 1941.

In August 1944, Orsbon was seriously wounded during the assault on Troyes, France, and in November of that year, he was wounded again near

Sarre-Union, France. He returned to duty in time to accompany his unit in the assault that relieved the siege of Bastogne, Belgium, only to be killed by artillery fire inside the city.

His Silver Star citation for action during World War II reads as follows:

On July 19, 1944, at Raids, France, Sergeant Orsbon assumed command of an infantry company after its officers had been either killed or captured during a strong enemy counter attack. Orsbon reorganized the company and led it back to the American lines under the cover of darkness.

Patch Barracks

Location: Stuttgart, Germany
Status: Active
Named for: General Alexander McCarrell Patch, Jr.
Date of Birth: November 23, 1889
Place of Birth: Fort Huachuca in Arizona
Date of Death: November 21, 1945
Place of Death: Fort Sam Houston in San Antonio, Texas
Decorations and Honors: Distinguished Service Medal with oak leaf cluster
Place of Burial: West Point Cemetery in New York, Section 2

General Alexander McCarrell Patch, Jr., was commander of XIV Corps and achieved the distinction of winning the first American land victory on Guadalcanal in early 1943 with the 1st Marine Division.

In March of 1944, Patch took command of the U.S. Seventh Army, which participated in the invasion of Southern France during the Overlord landings in Operation Anvil, later renamed Dragoon.

His Distinguished Service Medal citation reads as follows:

Landing in southern France, his troops drove through enemy opposition braving adverse weather, negotiating forbidding terrain and crushing enemy resistance until they had swung a tremendous arc to the east and south, reaching the Brannier Pass and accomplishing an advance of more than nine hundred miles in less than nine months. Under General Patch's masterful direction, the 7th Army Forces defeated the Germans in the Vosges Mountains and pressed on toward the Rhine, successfully aiding in halting the enemy's powerful December 1944 counteroffensive in the Hardt Mountains and along the Moder River Line. Resuming the advance in March 1945, his men fought through desperate hostile resistance, crossed the Rhine, and rapidly pushed to the Austrian-Italian border in the Brannier Pass, taking thousands of prisoners and accomplishing the destruction of prodigious amount of material and enemy troops. With bold tenacious aggressiveness and great tactical ability, General Patch led his 7th Army to victory and contributed in great measure to the Allied success in Europe.

Patton Barracks

Location: Heidelberg, Germany
Status: Active
Named for: General George Smith Patton, Jr.
Date of Birth: November 11, 1885
Place of Birth: San Gabriel, California
Date of Death: December 21, 1945
Place of Death: Heidelberg, Germany
Decorations and Honors: Distinguished Service Cross with oak leaf cluster; Distinguished Service Medal with two oak leaf clusters; Silver Star with oak leaf cluster; Legion of Merit; Bronze Star; Purple Heart; Congressional Life Saving Medal; Mexican Service Medal; World War I Victory Medal with five battle clasps; European-African-Middle Eastern Campaign Medal with one silver and two bronze service stars; American Defense Service Medal; World War II Victory Medal
Place of Burial: Luxembourg American Cemetery and Memorial in Luxembourg City, Luxembourg

General George Smith Patton, Jr., is considered by many to be the greatest military commander in U.S. military history, serving in the Mexican Expedition, World Wars I and II, in which he was famous for his "blood and guts" speeches.

Patton graduated from West Point with the class of 1909. During his long military career, he commanded II Corps, Seventh Army, Third Army, II Armored Corps, 2nd Armored Division, 3rd Cavalry Regiment, and the Fifteenth Army.

Patton was an outspoken proponent of the tank as a modern combat weapon. He carried out experiments to improve radio communications between tanks and helped invent the coaxial tank mount for cannons and machine guns.

His superiors in Washington requested that Patton be relieved of duty after he slapped a soldier he considered to be a coward and malingerer. Fortunately, General Dwight D. Eisenhower and Chief of Staff George C. Marshall refused to dismiss him, and Patton made a courageous public apology for the incident.

He was gravely injured in a traffic accident on December 7 and died twelve days later in an army hospital. He was married to Beatrice Ayer.

"The most vital quality a soldier can possess is self-confidence—utter, complete, and bumptious." —*General George Smith Patton, Jr.*

Peden Barracks

Location: Wertheim, Germany
Status: Closed
Named for: Technician Fifth Grade Forrest E. Peden
Date of Birth: No Data Found
Place of Birth: St. Joseph, Missouri
Date of Death: February 3, 1945
Place of Death: Bischheim, France
Decorations and Honors: Medal of Honor, posthumously
Place of Burial: Mount Olive Cemetery in Troy, Kansas

Technician Fifth Grade Forrest E. Peden served with Battery C, 10th Field Artillery Battalion, 3rd Infantry Division.

His Medal of Honor citation for action during World War II reads as follows:

He was a forward artillery observer when the group of about forty-five infantrymen with whom he was advancing was ambushed in the uncertain light of a waning moon. Enemy forces outnumbering the Americans by four to one poured withering artillery, mortar, machine-gun, and small-arms fire into the stricken unit from the flanks, forcing our men to seek the cover of a ditch which they found already occupied by enemy foot troops. As the opposing infantrymen struggled in hand-to-hand combat, Technician Peden courageously went to the assistance of two wounded soldiers and rendered first aid under heavy fire. With radio communications inoperative, he realized that the unit would be wiped out unless help could be secured from the rear. On his own initiative, he ran 800 yards to the battalion command post through a hail of bullets, which pierced his jacket and there secured two light tanks to go to the relief of his hard-pressed comrades. Knowing the terrible risk involved, he climbed upon the hull of the lead tank and guided it into battle. Through a murderous concentration of fire the tank lumbered onward, bullets and shell fragments ricocheting from its steel armor within inches of the completely exposed rider, until it reached the ditch. As it was about to go into action it was turned into a flaming pyre by a direct hit which killed Technician Peden. However, his intrepidity and gallant sacrifice was not in vain. Attracted by the light from the burning tank, reinforcements found the beleaguered Americans and drove off the enemy.

Pendleton Barracks

Location: Giessen, Germany
Status: Unknown
Named for: Staff Sergeant Jack James Pendleton
Date of Birth: March 31, 1918
Place of Birth: Sentinel Butte, North Dakota
Date of Death: October 12, 1944
Place of Death: Bardenberg, Germany
Decorations and Honors: Medal of Honor, posthumously
Place of Burial: Tahoma Cemetery in Yakima, Washington

Staff Sergeant Jack James Pendleton served with Company I, 120th Infantry Regiment, 30th Infantry Division.

His Medal of Honor citation for action during World War II reads as follows:

For conspicuous gallantry and intrepidity at the risk of his life above and beyond the call of duty on October 12, 1944. When Company I was advancing on the town of Bardenberg, Germany, they reached a point approximately two-thirds of the distance through the town when they were pinned down by fire from a nest of enemy machine guns. This enemy strong point was protected by a lone machine gun strategically placed at an intersection and firing down a street, which offered little or no cover or concealment for the advancing troops. The elimination of this protecting machine gun was imperative in order that the stronger position it protected could be neutralized. After repeated and unsuccessful attempts had been made to knock out this position, Staff Sergeant Pendleton volunteered to lead his squad in an attempt to neutralize this strongpoint. Staff Sergeant Pendleton started his squad slowly forward, crawling about ten yards in front of his men in the advance toward the enemy gun. After advancing approximately 130 yards under the withering fire, Staff Sergeant Pendleton was seriously wounded in the leg by a burst from the gun he was assaulting. Disregarding his grievous wound, he ordered his men to remain where they were, and with a supply of handgrenades he slowly and painfully worked his way forward alone. With no hope of surviving the veritable hail of machine-gun fire, which he deliberately drew onto himself, he succeeded in advancing to within ten yards of the enemy position when he was instantly killed by a burst from the enemy gun. By deliberately diverting the attention of the enemy machine gunners upon himself, a second squad was able to advance, undetected, and with the help of Staff Sergeant Pendleton's squad, neutralized the lone machine gun, while another platoon of his company advanced up the intersecting street and knocked out the machine-gun nest, which the first gun had been covering. Staff Sergeant Pendleton's sacrifice enabled the entire company to continue the advance and complete their mission at a critical phase of the action.

Peterson Kaserne

Location: Munich, Germany
Status: Unknown
Named for: Staff Sergeant George Peterson
Date of Birth: No Data Found
Place of Birth: Brooklyn, New York
Date of Death: March 30, 1945
Place of Death: Near Eisern, Germany
Decorations and Honors: Medal of Honor, posthumously
Place of Burial: Netherlands American Cemetery and Memorial in Margraten, Netherlands

Staff Sergeant George Peterson served with the 3rd Platoon, Company K, 18th Infantry Regiment.

His Medal of Honor citation for action during World War II reads as follows:

He was an acting platoon sergeant with Company K, near Eisern, Germany. When his company encountered an enemy battalion and came under heavy small-arms, machine-gun, and mortar fire, the 2nd Platoon was given the mission of flanking the enemy positions while the remaining units attacked frontally. Staff Sergeant Peterson crept and crawled to a position in the lead and motioned for the 2nd Platoon to follow. A mortar shell fell close by and severely wounded him in the legs, but, although bleeding and suffering intense pain, he refused to withdraw and continued forward. Two hostile machine guns went into action at close range. Braving this grazing fire, he crawled steadily toward the guns and worked his way alone to a shallow draw, where, despite the hail of bullets, he raised himself to his knees and threw a grenade into the nearest machine-gun nest, silencing the weapon and killing or wounding all its crew. The second gun was immediately turned on him, but he calmly and deliberately threw a second grenade, which rocked the position and killed all four Germans who occupied it. As he continued forward he was spotted by an enemy rifleman, who shot him in the arm. Undeterred, he crawled some twenty yards until a third machine gun opened fire on him. By almost superhuman effort, weak from loss of blood and suffering great pain, he again raised himself to his knees and fired a grenade from his rifle, killing three of the enemy guncrew and causing the remaining one to flee. With the first objective seized, he was being treated by the company aid man when he observed one of his outpost men seriously wounded by a mortar burst. He wrenched himself from the hands of the aid man and began to crawl forward to assist his comrade, whom he had almost reached when he was struck and fatally wounded by an enemy bullet. Staff Sergeant Peterson, by his gallant, intrepid actions, unrelenting fighting spirit, and outstanding initiative, silenced three enemy machine guns against great odds and while suffering from severe wounds, enabling his company to advance with minimum casualties.

Pinder Barracks

Location: Zirndorf, Germany
Status: Closed
Named for: Technician Fifth Grade John J. Pinder, Jr.
Date of Birth: June 6, 1912
Place of Birth: McKees Rocks, Pennsylvania
Date of Death: June 6, 1944
Place of Death: Colleville-sur-Mer, France
Decorations and Honors: Medal of Honor, posthumously
Place of Burial: Grandview Cemetery in Florence, Pennsylvania

Technician Fifth Grade John J. Pinder, Jr., served with the 16th Infantry, 1st Infantry Division.

His Medal of Honor citation for action during World War II reads as follows:

For conspicuous gallantry and intrepidity above and beyond the call of duty on June 6, 1944, near Colleville-sur-Mer, France. On D-day, Technician 5th Grade Pinder landed on the coast 100 yards off shore under devastating enemy machine gun and artillery fire which caused severe casualties among the boatload. Carrying a vitally important radio, he struggled towards shore in waist-deep water. Only a few yards from his craft he was hit by enemy fire and was gravely wounded. Technician 5th Grade Pinder never stopped. He made shore and delivered the radio. Refusing to take cover afforded, or to accept medical attention for his wounds, Technician 5th Grade Pinder, though terribly weakened by loss of blood and in fierce pain, on three occasions went into the fire-swept surf to salvage communication equipment. He recovered many vital parts and equipment, including another workable radio. On the third trip he was again hit, suffering machine-gun bullet wounds in the legs. Still this valiant soldier would not stop for rest or medical attention. Remaining exposed to heavy enemy fire, growing steadily weaker, he aided in establishing the vital radio communication on the beach. While so engaged this dauntless soldier was hit for the third time and killed. The indomitable courage and personal bravery of Technician 5th Grade Pinder was a magnificent inspiration to the men with whom he served.

Pirie Barracks

Location: Deggendorf, Germany
Status: Unknown
Named for: Captain James M. Pirie
Date of Birth: No Data Found

Place of Birth: No Data Found
Date of Death: September 28, 1944
Place of Death: Richecourt, France
Place of Burial: Wiltwyck Cemetery in Kingston, New York

Captain James M. Pirie was commanding officer of Service Company, 8th Tank Battalion, from September 1943 to July 20, 1944, and with Battalion S-4 in July 1944. He was the first officer of that battalion killed in action.

Pirie graduated from Kingston High School and Cornell University in New York. He joined the army in March 1941; graduated from the Armored Force Officer Candidate School at Fort Knox in Radcliff, in May 1942; and was commissioned a second lieutenant.

Pitman Barracks

Location: Weiden, Germany
Status: Unknown
Named for: Major James H. Pitman
Date of Birth: February 18, 1915
Place of Birth: Camden, New Jersey
Date of Death: September 18, 1944
Place of Death: Lunéville, France
Decorations and Honors: Silver Star, posthumously
Place of Burial: Lorraine American Cemetery and Memorial in Saint Avold, France

Major James H. Pitman graduated from West Point in June 1940 and was commissioned a second lieutenant. Pitman attended the Cavalry School and the Command and General Staff College from 1940 to 1943. He was later assigned to the 2nd Cavalry where he served as the regimental supply officer, and later as motor officer. In December of 1943, he assumed the duties of executive officer, commanding the 42nd Cavalry Reconnaissance Squadron.

His Silver Star citation for action during World War II reads as follows:

In 1944, while serving in France, Pitman disposed his squadron through the Forest de Mondon and the Villages of Gerberville and Chennevieres to protect the city of Lunéville and the left flank of XII Corps when he was attacked by the 11th Panzer Division in overwhelming strength. Pitman skillfully and courageously directed the defense of his positions six hours until elements of the 4th Armored Division arrived for his assistance. While reporting the situation to his group commander, he personally directed the placement of his units and directed the tanks until he was killed by enemy tank gunfire. His heroic efforts to keep the enemy from the outer defense of the town were successful and above and beyond the call of duty.

Ray Barracks

Location: Friedberg, Germany
Status: Closed
Named for: First Lieutenant Bernard James Ray
Date of Birth: June 9, 1921
Place of Birth: Brooklyn, New York
Date of Death: November 17, 1944
Place of Death: Schevenhutte, Germany
Decorations and Honors: Medal of Honor, posthumously
Place of Burial: Long Island National Cemetery in Farmingdale, New York

First Lieutenant Bernard James Ray served with Company F, 8th Infantry Regiment, 4th Infantry Division.

His Medal of Honor citation for action during World War II reads as follows:

He was platoon leader with Company F, 8th Infantry, on November 17, 1944, during the drive through the Hurtgen Forest near Schevenhutte, Germany. The American forces attacked in wet, bitterly cold weather over rough, wooded terrain, meeting brutal resistance from positions spaced throughout the forest behind minefields and wire obstacles. Small-arms, machine-gun, mortar, and artillery fire caused heavy casualties in the ranks when Company F was halted by a concertina-type wire barrier. Under heavy fire, First Lieutenant Ray reorganized his men and prepared to blow a path through the entanglement, a task, which appeared impossible of accomplishment and from which others tried to dissuade him. With implacable determination to clear the way, he placed explosive caps in his pockets, obtained several bangalore torpedoes, and then wrapped a length of highly explosive primer cord about his body. He dashed forward under direct fire, reached the barbed wire and prepared his demolition charge as mortar shells, which were being aimed at him alone, came steadily nearer his completely exposed position. He had placed a torpedo under the wire and was connecting it to a charge he carried when he was severely wounded by a bursting mortar shell. Apparently realizing that he would fail in his self-imposed mission unless he completed it in a few moments he made a supremely gallant decision. With the primer cord still wound about his body and the explosive caps in his pocket, he completed a hasty wiring system and unhesitatingly thrust down on the handle of the charger, destroying himself with the wire barricade in the resulting blast. By the deliberate sacrifice of his life, First Lieutenant Ray enabled his company to continue its attack, resumption of which was of positive significance in gaining the approaches to the Cologne Plain.

Ready Barracks

Location: Aschaffenburg, Germany
Status: Closed
Named for: Sergeant John P. Ready
Date of Birth: No Data Found
Place of Birth: No Data Found
Date of Death: June 8, 1945
Place of Death: Normandy, France
Decorations and Honors: Silver Star, posthumously
Place of Burial: Normandy American Cemetery and Memorial in Colleville-sur-Mer, France

Sergeant John P. Ready served with Headquarters Battery, 32nd Field Artillery Battalion.
Ready was killed when an enemy reconnaissance unit penetrated his command post and took him prisoner.
His Silver Star citation reads in part as follows:

Unarmed and facing certain death, Ready encouraged and led his fellow captives in a bold attempt to escape. Although he was mortally wounded, Sergeant Ready's courage and aggressiveness resulted in the capture of the entire enemy patrol.

Reese Barracks

Location: Augsburg, Germany
Status: Closed
Named for: Private James William Reese
Date of Birth: 1920
Place of Birth: Chester, Pennsylvania
Date of Death: August 5, 1943
Place of Death: Mt. Vassilio, Sicily
Decorations and Honors: Medal of Honor, posthumously
Place of Burial: Chester Rural Cemetery in Chester, Pennsylvania

Private James William Reese served with the 26th Infantry, 1st Infantry Division.
His Medal of Honor citation for action during World War II reads as follows:

For conspicuous gallantry and intrepidity at the risk of life above and beyond the call of duty in action involving actual conflict with the enemy. When the enemy launched a counterattack which threatened the position of his company, Private Reese, as the acting squad leader of a 60-mm mortar squad, displaying superior leadership on his own initiative, maneuvered his squad forward to a favorable position, from which, by skillfully directing the fire of his weapon, he caused many casualties in the enemy ranks, and aided materially in repulsing the counterattack. When the enemy fire became so severe as to make his position untenable, he ordered the other members of his squad to withdraw to a safer position, but declined to seek safety for himself. So as to bring more effective fire upon the enemy, Private Reese, without assistance, moved his mortar to a new position and attacked an enemy machine-gun nest. He had only three rounds of ammunition but secured a direct hit with his last round, completely destroying the nest and killing the occupants. Ammunition being exhausted, he abandoned the mortar, seized a rifle and continued to advance, moving into an exposed position overlooking the enemy. Despite a heavy concentration of machine-gun, mortar, and artillery fire, the heaviest experienced by his unit throughout the entire Sicilian campaign, he remained at this position and continued to inflict casualties upon the enemy until he was killed. His bravery, coupled with his gallant and unswerving determination to close with the enemy, regardless of consequences and obstacles which he faced, are a priceless inspiration to our armed forces.

Rivers Barracks

Location: Giessen, Germany
Status: Unknown
Named for: Staff Sergeant Rubin Rivers
Date of Birth: October 31, 1918
Place of Birth: Tecumseh, Oklahoma
Date of Death: November 19, 1944
Place of Death: Guébling, France
Decorations and Honors: Medal of Honor, posthumously; Silver Star; Purple Heart
Place of Burial: Lorraine American Cemetery and Memorial in Saint Avold, France

Staff Sergeant Rubin Rivers served with Company A, 761st Tank Battalion.
    His Medal of Honor citation for action during World War II reads as follows:

For extraordinary heroism in action during the November 15-19, 1944, toward Guebling, France. Though severely wounded in the leg, Sergeant Rivers refused medical treatment and evacuation, took command of another tank, and advanced with his company in Guebling the next day. Repeatedly refusing evacuation, Sergeant Rivers continued to direct his tank's fire at enemy positions through the morning of November 19, 1944. At dawn, Company A's tanks began to advance towards Bougaktroff, but were stopped by enemy fire. Sergeant Rivers, joined by another tank, opened fire on the enemy tanks, covering company A as they withdrew. While doing so, Sergeant Rivers' tank was hit, killing him and wounding the crew. Staff Sergeant Rivers' fighting spirit and daring leadership were an inspiration to his unit and exemplify the highest traditions of military service.

His Silver Star citation reads as follows:

For gallantry in action during a daylight attack on an objective Sergeant Rivers, a tank platoon sergeant, was in the leading tank when a road block was encountered which held up the advance. With disregard for his personal safety, he dismounted from his tank in the face of direct enemy small arms fire, attached a cable to the road block and had it moved off the road, permitting the combat team to proceed. His prompt action prevented a serious delay in this offensive operation and was instrumental in the successful assault and capture of the town. This brilliant display of initiative, courage, and devotion to duty reflected the highest credit upon Staff Sergeant Rivers and the armed forces of the United States.

Robinson Barracks

Location: Stuttgart, Germany
Status: Active
Named for: First Lieutenant James E. Robinson, Jr.
Date of Birth: July 10, 1918
Place of Birth: Toledo, Ohio
Date of Death: April 6, 1945
Place of Death: Untergriesheim, Germany
Decorations and Honors: Medal of Honor, posthumously
Place of Burial: Fort Sam Houston National Cemetery in San Antonio, Texas

First Lieutenant James E. Robinson, Jr., served with Battery A, 861st Field Artillery Battalion, 63rd Infantry Division.

His Medal of Honor citation for action during World War II reads as follows:

He was a field artillery forward observer attached to Company A, 253rd Infantry, near Untergriesheim, Germany, on April 6, 1945. Eight hours of desperate fighting over open terrain swept by German machine-gun, mortar, and small-arms fire had decimated Company A, robbing it of its commanding officer and most of its key enlisted personnel when First Lieutenant Robinson rallied the twenty-three remaining uninjured riflemen and a few walking wounded, and, while carrying his heavy radio for communication with American batteries, led them through intense fire in a charge against the objective. Ten German infantrymen in foxholes threatened to stop the assault, but the gallant leader killed them all at point-blank range with rifle and pistol fire and then pressed on with his men to sweep the area of all resistance. Soon afterward he was ordered to seize the defended town of Kressbach. He went to each of the nineteen exhausted survivors with cheering words, instilling in them courage and fortitude, before leading the little band forward once more. In the advance he was seriously wounded in the throat by a shell fragment, but, despite great pain and loss of blood, he refused medical attention and continued the attack, directing supporting artillery fire even though he was mortally wounded. Only after the town had been taken and he could no longer speak did he leave the command he had inspired in victory and walk nearly two miles to an aid station where he died from his wound. By his intrepid leadership First Lieutenant Robinson was directly responsible for Company's accomplishing its mission against tremendous odds.

In additional to Robinson Barracks in Stuttgart Germany, Robinson Hall at the Los Alamitos, California Reserve Center and a barracks building at Fort Sill in Lawton, Oklahoma, are also named in his honor.

Rose Barracks

Location: Bad Kreuznach, Germany
Status: Active
Named for: Major General Maurice Rose
Date of Birth: November 26, 1899
Place of Birth: Middletown, Connecticut
Date of Death: March 30, 1945
Place of Death: Hamborn, Germany
Decorations and Honors: Distinguished Service Cross; Distinguished Service
    Medal; Silver Star with two oak leaf clusters; Legion of Merit with oak leaf
    cluster; Bronze Star with oak leaf cluster; Purple Heart with oak leaf cluster; French Legion of Honor; French Croix de Guerre with palm; Belgian
    Croix de Guerre with palm
Place of Burial: Netherlands American Cemetery and Memorial in Margraten,
    Netherlands, Plot C, Grave 1

Major General Maurice Rose was the highest-ranking Jewish American officer killed in battle during World War II.

During his military career, which spanned thirty-nine years, Rose served in both World Wars I and II. Rose joined the U.S. Army in 1916 as a private and served on the Mexican border. After graduating from officer's training school, he was commissioned in the infantry and sent overseas. During World War I, he saw combat as a nineteen-year-old first lieutenant with the 89th Infantry Division in Argonne and at Saint Mihiel in France where he was wounded but continued to fight through the entire Meuse-Argonne offensive.

During World War II, Rose served with the 1st Division, "Old Ironsides," in Africa and Italy; the 2nd Division, "Hell on Wheels," in Normandy; and the 3rd Armored Division, "Spearhead," in Germany.

Among his significant achievements were: negotiating the 1943 German surrender in Tunisia; saving the 506th Parachute Infantry at the Battle of Carentan; playing an important role against the Germans in northern France, Belgium, and Germany in the Battle of the Bulge; and executing the greatest encirclement battle in American history by capturing 360,000 German soldiers in the "Ruhr Pocket," later renamed "The Rose Pocket."

On March 29, 1945, in central Germany, Rose's troops made the longest one-day advance by any Allied division during the war. Tragically, the next day, Rose was killed in action while trying to locate a forward 3rd Armored unit that had been cut off by German tanks. Rounding a corner in his jeep, he found himself surrounded by several German tanks. As he withdrew his pistol to surrender, a young German tank commander, apparently misunderstanding Rose's intentions, shot the general. Later, the Werwolf movement—a German guerilla group—claimed to have assassinated him.

His Distinguished Service Cross citation for action during World War II reads as follows:

With complete disregard for his own safety, he proceeded to the head of his column. Inspired by his leadership and gallantry, the troops seized the bridge intact. Before allowing troops or vehicles to cross the bridge, General Rose made a fearless personnel reconnaissance to determine if it had been mined or prepared for demolition by the enemy. On September 9, 1944, he again advanced to the point of the most intense action in full view of the enemy. Despite heavy mortar fire, he unhesitatingly took a position on the forward slope of a hill. While in this position, mortar shells landed nearby, killing an officer and wounding four other men. After assisting in the evacuation of the wounded men, he courageously returned to his former position and continued his observation. He was later killed in action. By his valor, undaunted leadership, and great personal courage, General Rose exemplified the highest traditions of the Armed Forces.

Sadowski Barracks

Location: Weilburg, Germany
Status: Unknown
Named for: Sergeant Joseph J. Sadowski
Date of Birth: 1916

Place of Birth: Perth Amboy, New Jersey
Date of Death: September 14, 1944
Place of Death: Valhey, France
Decorations and Honors: Medal of Honor, posthumously
Place of Burial: Saint Stephens Cemetery in Keasbey, New Jersey, Section N

Sergeant Joseph J. Sadowski served with Company A, 37th Tank Battalion, 4th Armored Division.

His Medal of Honor citation for action during World War II reads as follows:

For conspicuous gallantry and intrepidity at the risk of his life above and beyond the call of duty at Valhey, France. On the afternoon of September 14, 1944, Sergeant Sadowski as a tank commander was advancing with the leading elements of Combat Command A, 4th Armored Division, through an intensely severe barrage of enemy fire from the streets and buildings of the town of Valhey. As Sergeant Sadowski's tank advanced through the hail of fire, it was struck by a shell from an 88-mm gun fired at a range of twenty yards. The tank was disabled and burst into flames. The suddenness of the enemy attack caused confusion and hesitation among the crews of the remaining tanks of our forces. Sergeant Sadowski immediately ordered his crew to dismount and take cover in the adjoining buildings. After his crew had dismounted, Sergeant Sadowski discovered that one member of the crew, the bow gunner, had been unable to leave the tank. Although the tank was being subjected to a withering hail of enemy small-arms, bazooka, grenade, and mortar fire from the streets and from the windows of adjacent buildings, Sergeant Sadowski unhesitatingly returned to his tank and endeavored to pry up the bow gunner's hatch. While engaged in this attempt to rescue his comrade from the burning tank, he was cut down by a stream of machine-gun fire, which resulted in his death. The gallant and noble sacrifice of his life in the aid of his comrade, undertaken in the face of almost certain death, so inspired the remainder of the tank crews that they pressed forward with great ferocity and completely destroyed the enemy forces in this town without further loss to themselves. The heroism and selfless devotion to duty displayed by Sergeant Sadowski, which resulted in his death, inspired the remainder of his force to press forward to victory, and reflect the highest tradition of the armed forces.

Sheridan Barracks

Location: Garmisch, Germany
Status: Closed
Named for: Private First Class Carl Vernon Sheridan
Date of Birth: January 5, 1925
Place of Birth: Baltimore, Maryland

Date of Death: November 26, 1944
Place of Death: Frenzenberg Castle in Weisweiler, Germany
Decorations and Honors: Medal of Honor, posthumously
Place of Burial: Druid Ridge Cemetery in Pikesville, Maryland

Private First Class Carl Vernon Sheridan served with Company K, 47th Infantry, 9th Infantry Division.

His Medal of Honor citation for action during World War II reads as follows:

Attached to the 2nd Battalion of the 47th Infantry on November 26, 1944, for the attack on Frenzenberg Castle, in the vicinity of Weisweiler, Germany, Company K, after an advance of 1,000 yards through a shattering barrage of enemy artillery and mortar fire, had captured two buildings in the courtyard of the castle but was left with an effective fighting strength of only thirty-five men. During the advance, Private First Class Sheridan, acting as a bazooka gunner, had braved the enemy fire to stop and procure the additional rockets carried by his ammunition bearer who was wounded. Upon rejoining his company in the captured buildings, he found it in a furious fight with approximately seventy enemy paratroopers occupying the castle gate house. This was a solidly built stone structure surrounded by a deep water-filled moat twenty feet wide. The only approach to the heavily defended position was across the courtyard and over a drawbridge leading to a barricaded oaken door. Private First Class Sheridan, realizing that his bazooka was the only available weapon with sufficient power to penetrate the heavy oak planking, with complete disregard for his own safety left the protection of the buildings and in the face of heavy and intense small-arms and grenade fire, crossed the courtyard to the drawbridge entrance where he could bring direct fire to bear against the door. Although handicapped by the lack of an assistant, and a constant target for the enemy fire that burst around him, he skillfully and effectively handled his awkward weapon to place two well-aimed rockets into the structure. Observing that the door was only weakened, and realizing that a gap must be made for a successful assault, he loaded his last rocket, took careful aim, and blasted a hole through the heavy planks. Turning to his company he shouted, "Come on, let's get them!" With his .45 pistol blazing, he charged into the gaping entrance and was killed by the withering fire that met him. The final assault on Frenzenberg Castle was made through the gap which Private First Class Sheridan gave his life to create.

Sherwood Young Barracks

Location: Eschwege, Germany
Status: Unknown
Named for: First Lieutenant Sherwood M. Young, Jr.

Date of Birth: No Data Found
Place of Birth: Georgia
Date of Death: November 25, 1944
Place of Death: France
Decorations and Honors: Silver Star, posthumously
Place of Burial: Lorraine American Cemetery and Memorial in Saint Avold, France

First Lieutenant Sherwood M. Young, Jr., served with Company B, 128th Armored Ordnance Battalion.
His Silver Star citation for action during World War II reads as follows:

Lieutenant Young made repeated trips into areas swept by enemy fire and courageously entered known mine fields in order to retrieve disabled vehicles. He was killed by an enemy mine while attempting to find a route of access to a disabled tank.

Smith Barracks

Location: Baumholder, Germany
Status: Active
Named for: Captain Harold D. Smith
Date of Birth: No Data Found
Place of Birth: Kansas
Date of Death: September 13, 1944
Place of Death: No Data Found
Decorations and Honors: Distinguished Service Cross, posthumously
Place of Burial: Henri-Chapelle American Cemetery and Memorial in Henri-Chapelle, Belgium

Captain Harold D. Smith served with Infantry Reconnaissance Company, 67th Armored Regiment.
His Distinguished Service Cross citation for action during World War II reads as follows:

Captain Smith, due to the tactical situation at hand, left his company and went forward on foot to scout the enemy's positions. Approaching a crossroad held by the enemy, he was met by heavy fire. Friendly infantry, which had been attacking these positions had suffered severe casualties. He carried a number of the wounded infantrymen to safety and continued do so after all friendly troops had withdrawn.

Spinelli Barracks

Location: Mannheim, Germany
Status: Active
Named for: Private First Class Dominic Vito Spinelli
Date of Birth: July 23, 1923
Place of Birth: Hamilton, Ohio
Date of Death: April 14, 1945
Place of Death: Willsbach, Germany
Decorations and Honors: Silver Star; Purple Heart; Bronze Star with three oak leaf clusters; World War II Victory Medal, posthumously
Place of Burial: Saint Mary's Cemetery in Hamilton, Ohio

Private First Class Dominic Vito Spinelli was a medic with the 398th Infantry Regiment, 100th Infantry Division, Seventh Army, Medical Detachment.

Spinelli attended Hamilton Boys' Catholic High School and graduated in 1940 at the age of sixteen. He worked at the local grocery store, played many sports and loved music. He graduated from the University of Dayton in 1943, and had attended the University of Cincinnati for six months before being accepted for medical school at St. Louis University in Missouri.

He joined the service in September 1944 and received basic training at Camp Grant in Rockford, Illinois, and was sent to Lawson General Hospital in Atlanta, Georgia, for advanced training as a surgical technician where he graduated with honors. He participated in battles at Ardennes-Alsace Rhineland and throughout Central Europe.

His Silver Star citation for action during World War II reads as follows:

When the platoon to which Private Spinelli was attached was attacking across an open field, heavy enemy fire isolated five men. When word was received that four of those men were wounded, Private Spinelli left his own sheltered position in an attempt to aid the injured men, despite the enemy fire which raked the ground in front of him. After sniper fire forced him to the ground once, he heroically rose but went only a few feet when he was hit twice by small arms fire and was killed instantly. Private Spinelli gave his life in an effort to rescue his wounded comrades and his gallant action is in keeping with the high traditions of the Medical Department.

Stem Kaserne

Location: Heidelberg, Germany
Status: Unknown
Named for: Brigadier General David H. Stem

Date of Birth: January 23, 1938
Place of Birth: Easton, Pennsylvania
Date of Death: January 21, 1987
Place of Death: Independence, Missouri

Brigadier General David H. Stem was a 1960 graduate of West Point and the commandant of the Military Police Corps Regiment.

Stem earned a masters of art degree in business administration from Fairleigh Dickinson University in New Jersey. He graduated from the FBI National Academy at Quantico, Virginia, and the U.S. Army War College.

Stem was commander of the Military Police School at Fort McClellan in Alabama and served as commander of the 2nd Region Criminal Investigation Command in Europe. He was also the first chief of the Military Police Corps Regiment and commander of the 95th Military Police Battalion in Mannheim, Germany. During his twenty-seven years of active army service, Stem served ten years with the U.S. Army, Europe, (USAREUR) and Seventh Army. He was killed in a mid-air collision between an army plane and a Piper Navaho.

The Brigadier General David H. Stem Award was established in his name in 1985, which is presented annually to the best military police unit, company size or smaller, in the U.S. Army Training and Doctrine Command (TRADOC).

Storck Barracks

Location: Illesheim, Germany
Status: Active
Named for: Colonel Louis J. Storck
Date of Birth: July 1, 1897
Place of Birth: Pennsylvania
Date of Death: July 30, 1944
Place of Death: Raids, France
Decorations and Honors: Silver Star; Legion of Merit; Purple Heart, posthumously
Place of Burial: Normandy American Cemetery and Memorial in Colleville-sur-Mer, France

Colonel Louis J. Storck served as executive officer with the 4th Armored Division, commander of Combat Command A and the 37th Armored Regiment, and commander of the 704th Tank Destroyer Battalion during World War II.

Storck enlisted the U.S. Army in June 1918 and achieved the rank of corporal by December of that year. In 1919, he was appointed to West Point and graduated with the class of 1923.

Storck was killed in action while serving as commanding officer, Reserve

Command, 4th Armored Division. His Silver Star was awarded for his gallantry in action near Raids, France, from July 17 to 25, 1944.

Sullivan Barracks

Location: Käfertal, Germany
Status: Active
Named for: Private First Class George F. Sullivan
Date of Birth: No Data Found
Place of Birth: No Data Found
Date of Death: April 10, 1945
Place of Death: Near Heilbronn, Germany
Decorations and Honors: Silver Star; Bronze Star; Purple Heart, posthumously
Place of Burial: Ardennes American Cemetery and Memorial in Neupre, Belgium

Private First Class George F. Sullivan served with the 397th Infantry Regiment, 100th Division.

His Silver Star citation for action during World War II reads as follows:

Private Sullivan, a member of an antitank platoon, was serving as a provisional rifleman while his unit was assigned to clear a residential section of enemy resistance. When he observed that his squad was in danger of being annihilated by close range fire, he charged the German machine-gun nest single-handedly, killing the entire crew with rifle fire and silencing the machine gun but was killed in the act. The gallantry and magnificent courage displayed by Private Sullivan was directly responsible for saving his comrades from disaster and is in keeping with the highest traditions of the United States Army.

Taukkunen Barracks

Location: Worms, Germany
Status: Closed
Named for: Staff Sergeant Ernest Taukkunen
Date of Birth: No Data Found
Place of Birth: No Data Found
Date of Death: March 2, 1945
Place of Death: Schiefbahn, Germany

Staff Sergeant Ernest Taukkunen served with the 41st Armored Infantry Regiment, 2nd Armored Division. Taukkunen was killed by enemy machine-gun fire while attempting to find an escape route for his men who were trapped in a burning building.

Taylor Barracks

Location: Käfertal, Germany
Status: Active
Named for: Private First Class Cecil V. Taylor
Date of Birth: No Data Found
Place of Birth: No Data Found
Date of Death: April 18, 1945
Place of Death: Beilstein, Germany
Decorations and Honors: Silver Star, posthumously

Private First Class Cecil V. Taylor served with the 399th Infantry Regiment, 100th Division.
  His Silver Star citation for action during World War II reads as follows:

Private Taylor, an assistant machine gunner, was with his unit when his battalion drove the enemy from high ground overlooking Beilstein. When his weapon was emplaced on the crest of the hill, however, the enemy counter-attacked in considerable strength under cover of an intense artillery and mortar barrage. Although his severe wounds later proved fatal, Private Taylor remained at his gun killing three enemy and wounding many more before the enemy attack was broken. Private Taylor's gallantry in manning his weapon while mortally wounded gained him the admiration and respect of all those who fought with him.

Tompkins Barracks

Location: Schwetzingen, Germany
Status: Active
Named for: Private First Class George S. Tompkins, Jr.
Date of Birth: No Data Found
Place of Birth: No Data Found
Date of Death: April 3, 1945
Place of Death: No Data Found
Decorations and Honors: Silver Star, posthumously

Private First Class George S. Tompkins, Jr., served with the 397th Infantry Regiment, 100th Infantry Division.
  His Silver Star citation for action during World War II reads as follows:

While his platoon was covering the withdrawal of another immobilized platoon, the enemy unleashed a terrific concentration of fire upon the position. Private Tompkins firing from an exposed position was mortally wounded. He refused medical care, however, and continued to fire into the enemy tanks, enabling his harassed comrades to withdraw, regroup and retake the lost ground. Private Tompkins' gallant sacrifice reflected the noblest traditions of the United States Army.

Towle Barracks

Location: Kassel, Germany
Status: Unknown
Named for: Private John Roderick Towle
Date of Birth: October 19, 1924
Place of Birth: Cleveland, Ohio
Date of Death: September 21, 1945
Place of Death: Near Oosterhout, Holland
Decorations and Honors: Medal of Honor, posthumously
Place of Burial: Calvary Cemetery in Cleveland, Ohio

Private John Roderick Towle served as a rocket launcher gunner with Company C, 504th Parachute Infantry, 82nd Airborne Division.

His Medal of Honor citation for action during World War II reads as follows:

For conspicuous gallantry and intrepidity at the risk of life above and beyond the call of duty on September 21, 1944, near Oosterhout, Holland. The rifle company in which Private Towle served as rocket launcher gunner was occupying a defensive position in the west sector of the recently established Nijmegen bridgehead when a strong enemy force of approximately 100 infantry supported by two tanks and a half-track formed for a counterattack. With full knowledge of the disastrous consequences resulting not only to his company but to the entire bridgehead by an enemy breakthrough, Private Towle immediately and without orders left his foxhole and moved 200 yards in the face of intense small-arms fire to a position on an exposed dike roadbed. From this precarious position Private Towle fired his rocket launcher at and hit both tanks to his immediate front. Armored skirting on both tanks prevented penetration by the projectiles, but both vehicles withdrew slightly damaged. Still under intense fire and fully exposed to the enemy, Private Towle then engaged a nearby house which nine Germans had entered and were using as a strongpoint and with one round killed all nine. Hurriedly replenishing his supply of ammunition, Private Towle, motivated only by his high conception of duty, which called for the destruction of the enemy at any cost, then rushed approximately 125 yards through grazing enemy fire to an exposed position from which he could engage the enemy half-track with his rocket launcher. While in a kneeling position preparatory to firing on the enemy vehicle, Private Towle was mortally wounded by a mortar shell. By his heroic tenacity, at the price of his life, Private Towle saved the lives of many of his comrades and was directly instrumental in breaking up the enemy counterattack.

Turley Barracks

Location: Mannheim, Germany
Status: Closed
Named for: First Sergeant Samuel J. Turley
Date of Birth: No Data Found
Place of Birth: Minnesota
Date of Death: November 9, 1944
Place of Death: Metz, France
Decorations and Honors: Silver Star, posthumously
Place of Burial: Lorraine American Cemetery and Memorial in Saint Avold, France

First Sergeant Samuel J. Turley served with Company C, 761st Tank Battalion. His Silver Star citation for action during World War II reads as follows:

Sergeant Turley displayed supreme courage when he gave his life protecting the men in his company. He was killed in action when his company was pinned down by enemy fire. Sergeant Turley stood erect with a machine gun in his hands and fired at the enemy while his Company withdrew. He continued firing until he was struck by enemy machine-gun fire and a moment later a German 80 mm artillery shell hit the spot where he was lying.

Turner Barracks

Location: Berlin, Germany
Status: Unknown
Named for: Sergeant First Class Charles William Turner
Date of Birth: May 28, 1921
Place of Birth: Boston, Massachusetts
Date of Death: September 2, 1950
Place of Death: Yongsan, South Korea
Decorations and Honors: Medal of Honor, posthumously
Place of Burial: Arlington National Cemetery, Section 12, Lot 7762

Sergeant First Class Charles William Turner served with the 2nd Reconnaissance Company, 2nd Infantry Division.

His Medal of Honor citation for action during the Korean War reads as follows:

Sergeant First Class Turner distinguished himself by conspicuous gallantry and intrepidity above and beyond the call of duty in action against the enemy. A large enemy force launched a mortar and automatic weapon supported assault against his platoon. Sergeant First Class Turner, a section leader, quickly organized his unit for defense and then observed that the attack was directed at the tank section 100 yards away. Leaving his secured section he dashed through a hail of fire to the threatened position and, mounting a tank, manned the exposed turret machine gun. Disregarding the intense enemy fire he calmly held this position delivering deadly accurate fire and pointing out targets for the tank's 75 mm gun. His action resulted in the destruction of seven enemy machine-gun nests. Although severely wounded he remained at the gun shouting encouragement to his comrades. During the action the tank received over fifty direct hits; the periscopes and antenna were shot away and three rounds hit the machine-gun mount. Despite this fire he remained at his post until a burst of enemy fire cost him his life. This intrepid and heroic performance enabled the platoon to withdraw and later launch an attack, which routed the enemy. Sergeant First Class Turner's valor and example reflect the highest credit upon himself and are in keeping with the esteemed traditions of the U.S. Army.

Valdez Barracks

Location: Stuttgart, Germany
Status: Unknown
Named for: Private First Class Jose F. Valdez
Date of Birth: January 3, 1925
Place of Birth: Governador, New Mexico
Date of Death: January 25, 1945
Place of Death: Near Rosenkrantz, France
Decorations and Honors: Medal of Honor, posthumously
Place of Burial: Santa Fe National Cemetery in Santa Fe, New Mexico

Private First Class Jose F. Valdez served with Company B, 7th Infantry, 3rd Infantry Division.

His Medal of Honor citation for action during World War II reads as follows:

He was on outpost duty with five others when the enemy counterattacked with overwhelming strength. From his position near some woods 500 yards beyond the American lines he observed a hostile tank about seventy-five yards away, and raked it with automatic rifle fire until it withdrew. Soon afterward he saw three Germans stealthily approaching through the woods. Scorning cover as the enemy soldiers opened up with heavy automatic weapons fire from a range of thirty yards, he engaged in a fire fight with the attackers until he had killed all three. The enemy quickly launched an attack with two full companies of infantrymen, blasting the patrol with murderous concentrations of automatic and rifle fire and beginning an encircling movement, which forced the patrol leader to order a withdrawal. Despite the terrible odds, Private First Class Valdez immediately volunteered to cover the maneuver, and as the patrol one by one plunged through a hail of bullets toward the American lines, he fired burst after burst into the swarming enemy. Three of his companions were wounded in their dash for safety and he was struck by a bullet that entered his stomach and, passing through his body, emerged from his back. Overcoming agonizing pain, he regained control of himself and resumed his firing position, delivering a protective screen of bullets until all others of the patrol were safe. By field telephone he called for artillery and mortar fire on the Germans and corrected the range until he had shells falling within fifty yards of his position. For fifteen minutes he refused to be dislodged by more than 200 of the enemy; then, seeing that the barrage had broken the counter attack, he dragged himself back to his own lines. He died later as a result of his wounds. Through his valiant, intrepid stand and at the cost of his own life, Private First Class Valdez made it possible for his comrades to escape, and was directly responsible for repulsing an attack by vastly superior enemy forces.

Wallace Barracks

Location: Bad Cannstatt, Germany
Status: Unknown
Named for: Private First Class Herman C. Wallace
Date of Birth: 1924
Place of Birth: Marlow, Oklahoma
Date of Death: February 27, 1945
Place of Death: Near Prümzurlay, Germany
Decorations and Honors: Medal of Honor, posthumously
Place of Burial: City of Lubbock Cemetery in Lubbock, Texas

Private First Class Herman C. Wallace served with Company B, 301st Engineer Combat Battalion, 76th Infantry Division.

His Medal of Honor citation for action during World War II reads as follows:

He displayed conspicuous gallantry and intrepidity. While helping clear enemy mines from a road, he stepped on a well-concealed S-type antipersonnel mine.

Hearing the characteristic noise indicating that the mine had been activated and, if he stepped aside, would be thrown upward to explode above ground and spray the area with fragments, surely killing two comrades directly behind him and endangering other members of his squad, he deliberately placed his other foot on the mine even though his best chance for survival was to fall prone. Private First Class Wallace was killed when the charge detonated, but his supreme heroism at the cost of his life confined the blast to the ground and his own body and saved his fellow soldiers from death or injury.

Warner Barracks / Warner Kaserne

Location: Bamberg / Munich, Germany
Status: Active / Closed
Named for: Corporal Henry F. Warner
Date of Birth: August 23, 1923
Place of Birth: Troy, North Carolina
Date of Death: December 21, 1944
Place of Death: Bütgenbach, Belgium
Decorations and Honors: Medal of Honor, posthumously
Place of Burial: Southside Cemetery in Troy, North Carolina, Lot 813

Corporal Henry F. Warner served with Antitank Company, 2nd Battalion, 26th Infantry, 1st Infantry Division.
    His Medal of Honor citation for action during World War II reads as follows:

Serving as 57-mm antitank gunner with the 2nd Battalion, he was a major factor in stopping enemy tanks during heavy attacks against the battalion position near Dom Bütgenbach, Belgium, on December 20–21, 1944. In the first attack, launched in the early morning of the 20th, enemy tanks succeeded in penetrating parts of the line. Corporal Warner, disregarding the concentrated cannon and machine-gun fire from two tanks bearing down on him, and ignoring the imminent danger of being overrun by the infantry moving under tank cover, destroyed the first tank and scored a direct and deadly hit upon the second. A third tank approached to within five yards of his position while he was attempting to clear a jammed breach lock. Jumping from his gun pit, he engaged in a pistol duel with the tank commander standing in the turret, killing him and forcing the tank to withdraw. Following a day and night during which our forces were subjected to constant shelling, mortar barrages, and numerous unsuccessful infantry attacks, the enemy struck in great force on the early morning of the 21st. Seeing a Mark IV tank looming out of the mist and heading toward his position, Corporal Warner scored a direct hit. Disregarding his injuries, he endeavored to finish the loading and again fire at the tank whose motor was now aflame, when a second machine gun burst killed him. Corporal Warner's gallantry and intrepidity at the risk of life above and beyond the call of duty contributed materially to the successful defense against the enemy attacks.

Wharton Barracks

Location: Heilbronn, Germany
Status: Closed
Named for: Brigadier General James E. Wharton
Date of Birth: December 12, 1894
Place of Birth: Elk, New Mexico
Date of Death: August 12, 1944
Place of Death: Normandy, France
Decorations and Honors: Distinguished Service Medal; Purple Heart
Place of Burial: Arlington National Cemetery, Section 34, Site 1198

Brigadier General James E. Wharton was commanding general of the 1st Engineer Special Brigade and assistant division commander of the 9th Infantry Division.

While leading VII Corps, Wharton planned and coordinated the landing of supplies at Cherbourg, France. The success of the mission was due mainly to his efforts in preventing essential supply shortages. Landing early on June 6, 1944, he personally directed, while under fire, the organization of the work ashore so that during the extremely critical initial hours of the difficult operation supplies were handled promptly and efficiently.

As assistant division commander of the 9th Infantry Division, Wharton helped plan the breakthrough at Marigny, France. Wharton was killed by a German sniper as he assumed command of the 28th Infantry Division.

Whitson Kaserne

Location: Schwabach, Germany
Status: Unknown
Named for: Private William H. "Red" Whitson
Date of Birth: No Data Found
Place of Birth: No Data Found
Date of Death: July 31, 1944
Place of Death: Avranches, France
Decorations and Honors: Distinguished Service Cross, posthumously

Private William H. Whitson served with Company B, 53rd Armored Infantry Battalion.

His Distinguished Service Cross citation for action during World War II reads as follows:

Private Whitson's company was ordered to move to the south of Avranches to cut off the withdrawal of the enemy which were being forced southward by concentrated tank, artillery and air support. Private Whitson manned a machine gun, and as the enemy column approached, he opened fire, knocking out twenty-four vehicles and killing forty-eight of the enemy single handedly. He continued to fire until he was mortally wounded.

Wilkin Barracks

Location: Stuttgart, Germany
Status: Unknown
Named for: Corporal Edward G. Wilkin
Date of Birth: May 25, 1917
Place of Birth: Burlington, Vermont
Date of Death: April 18, 1944
Place of Death: Siegfried Line in Germany
Decorations and Honors: Medal of Honor, posthumously
Place of Burial: Longmeadow Cemetery in Longmeadow, Massachusetts

Corporal Edward G. Wilkin served with Company C, 157th Infantry, 45th Infantry Division.

His Medal of Honor citation for action during World War II reads as follows:

He spearheaded his unit's assault of the Siegfried Line in Germany. Heavy fire from enemy riflemen and camouflaged pillboxes had pinned down his comrades when he moved forward on his own initiative to reconnoiter a route of advance. He cleared the way into an area studded with pillboxes, where he repeatedly stood up and walked into vicious enemy fire, storming one fortification after another with automatic rifle fire and grenades, killing enemy troops, taking prisoners as the enemy defense became confused, and encouraging his comrades by his heroic example. When halted by heavy barbed wire entanglements, he secured bangalore torpedoes and blasted a path toward still more pillboxes, all the time braving bursting grenades and mortar shells and direct rifle and automatic-weapons fire. He engaged in fierce fire fights, standing in the open while his adversaries fought from the protection of concrete emplacements, and on one occasion pursued enemy soldiers across an open field and through interlocking trenches, disregarding the crossfire from two pillboxes until he had penetrated the formidable line 200 yards in advance of any American element. That night, although terribly fatigued, he refused to rest and insisted on distributing rations and supplies to his comrades. Hearing that a nearby company was suffering heavy casualties, he secured permission to guide litter bearers and assist them in evacuating the wounded. All that night he remained in the battle area on his mercy missions, and for the following two days he continued to remove casualties, venturing into enemy-held territory, scorning cover and braving devastating mortar and artillery bombardments. In three days he neutralized and captured six pillboxes single-handedly, killed at least nine Germans, wounded thirteen, took thirteen prisoners, aided in the capture of fourteen others, and saved many American lives by his fearless performance as a litter bearer. Through his superb fighting skill, dauntless courage, and gallant, inspiring actions, Corporal Wilkin contributed in large measure to his company's success in cracking the Siegfried Line. One month later he was killed in action while fighting deep in Germany.

Will Kaserne

Location: Munich, Germany
Status: Closed
Named for: First Lieutenant Walter J. Will
Date of Birth: No Data Found
Place of Birth: Pittsburgh, Pennsylvania
Date of Death: March 30, 1945
Place of Death: Near Eisern, Germany
Decorations and Honors: Medal of Honor, posthumously
Place of Burial: Netherlands American Cemetery and Memorial in Margraten, Netherlands

First Lieutenant Walter J. Will served with Company K, 18th Infantry Regiment, 1st Infantry Division.
 His Medal of Honor citation for action during World War II reads as follows:

He displayed conspicuous gallantry during an attack on powerful enemy positions. He courageously exposed himself to withering hostile fire to rescue two wounded men and then, although painfully wounded himself, made a third trip to carry another soldier to safety from an open area. Ignoring the profuse bleeding of his wound, he gallantly led men of his platoon forward until they were pinned down by murderous flanking fire from two enemy machine guns. He fearlessly crawled alone to within thirty feet of the first enemy position, killed the crew of four and silenced the gun with accurate grenade fire. He continued to crawl through intense enemy fire to within twenty feet of the second position where he leaped to his feet, made a lone, ferocious charge and captured the gun and its nine-man crew. Observing another platoon pinned down by two more German machine guns, he led a squad on a flanking approach and, rising to his knees in the face of direct fire, coolly and deliberately lobbed three grenades at the Germans, silencing one gun and killing its crew. With tenacious aggressiveness, he ran toward the other gun and knocked it out with grenade fire. He then returned to his platoon and led it in a fierce, inspired charge, forcing the enemy to fall back in confusion. First Lieutenant Will was mortally wounded in this last action, but his heroic leadership, indomitable courage, and unflinching devotion to duty live on as a perpetual inspiration to all those who witnessed his deeds.

Wilson Barracks

Location: Landstuhl, Germany
Status: Unknown
Named for: Technician Fifth Grade Alfred Leonard Wilson
Date of Birth: September 18, 1919
Place of Birth: Fairchance, Pennsylvania
Date of Death: November 8, 1944
Place of Death: Near Bezange-la-Petite, France
Decorations and Honors: Medal of Honor, posthumously
Place of Burial: Maple Grove Cemetery in Fairchance, Pennsylvania

Technician Fifth Grade Alfred Leonard Wilson served with Medical Detachment, 328th Infantry, 26th Infantry Division.
   His Medal of Honor citation for action during World War II reads as follows:

He volunteered to assist as an aid man a company other than his own, which was suffering casualties from constant artillery fire. He administered to the wounded and returned to his own company when a shellburst injured a number of its men. While treating his comrades he was seriously wounded, but refused to be evacuated by litter bearers sent to relieve him. In spite of great pain and loss of blood, he continued to administer first aid until he was too weak to stand. Crawling from one patient to another, he continued his work until excessive loss of blood prevented him from moving. He then verbally directed unskilled enlisted men in continuing the first aid for the wounded. Still refusing assistance himself, he remained to instruct others in dressing the wounds of his comrades until he was unable to speak above a whisper and finally lapsed into unconsciousness. The effects of his injury later caused his death. By steadfastly remaining at the scene without regard for his own safety, Corporal Wilson through distinguished devotion to duty and personal sacrifice helped to save the lives of at least ten wounded men.

Army Camps
South Korea

They'll build for us a monument
Young boys will come to stare
And they will be the next to go
To shed their blood somewhere.

—*Ella Wheeler Wilcox*

CHAPTER 7

Army Camps South Korea

Camp Bonifas

Location: Panmunjom, South Korea
Status: Active
Named for: Captain Arthur George Bonifas
Date of Birth: April 22, 1943
Place of Birth: Newburgh, New York
Date of Death: August 18, 1976
Place of Death: Panmunjom, South Korea
Decorations and Honors: Bronze Star with oak leaf cluster; Commendation Medal; Purple Heart; Vietnam Service Medal

Captain Arthur George Bonifas served with the 2nd Infantry Division. He was slain by North Korean KPA guards inside the demilitarized zone (DMZ) during an event known as the Axe Murder Incident.*

Bonifas graduated from West Point in 1966. He attended Airborne and Ranger School and served with the 4th Infantry Division. Bonifas was promoted to major, posthumously.

---

* The Axe Murder Incident occurred when North Korean guards, using pick handles, knives, clubs, and axes, attacked the United Nations Command soldiers inside the Joint Security Area as they attempted to prune a tree blocking the view between two outposts near the Bridge of No Return.

★★★

Camp Carroll

Location: Waegwan, Korea
Status: Active
Named for: Sergeant First Class Charles F. Carroll
Date of Birth: 1927
Place of Birth: Jefferson, Oklahoma
Date of Death: September 26, 1950
Place of Death: Kumchon, Korea
Decorations and Honors: Distinguished Service Cross, posthumously

Sergeant First Class Charles F. Carroll served with the 72nd Combat Engineer Company, 5th Infantry Regiment, 24th Infantry Division. He was killed on the Pusan perimeter.

His Distinguished Service Cross citation for action during the Korean War reads as follows:

To Sergeant First Class Charles F. Carroll, United States Army, for extraordinary heroism in action during a combined infantry-tank attack against fierce enemy opposition, the tanks were held up by a roadblock consisting of antitank mines and enemy machine-gun emplacements. Voluntarily and with complete disregard for his own personal safety, Sergeant Carroll made his way out in front of the lead tank and began to remove the mines, heedless of the heavy volume of enemy fire. Tenaciously, he continued to remove the mines until he was mortally wounded by a burst of enemy machine-gun fire. His courage and devotion to duty in the face of grave danger were an inspiration to the men and enabled them to continue their attack and destroy the enemy without undue casualties to themselves.

Camp Casey

Location: Dongducheon, Gyeonggi-do Province, South Korea
Status: Active
Named for: Major Hugh Boyd Casey
Date of Birth: November 30, 1925
Place of Birth: Kansas
Date of Death: January 11, 1952
Place of Death: Near Dongducheon, South Korea
Decorations and Honors: Distinguished Service Cross; Combat Infantryman's Badge; Service Medal (Korea); United Nations Service Medal
Place of Burial: Arlington National Cemetery, Section 3

Major Hugh Boyd Casey served during World War II and in Korea as a company commander in the 2nd Battalion, 7th Infantry Regiment, 3rd Infantry Division, where he received the nation's second highest award for valor and heroism at the Hungnam Beachhead.

According to Lieutenant Colonel Roy E. Lewis, then executive officer of the 7th Infantry Division Support Command, Casey was ordered to put his company in a blocking position west of Hungnam Beachhead by sunrise. He had to cross a snow-covered mountain pass. Force-marching his men, he had them only halfway to the objective. He pressed forward, refusing to give up despite the fatigue and hopelessness of the mission. He didn't stop marching until ordered to. To Lewis, this was what made Casey an extraordinary soldier. "He gave little thought to himself," Lewis said.

Casey was killed when his light observation plane was hit by ground fire. The plane crashed near the 2nd Infantry Division Headquarters.

A white wooden cross was erected to mark the spot where he died. In 1960, it was replaced by a white concrete cross inscribed with "Lest we forget." The cross and camp now stand in his memory.

Camp Coiner

Location: Yongsan-gu, Seoul, South Korea
Status: Active
Named for: Second Lieutenant Randall E. Coiner
Date of Birth: September 19, 1927
Place of Birth: Hillsborough, Florida
Date of Death: April 16, 1953
Place of Death: Sokkagae, South Korea
Decorations and Honors: Silver Star, posthumously

Second Lieutenant Randall E. Coiner was assigned to the 3rd Battalion, 31st Infantry Regiment, 7th Division.

Camp Edwards

Location: Paju, Gyeonggi-do Province, South Korea
Status: Active
Named for: Sergeant First Class Junior D. Edwards
Date of Birth: October 7, 1926
Place of Birth: Indianola, Iowa
Date of Death: January 2, 1951

Place of Death: Near Changsong-ni, North Korea
Decorations and Honors: Medal of Honor, posthumously
Place of Burial: Indianola, Iowa

Sergeant First Class Junior D. Edwards served with Company E, 23rd Infantry Regiment, 2nd Infantry Division.

His Medal of Honor citation for action during the Korean War reads as follows:

Sergeant First Class Edwards, Company E, distinguished himself by conspicuous gallantry and intrepidity above and beyond the call of duty in action against the enemy. When his platoon, while assisting in the defense of a strategic hill, was forced out of its position and came under vicious raking fire from an enemy machine gun set up on adjacent high ground, Sergeant First Class Edwards individually charged the hostile emplacement, throwing grenades as he advanced. The enemy withdrew but returned to deliver devastating fire when he had expended his ammunition. Securing a fresh supply of grenades, he again charged the emplacement, neutralized the weapon and killed the crew, but was forced back by hostile small-arms fire. When the enemy emplaced another machine gun and resumed fire, Sergeant First Class Edwards again renewed his supply of grenades, rushed a third time through a vicious hail of fire, silenced this second gun and annihilated its crew. In this third daring assault he was mortally wounded but his indomitable courage and successful action enabled his platoon to regain and hold the vital strongpoint. Sergeant First Class Edwards' consummate valor and gallant self-sacrifice reflect the utmost glory upon himself and are in keeping with the esteemed traditions of the infantry and military service.

Camp George

Location: Daegu (or Taegu), South Korea
Status: Active
Named for: Private First Class Charles George
Date of Birth: August 23, 1932
Place of Birth: Cherokee, North Carolina
Date of Death: November 30, 1952
Place of Death: Songnam-dong, South Korea
Decorations and Honors: Medal of Honor, posthumously
Place of Burial: Yellow Hill Cemetery in Cherokee, North Carolina

Private First Class Charles George served with Company C, 179th Infantry Regiment, 45th Infantry Division.

His Medal of Honor citation for action during the Korean War reads as follows:

Private First Class George, a member of Company C, distinguished himself by conspicuous gallantry and outstanding courage above and beyond the call of duty in action against the enemy on the night of November 30, 1952. He was a member of a raiding party committed to engage the enemy and capture a prisoner for interrogation. Forging up the rugged slope of the key terrain feature, the group was subjected to intense mortar and machine-gun fire and suffered several casualties. Throughout the advance, he fought valiantly and, upon reaching the crest of the hill, leaped into the trenches and closed with the enemy in hand-to-hand combat. When friendly troops were ordered to move back upon completion of the assignment, he and two comrades remained to cover the withdrawal. While in the process of leaving the trenches, a hostile soldier hurled a grenade into their midst. Private First Class George shouted a warning to one comrade, pushed the other soldier out of danger, and, with full knowledge of the consequences, unhesitatingly threw himself upon the grenade, absorbing the full blast of the explosion. Although seriously wounded in this display of valor, he refrained from any outcry, which would divulge the position of his companions. The two soldiers evacuated him to the forward aid station and shortly thereafter he succumbed to his wound. Private First Class George's indomitable courage, consummate devotion to duty, and willing self-sacrifice reflect the highest credit upon himself and uphold the finest traditions of the military service.

Camp Greaves

Location: Paju, Gyeonggi-do Province, South Korea
Status: Active
Named for: Corporal Clinton Greaves
Date of Birth: August 12, 1855
Place of Birth: Madison County, Virginia
Date of Death: August 18, 1906
Place of Death: No Data Found
Decorations and Honors: Medal of Honor
Place of Burial: Greenlawn Cemetery in Columbus, Ohio

Corporal Clinton Greaves was a Buffalo Soldier.

Greaves, born into slavery, was a laborer when he first enlisted in the U.S. Army on November 21, 1872. He could not write so he signed his name with a mark. Greaves spent more than twenty years in the army, most of it in the 9th Cavalry, fighting during the Indian wars.

His Medal of Honor citation for action during the Indian War campaigns reads as follows:

While part of a small detachment to persuade a band of renegade Apache Indians to surrender, his group was surrounded. Corporal Greaves in the center of the savage hand-to-hand fighting, managed to shoot and bash a gap through the swarming Apaches, permitting his companions to break free.

Camp Henry

Location: Daegu (or Taegu), South Korea
Status: Active
Named for: First Lieutenant Frederick F. Henry
Date of Birth: No Data Found
Place of Birth: Vian, Oklahoma
Date of Death: September 1, 1950
Place of Death: Am-Dong, Korea
Decorations and Honors: Medal of Honor, posthumously

First Lieutenant Frederick F. Henry served with Company F, 38th Infantry Regiment.

His Medal of Honor citation for action during the Korean War reads as follows:

First Lieutenant Henry, Company F, distinguished himself by conspicuous gallantry and intrepidity above and beyond the call of duty in action. His platoon was holding a strategic ridge near the town when they were attacked by a superior enemy force, supported by heavy mortar and artillery fire. Seeing his platoon disorganized by this fanatical assault, he left his foxhole and moving along the line ordered his men to stay in place and keep firing. Encouraged by this heroic action the platoon reformed a defensive line and rained devastating fire on the enemy, checking its advance. Enemy fire had knocked out all communications and First Lieutenant Henry was unable to determine whether or not the main line of resistance was altered to this heavy attack. On his own initiative, although severely wounded, he decided to hold his position as long as possible and ordered the wounded evacuated and their weapons and ammunition brought to him. Establishing a one-man defensive position, he ordered the platoon's withdrawal and despite his wound and with complete disregard for himself remained behind to cover the movement. When last seen he was single-handedly firing all available weapons so effectively that he caused an estimated fifty enemy casualties. His ammunition was soon expended and his position overrun, but this intrepid action saved the platoon and halted the enemy's advance until the main line of resistance was prepared to throw back the attack. First Lieutenant Henry's outstanding gallantry and noble self-sacrifice above and beyond the call of duty reflect the highest honor on him and are in keeping with the esteemed traditions of the U.S. Army.

Camp Hovey

Location: Dongducheon, Gyeonggi-do Province, South Korea
Status: Active
Named for: Master Sergeant Howard Cleasby Hovey
Date of Birth: June 25, 1911
Place of Birth: St. Johnsbury, Vermont
Date of Death: July 6, 1953
Place of Death: Pork Chop Hill, Sokkagae, South Korea
Decorations and Honors: Distinguished Service Cross, posthumously
Place of Burial: Arlington National Cemetery, Section MC, Site 25J

Master Sergeant Howard Cleasby Hovey was a rifleman attached to a unit in General George S. Patton's Third Army during World War II that helped liberate prisoners from several German Concentration Camps. He returned from serving in the European Theater of Operations for a four-year tour at Camp Drum, now Fort Drum in Watertown, New York. He was forty-two years old when he was killed in action during one of the final battles for Pork Chop Hill. He was married to Evelyn Seymour.

His Distinguished Service Cross citation for action during the Korean War reads as follows:

The Distinguished Service Cross is awarded to Master Sergeant Howard C. Hovey, United States Army, for extraordinary heroism in connection with military operations involving conflict with an armed hostile force in the Republic of Korea. Master Sergeant Hovey, Infantry, United States Army, a member of Company A, 17th Infantry Regiment, 7th Infantry Division, distinguished himself by extraordinary heroism in action against an armed enemy of the United Nations in the vicinity of Sokkagae, Korea, on July 6, 1953. Master Sergeant Hovey and other members of the company were on duty in the company command post when their position was suddenly attacked by a vicious, numerically superior enemy force. With total disregard for his own life, Sergeant Hovey left the comparative safety of his bunker, moved into a nearby trench and directed a hail of fire at hostile troops, temporarily repulsing several attempts to overrun friendly positions. Aware that the dangerous proximity of the determined, reinforced enemy posed an imminent threat to the defense of the entire post, Sergeant Hovey, arming himself with a carbine and hand grenades, moved from the cover of the trench, spotted the enemy advancing within about fifty yards of the post and charged the enemy, pouring crippling fire and throwing grenades at the assailants, inflicting numerous casualties and checking their advance. Although wounded by automatic weapons during the ensuing action, he continued firing until he was again critically wounded by a napalm grenade. Feeling that the lives of other members were still endangered, he grabbed another carbine and grenades and again left the bunker area, maintaining his stand and firing his weapon and throwing grenades until he was mortally wounded by a direct hit from another enemy grenade. Through his indomitable fighting spirit and courageous actions, he enabled other members of the command post to evacuate the bunker, establish operations in another position, and eventually stem the onslaught. Master Sergeant Hovey's extraordinary heroism and devotion to duty were in keeping with the highest traditions of the military service and reflect great credit upon himself, his unit, and the United States Army.

Camp Howze

Location: Paju, Gyeonggi-do Province, South Korea
Status: Active
Named for: Major General Robert Lee Howze
Date of Birth: August 22, 1864
Place of Birth: Overton, Rush County, Texas
Date of Death: September 19, 1926
Place of Death: Columbus, Ohio
Decorations and Honors: Medal of Honor; Distinguished Service Medal; Silver Star with oak leaf cluster; French Croix de Guerre; French Legion of Honor
Place of Burial: West Point Cemetery in New York

Major General Robert Lee Howze served in the Philippine Insurrection, the Spanish-American War, and World War I.

Howze graduated from West Point in 1888, was commissioned a second lieutenant in the cavalry, and served with the 6th Cavalry where he fought off a Sioux attack on January 1, 1891. At the beginning of the Spanish-American War in 1898, Howze was appointed adjutant general of the cavalry in Cuba, and later he commanded the 34th Volunteer Infantry during the Philippine Insurrection. Following a tour of duty in Puerto Rico, he was appointed commandant of cadets at West Point from 1905 to 1909. Later, he returned to active military command in 1916 as a major in John J. Pershing's Punitive Expedition into Mexico.

In 1917, he was assigned to Fort Bliss in El Paso, Texas, and in October 1918, he commanded the 38th Division, which participated in the Meuse-Argonne offensive. He commanded the 3rd Division in its march on the Rhine River and the Third Army of Occupation in Germany until 1919. On July 3, 1920, he helped organize and train the 1st Cavalry Division.

Camp Howze in Gainesville, Texas, was also named in his honor. He was married to Anne Chiffelle Hawkins.

His Medal of Honor citation for action during the Indian War campaigns reads as follows: "Bravery in action."

Camp Kyle

Location: near Uijeongbu-si, Gyeonggi-do Province, South Korea
Status: Unknown
Named for: Second Lieutenant Darwin Keith Kyle
Date of Birth: June 1, 1918
Place of Birth: Jenkins, Kentucky
Date of Death: February 16, 1951
Place of Death: Kamil-ni, South Korea
Decorations and Honors: Medal of Honor, posthumously
Place of Burial: Sunset Memorial Cemetery in South Charleston, West Virginia, Section H, Lot 898

Second Lieutenant Darwin Keith Kyle served with Company K, 7th Infantry Regiment, 3rd Infantry Division.

His Medal of Honor citation for action during the Korean War reads as follows:

Second Lieutenant Kyle distinguished himself by conspicuous gallantry and intrepidity above and beyond the call of duty in action against the enemy. When his platoon had been pinned down by intense fire, he completely exposed himself to move among and encourage his men to continue the advance against enemy forces strongly entrenched on Hill 185. Inspired by his courageous leadership, the platoon resumed the advance but was again pinned down when an enemy machine gun opened fire, wounding six of the men. Second Lieutenant Kyle immediately charged the hostile emplacement alone, engaged the crew in hand-to-hand combat, killing all three. Continuing on toward the objective, his platoon suddenly received an intense automatic-weapons fire from a well-concealed hostile position on its right flank. Again leading his men in a daring bayonet charge against this position, firing his carbine and throwing grenades, Second Lieutenant Kyle personally destroyed four of the enemy before he was killed by a burst from an enemy submachine gun. The extraordinary heroism and outstanding leadership of Second Lieutenant Kyle, and his gallant self-sacrifice, reflect the highest credit upon himself and are in keeping with the esteemed traditions of the military service.

Camp Libby (see Libby Army Airfield)

★★★

Camp Long

Location: Wonju, Gangwon (Kangwon) Province, South Korea
Status: Active
Named for: Sergeant Charles R. Long
Date of Birth: December 10, 1923
Place of Birth: Kansas City, Missouri
Date of Death: February 12, 1951
Place of Death: Near Hoengseon, South Korea
Decorations and Honors: Medal of Honor, posthumously
Place of Burial: Mount Washington Cemetery in Independence, Missouri, Garden of Valor Section

Sergeant Charles R. Long served with Company M, 38th Infantry Regiment, 2nd Infantry Division.

His Medal of Honor citation for action during the Korean War reads as follows:

Sergeant Long, a member of Company M, distinguished himself by conspicuous gallantry and intrepidity above and beyond the call of duty in action against an armed enemy of the United Nations. When Company M, in a defensive perimeter on Hill 300, was viciously attacked by a numerically superior hostile force at approximately 0300 hours and ordered to withdraw, Sergeant Long, a forward observer for the mortar platoon, voluntarily remained at his post to provide cover by directing mortar fire on the enemy. Maintaining radio contact with his platoon, Sergeant Long coolly directed accurate mortar fire on the advancing foe. He continued firing his carbine and throwing hand grenades until his position was surrounded and he was mortally wounded. Sergeant Long's inspirational, valorous action halted the onslaught, exacted a heavy toll of enemy casualties, and enabled his company to withdraw, reorganize, counterattack, and regain the hill strongpoint. His unflinching courage and noble self-sacrifice reflect the highest credit on himself and are in keeping with the honored traditions of the military service.

Camp Page

Location: Chuncheon, Gangwon Province, South Korea
Status: Active
Named for: Lieutenant Colonel John Upshur Dennis Page
Date of Birth: February 8, 1904
Place of Birth: Luzon, Philippines
Date of Death: December 10, 1950
Place of Death: near Chosin Reservoir in Korea

Decorations and Honors: Medal of Honor; Navy Cross, both posthumously
Place of Burial: Arlington National Cemetery, Section 4, Lot 2743

Lieutenant Colonel John Upshur Dennis Page served with X Corps Artillery, attached to the 52nd Transportation Truck Battalion.

His Medal of Honor citation for action during the Korean War reads as follows:

Lieutenant Colonel Page, a member of X Corps Artillery, distinguished himself by conspicuous gallantry and intrepidity in action above and beyond the call of duty in a series of exploits. On November 29, Lieutenant Colonel Page left X Corps Headquarters at Hamhung with the mission of establishing traffic control on the main supply route to 1st Marine Division positions and those of some Army elements on the Chosin Reservoir plateau. Having completed his mission, Lieutenant Colonel Page was free to return to the safety of Hamhung but chose to remain on the plateau to aid an isolated signal station, thus being cut off with elements of the marine division. After rescuing his jeep driver by breaking up an ambush near a destroyed bridge Lieutenant Colonel Page reached the lines of a surrounded marine garrison at Koto-ri. He then voluntarily developed and trained a reserve force of assorted army troops trapped with the marines. By exemplary leadership and tireless devotion he made an effective tactical unit available. In order that casualties might be evacuated, an airstrip was improvised on frozen ground partly outside of the Koto-ri defense perimeter, which was continually under enemy attack. During two such attacks, Lieutenant Colonel Page exposed himself on the airstrip to direct fire on the enemy, and twice mounted the rear deck of a tank, manning the machine gun on the turret to drive the enemy back into a no man's land. On December 3 while being flown low over enemy lines in a light observation plane, Lieutenant Colonel Page dropped hand grenades on Chinese positions and sprayed foxholes with automatic fire from his carbine. After ten days of constant fighting, the marine and army units in the vicinity of the Chosin Reservoir had succeeded in gathering at the edge of the plateau and Lieutenant Colonel Page was flown to Hamhung to arrange for artillery support of the beleaguered troops attempting to break out. Again Lieutenant Colonel Page refused an opportunity to remain in safety and returned to give every assistance to his comrades. As the column slowly moved south, Lieutenant Colonel Page joined the rear guard. When it neared the entrance to a narrow pass it came under frequent attacks on both flanks. Mounting an abandoned tank, Lieutenant Colonel Page manned the machine gun, braved heavy return fire, and covered the passing vehicles until the danger diminished. Later, when another attack threatened his section of the convoy, then in the middle of the pass, Lieutenant Colonel Page took a machine gun to the hillside and delivered effective counterfire, remaining exposed while men and vehicles passed through the ambuscade. On the night of December 10, the convoy reached the bottom of the pass but was halted by a strong enemy force at the front and on both flanks. Deadly small-arms fire poured into the column. Realizing the danger to the column as it lay motionless, Lieutenant Colonel Page fought his way to the head of the column and plunged forward into the heart of the hostile position. His intrepid action so surprised the enemy that their ranks became disordered and suffered heavy casualties. Heedless of his safety, as he had been throughout the preceding ten days, Lieutenant Colonel Page remained forward, fiercely engaging the enemy single-handed until mortally wounded. By his valiant and aggressive spirit Lieutenant Colonel Page enabled friendly forces to stand off the enemy. His outstanding courage, unswerving devotion to duty, and supreme self-sacrifice reflect great credit upon Lieutenant Colonel Page and are in the highest tradition of the military service.

Camp Red Cloud

Location: Uijeongbu-si, Gyeonggi-do Province, South Korea
Status: Active
Named for: Corporal Mitchell Red Cloud, Jr.
Date of Birth: July 2, 1924
Place of Birth: Hatfield, Wisconsin
Date of Death: November 5, 1950
Place of Death: Chonghyon-dong, Korea
Decorations and Honors: Medal of Honor, posthumously
Place of Burial: Decorah Cemetery in Black Rivers Falls, Wisconsin

Corporal Mitchell Red Cloud, Jr., served with Company E, 19th Infantry Regiment, 24th Infantry Division. He also served with the U.S. Marines during World War II.
    His Medal of Honor citation for action during the Korean War reads as follows:

Corporal Red Cloud, Company E, distinguished himself by conspicuous gallantry and intrepidity above and beyond the call of duty in action against the enemy. From his position on the point of a ridge immediately in front of the company command post he was the first to detect the approach of the Chinese Communist forces and give the alarm as the enemy charged from a brush-covered area less than 100 feet from him. Springing up he delivered devastating pointblank automatic rifle fire into the advancing enemy. His accurate and intense fire checked this assault and gained time for the company to consolidate its defense. With utter fearlessness he maintained his firing position until severely wounded by enemy fire. Refusing assistance he pulled himself to his feet and wrapping his arm around a tree continued his deadly fire again, until he was fatally wounded. This heroic act stopped the enemy from overrunning his company's position and gained time for reorganization and evacuation of the wounded. Corporal Red Cloud's dauntless courage and gallant self-sacrifice reflects the highest credit upon himself and upholds the esteemed traditions of the U.S. Army.

General Omar N. Bradley presented his Medal of Honor award to Red Cloud's mother at the Pentagon on April 3, 1951.

Camp Sears

Location: Uijeongbu-si, Gyeonggi-do Province, South Korea
Status: Active
Named for: Sergeant First Class Jerome F. Sears
Date of Birth: 1928
Place of Birth: Buffalo, New York
Date of Death: June 9, 1952
Place of Death: Sidamak, Korea
Decorations and Honors: Distinguished Service Cross; Silver Star, both posthumously

Sergeant First Class Jerome F. Sears, a platoon sergeant, was taken prisoner and killed in the battle of Old Baldy. He was found shot in cold blood with his hands tied behind his back with commo wire.

Sears attended Grant and Cleveland high schools in Portland, Oregon. He enlisted in the U.S. Army after college in 1950 and was assigned to the Far East Command in 1951 where he saw combat in Korea. Sears Hall at the U.S. Army Reserve Center at the National Guard Armory in Portland, Oregon, is also named in his honor.

His Distinguished Service Cross citation for action during the Korean War reads as follows:

The Distinguished Service Cross is awarded to Sergeant First Class Jerome F. Sears, United States Army, for extraordinary heroism in action while serving with an infantry company in the vicinity of Sidamak, Korea, on June 8, 1952. On that date, the company of which Sergeant Sears was a member was ordered to occupy and hold a hill recently captured by friendly forces. Sergeant Sears acted as an artillery observer with a small screening party located in positions approximately two hundred yards forward of the friendly perimeter. That evening, although he could have returned to the main unit, Sergeant Sears voluntarily remained with the small party in its advance position. Early the following morning, the friendly troops were hit by an intense hostile artillery and mortar bombardment. Painfully wounded by flying shrapnel, Sergeant Sears nevertheless remained at his post, offering advice and encouragement to his men. Suddenly he saw an enemy force advancing recklessly through the exploding shells and shouted to his comrades to get ready to meet the attack. As wave after wave of enemy troops appeared, charging fanatically toward the friendly positions, Sergeant Sears realized his small party would be engulfed and annihilated if they attempted to overcome the vast numerical superiority of the enemy. Shouting to his men to move back, he remained at his post and began to fire rapidly and accurately into the ranks of the advancing enemy. With complete disregard for his personal safety, he continued to cover the withdrawal of his men until the foe overran his position and ended his courageous stand.

Camp Walker

Location: Taegu (or Daegu), South Korea
Status: Unknown
Named for: Lieutenant General Walton Harris Walker
Date of Birth: December 3, 1889
Place of Birth: Belton, Texas
Date of Death: December 23, 1950
Place of Death: Uijeongbu-si, South Korea
Decorations and Honors: Distinguished Service Cross with bronze oak leaf cluster; Distinguished Service Medal with bronze oak leaf cluster; Silver Star with two bronze oak leaf clusters; Legion of Merit; Distinguished Flying Cross with bronze oak leaf cluster; Bronze Star; Air Medal with two silver oak leaf clusters and one bronze oak leaf cluster; American Defense Service Medal; American Campaign Medal; National Defense Service Medal; World War I Victory Medal with five stars and two clasps; World War II Victory Medal; Honorary Citizen of Angers, City of Luxembourg, Chartres, Chateau-Thierry, Epernay, Fontainebleau, Mélun, Metz, Reims, Saint Symphorien, Thionville, Verdun
Place of Burial: Arlington National Cemetery, Section 34, Site 86-A

Lieutenant General Walton Harris Walker served in the Veracruz Expedition, World War I, World War II, and in Korea. He commanded the 3rd Armored Division, Fifth and Eighth Army, and IV Armored Corps and XX Corps.

Walker graduated from West Point in 1912. In 1917, he organized Company A, 13th Machine Gun Battalion, and fought at Saint Mihiel and Meuse-Argonne where he was cited twice for gallantry.

During World War II, he took part in the Normandy Invasion, the capture of Metz, and the liberation of Buchenwald. On July 1950, Walker was placed in charge of all U.S. Army and South Korean forces in Korea. As commander, he led the Eighth Army across the 38th Parallel into North Korea and captured the North Korean capital of Pyongyang on October 20. During his service in Korea, he fought in the defense of the Naktong Line and was responsible for holding the Pusan Perimeter, a small corner on the southeast side of the Korean peninsula.

He was killed while on his way to an awards ceremony to decorate soldiers of his Eighth Army when his jeep collided with a civilian truck as he tried passing a stalled column of South Korean Army vehicles near Seoul.

He carried the nickname "Johnnie Walker" for the brand of scotch whiskey he drank. He was promoted to lieutenant general in 1945, with the same stars, which General George S. Patton, Jr. had received from General Dwight D. Eisenhower on his own promotion. He was promoted to general, posthumously.

Walker was married to Caroline Victoria Emerson of Baltimore.

His Distinguished Service Cross citation for action during the battles of Saint Mihiel and Meuse-Argonne reads as follows:

Major General Walton H. Walker, United States Army, for extraordinary heroism in connection with military operations against an armed enemy of the United States. On August 23, 1944, Major General Walton H. Walker, Commanding General, XX United States Army Corps, with complete disregard for his own safety, personally directed the successful operation, which established a bridgehead across the Seine River near Melun, France. By his continuous presence with the forward elements of his command, as well as exemplary judgment and leadership, he inspired his command in effecting an early crossing of the Seine River and the continuance of the attack eastward. General Walker's contact with the forward combat troops was maintained in the face of heavy enemy fire. He repeatedly exposed himself to this enemy fire, encouraging the troops to move forward and by doing so gave them the required confidence to continue their advance. When certain elements were halted by intense enemy fire, he courageously assumed personal command and through his own supervision, force and persuasion, although he himself was in complete view of the enemy, caused the troops to effect the crossing of the river. By his intrepid direction, heroic leadership and superior tactical knowledge and ability, General Walker set an inspiring example for his command, reflecting the highest traditions of the armed forces.

His second Distinguished Service Cross citation for action during the Korean War reads as follows:

The Distinguished Service Cross is awarded to Lieutenant General Walton H. Walker, United States Army, for extraordinary heroism in action while serving as Commanding General of the 8th United States Army from July 14 to September 28, 1950. During this campaign, General Walker personally, and at great risk to his own life from enemy ground fire, performed repeated aerial reconnaissance flights in unarmed plane deep into enemy territory. The knowledge gained by General Walker from these flights was of inestimable value to him in making tactical decisions, and contributed greatly to the accomplishment of his mission in spite of the preponderance of force possessed by the enemy. In addition to the above, and with personal disregard, not only of health of, but life itself, he spent hour after hour and day after day on the battlefield, inspiring the United Nations forces with his own courage and his will to fight. Where acts of personal courage were common, General Walker's fearlessness and courageous leadership were outstanding.

United States Marine Corps

The Soldier's Prayer

"And When He Gets To Heaven,
To Saint Peter He Will Tell;
One More Marine Reporting Sir,
I've Served My Time In Hell."

—*Marine grave inscription on Guadalcanal, 1942*

CHAPTER 8

United States Marine Corps

Archibald Field

Location: Managua, Nicaragua
Status: Closed
Named for: Captain Robert James Archibald
Date of Birth: April 27, 1892
Place of Birth: Wheeling, West Virginia
Date of Death: November 1, 1928
Place of Death: Managua, Nicaragua
Decorations and Honors: Navy Cross; Purple Heart
Place of Burial: Arlington National Cemetery, Section 6, Site 8426

Captain Robert James Archibald was an aviator who selected the location for airfields in Nicaragua. He was killed in the line of duty.

His Navy Cross citation reads as follows:

The Navy Cross is presented to Robert J. Archibald, Captain, U.S. Marine Corps, for distinguished service in the line of his profession as an aviator attached to the Second Brigade, U.S. Marine Corps operating in the Republic of Nicaragua from March 1927 to July 1928. Captain Archibald worked unceasingly under the most trying weather conditions, keeping the material in his charge in order and operating against armed groups of bandits in the vicinity of Nueva Segovia. He assisted and cooperated with the ground forces in every way possible, and by his acts of valor inspired all members of the Brigade.

★★★

Bauer Field

Location: Vila, New Hebrides Island
Status: Closed
Named for: Lieutenant Colonel Harold William "Indian Joe" Bauer
Date of Birth: November 20, 1908
Place of Birth: Woodruff, Kansas
Date of Death: November 14, 1942
Place of Death: Near the Solomon Islands
Decorations and Honors: Medal of Honor, posthumously; Purple Heart; Presidential Unit Citation; American Defense Service Medal; Asiatic-Pacific Campaign Medal with battle star; World War II Victory Medal; Letter of Commendation Ribbon
Place of Burial: Memorialized at Manila American Cemetery and Memorial in Manila, Philippines

Lieutenant Colonel Harold William Bauer was a Marine Corps aviator who shot down eleven Japanese planes over Guadalcanal.

Bauer graduated from the United States Naval Academy at Annapolis, Maryland, on June 5, 1930, where he was considered an outstanding athlete, playing football, basketball, and lacrosse. He later became an assistant basketball and lacrosse coach and a marksmanship instructor at the academy.

His first sea duty was aboard the cruiser USS *San Francisco*. He was assigned to Naval Air Station Pensacola, Florida, in December 1934 for flight training. As a major, he was assigned to Hawaii to take command of VMF 212, the first U.S. Marine fighter unit to reach the South Pacific.

He was shot down while engaged in an air battle and was last seen in the water wearing a Mae West life preserver. Days of searching the sea and nearby islands failed to locate any trace of him. In May 1947, Bauer was posthumously promoted to the rank of colonel.

He got the nickname "Indian Joe" from the chaplain at the United States Naval Academy who referred to Harold as "Holy Joe." He was married to Harriette Hemman.

His Medal of Honor citation for action during World War II reads as follows:

For extraordinary heroism and conspicuous courage as Squadron Commander of Marine Fighting Squadron 212 in the South Pacific Area during the period May 10 to November 14, 1942. Volunteering to pilot a fighter plane in defense of our positions on Guadalcanal, Lieutenant Colonel Bauer participated in two air battles against enemy bombers and fighters outnumbering our force more than two to one, boldly engaged the enemy and destroyed one Japanese bomber in the engagement of September 28 and shot down four enemy fighter planes in flames on October 3, leaving a fifth smoking badly. After successfully leading twenty-six planes on an over-water ferry flight of more than 600 miles on October 16, Lieutenant Colonel Bauer, while circling to land, sighted a squadron of enemy planes attacking the USS *McFarland*. Undaunted by the formidable opposition and with valor above and beyond the call of duty, he engaged the entire squadron and, although alone and his fuel supply nearly exhausted, fought his plane so brilliantly that four of the Japanese planes were destroyed before he was forced down by lack of fuel. His intrepid fighting spirit and distinctive ability as a leader and an airman, exemplified in his splendid record of combat achievement, were vital factors in the successful operations in the South Pacific Area.

Byrd Field

Located: Puerto Cabezas, Nicaragua
Status: Closed
Named for: Captain William Carl Byrd
Date of Birth: September 29, 1896
Place of Birth: Greenwood, South Carolina
Date of Death: March 8, 1928
Place of Death: Esteli, Nicaragua
Place of Burial: Arlington National Cemetery, Section 5-E, Site 2830

Captain William Carl Byrd was a naval aviator.
   Byrd was a graduate of the Citadel in Charleston, South Carolina, and was commissioned in the U.S. Marine Corps on October 29, 1916. During his career, he served in Santiago, Chile; at the U.S. Marine Barracks in Quantico, Virginia; Santo Domingo; and with the American Legation in Managua, Nicaragua. He was also assigned as the adjutant of Company Headquarters, Aircraft Squadron, where he was an instructor. In 1927, after flight training, he received his pilot wings as naval aviator number 30. Byrd died in an airplane crash while attached to an observation squadron.

Camp Butler

Location: Okinawa
Status: Active
Named for: Major General Smedley Darlington Butler
Date of Birth: July 30, 1881
Place of Birth: West Chester, Pennsylvania
Date of Death: June 21, 1940
Place of Death: U.S. Naval Hospital in Philadelphia, Pennsylvania

Decorations and Honors: Two Medals of Honor; Army Distinguished Service Medal; Navy Distinguished Service Medal; French Order of the Black Star; Marine Corps Brevet Medal*
Place of Burial: West Chester, Pennsylvania

Major General Smedley Darlington Butler, whose military career spanned thirty-three years, was known by thousands of U.S. Marines as "Ol' Gimlet Eye" and was one of only two U.S. Marines to receive the Medal of Honor twice.

Butler served during the Boxer Rebellion in China in 1900, the Philippine Insurrection, and World War I.

His first Medal of Honor citation for action at Veracruz reads as follows:

For distinguished conduct in battle, engagement of Veracruz, April 22, 1914. Major Butler was eminent and conspicuous in command of his battalion. He exhibited courage and skill in leading his men through the action of the 22nd and in the final occupation of the city.

His second Medal of Honor citation for action in Haiti reads as follows:

As Commanding Officer of detachments from the 5th, 13th, 23rd Companies and the marine and sailor detachment from the USS *Connecticut*, Major Butler led the attack on Fort Riviere, Haiti, November 17, 1915. Following a concentrated drive, several different detachments of marines gradually closed in on the old French bastion fort in an effort to cut off all avenues of retreat for the Caco bandits. Reaching the fort on the southern side where there was a small opening in the wall, Major Butler gave the signal to attack and marines from the 15th Company poured through the breach, engaged the Cacos in hand-to-hand combat, took the bastion, and crushed the Caco resistance. Throughout this perilous action, Major Butler was conspicuous for his bravery and forceful leadership.

"War is a racket. It always has been. It is possibly the oldest, easily the most profitable, surely the most vicious." —*General Smedley Butler*

* Marine Corps Brevet Medal is awarded to U.S. Marine officers who displayed bravery under fire. At that time, officers were not authorized the Medal of Honor. Only twenty-two of these medals were ever issued.

Camp Courtney

Location: Okinawa
Status: Active
Named for: Major Henry Alexius Courtney, Jr.
Date of Birth: January 6, 1916
Place of Birth: Duluth, Minnesota

Date of Death: May 15, 1945
Place of Death: Okinawa in the Ryukyu Islands
Decorations and Honors: Medal of Honor, posthumously; Purple Heart; Gold Star
Place of Burial: Calvary Cemetery in Duluth, Minnesota

Major Henry Alexius Courtney, Jr., was an executive officer with the 22nd Marines, 6th Marine Division.

Courtney received a bachelor's degree from the University of Minnesota and a doctoral degree from Loyola University in Chicago, Illinois, and was admitted to the bar in Minnesota and Illinois. He was commissioned a second lieutenant in the Marine Corps Reserve and commanded the Duluth unit of the Marine Corps Reserve. He also served at Guadalcanal in the Solomon Islands, participated in the first United States offensive of World War II, and commanded a company of the 1st Marine Division.

His Medal of Honor citation for action during World War II reads as follows:

For conspicuous gallantry and intrepidity at the risk of his life above and beyond the call of duty as Executive Officer of the 2nd Battalion, 22nd Marines, 6th Marine Division, in action against enemy Japanese forces on Okinawa Shima in the Ryukyu Islands, May 14 and 15, 1945. Ordered to hold for the night in static defense behind Sugar Loaf Hill after leading the forward elements of his command in a prolonged fire fight, Major Courtney weighed the effect of a hostile night counterattack against the tactical value of an immediate marine assault, resolved to initiate the assault, and promptly obtained permission to advance and seize the forward slope of the hill. Quickly explaining the situation to his small remaining force, he declared his personal intention of moving forward and then proceeded on his way, boldly blasting nearby cave positions and neutralizing enemy guns as he went. Inspired by his courage, every man followed without hesitation, and together the intrepid marines braved a terrific concentration of Japanese gunfire to skirt the hill on the right and reach the reverse slope. Temporarily halting, Major Courtney sent guides to the rear for more ammunition and possible replacements. Subsequently reinforced by 26 men and an LVT load of grenades, he determined to storm the crest of the hill and crush any planned counterattack before it could gain sufficient momentum to effect a breakthrough. Leading his men by example rather than by command, he pushed ahead with unrelenting aggressiveness, hurling grenades into cave openings on the slope with devastating effect. Upon reaching the crest and observing large numbers of Japanese forming for action less than 100 yards away, he instantly attacked, waged a furious battle and succeeded in killing many of the enemy and in forcing the remainder to take cover in the caves. Determined to hold, he ordered his men to dig in and, coolly disregarding the continuous hail of flying enemy shrapnel to rally his weary troops, tirelessly aided casualties and assigned his men to more advantageous positions. Although instantly killed by a hostile mortar burst while moving among his men, Major Courtney, by his astute military acumen, indomitable leadership and decisive action in the face of overwhelming odds, had contributed essentially to the success of the Okinawa campaign. His great personal valor throughout sustained and enhanced the highest traditions of the U.S. Naval Service. He gallantly gave his life for his country.

Camp Elliott (formerly, Camp Holcomb)

Location: San Diego, California
Status: Now, belongs to the city of San Diego
Named for: Major General George Frank Elliott
Date of Birth: November 30, 1846
Place of Birth: Eutaw, Alabama
Date of Death: November 4, 1931
Place of Death: Washington, D.C.
Date of Retirement: November 1910
Place of Burial: Arlington National Cemetery, Section 2, Site 845

Major General George Frank Elliott was the U.S. Marine Corps' tenth commandant.

Elliott was appointed to the rank of second lieutenant in the Marine Corps in October 1870. His first assignment was at the Marine Barracks in Washington, D.C. His early sea duty was aboard the battleship USS *Vermont*; the schooner USS *Frolic*; and the sloop USS *Monongahela*. He served with the U.S. Marine battalion sent to the Isthmus of Panama in 1885.

In 1894, as a U.S. Marine fleet officer aboard the cruiser USS *Baltimore*, he was sent to China to protect the U.S. Legation in Seoul, Korea, where the Chinese-Japanese War threatened neutral countries. He served in Cuba during the Spanish-American War and distinguished himself at Guantanamo. In March 1899, he commanded the 2nd Battalion during the Philippine Insurrection and from October to January 1900, he led the 1st Brigade to victory at the battle of Noveleta.

In October 1903, he was appointed commandant of the Marine Corps with the rank of brigadier general. From December 1903 to January 1904, he commanded the Marine Corps Expeditionary Force on the Isthmus of Panama following the Panamanian revolt against Colombia. Afterward, he relinquished command of the brigade and resumed his duties at Headquarters Marine Corps.

On May 21, 1908, he was appointed major general commandant of the Marine Corps. During his tenure as commandant, he was successful in preventing the merging of seagoing marines into the U.S. Army. Elliott died at his home after a brief illness.

The USS *George F. Elliott* (AP-13), a Heywood-class transport, was also named in his honor.

Camp Elmore

Location: Norfolk, Virginia
Status: Active
Named for: Private First Class George William Elmore
Date of Birth: ca. 1931
Place of Birth: Plasterco, Virginia
Date of Death: February 26, 1951
Place of Death: Korea
Decorations and Honors: Navy Cross, posthumously

Private First Class George William Elmore was an automatic rifleman with Company G, 3rd Battalion, 5th Marines, 1st Marine Division, that was cut off by Communist forces in Korea.

His Navy Cross citation for action during the Korean War reads as follows:

For extraordinary heroism in action against the enemy. Private First Class Elmore was serving as an automatic rifleman with a combat patrol, which was subjected to intense and accurate enemy automatic weapons, small arms, and hand grenade fire, causing numerous casualties. With complete disregard for his personal safety, he fearlessly exposed himself to the heavy enemy fire to reach a position from which he could effectively engage the enemy and permit the wounded to be evacuated. Courageously refusing to seek safely for himself until his wounded comrades had reached safety, he was seriously wounded by enemy fire, and later died, gallantly giving his life for his country. His great personal bravery was an inspiration to all members of the command. Private First Class Elmore's display of outstanding courage and devotion to duty were in keeping with the highest traditions of the United States Naval Service.

Camp Foster

Location: Okinawa
Status: Active
Named for: Private First Class William Adelbert Foster
Date of Birth: February 17, 1917
Place of Birth: Cleveland, Ohio
Date of Death: May 2, 1945
Place of Death: Okinawa
Decorations and Honors: Medal of Honor; Purple Heart; Presidential Unit Citation with star; Asiatic-Pacific Campaign Medal with bronze star; World War II Victory Medal, posthumously
Place of Burial: Calvary Cemetery in Cleveland, Ohio

Private First Class William Adelbert Foster was a six-year veteran of the Ohio National Guard when he enlisted in the Marine Corps Reserve in 1944. After combat training at Camp Pendleton in California, he was assigned to overseas duty aboard the USS *General C. G. Morton* bound for the Russell Islands. There, he joined Company K, 3rd Battalion, 1st Marines, 1st Marine Division, on Okinawa on April 1, 1945, the first anniversary of his enlistment in the Marine Corps.

His Medal of Honor citation for action during World War II reads as follows:

For conspicuous gallantry and intrepidity at the risk of his life above and beyond the call of duty while serving as a rifleman with the 3rd Battalion, 1st Marines, 1st Marine Division, in action against enemy Japanese forces on Okinawa Shima in the Ryukyu Chain May 2, 1945. Dug in with another marine on the point of the perimeter defense after waging a furious assault against a strongly fortified Japanese position, Private First Class Foster and his comrade engaged in a fierce hand grenade duel with infiltrating enemy soldiers. Suddenly an enemy grenade landed beyond reach in the foxhole. Instantly diving on the deadly missile, Private First Class Foster absorbed the exploding charge in his own body, thereby protecting the other marine from serious injury. Although mortally wounded as a result of his heroic action, he quickly rallied, handed his own remaining two grenades to his comrade and said, "Make them count." Stouthearted and indomitable, he had unhesitatingly relinquished his own chance of survival that his fellow marine might carry on the relentless fight against a fanatic enemy, and his dauntless determination, cool decision and valiant spirit of self-sacrifice in the face of certain death reflect the highest credit upon Private First Class Foster and upon the U.S. Naval Service. He gallantly gave his life in the service of his country.

Camp Geiger

Location: Jacksonville, North Carolina
Status: Active
Named for: Lieutenant General Roy Stanley Geiger
Date of Birth: January 25, 1885
Place of Birth: Middleburg, Florida
Date of Death: January 23, 1947
Place of Death: National Naval Medical Center in Bethesda, Maryland
Decorations and Honors: Navy Cross with gold star; Navy Distinguished Service Medal with gold star; Army Distinguished Service Medal (Okinawa); Presidential Unit Citation (Guadalcanal, 1942); Nicaraguan Campaign Medal (1912); Expeditionary Medal with two bronze stars (Nicaragua, 1912, China, 1914, Haiti 1919 and 1929); World War I Victory Medal with

Ypres Lys clasp (1918); Haitian Campaign Medal (1919 and 1920); Second Nicaraguan Campaign Medal (1931); American Defense Service Medal; Asiatic-Pacific Campaign Medal; American Campaign Medal; World War II Victory Medal; Dominican Medal of Military Merit; Nicaraguan Medal of Distinction and Diploma

Place of Burial: Arlington National Cemetery, Section 2, Lot 4954

Lieutenant General Roy Stanley Geiger, commanding both air and ground units during World War II, directed the III Amphibious Corps during the battle of Okinawa, and was the first U.S. Marine to command the Tenth Army during World War II.

Geiger was commissioned a second lieutenant in 1909 and served as a member of the Marine Detachments aboard the battleships USS *Wisconsin* and the USS *Delaware*. In Nicaragua, he participated in the capture of Coyotepe and Barranca. He also saw duty in the Philippines and China with the 1st Brigade and with the Marine Detachment, American Legation in Peking, China, from 1913 to 1916. He was promoted to four-star general posthumously by the Eightieth Congress

His Navy Cross citation for action during World War I reads as follows:

The Navy Cross is presented to Roy Stanley Geiger, Captain, U.S. Marine Corps, for distinguished service in the line of his profession as Commanding Officer of Airplane Squadron No. 2, 1st Marine Aviation Force, attached to the Northern Bomb Group (USN), in which capacity he trained and led this Squadron on bombing raids against the enemy. His conduct throughout was in keeping with the highest traditions of the Navy of the United States.

His Distinguished Service Medal citation reads in part:

Going ashore with the early landing elements on April 1, 1945, he began a bitter three-month campaign . . . with outstanding professional skill, forceful leadership and unswerving determination, he directed his units . . . repeatedly disregarding personal safety to secure a first hand estimate of the battle situation and inspiring his men to heights of bravery and accomplishment.

His Gold Star citation reads as follows:

Despite almost continuous bombardment by enemy aircraft, hostile naval gunfire and shore-based artillery, the combined total of Army, Navy and Marine Corps units stationed at Guadalcanal under Major General Geiger's efficiently coordinated command succeeded in shooting down 268 Japanese planes in aerial combat and inflicting damage on a number estimated to be as great. . . . Sank six enemy vessels, including one heavy cruiser, possibly sank three destroyers and one heavy cruiser, and damaged eighteen other ships, including one heavy cruiser and five light cruisers.

Camp Gonsalves

Location: Okinawa
Status: Active
Named for: Private First Class Harold Gonsalves
Date of Birth: January 28, 1926
Place of Birth: Alameda, California
Date of Death: April 15, 1945
Place of Death: Okinawa
Decorations and Honors: Medal of Honor, posthumously
Place of Burial: Golden Gate National Cemetery in San Bruno, California

Private First Class Harold Gonsalves enlisted in the Marine Corps Reserve and was classified as a cannoneer. He was transferred to Hawaii and assigned to the 2nd Pack Howitzer Battalion, 22nd Marines. He participated in the assault, capture, and occupation of Engebi and Parry Islands in the Marshall Islands.

His Medal of Honor citation for action during World War II reads as follow:

For conspicuous gallantry and intrepidity at the risk of his life above and beyond the call of duty while serving as Acting Scout Sergeant with the 4th Battalion, 15th Marines, 6th Marine Division, during action against enemy Japanese forces on Okinawa Shima in the Ryukyu Chain, April 15, 1945. Undaunted by the powerfully organized opposition encountered on Motobu Peninsula during the fierce assault waged by his battalion against the Japanese stronghold at Mount Yaetake, Private First Class Gonsalves repeatedly braved the terrific enemy bombardment to aid his forward observation team in directing well-placed artillery fire. When his commanding officer determined to move into the front lines in order to register a more effective bombardment in the enemy's defensive position, he unhesitatingly advanced uphill with the officer and another Marine despite a slashing barrage of enemy mortar and rifle fire. As they reached the front and a Japanese grenade fell close within the group, instantly Private First Class Gonsalves dived on the deadly missile, absorbing the exploding charge in his own body and thereby protecting the others from serious and perhaps fatal wounds. Stouthearted and indomitable, Private First Class Gonsalves readily yielded his own chances of survival that his fellow marines might carry on the relentless battle against a fanatic enemy and his cool decision, prompt action and valiant spirit of self-sacrifice in the face of certain death reflect the highest credit upon himself and upon the U.S. Naval Service.

Camp H. M. Smith

Location: Oahu, Hawaii
Status: Active, Home of the Fleet Marine Force Pacific
Named for: General Holland McTyeire "Howling Mad" Smith
Date of Birth: April 20, 1882
Place of Birth: Seale, Alabama
Date of Death: January 12, 1967
Place of Death: U.S. Naval Hospital in San Diego, California
Decorations and Honors: Distinguished Service Medal with three gold stars; Purple Heart; French Croix de Guerre with palm (Belleau Wood); Meritorious Service Citation; Marine Corps Expeditionary Medal with three bronze stars; Mexican Service Medal; Dominican Campaign Medal; World War I Victory Medal with five sector clasps; Army of Occupation Medal (Germany); American Defense Service Medal with base clasp; American Campaign Medal; Asiatic-Pacific Campaign Medal with one silver star in lieu of five bronze stars; World War II Victory Medal; Dominican Order of the First Merit; British Order of Commander of the Bath
Date of Retirement: April 1946
Place of Burial: Fort Rosecrans National Cemetery in San Diego, California

General Holland McTyeire Smith, known as "the father of modern U.S. amphibious warfare," was considered one of America's top commanders in the Pacific during World War II.

Smith received a bachelor of science degree from Alabama Polytechnic Institute in 1901, obtained his bachelor of law degree from the University of Alabama in 1903, and practiced law in Montgomery, Alabama, before being appointed to the rank of second lieutenant in the Marine Corps on March 20, 1905. Smith served in the Philippines, Nicaragua, Santo Domingo, and with a marine brigade in France during World War I.

Smith commanded all expeditionary troops in the Mariana Islands, including those that recaptured Guam. He headed Task Force 56 at Iwo Jima where he commanded American ground forces at Iwo Jima and the Fleet Marine Forces.

His development of amphibious warfare concepts and his ability to direct the army, navy, and marine amphibious training was a major factor in the successful U.S. landings in both the Atlantic and Pacific. He also was responsible for preparing U.S. Army and Canadian troops for the Kiska and Attu landings.

Smith led the V Amphibious Corps in the assaults on the Gilbert and Marshall Islands and on Saipan and Tinian in the Marianas on November 20, 1943. He coauthored *Coral and Brass* (New York: C. Scribner's Sons, 1949). He was married to Ada Wilkinson.

Camp Hansen

Location: Okinawa
Status: Active
Named for: Private Dale Merlin Hansen
Date of Birth: December 13, 1922
Place of Birth: Wisner, Nebraska
Date of Death: May 11, 1945
Place of Death: Wana-Dakeshi Ridge, Okinawa
Decorations and Honors: Medal of Honor; Purple Heart, posthumously
Place of Burial: Wisner Cemetery in Wisner, Nebraska

Private Dale Merlin Hansen served with Company E, 2nd Battalion, 1st Marines, at Pavuvu in the Russell Islands.

He received bazooka training before sailing with the 1st Marine Division for maneuvers at Banika Island and Guadalcanal in February 1945. He landed on Okinawa with his unit on Easter Sunday, April 1.

Hansen lost his life on the first anniversary of his enlistment into the Marine Corps in the battle for Hill 60 on the southern part of the island.

His Medal of Honor citation for action during World War II reads as follows

For conspicuous gallantry and intrepidity at the risk of his life above and beyond the call of duty while serving with Company E, 2d Battalion, 1st Marines, 1st Marine Division, in action against enemy Japanese forces on Okinawa Shima in the Ryukyu Chain, May 7, 1945. Cool and courageous in combat, Private Hansen unhesitatingly took the initiative during a critical stage of the action and, armed with a rocket launcher, crawled to an exposed position where he attacked and destroyed a strategically located hostile pillbox. With his weapon subsequently destroyed by enemy fire, he seized a rifle and continued his one-man assault. Reaching the crest of a ridge, he leaped across, opened fire on six Japanese and killed four before his rifle jammed. Attacked by the remaining two Japanese, he beat them off with the butt of his rifle and then climbed back to cover. Promptly returning with another weapon and supply of grenades, he fearlessly advanced, destroyed a strong mortar position and annihilated eight more of the enemy. In the forefront of battle throughout this bitterly waged engagement, Private Hansen, by his indomitable determination, bold tactics and complete disregard of all personal danger, contributed essentially to the success of his company's mission and to the ultimate capture of this fiercely defended outpost of the Japanese Empire. His great personal valor in the face of extreme peril reflects the highest credit upon himself and the U.S. Naval Service.

Camp Holcomb

Location: San Diego, California
Status: Closed
Named for: General Thomas Holcomb
Date of Birth: August 5, 1879
Place of Birth: New Castle, Delaware
Date of Death: May 24, 1965
Place of Death: New Castle, Delaware
Decorations and Honors: Navy Cross; Distinguished Service Medal; Silver Star with three oak leaf clusters; Purple Heart; Expeditionary Medal (China); World War I Victory Medal; Army of Occupation Medal (Germany); American Defense Service Medal with base clasp; Asiatic-Pacific Campaign Medal with bronze star (Guadalcanal); American Campaign Medal; World War II Victory Medal; Legion of Honor; French Croix de Guerre with three palms; Knight Grand Cross (Netherlands); French Fourragère
Date of Retirement: January 1, 1944
Place of Burial: Arlington National Cemetery, Section 3, Site 2501

General Thomas Holcomb was the seventeenth commandant of the United States Marine Corps.

Holcomb received a direct commission to second lieutenant in the Marine Corps on April 13, 1900, and was assigned to the North Atlantic Fleet from September 1902 to April 1903. He served in the Philippine Islands and saw duty with the Legation Guard in Peking, China, from 1905 to 1906, and again from 1908 to 1910, where he served as attaché on the staff of the American Minister for study of the Chinese language. He served again in China from 1911 to 1914.

During World War I, Holcomb commanded the 2nd Battalion, 6th Marine Regiment, at the Marine Barracks in Quantico, Virginia. From February 1918 to July 1919, he served with the American Expeditionary Force in France, commanding the 2nd Battalion and the 6th Marine Regiment where he saw action in the Aisne defensive (Chateau Thierry), the Aisne-Marne offensive (Soissons), the Marbache Sector, the Saint Mihiel offensive, the Meuse-Argonne offensive (Champagne), and the Meuse-Argonne offensive (Argonne Forest).

Following his duties as commander of the Marine Barracks at the Naval Station at Guantanamo Bay, Cuba, from 1922 to 1924, he attended the Command and General Staff College at Fort Leavenworth in Kansas City, Kansas, where he was a distinguished graduate. From June 1925 to June 1927, he was assigned to Headquarters Marine Corps for duty in the Division of Operations and Training. From August 1927 to February 1930, he returned to China where he commanded the Marine Detachment, American Legation, in Peking. In June 1930, he attended the Naval War College, and, in June 1931, the Army War

College. From June 1932 to January 1935, he served in the Office of Naval Operations, Navy Department.

Holcomb was promoted to lieutenant general on January 20, 1942, to become the highest-ranking officer ever to command the Marine Corps. In that position, he increased the strength of the Marine Corps from 16,000 to 300,000 members, and in February 1943, under his leadership, women became eligible to serve in the Marine Corps. By a special act of Congress, he was promoted to the rank of general, the first marine ever to hold that rank.

After retiring, he was nominated for the position of United States Minister to the Union of South Africa and served in that position from March 9, 1944, to June 15, 1948. He was married to Beatrice Miller Clover of Washington, D.C.

Camp Howard

Location: San Diego, California
Status: Closed
Named for: Admiral Thomas Benton Howard, USN
Date of Birth: August 10, 1854
Place of Birth: Illinois
Date of Death: November 10, 1920
Place of Death: Annapolis, Maryland
Date of Retirement: August 10, 1916

Admiral Thomas Benton Howard was commander in chief of the Pacific Fleet in 1914.

Howard graduated from the United States Naval Academy at Annapolis, Maryland, in 1873. During his career, he served at the battle of Manila Bay and was the commander of the frigate USS *Chesapeake*, monitor USS *Nevada*, cruiser USS *Olympia*, and battleships USS *Tennessee* and USS *Ohio*. As captain of the USS *Ohio*, he sailed around the world with the 3rd Division of the Great White Fleet from 1908 to 1909.

In 1915, he became the fifth full admiral in the history of the U.S. Navy. From March 31, 1917, to March 4, 1919, Howard was superintendent of the U.S. Naval Observatory.

Camp Johnson

Location: Jacksonville, North Carolina
Status: Active
Named for: Sergeant Major Gilbert Hubert "Hashmark" Johnson

Date of Birth: October 30, 1905
Place of Birth: Mount Hebron, Alabama
Date of Death: August 5, 1972
Place of Death: Jacksonville, North Carolina
Date of Retirement: 1959
Place of Burial: Arlington national Cemetery, Section S2, Site 288

Sergeant Major Gilbert Hubert Johnson was one of the first African Americans to enlist in the U.S. Marine Corps who went on to become one of the first black marine drill instructors and the first sergeant major in the U.S. Marine Corps.

Johnson attended Stillman College in 1922, but left college to join the army. He was discharged in October 1929, and reenlisted in the navy four years later and was assigned to the Steward's Branch, the only branch available to blacks at that time. He served there for nearly ten years before serving aboard the battleship USS *Wyoming,* during the bombing of Pearl Harbor.

When the armed forces were integrated in 1954, Johnson requested transfer from the navy to the Marine Corps where he served the last seventeen years of his thirty-two-year military career. He served as field sergeant in charge of all recruit training at Montford Point in North Carolina. As a member of the 52nd Defense Battalion on Guam in World War II, Johnson requested that black marines be assigned to combat patrols. With approval, he personally led patrols in twenty-five combat missions.

During his assignment in Korea, Johnson served with the 1st Shore Party Battalion; the 2nd Battalion, 1st Marines; and, finally, as administrative advisor at the headquarters of the Republic of Korea Marine Corps. He died of a heart attack while addressing an annual meeting of the Montford Point Marine Association.

He was given the nickname "Hashmark" because of the number of stripes he wore on his sleeve representing his many years of service.

Camp Kinser

Location: Okinawa
Status: Active
Named for: Sergeant Elbert Luther Kinser
Date of Birth: October 21, 1922
Place of Birth: Greenville, Tennessee
Date of Death: May 4, 1945
Place of Death: Okinawa
Decorations and Honors: Medal of Honor, posthumously; Purple Heart; Presidential Unit Citation (awarded the 1st Marine Division); Asiatic-Pacific Campaign Medal; the World War II Victory Medal

Place of Burial: Greenville, Tennessee

Sergeant Elbert Luther Kinser enlisted in the U.S. Marine Corps in December 1942, and after boot training at Parris Island, South Carolina, he was assigned to the 7th Replacement Battalion in Pago Pago, Tutuila, American Samoa. He was later assigned to Company I, 1st Marines, and saw action with the 1st Marines at Cape Gloucester, New Britain, and later at Peleliu in the Palau Islands, and Okinawa.

His Medal of Honor citation for action during World War II reads as follows:

For conspicuous gallantry and intrepidity at the risk of his life above and beyond the call of duty while acting as leader of a Rifle Platoon, serving with Company I, 3rd Battalion, 1st Marines, 1st Marine Division, in action against Japanese forces on Okinawa Shima in the Ryukyu Chain, May 4, 1945. Taken under sudden, close attack by hostile troops entrenched on the reverse slope while moving up a strategic ridge along which his platoon was holding newly won positions, Sergeant Kinser engaged the enemy in a fierce hand grenade battle. Quick to act when a Japanese grenade landed in the immediate vicinity, Sergeant Kinser unhesitatingly threw himself on the deadly missile, absorbing the full charge of the shattering explosion in his own body and thereby protecting his men from serious injury and possible death. Stouthearted and indomitable, he had yielded his own chance of survival that his comrades might live to carry on the relentless battle against a fanatic enemy. His courage, cool decision and valiant spirit of self-sacrifice in the face of certain death sustained and enhanced the highest traditions of the U.S. Naval Service. He gallantly gave his life for his country.

Camp Lejeune

Location: Jacksonville, North Carolina
Status: Active
Named for: Lieutenant General John Archer Lejeune
Date of Birth: January 10, 1867
Place of Birth: Pointe Coupee, Louisiana
Date of Death: November 20, 1942
Place of Death: Union Memorial Hospital in Baltimore, Maryland
Decorations and Honors: Navy Distinguished Service Medal; Army Distinguished Service Medal; Sampson Medal (USS *Cincinnati*); Spanish Campaign Medal; Marine Corps Expeditionary Medal with three bronze stars (Panama, Cuba, and the Dominican Republic); Mexican Service Medal; World War I Victory Medal with defensive sector clasp (Saint Mihiel, Champagne, Meuse-Argonne); Second Nicaraguan Campaign Medal;

French Legion of Honor (Commander); French Croix de Guerre with palm
Place of Burial: Arlington National Cemetery, Section 6, Lot 5682

Lieutenant General John Archer Lejeune, known as "the greatest of all Leathernecks," served for more than forty years with the U.S. Marine Corps and was the first marine officer to command an army division in combat and was the thirteenth commandant of the Marine Corps.

Lejeune graduated from the United States Naval Academy at Annapolis, Maryland, in 1888 and was commissioned a second lieutenant in the Marine Corps in 1890. He was a superintendent of the Virginia Military Institute and is credited with making scarlet and gold the Marine Corps' official colors. He saw action in the Spanish-American War aboard the cruiser USS *Cincinnati*; was sent to Panama in 1903; commanded the Marine Barracks, Navy Yard at Cavite in the Philippine Islands; and later, commanded the 1st Brigade of Marines in the Philippines.

As a lieutenant colonel, he served in Cuba with the 2nd Provisional Brigade Marines in 1912, and then in Veracruz, Mexico, with the 2nd Advanced Base Regiment. Lejeune assumed command of the Marine Barracks in Quantico, Virginia, in 1917 and again in 1919.

Camp Lester

Location: Okinawa
Status: Active
Named for: Hospital Apprentice First Class Fred Faulkner Lester, USN
Date of Birth: April 29, 1926
Place of Birth: Downers Grove, Illinois
Date of Death: June 8, 1945
Place of Death: Okinawa
Decorations and Honors: Medal of Honor, posthumously

Hospital Apprentice First Class Fred Faulkner Lester served as a hospital corpsman during the Okinawa campaign.

Lester enlisted in the U.S. Naval Reserve as an Apprentice Seaman. After basic and advanced training, he enrolled as a student at the Hospital Corps School in San Diego, California. After completing his training there, he reported to Fleet Marine Force at Camp Elliott in California where he joined the 1st Battalion, 22nd Marines, 6th Marine Division.

His Medal of Honor citation for action during World War II reads as follows:

For conspicuous gallantry and intrepidity at the risk of his life above and beyond the call of duty while serving as a Medical Corpsman with an Assault Rifle Platoon, attached to the 1st Battalion, 22nd Marines, 6th Marine Division, during action against enemy Japanese forces on Okinawa Shima in the Ryukyu Chain, June 8, 1945. Quick to spot a wounded marine lying in an open field beyond the front lines following the relentless assault against a strategic Japanese hill position, Lester unhesitatingly crawled toward the casualty under a concentrated barrage from hostile machine guns, rifles, and grenades. Torn by enemy rifle bullets as he inched forward, he stoically disregarded the mounting fury of Japanese fire and his own pain to pull the wounded man toward a covered position. Struck by enemy fire a second time before he reached cover, he exerted tremendous effort and succeeded in pulling his comrade to safety where, too seriously wounded himself to administer aid, he instructed two of his squad in proper medical treatment of the rescued marine. Realizing that his own wounds were fatal, he staunchly refused medical attention for himself and, gathering his fast-waning strength with calm determination, coolly and expertly directed his men in the treatment of two other wounded marines, succumbing shortly thereafter. Completely selfless in his concern for the welfare of his fighting comrades, Lester, by his indomitable spirit, outstanding valor, and competent direction of others, had saved the life of one who otherwise must have perished and had contributed to the safety of countless others. Lester's fortitude in the face of certain death sustains and enhances the highest traditions of the U.S. Naval Service. He gallantly gave his life for his country.

The USS *Lester* (DE-1022) a Dealey-class destroyer escort was also named in his honor.

Camp McCutcheon

Location: New River, North Carolina
Status: Active
Named for: General Keith Barr McCutcheon
Date of Birth: August 10, 1915
Place of Birth: East Liverpool, Ohio
Date of Death: July 13, 1971
Place of Death: National Naval Medical Center in Bethesda, Maryland
Decorations and Honors: Distinguished Service Medal with two gold stars; Silver Star; Legion of Merit with combat V device and two gold stars; Distinguished Flying Cross; Air Medal with nine oak leaf clusters; three Navy Unit Commendations; American Defense Service Medal with base clasp; American Campaign Medal; Asiatic-Pacific Campaign Medal with three bronze stars; World War II Victory Medal; Navy Occupation Service Medal with Europe clasp; National Defense Service Medal with bronze star; Korean Service Medal with three bronze stars; Vietnam Service

Medal with four bronze stars; Vietnam Cross of Gallantry with palm; Vietnamese Medal of Honor (First Class); United Nations Service Medal; Philippine Liberation Medal with bronze star; Korean Presidential Unit Citation; Republic of Vietnam Campaign Medal
Place of Burial: Arlington National Cemetery, Section 5

General Keith Barr McCutcheon resigned his U.S. Army Reserve commission to accept an appointment as a U.S. Marine second lieutenant. He served aboard the aircraft carriers USS *Ranger*, USS *Wasp*, and USS *Yorktown*. His many assignments included: operations officer of Marine Aircraft Group 24 at Bougainville in Papua New Guinea, and at Luzon and Mindanao in the Philippine Islands; operations officer of Marine Aircraft Groups at Dagupan, Luzon, and Zamboanga on Mindanao Island; instructor in the aviation section of the Marine Corps schools at Quantico, Virginia; commanding officer of Marine Helicopter Squadron One (HMX-One); commander of the Hawaii-based 1st Marine Brigade; deputy chief of staff (air) at Headquarters Marine Corps.

McCutcheon completed aeronautical engineering courses at the U.S. Naval Postgraduate School and the Massachusetts Institute of Technology, earning a master's degree in 1944.

Camp McTureous

Location: Okinawa
Status: Active
Named for: Private Robert Miller McTureous, Jr.
Date of Birth: March 26, 1924
Place of Birth: Altoona, Florida
Date of Death: June 11, 1945
Place of Death: At sea aboard the USS *Relief*
Decorations and Honors: Medal of Honor, posthumously
Place of Burial: Glendale Cemetery in Umatilla, Florida

Private Robert Miller McTureous, Jr., worked as a rodman on a survey team for the Florida State Highway Department before enlisting in the Marine Corps in August 1944 where he was assigned to the 46th Replacement Draft.

His Medal of Honor citation for action during World War II reads as follows:

For conspicuous gallantry and intrepidity at the risk of his life above and beyond the call of duty, while serving with the 3rd Battalion, 29th Marines, 6th Marine Division, during action against enemy Japanese forces on Okinawa in the Ryukyu Chain, June 7, 1945. Alert and ready for any hostile counteraction following his company's seizure of an important hill objective, Private McTureous was quick to observe the plight of company stretcher bearers who were suddenly assailed by slashing machine-gun fire as they attempted to evacuate wounded at the rear of the newly won position. Determined to prevent further casualties, he quickly filled his jacket with hand grenades and charged the enemy-occupied caves from which the concentrated barrage was emanating. Coolly disregarding all personal danger as he waged his furious one-man assault, he smashed grenades into the cave entrances, thereby diverting the heaviest fire from the stretcher bearers to his own person and, resolutely returning to his own lines under a blanketing hail of rifle and machine-gun fire to replenish his supply of grenades, dauntlessly continued his systematic reduction of Japanese strength until he himself sustained serious wounds after silencing a large number of the hostile guns. Aware of his own critical condition and unwilling to further endanger the lives of his comrades, he stoically crawled a distance of 200 yards to a sheltered position within friendly lines before calling for aid. By his fearless initiative and bold tactics, Private McTureous had succeeded in neutralizing the enemy fire, killing six Japanese troops and effectively disorganizing the remainder of the savagely defending garrison. His outstanding valor and heroic spirit of self-sacrifice during a critical stage of operations reflect the highest credit upon himself and the U.S. Naval Service.

McTureous died four days later of massive wounds and loss of blood.

Camp Pendleton

Location: Oceanside, California
Status: Active
Named for: Major General Joseph Henry Pendleton
Date of Birth: June 2, 1860
Place of Birth: Rochester, Pennsylvania
Date of Death: February 4, 1942
Place of Death: Coronado, California
Decorations and Honors: Navy Cross; Distinguished Service Medal
Date of Retirement: June 2, 1924
Place of Burial: Fort Rosecrans National Cemetery in San Diego, California, Site 191

Major General Joseph Henry Pendleton is credited with establishing the Marine Corps base at San Diego, California.

Pendleton attended the United States Naval Academy at Annapolis, Maryland, graduated in 1878, and was commissioned a second lieutenant in the U.S. Marine Corps on July 1, 1884. In 1914, recognizing the value of San Diego as an ideal place for a military base, he established what would later become Camp Pendleton there.

His many assignments included service aboard the heavy cruiser USS *Pensacola*, battleship USS *South Dakota*, and the cruiser USS *Yankee*. He served at the Marine Barracks in Sitka, Alaska; Marine Barracks in Washington, D.C.; New York and Annapolis; and Marine Barracks, Mare Island, California.

He was commander of the U.S. Marines on the island of Guam; commanding officer and post commander of the 1st Brigade; commanding officer of the 1st Regiment at Olongapo in the Philippines; and commander of the Marine Barracks at Puget Sound, Washington.

He served during the skirmishes at Massaya, Guinea, and Chichigalpa, Nicaragua, and in the capture of Coyotepe and Leon in Mexico. He also served with an expeditionary force at Guantanamo Bay, Cuba, from February to June 1913. He was married to Mary Helen Fay.

Camp Schwab

Location: Okinawa
Status: Active
Named for: Private First Class Albert Earnest Schwab
Date of Birth: July 17, 1920
Place of Birth: Washington, D.C.
Date of Death: May 7, 1945
Place of Death: Ryukyu Islands, Okinawa
Decorations and Honors: Medal of Honor; Purple Heart, both posthumously
Place of Burial: Memorial Park in Tulsa, Oklahoma

Private First Class Albert Earnest Schwab was a flame thrower operator.

Schwab graduated from Tulsa High School in 1937, attended one semester at Tulsa University (now, University of Tulsa) before enlisting in the U.S. Marine Corps on May 12, 1944. After basic training, he was assigned to the 1st Marine Division at Pavuvu Island in the Russell Islands. He was just five days short of having served one year in the Marine Corps when he was killed.

The Medal of Honor was presented to Private First Class Schwab's three-year-old son at Boulder Park in Tulsa on Memorial Day, 1946. He was married to Kathryn Ellen Schlosser of Tulsa.

His Medal of Honor citation for action during World War II reads as follows:

For conspicuous gallantry and intrepidity at the risk of his life above and beyond the call of duty as a flamethrower operator in action against enemy Japanese forces on Okinawa Shima in the Ryukyu Islands, May 7, 1945. Quick to take action when his company was pinned down in a valley and suffered resultant heavy casualties under blanketing machine-gun fire emanating from a high ridge to the front, Private First Class Schwab, unable to flank the enemy emplacement because of steep cliffs on either side, advanced up the face of the ridge in bold defiance of the intense barrage and, skillfully directing the fire of his flamethrower, quickly demolished the hostile gun position, thereby enabling his company to occupy the ridge. Suddenly a second enemy machine gun opened fire, killing and wounding several marines with its initial bursts. Estimating with split-second decision the tactical difficulties confronting his comrades, Private First Class Schwab elected to continue his one-man assault despite a diminished supply of fuel for his flamethrower. Cool and indomitable, he moved forward in the face of a direct concentration of hostile fire, relentlessly closed the enemy position and attacked. Although severely wounded by a final vicious blast from the enemy weapon, Private First Class Schwab had succeeded in destroying two highly strategic Japanese gun positions during a critical stage of the operation and, by his dauntless, single-handed efforts, had materially furthered the advance of his company. His aggressive initiative, outstanding valor and professional skill throughout the bitter conflict sustain and enhance the highest traditions of the U.S. Naval Service.

Camp Shields

Location: Okinawa
Status: Active
Named for: Construction Mechanic Third Class Marvin Glen Shields, USN
Date of Birth: December 30, 1939
Place of Birth: Port Townsend, Washington
Date of Death: June 10, 1965
Place of Death: Dong Xoai, South Vietnam
Decorations and Honors: Medal of Honor, posthumously

Construction Mechanic Third Class Marvin Glen Shields enlisted in the U.S. Navy on January 8, 1962. After training, he served with Mobile Construction Battalion 11 and with Seabee Team 1104.
 His Medal of Honor citation for action in South Vietnam reads as follows:

For conspicuous gallantry and intrepidity at the risk of his life above and beyond the call of duty. Although wounded when the compound of Detachment A342, 5th Special Forces Group (Airborne), 1st Special Forces, came under intense fire from an estimated reinforced Viet Cong regiment employing machine guns, heavy weapons and small arms, Shields continued to resupply his fellow Americans who needed ammunition and to return the enemy fire for a period of approximately three hours, at which time the Viet Cong launched a massive attack at close range with flame-throwers, hand grenades and small-arms fire. Wounded a second time during this attack, Shields nevertheless assisted in carrying a more critically wounded man to safety, and then resumed firing at the enemy for four more hours. When the commander asked for a volunteer to accompany him in an attempt to knock out an enemy machine-gun emplacement which was endangering the lives of all personnel in the compound because of the accuracy of its fire, Shields unhesitatingly volunteered for this extremely hazardous mission. Proceeding toward their objective with a 3.5-inch rocket launcher, they succeeded in destroying the enemy machine-gun emplacement, thus undoubtedly saving the lives of many of their fellow servicemen in the compound. Shields was mortally wounded by hostile fire while returning to his defensive position. His heroic initiative and great personal valor in the face of intense enemy fire sustain and enhance the finest traditions of the U.S. Naval Service.

Cunningham Field

Location: Cherry Point, North Carolina
Status: Active
Named for: Lieutenant Colonel Alfred Austell Cunningham
Date of Birth: March 8, 1882
Place of Birth: Atlanta, Georgia
Date of Death: May 27, 1939
Place of Death: Sarasota, Florida
Decorations and Honors: Navy Cross; inducted into the National Aviation Hall of Fame (1965)
Date of Retirement: August 1, 1935
Place of Burial: Arlington National Cemetery, Section 7, Site 10177

Lieutenant Colonel Alfred Austell Cunningham, whose career spanned twenty-six years, was an aviation pioneer and the first aviator of the U.S. Marine Corps.

Cunningham was commissioned a second lieutenant on January 25, 1909, and entered flight training at Annapolis, Maryland, on May 22, 1912. He made his first solo flight on August 20, 1912, and was designated naval aviator number 5 on September 17, 1915. He made more than four hundred test flights in the Curtiss B-1 aircraft. Early in his career, he served aboard the battleships USS *New Jersey*, USS *North Dakota*, and the cargo ship USS *Lancaster*.

On February 26, 1917, Cunningham received orders to organize the Aviation Company for the Advanced Base Force at the Philadelphia Navy Yard where he became the unit's commander and director of Marine Corps Aviation. He also served on a joint Army-Navy board that selected sites for naval air stations in seven naval districts and on the east and gulf coasts that resulted in the establishment of the Naval Aeronautical Station at Pensacola, Florida.

In January 1918, after observing British and French aviation practices in Europe, he presented a plan for using Marine Corps aircraft against submarines off the Belgian coast and against submarine bases at Zeebrugge, Ostend, and Bruges, Belgium. During his career, Cunningham became officer-in-charge of Marine Corps aviation; commander of the 1st Air Squadron in Santo Domingo, Dominican Republic; division Marine Corps officer and aide on the staff of commander, Battleship Division 3; and executive officer of the Western Area at Leon, Nicaragua, with the 2nd Brigade of Marines.

The destroyer USS *Alfred A. Cunningham* (DD-752) was also named in his honor.

Dowdell Field

Location: Apali, Nicaragua
Status: Closed
Named for: Sergeant Frank E. Dowdell
Date of Birth: No Data Found
Place of Birth: No Data Found
Date of Death: October 8, 1927 (declared dead on October 20, 1928)
Place of Death: Sapotilla Ridge, Nicaragua

Sergeant Frank E. Dowdell was a U.S. Marine Corps observer.

While flying over the mountains of Nueva Segovia in Nicaragua, the flight crew observed enemy activity on the trails below. During the patrol, the plane, piloted by Lieutenant Earl A. Thomas, with Sergeant Frank E. Dowdell as his observer, was attacked and shot down. Dowdell and Thomas were seen escaping from the wreckage, however, an air search of the area found no signs of the two airmen.

The following morning a search party, after marching for more than three hours through treacherous Nicaragua terrain, reached the base of the ridge where the plane went down. They found nothing but the burned out plane. Neither Thomas nor Dowdell was seen again and are still listed as missing in action. Marine intelligence officers later learned that Sandinistas had killed Thomas and Dowdell after they had taken shelter in a cave.

★★★

Dyess Field

Location: Roi Island, Kwajalein Atoll, Marshall Islands
Status: Closed
Named for: Lieutenant Colonel Aquilla James "Jimmy" Dyess
Date of Birth: January 11, 1909
Place of Birth: Andersonville, Georgia
Date of Death: February 2, 1944
Place of Death: Namur Island, Marshall Islands
Decorations and Honors: Medal of Honor, posthumously; Bronze Star; Purple Heart; Carnegie Medal
Place of Burial: Westover Memorial Park Cemetery in Augusta, Georgia

Lieutenant Colonel Aquilla James Dyess was the highest-ranking officer killed during the assault on Roi Namur while leading an attack on a Japanese bunker in Operation Flintlock.

Dyess graduated from Clemson College in South Carolina in 1932 with a bachelor of science degree in architecture.

His Medal of Honor citation for action during World War II reads as follows

For conspicuous gallantry and intrepidity at the risk of his life above and beyond the call of duty as Commanding Officer of the 1st Battalion, 24th Marines (Rein), 4th Marine Division, in action against enemy Japanese forces during the assault on Namur Island, Kwajalein Atoll, Marshall Islands, February 1 and 2, 1944. Undaunted by severe fire from automatic Japanese weapons, Lieutenant Colonel Dyess launched a powerful final attack on the second day of the assault, unhesitatingly posting himself between the opposing lines to point out objectives and avenues of approach and personally leading the advancing troops. Alert, and determined to quicken the pace of the offensive against increased enemy fire, he was constantly at the head of advance units, inspiring his men to push forward until the Japanese had been driven back to a small center of resistance and victory assured. While standing on the parapet of an antitank trench directing a group of infantry in a flanking attack against the last enemy position, Lieutenant Colonel Dyess was killed by a burst of enemy machine-gun fire. His daring and forceful leadership and his valiant fighting spirit in the face of terrific opposition were in keeping with the highest traditions of the U.S. Naval Service. He gallantly gave his life for his country.

The USS *Dyess* (DD-880) was also named in his honor.

★★★

Hawkins Field

Location: Tarawa, Gilbert Islands
Status: Closed
Named for: First Lieutenant William Deane Hawkins
Date of Birth: April 19, 1914
Place of Birth: Fort Scott, Kansas
Date of Death: November 21, 1943
Place of Death: Tarawa, Gilbert Islands
Decorations and Honors: Medal of Honor, posthumously
Place of Burial: National Memorial Cemetery of the Pacific in Honolulu, Hawaii

First Lieutenant William Deane Hawkins served with the 2nd Battalion, 2nd Marine Division.

Hawkins enlisted in the Marine Corps Reserve on January 5, 1942, and was assigned to the 7th Recruit Battalion, Marine Corps Recruit Depot, in San Diego. He was commissioned a second lieutenant while taking part in the Guadalcanal campaign during the battle for the Solomon Islands.

His Medal of Honor citation for action during World War II reads as follows:

For valorous and gallant conduct above and beyond the call of duty as commanding officer of a Scout Sniper Platoon attached to the Assault Regiment in action against Japanese-held Tarawa in the Gilbert Island, November 20 and 21, 1943. The first to disembark from the jeep lighter, First Lieutenant Hawkins unhesitatingly moved forward under heavy enemy fire at the end of the Betio Pier, neutralizing emplacements in coverage of troops assaulting the main beach positions. Fearlessly leading his men on to join the forces fighting desperately to gain a beachhead, he repeatedly risked his life throughout the day and night to direct and lead attacks on pillboxes and installations with grenades and demolitions. At dawn on the following day, First Lieutenant Hawkins resumed the dangerous mission of clearing the limited beachhead of Japanese resistance, personally initiating an assault on a hostile position fortified by five enemy machine guns, and, crawling forward in the face of withering fire, boldly fired pointblank into the loopholes and completed the destruction with grenades. Refusing to withdraw after being seriously wounded in the chest during this skirmish, First Lieutenant Hawkins steadfastly carried the fight to the enemy, destroying three more pillboxes before he was caught in a burst of Japanese shellfire and mortally wounded. His relentless fighting spirit in the face of formidable opposition and his exceptionally daring tactics served as an inspiration to his comrades during the most crucial phase of the battle and reflect the highest credit upon the U.S. Naval Service. He gallantly gave his life for his country.

Henderson Field

Location: Guadalcanal
Status: Now, Honiara International Airport
Named for: Major Lofton R. Henderson
Date of Birth: May 24, 1903
Place of Birth: Lorain, Ohio
Date of Death: June 4, 1942
Place of Death: Battle of Midway
Decorations and Honors: Navy Cross, posthumously
Place of Burial: Memorialized at the National Memorial Cemetery of the Pacific in Honolulu, Hawaii

Major Lofton R. Henderson was the first U.S. Marine aviator to die during the Battle of Midway.

Henderson graduated from the United States Naval Academy at Annapolis, Maryland, in 1926. Prior to World War II, he served in China and various Caribbean stations and on the aircraft carriers USS *Langley*, USS *Ranger*, and USS *Saratoga*. He was the commanding officer of Marine Scout-Bombing Squadron (VMSB-241) during the Battle of Midway.

He was killed while leading sixteen Marine Corps planes in a glide bombing attack on the Japanese aircraft carrier *Hiryu*. Although the left wing of his plane had burst into flames as he began his final approach, he continued the attack and perished as his plane dove toward the enemy carrier.

His Navy Cross citation reads as follows:

The Navy Cross is presented to Lofton R. Henderson, Major, U.S. Marine Corps, for extraordinary heroism as Squadron Commander of Marine Scout-Bombing Squadron Two Hundred Forty-one (VMSB-241), during action against enemy Japanese forces in the Battle of Midway on June 4, 1942. With utter disregard for his own personal safety, Major Henderson, with keen judgment and courageous aggressiveness in the face of strong enemy fighter opposition, led his squadron in an attack which contributed materially to the defeat of the enemy. He was subsequently reported as missing it action. It is believed he gallantly gave up his life in the service of his country.

The Gearing class destroyer, USS *Henderson* (DD-785), was also named in his honor.

Henderson Hall

Location: Arlington, Virginia
Status: Active
Named for: Colonel Archibald Henderson
Date of Birth: January 21, 1783
Place of Birth: Colchester, Virginia
Date of Death: January 6, 1859
Place of Death: Stanford, Kentucky
Decorations and Honors: Silver Star; a jeweled sword from the State of Virginia
Place of Burial: Congressional Cemetery in Washington, D.C.

Colonel Archibald Henderson was the fifth commandant of the U.S. Marine Corps from October 17, 1820, to January 6, 1859, the longest term held by any officer in that position.

Henderson, often referred to as the "Grand old man of the Marine Corps," served during the War of 1812 on board the U.S. frigate *Constitution*. He also served during the Indian Wars and the Mexican-American War. He served at posts and stations in Boston, Massachusetts; Portsmouth, New Hampshire; Headquarters, U.S. Marine Corps; and in New Orleans, Louisiana.

Henderson was responsible for Congress passing the Act for the Better Organization of the Marine Corps in 1834, which ensured the Marine Corps would remain part of the U.S. Department of the Navy instead of becoming part of the U.S. Army.

He served during the 1836–37 war with the Seminole Indians in Florida and Creek Indians in Georgia. He was promoted to the brevet rank of brigadier general for his services in stopping the Indian hostilities.

A sword presented to Henderson after the Mexican-American War was inscribed with the words, "From the Halls of Montezuma, to the Shores of Tripoli," which became the opening words to the Marine Corps hymn.

In 1857, during the Know-Nothing riots in Washington, D.C., Henderson demonstrated his leadership and courage by deliberately placing his body against the muzzle of a cannon, preventing it from being aimed at the marines.

The navy transport USS *Henderson* was also named in his memory.

★★★

Merritt Field

Located: Beaufort Marine Corps Air Station in Beaufort, South Carolina
Status: Active
Named for: Major General Lewis Griffith Merritt
Date of Birth: June 26, 1897
Place of Birth: Ridge Spring, South Carolina
Date of Death: March 24, 1974
Place of Death: Brooke Army Medical Center at San Antonio, Texas
Decorations and Honors: Bronze Star; Legion of Merit
Date of Retirement: June 1, 1947

Major General Lewis Griffith Merritt was a pioneer in U.S. Marine Corps aviation.

Merritt graduated from the Citadel in Charleston, South Carolina, in 1917 with a bachelor of science degree and was commissioned a lieutenant that same year. He was accepted for flight training at Pensacola, Florida, and was awarded his pilot wings as a naval aviator in January 1924.

During his career, he served with the American Expeditionary Force in France and aboard the battleship USS *New Mexico*. While attached to the office of the Judge Advocate General in 1925, he studied law and was admitted to the bar in South Carolina in 1928. Later, he commanded the Observation Squadron 9-M in Haiti.

He attended the Army Air Corps Tactical School at Langley Field in Virginia and the Command and General Staff College at Fort Leavenworth in Kansas. He served on the staff of Aircraft 1, Fleet Marine Force, in June 1933 and again in July 1937. Between those years, he was assigned to the Naval Operating Base in San Diego, California, with Aircraft 2, Fleet Marine Force.

During World War II, Merritt was commander of the Service Group, Marine Air Wings, in the Pacific. He had been serving with the Royal Air Force when his plane was shot down while en route to Cairo from El Adam. He survived the crash and was rescued by the British while under enemy fire. After the war, he returned to South Carolina to practice law.

His Bronze Star citation for action from September 1942 to August 1943 reads in part as follows:

Merritt skillfully employed his squadron in neutralization aircraft strikes against enemy positions on New Ireland and New Britain Islands and, in addition, personally directed close air support missions in aid of the First Australian Army against Japanese forces on New Britain Island. During the early part of this period, as Commander, Aircraft, Northern Solomons, he was in operational and tactical control of units of the Royal New Zealand Air Force at Bougainville, and directed close air support missions in aid of the Second Australian Corps against enemy positions on Bougainville. Throughout this period, (the then) Brigadier General Merritt rendered invaluable service as a tactical aircraft commander.

Moret Field

Located: Zamboanga, Philippine Islands
Status: Closed
Named for: Lieutenant Colonel Paul Moret
Date of Birth: No Data Found
Place of Birth: Jackson, Michigan
Date of Death: June 8, 1943
Place of Death: Nouméa, New Caledonia in the South Pacific
Decorations and Honors: Legion of Merit, posthumously
Place of Burial: Fort Rosecrans National Cemetery in San Diego, California

Lieutenant Colonel Paul Moret was a U.S. Marine aviator and the youngest squadron commander in Marine Corps aviation.

Moret graduated from the United States Naval Academy at Annapolis, Maryland, in 1930 where he was a football, basketball, boxing and football coach from 1930 to 1935. After graduation, he was assigned to Naval Air Station Pensacola, Florida, where he received his pilot wings in 1932. He was commander of Marine Scout Bombing Squadron 131. Moret was killed when the plane in which he was a passenger crashed.

The Legion of Merit was awarded to him for his outstanding service in directing operations by army, navy, and marine aircraft in bombing, torpedo, reconnaissance, search, antisubmarine, and ground support operations on Guadalcanal from November 12, 1942, to January 20, 1943.

The Legion of Merit citation reads as follows:

Throughout an exceedingly grave period, Lieutenant Colonel Moret displayed courage, foresight and unusual ability. His skillful employment of aircraft caused severe losses to be inflicted on the enemy in surface vessels, aircraft personnel and vital materials. Determined to keep our operational losses at a minimum, he worked tirelessly and with great success toward airdrome control and the training and indoctrination of pilots. He contributed invaluable service toward the success of our armed forces in the Solomon Islands.

Munn Field

Location: Adjacent to Camp Pendleton in Oceanside, California
Status: Active
Named for: Lieutenant General John Calvin Munn
Date of Birth: October 17, 1906
Place of Birth: Prescott, Arkansas
Date of Death: April 14, 1986

Place of Death: Encinitas, California
Decorations and Honors: Silver Star; Legion of Merit with combat V device and gold star; Navy Commendation Medal with combat V device and gold star; Presidential Unit Citation; Navy Unit Commendation; Second Nicaraguan Campaign Medal; American Defense Service Medal with base clasp; Asiatic-Pacific Campaign Medal with three bronze stars; American Campaign Medal; World War II Victory Medal; Navy Occupation Service Medal with Asia clasp
Date of Retirement: July 1, 1964
Place of Burial: Fort Rosecrans National Cemetery in San Diego, California

Lieutenant General John Calvin Munn served as assistant commandant of the U.S. Marine Corps from 1960 to 1963 and was the first U.S. Marine aviator to command Camp Pendleton.

Munn was a 1927 graduate of the United States Naval Academy at Annapolis, Maryland. His long list of assignments included serving with Scouting Squadron 14-M aboard the aircraft carrier USS *Saratoga*; Bombing Squadron 4-M aboard the aircraft carriers USS *Lexington* and USS *Langley*; naval attaché at the American embassies in Colombia, Panama, Venezuela, Ecuador, and Peru; and Marine Observation Squadron 151 of Marine Aircraft Group 11, 1st Marine Aircraft Wing, at Quantico, Virginia. He also served as assistant chief of staff, G-2, 1st Marine Aircraft Wing; assistant chief of staff, G-3, 2nd Marine Aircraft Wing; commander of the Marine Aircraft Group 11 in the New Hebrides; assistant head of the Aviation Planning Section, Headquarters; commander in chief, U.S. Fleet; commander of the Marine Aircraft Group 31; executive officer of the Division of Aviation at Headquarters Marine Corps; assistant commanding general, Aircraft, Fleet Marine Force, Atlantic; Marine Corps liaison officer to the Office of the Vice Chief of Naval Operations; inspector general of the Marine Corps; commander of the 2nd Marine Aircraft Wing; and director of aviation at Headquarters Marine Corps.

Page Field

Located: Parris Island, South Carolina
Status: Closed
Named for: Captain Arthur Hallet Page, Jr.
Date of Birth: September 17, 1895
Place of Birth: St. Paul, Minnesota
Date of Death: September 1, 1930
Place of Death: Chicago, Illinois
Decorations and Honors: Distinguished Flying Cross, posthumously
Place of Burial: Arlington National Cemetery, Section 7, Site 9059

Captain Arthur Hallet Page, Jr., pioneered instrument flying techniques.

Page graduated from the United States Naval Academy at Annapolis, Maryland, on June 28, 1917, and received his pilot wings on March 14, 1918. He attended the Army Balloon School at Fort Omaha, Nebraska, and later specialized in balloons during World War I. He served with the Marine Aeronautic Detachment in Miami, Florida, and in Philadelphia, Pennsylvania. In the spring of 1930, he flew a heavy transport plane from Washington to Managua, Nicaragua, and back, setting a record of six days and twenty minutes, of which fifty-five hours was actual flying time.

He won the Curtiss Marine Trophy Race on May 31, 1930, for flying five times around a 20-mile course at an average speed of 164 miles per hour in a Curtiss F6C-3 Blackhawk, equipped with pontoons. He died in a crash while leading in the Thompson Trophy Race.

His Distinguished Flying Cross citation reads as follows:

For extraordinary achievement while participating in an aerial flight on July 21, 1930. Captain Page successfully completed the longest recorded blind flight as pilot in an 02U-1 airplane from Omaha, Nebraska, to Anacostia, Washington, D.C., a distance of approximately one thousand miles flying blind the entire distance, at time through rain storms and clouds, and negotiating the entire flight in one day. Captain Page's pioneering, scientific study and successful accomplishment in the art of blind flying have contributed much towards the advancement of aeronautics.

Sailer Field

Location: Guadalcanal
Status: Closed
Named for: Major Joseph Sailer, Jr.
Date of Birth: August 14, 1907
Place of Birth: Jamestown, Rhode Island
Date of Death: December 7, 1942
Place of Death: At sea near the Solomon Islands
Decorations and Honors: Navy Cross
Place of Burial: Memorialized at the Manila American Cemetery and Memorial in Manila, Philippines

Major Joseph Sailer, Jr., was considered one of the best dive-bomber pilots and squadron leaders in the U.S. Marine Corps.

Sailer graduated from Princeton University in 1930 with a degree in mechanical engineering. He flew for the Marine Corps Reserve prior to World War II, worked for United Air Lines, and then became an engineer with the Sperry Gyroscope Company where he worked on the Norden top secret bombsight project and trained the Royal Air Force in its use. He was called to active duty in 1941 and was a squadron leader of Marine Scout Bombing Squadron (VMSB-132).

He, along with his gunner, Private First Class J. W. Alexander, died while leading a squadron of Douglas SBD-Dauntless aircraft in the defense of Henderson Field on Guadalcanal that was being attacked by a Japanese convoy. When he discovered that the plane's dive brakes would not retract, he radioed that he was unable to make the 160-mile flight back to Henderson Field and that a Japanese air force F1M2 had attacked him. Members of his squadron saw his Dauntless roll inverted and crash into the water.

Thomas Field

Located: Ocotal, Nicaragua
Status: Closed
Named for: Second Lieutenant Earl Albert Thomas
Date of Birth: August 3, 1900
Place of Birth: Richmond, Indiana
Date of Death: October 8, 1927
Place of Death: Sapotilla Ridge, Nicaragua
Decorations and Honors: Distinguished Flying Cross

Second Lieutenant Earl Albert Thomas was a U.S. Marine Corps aviator.

Thomas enlisted in the U.S. Navy on June 14, 1918, then reenlisted in the Marine Corps on October 20, 1921, and was commissioned in April 1924. He completed flight training at Naval Air Station Pensacola, Florida. He was assigned to the 5th Regiment, 2nd Brigade, as an operations, parachute, and aerological officer in Managua, Nicaragua, in August 1927.

He and his observer, Sergeant Frank E. Dowdell, disappeared while on a patrol flight. They were last seen leaving their downed plane as it burst into flames. A rescue patrol attempted to find Thomas and his observer, but hostile Sandinistas killed the patrol. Both men were reported missing in action and Thomas was officially declared dead on October 20, 1928.

His Distinguished Flying Cross citation reads as follows:

On July 16, 1927, he served as a gunner in one of the five airplanes which by a daring ground attack accomplished the rescue of the besieged garrison of Marines and native troops at Ocotal, Nicaragua. He displayed great coolness and courage in the face of hostile fire and made use of every opportunity to attack the enemy with telling effect. He contributed materially to the victory, which resulted in the complete rout of the enemy and saved the little garrison from great loss of life and almost certain destruction. The achievement was extraordinary.

Turner Field

Location: Quantico, Virginia
Status: Active
Named for: Colonel Thomas Caldwell Turner
Date of Birth: March 29, 1882
Place of Birth: No Data Found
Date of Death: October 28, 1931
Place of Death: Haiti
Decorations and Honors: Distinguished Flying Cross; Purple Heart
Place of Burial: Arlington National Cemetery, Section 3, Site 4221-A

Colonel Thomas Caldwell Turner was a naval aviator and director of U.S. Marine Corps Aviation from December 13, 1920, to March 2, 1925, and again from May 10, 1929, to October 28, 1931.

Turner set a record when he led two British de Havilland DH-4 airplanes from Washington, D.C., to Santo Domingo in the Dominican Republic, making the longest unguarded flight over land and water at that time. He was killed in the line of duty.

United States Navy

Lest We Forget

Engraved in bronze upon a marble stand,
Rows of white crosses bowing across the land,
But for you Sailor to be,
Let no epitaph be written upon the sea.

—*L. Deloma*

CHAPTER 9

United States Navy

Alvin Callender Field

Location: New Orleans, Louisiana
Status: Now, Naval Air Station Joint Reserve Base
Named for: Captain Alvin Andrew Callender
Date of Birth: July 4, 1893
Place of Birth: New Orleans, Louisiana
Date of Death: October 30, 1918
Place of Death: Ghislain, France
Place of Burial: Valenciennes Cemetery (St. Roch) Communal in Nord, France, Grave II. E. 5

Captain Alvin Andrew Callender was a World War I ace pilot, credited with fourteen air victories.

Callender graduated from Tulane University in 1914 with a degree in architecture. He served on the Mexican border with the Louisiana National Guard in 1916. The following year he joined the Royal Flying Corps in Canada and received a commission, and later became a flight instructor. He was assigned to the 32nd Squadron of the Royal Canadian Air Force where he saw action in German, British, and French offensives. On July 6, 1918, while serving with this unit, he was shot down but was uninjured. He was killed three months later when his S.E.5a aircraft was shot down by members of Jasta 2.

Callender's descendants published a collection of his letters and photographs titled *War in an Open Cockpit: The Wartime Letters of Captain Alvin Andrew Callender, RAF,* (1978).

Armitage Field

Location: China Lake Naval Air Weapons Station in California
Status: Active
Named for: Lieutenant John Murray Armitage
Date of Birth: December 14, 1919
Place of Birth: Zamboanga, Philippine Islands
Date of Death: August 21, 1944
Place of Death: China Lake, California
Decorations and Honors: Distinguished Flying Cross, posthumously; Silver Star; Air Medal; American Defense Service Medal; Asiatic-Pacific Campaign Medal
Place of Burial: Golden Gate National Cemetery in San Bruno, California

Lieutenant John Murray Armitage attended Purdue University and enlisted in the Naval Reserve in January 1941. He accepted an appointment as an aviation cadet in April 1941 and was assigned to the Advanced Carrier Training Group, Pacific Fleet, in November of that year.

Armitage was appointed lieutenant junior grade in October 1942. In March 1943, he was assigned to Fleet Air Seattle for flight duty with Carrier Aircraft Service Unit 7 and in fitting out of Composite Squadron 41. His last assignment was with the U.S. Naval Ordnance Test Station. He was killed while conducting air-firing tests of a Tiny Tim rocket.

His Distinguished Flying Cross citation reads as follows:

For distinguished service above and beyond the call of duty in the testing and development of aircraft rockets. Being among the first to volunteer for hazardous test flights without regard for the personal danger involved, Lieutenant Armitage gave his life while testing an early development of the navy's largest aircraft rocket. Lieutenant Armitage soloed in twenty-two single-engine and seven multi-engine aircraft. While with this command since November 30, 1942, he logged 488.8 hours, of which 111.7 were experimental flights. Holding an admirable record for combat flights in the South Pacific and Southwest Pacific, Lieutenant Armitage was thoroughly convinced that rockets increased the striking power of aircraft, and would be of great value to the fleet, and worked untiringly in the development of the weapon.

His Silver Star citation reads as follows:

For distinguished service in the line of his profession as pilot of a torpedo bomber in the successful aerial action against Japanese naval forces on October 26, 1942, near Santa Cruz Islands. In the face of extremely heavy enemy antiaircraft fire, Lieutenant Armitage, with conspicuous gallantry and intrepidity, pressed home a torpedo attack on a Japanese heavy cruiser. His courageous action was in keeping with the highest traditions of the Naval Service.

His Air Medal citation reads as follows:

For meritorious achievement in the line of his profession as leader of a section of torpedo bombers in the successful aerial attack on Japanese shipping in the Solomon Islands area on October 5, 1942. Despite extremely bad weather and in the face of heavy antiaircraft fire, Lieutenant Armitage located the enemy ships, making four dives and obtaining one direct bomb hit amidship on a large Japanese transport. His courageous action was in keeping with the highest tradition of the Naval Service.

Ault Field

Location: Whidbey Island Naval Air Station in Oak Harbor, Washington
Status: Active
Named for: Commodore William B. Ault
Date of Birth: October 6, 1898
Place of Birth: Enterprise, Oregon
Date of Death: May 8, 1942
Place of Death: Coral Sea, reported missing in action. Officially declared dead on May 9, 1943
Decorations and Honors: Navy Cross, posthumously; Purple Heart, posthumously; World War I Victory Medal; American Defense Service Medal with fleet clasp; Asiatic-Pacific Campaign Medal; World War II Victory Medal
Place of Burial: Memorialized at the Manila American Cemetery and Memorial in Manila, Philippines

Commodore William B. Ault graduated from the United States Naval Academy at Annapolis, Maryland, in 1922 with a bachelor of science degree and was commissioned an ensign on June 3, 1922.

In 1925, Ault reported to Naval Air Station Pensacola, Florida, for flight training and was assigned to Aircraft Squadrons Scouting Fleet in Hampton Roads, Virginia. He later joined the Aviation Unit attached to the cruiser USS *Cincinnati*. In August 1939, he took command of the Naval Reserve Aviation Base in Kansas City, Missouri, and served as commander of an air group attached to the aircraft carrier USS *Lexington* during the early years of World War II.

While engaged in an attack on the Japanese fleet carrier *Shokaku*, Ault and his radio-gunner, Aviation Radioman 1st Class William T. Butler, were hit by Zero fighters. Ault tried to make radio communication with his ship but was unaware that it had been hit and its communication system had been put out of commission. The aircraft carrier USS *Yorktown*, which had taken over communications for the aircraft carrier USS *Lexington*, told him that he was on his own and wished him "Good luck." Ault changed course in an attempt to be picked up on radar. Ault radioed, "O.K. So long, people. We got a 1,000 pound hit on the flat top." No further word was received, and neither he nor his radioman was ever seen again. Ault was officially reported missing in action.

His Navy Cross citation reads as follows:

For heroic and distinguished service in the line of his profession as Air Group Commander of the USS *Lexington* in action against Japanese forces in the Coral Sea, May 7 and 8, 1942. He led the air attacks, carried out in the face of heavy antiaircraft fire and opposed by enemy fighters, which resulted in the destruction of an enemy carrier on May 7 and major damage to another on May 8. He failed to return from the last attack. His conduct during these attacks was an inspiration to the entire air group.

The destroyer, USS *Ault,* was also named in his honor.

Barin Field

Location: Foley, Alabama
Status: Active
Named for: Lieutenant Louis T. Barin, USNRF
Date of Birth: August 20, 1890
Place of Birth: San Diego, California
Date of Death: June 12, 1920
Place of Death: No Data Found
Decorations and Honors: Navy Cross, posthumously
Place of Burial: Fort Rosecrans National Cemetery in San Diego, California

Lieutenant Louis T. Barin was a test pilot and pilot of the seaplane NC-1 on the U.S. Navy's 1919 transatlantic flight from Newfoundland to the Azore Islands.

Barin completed flight training at Naval Air Station Pensacola, Florida, in 1916 and was designated aviator number 56. He was one of two hundred aviators classified as a National Naval Volunteer (NNV).

His Navy Cross citation reads as follows:

The Navy Cross is awarded to Lieutenant Louis T. Barin, United States Navy (Reserve Forces), for distinguished service in the line of his profession as a member of the crew of the seaplane NC-1, which made a long overseas flight from Newfoundland to the vicinity of the Azores in May 1919. Also for extraordinary heroism as pilot of a sea plane which was being utilized for the test of a new method of aerodynamic control. Realizing from the performance of this device when on the water, that as a pilot, he was practically helpless to control the machine, he nevertheless took it into the air, and continued the experiment in order that the test might be complete.

Bordelon Field

Location: Hilo, Hawaii
Status: Closed
Named for: Staff Sergeant William James Bordelon, USMC
Date of Birth: December 25, 1920
Place of Birth: San Antonio, Texas
Date of Death: November 20, 1943
Place of Death: Tarawa, Gilbert Islands
Decorations and Honors: Medal of Honor, posthumously; Purple Heart; Presidential Unit Citation; Asiatic-Pacific Campaign Medal; the World War II Victory Medal
Place of Burial: Fort Sam Houston National Cemetery in San Antonio, Texas, Section A-1, Grave 558

Staff Sergeant William James Bordelon joined the U.S. Marine Corps in December 1941 and was promoted through the ranks to staff sergeant on May 13, 1943. He served with Company D, 2nd Engineer Battalion, 2nd Marine Division, and later with Company C, 18th Marines.

His Medal of Honor citation for action during World War II reads as follows:

For valorous and gallant conduct above and beyond the call of duty as a member of an assault engineer platoon of the 1st Battalion, 18th Marines, tactically attached to the 2nd Marine Division, in action against the Japanese-held atoll of Tarawa in the Gilbert Islands on November 20, 1943. Landing in the assault waves under withering enemy fire, which killed all but four of the men in his tractor, Staff Sergeant Bordelon hurriedly made demolition charges and personally put two pillboxes out of action. Hit by enemy machine-gun fire just as a charge exploded in his hand while assaulting a third position, he courageously remained in action and, although out of demolition, provided himself with a rifle and furnished fire coverage for a group of men scaling the seawall. Disregarding his own serious condition, he unhesitatingly went to the aid of one of his demolition men, wounded and calling for help in the water, rescuing this man and another who had been hit by enemy fire while attempting to make the rescue. Still refusing first aid for himself, he again made up demolition charges and single-handedly assaulted a fourth Japanese machine-gun position but was instantly killed when caught in a final burst of fire from the enemy. Staff Sergeant Bordelon's great personal valor during a critical phase of securing the limited beachhead was a contributing factor in the ultimate occupation of the island, and his heroic determination throughout three days of violent battle reflects the highest credit upon the U.S. Naval Service. He gallantly gave his life for his country.

Bristol Field

Location: Argentia, Newfoundland
Status: Closed
Named for: Vice Admiral Arthur LeRoy Bristol, Jr.
Date of Birth: July 15, 1886
Place of Birth: Charleston, South Carolina
Date of Death: April 27, 1942
Place of Death: Argentia, Newfoundland
Decorations and Honors: Navy Cross; Navy Distinguished Service Medal, posthumously; Army Distinguished Service Medal; Order of St. Stanislav, III Class
Place of Burial: Magnolia Cemetery in Charleston, South Carolina

Vice Admiral Arthur LeRoy Bristol, Jr., was the first commander of the Support Force, which helped escort convoys across the Atlantic to aid the British in 1941.

Bristol graduated from the United States Naval Academy at Annapolis, Maryland, in 1906 and received a commission as an ensign in 1908.* In January 1912, he served as a naval attaché. He became commander of the destroyers USS *Cummings*, USS *Terry*, and USS *Jarvis*. He also commanded the 2nd Division, Reserve Torpedo Flotilla, U.S. Atlantic Fleet.

During World War I, he was assigned as a torpedo officer on the staff of commander, Torpedo Flotilla, Atlantic Fleet, and, in 1916, he became aide and flag secretary to the commander, Destroyer Force, Atlantic Fleet. He was also aide and flag secretary to the commander, Cruiser Force, Atlantic Fleet. During the Russian Civil War of 1918–20, he commanded the destroyers USS *Breckinridge* and USS *Overton* where he oversaw the ship's operations in the Black Sea in November 1920.

Bristol attended the Naval War College in Newport, Rhode Island, from July 1922 to May 1923, and he served as an instructor on the staff there from May 1923 until May 1924. Bristol served as executive officer on the battleship USS *Arizona* from February 1927 until April 1928. He received aviation training at Naval Air Station San Diego, California, and flight training at Naval Air Station Pensacola, Florida. As a naval aviator, he was assigned to the Asiatic Fleet where he served as commanding officer of the seaplane tender USS *Jason*. Later, he was assigned commander, Aircraft Squadrons, Asiatic Fleet.

In 1931, he was assigned to the United Kingdom as naval attaché in London. As commanding officer of the new aircraft carrier USS *Ranger*, Bristol took the ship to South America on shakedown and commanded her until June 1936, when he became commanding officer of Naval Air Station San Diego.

During World War II, Bristol commanded Patrol Wing 2 at Pearl Harbor, and was given flag rank and became commander of Carrier Division 1. He became commander of the Aircraft, Scouting Force, in 1940, and of Patrol Wings, United States Fleet, in 1941.

As a rear admiral, he held the position of commander of Support Force during the summer and autumn of 1941 until the United States entered World War II on December 7, 1941. He remained in that command until he suffered a fatal heart attack.

His Navy Cross citation reads as follows:

The Navy Cross is presented to Arthur L. Bristol, Commander, U.S. Navy, for distinguished service in the line of his profession as flag secretary on staff of commander Cruiser and Transport Force and also temporarily as acting chief of staff.

The destroyer USS *Arthur L. Bristol* (DE-281) was also named in his honor.

---

* Until 1912, a midshipman graduating from the Naval Academy had to serve two years sea duty before receiving a commission.

Bronson Field

Location: Pensacola, Florida
Status: Closed (now, Blue Angel Recreation Park)
Named for: Lieutenant Junior Grade Clarence King Bronson
Date of Birth: July 21, 1888
Place of Birth: Bushnell, Illinois
Date of Death: November 8, 1916
Place of Death: Naval Proving Ground in Indianhead, Maryland
Place of Burial: Arlington National Cemetery, Section 2, Site 3698

Lieutenant Junior Grade Clarence King Bronson was a naval aviation pioneer.

Bronson graduated from the United States Naval Academy at Annapolis, Maryland, in 1910. He trained to be a pilot in 1914 at the Curtiss Aeroplane and Motor Company in Hammondsport, New York, and Pensacola, Florida.

He was killed while testing an experimental aerial bomb when it prematurely exploded during a bomb dropping test.

The destroyer USS *Clarence King Bronson* was also named in his honor.

Brown Field

Location: Otay Mesa, California
Status: Closed
Named for: Commander Melville Stuart Brown

Date of Birth: March 8, 1889
Place of Birth: Chicago, Illinois
Date of Death: November 2, 1936
Place of Death: Descanso, California
Decorations and Honors: Mexican Service Medal; World War I Victory Medal; Order of Avis
Place of Burial: Fort Rosecrans National Cemetery in San Diego, California

Commander Melville Stuart Brown was a naval aviator.

Brown graduated from the United States Naval Academy at Annapolis, Maryland, in 1910 and was assigned to the battleship USS *Nebraska*. During the summer of 1914, he had duty at the rifle matches held at Wakefield, Massachusetts. In May 1919, after a tour of duty with the Bureau of Navigation, he served with Commander, Destroyer Squadron 3, Atlantic Fleet, where he helped guard the first U.S. Navy transatlantic flight of the seaplane NC-4. He served aboard the destroyer USS *MacDonough* in June 1924.

He attended the Naval War College in Newport, Rhode Island, in May 1928, and then served on the staff there for two years. He served as gunnery officer aboard the aircraft carrier USS *Saratoga* from June 1930 until June 1932 and had duty in the Division of Fleet Training, Office of the Chief of Naval Operations, until December 1934.

After flight training at Naval Air Station Pensacola, Florida, Brown qualified as a naval aviator in February 1936 and was assigned to duty on the staff of Vice Admiral Frederick J. Horne. At the time of his death in a plane crash, he was the executive officer of the aircraft carrier USS *Lexington*.

Cabaniss Field

Location: Corpus Christi, Texas
Status: Closed
Named for: Commander Robert Wright Cabaniss
Date of Birth: January 3, 1884
Place of Birth: Union Springs, Alabama
Date of Death: March 31, 1927
Place of Death: Navassa Island in the West Indies

Commander Robert Wright Cabaniss graduated from the United States Naval Academy at Annapolis, Maryland, in 1906. He served at the Asiatic Station and on the Pacific Coast until 1915. He was designated naval aviator number 36 after training at Naval Air Station Pensacola, Florida.

During World War I, Cabaniss commanded the aviation detachment at the Massachusetts Institute of Technology. In 1918, he was sent to France where he commanded Naval Air Station Moutchic-Lacanau. He also served at Pauillac and at Bordeaux.

After the war, he was the commanding officer of Naval Air Station Rockaway, Long Island, New York; the executive officer aboard the aircraft tender USS *Wright* in 1921; and the commander of the USS *Aroostook* in 1926. He was killed in the crash of the navy seaplane, PN-9, which he was piloting.

Cecil Field

Location: Jacksonville, Florida
Status: Closed (now, Cecil Commerce Center)
Named for: Commander Henry Barton Cecil
Date of Birth: February 17, 1888
Place of Birth: New River, Tennessee
Date of Death: April 4, 1933
Place of Death: Lakehurst, New Jersey
Decorations and Honors: World War I Victory Medal with aviation clasp; Letter of Commendation from the Secretary of the Navy for his World War I service

Commander Henry Barton Cecil graduated from the United States Naval Academy at Annapolis, Maryland, in June 1910 and reported to Naval Air Station Pensacola, Florida, for flight training in 1915 where he received the designation of naval aviator number 42, qualifying in both heavier-than-air and lighter-than-air craft.

In January 1918, Cecil reported for duty with the United States Naval Aviation Forces in France where he served as commander of Naval Air Station Pauillac, France, until April 1918, and later in L'Aber Vrach, France.

After flight training in seaplanes, Cecil was assigned to the tender USS *Harding* for duty in command of the Atlantic NC Seaplane Division. In 1921, he was transferred to Aircraft Squadron, Atlantic Fleet, and served there until May 1922.

His other duties included assistant naval attaché at the American Embassy in Rome, Italy; aide on the staff of commander in chief of Battle Fleet; fleet aviation officer; executive officer of the aircraft carrier USS *Wright*; and head of the Flight Division for the Bureau of Aeronautics.

During his career, he served aboard the battleships USS *Idaho*, USS *California*, USS *West Virginia, and* USS *Montana*; the monitor USS *Monadnock;* the heavy cruiser USS *Albany*; aircraft carriers USS *Monterey* and USS *Saratoga;* the gunboat USS *Palos*; and the aircraft tender and minelayer USS *Shawmut*.

He died while a passenger aboard the dirigible, *Akron,* which crashed off the coast of New Jersey.

Chambers Field

Location: Norfolk, Virginia
Status: Now, Norfolk Naval Station
Named for: Captain Washington Irving Chambers
Date of Birth: 1856
Place of Birth: Kingsport, New York
Date of Death: September 23, 1934
Place of Death: No Data Found
Decorations and Honors: Medal of the Aeronautical Society (1912)
Place of Burial: Arlington National Cemetery, Section South, Site 3936

Captain Washington Irving Chambers was a staunch promoter of aviation in the naval fleet.

Chambers graduated from the United States Naval Academy at Annapolis, Maryland, in 1876 and became assistant chief of the Bureau of Ordnance from 1907 to 1909 where he studied the potential use of Professor Samuel P. Langley's flying machine. Believing that airplanes could take off from ships, he worked closely with aircraft manufacturer, Glenn Curtiss and Lieutenant Theodore Ellyson, in demonstrating the advantages of aviation to the navy. After proving his theory a success with the first test at the naval yards at Norfolk, Virginia, on November 1910, Chambers ordered the navy's first airplane, the Curtiss A-1 on May 8, 1911.

Chambers also participated in the rescue of General Adolphus Washington Greely and seven of his crewmembers during the Greely Relief Expedition of 1881.

Chase Field

Location: Beeville, Texas
Status: Closed
Named for: Lieutenant Commander Nathan Brown Chase
Date of Birth: September 3, 1889
Place of Birth: Washington, D.C.
Date of Death: June 23, 1925
Place of Death: Pearl Harbor, Hawaii
Decorations and Honors: Mexican Service Medal; World War I Victory Medal
Place of Burial: Arlington National Cemetery, Section E, Site 3886

Lieutenant Commander Nathan Brown Chase was a naval aviator.

Chase graduated from the United States Naval Academy at Annapolis, Maryland, in 1912 and was assigned to the battleship USS *Georgia* with the 3rd

Division, Atlantic Fleet, until 1915. From January to March 1916, he was assigned to the battleship USS *North Carolina*. Following flight training at Naval Air Station Pensacola, Florida, he received his pilot wings and was designated naval aviator number 37.

Chase commanded Naval Air Stations Bay Shore, Long Island; Brunswick, Georgia; and Chatham, Massachusetts. In October 1919, he served as an instructor at Carlstrom Field in Arcadia, Florida. In 1920, he served in the Bureau of Construction and Repair, Aircraft Branch, in Washington, D.C. He served aboard the USS *Aroostook* as commanding officer of Fighting Squadron 2. He was promoted to the rank of lieutenant commander in December 1922. Chase was killed in an air collision while leading his squadron in fighter tactics.

Chevalier Field

Location: Pensacola, Florida
Status: Now, Naval Air Technical Training Center
Named for: Lieutenant Commander Godfrey DeCourcelles Chevalier
Date of Birth: March 7, 1889
Place of Birth: Providence, Rhode Island
Date of Death: November 14, 1922
Place of Death: U.S. Naval Hospital in Norfolk, Virginia
Decorations and Honors: Distinguished Service Medal; Mexican Service Medal; World War I Victory Medal with overseas clasp; French Legion of Honor, rank of Chevalier; French Croix de Guerre with palm
Place of Burial: Arlington National Cemetery, Section 3, Site 4646

Lieutenant Commander Godfrey DeCourcelles Chevalier was an aviator who made naval history when he successfully landed the first plane on a moving ship.

Chevalier graduated from the United States Naval Academy at Annapolis, Maryland, in June 1910 and was assigned to the battleship USS *New Hampshire* with the 2nd Division, Atlantic Fleet, where on October 10, 1910, he swam the frigid waters of the Hudson River to rescue twenty men when the barge carrying them to their ship overturned in high waves. He was promoted several ranks for his heroism. He showed his courage again in March 1911, when a valve sprung a leak and began filling the engine room of his ship with water. He dove into the water and sealed the leak with a bucket of red lead, saving the navy more than a million dollars in damage.

On March 19, 1913, he made a record flight with Lieutenant John H. Towers during Atlantic Fleet Maneuvers over Cuba. Chevalier served as an instructor at the United States Naval Academy until 1914. Afterward, he was sent with the Aviation Detachment on board the cruiser USS *Birmingham* to Tampico,

Mexico, for aviation maneuvers, and later to Pensacola, Florida, for duty in experimental aviation, with additional duty as inspector of hydroaeroplanes.

He received flight training and was designated naval aviator number 7 in March 1915. In 1916, he was assigned to the battleship USS *North Carolina* where he participated in the installation of the first catapult on a naval ship and piloted the first plane shot off a catapult. Chevalier died from multiple injuries received in a plane crash near Norfolk, Virginia.

His Distinguished Service Medal citation reads as follows:

For exceptional meritorious service in a duty of great responsibility in connection with the first aeronautical detachment to reach France, and as Commander of the U.S. Naval Air Station at Dunkirk, which was established and maintained in spite of constant bombing by the enemy.

Corry Field

Location: Pensacola, Florida
Status: Now, Naval Technical Training Center
Named for: Lieutenant Commander William Merrill Corry, Jr.
Date of Birth: October 5, 1889
Place of Birth: Quincy, Florida
Date of Death: October 6, 1920
Place of Death: Hartford, Connecticut
Decorations and Honors: Medal of Honor, posthumously; Navy Cross
Place of Burial: Eastern Cemetery in Quincy, Florida

Lieutenant Commander William Merrill Corry, Jr., was a naval aviator.

Corry graduated from the United States Naval Academy at Annapolis, Maryland, in 1910 and spent five years serving on the battleship USS *Kansas*. In 1915, he began pilot training at Naval Air Station Pensacola, Florida, and was designated naval aviator number 23 in March 1916. He was then assigned to the armored cruiser USS *Seattle*, and later to the battleship USS *North Carolina*.

From 1918 to 1920, Corry commanded naval air stations at La Croisic and Brest, France, where he was promoted to lieutenant commander and helped remove U.S. Naval Aviation forces from Europe as part of the postwar demobilization. In mid-1920, Corry served on the battleship USS *Pennsylvania* as aviation aide to the commander in chief, Atlantic Fleet.

His Medal of Honor citation reads as follows:

For heroic service in attempting to rescue a brother officer from a flame-enveloped airplane. On October 2, 1920, an airplane in which Lieutenant Commander Corry was a passenger crashed and burst into flames. He was thrown thirty feet clear of the plane and, though injured, rushed back to the burning machine and endeavored to release the pilot. In so doing he sustained serious burns, from which he died four days later.

His Navy Cross citation for action during World War I reads as follows:

The Navy Cross is awarded to Lieutenant Commander William M. Corry, U.S, Navy, for distinguished and heroic service as an air pilot making many daring flights over the enemy's lines, also for untiring and efficient efforts toward the organization of U.S. Naval Aviation, foreign service, and the building up of the northern bombing project.

Cuddihy Field

Location: Corpus Christi, Texas
Status: Closed
Named for: Lieutenant George Thomas Cuddihy
Date of Birth: February 22, 1896
Place of Birth: Alto, Michigan
Date of Death: November 25, 1929
Place of Death: Anacostia, D.C.
Decorations and Honors: Distinguished Flying Cross, posthumously; World War I Victory Medal with Atlantic Fleet clasp
Place of Burial: Arlington national Cemetery, Section 6, Site 8477

Lieutenant George Thomas Cuddihy was a test pilot who established a world's record flying a navy CR-3 seaplane at a speed of 188.82 mph during the Naval Air Meet at Bay Shore, Maryland, in October 1924.

Cuddihy graduated from the United States Naval Academy at Annapolis, Maryland, in 1918. He was assigned to the battleship USS *Mississippi*, and later to Naval Air Station Pensacola, Florida, for aviation training. He was assigned to Aircraft Squadron, Battle Fleet, on the West Coast and commanded the high-speed aviation gunnery unit from 1922 to 1924. Cuddihy was the head of the Flight Test Division when he was killed in a crash while testing a Bristol airplane.

His Distinguished Flying Cross citation reads as follows:

For extraordinary achievements while participating in an aerial flight on August 7, 1929, for the purpose of determining the "flat" spinning characteristics of the type F-4B-L airplanes (fighting land planes). During this flight, Lieutenant Cuddihy put the airplane in a tailspin at an altitude of 10,000 feet. It soon assumed the position of a "flat" spin, and apparently could not be again brought under control until Lieutenant Cuddihy discovered a method of altering the head resistance, which resulted in control being regained and a safe landing effected. This principal of regaining control is one that applies to all types of airplanes and will undoubtedly be the means of preventing many crashes. Lieutenant Cuddihy's entire service in the aeronautical forces of the Navy has been marked by conscientious hard work and crowned by notable achievements, some of which are his services as a test pilot, as a pilot of racing craft and in successfully making a flight from Buenos Aires, Argentina, to Santiago, Chile over the Andes Mountains. The interest and efficiency displayed by Lieutenant Cuddihy in the performance of his duty, and his willingness to undertake the most hazardous feats have contributed much toward the advancement of the science of aeronautics while his modesty, earnestness and courage have been an inspiration to his comrades.

Earle Naval Weapons Station

Location: Colts Neck, New Jersey
Status: Active
Named for: Rear Admiral Ralph Earle
Date of Birth: May 3, 1874
Place of Birth: Worcester, Massachusetts
Date of Death: February 13, 1939
Place of Death: No Data Found
Date of Retirement: 1927

Rear Admiral Ralph Earle was considered an expert on guns and explosives and was chief of the Bureau of Ordnance during World War I.

Earle graduated from the United States Naval Academy at Annapolis, Maryland, in 1896 and served at sea aboard the USS *Massachusetts,* USS *Essex,* and USS *Hornet.* He commanded the cruiser USS *Dolphin* during the occupation of Veracruz, Mexico, and later the USS *Connecticut.* He received praise from President William Howard Taft and Secretary of the Navy George Meyer for his conduct during the disastrous turret explosion board the battleship USS *Missouri* on April 13, 1909.

Earle served at the United States Naval Academy and the Naval Proving Ground and was instrumental in designing long-range artillery mounted 14-inch guns on railway cars that were used on the Western Front.

After his retirement, Earle served as the sixth president of Worcester Polytechnic Institute and chair of the Board of Trustees from 1925 until his death. The destroyer USS *Earle* was also named in his honor.

★★★

Ellyson Field

Location: Pensacola, Florida
Status: Closed (now, Ellyson Industrial Park)
Named for: Commander Theodore Gordon "Spuds" Ellyson
Date of Birth: February 27, 1885
Place of Birth: Richmond, Virginia
Date of Death: February 27, 1928
Place of Death: Enroute to Annapolis from Norfolk, Virginia
Decorations and Honors: Navy Cross; World War I Victory Medal with submarine chaser clasp; inducted in the National Aviation Hall of Fame (1964)
Place of Burial: United States Naval Academy Cemetery, Section 04-0557

Commander Theodore Gordon Ellyson was the first U.S. Navy officer to qualify as an airplane pilot, becoming the first naval aviator.

Ellyson graduated from the United States Naval Academy at Annapolis, Maryland, in 1905. During his early career he served aboard the battleships USS *Texas*, USS *Missouri*, USS *Pennsylvania*, USS *Colorado*, and USS *West Virginia*; the tender USS *Rainbow*; and the submarine USS *Shark*. He commanded the patrol boat USS *Tarantula*, and served during the fitting out of the submarine USS *Seal* at Newport News, Virginia.

Ellyson worked with Glenn Curtiss in designing a pontoon for aircraft and became the first passenger to fly in a float plane. With Navy Lieutenant John H. Towers as pilot, Ellyson made the longest over-water flight on January 26, 1911, flying from Annapolis, Maryland, to within two miles of Fort Monroe in Virginia, traveling over the Chesapeake Bay nearly the entire flight.

He piloted the Curtiss A-1 flying boat in its first successful catapult launch from an anchored barge at the Washington Navy Yard in November 1912. On February 14, 1918, he was assigned to the Submarine Chaser Base in New London, Connecticut, and in June, he was transferred to England for duty with a submarine chaser squadron at U.S. Naval Base 27 in Plymouth.

After the war, he remained in Europe commanding Nucleus Crew 14 (zeppelin) until May 1919. In January 1921, he served as executive officer of the Naval Operating Base at Hampton Roads, Virginia, and on October 21, 1921, he was put in charge of the Plans Division there. In December 1922, he was assigned to the U.S. Naval Mission in Brazil where he helped reorganize the Brazilian navy. In July 1925, he assumed command of Torpedo Squadron 1, and from March to June 1926, he was executive officer of the seaplane tender USS *Wright*. He was married to Helen Mildred Lewis Glenn. Ellyson was killed in a plane crash while on a night flight.

His Navy Cross citation reads as follows:

For distinguished service in the line of his profession as Assistant for Operations to the Commander, Submarine Chaser Detachment One, and was largely responsible for the development of successful submarine chaser tactics and doctrine.

Flatley Field

Location: Olathe, Kansas
Status: Closed
Named for: Vice Admiral James Henry "Jimmy" Flatley, Jr.
Date of Birth: June 17, 1906
Place of Birth: Green Bay, Wisconsin
Date of Death: July 9, 1958
Place of Death: U.S. Naval Hospital in Bethesda, Maryland
Decorations and Honors: Navy Cross; Distinguished Service Medal; Legion of Merit with combat V device; Distinguished Flying Cross with gold star; Bronze Star; Presidential Unit Citation with five blue stars; American Defense Service Medal with fleet clasp; Asiatic-Pacific Campaign Medal with two silver stars; American Campaign Medal; World War II Victory Medal; National Defense Service Medal; Philippine Liberation Medal with bronze star
Place of Burial: Arlington National Cemetery, Section 30, Site 337

Vice Admiral James Henry Flatley, Jr., was an ace fighter pilot and aircraft carrier commander.

Flatley graduated from the United States Naval Academy at Annapolis, Maryland, in 1929 and received his pilot wings in 1931. At the beginning of World War II, he was assigned as the executive office of Fighting Squadron 5 based aboard the aircraft carrier USS *Lexington*. In 1942, he trained and commanded Fighting Squadron 10, known as "The Grim Reapers," that fought Japanese aircraft in the Pacific. In October 1945, he became director of training at Naval Air Station Corpus Christi, Texas.

In 1950, Flatley commanded Naval Air Station Olathe, Kansas; the escort carrier USS *Block Island*; and the aircraft carrier USS *Lake Champlain*. He was also the director of the Air Warfare Division in the office of the chief of Naval Operations at the Pentagon. He was married to Dorothy McMurray of Bartow, Florida.

His Navy Cross citation reads, in part, as follows:

For extraordinary heroism and conspicuous courage in action against enemy Japanese forces in the Battle of the Coral Sea on May 7 and 8, 1942. As leader of the fighting escort of our own planes attacking an enemy Japanese carrier, Lieutenant Commander Flatley fearlessly engaged enemy fighters, destroying one and assisting in the destruction of another with no loss to his own escort group. That evening, he led a seven plane division on combat air patrol in a fierce attack and resultant dispersal of a formation of enemy scouting planes, assisting in the destruction of two of them. On May 8, fighting persistently, and at great odds, he again led a division of the combat air patrol in a courageous attack against enemy aircraft attacking our surface forces and destroyed an enemy fighter harassing our anti-torpedo plane patrol and assisted in the destruction of two others. On all these occasions, Lieutenant Commander Flatley displayed the highest qualities of leadership, aggressiveness and complete disregard for his own personal safety.

Fleming Field

Location: Minneapolis, Minnesota
Status: Closed (now, civilian airport)
Named for: Captain Richard E. Fleming, USMC
Date of Birth: November 2, 1917
Place of Birth: St. Paul, Minnesota
Date of Death: June 5, 1942
Place of Death: Pacific Ocean
Decorations and Honors: Medal of Honor, posthumously
Place of Burial: Fort Snelling National Cemetery in Minneapolis, Minnesota, Section F-1, Site 111

Captain Richard E. Fleming was a Marine Corps aviator.

Captain Fleming attended the University of Minnesota and received a bachelor of arts degree in 1939. He enlisted in the Marine Corps, and was assigned to Naval Air Station San Diego, California. He arrived at Midway Island ten days after the Japanese attack on Pearl Harbor.

His Medal of Honor citation for action during World War II reads as follows:

For extraordinary heroism and conspicuous intrepidity above and beyond the call of duty as Flight Officer, Marine Scout Bombing Squadron 241, during action against enemy Japanese forces in the Battle of Midway on June 4 and 5, 1942. When his Squadron Commander was shot down during the initial attack upon an enemy aircraft carrier, Captain Fleming led the remainder of the division with such fearless determination that he dived his own plane to the perilously low altitude of 400 feet before releasing his bomb. Although his craft was riddled by 179 hits in the blistering hail of fire that burst upon him from Japanese fighter guns and antiaircraft batteries, he pulled out with only two minor wounds inflicted upon himself. On the night of June 4, when the squadron commander lost his way and became separated from the others, Captain Fleming brought his own plane in for a safe landing at its base despite hazardous weather conditions and total darkness. The following day, after less than four hours' sleep, he led the second division of his squadron in a coordinated glide-bombing and dive-bombing assault upon a Japanese battleship. Undeterred by a fateful approach glide, during which his ship was struck and set afire, he grimly pressed home his attack to an altitude of 500 feet, released his bomb to score a near miss on the stern of his target, then crashed to the sea in flames. His dauntless perseverance and unyielding devotion to duty were in keeping with the highest traditions of the U.S. Naval Service.

Floyd Bennett Field

Location: Brooklyn, New York
Status: Closed (now, under control of the National Park Service)
Named for: Warrant Officer Floyd Bennett
Date of Birth: October 25, 1890
Place of Birth: Warrensburg, New York
Date of Death: April 25, 1928
Place of Death: Quebec, Canada
Decorations and Honors: Medal of Honor; Distinguished Service Medal; Medal of the National Geographic Society
Place of Burial: Arlington National Cemetery, Section 3, Site 1852

Warrant Officer Floyd Bennett was a test pilot and explorer.

Bennett enlisted in the U.S. Navy in 1917 and became chief machinists mate aboard the sloop USS *Richmond*. In 1925, he accompanied Admiral Richard E. Byrd on the MacMillan Expedition to the Arctic. On May 9, 1926, they made history by being the first men to fly over the North Pole in a 3-engine Fokker monoplane, the *Josephine Ford*.

He contracted influenza and died of pneumonia while attempting to rescue the Irish-German crew of the *Bremen*, which was forced down on Greenly Island, Quebec.

His Medal of Honor citation reads as follows:

For distinguishing himself conspicuously by courage and intrepidity at the risk of his life as a member of the Byrd Antarctic Expedition and thus contributing largely to the success of the first heavier-than-air flight to the North Pole and return.

Forrest Sherman Field (formerly, Fort Barrancas Airfield)

Location: Pensacola, Florida
Status: Active
Named for: Admiral Forrest Percival Sherman
Date of Birth: October 30, 1896
Place of Birth: Merrimack, New Hampshire
Date of Death: July 22, 1951
Place of Death: Naples, Italy

Decorations and Honors: Navy Cross
Place of Burial: Arlington National Cemetery, Section 30, Lot 633

Admiral Forrest Percival Sherman was chief of Naval Operations from 1949 to 1951.

Sherman graduated from the United States Naval Academy at Annapolis, Maryland, in 1917. During World War I, he served in Europe as an officer on the gunboat USS *Nashville* and the destroyer USS *Murray*. From 1919 to 1921, Sherman was assigned to the battleship USS *Utah,* and then to the destroyer USS *Reid*, and later he served as commanding officer of the destroyer USS *Barry*.

He received flight training at Naval Air Station Pensacola, Florida, and was designated a naval aviator in December 1922. In 1927, he served aboard the aircraft carrier USS *Lexington*. While serving on the carrier USS *Saratoga*, he commanded Scouting Squadron 2, and was assigned as flag secretary to Commander Aircraft Squadrons, Battle Fleet.

From 1930 to 1937, Sherman served at the Naval Academy, commanded Fighting Squadron 1, led the Aviation Ordnance Section of the Bureau of Ordnance, and was navigator of the aircraft carrier USS *Ranger*.

From 1941 to 1942, Sherman served with the Office of the Chief of Naval Operations and was a member of the Permanent Joint Board on Defense in Canada and the United States. In May 1942, he took command of the aircraft carrier USS *Wasp* where he participated in the Solomon Islands campaign. Later, Sherman became chief of staff to Commander Air Force, Pacific Fleet.

In November 1943, Sherman was assigned as deputy chief of staff to Admiral Chester W. Nimitz and held that position for the remainder of World War II, during which time he played a critical role in planning the offensives that helped win the war in the Pacific. He was present at the surrender of Japan aboard the battleship USS *Missouri* on September 2, 1945. In December 1945, he became deputy chief of Naval Operations and, in January 1948, he was placed in command of Naval Operations in the Mediterranean Sea. In October 1949, he became chief of Naval Operations, with the rank of admiral. While on a military and diplomatic trip to Europe, Sherman died of heart attack.

The destroyer USS *Forrest Sherman* was also named in his honor.

Frederick C. Sherman Field

Location: San Clemente Island, California
Status: Now, Naval Air Landing Field
Named for: Vice Admiral Frederick Carl "Ted" Sherman
Date of Birth: May 27, 1888
Place of Birth: Port Huron, Michigan

Date of Death: July 27, 1957
Place of Death: San Diego, California
Decorations and Honors: Navy Cross
Date of Retirement: 1947
Place of Burial: Fort Rosecrans National Cemetery in San Diego, California

Vice Admiral Frederick Carl Sherman served during World War I and World War II.

Sherman was a 1910 graduate of the United States Naval Academy at Annapolis, Maryland, and served as a submarine commander during World War I. He became an aviator and served as executive officer aboard the aircraft carrier USS *Saratoga* in 1937, and in 1938, he commanded Naval Air Station San Diego, California.

He was assigned captain of the aircraft carrier USS *Lexington* where he directed the air operations during the raid on Rabaul in February 1942, and where he lost the ship in the battle of the Coral Sea. He served as commander, Carrier Division 2, on board the aircraft carrier USS *Essex,* in 1943.

Sherman led fast carriers from 1942 to 1945 and participated in battles of Rabaul, Leyte Gulf, Iwo Jima, and Okinawa. As a rear admiral, he commanded the aircraft carrier USS *Enterprise*. On June 14, 1945, he was promoted to vice admiral and became commander of the 5th Fleet.

Sherman's motto was "Kill the bastards scientifically." He was the author of *Combat Command: The American Aircraft Carriers in the Pacific War* (New York: Dutton, 1950).

Frederick M. Trapnell Field

Location: Naval Air Station Patuxent River, Maryland
Status: Active
Named for: Vice Admiral Frederick M. Trapnell
Date of Birth: 1903
Place of Birth: Elizabeth, New Jersey
Date of Death: January 1975
Place of Death: San Diego, California
Decorations and Honors: Octave Chanute Award*

Vice Admiral Frederick M. Trapnell was the navy's first test pilot.

Trapnell graduated from the United States Naval Academy at Annapolis, Maryland, in 1923 and completed flight training at Naval Air Station Pensacola, Florida, and received his pilot wings in 1927. He was assigned to the airship *Akron*, the navy's airplane-carrying dirigible. After the crash of the *Akron* in 1933, he was assigned to her sister ship, *Macon*, where he was responsible for redesigning and testing the gear and airplane hookup methods.

From 1940 to 1943, Trapnell was assigned to the Flight Test Section in Maryland where he helped develop and test modifications on two high-performance navy fighters, one being the Corsair that was used during the war.

In early 1943, Trapnell was assigned to the Army Air Force's new secret test base at Muroc Dry Lake, California, where he flew and evaluated the Bell XP-59A. He test-flew the Grumman F9F Panther, McDonnell F2H Banshee, and the North American Fury. He helped establish a formalized course of instruction for test pilots and formed the U.S. Navy Test Pilot School. He took command of the aircraft carrier USS *Coral Sea* in 1950 where he participated in the first deployment of jet fighters aboard ship.

* The Octave Chanute Award, given in 1949, was from the Institute of Aeronautical Sciences for the pilot who had contributed most to aviation in that year.

Halsey Field

Location: North Island Naval Air Station in California
Status: Active
Named for: Fleet Admiral William Frederick "Bull" Halsey, Jr.
Date of Birth: October 30, 1882
Place of Birth: Elizabeth, New Jersey
Date of Death: August 16, 1959
Place of Death: Fishers Island Country Club in New York
Decorations and Honors: Navy Cross; Navy Distinguished Service Medal with three gold stars; Army Distinguished Service Medal; Presidential Unit Citation; World War I Victory Medal with destroyer clasp; American Campaign Medal; Asiatic-Pacific Campaign Medal; World War II Victory Medal; Mexican Service Medal; American Defense Service Medal with fleet clasp; National Defense Service Medal; Philippine Liberation Medal
Date of Retirement: March 1, 1947
Place of Burial: Arlington National Cemetery, Section 2, Site 1184

Fleet Admiral William Frederick Halsey, Jr., was the fourth and last officer to hold the rank of Fleet Admiral.

Halsey graduated from the United States Naval Academy at Annapolis, Maryland, in February 1904 and was commissioned an ensign. In 1907, Halsey made the famous World Cruise aboard the battleship USS *Kansas*.

He spent most of his twenty-five years of sea duty commanding the destroyers USS *DuPont*, USS *Lamson*, USS *Flusser*, USS *Jarvis*, USS *Benham*, USS *O'Brien*, USS *Shaw*, USS *Chauncey*, USS *John Francis Burnes*, USS *Wickes*, USS *Dale*, and USS *Osborne*.

Halsey served in the Office of Naval Intelligence in Washington, D.C., and as naval attaché at the American Embassy in Berlin, Germany; Christiana, Norway; Copenhagen, Denmark; and Stockholm, Sweden. He served one year as executive officer of the battleship USS *Wyoming*.

He served in Carrier Division 2 aboard the aircraft carrier USS *Yorktown* and, in Carrier Division 1 aboard the aircraft carrier USS *Saratoga*, and later he was placed in command of her. He was commander, Task Force 16 aboard the aircraft carrier USS *Enterprise*, which escorted the aircraft carrier USS *Hornet* to within eight hundred miles of Tokyo to launch the army planes for Colonel Jimmy Doolittle's raid on Japan on April 18, 1942. In October 1942, Halsey participated in the Guadalcanal campaign, and later he saw action in the Solomon Islands and the Japanese stronghold at Rabaul. In June 1944, as commander of the 3rd Fleet, he was designated Commander, Western Pacific, Task Forces, where he fought the Japanese in the Palais, Philippines, Formosa, Okinawa and South China Sea.

Halsey was on the battleship USS *Missouri* on September 2, 1945, in Tokyo Bay when the Japanese signed the surrender. After retiring, Halsey tried to preserve the aircraft carrier USS *Enterprise* as a national shrine, but was unsuccessful. He was elected honorary vice president of the Naval Historical Foundation.

His Navy Cross citation for action during World War I reads as follows:

The Navy Cross is awarded to Commander William F. Halsey, Jr., U.S. Navy, for distinguished service in the line of his profession as commanding officer of the USS *O'Brien* and the USS *Shaw*, engaged in the important, exacting and hazardous duty of patrolling the waters infested with enemy submarines and mines, in escorting and protecting vitally important convoys of troops and supplies through these waters and in offensive and defensive action, vigorously and unremittingly prosecuted against all forms of enemy naval activity.

Harvey Field

Location: Inyokern, California
Status: Closed
Named for: Lieutenant Commander Warren Wallace Harvey
Date of Birth: May 9, 1901
Place of Birth: Garrett, Indiana
Date of Death: December 12, 1940
Place of Death: Naval Air Station in Anacostia, D.C.
Place of Burial: Arlington National Cemetery, Section S, Site 5038

Lieutenant Commander Warren Wallace Harvey contributed to the development of aviation ordnance and fighter tactics.

Harvey graduated from the United States Naval Academy at Annapolis, Maryland, in 1924. He qualified as a naval aviator in November 1926 and served in Fighting Squadron 1 and Scouting Squadron 6 at San Diego, California.

After flight training at Naval Air Station Pensacola, Florida, in 1927, he served in Aircraft Squadron Battle Force and in Patrol Squadrons based at Pearl Harbor, Hawaii. He also was in command of the patrol seaplane assigned to search for Amelia Earhart's missing plane in the vicinity of Howland Island on July 3, 1937.

Hensley Field

Location: Dallas, Texas
Status: Now, Texas Air National Guard Base
Named for: Major William Nicholas Hensley, USMC
Date of Birth: August 14, 1918
Place of Birth: Pasadena, California
Date of Death: May 10, 1951
Place of Death: Houston, Texas
Decorations and Honors: Distinguished Flying Cross; Air Medal
Place of Burial: Arlington National Cemetery, Section 6, Site 5788

Major William Nicholas Hensley made the first transatlantic dirigible crossing in 1919.

Hensley graduated from Cumberland University, and later he taught there before taking the Texas bar exams in 1939. He joined the army's Enlisted Reserve Corps in 1937, received a commission and pilot wings in 1941, and was called to active duty after the bombing of Pearl Harbor. While serving in Guam, he commanded the 16th Bombardment Squadron and led bombing missions against Japan, flying 105 combat hours.

After the war, Hensley became district attorney for Bexar County in Texas. In 1947, he helped organize the 182nd Fighter Squadron and was its commander. When his unit was called to active duty during the Korean Conflict, he completed flight training in the Republic F-84 Thunderjet at Langley Air Force Base in Virginia.

Hensley was killed in a plane crash while returning on a flight from San Antonio, Texas, en route to Virginia. A small Bible and Texas flag were found in his pocket when he died.

Isely Field

Location: Aslito on Saipan, Mariana Islands
Status: Closed (now, Saipan International Airport)
Named for: Commander Robert Henry Isely, USN*
Date of Birth: December 25, 1909
Place of Birth: Cimarron, Kansas
Date of Death: June 13, 1944
Place of Death: Aslito Field in Saipan, Mariana Island
Decorations and Honors: Navy Cross; Distinguished Flying Cross, both posthumously

Commander Robert Henry Isely served during World War II in the Pacific, Atlantic, and Caribbean areas.

Isely graduated from the United States Naval Academy at Annapolis, Maryland, in 1933. In 1937, he received flight training at Naval Air Station Pensacola, Florida, and was designated a naval aviator.

In 1943, he was promoted to the rank of commander and became the commanding officer of VT-16 (Torpedo Squadron), part of Task Force 58, aboard the aircraft carrier USS *Lexington,* which carried out bombing raids against the Japanese at Tarawa, Wake, Kwajalein, Mille, Palau, Truk, and Hollandia.

Isely was killed while leading his squadron in a low altitude, preinvasion bombing strafing attack against the Japanese on Aslito Airfield on Saipan. While flying a Grumman TBF Avenger, he was hit by Japanese antiaircraft fire and crashed in flames at the south edge of the runway.

* Many sources refer to the field as Isley, others as Isely. The name was misspelled.

John Rodgers Field

Location: Barber Point, Hawaii
Status: Closed (now, Honolulu International Airport)
Named for: Commander John Rodgers
Date of Birth: January 15, 1881
Place of Birth: Washington, D.C.
Date of Death: August 26, 1926
Place of Death: U.S. Naval Hospital in Bethesda, Maryland
Place of Burial: Arlington National Cemetery, Section 1, Site 130

Commander John Rodgers was an aviation pioneer, and the great-grandson of John Rodgers (1773–1838) and the grandson of Sarah (Perry) Rodgers, daughter of Commodore Matthew C. Perry.

Rodgers graduated from the United States Naval Academy at Annapolis, Maryland, in 1903 and received flying lessons at a school operated by the Wright brothers, to become the second naval officer to be licensed as an aviator. During World War I, he served in the submarine service. He was also responsible for establishing the naval air station at San Diego, California.

He was commander of the Naval Air Station Pearl Harbor, Hawaii, where, with a four-man crew, he made the first transpacific flight from San Francisco to Hawaii in 1925, using a navy-designed seaplane. Low on fuel, he had to land on the sea but was spotted and rescued eight days later.

On August 16, 1926, while serving as assistant chief of the Bureau of Aeronautics, Rogers was placed in command of a newly created experimental scouting seaplane squadron in San Diego, California. Rogers was killed while en route to Philadelphia when his plane crashed into the shallow water of the Delaware River.

Maxfield Field

Located: Lakehurst, New Jersey
Status: Active
Named for: Commander Louis Henry Maxfield
Date of Birth: November 19, 1883
Place of Birth: St. Paul, Minnesota
Date of Death: August 24, 1921
Place of Death: East Coast of Northern England
Place of Burial: Arlington National Cemetery, Site 4560

Commander Louis Henry Maxfield was commander of the Rigid Air Detachment for the United States Navy.

Maxfield graduated from the United States Naval Academy at Annapolis, Maryland, in 1907. He received aviation training at Pensacola, Florida, and was designated a pilot in the heavier-than-air branch. In September 1917, he went to Akron, Ohio, where he qualified as a pilot in lighter-than-air dirigibles. Later that year, he became commander of U.S. Naval Air Station Paimboeuf, France. He was killed in the crash of the Short Brothers' dirigible R-38, a British rigid airship that was built for the U.S. Navy as the ZR-2, the world's largest airship at that time.

McCain Field

Location: Meridian, Mississippi
Status: Active
Named for: Admiral John Sidney McCain, Sr.
Date of Birth: August 9, 1884
Place of Birth: Teoc, Mississippi
Date of Death: September 6, 1945
Place of Death: United States
Decorations and Honors: Navy Cross; Distinguished Service Medal with two gold stars
Place of Burial: Arlington National Cemetery, Section 3, Grave 4356

Admiral John Sidney McCain, Sr., served as chief of the Naval Bureau of Aeronautics; deputy chief of Naval Operations for Air; and commander, Carrier Task Force 38.

McCain graduated from the United States Naval Academy at Annapolis, Maryland, in 1906 and served in the American occupation of Veracruz during the Mexican Revolution. He served aboard many ships, including the USS *Maryland*, USS *New Mexico*, and the communication ship USS *Nitro*. After flight training in 1936, he was designated a Naval Aviator, and from 1937 to 1939 he commanded the USS *Ranger*.

During World War II, he served as commander of air forces for Western Sea Frontier and the South Pacific Force where he commanded all Allied air operations during the Guadalcanal campaign.

In 1944, after a brief assignment in Washington, D.C., he returned to the Pacific Theater to command a fast carrier task force that saw action over Peleliu, Leyte Gulf, Philippine Sea, Mindoro, Luzon, Formosa, and Ryukyus where his planes sank forty-nine Japanese ships. McCain was aboard the USS *Missouri* for the signing of the Japanese the surrender on September 2, 1945. He was married to Katherine Vaulx.

McCalla Field

Location: Guantanamo Bay, Cuba
Status: Closed
Named for: Captain Bowman Henry McCalla
Date of Birth: June 19, 1844
Place of Birth: Camden, New Jersey
Date of Death: May 6, 1910
Place of Death: Santa Barbara, California
Place of Burial: Arlington National Cemetery, Section E, Site 857

Captain Bowman Henry McCalla graduated from the United States Naval Academy at Annapolis, Maryland, in 1865 and was the captain of the cruiser USS *Marblehead* during the capture of Guantanamo Bay in 1898, and later he became the first commander of the base established there during the Spanish-American War. He also participated in the China Relief Expedition on June 10, 1900.

He commanded the USS *Newark* during the Boxer Rebellion in 1901, where he led a force of English blue jackets from Tientsin to Peking. McCalla also commanded naval troops immediately following the 1906 San Francisco earthquake where he helped restore order to the city.

The USS *McCalla* (DD-253) was also named in his honor.

Mitscher Field

Location: Miramar, California
Status: Active
Named for: Admiral Marc Andrew "Pete" Mitscher
Date of Birth: January 26, 1887
Place of Birth: Hillsboro, Wisconsin
Date of Death: February 3, 1947
Place of Death: Norfolk, Virginia
Decorations and Honors: Navy Cross with two gold stars; inducted into the International Aerospace Hall of Fame (1989); inducted into the National Aviation Hall of Fame (1989)
Place of Burial: Arlington National Cemetery, Section 2, Site 4942

Admiral Marc Andrew Mitscher was commander in chief of the U.S. Atlantic Fleet in 1946.

Mitscher graduated from the United States Naval Academy at Annapolis, Maryland, in 1910. In August 1913, he served aboard the destroyer USS *California* during the Mexican campaign. After flight training at Naval Air Station Pensacola, Florida, he was designated naval aviator number 33 on June 2, 1916. On April 6, 1917, he reported for duty aboard the cruiser USS *Huntington* where he experimented with catapulting aircraft from ships. In 1919, he was transferred to the aviation section in the Office of the Chief of Naval Operations and, in 1922, was assigned to the Plans Division, Bureau of Aeronautics.

He was captain of the aircraft carrier USS *Hornet* during the attack on Pearl Harbor, Hawaii, and during Colonel Jimmy Doolittle's raid against Tokyo on April 18, 1942, and also during the Battle of Midway from June 3 to 7, 1942. In 1943, he was the commander of Fleet Air in the Solomon Islands and was the commander of Operations when the aircraft carrying Japanese admiral Isoruku Yamamoto was shot down on April 18, 1943.

In January 1944, Mitscher became commander of Carrier Division 3. He fought in the battle of the Philippine Sea from June 19 to 20, 1944, and in the battle of Leyte Gulf from October 24 to 25, 1944. He was responsible for the defeat of the Japanese kamikazes in the Okinawa campaign in 1945. He became deputy chief of Naval Operations, was appointed to the rank of admiral, and assumed command of the 8th Fleet in 1946. He gave forty-one years of continuous service to the navy.

His Navy Cross citation reads as follows:

The Navy Cross is presented to Marc Andrew Mitscher, Lieutenant Commander, U.S. Navy, for distinguished service in the line of his profession as a member of the crew of the Seaplane NC-1, which made a long overseas flight from Newfoundland to the vicinity of the Azores, in May 1919.

Moffett Field

Location: Sunnyvale, California
Status: Closed (now, privatized federal airfield)
Named for: Rear Admiral William Adger Moffett
Date of Birth: October 31, 1869
Place of Birth: Charleston, South Carolina
Date of Death: April 4, 1933
Place of Death: Coast of New Jersey
Decorations and Honors: Medal of Honor; Distinguished Service Medal; inducted into the National Aviation Hall of Fame (2008)
Place of Burial: Arlington National Cemetery, Section 3, Lot 1655-A

Rear Admiral William Adger Moffett helped in the creation of an aeronautical bureau in the U.S. Navy.

Moffett graduated from the United States Naval Academy at Annapolis, Maryland, in 1898 and served aboard the amphibious cargo ship USS *Charleston* in Commodore George Dewey's fleet in the battle of Manila Bay during the Spanish-American War.

Moffett commanded the cruiser USS *Chester* that was involved in the Tampico Affair during the Mexican Revolution on April 9, 1914; took part in the occupation of Veracruz, Mexico; commanded the Great Lakes Naval Training Center and the 9th, 10th, and 11th naval districts; commanded the battleship USS *Mississippi*; was appointed director of Naval Aviation; and qualified as an aerial observer in June 1921.

During his career he helped organize the U.S. Navy's aviation program; helped plan the expansion of sites and buildings of naval air stations; and oversaw the installation of aircraft landing catapults on battleships and cruisers of the Fleet.

Moffett was killed, and most of the crew lost, in the crash of the airship, *Akron,* when it went down in a severe storm during a flight from Lakehurst to Newport, New Jersey. He was married to Jeanette Whitton. His son, William Adger Moffett, Jr., was also a rear admiral and is buried in Arlington National Cemetery.

His Medal of Honor citation for action during the Mexican campaign (Veracruz) reads as follows:

For distinguished conduct in battle, engagements of Vera Cruz, [sic] April 21 and 22, 1914. Commander Moffett brought his ship into the inner harbor during the nights of the 21st and 22nd without the assistance of a pilot or navigational lights, and was in a position on the morning of the 22nd to use his guns at a critical time with telling effect. His skill in mooring his ship at night was especially noticeable. He placed her nearest to the enemy and did most of the firing and received most of the hits.

Mullinnix Field

Location: Tarawa, Gilbert Islands
Status: Closed
Named for: Rear Admiral Henry Maston Mullinnix
Date of Birth: July 4, 1892
Place of Birth: Spencer, Indiana
Date of Death: November 24, 1943
Place of Death: Aboard the USS *Liscombe Bay* in the Gilbert Islands
Decorations and Honors: Legion of Merit; Purple Heart, posthumously; World War I Victory Medal with destroyer clasp; Asiatic-Pacific Area Campaign Medal; World War II Victory Medal
Place of Burial: Memorialized at the National Memorial Cemetery of the Pacific in Honolulu, Hawaii

Rear Admiral Henry Maston Mullinnix was a naval aviator and commander of the Air Support Group, Carrier Division, during World War II.

Mullinnix graduated from the United States Naval Academy at Annapolis, Maryland, in 1916. During his career, he served aboard destroyers USS *Balch,* USS *Brooks,* and USS *Gridley;* aircraft carriers USS *Saratoga* and USS *Wright*; and was commander of the aircraft tender USS *Albemarle* and the escort carrier USS *Liscombe Bay.*

Mullinnix attended the Massachusetts Institute of Technology in Cambridge, Massachusetts, where he earned a master of science degree in aeronautical engineering in 1923 and went on to help in the development of the air-cooled engine for naval aircraft.

Mullinnix died along with 53 other officers and 591 enlisted men when the escort carrier USS *Liscombe Bay* was torpedoed. Only 272 of the ship's crew were rescued. The USS *Mullinnix* (DD-944) was also named in his honor.

His Legion of Merit citation reads as follows:

For exceptionally meritorious conduct in the performance of outstanding service to the Government of the United States as Commander of a Carrier Air Support Group prior to and during the amphibious invasion of Japanese-held Makin Atoll, Gilbert Islands, from November 1 to 24, 1943. Displaying outstanding initiative and superior executive ability, Rear Admiral Mullinnix skillfully conducted antisubmarine and combat air patrols supporting our landing operations on this strongly defended island, and through his brilliant leadership, enabled escort carriers to carry out a well coordinated, aggressive attack against the enemy. Rear Admiral Mullinnix's tireless efforts, meticulous attention to detail and loyal devotion to the accomplishment of an extremely difficult and hazardous mission contributed materially to our subsequent capture of this strategic area.

Mustin Field

Location: Philadelphia, Pennsylvania
Status: Closed
Named for: Captain Henry Croskey Mustin
Date of Birth: February 6, 1874
Place of Birth: Pennsylvania
Date of Death: August 23, 1923
Place of Death: Naval Hospital, Washington, D.C.
Decorations and Honors: Gold Life Saving Medal
Place of Burial: Arlington National Cemetery, Section S, Site 1332

Captain Henry Croskey Mustin was a pioneer naval aviator who developed a method for launching aircraft from ships. He helped establish the naval air station at Pensacola, Florida, as a naval training center, and also designed the insignia worn by U.S. naval aviators.

Mustin was an 1896 graduate of the United States Naval Academy at Annapolis, Maryland, and served during the Spanish-American War where he sought to improve naval gunnery operations. He earned several patents to improve naval range finding equipment.

He was designated naval aviator number 11, and was commander of the freighter USS *Samar* during the capture of Vigan, Philippines, in 1899. He earned the distinction of being the first pilot to be catapulted from a ship during action at Veracruz in 1914.

In 1915, piloting a Curtiss AB-2 flying boat, Mustin made the first underway catapult launch from the battleship USS *North Carolina* at Pensacola Bay, Florida, and commanded the first catapult launch during hostile fire. He flew the first combat missions of American aircraft from the battleship USS *Mississippi* and was the first commander of Aircraft Squadrons, Battle Fleet.

The destroyer USS *Mustin* was also named in his honor.

Nimitz Field

Location: Alameda, California
Status: Closed
Named for: Fleet Admiral Chester William Nimitz
Date of Birth: February 24, 1885
Place of Birth: Fredericksburg, Texas
Date of Death: February 20, 1966
Place of Death: Treasure Island, San Francisco Bay
Decorations and Honors: Navy Distinguished Service Medal with two gold stars; Army Distinguished Service Medal; Silver Life Saving Medal; World War I Victory Medal with escort clasp and star; American Defense Service Medal; Asiatic-Pacific Campaign Medal; World War II Victory Medal; National Defense Service Medal; numerous foreign medals
Place of Burial: Golden Gate National Cemetery in San Bruno, California

Fleet Admiral Chester William Nimitz signed the Japanese surrender document on behalf of the United States aboard the battleship USS *Missouri* in Tokyo Bay on September 2, 1945.

Nimitz graduated from the United States Naval Academy at Annapolis, Maryland, in 1905, seventh in a class of 114. During World War I, Nimitz served on the staff of the commander of submarines in the Atlantic. He commanded the battleship USS *South Carolina* and cruisers USS *Augusta* and USS *Chicago*. He was chosen by President Theodore Roosevelt to relieve Admiral Husband E. Kimmel at Pearl Harbor after its attack.

Nimitz was promoted to fleet admiral in 1944 and appointed commander in chief of Naval Operations of the Pacific during World War II where he commanded more than two million troops, five thousand ships, and twenty thousand planes during the Battle of Midway, which was considered the greatest victory of the United States Navy.

After the war, he was decorated by fourteen nations and became a goodwill ambassador of the United Nations. He also worked to restore good will with Japan by raising funds for the restoration of the Japanese memorial ship *Mikasa* and urging return of ancestral samurai swords. He was married to Catherine Vance Freeman.

"The Battle of Iwo Jima has been won. Among the Americans who served on Iwo, uncommon valor was a common virtue."—*Fleet Admiral Chester W. Nimitz,* March 17, 1945.

O'Hare Field

Location: Abemama, Gilbert Islands
Status: Closed
Named for: Lieutenant Commander Edward Henry "Butch" O'Hare
Date of Birth: March 13, 1914
Place of Birth: St. Louis, Missouri
Date of Death: November 26, 1943
Place of Death: At sea
Decorations and Honors: Medal of Honor; Navy Cross; Distinguished Flying Cross with gold star; Purple Heart
Place of Burial: Memorialized at the National Memorial Cemetery of the Pacific in Honolulu, Hawaii

Lieutenant Commander Edward Henry O'Hare was the navy's first ace pilot of World War II and the navy's first fighter pilot to receive the Medal of Honor.

O'Hare graduated from the United States Naval Academy at Annapolis, Maryland, in 1937. He received flight training in 1939 at Naval Air Station Pensacola, Florida, and was assigned to Fighter Squadron VF-3 aboard the aircraft carrier USS *Saratoga* in May 1940 and later aboard the carrier USS *Lexington.*

O'Hare's most famous flight occurred on February 20, 1942. Flying a Grumman F-4F Wildcat, he was one of several pilots that intercepted nine Japanese Mitsubishi G4M "Betty" bombers, shot down five, and damaged a sixth, making him an ace pilot. His actions were credited for saving an aircraft carrier from serious damage and loss.

On October 10, 1943, O'Hare flew air strikes against Wake Island and was placed in command of Air Group 6 aboard the aircraft carrier USS *Enterprise* where he supervised three squadrons. On November 26, 1943, he volunteered to lead a mission to conduct the first U.S. Navy nighttime fighter attack from an aircraft carrier to intercept a large force of enemy torpedo bombers. The night-fighter unit, called the Black Panthers, consisting of 1 VT and 2 VF, was catapulted from the ship and flew out into the incoming mass of Japanese planes. O'Hare was last seen as his Grumman F6F Hellcat flew into the darkness and vanished. A three-plane search made at dawn found no trace of O'Hare or his plane.

His Medal of Honor citation for action during World War II reads as follows:

For conspicuous gallantry and intrepidity in aerial combat, at grave risk of his life above and beyond the call of duty, as section leader and pilot of Fighting Squadron 3 on February 20, 1942. Having lost the assistance of his teammates, Lieutenant O'Hare interposed his plane between his ship and an advancing enemy formation of nine attacking twin-engine heavy bombers. Without hesitation, alone and unaided, he repeatedly attacked this enemy formation, at close range in the face of intense combined machine-gun and cannon fire. Despite this concentrated opposition, Lieutenant O'Hare, by his gallant and courageous action, his extremely skillful marksmanship in making the most of every shot of his limited amount of ammunition, shot down five enemy bombers and severely damaged a sixth before they reached the bomb release point. As a result of his gallant action–one of the most daring, if not the most daring, single action in the history of combat aviation—he undoubtedly saved his carrier from serious damage.

The Chicago-area Orchard Depot Airport was renamed O'Hare International Airport in his honor.

Ofstie Field

Located: Roosevelt Roads Naval Station in Puerto Rico
Status: Active
Named for: Vice Admiral Ralph Andrew Ofstie
Date of Birth: November 16, 1897
Place of Birth: Eau Claire, Wisconsin
Date of Death: November 19, 1956
Place of Death: National Naval Medical Center in Bethesda, Maryland
Decorations and Honors: Navy Cross; Republic of Korea Order of Military Merit (Taiguk)
Place of Burial: Arlington National Cemetery, Section 30, Grave 2138

Vice Admiral Ralph Andrew Ofstie was a test pilot, Fleet commander, and deputy chief of Naval Air Operations.

Ofstie graduated from the United States Naval Academy at Annapolis, Maryland, in 1918 and was commissioned an ensign. During his career, he served aboard the torpedo boat destroyer USS *Whipple*; cruiser USS *Chattanooga;* destroyer USS *O'Bannon*; and aircraft carriers USS *Saratoga*, USS *Enterprise*, and USS *Yorktown*. He received his pilot wings after flight training at Naval Air Station Pensacola, Florida.

His many assignments included: commander, Scouting Squadron VS-6; aviation officer aboard the cruiser USS *Detroit*; commander, Fighter Squadron VF-6; assistant naval attaché, Tokyo, Japan; assistant naval attaché, London, England; commander, amphibious assault ship USS *Essex*; commander, Task

Group 32.7, Carrier Division 26.

During World War II, he served as commander on the staff of Admiral Chester W. Nimitz, commander United States Pacific Fleet, at Pearl Harbor, Hawaii. After the war, he was assigned to the Joint Chiefs of Staff Evaluation Group. While serving as commander of the 6th Fleet in European waters, he became ill and was flown back to the United States where he died.

Radford Field

Location: Cubi Point, Philippines
Status: Closed
Named for: Admiral Arthur William Radford
Date of Birth: February 27, 1896
Place of Birth: Chicago, Illinois
Date of Death: August 17, 1973
Place of Death: U.S. Naval Hospital in Bethesda, Maryland
Decorations and Honors: Distinguished Service Medal with three oak leaf clusters; Legion of Merit with oak leaf cluster; Presidential Unit Citation; Navy Unit Commendation; World War I Victory Medal with Atlantic fleet clasp; American Defense Service Medal with fleet clasp; American Defense Service Medal; American Campaign Medal; Asiatic-Pacific Campaign Medal; World War II Victory Medal; National Defense Service Medal; Philippine Liberation Medal with bronze star
Date of Retirement: August 1, 1957
Place of Burial: Arlington National Cemetery, Section 3

Admiral Arthur William Radford was an outspoken opponent of what was known as the "Admirals Revolt," which took a stand against the creation of an independent air force.

Radford graduated from the United States Naval Academy at Annapolis, Maryland, in 1916 and completed flight training at Naval Air Station Pensacola, Florida, in November 1920. During World War I, he served aboard the guided missile carrier USS *South Carolina*; USS *Aroostook*; and battleships USS *Colorado* and USS *Pennsylvania*.

In 1929, he supervised the Alaskan aerial survey operation where he conducted aerial surveys of forest and mineral resources in Alaska. From 1931 to 1932, he was an aide and flag secretary to the commander of Aircraft, Battle Fleet. From 1937 to 1941, he served aboard the aircraft carriers USS *Wright* and USS *Saratoga*; commanded Naval Air Station Seattle, Washington; was executive officer of the aircraft carrier USS *Yorktown*; and commanded the Naval Air Station Trinidad.

In December 1941, he was named director of aviation training in the

Bureau of Aeronautics. From July 1943 to May 1944, he commanded the Northern Carrier Group, that included the aircraft carrier USS *Enterprise*; amphibious assault ship USS *Belleau Wood*; and the aircraft carrier USS *Monterey*. While with the 5th Fleet, he participated in campaigns in the Gilbert and Marshall Islands.

From 1944 to 1949, he commanded Carrier Division 6 and participated in operations at Iwo Jima and Okinawa; became deputy commander of Naval Operations; and later vice chief of Naval Operations; commander, 2nd Task Fleet, Atlantic; commander, Pacific Fleet; and high commissioner of Trust Territory of the Pacific Islands.

In August 1953, he was appointed chairman of the Joint Chiefs of Staff, and reappointed to that position in 1955. He was also involved in the strategy, planning, and execution of the most critical operations of the Korean War.

His Distinguished Service Medal citation reads in part:

Through his courageous initiative and aggressive determination, the first carrier-borne Night Fighter teams were organized and trained at sea, later proving their value by effectively dispersing a hostile night torpedo attack.

Ramey Field

Location: Sanford, Florida
Status: Closed (now, Orlando Sanford International Airport)
Named for: Lieutenant Commander Robert Winford Ramey
Date of Birth: No Data Found
Place of Birth: No Data Found
Date of Death: June 2, 1958
Place of Death: No Data Found
Decorations and Honors: Air Medal with five gold stars; Navy and Marine
    Corps Medal, posthumously

Lieutenant Commander Robert Winford Ramey distinguished himself while participating in aerial flights against the enemy in the Okinawa Gunto Area on March 25, 1945, and while participating in five aerial flights against the enemy at Iwo Jima from February 16, 1945, to March 8, 1945.

Ramey died while guiding his crippled A3D Skywarrior plane away from a residential area.

The citation accompanying his gold star, in lieu of a second Air Medal, reads as follows:

For distinguishing himself by meritorious acts in aerial flight. He served as pilot of a carrier-based fighter plane in destroying an enemy aircraft on January 5, 1945, in the vicinity of Mindoro, Philippine Islands. As leader of the second section of a four-plane division in Composite Squadron 85 aboard the escort carrier, USS *Lunga Point,* he intercepted and engaged an enemy fighter plane. By exhibiting great skill and daring, he shot it down. So closely did he pursue the enemy in a series of radical maneuvers and so daringly did he press the attack that he placed himself in the dangerous position of pulling out of a steep dive at the high speed and at an extremely low altitude. Throughout the action his skill and conduct distinguished him among those performing duties of the same character.

Reeves Field

Location: Lemoore, California
Status: Closed
Named for: Admiral Joseph Mason "Bull" Reeves
Date of Birth: November 20, 1872
Place of Birth: Tampico, Illinois
Date of Death: March 25, 1948
Place of Death: U.S. Naval Hospital in Bethesda, Maryland
Decorations and Honors: Navy Cross; Distinguished Service Medal
Place of Burial: United States Naval Academy Cemetery in Annapolis, Maryland

Admiral Joseph Mason Reeves was responsible for the formation of the modern U.S. carrier strike force.

Reeves graduated from the United States Naval Academy at Annapolis, Maryland, in 1894 and served aboard the battleship USS *Oregon* in operations against Admiral D. Pascual Cervera's fleet in Santiago Harbor in 1898 during the battle of Santiago. During World War I, he was commanding officer of the battleships USS *Maine,* USS *Kansas,* USS *Pittsburgh,* and USS *North Dakota.*

Reeves became a naval aviator at the age of fifty-two and retired at the age of seventy-four. Between those years, he was commander of Aircraft Squadron, Battle Fleet, and served on the experimental aircraft carrier USS *Langley* where he developed revolutionary fleet air tactics that reduced the time it took to launch and recover aircraft from a ship.

He wrote the manual *Aircraft Squadrons, Battle Fleet Tactical Instructions* (1928). He is credited for the origin of the modern football helmet that later became the leather football helmet first worn in an 1893 Army-Navy game. He was married to Eleanor Watkins.

His Navy Cross citation reads as follows:

The Navy Cross is awarded to Captain Joseph M. Reeves, U.S. Navy, for exceptionally meritorious service in a duty of great responsibility as commanding officer of the USS *Maine* in the Atlantic Fleet.

Rodd Field

Location: Corpus Christi, Texas
Status: Closed
Named for: Ensign Herbert Charles Rodd, USNRF
Date of Birth: September 7, 1894
Place of Birth: No Data Found
Date of Death: June 15, 1932
Place of Death: Hampton Roads, Virginia
Decorations and Honors: Navy Cross; NC-4 Medal; Royal Air Force Cross from King George V of England
Place of Burial: Arlington National Cemetery, Section 7, Site 9875

Ensign Herbert Charles Rodd was the radio officer in the seaplane NC-4 on the first transatlantic flight on February 9, 1919.

When the NC-4 seemed to be lost at sea, Rodd successfully picked up radio bearings and weather information from the destroyers hidden below by fog and clouds. After more than fifteen hours in the air, Rodd's radio reports gave assurance that NC-4 was very near the Azores.

His Navy Cross citation reads as follows:

The Navy Cross is presented to Herbert C. Rodd, Lieutenant (JG), U.S. Navy (Reserve Force), for distinguished service in the line of his profession as a member of the crew of Seaplane NC-4, in making the first successful transatlantic flight.

Saufley Field

Location: Pensacola, Florida
Status: Active
Named for: Lieutenant JG Richard Caswell Saufley
Date of Birth: September 1, 1884
Place of Birth: Stanford, Kentucky
Date of Death: June 9, 1916
Place of Death: Pensacola, Florida

Lieutenant JG Richard Caswell Saufley was a pioneer naval aviator.

Saufley graduated from the United States Naval Academy at Annapolis, Maryland, in June 1908 and served aboard the gunboat USS *Kansas*; torpedo boat USS *Biddle*; and destroyer USS *Terry*. On June 6, 1913, after flight training at the United States Naval Academy, he was designated naval aviator number 14. During the Mexican campaign of 1914, he served aboard the battleships

USS *Mississippi* and USS *North Carolina*.

He was killed when his plane crashed while attempting to set an altitude and endurance record. He had flown for eight hours and fifty-one minutes before his plane crashed.

The destroyer USS *Saufley* was also named in his honor.

Shea Field

Location: South Weymouth, Massachusetts
Status: Closed
Named for: Lieutenant Commander John Joseph Shea
Date of Birth: January 13, 1898
Place of Birth: Cambridge, Massachusetts
Date of Death: September 15, 1942
Place of Death: Aboard the USS *Wasp* in the South Pacific
Decorations and Honors: Navy Cross; Purple Heart, posthumously

Lieutenant Commander John Joseph Shea enlisted in the Naval Reserve Force on June 11, 1918. When the Naval Reserve Force was disbanded in 1925, he was transferred to the Fleet Reserve. In 1941, he was transferred to active duty and promoted to lieutenant commander.

Shea was killed when the USS *Wasp* was torpedoed and sunk by the Japanese. As fires caused explosions on deck, he fought to save the carrier. He was leading out a hose near the ammunition room when an explosion ripped through the ship. Shea was declared missing in action and declared legally dead a year later.

Smartt Field

Location: St. Charles, Missouri
Status: Closed
Named for: Ensign Joseph Gillespie Smartt, USNR
Date of Birth: March 19, 1917
Place of Birth: Austin, Texas
Date of Death: December 7, 1941
Place of Death: Kaneohe, Hawaii
Place of Burial: National Memorial Cemetery of the Pacific in Honolulu, Hawaii

Ensign Joseph Gillespie Smartt served with the VP11 Naval Air Transport

Squadron at Kaneohe, Hawaii.

Smartt enlisted in the Naval Reserve on October 8, 1940, and was appointed an aviation cadet on January 28, 1941. He completed aviation training at Naval Air Station Pensacola, Florida, and was promoted to ensign on September 17, 1941.

Smartt was killed during the Japanese attack on Pearl Harbor. He was posthumously commended by the commander in chief, Pacific Fleet, for his effort to repel the attack on the air station.

Towers Field

Location: Jacksonville Naval Air Station in Florida
Status: Active
Named for: Admiral John Henry Towers
Date of Birth: January 30, 1885
Place of Birth: Rome, Georgia
Date of Death: April 30, 1955
Place of Death: St. Albans Naval Hospital in Queens, New York
Decorations and Honors: Navy Cross; Distinguished Service Medal; Legion of Merit; Congressional Gold Medal; NC-4 Medal; Royal Air Force Cross from King George V of England; inducted into the International Aerospace Hall of Fame 1973; Gray Eagle Award, posthumously; inducted into the National Aviation Hall of Fame (1966)
Date of Retirement: 1947
Place of Burial: Arlington National Cemetery, Section 30, Grave 676

Admiral John Henry Towers was the commander of the seaplane NC-4, which made the first transatlantic flight on February 9, 1919.

Towers graduated from the United States Naval Academy at Annapolis, Maryland, in 1906. He received flight training at the Curtiss Flying School and became naval aviator number 3.

As a proponent for the use of the airplanes in the navy's fleet, he was put in charge of the aviation unit that began operations with the fleet off Guantanamo Bay, Cuba, exploring the potential of airplanes in aerial reconnaissance, bombing, aerial photography, and wireless communications. In 1914, Towers participated in establishing the first naval air station at Pensacola, Florida.

One of the most noted events of his career was his attempt to fly from Newfoundland across the Atlantic in 1919. When Towers was forced to land his plane in rough seas, he had to taxi the aircraft 205 miles to the Azores. He reached the Azores and then flew on to Portugal and England to become first to reach England.

During World War II, Towers commanded the 2nd Carrier Task Force, Task

Force 38, 5th Fleet, and USS *Langley*, the navy's first aircraft carrier. Following World War II, he was appointed commander in chief of the Pacific Fleet.

His Navy Cross citation for action during World War I reads as follows:

The Navy Cross is presented to John H. Towers, Commander, U.S. Navy, for distinguished service in the line of his profession while serving as assistant to the director of naval aviation, for his thorough knowledge of Naval Aviation, and his successful application of this knowledge to the work of making naval aircraft effective war weapons; for his distinguished service in assisting and devising plans for the use of naval aircraft during the war.

Van Voorhis Field

Location: Fallon, Nevada
Status: Active
Named for: Lieutenant Commander Bruce Avery Van Voorhis
Date of Birth: January 29, 1908
Place of Birth: Aberdeen, Washington
Date of Death: July 6, 1943
Place of Death: Solomon Islands
Decorations and Honors: Medal of Honor, posthumously
Place of Burial: Jefferson Barracks National Cemetery in St. Louis, Missouri

Lieutenant Commander Bruce Avery Van Voorhis was killed while on a low-level bombing attack during the battle of the Solomon Islands.

Van Voorhis graduated from the United States Naval Academy at Annapolis, Maryland, on June 6, 1929. His first sea duty was aboard the battleship USS *Mississippi*. In November 1930, he was assigned to Naval Air Station Pensacola, Florida, for flight training and received his pilot wings on September 3, 1931. Later, he was assigned to the battleship USS *Maryland* as a member of Observation Squadron 4B. During his career, he served aboard the aircraft carriers USS *Ranger*, USS *Saratoga*, USS *Enterprise*, and USS *Yorktown* and light cruiser USS *Honolulu*.

His Medal of Honor citation for action during World War II reads as follows:

For conspicuous gallantry and intrepidity at the risk of his life above and beyond the call of duty as Squadron Commander of Bombing Squadron 102 and as Plane Commander of a PB4Y-I Patrol Bomber operating against the enemy on Japanese-held Greenwich Island during the battle of the Solomon Islands, July 6, 1943. Fully aware of the limited chance of surviving an urgent mission, voluntarily undertaken to prevent a surprise Japanese attack against our forces, Lieutenant Commander Van Voorhis took off in total darkness on a perilous 700-mile flight without escort or support. Successful in reaching his objective despite treacherous and varying winds, low visibility and difficult terrain, he fought a lone but relentless battle under fierce antiaircraft fire and overwhelming aerial opposition. Forced lower and lower by pursuing planes, he coolly persisted in his mission of destruction. Abandoning all chance of a safe return he executed six bold ground-level attacks to demolish the enemy's vital radio station, installations, antiaircraft guns and crews with bombs and machine-gun fire, and to destroy one fighter plane in the air and three on the water. Caught in his own bomb blast, Lieutenant Commander Van Voorhis crashed into the lagoon off the beach, sacrificing himself in a single-handed fight against almost insuperable odds, to make a distinctive contribution to our continued offensive in driving the Japanese from the Solomons and, by his superb daring, courage and resoluteness of purpose, enhanced the finest traditions of the U.S. Naval Service. He gallantly gave his life for his country.

Waldron Field

Location: Corpus Christi, Texas
Status: Active
Named for: Lieutenant Commander John Charles Waldron
Date of Birth: August 24, 1900
Place of Birth: Fort Pierre, South Dakota
Date of Death: June 4, 1942
Place of Death: Midway Island in the Pacific
Decorations and Honors: Navy Cross, posthumously

Lieutenant Commander John Charles Waldron was a naval aviator who led a squadron of torpedo bombers in World War II.

Waldron graduated from the United States Naval Academy at Annapolis, Maryland, in 1924. He received his pilot wings in 1927 following sea duty aboard the support ship USS *Seattle*. During his career, he served with Scouting Squadron 3B and Patrol Squadron 1B. In the summer of 1941, he took command of Torpedo Squadron 8, part of the newly formed air group being assembled for the new fleet carrier USS *Hornet* at Newport News, Virginia.

Waldron received the Navy Cross for his action when, unprotected, he lead Torpedo Squadron 8 into an attack against the combat air patrol of Mitsubishi "Zero" fighters at the Battle of Midway.

The destroyer USS *Waldron* was also named in his honor. In addition, a street in Fort Pierre, South Dakota, is named for him.

Webster Field

Location: Priest Point, Maryland
Status: Active
Named for: Captain Walter Wynne Webster
Date of Birth: July 28, 1888
Place of Birth: Fargo, North Dakota
Date of Death: March 16, 1943
Place of Death: Chester, Pennsylvania
Decorations and Honors: Legion of Merit, posthumously; World War I Victory Medal; American Defense Service Medal; American Campaign Medal; World War II Victory Medal
Place of Burial: Arlington National Cemetery, Section South, Site 1859

Captain Walter Wynne Webster was a pioneer naval aviator.

Webster graduated from the United States Naval Academy at Annapolis, Maryland, in 1911 and was commissioned an assistant naval constructor with the rank of lieutenant (JG) on May 15, 1914, and on June 6, 1922, he was commissioned a naval constructor with the rank of lieutenant commander and earned his naval observer wings in July of that year.

Webster was assigned to the Naval Aircraft Factory in the Philadelphia Navy Yard on November 2, 1925. In 1933, he received instruction at Naval Air Station Pensacola, Florida, in heavier-than-air flight and was assigned to the Bureau of Aeronautics to become Force Materiel Officer.

In June 25, 1936, he returned to the Naval Aircraft Factory in Pennsylvania as manager and served there until June 1940. After the Japanese attack on Pearl Harbor, Webster returned to the Naval Aircraft Factory where he was killed in a plane crash there.

His Legion of Merit citation reads as follows:

For exceptional meritorious conduct as Manager of the United States Aircraft Factory from December 6, 1941, to March 16, 1943. Charged with the administration of this important activity during a period of unprecedented Naval expansion, Captain Webster skillfully developed his command as an essential part of the overall aircraft manufacturing program, working tirelessly to meet the increasing requirements of the Fleet and rendered invaluable service in providing vital services and materials to our operation forces in spite of inadequate facilities, drastic changes in planning and specifications and the competition of other projects of high priority. Under his expert direction, the Naval Aircraft Factory designed, manufactured, tested and supplied catapults and arresting gear with the necessary spare parts; trained crews for the operation of this gear; conducted unusual test and development in experimental laboratories; and made many advances in the field of radio-controlled aircraft and special weapons.

Whiting Field

Location: Milton, Florida
Status: Active
Named for: Captain Kenneth Whiting
Date of Birth: July 22, 1881
Place of Birth: Stockbridge, Massachusetts
Date of Death: April 24, 1943
Place of Death: U.S. Naval Hospital in Bethesda, Maryland
Decorations and Honors: Navy Cross; inducted into the National Museum of Naval Aviation
Date of Retirement: June 30, 1940

Captain Kenneth Whiting was a pioneer naval aviator who was taught to fly by Orville Wright.

Whiting graduated from the United States Naval Academy at Annapolis, Maryland, in 1905 and was commissioned an ensign February 25, 1908, qualifying in submarines. He commanded the submarines USS *Porpoise*, USS *Shark*, USS *Tarpon*, and USS *Seal*.

In 1914, he was designated naval aviator number 16 and, in 1917, he commanded the 1st Aeronautic Detachment in France where he established several air stations. While at Killingholm, England, he commanded Naval Air Stations 14 and 15.

After the war, he worked on the conversion of the collier USS *Jupiter* into the navy's first aircraft carrier, the USS *Langley*. In November 1922, Whiting made the first catapult launch in a PT seaplane from the aircraft carrier USS *Langley* anchored in the York River.

He was one of the last persons to see Amelia Earhart before she disappeared in 1937. As the commanding officer of Fleet Air Base, he was also involved in the search for her plane.

After retirement, he was retained on active duty as general inspector of Naval Aircraft, Eastern Division, until 1943, when he was assigned commander of Naval Air Station New York.

His Navy Cross citation for action during World War I reads as follows:

The Navy Cross is awarded to Commander Kenneth Whiting, U.S. Navy, for exceptionally meritorious service in a duty of great responsibility as commanding officer of the first U.S. aeronautical detachment to reach France, and later in command of the important U.S. naval air station at Killingholme, England.

The seaplane tender USS *Kenneth Whiting* was also named in his honor.

Williams Field

Location: McMurdo Sound, Antarctica
Status: Active
Named for: Petty Officer Richard Thomas Williams
Date of Birth: August 30, 1933
Place of Birth: Oppenheim, New York
Date of Death: January 6, 1956
Place of Death: McMurdo Sound, Antarctica

Petty Officer Richard Thomas Williams was a Seabee construction driver who was killed supporting of the scientific exploration of Antarctica.

Williams was a member of U.S. Naval Mobile Construction Battalion (Special), Task Force 43, Byrd Antarctic Expedition V, under command of Rear Admiral Richard E. Byrd and Rear Admiral George J. Dufek.

Williams was bringing in supplies for Seabees to begin construction at McMurdo Sound during Operation Deep Freeze I where the United States was building stations at the South Pole and on Ross Island. About forty miles from McMurdo, the ship became stuck in the thick sea ice. Icebreakers cut short paths but were unable to plow through the heavy ice. On foot and in tractors, the men started moving across the bay ice. With tractors pulling the sleds that carried the building supplies, they were soon standing in front of a water-filled crack about three-feet wide. The men built a bridge with heavy timber. Suddenly, the tractor broke through the ice, and Williams, the driver, plunged 250 fathoms to the bottom of McMurdo Sound. His body was never recovered.

The crew placed the memorial, Our Lady of the Snows, for him at McMurdo Station above Hut Point, overlooking McMurdo Sound where Williams was lost. On January 6, 1996, the CEC/Seabee Historical Foundation rededicated the shrine with a bronze tablet to Petty Officer Williams and others who gave their lives in order to provide a better understanding of the Antarctica.

Appendix A

Installations Listed by Branch of Service

Air Force

Albrook AFB
Andersen AFB
Andrews AFB
Arnold AFB
Bakalar AFB
Barksdale AFB
Beale AFB
Bellows AFB
Bergstrom AFB
Bolling AFB
Brookley AFB
Brooks AFB
Buckley AFB
Cannon AFB
Carswell AFB
Castle AFB
Chanute AFB
Chennault AFB
Clark AB
Connally AFB
Craig AFB
Davis-Monthan AFB
Dobbins AFB
Donaldson AFB
Dow AFB
Duke Field
Dyess AFB
Eaker AFB
Eareckson AFB
Edwards AFB

Eglin AFB
Eielson AFB
Ellington AFB
Ellsworth AFB
Elmendorf AFB
England AFB
Ent AFB
Epler Field
Fairchild AFB
Forbes AFB
Foster AFB
Francis E. Warren AFB
Gary AFB
Geiger AFB
George AFB
Goodfellow AFB
Grenier AFB
Griffiss AFB
Grissom AFB
Hamilton AFB
Hancock AFB
Hanscom AFB
Harmon AFB
Harmon AFB
Hickam AFB
Hill AFB
Holloman AFB
Hurlburt Field
Johnson AB
K.I. Sawyer AFB
Keesler AFB
Kelly AFB

Kincheloe AFB
Kindley AFB
Kirtland AFB
Lackland AFB
Langley AFB
Larson AFB
Laughlin AFB
Lawson AFB
Loring AFB
Lowry AFB
Luke AFB
MacDill AFB
Malmstrom AFB
March AFB
Mather AFB
Maxwell-Gunter AFB
McChord AFB
McClellan AFB
McConnell AFB
McCoy AFB
McEntire AFB
McGhee Tyson AFB
McGuire AFB
Moody AFB
Nellis AFB
Norton AFB
Offutt AFB
Olmsted AFB
Onizuka AS
Otis AFB
Paine AFB
Patrick AFB
Pease AFB
Perrin AFB
Peterson AFB
Piccolo Field
Pope AFB
Ramey AFB
Randolph AFB
Reese AFB
Richard Bong AFB
Richards-Gebaur AFB
Rickenbacker AFB
Robins AFB
Sampson AFB
Schilling AFB
Schriever AFB
Scott AFB
Selfridge AFB
Sewart AFB

Seymour Johnson AFB
Shaw AFB
Sheppard AFB
Slocum AFB
Stead AFB
Thornbrough AFB
Tinker AFB
Travis AFB
Tyndall AFB
Vance AFB
Vandenberg AFB
Walker AFB
Walseth AFB
Weaver AFB
Westover AFB
Wheeler AFB
Whiteman AFB
Williams AFB
Wright-Patterson AFB
Wurtsmith AFB

Air National Guard

Bluethenthal Field
Bradley Field
Byrd Field
Dannelly Field
Francis S. Gabreski Field
General Billy Mitchell Field
Gowen Field
Joe Foss Field
Kegelman AF Auxiliary Field
Key Field
Kingsley Field
Kulis Field
Lambert Field
Mansfield-Lahm Field
Morris Field
Phelps Collins Field
Rosecrans Field
Stewart Field
Stratton Air National Guard Base
Truax Field
Volk Field
Yeager Field

U.S. Army

Brann Barracks
Camp Barkeley

Camp Bondsteel
Camp Claiborne
Camp Cooke
Camp Croft
Camp Funston
Camp Gordon Johnston
Camp Grant
Camp Livingston
Camp Mackall
Camp Monteith
Camp Sherman
Camp Taliaferro
Camp Truscott
Camp Wallace AS
Fort A. P. Hill
Fort Benjamin Harrison
Fort Benning
Fort Bliss
Fort Bragg
Fort Buchanan
Fort Buckner
Fort Campbell
Fort Carson
Fort Chaffee
Fort Detrick
Fort Devens
Fort Dix
Fort Drum
Fort Eustis
Fort George Wright
Fort Gillem
Fort Gordon
Fort Greely
Fort Holabird
Fort Hood
Fort Hunter Liggett
Fort Irwin
Fort Jackson
Fort Knox
Fort Kobbe
Fort Leavenworth
Fort Lee
Fort Leonard Wood
Fort Lewis
Fort McClellan
Fort McCoy
Fort McDowell
Fort McNair
Fort McPherson
Fort Meade
Fort Monroe
Fort Myer
Fort Ord
Fort Pickett
Fort Polk
Fort Richardson
Fort Riley
Fort Rucker
Fort Sam Houston
Fort Shafter
Fort Sheridan
Fort Sill
Fort Stewart
Fort Story
Fort Wainwright
Fort Wint
Fort Wolters
Schofield Barracks

Army Airfields, Stagefields, and Heliports

Allen Army Airfield
Biggs Army Airfield
Brown Stagefield
Butts Army Airfield
Cairns Army Airfield
Carlstrom Field
Charles L. Kelly Heliport
Cochran Army Airfield
Condron Army Airfield
Davison Army Airfield
Dodd Field
Dorr Army Airfield
Felker Army Airfield
Forney Army Airfield
Fort MacArthur Airfield
Freeman Army Airfield
Godman Army Airfield
Goldberg Stagefield
Gray Army Airfield
Guthrie Stagefield
Hagler Army Airfield
Hanchey Army Heliport
Hancock Army Airfield
Hatch Stagefield
Henry J. Reilly Army Airfield
Henry Post Army Airfield
Hunt Heliport
Hunter Army Airfield

Joseph G. LaPointe Heliport
Ladd Field
Lawson Army Airfield
Libby Army Airfield
Lowe Army Airfield
Lucas Army Airfield
Marshall Army Airfield
McCook Field
Moore Army Airfield
Muir Army Airfield
Phillips Army Airfield
Ray S. Miller Army Airfield
Robert Gray Army Airfield
Robinson Army Airfield
Runkle Tactical Site
Shell Army Heliport
Sherman Army Airfield
Simmons Army Airfield
Skelly Stagefield
Strother Army Airfield
Toth Stagefield
Tusi Army Heliport
Wheeler-Sack Army Airfield
Wright Army Airfield

Army National Guard

Camp Abbot
Camp Adair
Camp Atterbury
Camp Beauregard
Camp Blanding
Camp Bowie
Camp Bullis
Camp Clark
Camp Cook
Camp Crowder
Camp Curtis Guild
Camp Dawson
Camp Dodge
Camp Edsall
Camp Edwards
Camp G. C. Grafton
Camp George West
Camp Greene
Camp Gruber
Camp Hartell
Camp Johnson
Camp Keyes
Camp Labonte

Camp Mabry
Camp Maxey
Camp McCain
Camp Pendleton
Camp Perry
Camp Pike
Camp Rilea
Camp Ripley
Camp Roberts
Camp Shelby
Camp Stanley
Camp Swift
Camp Varnum
Camp Villere
Camp W. G. Williams
Camp White
Camp Williams
Camp Withycombe
Charles E. Kelly Sup. Fac.
Fort Custer Training Center
Fort William Henry Harrison
Fraine Barracks
Greenlief Training Site
Nickell Hall

Army Barracks and Kasernes, Germany

Adams Barracks
Anderson Barracks
Armstrong Barracks
Azbill Barracks
Baker Barracks
Barton Barracks
Camp Bloomquist
Camp Clarke
Camp Gates
Camp Lindsey
Camp Pieri
Camp Whalen
Campbell Barracks
Cawley Kaserne
Christensen Barracks
Coffey Barracks
Coleman Barracks
Coleman Barracks
Cooke Barracks
Daley Barracks
Darby Barracks
Downs Barracks

Eastman Barracks
Emery Barracks
Ferris Barracks
Fiori Barracks
Ford Barracks
Funari Barracks
George C. Marshall Kaserne
Gerszewski Barracks
Graves Barracks
Hammonds Barracks
Harris Barracks
Harvey Barracks
Henry Kaserne
Jenson Barracks
Johnson Barracks
Kapaun Barracks
Kelley Barracks
Kilbourne Barracks
Kimbro Kaserne
Knight Barracks
Larson Barracks
Ledward Barracks
Lee Barracks
Leighton Barracks
Lloyd Barracks
Lucius D. Clay Kaserne
Mansfield Kaserne
McCully Barracks
McGee Barracks
McGraw Kaserne
McKee Barracks
McPheeters Barracks
Merrell Barracks
Miller Barracks
Minick Kaserne
Murphy Barracks
Nelson Barracks
O'Brien Barracks
Oliver Barracks
Orsbon Barracks
Patch Barracks
Patton Barracks
Peden Barracks
Pendleton Barracks
Peterson Kaserne
Pinder Barracks
Pirie Barracks
Pitman Barracks
Ray Barracks
Ready Barracks
Reese Barracks
Rivers Barracks
Robinson Barracks
Rose Barracks
Sadowski Barracks
Sheridan Barracks
Sherwood Young Barracks
Smith Barracks
Spinelli Barracks
Stem Kaserne
Storck Barracks
Sullivan Barracks
Taukkunen Barracks
Taylor Barracks
Tompkins Barracks
Towle Barracks
Turley Barracks
Turner Barracks
Valdez Barracks
Wallace Barracks
Warner Barracks
Wharton Barracks
Whitson Kaserne
Wilkin Barracks
Will Kaserne
Wilson Barracks

Army Camps, Korea

Camp Bonifas
Camp Carroll
Camp Casey
Camp Coiner
Camp Edwards
Camp George
Camp Greaves
Camp Henry
Camp Hovey
Camp Howze
Camp Kyle
Camp Long
Camp Page
Camp Red Cloud
Camp Sears
Camp Walker

U.S. Marine Corps

Archibald Field
Bauer Field

Byrd Field
Camp Butler
Camp Courtney
Camp Elliott
Camp Elmore
Camp Foster
Camp Geiger
Camp Gonsalves
Camp H. M. Smith
Camp Hansen
Camp Holcomb
Camp Howard
Camp Johnson
Camp Kinser
Camp Lejeune
Camp Lester
Camp McCutcheon
Camp McTureous
Camp Pendleton
Camp Schwab
Camp Shields
Cunningham Field
Dowdell Field
Dyess Field
Hawkins Field
Henderson Field
Henderson Hall
Merritt Field
Moret Field
Munn Field
Page Field
Sailer Field
Thomas Field
Turner Field

U.S. Navy

Alvin Callender Field
Armitage Field
Ault Field
Barin Field
Bordelon Field
Bristol Field
Bronson Field
Brown Field
Cabaniss Field
Cecil Field
Chambers Field
Chase Field
Chevalier Field
Corry Field
Cuddihy Field
Earle NWS
Ellyson Field
Flatley Field
Fleming Field
Floyd Bennett Field
Forrest Sherman Field
Frederick C. Sherman Field
Frederick M. Trapnell Field
Halsey Field
Harvey Field
Hensley Field
Isely Field
John Rodgers Field
Maxfield Field
McCain Field
McCalla Field
Mitscher Field
Moffett Field
Mullinnix Field
Mustin Field
Nimitz Field
Ofstie Field
O'Hare Field
Radford Field
Ramey Field
Reeves Field
Rodd Field
Saufley Field
Shea Field
Smartt Field
Towers Field
Van Voorhis Field
Waldron Field
Webster Field
Whiting Field
Williams Field

Appendix B

Installations Listed by Location

ALABAMA

Air Force

Brookley AFB
Craig AFB
Dannelly Field
Maxwell-Gunter AFB

Army

Brown Stagefield
Fort McClellan
Fort Rucker
Cairns AAF
Goldberg Stagefield
Guthrie Stagefield
Hanchey AH
Hatch Stagefield
Henry J. Reilly AAF
Hunt AH
Lowe AAF
Lucas AAF
Runkle Tactical Site
Shell AH
Skelly Stagefield
Toth Stagefield

Navy

Barin Field

ALASKA

Air Force

Eareckson AFB
Eielson AFB
Elmendorf AFB
Kulis Field
Thornbrough AFB
Walseth AFB

Army

Allen AAF
Fort Greely
Fort Richardson
Fort Wainwright
Ladd Field

ARIZONA

Air Force

Davis-Monthan AFB
Luke AFB
Williams AFB

Army

Libby AAF

ARKANSAS

Air Force

Eaker AFB

Army

Camp Pike
Fort Chaffee
Robinson AAF

CALIFORNIA

Air Force
Beale AFB
Castle AFB
Edwards AFB
George AFB
Hamilton AFB
March AFB
Mather AFB
McClellan AFB
Norton AFB
Onizuka AS
Travis AFB
Vandenberg AFB

Army
Camp Cooke
Camp Roberts
Fort Hunter Liggett
Fort Irwin
Fort MacArthur AAF
Fort McDowell
Fort Ord
Hancock AAF
Tusi AH

Marines
Camp Elliott
Camp Holcomb
Camp Howard
Camp Pendleton
Munn Field

Navy
Armitage Field
Brown Field
Frederick C. Sherman Field
Halsey Field
Harvey Field
Mitscher Field
Moffett Field
Nimitz Field
Reeves Field

COLORADO

Air Force
Buckley AFB
Ent AFB
Lowry AFB
Peterson AFB
Schriever AFB

Army
Butts AAF
Camp George West
Fort Carson

CONNECTICUT

Air Force
Bradley Field

Army
Camp Hartell

FLORIDA

Air Force
Duke Field
Eglin AFB
Epler Field
Hurlburt Field
MacDill AFB
McCoy AFB
Patrick AFB
Piccolo Field
Tyndall AFB

Army
Carlstrom Field
Camp Blanding
Camp Gordon Johnston
Dorr AAF

Navy
Bronson Field
Cecil Field
Chevalier Field
Corry Field
Ellyson Field
Forrest Sherman Field
Ramey Field
Saufley Field
Towers Field
Whiting Field

GEORGIA

Air Force
Dobbins AFB
Lawson AFB

Moody AFB
Robins AFB

Army

Cochran AAF
Fort Benning
Fort Gillem
Fort Gordon
Fort McPherson
Fort Stewart
Hunter AAF
Joseph G. LaPointe AH
Lawson AAF
Wright AAF

HAWAII

Air Force

Bellows AFB
Hickam AFB
Wheeler AFB

Army

Fort Shafter
Schofield Barracks

Marines

Camp H. M. Smith

Navy

Bordelon Field
John Rodgers Field

IDAHO

Air Force

Gowen Field

ILLINOIS

Air Force

Chanute AFB
Scott AFB

Army

Camp Grant
Fort Sheridan

INDIANA

Air Force

Bakalar AFB

Grissom AFB

Army

Camp Atterbury
Fort Benjamin Harrison
Freeman AAF

IOWA

Army

Camp Dodge

KANSAS

Air Force

Forbes AFB
McConnell AFB
Schilling AFB

Army

Camp Funston
Fort Leavenworth
Fort Riley
Marshall AAF
Nickell Hall
Sherman AAF
Strother AAF

Navy

Flatley Field

KENTUCKY

Army

Fort Campbell
Fort Knox
Godman AAF

LOUISIANA

Air Force

Barksdale AFB
Chennault AFB
England AFB

Army

Camp Beauregard
Camp Claiborne
Camp Cook
Camp Livingston
Camp Villere
Fort Polk

Navy

Alvin Callender Field

MAINE

Air Force
Dow AFB
Loring AFB

Army
Camp Keyes

MARYLAND

Air Force
Andrews AFB

Army
Fort Detrick
Fort Holabird
Fort Meade
Phillips AAF

Navy
Frederick M. Trapnell Field
Webster Field

MASSACHUSETTS

Air Force
Hanscom AFB
Otis AFB
Westover AFB

Army
Camp Curtis Guild
Camp Edwards
Fort Devens
Moore AAF

Navy
Shea Field

MICHIGAN

Air Force
K.I. Sawyer AFB
Kincheloe AFB
Phelps Collins Field
Selfridge AFB
Wurtsmith AFB

Army
Fort Custer Training Center

MINNESOTA

Army
Camp Ripley
Ray S. Miller AAF

Navy
Fleming Field

MISSISSIPPI

Air Force
Keesler AFB
Key Field

Army
Camp McCain
Camp Shelby
Hagler AAF

Navy
McCain Field

MISSOURI

Air Force
Lambert Field
Richards-Gebaur AFB
Rosecrans Field
Whiteman AFB

Army
Camp Clark
Camp Crowder
Forney AAF
Fort Leonard Wood

Navy
Smartt Field

MONTANA

Air Force
Malmstrom AFB

Army
Fort William Henry Harrison

NEBRASKA

Air Force

Offutt AFB

Army

Greenlief Training Site

NEVADA

Air Force

Nellis AFB
Stead AFB

Army

Camp Edsall

Navy

Van Voorhis Field

NEW HAMPSHIRE

Air Force

Grenier AFB
Pease AFB

Army

Camp Labonte

NEW JERSEY

Air Force

McGuire AFB

Army

Fort Dix

Navy

Earle NWS
Maxfield Field

NEW MEXICO

Air Force

Cannon AFB
Holloman AFB
Kirtland AFB
Walker AFB

Army

Condron AAF

NEW YORK

Air Force

Francis S. Gabreski Field
Griffiss AFB
Hancock AFB
Sampson AFB
Slocum AFB
Stewart Field
Stratton Field

Army

Fort Drum
Wheeler-Sack AAF

Navy

Floyd Bennett Field

NORTH CAROLINA

Air Force

Bluethenthal Field
Morris Field
Pope AFB
Seymour Johnson AFB

Army

Camp Mackall
Fort Bragg
Simmons AAF

Marines

Camp Geiger
Camp Johnson
Camp Lejeune
Camp McCutcheon
Cunningham Field

NORTH DAKOTA

Army

Camp G. C. Grafton
Fraine Barracks

OHIO

Air Force

Mansfield-Lahm Field
Rickenbacker AFB
Wright-Patterson AFB

Army
Camp Perry
Camp Sherman
McCook Field

OKLAHOMA
Air Force
Kegelman AF Auxiliary Field
Tinker AFB
Vance AFB
Army
Camp Gruber
Fort Sill
Henry Post AAF

OREGON
Air Force
Kingsley Field
Army
Camp Abbot
Camp Adair
Camp Rilea
Camp White
Camp Withycombe

PENNSYLVANIA
Air Force
Olmsted AFB
Army
Charles E. Kelly Sup. Fac.
Muir AAF
Navy
Mustin Field

RHODE ISLAND
Army
Camp Greene
Camp Varnum

SOUTH CAROLINA
Air Force
Donaldson AFB
McEntire AFB
Shaw AFB
Army
Camp Croft
Fort Jackson
Marines
Merritt Field
Page Field

SOUTH DAKOTA
Air Force
Ellsworth AFB
Joe Foss Field
Weaver AFB

TENNESSEE
Air Force
Arnold AFB
McGhee Tyson AFB
Sewart AFB

TEXAS
Air Force
Bergstrom AFB
Brooks AFB
Carswell AFB
Connally AFB
Dyess AFB
Ellington AFB
Foster AFB
Gary AFB
Goodfellow AFB
Kelly AFB
Lackland AFB
Laughlin AFB
Perrin AFB
Randolph AFB
Reese AFB
Sheppard AFB
Army
Biggs AAF
Camp Barkeley
Camp Bowie
Camp Bullis
Camp Mabry
Camp Maxey

Camp Stanley
Camp Swift
Camp Taliaferro
Charles L. Kelly AH
Dodd Field
Fort Bliss
Fort Hood
Fort Sam Houston
Fort Wolters
Robert Gray AAF

Navy

Cabaniss Field
Chase Field
Cuddihy Field
Hensley Field
Rodd Field
Waldron Field

UTAH

Air Force

Hill AFB

Army

Camp W. G. Williams

VERMONT

Army

Camp Johnson

VIRGINIA

Air Force

Byrd Field
Langley AFB

Army

Camp Pendleton
Davison AAF
Felker AAF
Fort A.P. Hill
Fort Eustis
Fort Lee
Fort Monroe
Fort Myer
Fort Pickett
Fort Story

Marines

Camp Elmore

Henderson Hall
Turner Field

Navy

Chambers Field

WASHINGTON

Air Force

Fairchild AFB
Geiger AFB
Larson AFB
McChord AFB
Paine AFB

Army

Fort George Wright
Fort Lewis
Gray AAF

Navy

Ault Field

WASHINGTON, D.C.

Air Force

Bolling AFB

Army

Fort McNair

WEST VIRGINIA

Air Force

Yeager Field

Army

Camp Dawson

WISCONSIN

Air Force

General Billy Mitchell Field
Richard Bong AFB
Truax Field
Volk Field

Army

Fort McCoy
Camp Williams

WYOMING

Air Force

Francis E. Warren AFB

Overseas Bases

ANTARCTICA

Navy

Williams Field

AUSTRIA

Army

Brann Barracks
Camp Truscott

BERMUDA

Air Force

Kindley AFB

CUBA

Navy

McCalla Field

GERMANY

Army

Adams Barracks
Anderson Barracks
Armstrong Barracks
Azbill Barracks
Baker Barracks
Barton Barracks
Camp Bloomquist
Camp Clarke
Camp Gates
Camp Lindsey
Camp Pieri
Camp Whalen
Campbell Barracks
Cawley Kaserne
Christensen Barracks
Coffey Barracks
Coleman Barracks
Coleman Barracks
Cooke Barracks
Daley Barracks
Darby Barracks
Downs Barracks
Eastman Barracks
Emery Barracks
Ferris Barracks
Fiori Barracks
Ford Barracks
Funari Barracks
George C. Marshall Kaserne
Gerszewski Barracks
Graves Barracks
Hammonds Barracks
Harris Barracks
Harvey Barracks
Henry Kaserne
Jenson Barracks
Johnson Barracks
Kapaun Barracks
Kelley Barracks
Kilbourne Barracks
Kimbro Kaserne
Knight Barracks
Larson Barracks
Ledward Barracks
Lee Barracks
Leighton Barracks
Lloyd Barracks
Lucius D. Clay Kaserne
Mansfield Kaserne
McCully Barracks
McGee Barracks
McGraw Kaserne
McKee Barracks
McPheeters Barracks
Merrell Barracks
Miller Barracks
Minick Kaserne
Murphy Barracks
Nelson Barracks
O'Brien Barracks
Oliver Barracks
Orsbon Barracks
Patch Barracks
Patton Barracks
Peden Barracks
Pendleton Barracks
Peterson Kaserne
Pinder Barracks

Pirie Barracks
Pitman Barracks
Ray Barracks
Ready Barracks
Reese Barracks
Rivers Barracks
Robinson Barracks
Rose Barracks
Sadowski Barracks
Sheridan Barracks
Sherwood Young Barracks
Smith Barracks
Spinelli Barracks
Stem Kaserne
Storck Barracks
Sullivan Barracks
Taukkunen Barracks
Taylor Barracks
Tompkins Barracks
Towle Barracks
Turley Barracks
Turner Barracks
Valdez Barracks
Wallace Barracks
Warner Barracks
Wharton Barracks
Whitson Kaserne
Wilkin Barracks
Will Kaserne
Wilson Barracks

GILBERT ISLANDS

Marines

Hawkins Field

Navy

Mullinnix Field
O'Hare Field

GUADALCANAL

Marines

Henderson Field
Sailer Field

GUAM

Air Force

Andersen AFB
Harmon AFB

KOREA

Army

Camp Bonifas
Camp Carroll
Camp Casey
Camp Coiner
Camp Edwards
Camp George
Camp Greaves
Camp Henry
Camp Hovey
Camp Howze
Camp Kyle
Camp Long
Camp Page
Camp Red Cloud
Camp Sears
Camp Walker

KOSOVO

Army

Camp Bondsteel
Camp Monteith

JAPAN

Air Force

Johnson AB

MARIANA ISLAND

Navy

Isely Field

MARSHALL ISLANDS

Marines

Dyess Field

NEWFOUNDLAND

Air Force

Harmon AFB

Navy

Bristol Field

NEW HEBRIDES ISLAND

Marines

Bauer Field

NICARAGUA

Marines

Archibald Field
Byrd Field
Dowdell Field
Thomas Field

OKINAWA

Army

Fort Buckner

Marines

Camp Butler
Camp Courtney
Camp Foster
Camp Gonsalves
Camp Hansen
Camp Kinser
Camp Lester
Camp McTureous
Camp Schwab
Camp Shields

PANAMA

Air Force

Albrook AFB

Army

Fort Kobbe

PHILIPPINE ISLANDS

Air Force

Clark AB

Army

Camp Wallace AS
Fort Wint

Marines

Moret Field

Navy

Radford Field

PUERTO RICO

Air Force

Ramey AFB

Army

Fort Buchanan

Navy

Ofstie Field

Selected Bibliography

A History of Military Aviation in San Antonio. [San Antonio, Tex. (?)]: 2000.
Abilene Reporter-News. January 12, 1941.
Admiral Flatley Memorial Committee of Green Bay, Wisconsin. Frank A. Wood: n.d. A six-page insert into the *Brown County Chronicle-Shoppers Guide.*
Air Force Historical Research Agency. "Personal Papers." *Air Force Historical Research Agency.* http://www.afhra.af.mil/documents/personalpapers.asp/.
Air Force Materiel Command News Service. *The Integrator* 4, no. 12 (March 25, 2002).
Allen, Mary Moore. *Origin and Names of Army and Air Corps Posts, Camps, and Stations in World War II in Georgia.* Goldsboro, N.C.: n.d.
Allies. Military Historical Society of Minnesota. Newsletter. Spring 2004.
Alpena News, March 20, 1918.
The American Fighter Aces Association. *American Fighter Aces Album,* Mesa, Ariz.: American Fighter Aces Association, 1996.
Andrews Air Force Base. www.andrews.af.mil/library.
Appleton's Cyclopedia of American Biography. New York: D. Appleton and Company, 1887–1889.
Arlington National Cemetery. http://www.arlingtonnationalcemetery.org/.
The Army Historical Foundation. *The Army Historical Foundation.* http://www.armyhistory.org/.
Austin File. Austin History Center. Austin Public Library, Texas.
Baer, Sandra. "Vandalia VFW Post 9582 Gives Memorial Award." *Dayton Daily News*, May 19, 2005, section northeast, Z5-1.
Bangor Daily News, January 22, 1942. p. 1.
———, February 27, 1958. p. 13.
———, November 27, 1959. p. 8.
———, November 30, 1959. p. 11.
———, February 28, 1968. p.10.
Barnes, Betty. *Diggin' Up Bones: Obituaries of Lakin and Hartland Cemeteries, Kearny County, Kansas.* Bowie, Md.: Heritage Books, Inc., 1995.
Benton, Jeffrey C. *They Served Here: Thirty-three Maxwell Men.* Maxwell Air Force Base, Ala.: Air University Press, 1999.

Bergstrom, J. A. Austin File. Austin History Center. Austin Public Library, Texas.
Biographical Directory of the United States Congress. http://bioguide.congress.gov/biosearch/biosearch.asp.
Boyne, Walter J. "The Man Who Built the Missiles." *Air Force Magazine* 83 (October 2000).
Bradfield, Bill. "Ira Eaker: From Covered Wagon to Jet-Age Air Power, Four Stars." *Texas Escapes Online Magazine* (February 2001). http://www.texasescapes.com/Features/Bill_Bradfield/GeneralIraEaker.htm.
Brashear, John A., *Miscellaneous Scientific Papers of the Allegheny Observatory—New Series.* No. 19. Reprinted from *Popular Astronomy* 14 (1906).
Brian, Lindne. *Nutley Sun,* August 25, 1917.
———. *The Toronto Globe,* August 18, 1917.
Brown, Kent B. "Lt. Col. Harold William 'Indian Joe' Bauer." *Amazon.com.* http://www.acepilots.com/bauer/usmc_bauer1.html.
Bruning, John R. Jungle Ace: Col. Gerald R. Johnson, the USAF's Top Fighter Leader of the Pacific War. Dullas, Va.: Brassey's Inc., 2001.
"California State Military Department: Lieutenant General Hunter Liggett, (1857–1937)." *California State Military Department: The California Military Museum: Preserving California's Military Heritage.* http://www.militarymuseum.org/Liggett.html.
California State Military Museum, Sacramento.
Callender, Alvin Andrew and Gordon W Callender. *Callender, War in an Open Cockpit.* West Roxbury, Mass.: World War I Aero Publishers, 1978.
Cannon, Doris Rollins. *Cold Mountain Bomber Crash: The Enduring Legacy.* Ann Arbor, Mich.: Edwards Brothers, Inc., 2005.
Card, Linda J. "Family Musters for Fallen Aviation Pioneer." August 6, 2004. Found on
Paterson, Michael Robert. "Wendell Holsworth Brookley." *Arlington National Cemetery Website: Where Valor Proudly Sleeps.* http://www.arlingtoncemetery.net/whbookley.htm.
Carlson, Erik. *Ellington Field: A Short History, 1917–1963.* NASA/CR-1999-20892.1. National Aeronautics and Space Administration. Houston, Tex.: Lyndon B. Johnson Space Center, February 1999. http://www.jsc.nasa.gov/history/ellington/Ellington.pdf.
Chanute, Octave. *Progress in Flying Machines.* New York: The American Engineer and Railroad Journal, 1894.
Chapman Publishing Co. *Portrait and biographical Record of Denver and Vicinity. . . .* Chicago: Chapman Pub. Co., 1898.
Citadel Archives & Museum. Charleston, South Carolina.
Close, Dan. "Wichita Base Borrows Flying Brothers' name." *The Wichita Eagle,* May 20, 1985. As found on Carl Chance, Chance Communications, Inc. "Aviation History: McConnell has grown." *Wings Over Kansas.* http://www.wingsoverkansas.com/history/article.asp?id=113.
Coletta, Paolo E. *McCalla, Bowman Hendry: A Fighting Sailor.* Washington: University Press of America, 1979.
The Columbia Encyclopedia. 5th ed. N.p.: Columbia University Press, 1994.
Commonwealth of Massachusetts. "Curtis Guild, Jr." *Mass.gov.* http://www.mass.gov.
Crowder, James L. Jr., *Osage General: Major General Clarence L. Tinker.* Tinker Air Force Base, Okla.: Office of History, Oklahoma City Air Logistics Center, 1987.
Daily Record (San Marcos, Tex.), May 26, 2002.

Dameron, J. David. *General Henry Lewis Benning: This Was a Man: A Biography of Georgia's Supreme Court Justice and Confederate General.* Bowie, Md.: Heritage Books, Inc., 2004.
Darst, James E., "Gen. Leonard Wood Says 89th Was Second to None." *St. Louis Globe Democrat*, April 7, 1919.
Davis, David J. and E. C. Shannon, eds. *Pennsylvania Guardsman.* April 12, 1941.
Davis, Henry Blaine, Jr. *Generals in Khaki.* Raleigh, N.C.: Pentland Press, Inc., 1998.
Defense News. Springfield, Va.: Army Times Publishing Company, 1997.
Denfeld, Duane and Michele Michael. *Simmons Army Airfield Inventory and National Register of Historic Places Evaluation.* N.p.: Fort Bragg Cultural Resources Management Program, June 2004.
Denger, Mark J. "California State Military Department: Major General Joseph H. Pendleton, USMC (1860–1942)." *California State Military Department: The California Military Museum: Preserving California's Military Heritage.* http://www.militarymuseum.org/Pendleton.html.
Denger, Mark J. and Norman S. Marshall. "California State Military Department: Admiral Joseph Mason "Bull" Reeves, USN, (1872–1948)." *California State Military Department: The California Military Museum: Preserving California's Military Heritage.* http://www.militarymuseum.org/Reeves.html.
Denslo, William R. *10,000 Famous Freemasons.* vol. 1. Richmond, Va.: Macoy Publishing & Masonic Supply Co., Inc., 1957.
Devlin, Gerard M. *Paratrooper! The Saga of the US Army and Marine Parachute and Glider Combat Troops During World War II.* Foreword by William P. Yarborough. New York: St. Martin's Press. 1979.
Diamond, Beryl I. "Dobbins Air Reserve Base." *The New Georgia Encyclopedia.* http:www.georgiaencyclopedia.org/nge/Article.jsp?id=h-764.
Dorland, Peter and James Nanney. *Dust Off: Army Aaeromedical Evacuation in Vietnam.* Washington, D.C.: Center of Military History, U.S. Army; For sale by the Supt. of Docs., U.S.G.P.O., 1982.
Dorr, Robert F. *Korean War Aces.* Aircraft of the Aces Series 4. Colchester, Esssex, UK: Osprey Publishing, April 1995. http://www.acepilots.com/korea_aces.html.
Duffy, Michael. *Who's Who: Lloyd Hamilton.* First World War.com. 2002. http://www.firstworldwar.com/bio/hamilton_lloyd.htm.
DuPre, Flint 0., *U.S. Air Force Biographical Dictionary.* New York: F. Watts, 1965.
Edwards, Harry W. "A Different War: Marines in Europe and North Africa." *Marines in World War II Commemorative Series.* http://www.nps.gov/archive/wapa/indepth/extContent/usmc/pcn-190-003125-00/index.htm.
El Reno Tribune, March 28, 1945. Obituary.
Ent, Uzal W. *Fighting on the Brink: Defense of the Pusan Perimeter.* Paducah, Ky.: Turner Publishing Co., c1996.
Evans, Clement Anselm. *Confederate Military History.* Vol. 3. Atlanta, Ga.: Confederate Pub. Co., 1899.
FamilyLink.com, Inc. "Report of the Adjutant General of Missouri. January 10, 1921–December 31,1924." *World Vital Records.com.* http://www.worldvitalrecords.com/indexinfo.aspx?ix=qcd_reportoftheadjutantgeneralofmissiouri.
Faust, Patricia L. *Historical Times Illustrated Encyclopedia Of The Civil War.* New York: Harper & Row, 1986.
Feeny, William D. "In Their Honor." *Model Airplanes News*, February 1969.

Fifteenth Air Base Wing History Office, personal communication.
Fifty-fourth Annual Report of the Association of Graduates of the United States Military Academy. June 11, 1923, pp. 110–114.
Finley, James P. "The Buffalo Soldiers at Fort Huachuca." *Huachuca Illustrated* 1 (1993), http://net.lib.byu.edu/estu/wwi/comment/huachuca/HI1-22.htm.
Fort Wolters Trumpet. July 27, 1973.
Frisbee, John L., "China Bomber." *Air Force Magazine,* April 1988.
———, "The Quiet Hero." *Air Force Magazine* 17 (March 1988).
———, "Hero of the Philippines." *Air Force Magazine* 73, no. 5 (May 1990).
———, "Eareckson of the Aleutians." *Air Force Magazine* 74, no. 6 (June 1991).
———, "AACMO—Fiasco or Victory?" *Air Force Magazine* (March 1995).
———, "The Bravest Man I Ever Knew." *Air Force Magazine* 74, no. 3 (March 1991).
———, "Sacrifice at Sniper Ridge." *Air Force Magazine* 73, no. 7 (July 1990).
———, "Rabaul on a Wing and a Prayer." *Air Force Magazine* 73, no. 7 (July 1990).
———, "Courage, Heroism, Valor." *Air Force Magazine* 71, no. 12 (December 1988).
———, "The Iron Hand of Fate." *Air Force Magazine* 72, no. 9 (September 1989).
———, "Forgotten Firsts." *Air Force Magazine* 74, no. 5 (May 1991).
———, "A Rather Special Award." *Air Force Magazine* 73, no. 8 (August 1990).
———, "Always a Fighter Pilot." *Air Force Magazine* 74, no. 2 (February 1991).
———, "Valor." *Air Force Magazine* 80, no. 7 (July 1997).
Golden, Randy. "Death of a Bishop (Leonidas Polk)." *About North Georgia*, 1994. http://ngeorgia.com.
Grandstaff, Dr. Mark R. "Muir Fairchild and the Origins of Air University 1945–46." *Aerospace Power Journal*, Winter 1997.
Granger, John Tileston. *A Brief Biographical Sketch of the Like of Major-General Grenville M. Dodge.* New York: Press of Styles & Cash, 1893.
Green, Peyton. "50 years of Aerospace Medicine." *AFSC Historical Publications*, 1968.
Greguras, Fred. "Spanish American War Camps, 1898–99." *NEGenWeb Project. Spanish American War.* 2005. http://www.usgennet.org/usa/ne/topic/military/SpanishAmericanWar/span_am_camps/pg1.htm.
Guttman, Jon. "Japan's Feisty Floatplane." *Aviation History Magazine,* January 2001.
Harrington, Dwight D. *A History of the Vermont National Guard.* 145, 161, 180, 183, 187.
Haskins, Harold W. *A History of Bradford Vermont Covering its Period From its Beginning in 1765 to the Middle of 1968.* Littleton, N.H.: Printed by Courier Print. Co. 1966.
Headquarters First Army Camp Drum. Dedication booklet. August 22, 1952.
Headquarters, U.S. Army, Europe, and Seventh Army. *USAREUR: United States Army, Europe, and 7th Army.* http://www.hqusareur.army.mil/leaders1.asp.
Hendrickson, Kenneth E. Jr., Michael L. Collins, and Patrick Cox, eds. *Profiles in Power: Twentieth-Century Texans in Washington.* Austin, Tex.: University of Texas Press, c2004.
Herwig, George J. Collection, Missouri Historical Society, St. Louis.
Historical Holding and Archives, May 1994. "Joint Force: History of Fraine Barracks." Letter. *North Dakota ARNG.* http://www.guard.bismarck.nd.us/jointforces/default.asp?ID=378.
House, Dawn. "Camp Williams a Mainstay for Guard Training." *Salt Lake Tribune* 265, no. 80 (January 1, 2003).

Hudson, Dr. James J. "Lieutenant John O. Donaldson: World War I Air Ace and Escape Artist." *Air University Review,* January–February 1986.
Hunt, John M., Jr. "James Mitchell Varnum, 1748-89." Society of Mayflower Descendants in the Commonwealth of Pennsylvania. *Sail 1620.* http://www.sail1620.org/history/notable-mayflower-descendants/95-james-mitchell-varnum.html.
Idaho Military Historical Society. "Pass In Review." *Idaho Military Historical Society.* http://museum.mil.idaho.gov/newsltr.htm.
Independence Hall Association. "Historic Valley Forge: Who Served Here?" *US History.org.* http://www.ushistory.org/valleyforge/served.
International Journal of Naval History. *These We Honor: The International Hall of Fame.* San Diego, Calif.: San Diego Aerospace Museum, 1984.
"John Donaldson." *The Aerodrome Forum.* http://www.theaerodrome.com/aces/usa/donaldson.html.
Johnson, Suzanne P., et al. *An American Legacy in Panama: A Brief History of the Department of Defense Installations and Properties: the Former Panama Canal Zone, Republic of Panama.* [S.l.: s.m., 1994?].
Kelley, Dayton, ed. *The Handbook of Waco and McLennan County, Texas.* Waco, Tex.: Texian Press, 1972.
Kingston Daily Freeman, May 26, 1942, p. 128.
———, June 4, 1942, p. 132.
Kimball, Neil W. "George West." *Colorado Magazine* 27, no. 3 (July 1950).
Kline, Gregg. "Love that Soars: A Story of Romance, Tragedy and Chanute." *News-Gazette,* May 29, 1998.
Knox, Henry. *General Washington's General.* New York: A. S. Barnes and Co., 1958.
Lake, James. "County to Retain Sawyer Name." *Mining Journal,* November 5, 2002.
Levin, Steve. "North Side's Battlefield Hero Found Life's Wounds Too Deep." *Post Gazette,* May 31, 1999.
"Lloyd Hamilton." *The Aerodrome Forum.* http://www.theaerodrome.com/aces/usa/hamilton3.php.
Longmont Ledger, February 15, 1918.
Lubbock Avalanche-Journal, September 30, 1997.
Lundberg, Murray, et al. "Carl Ben Eielson, Alaska Aviation Pioneer." *ExploreNorth.* http://www.explorenorth.com/library/weekly/aa022800a.htm.
Marshall, R. Jackson. *Memories of World War I: North Carolina Doughboys on the Western Front.* North Carolina Office of Archives I History. Raleigh: Division of Archives and History, North Carolina Department of Cultural Resources, 1998.
Martin, Charles A. *The Last Great Ace: The Life of Major Thomas B. McGuire, Jr.* Jacksonville, Fla.: Fruit Cove Publishing, 1998.
McCartney, William F. *The Jungleers: A History of the 41st Infantry Division.* Washington, D.C.: Infantry Journal Press, 1948.
Meilinger, Phillip S. *American Airpower Biography: A Survey of the Field.* Maxwell Air Force Base, Ala.: Air University Press, [1997].
———. *Hoyt S. Vandenberg, The Life of a General.* Bloomington: Indiana University Press, c.1989.
Metz, Leon C. *Desert Army: Fort Bliss on the Texas Border.* El Paso, Tex.: Mangan Books, 1988.
Miller, Francis Trevelyn. *The Armies and the Leaders.* New York: Castle Books, 1957.
Minneci, Beth. "A life on The Ice." *Antarctic Sun,* October 2000.

Mooney, James L. "Dictionary of American Naval Fighting Ships." *Haze Gray & Underway*. http://www.hazegray.org/danfs/.
Muckenfuss, Mark. "Let This Honor Stay." *The Press-Enterprise*, May 15, 2004.
Naval Aviation Hall of Fame. http://www.nationalaviation.org/.
Navarre, Joanne. "Irony: to be famous, but forgotten at home." *Daily News*, June 5, 1974.
Navy Department News Release, "Four Navy Air Fliers Named for Deceased Aviators," June 29, 1943.
———, "Funeral Services for Lieutenant Commander Warren Wallace Harvey, US Navy," December 12, 1940.
Neely, Jack. "Of a Foggy October Morning and The Naming of an Airport." *Metro Pulse* 8, no. 48 (October 22, 1998).
Nevada State Journal. August 30, 1942. p. 20.; December 13, 15, 1949.
New York Times, April 7, 1915, p. 13. Archives.
———, "Uzal Ent." March 7, 1948. Obituary.
1910 United States Bureau of the Census.
O'Conner, Richard. "Mr. Coolidge's Jungle War." *American Heritage Magazine* 19, no. 1 (December 1967).
Ossad, Steven L., Don R. Marsh, and Martin Blumenson. *Major General Maurice Rose: World War II's Forgotten Commander.* Landham, Md.: Taylor Trade Pub., 2003.
Parkinson, Russell J. "Foreign Command of U.S. Forces, 25 February 1993." http://www.dtic.mil/doctrine/jel/research_pubs/p176.pdf.
Parrish, Deanie Bishop. "Hap Arnold Biography." *National WASP World War II Museum.* http://waspmuseum.org/hap-arnold biography.
Paterson, Michael Robert. "Wendell Holsworth Brookley." *Arlington National Cemetery Website: Where Valor Proudly Sleeps*. http://www.arlingtoncemetery.net/whbookley.htm.
Person, Gustav. "Davison Airfield Named in Honor of Army Engineer." *Belvoir Eagle,* September 23, 2004.
Peyton, Green. "50 Years of Aerospace Medicine." AFSC Historical Publication. Series 67-180. As found on "Sidney Johnson Brooks, Jr." *The Early Birds of Aviation*. http://www.earlyaviators.com/ebrooks.htm.
Philadelphia Navy Yard Beacon, "Captain WW Webster Mourned; Services Here Today," March 19, 1943.
Pine, Dan. "Tales of Bravery and Mystery Surround WW II Jewish General." *News Weekly of Northern California,* September 12, 2003.
The Pride. "A Native Son Deserves Overdue Recognition." June 9, 1966.
———, "A Born Leader Whose Courage Made History." June 23, 1966.
Pulaski County Democrat (Winamac, Ind.), February 13, 1941.
Putman, Eben. *Report of the Commission Massachusetts' Part in the World War.* Vol. 1. Boston, Mass.: Commonwealth of Massachusetts, 1931.
Rantol Weekly Press, August 4, 1924, p. 1.
Sarantakes, Nicholas Evan, ed. *Seven Stars The Okinawa Battle Diaries of Simon Bolivar Buckner, Jr. and Joseph Stilwell,* by Simon Bolivar Buckner. College Station: Texas A&M University Press, 2004.
Scarbrough, Clara Stearns. *Land of Good Water: Takachue Pouetsu: a Williamson County, Texas History.* Georgetown, Tex.: Williamson County Sun Publishers, 1973.
Schultz, Duane. *Hero of Bataan, The Story of General Jonathan M. Wainwright.* New York: St. Martin's Press, 1981.

Scutts, Jerry. *Mustang Aces of the Eighth Air Force*. Colchester, Essex, UK: Osprey Publishing, 2004.
———. *Thunderbolt Aces of the Eighth Air Force*. London: Osprey Aerospace, 1998.
Sevigny, Arthur. Major Clarence L. Tinker, "US Army, Camp Gerle Commanding Officer." http://www.gerlecreek.com/documents/tinker.htm. Excerpt from Crowder, James L., Jr. *Osage General: Maj. Gen. Clarence L. Tinker*.
Sherman, William C. *Air Warfare*. Maxwell, Ala.: Air University Press, 2002.
Schroder, Walter K. *Defenses of Narragansett Bay in World War II*. Providence, R.I.: Rhode Island Bicentennial Foundation, 1980.
Sherwood, Adiel, *A Gazetteer of the State of Georgia*. Washington City: Printed by P. Force, 1837.
Sifakis, Stewart. *Who Was Who In The Civil War*. New York: Facts On File, Inc., 1988.
Smithsonian Institution. *Smithsonian National Air and Space Museum*. http://www.nasm.si.edu/.
Spanish American War Centennial. http://www.spanamwar.com/iowa.htm.
Sparks Tribune, February 9, 1966.
State Archives of Florida. *Florida Memory: State Library and Archives of Florida*. http://www.floridamemory.com/.
The State Historical Society of Colorado. *Colorado Magazine* 27, no. 3 (July 1950).
Sweeney, James B. *Famous Aviators of World War II*. New York: F. Watts, 1987.
Tampa Tribune, n.d. Coiner Obituary.
Taylor, Theodore. *The Magnificent Mitscher*. 1954. Reprint, Annapolis, Md.: Naval Institute Press, 1991.
Texas Historical Commission. *National Museum of the Pacific War*. http://www.nimitz-museum.org/.
Texas Military Forces Museum, Austin.
Texas State Historical Association. "The Handbook of Texas Online." *TSHA Online: A Digital Gateway to Texas History*. www.tshaonline.org.
Thole, Lou. "Building An Airfield: Atterbury Army Air Field." *Friends Journal* 23 no. 3 (2000).
Tillman, Barrett. *Wildcat Aces of World War 2*. Osprey Aircraft of the Aces 3. London: Osprey, 1995.
Tufts, Ellen. "He honored the man, not the battlefield." *News-Chronicle*, June 29, 1976.
U.S. Air Force. "Air Force Search." *Air Force Historical Research Agency*. http://www.afhra.af.mil/index.asp.
U.S. Army Center of Military History. *Medal of Honor*. www.history.army.mil/moh.html.
U.S. Executive Branch. *American Battle Monument Commission*. http://www.abmc.gov.
U.S. Naval Academy, Class of 1906 Anniversary Book.
U.S. Navy. *Naval History & Heritage Command*. http://www.history.navy.mil/.
U.S. Veterans. "Burial & Memorials." *United States Department of Veterans Affairs*. http://www.gravelocator.cem.va.gov.
Wallace, Patricia Ward. *Waco: Texas Crossroads*. Woodland Hills, Calif.: Windsor Publications, 1983.
Warner, Ezra J. *Generals in Blue: Lives of the Union Commanders*. [Baton Rouge]: Louisiana State University Press, 1964.
Weider History Group. *HistoryNet.com*. http://www.historynet.com/a-stupid-old-useless-fool.htm#high_1.
West Virginia Archives and History, Charleston.

White, Alexander S. *Dauntless Marine: Joseph Sailer Jr., Dive-Bombing Ace of Guadalcanal*. Pacifica, Calif.: Pacific Press, 1997.

Whitley, Charles G. Jr. *Colorado Pride: A Commemorative History of the Colorado Air National Guard 1923–1988*. Dallas, Tex.: Taylor Publishing Co, 1989.

Wichita Beacon, May 5, 1941.

Wichita Eagle, May 5, 1941.

Wilson, James Grant and John Fiske. *Appleton's Cyclopedia of American Biography*. New York: D. Appleton and Company, 1887–1889. Reprint edited by Stanley L. Klos, 1999.

Wright Brothers Collection. Wright State University Library, Dayton, Ohio.

Yakima Daily Republic, August 4, 5, 10, 15 & 21, 1944; September 15, 1944.

Index

A

A Commentary on the Campaign and Battle of Manassas (Beauregard) 234
A Winter in Madeira, and a Summer in Spain and Florence (Dix) 155
A.P. Hill Monument (Richmond, Va.) 146
Aachen, Germany 312
Abbot, Henry Larcom 231–232
Abemama, Gilbert Islands 430
Aberdeen Proving Ground 218
Aberdeen, Wash. 438
Abilene, Tex. 24, 134
Abingdon, Va. 151
Acacia Park Cemetery (St. Paul, Minn.) 219
Act for the Better Organization of the Marine Corps 390
Adair, Henry Rodney 232
Adams Barracks 269, 446, 456
Adams, John 141
Adams, John Quincy 259
Adams, John W. 269
Admirals Revolt 432
Aerial Experiment Association 92
    Aerodrome no. 1 Red Wing 92
    Aerodrome no. 2 White Wing 92
aerial map 223
Aerial Observers School 82
aeronautics
    regaining control 412
African American
    first accomplishments 377
Afua, Dutch New Guinea 279
Agricultural Experiment Station 261
agriculture 141
    merino sheep 141
    powdered gypsum 141
Aguadilla, Puerto Rico 82
Aiken, S.C. 57
Air Corps Mail Service 41
Air Corps Newsletter 48
Air Corps Tactical School 103
air force
    establishment of 5
Air Force Base High School 204
Air Force Commendation Medal 76, 128
Air Force Meritorious Service Medal 76
Air Medal 4, 7, 13, 15, 20, 22, 25, 27, 30, 32, 35, 42, 50, 51, 53, 58, 60, 69, 70, 72, 74, 78, 84, 85, 89, 92, 98, 101, 108, 114, 119, 120, 128, 191, 195, 200, 207, 217, 221, 225, 226, 227, 270, 271, 273, 275, 358, 380, 400, 421, 433
Air National Guard Base 13, 23, 29, 35, 70, 71, 77, 78, 86
Air Offensive Europe Campaign 50
air position indicator 49
air refueling system 70
Air Reserve Base 42, 115
Air University 35
Air Warfare (Sherman) 224

Airco
  DH.4 3, 11, 28, 39, 66, 107, 396
air-cooled engine 427
aircraft carrier
  first deployment of jet fighters aboard ship 419
aircraft landing
  catapults 426
  first on moving ship 409
Aircraft Squadrons, Battle Fleet Tactical Instructions (Reeves) 434
airmail 19, 29, 82
airplane race 195
Airport Approval Board 302
airspeed indicator 49
air-to-air refueling 119
Akron 407, 418, 427
Alabama 21, 149, 185, 449
Alabama Polytechnic Institute 373
Alameda, Calif. 372, 429
Alamo 134, 138, 235
Alamo Masonic Cemetery 12
Alamogordo Army Air Base 50
Alamogordo, N.Mex. 49
Alaska 134, 449
  first airmail route 29
Alaska Air National Guard 121
Alaska Road Commission 178
Albana, Italy 300
Albany, N.Y. 126, 182
Albany, Tex. 24
Albemarle Co., Va. 168
Albrook AFB 3, 90, 117, 443, 458
Albrook, Frank P. 3
Albuquerque, N.Mex. 56, 120, 275
Alcoa, Tenn. 71
Alcolu, S.C. 93
Aldrich, Margaret Sexton 89
Aldrin, Edwin "Buzz" 54
Alexander, J. W. 395
Alexandria, La. 32, 135, 177, 237
Alexandria, Va. 197
Algeria 285
Allegheny Observatory 58
Allen AAF 191, 445, 449
Allen, Jeanette 5
Allen, Robert Lloyd 191
Alone (Byrd) 113

Alpena County Regional Airport (Mich.) 124
Alpena, Mich. 124
Alpha Delta Phi fraternity 75
Altadena, Calif. 214
altitude formation flying 31
altitude record 6, 54
Alto, Mich. 411
Altoona, Fla. 381
Alvin Callender Field 399, 448, 452
Am-Dong, Korea 350
American Academy of Fine Arts 141
American Airlines 21, 87
American Campaign Medal 25, 101, 105, 191, 241, 285, 302, 358, 371, 373, 375, 380, 393, 414, 419, 432, 440
American Civil War 37, 88, 95, 131, 136, 137, 143, 146, 149, 150, 152, 154, 155, 158, 159, 160, 165, 166, 167, 169, 171, 172, 173, 176, 177, 181, 182, 183, 184, 186, 188, 200, 201, 214, 216, 231, 236, 240, 243, 247, 249, 251, 256, 257
American Combat Airman Hall of Fame 117
American Defense Service Medal 25, 50, 57, 58, 101, 105, 208, 285, 302, 315, 358, 364, 371, 373, 375, 380, 393, 400, 401, 414, 419, 429, 432, 440
American Ethnological Society 148
American Expeditionary Force 62, 87, 99, 115, 123, 139, 162, 172, 198, 223, 289, 375, 391
  first chief of staff 155
American Flying Corps 125
American Football League 117, 118
American Legion 23, 127, 234, 260
American Legion Aviation Award for Valor 226
American Legion Magazine 260
American Military Mission 257
American Philosophical Society 174
American Railway Union strike of 1894 233
American Revolution 164, 184, 256, 258
The American Sportsman 118
American Theater Medal 57, 58
American Volunteer Group 18
  Flying Tigers 18

Ames, Iowa 3, 127
Amiens offensive 8
Amiens, France 74
Amiens-Saint-Quentin, France 11
amphibious warfare 373
Amvets 127
Anacostia, Washington, D.C. 64, 411
Anchorage, Alaska 31, 121, 134, 178
Andersen AFB 4, 443, 457
Andersen, James Roy 4, 46
Anderson Barracks 270, 446, 456
Anderson, Ameth 270
Andersonville, Ga. 387
Andrews AFB 4, 25, 443, 452
Andrews, Frank Maxwell 4–5
Angel Island, San Francisco Bay, Calif. 171
Anna, Ill. 198
Annapolis, Md. 376, 413, 434
Anniston, Ala. 28, 169, 206
Ansbach, Germany 272
Antarctica 456
Antler, Okla. 112
Anzio Beachhead, Italy 270, 299, 307
Apali, Nicaragua 386
Apollo 1 43
Apollo 11 54
Appomattox Court House 147
Aquinaldo, Emilio 138
Arcadia, Calif. 13
Arcadia, Fla. 21, 194, 199
Archibald Field 363, 447, 458
Archibald, Robert James 363
Arctic Ocean
 first aviator 29
Ardennes American Cemetery and Memorial (Neupre, Belgium) 58, 275, 332
Argentia, Newfoundland 404
Argonne, France 13
Arizona 449
Arizona Aviation Hall of Fame 117
Arizona Balloon Buster. *See also,* Luke, Frank, Jr. 62
Arizona Veterans Hall of Fame 117
Arkansas 221, 283, 449
Arkansas National Guard 222
Arlington National Cemetery 4, 5, 6, 7, 11, 13, 18, 19, 25, 26, 31, 32, 34, 38, 39, 42, 47, 49, 53, 57, 60, 64, 65, 72, 78, 80, 88, 89, 90, 91, 92, 98, 99, 101, 102, 103, 104, 108, 112, 117, 120, 124, 126, 133, 137, 139, 152, 155, 157, 159, 167, 175, 182, 184, 185, 186, 187, 191, 197, 200, 207, 211, 213, 218, 238, 242, 250, 257, 265, 281, 285, 288, 297, 335, 339, 346, 351, 355, 358, 363, 365, 368, 371, 375, 379, 381, 385, 393, 396, 405, 408, 409, 414, 416, 417, 419, 420, 421, 422, 423, 424, 425, 426, 427, 428, 432, 435, 437, 440
Arlington, Va. 92, 175, 390
Armed Forces Reserve Medal 253, 285
Armitage Field 400, 448, 450
Armitage, John Murray 400
Armstrong Barracks 270, 446, 456
Armstrong, Eugene M. 270
Armstrong, Neil 54
Army Achievement Medal 192
Army Aerial Forest Fire Patrol 6
Army Air Corps Tactical School (Langley Field, Va.) 391
Army Air Force Combat Crew School (Hendricks Field in Florida) 15
Army Air Forces Technical Training Command 104
Army Aviation Hall of Fame 210, 226
Army Aviator of the Year 273
Army Balloon School 394
Army Commendation Medal 192, 195, 208, 221, 227, 237, 241, 271
Army Flyer (Arnold & Eaker) 26
Army National Guard Base 113, 152, 169, 176, 217, 251
Army of Occupation Medal 222, 302
 (Germany) 5, 253, 373, 375
army officer
 first to die in airplane accident 92
Army War College 56, 152, 162, 172, 259, 289
Arnold AFB 6, 443, 454
Arnold Trophy 90
Arnold, Henry Harley "Hap" 3, 6, 26, 68
around-the-world flight 70
Arsenal Technical High School 307
Articles of Confederation 165
Aschaffenburg, Germany 286, 290, 322

Asheville, N.C. 108
Asiatic-Pacific Campaign Medal 105, 191,
    364, 369, 371, 373, 375, 377, 380, 393,
    400, 401, 403, 414, 419, 427, 429, 432
Aslito Field (Saipan, Mariana Island) 422
Aslito, Saipan, Mariana Islands 422
Assam, India 220
Astoria, Ore. 232
Atlanta, Ga. 22, 157, 158, 172, 385
Atlantic and Great Western Railroad 170
Atlantic Coast Aeronautical Station (Newport News, Va.) 195
Atlantic-Fokker
    C-2A Question Mark 26
Atterbury AAF 7
Atterbury, William Wallace 232–233
Audie Murphy Award 117
Audie Murphy Program 237, 238
Augsburg, Germany 322
Augusta, Ga. 158, 223, 387
Augusta, Maine 247
Augusta, Mich. 263
Ault Field 401, 448, 455
Ault, William B. 401
Austin National Bank 10
Austin, Tex. 10, 83, 248, 436
Austin-Bergstrom International Airport 10
Austria 456
automatic landing gear 49
Aviation Cross (Peru) 32, 33
aviation records
    altitude 144
Aviator's wings and commission 12
Avranches, France 339
Axe Murder Incident 345
Ayer High School (Mass.) 217
Ayer, Beatrice 315
Ayer, Mass. 217
Azbill Barracks 271, 446, 456
Azbill, Roy Gordon 271

B

Bad Cannstatt, Germany 304, 337
Bad Kissingen, Germany 283
Bad Kreuznach, Germany 288, 310, 325
Bad Tolz, Germany 271
Bagstone, Belgium 74
Bainbridge, Adelaide 104

Bakalar AFB 7, 443, 451
Bakalar, Dorothea 7
Bakalar, John Edmond "Buck" 7
Baker Barracks 271, 446, 456
Baker, A. J. "Bo" 271–272
Bakersfield, Calif. 181
Balboa Field 3, 19
Ball, La. 237
Ballistic Missile Defense Organization
    Advisory Committee 91
Balloon Corps 159
balloon flight
    Explorer I 35
balloons 214
Baltimore, Md. 80, 137, 153, 160, 173, 218, 327, 359
Bamberg Co., Ga. 244
Bamberg, Germany 338
Bangalore, India 197
Bangor, Maine 23
Barbary Wars 252
Barber Point, Hawaii 422
Bardenberg, Germany 317
Barin Field 402, 448, 449
Barin, Louis T. 402
Bark(e)ley, David Bennes 134
Barksdale AFB 7, 14, 30, 46, 65, 117, 443, 451
Barksdale Field 278
Barksdale, Eugene Hoy 7–8
Barrow, Fla. 234
Barstow, Calif. 163
Barton Barracks 272, 446, 456
Barton, David B. 272
Bartow, Fla. 414
Bastogne, Belgium 313
Bastrop, Tex. 257
Bataan Death March 24, 25, 185
Bates Field 11
Battle of Midway 389
    first marine aviator death 389
Bauer Field 364, 447, 458
Bauer, Harold William "Indian Joe" 364–365
Baumholder, Germany 329
Bay City, Mich. 104
Beale AFB 8, 443, 450
Beale, Edward Fitzgerald "Ned" 8–9

Beaufort Marine Corps Air Station (Beaufort, S.C.) 391
Beaufort, S.C. 391
Beauregard, Pierre Gustave Toutant 233–234
Bedford, Mass. 45
Beebe, David C. 9
Beech Aircraft Co. 73
Beechcraft
    AT-10 73
Beeville, Tex. 408
Beilstein, Germany 333
Belgian Fourragere 285
Belgium 286, 290
Belgium Order of Leopold 161
Bell
    AH-1 Cobra 226
    CH-21 Shawnee 204, 225
    H-13 Sioux 194
    H-29B 224
    P-39 Airacobra 51, 61
    UH-1 Huey 192
    UH-1B Huey 196, 271
    UH-60 Blackhawk 192
    X-1 129
    X-1A 129
    X-2 54
    XP-59A 419
Bellefontaine Cemetery (St. Louis, Mo.) 122
Belleville, Ill. 91, 203
Bellingham, Wash. 34
Bellows AFB 9, 106, 443, 451
Bellows Falls, Vt. 247
Bellows, Franklin Barney 9–10
Belton, Tex. 358
Beltran, France 192
Ben Tre, Vietnam 225
Bend, Ore. 231
Bennet, May 218
Bennett, Floyd 416
Benning, Henry Lewis "Old Rock" 147
Bentley, Mary T. 180
Bergstrom AFB 10, 443, 454
Bergstrom family 10
Bergstrom, John August Earl 10
Bering Sea 96
Berlin Airlift 101, 302

Berlin, Germany 302, 313, 335
Bermuda 55, 456
Bermuda International Airport 54
Bernard Airport (Youngstown, Ohio) 81
Bethany College (W.Va.) 47
Bethesda, Md. 414, 422, 431, 432, 434
Beverly, Mass. 231
Bexar Co., Tex. 421
Bezange-la-Petite, France 342
Biffle, Jacob B. 180
Biggs AAF 10, 192, 197, 445, 454
Biggs AFB 10, 192
Biggs Field 15, 65, 197
Biggs, James Berther "Buster" 192
Bigler, John 8
Biloxi, Miss. 52, 205
Binh Gia, Vietnam 271
Birmingham, Ala. 179, 180, 205
Bischheim, France 316
Bismarck, N.Dak. 264
bituminous surface treatments 52
Bivalue, N.J. 294
Black Hills National Cemetery (Sturgis, S. Dak.) 30
Black Panthers 430
Black Rivers Falls, Wisc. 356
Black Seminole scouts 236
Blackerwick, Ann M. 112
Blackstone, Va. 176
Blanding, Albert Hazen 234–235
Blankart, Edna 138
Bliss, William Wallace Smith 148
Blood, Henry H. 259
Bloomington, Md. 240
Bloomquist, Paul A. 273
Blountville, Ind. 107
Blue Angel Recreation Park 405
Blue Lodge 36
Bluethenthal Field 111, 444, 453
Bluethenthal, Arthur "Bluey" 111
Blytheville, Ark. 25, 301
Blytheville, Miss. 301
Board of Police Commissioners 122
Boeing
    B-17 Flying Fortress 5, 36, 38, 49, 59, 79, 87, 102, 103, 115, 120, 201
    Pluto 82
    first mass formation flight 79

first sent to England 20
B-29 Superfortress 6, 20, 33, 36, 46, 49, 70, 98
   photo squadron 36
B-47 Stratojet 70, 102
   first operational flight 70
B-50 Superfortress 70
Model 15 99
Model 299 49
P-12 31, 90
PW-9A 106
Boerne, Tex. 80
Boise, Idaho 116
Bolling AFB 10, 31, 42, 47, 64, 68, 443, 455
Bolling Mission 11
Bolling, Raynal Cawthorne 10–11
bolometer 58
bomber
   first long-range, high-altitude strategic. *See,* Boeing, B-17 Flying Fortress
Bonaparte, Napoleon 141
Bondsteel, James Leroy 134–135
Bong, Richard Ira 72, 84–85
Bonifas, Arthur George 345
Bony, France 11
Bordelon Field 403, 448, 451
Bordelon, William James 403
Borland, Earl 29
Boscawen, N.H. 154
Boston City Hospital 77
Boston College 155
Boston Company 243
Boston Grenadier Corps 164
Boston Transcript. 243
Boston, Mass. 112, 137, 152, 153, 156, 164, 167, 182, 217, 239, 243, 250, 311, 335
Bougainville Island (Pacific) 69
Bountiful Memorial Park (Bountiful, Utah) 206
Bountiful, Utah 206
Bourne, Mass. 242
Bowden, England 242
Bowie, James 180, 235
Bowie, Rezin 235
Bowman, A. J. 80

Boxer Rebellion 207, 215, 218, 297, 366, 425
Braddock, Pa. 91
Bradford Town Cemetery (Vt.) 247
Bradford, Vt. 246
Bradley Field 112, 444, 450
Bradley International Airport (Windsor Locks, Conn.) 112
Bradley, Eugene Morris 112
Bradley, Omar N. 33, 197, 357
Brady, Matthew 214
Bragg, Braxton 148–149, 178
Braggs, Okla. 244
Brand, Germany 274
Brann Barracks 133, 444, 456
Brann, Donald Weldon 133
Brazil 6
Bremen 416
Bremen, Germany 90
Bremerhaven, Germany 302
Bridge of No Return 345
Bridges, Frances 39
Bridgeton, Maine 213
Bridgeton, Mo. 122
Brigadier General David H. Stem Award 331
Brimfield, Mass. 247
Bristol 107
   F.2 Brisfit 94
Bristol College (Pa.) 251
Bristol Field 404, 448, 457
Bristol, Arthur LeRoy, Jr. 404–405
British Air Force Cross 20
British Distinguished Flying Cross 54, 89
British Distinguished Service Cross 119
British Distinguished Service Order 118, 283
British Knight Commander of the Order of St. Michael and St. George 218
British Military Cemetery (Grandcourt, France) 93
British Military Medal 274
British Order of Commander of the Bath 373
British Order of St. Michael and St. George 250
Brittany American Cemetery, St. James, France 7

Bronson Field 405, 448, 450
Bronson, Clarence King 405
Bronze Star 13, 58, 64, 70, 101, 114, 119, 126, 128, 194, 195, 210, 217, 219, 221, 226, 227, 241, 253, 271, 274, 285, 295, 299, 302, 305, 306, 315, 325, 330, 332, 345, 358, 387, 391, 414
Brooke Army Medical Center (San Antonio, Tex.) 191, 391
Brookley AFB 11, 443, 449
Brookley, Wendell Holsworth 11–12
Brooklyn Collegiate and Polytechnic Institute 183
Brooklyn, Iowa 34
Brooklyn, N.Y. 95, 121, 318, 321, 416
Brooks AFB 12, 33, 36, 41, 57, 101, 197, 201, 443, 454
Brooks City Base 12
Brooks, Sidney Johnston, Jr. 12
Brookside Dairy 126
Brother Jonathan 157
Brown Field 405, 448, 450
Brown Stagefield 192, 445, 449
Brown University 48, 258
Brown, Jacob 254
Brown, Jerry L. 192
Brown, Melville Stuart 405–406
Brownwood, Tex. 235
Bryan, Tex. 42
Bryn Mawr Hospital (Pa.) 232
Buchanan, James 149
Buckley AFB 13, 443, 450
Buckley, John Harold 13
Buckner, Simon Bolivar, Jr. 150
Büdingen, Germany 270
Buffalo Medical College 175
Buffalo Soldier 349
Buffalo, N.Y. 21, 41, 175, 179, 357
Bullis, John Lapham 235–236
Bullis, Lydia Porter 186
Bundy, Gareth H. 117
Bunker Hill AFB 42
Bunton Bock Gun and Rod Club 278
Burbank, Calif. 24, 104
Burgess
    H Model 198
Burgess-Wright
    altitude record 6

Buring, Elizabeth Susan 89
Burlington, N.C. 204
Burlington, Vt. 105, 340
Burress, Withers A. 291
Bushnell, Ill. 405
Bustleton Field (Philadelphia, Pa.) 198
Busy Park (England) 42
Bütgenbach, Belgium 338
Butler University (Indianapolis, Ind.) 307
Butler, Mo. 236, 237
Butler, Smedley Darlington 365–366
Butler, William T. 401
Butts AAF 193, 445, 450
Butts, John Edward 193
Byrd Antarctic Expedition 416
Byrd Field 112, 444, 448, 455, 458
Byrd, Richard Evelyn 112–113, 416, 442
Byrd, William Carl 365

C

Cabaniss Field 406, 448, 455
Cabaniss, Robert Wright 406–407
Cadiz, Spain 173
Cairns AAF 193, 445, 449
Cairns, Bogardus Snowden 193–194
"The Caissons Go Rolling Along" 245
Caldwell, Idaho 116
California 171, 206, 450
California Bank 206
Callender, Alvin Andrew 399
Calumos Club 192
Calvary Cemetery
    (Cleveland, Ohio) 334, 369
    (Duluth, Minn.) 367
    (Grand Forks, N.Dak.) 289
    (Los Angeles, Calif.) 206
    (St. Louis, Mo.) 143
Calverton National Cemetery (N.Y.) 114
Calverton, N.Y. 114
Cambrai offensive 8
Cambridge American Cemetery and Memorial (England) 41, 99
Cambridge, England 41, 99
Cambridge, Mass. 154, 231, 436
Camden, N.J. 424
camels 8
Cameron Twp., Iowa 279
Cameron, Marjorie 21

Camilla, Ga. 196
Camp Abbot 231, 446, 454
Camp Adair 232, 446, 454
Camp Atterbury 232, 446, 451
Camp Barkeley 134, 444, 454
Camp Beauregard 178, 233, 238, 446, 451
Camp Blanding 204, 234, 446, 450
Camp Bloomquist 273, 446, 456
Camp Bondsteel 134, 445, 457
Camp Bonifas 345, 447, 457
Camp Bowie 235, 446, 454
Camp Bullis 235, 446, 454
Camp Butler 365, 448, 458
Camp Carroll 346, 447, 457
Camp Casey 346, 447, 457
Camp Claiborne 135, 227, 445, 451
Camp Clark 236, 446, 452
Camp Clarke 273, 446, 456
Camp Coiner 347, 447, 457
Camp Cook 237, 446, 451
Camp Cooke 20, 101, 136, 445, 450
Camp Courtney 366, 448, 458
Camp Croft 137, 445, 454
Camp Crowder 238, 446, 452
Camp Curtis Guild 239, 446, 452
Camp Custer 137
Camp Dawson 239, 446, 455
Camp Devens 137, 153, 250
Camp Dodge 240, 446, 451
Camp Drum 155, 351
Camp Edsall 241, 446, 453
Camp Edwards 242, 347, 446, 447, 452, 457
Camp Elliott 368, 448, 450
Camp Elmore 369, 448, 455
Camp Foster 369, 448, 458
Camp Fremont 162
Camp Funston 12, 138, 445, 451
Camp G. C. Grafton 242, 446, 453
Camp Gary 38, 222
Camp Gates 274, 446, 456
Camp Geiger 370, 448, 453
Camp George 348, 447, 457
Camp George West 243, 446, 450
Camp Gonsalves 372, 448, 458
Camp Gordon 257
Camp Gordon Johnston 139, 445, 450
Camp Grant 140, 245, 330, 445, 451
Camp Greaves 349, 447, 457
Camp Greene 244, 446, 454
Camp Griffiss (England) 42
Camp Gruber 244, 446, 454
Camp H. M. Smith 373, 448, 451
Camp Hancock 218
Camp Hansen 374, 448, 458
Camp Hartell 245, 446, 450
Camp Henry 350, 447, 457
Camp Holcomb 368, 375, 448, 450
Camp Hospital no. 24 (France) 243
Camp Hovey 351, 447, 457
Camp Howard 376, 448, 450
Camp Howze 352, 447, 457
Camp Jackson 82, 163
Camp Johnson 246, 376, 446, 448, 453, 455
Camp Keyes 247, 446, 452
Camp Kinser 377, 448, 458
Camp Kyle 353, 447, 457
Camp Labonte 248, 446, 453
Camp Lejeune 378, 448, 453
Camp Lester 379, 448, 458
Camp Lewis 99, 168
Camp Libby 213, 353
Camp Lindsey 275, 446, 456
Camp Livingston 141, 445, 451
Camp Long 354, 447, 457
Camp Mabry 248, 446, 454
Camp Mackall 141, 445, 453
Camp Maxey 249, 278, 446, 454
Camp McCain 250, 446, 452
Camp McCoy 170, 261
Camp McCutcheon 380, 448, 453
Camp McTureous 381, 448, 458
Camp Meade 137, 173
Camp Merritt 218
Camp Monteith 142, 445, 457
Camp Page 354, 447, 457
Camp Pendleton 251, 370, 382, 392, 393, 446, 448, 450, 455
Camp Perry 251, 446, 454
Camp Pieri 276, 446, 456
Camp Pike 106, 252, 446, 449
Camp Red Cloud 356, 447, 457
Camp Rilea 253, 446, 454
Camp Ripley 219, 254, 446, 452
Camp Roberts 255, 446, 450

Camp Robinson 221
Camp Schwab 383, 448, 458
Camp Sears 357, 447, 457
Camp Shelby 204, 227, 255, 446, 452
Camp Sherman 143, 445, 454
Camp Shields 384, 448, 458
Camp Stanley 256, 446, 455
Camp Swift 257, 446, 455
Camp Taliaferro 144, 445, 455
Camp Travis 83
Camp Truscott 144, 445, 456
Camp Varnum 257, 446, 454
Camp Villere 258, 446, 451
Camp W. G. Williams 259, 446, 455
Camp Wadsworth 153
Camp Walker 358, 447, 457
Camp Wallace AS 145, 445, 458
Camp Whalen 277, 446, 456
Camp Wheeler 245
Camp White 260, 446, 454
Camp Williams 260, 446, 455
Camp Withycombe 261, 446, 454
Camp Wolters 142, 186, 205
Campbell Barracks 277, 446, 456
Campbell Co., Ky. 144
Campbell, Charles L. 277–278
Campbell, Ohio 81
Campbell, William Bowen 150–151
Canaan, Litchfield Co., Conn. 160
Cannon AFB 13, 443, 453
Cannon, John Kenneth 13–14
Canyon Hill Cemetery (Caldwell, Idaho) 116
Cape Sabine 159
Cape Udak, Aleutian Islands, Alaska 103
Carberry, Joseph E. 144
Carbondale, Kans. 35
Caribbean Defense Command 5
Carlisle, Pa. 149, 310
Carlstrom Field 21, 31, 106, 409, 445, 450
Carlstrom, Victor 194–195
Carnegie Medal 387
Caroline Co., Va. 145
Carrabelle, Fla. 139
Carrizal, Mexico 232
Carroll, Charles F. 346
Carson, Christopher Houston "Kit" 8, 151–152

Carswell AFB 14, 443, 454
Carswell, Horace Seaver "Stump" Jr. 14–15
Carthage, Tenn. 151
Carthage, Tunisia 222, 285
Caruthersville, Mo. 32
Casey, Hugh Boyd 346–347
Castle AFB 16, 443, 450
Castle, Frederick Walker 16–17
catapult
    first from ship at Veracruz 428
    first under hostile fire 429
    first while underway 429
    launch 441
Caterpillar Club 38, 48, 117
Cawley Kaserne 278, 446, 456
Cawley, Arthur Nelson 278–279
CEC/Seabee Historical Foundation 442
Cecil Commerce Center 407
Cecil Field 407, 448, 450
Cecil, Henry Barton 407
Cedar Grove Cemetery (Lebanon, Tenn.) 151
Cedar Hill plantation 184
Cedar Hill, Ga. 184
Cedar Valley, Ohio 256
Cedartown, Ga. 224
Centerville, Ohio 68
ceremonial swords 236
Cerrillos, N.Mex. 102
Certificate of Valor 70
Cervantes, Ramiro 47
Cervera, D. Pascual 434
Chaffee, Adna Romanza, Jr. 152–153
Chaffee, Roger 43
Chambers Field 408, 448, 455
Chambers, Washington Irving 408
Chandler, Ariz. 106
Changsong-ni, N. Korea 348
Chanute AFB 3, 17, 67, 106, 443, 451
Chanute, Octave Alexandre 17
Chapman, Mary Sarah 158
Charles City County, Va. 264
Charles E. Kelly Sup. Fac. 262, 446, 454
Charles L. Kelly AH 195, 445, 455
Charleston, S.C. 103, 208, 365, 391, 404, 426
Charleston, W.Va. 128, 240

Charlestown, Mass. 153
Charlotte, N.C. 123, 124, 139
Chase Field 408, 448, 455
Chase, Nathan Brown 408–409
Chatham, Mass. 302
Chautauqua Co., N.Y. 50, 187
Chen, Ann 18
Cheney Award 32, 33
Chennault AFB 18, 443, 451
Chennault, Claire Lee 18
Cherokee, N.C. 348
Cherokee, Okla. 118
Cherry Point, N.C. 385
Chester Rural Cemetery (Chester, Pa.) 322
Chester, Pa. 322, 440
Chevalier Field 409, 448, 450
Chevalier, Godfrey DeCourcelles 409–410
Cheyenne, Wyo. 37
Chiang Kai-shek, Madame 18
Chicago Fire 182
Chicago, Ill. 17, 64, 77, 182, 239, 253, 367, 393, 406, 432
Chico Cemetery (Chico, Calif.) 60
Chico, Calif. 60
Child, Martha 258
Chillicothe, Ohio 143, 183
China Air Task Force 18
China Lake, Calif. 400
China Relief Expedition 215, 425
China Relief Expedition Medal 186
Chinese Air Force Wings 30
Chinese Army, Navy, and Air Corps Medal 60, 220
Chinese-Japanese War 368
Chonghyon-dong, Korea 356
Chosin Reservoir (Korea) 354
Christ Church Cathedral (New Orleans, La.) 177
Christ Lutheran Church 278
Christensen Barracks 279, 446, 456
Christensen, Dale Eldon 279–280
Chuncheon, Gangwon Province, S. Korea 354
Cimarron, Kans. 422
Cincinnati, Ohio 216, 244
Citadel 137, 208, 365, 391
City of Lubbock Cemetery (Tex.) 337
Civil War Campaign Medal 186, 200

Civilian Conservation Corps 112
Clackamas, Ore. 260, 261
Claiborne, William Charles Cole 135–136
Claremont, N.H. 243
Clarendon Bridge 82
Clark AB 19, 129, 443, 458
Clark Field 10, 20, 38, 73
Clark, Harold Melville 19
Clark, Harvey C. 236–237
Clark, William 169
Clarke, Denny T. 273–274
Clay, Lucius DuBignon 302–303
Clayton City Cemetery (N.C.) 29
Clemson College (S.C.) 387
Clermont, N.Y. 141
Cleveland High School (Portland, Ore.) 357
Cleveland, Grover 147
Cleveland, Ohio 242, 334, 369
Cline, Vera 40
Clover, Beatrice Miller 376
Clovis AFB 15
Clovis, N.Mex. 13
Clyde, Ohio 172
Coburg, Germany 291
Cochran AAF 196, 445, 451
Cochran, Kay 114
Cochran, Robert James 196
Cocoa Beach, Fla. 78
Coffey Barracks 280, 446, 456
Coffey, John W. 280
Coffeyville, Kans. 55
Coiner, Randall E. 347
Colchester, Va. 390
Colchester, Vt. 246
Cold Bay, Alaska 96, 97
Cold Mountain, N.C. 108
Coleman Barracks 280, 281, 446, 456
Coleman, Kenneth W. 280–281
Coleman, Wilson Dudley 281–282
College of William and Mary 174
College Park, Md. 91
Colleville-sur-Mer, France 142, 171, 319, 322, 331
Collier Trophy 128
Collins, Michael 54
Collins, Phelps 124–125
Colorado 62, 69, 450

Colorado Springs, Colo. 32, 80, 90, 151, 193
Colorado Transcript 243
Colts Neck, N.J. 412
Columbia Co., Ga. 147
Columbia, S.C. 70, 163, 202
Columbiana Co., Ohio 216
Columbus Municipal Airport 7
Columbus, Ga. 59, 147, 210, 212
Columbus, Ind. 7
Columbus, Ohio 86, 349, 352
Columbus, Tex. 187
Combat Command: The American Aircraft Carriers in the Pacific War (Sherman) 418
Combat Infantryman's Badge 346
Command and General Staff College 143, 152, 172, 245
Commander of the Belgian Order of the Crown 233
Commander of the Crown of Italy 4
Commander of the Legion of Honor 232
Commander of the Order of the British Empire 32
Commendation Medal 345
Commendation Ribbon 253
Commerce, Tex. 18
Commercial Airplane Reliability Tour for the Edsel B. Ford Trophy, The 12
Committee of Five 141
Commonwealth Edison 82
Companion of the Order of the Bath 232
concentration camp 25
Concord, N.H. 248
Condor of the Andes (Bolivia) 32, 33
Condron AAF 196, 445, 453
Condron, Max Henderson 196–197
Congressional Cemetery (Washington, D.C.) 390
Congressional Gold Medal 128, 140, 163, 251, 254, 256, 264, 288, 437
Congressional Life Saving Medal 315
Congressional Space Medal of Honor 42
Connally AFB 20, 443, 454
Connally, James Thomas 20
Connecticut 450
connecting inclined railroads 214
Consolidated

B-24 Liberator 4, 5, 15, 21, 33, 36, 46, 69, 70, 97, 99
P-30 49, 68
Y1P-25 31
Consolidated Aircraft Corporation 21
Continental army 174, 244
Continental Can Co. 303
Convair
  B-36 Peacemaker 31, 101
  F-102 Delta Dagger 54
  F-106 Delta Dart 54
Cook, Harold Bobby 237–238
Cooke AFB 20, 136
Cooke Barracks 282, 446, 456
Cooke, Charles H. 282
Cooke, Francis 258
Cooke, John R. 137
Cooke, Philip St. George 136–137
Cooley, Grace W. 78
Cooper Co., Mo. 236
Copley News Service 26
Coral and Brass (Smith) 373
Coral Sea 401
Cordova Airlines (Alaska) 122
Cordova, Alaska 122
Cornell University 22, 31, 320
Coronado, Calif. 382
Corpus Christi, Tex. 406, 411, 435, 439
Corry Field 410, 448, 450
Corry, William Merrill, Jr. 410–411
Corsair 419
Corvallis, Ore. 232
Cotner College 34
Council Bluffs, Iowa 240
County Road Association of Michigan 52
Courthouse Lawn (Blytheville, Miss.) 301
Courtney, Henry Alexius, Jr. 366–368
Covelo, Calif. 241
Craig AFB 20, 443, 449
Craig, Bruce Kilpatrick, Jr. 20–21
Crailsheim, Germany 306
Creighton University Law School 266
Crepion, France 62
Crimean War 136
Crissy Field 33
Croce Merito (Italy) 134
Crockett, David 180
Croft, Edward 137–138

Croix de Guerre 32, 86, 98, 111, 114, 134, 155, 163, 170, 194, 215, 218, 242, 255, 297, 325, 409
Croix de Guerre (Belgium) 16, 325
Croix de Guerre (French) 45, 89, 241, 352, 373, 375, 379
Croix de Guerre (Italy) 62
Crosher, Kenneth R. 117
Cross of Gallantry 195
Cross of the Black Star (French) 260
Cross of the Legion of Honor 11
Cross Timbers, Indian Territory (Okla.) 166
Crow Agency, Mont. 263
Crowder, Enoch Herbert 238–239
Crown Hill Cemetery
  (Indianapolis) 146
  (Winamac, Ind.) 201
Cruz Peruna de Aviacion of Peru 4
Cuba 149, 237, 456
Cuban Occupation 139
Cuban Pacification 163, 186
Cubi Point, Philippines 432
Cuddihy Field 411, 448, 455
Cuddihy, George Thomas 411–412
Culberson, Charles Allen 249
Culpeper, Va. 145
Cumberland University 421
Cumberland, Md. 175
Cunningham Field 385, 448, 453
Cunningham, Alfred Austell 385–386
Curtiss
  A-1 408, 413
  A-12 Shrike 41, 48
  AB-2 429
  AT-4 83
  B-1 385
  CR-3 411
  F6C-3 Blackhawk 394
  JN-4 Jenny 12, 65, 82, 227
    speed and distance record 195
  NC-1 113, 402, 426
  NC-3 113
  NC-4 113, 406
    first transatlantic flight 435
  P-1 Hawk 99
  P-40 Warhawk 51, 61, 106, 112, 127
  R-2
    altitude record 195
  R-6 11
  tractor #30 144
  Type-4 Pusher 53
Curtiss Aeroplane and Motor Co. 405
Curtiss Aviation Co. 219
Curtiss Flying School 437
Curtiss Marine Trophy Race 394
Curtiss, Glenn 408, 413
Custer, George Armstrong 263
Custer's Last Stand 263
Custis, Mary Anna Randolph 167
Cuyamaca Mountains (near San Diego, Calif.) 215

D

D'Angelo, Victoria Scott 129
Dachau, Germany 285
Daegu (Taegu), S. Korea 348, 350, 358
Daily Capital (Topeka, Kans.) 266
Daley Barracks 283, 446, 456
Daley, William T. 283
Dallas, Tex. 46, 421
Danbury, Conn. 246
Dannelly Field 113, 444, 449
Dannelly, Clarence Moore, Jr. 113
Danvers, Mass. 240
Darby Barracks 283, 446, 456
Darby, William Orlando 283–284
Darby's Rangers 283
Darling, Dorothy 50
Dartmouth College 89, 148
Darwin, Australia 39
Davids Island, N.Y. 95
Davidson College 52, 94, 124
Davis, Jefferson 167
Davis, Samuel Howard 21
Davis-Monthan AFB 15, 21, 57, 443, 449
Davison AAF 197, 445, 455
Davison, Donald Angus 197–198
Dawson, William Mercer Owens 239–240
Dayton, Ohio 7, 48, 107, 124, 201, 210, 212, 216, 219
D-Day 142, 313, 319
de Havilland
  DH-4. *See also,* Airco, DH.4 3, 11, 28, 39, 66, 107, 396
De Kooy Airfield 119

Decisions of the Superintendents of Common Schools (Dix) 155
Declaration of Independence 141, 174
  Committee of Five 141
Decorah Cemetery (Black Rivers Falls, Wisc.) 356
Decorations from
  France 13
  Great Britain 13
  Italy 13
  Morocco 13
  Poland 13
  Yugoslavia 13
Defense Science Board 91
Defiance, Ohio 36
Deggendorf, Germany 319
Del Rio High School 59
Del Rio, Tex. 59
Delhi, Iowa 3
Delhi, N.Y. 166
Delphi, Onondaga Co., N.Y. 95
Delta Junction, Alaska 159, 191
Denton, Marilda Cass 250
Denver University 80
Denver, Colo. 13, 32, 61, 69
Department of the Platte 238
Descanso, Calif. 406
Detrick, Frederick Louis 153
Detroit News Trophy 47
Detroit, Mich. 53, 108, 136
Devantave, Belgium 303
Devens Reserve Forces Training Area 153
Devens, Charles, Jr. 153–154
Devonshire, England 261
Dewey, George 426
Dewsbury, England 21
Dickhouse, Glennis Faye 129
Dickinson College (Pa.) 149, 257
Dinkins Military Academy 21
dirigible
  first qualified pilot 123
  first transatlantic crossing 421
Discovery, the Story of the Second Byrd Antarctic Expedition (Byrd) 113
Distinguished Flying Cross 4, 6, 15, 16, 18, 20, 22, 25, 27, 28, 30, 32, 34, 35, 42, 43, 49, 50, 51, 53, 54, 58, 60, 68, 70, 72, 74, 78, 84, 85, 89, 92, 97, 98, 101, 108, 112, 114, 117, 119, 128, 195, 201, 203, 207, 217, 220, 221, 225, 226, 227, 271, 273, 358, 380, 393, 395, 396, 400, 411, 414, 421, 422, 430
Distinguished Service Cross 6, 7, 9, 15, 16, 22, 24, 26, 32, 39, 43, 51, 52, 54, 62, 72, 82, 84, 85, 86, 89, 92, 96, 114, 115, 118, 119, 139, 195, 208, 212, 218, 225, 226, 269, 270, 277, 278, 281, 283, 284, 285, 286, 290, 292, 295, 297, 299, 304, 312, 315, 325, 329, 339, 346, 351, 357, 358
Distinguished Service Medal 4, 11, 13, 18, 25, 32, 33, 39, 41, 82, 97, 101, 104, 108, 112, 115, 123, 128, 139, 155, 161, 163, 170, 171, 178, 185, 208, 215, 218, 234, 237, 241, 242, 244, 250, 253, 260, 266, 271, 288, 297, 302, 314, 315, 325, 339, 352, 358, 366, 370, 373, 375, 378, 380, 382, 409, 414, 416, 419, 424, 426, 432, 434, 437
Distinguished Service Medal (Army) 404, 419, 429
Distinguished Service Medal (Navy) 404, 429
Dix, John Adams 154–155
Djebel Dardys, Tunisia 312
Dobbins AFB 22, 443, 450
Dobbins, Charles M. 22
Dodd Field 198, 445, 455
Dodd, Townsend Foster 198–199
Dodge, Grenville Mullen 240–241
Dominican Campaign Medal 373
Dominican Medal of Military Merit 371
Dominican Order of the First Merit 373
Donaldson AFB 22, 443, 454
Donaldson, John Owen 22–23
Donaldson, Marie 113
Donelson, Rachel 164
Dong Xoai, South Vietnam 384
Dongducheon, Gyeonggi-do Province, South Korea 346, 351
Doolittle Raid 60, 220
Doolittle, Jimmy 60, 420, 425
Dorr AAF 199, 445, 450
Dorr Field 48
Dorr, Stephen Higginson, Jr. 199

Douglas 28
   A-3 Skywarrior 24
   A3D Skywarrior 433
   A-20 75
   A-20 Havoc 27, 119
   BT2-B 12
   C-1 26
   C-29 Dolphin 68
   C-47 Skytrain 22, 303
   C-54 Skymaster 99
   0-2 8
   0-25C 47
   0-46A 77
   SBD-Dauntless 395
   XB-42
      Mixmaster
         transcontinental speed record 27
   YOA-5 amphibian 5
Douglas Aircraft Co. 26, 60
Douglas, Marian Amelia 153
Dover, Del. 311
Dow AFB 23, 443, 452
Dow, James Frederick 23
Dowdell Field 386, 448, 458
Dowdell, Frank E. 386, 395
Downers Grove, Ill. 379
Downs Barracks 284, 446, 456
Downs, Robert C. 284
Doyle, Madeline 97
Dracut, Mass. 258
Drane, Sally 187
Drew Field 120
Druid Ridge Cemetery (Pikesville, Md.) 328
Drum, Hugh Aloysius 155–156
Dufek, George J. 442
Duke Field 24, 443, 450
Duke, Robert Lewis 24
Duluth, Minn. 366, 367
Duncan Field 57, 123
Dunn, Lura Lee 8
Dupont Trophy 219
Durant, Elliot M., Jr. 40
Dustoff Hall of Fame 195, 273
Dyer County, Tenn. 21
Dyess AFB 24, 443, 454
Dyess Field 387, 448, 457
The Dyess Story (Dyess) 25

Dyess, Aquilla James "Jimmy" 387
Dyess, William Edwin 24–25

E

E. I. Du Pont de Nemours Co. 7
Eagles 127
Eaker AFB 25, 443, 449
Eaker, Ira Clarence 16, 25–26, 35
Eareckson AFB 26, 443, 449
Eareckson Air Station 26
Eareckson, William "Eric" Olmstead 26–27
Earhart, Amelia 421, 441
Earle NWS 412, 448, 453
Earle, Ralph 412
Early, Jubal A. 158
East Florida Seminary (now Univ. of Florida) 234
East Liverpool, Ohio 380
East Orange, N.J. 38
East Palestine, Ohio 142
East Pascagoula, Miss. 148
Eastern Airlines 87
Eastern Cemetery (Quincy, Fla.) 410
Eastman Barracks 285, 447, 456
Eastman, Tobias C. 285
Easton, Pa. 331
Eau Claire, Wisc. 431
Ede, Virginia 15
Edinburgh, Ind. 232
Edinburgh, Mo. 238
Edsall, Floyd L. 241
Edsel B. Ford Trophy 12
Edwards AFB 27, 42, 53, 129, 443, 450
Edwards, Clarence Ransom 242
Edwards, Glen Walter 27–28, 36
Edwards, Junior D. 347–348
Edwards, Mary 9
Egbert, Elizabeth Gordon 298
Eglin AFB 24, 28, 34, 50, 81, 443, 450
Eglin Field 34, 81
Eglin, Frederick Irving 28
Eielson AFB 28, 443, 449
Eielson, Carl Benjamin 28–29
Eighth Air Force Bomber Command 26
8th Fighter Command 208
Eisenhower, Dwight D. 31, 197, 303, 315, 359

Eisern, Germany 318, 341
El Paso, Tex. 148, 152, 192, 197
El Reno, Okla. 118
El Sol del Peru (Grand Officer) 5
Elba, Ala. 192
Elizabeth, N.J. 418, 419
Elk, N.Mex. 339
Elkhorn, Neb. 197
Ellington AFB 29, 31, 66, 67, 443, 454
Ellington, Eric Lamar 29
Elliott, George Frank 368
Ellsworth AFB 30, 103, 443, 454
Ellsworth, Richard Elmer 30–31
Ellyson Field 413, 448, 450
Ellyson Industrial Park 413
Ellyson,Theodore Gordon "Spuds" 408, 413
Elmendorf AFB 31, 150, 443, 449
Elmendorf, Hugh Merle 31
Elmendorf, Irene 31
Elmendorf, Virginia 31
Elmore, George William 369
Elmwood Cemetery (Detroit, Mich.) 136
Emblem of the Ejercito Argentino 5
Emerson, Caroline Victoria 359
Emery Barracks 285, 447, 456
Emery, Robert M. 285–286
Empire State Inc. 156
Encinitas, Calif. 393
Engineering Development Center 6
England 41, 264, 423
England AFB 32, 443, 451
England, John B. 32
Enid, Okla. 99, 118
Enlisted Reserve Corps 421
Ent AFB 32, 443, 450
Ent, Girard (son) 33
Ent, Uzal Girard 32–33
Enterprise, Ala. 113
Enterprise, Ore. 401
Epes, Carey 195
Epler Field 34, 443, 450
Epler, Robin Bruce 34
Erie, Mich. 218
Erie, Pa. 30
Eriswell, Suffolk, England 89
Erlangen, Germany 286
Eschwege, Germany 328

Esquennoy, Oise, France 111
Esteli, Nicaragua 365
Esterbrook, Merritt G. 12
Eureka Springs, Ark. 249
Europe 133, 274
    first strike on continental 26
European Railroad 233
European Theater of Operations 5, 158, 262, 351
European Theater Ribbon 58
European-African-Middle Eastern Campaign Medal 25, 50, 101, 222, 285, 302, 315
Eustis, Abraham 156
Eutaw, Ala. 368
Evanston, Ill. 9
Evening Gazette 45
Everett, Mary Susan 232
Everett, Wash. 77
Everglades National Park Commission 235
Evergreen Cemetery
    (Delhi, Iowa) 3
    (Paris, Tex.) 249
Evert, Paul 33
Expeditionary Medal 370
Expeditionary Medal (China) 375
Experiments in Aerodynamics (Langley) 58

F

Failor, Cindy 210
Fairbanks, Alaska 28, 185, 211
Fairchance, Pa. 342
Fairchild AFB 34, 443, 455
Fairchild, Muir Stephen 34–35
Fairfax Hospital (Va.) 265
Fairfield Air Intermediate Depot 3
Fairfield Aviation General Supply Depot 107
Fairfield, Calif. 98
Fairfield-Suisun AFB 30, 98
Fairleigh Dickinson University (N.J.) 331
Fairmount Cemetery (Denver, Colo.) 62
Fallon, Nev. 438
Falmouth, Mass. 77
Fargo, N.Dak. 242, 440
Farmingdale, N.Y. 286, 321
Farmington Grange 261

Farthest North Aviation Co. 29
Fater, J. G. 13
The Father of the Berlin Airlift 302
fatigue uniforms 160
Fauquier County, Va. 57
Fay, Mary Helen 383
Fayetteville Co., Tex. 187
Fayetteville, N.C. 81, 141, 148, 221, 224
FBI National Academy (Quantico, Va.) 331
Federal Credit Union Act 94
Felker AAF 199, 445, 455
Felker, Alfred Clinton 199
Ferris Barracks 286, 447, 456
Ferris, Geoffrey C. 286
Field Creek, Tex. 25
Field, Charles W. 147
Fifty Years' Observation of Men and Events (Keyes) 248
Fighting Bishop. *See also,* Polk, Rev. Leonidas 177
"The Fighting McCooks" 216
Fighting the Flying Circus (Rickenbacker) 87
Fiori Barracks 286, 447, 456
Fiori, Nanti J. 286–287
First Baptist Church (Searcy, Ark.) 272
first inter-island flight 19
first of the spacemen 54
first powered air flight 107
first transatlantic cable 214
Fishers Island Country Club (N.Y.) 419
Fisk, James 140
Fitzsimmons, Robert 249
Flatley Field 414, 448, 451
Flatley, James "Jimmy" Henry, Jr. 414–415
Fleet Marine Force Pacific 373
Fleetwings
    BT-12 117
Fleming Field 415, 448, 452
Fleming, Richard E. 415–416
Flemming, Walter 82
Fletcher, Shirley R. 74
flight training
    first at West Point 4
Florence, Pa. 319
Florida 450

Florida Cross 234
Florida Institute of Technology 42
Florida National Guard 234
Florida State Highway Department 381
Florida Wars 151
Floyd Bennett Field 416, 448, 453
Floyd Edsall Training Center 241
Flucker, Lucy 165
Flying Knights 51, 84
Flying McConnell Brothers 69
Flying Tigers
    founder 18
Focke-Wulf 16
Fokker 52, 55
    biplane 43, 44
    D.VII 208
    Josephine Ford 416
Foley, Ala. 402
football helmet 434
Forbes AFB 35, 443, 451
Forbes, Daniel Hugh, Jr. 28, 35–36
Forces Command's Sergeant Audie Murphy Program 237, 238
Ford Air Tour 12
Ford Barracks 287, 447, 456
Ford Island, Hawaii 31, 63
Ford, James C. 287
Foreign Intelligence Advisory Board 91
Forest Hills Cemetery
    (Boston, Mass.) 239
    (Jamaica Plain, Mass.) 58
Forest Home Cemetery (Milwaukee Country, Wisc.) 115
Forest Lawn Cemetery
    (Buffalo, N.Y.) 175, 179
    (Houston, Tex.) 187
    (Omaha, Neb.) 75
Forest Park, Ga. 157
formation of an independent air force 101
Forney AAF 200, 445, 452
Forney, Frank Hartman 200
Forrest Sherman Field 416, 448, 450
Forrest, Nathan 180
Fort A. P. Hill 145, 445, 455
Fort Barrancas Airfield 416
Fort Belvoir 197
Fort Benjamin Harrison 7, 146, 445, 451
Fort Benning 133, 142, 147, 150, 198, 199,

208, 210, 212, 241, 272, 289, 445, 451
Fort Benton, Mont. 56
Fort Bliss 18, 148, 152, 192, 352, 445, 455
Fort Bliss Post Cemetery (El Paso) 148
Fort Brady (Sault Ste. Marie, Mich.) 155
Fort Bragg 141, 142, 148, 222, 224, 248, 272, 445, 453
Fort Buchanan 149, 445, 458
Fort Buckner 150, 445, 458
Fort Campbell 150, 192, 445, 451
Fort Carson 151, 193, 272, 445, 450
Fort Chadbourne, Tex. 257
Fort Chaffee 152, 445, 449
Fort Clark 236
Fort Crockett 47, 48
Fort Crowder 238
Fort Custer Training Center 263, 446, 452
Fort Davis 242
Fort Defiance 8
Fort DeRussy (Hawaii) 106
Fort Des Moines 275
Fort Detrick 153, 445, 452
Fort Devens 153, 217, 445, 452
Fort Dix 154, 445, 453
Fort Donelson 173
Fort Douglas 39, 59
Fort Drum 155, 226, 351, 445, 453
Fort Egbert 178
Fort Eustis 156, 184, 199, 445, 455
Fort Francis E. Warren 37
Fort George Wright 40, 157, 445, 455
Fort Gillem 157, 445, 451
Fort Glenn 150
Fort Gordon 158, 445, 451
Fort Greely 159, 191, 445, 449
Fort Hamilton 137, 163
Fort Harrison 176
Fort Henry 173
Fort Holabird 160, 445, 452
Fort Hood 220, 445, 455
Fort Howard 157
Fort Huachuca 21, 106, 168, 213, 216, 314
Fort Humphreys 197
Fort Hunter Liggett 161, 226, 445, 450
Fort Indiantown Gap, Pa. 217
Fort Irwin 163, 445, 450
Fort Jackson 163, 222, 297, 445, 454
Fort Jay 137

Fort Kamehameha 19
Fort Knox 152, 164, 202, 270, 445, 451
Fort Kobbe 165, 445, 458
Fort Leavenworth 28, 39, 101, 105, 137, 143, 152, 156, 157, 162, 165, 166, 172, 197, 205, 217, 223, 244, 245, 260, 293, 375, 391, 445, 451
Fort Leavenworth National Cemetery (Kans.) 166
Fort Lee 166, 445, 455
Fort Leonard Wood 167, 200, 445, 452
Fort Lewis 168, 203, 272, 445, 455
Fort Logan 11, 125
Fort Logan H. Roots (Ark.) 281
Fort Logan National Cemetery (Denver, Colo.) 69
Fort Lyons, Colo. 151
Fort MacArthur AAF 200, 445, 450
Fort Mason, Calif. 45
Fort McClellan 169, 206, 254, 331, 445, 449
Fort McCoy 127, 170, 261, 445, 455
Fort McDowell 255, 445, 450
Fort McKinley (Manila, Philippines) 16
Fort McNair 171, 445, 455
Fort McPherson 66, 157, 158, 162, 172, 196, 445, 451
Fort Meade 173, 227, 445, 452
Fort Mills 55
Fort Monmouth 272
Fort Monroe 65, 174, 184, 208, 297, 445, 455
   Artillery School
      founder and first commandant 156
Fort Moultrie 95, 289
Fort Myer 34, 92, 175, 199, 445, 455
Fort Myer, Va. 297
Fort Omaha 394
Fort Ord 175, 445, 450
Fort Pickett 176, 445, 455
Fort Pierre, S.Dak. 439
Fort Polk 177, 445, 451
Fort Randall 97, 150
Fort Richardson 150, 178, 445, 449
Fort Richardson National Cemetery (Alaska) 134
Fort Riley 13, 69, 138, 145, 152, 179, 194, 197, 215, 245, 445, 451

Fort Riviere, Haiti 366
Fort Rosecrans National Cemetery (San Diego, Calif.) 293, 373, 382, 392, 393, 406, 418
Fort Rucker 179, 191, 192, 193, 194, 202, 204, 205, 206, 207, 213, 214, 217, 221, 222, 224, 225, 445, 449
Fort Sam Houston 30, 53, 57, 138, 144, 180, 195, 198, 210, 236, 285, 314, 445, 455
Fort Sam Houston National Cemetery (San Antonio, Tex.) 83, 84, 112, 324, 403
Fort Scott, Kans. 388
Fort Serican 9
Fort Shafter 181, 445, 451
Fort Sheridan 182, 250, 445, 451
Fort Sherman 272
Fort Sill 12, 52, 82, 107, 163, 172, 183, 197, 199, 205, 207, 208, 223, 227, 245, 307, 325, 445, 454
Fort Slocum 95
Fort Smith 243
Fort Smith National Cemetery (Ark.) 283
Fort Smith, Ark. 152, 283
Fort Snelling 75, 243
Fort Snelling National Cemetery (Minneapolis, Minn.) 222, 415
Fort Stedman 158
Fort Stewart 183, 208, 227, 289, 445, 451
Fort Stewart/Hunter AAF 227
Fort Story 184, 445, 455
Fort Totten 232
Fort Wainwright 185, 211, 445, 449
Fort William H. Seward 178
Fort William Henry Harrison 264, 446, 452
Fort William McKinley 162
Fort Winfield 105
Fort Wint 186, 445, 458
Fort Wolters 107, 186, 445, 455
Fort Worth, Tex. 14, 15, 40, 65, 144
Fort Yates, N.Dak. 22
Foss, Joseph Jacob 117–118
Foster AFB 36, 443, 454
Foster, Arthur Lee 36
Foster, William Adelbert 369–370
Foulois, Benjamin D. 198
Fraine Barracks 264, 446, 453

Fraine, John Henry 264–265
France 6, 85, 111, 124, 134, 155, 260, 275, 281, 329
France Field 3, 19, 34
Francis E. Warren AFB 37, 443, 456
Francis S. Gabreski Field 113, 444, 453
Frankfort Cemetery (Ky.) 150
Frankfort, Ky. 150
Frankfurt, Germany 273
Franklin Co., Va. 76
Franklin, Ark. 222
Franklin, Benjamin 141
Frederick C. Sherman Field 417, 448, 450
Frederick M. Trapnell Field 418, 448, 452
Frederick, Md. 153
Fredericksburg, Tex. 429
Fredericksburg, Va. 174
Freeman AAF 201, 445, 451
Freeman, Catherine Vance 429
Freeman, Richard Shafle 201
Freemasons 127
Frémont, John C. 151
French Fourragère 375
French Lafayette Flying Corps 111
French Legion of Honor 16, 41, 86, 114, 123, 139, 161, 163, 171, 218, 260, 297, 325, 352, 379, 409
French Military Medal 255
French Order of the Black Star 366
French Patriot Medallion 212
Frenzenberg Castle, Weisweiter, Germany 328
Fresno, Calif. 59
Friedberg, Germany 321
Frost, Adelaide 87
Fryeburg, Maine 285
Fulda, Germany 284, 307
Funari Barracks 288, 447, 456
Funari, Robert, Jr. 288
Funston, Frederick N. 138–139, 155
Furman University (S.C.) 22
Furth, Germany 144, 283, 294

G

G. Allan Hancock Community College 206
Gabby: A Fighter Pilot's Life (Gabreski & Molesworth) 114

Gabreski, Francis "Gabby" S. 113–114
Gael, France 7
Gainesville, Tex. 352
Galena, Ill. 215
Galveston, Tex. 47, 148, 149
Garcia, Calixto 138
Garden Plain Airport (Kans.) 69
Garmisch, Germany 327
Garner Field 197
Garrett, Ind. 420
Garrett, Maurine 124
Gary AFB 38, 443, 454
"Garry Owen" 263
Gary, Arthur Edward "Tex" 38
Garza, Catarino E. 249
Gates, Beecher J. 274–275
Gebaur, Arthur William, Jr. 85–86
Geiger AFB 38, 443, 455
Geiger, Harold C. 38–39, 48
Geiger, Roy Stanley 370–371
Gela, Sicily 282
Gelnhausen, Germany 280
General 233
General Billy Mitchell Field 115, 444, 455
General Billy Mitchell International Airport (Milwaukee, Wisc.) 115
General Mounted Service 186
General Service School 156, 172
Geneva, N.Y. 88
George AFB 39, 443, 450
George C. Marshall Kaserne 288, 447, 456
George Washington University 47
George Wright AFB 40
George, Charles 348–349
George, Harold Huston 39–40
Georgetown University 34
Georgetown, Tex. 36
Georgia 158, 313, 329, 450
Georgia Institute of Technology 72
Georgia School of Technology 21
Georgia Supreme Court 147
Georgia Tech University 99
German Riding Academy 139
German-Czechoslovakian border 277
Germany 93, 269, 285, 304, 456
Gerstner Field 124
Gerszewski Barracks 289, 447, 456
Gerszewski, Adolph C. 289

Gettysburg Monuments Commissioners 96
Gettysburg National Cemetery (Gettysburg, Pa.) 277
Gettysburg, Pa. 277
Ghislain, France 399
Gibraltar 142
Giesler, Marilynn 72
Giessen, Germany 317, 323
Gilbert Islands 427, 457
Gildner, Richard Watson 131
Gillem, Alvan Cullom, Jr. 157–158
Gillispie, Irene 108
Gladwyne, Pa. 6
Glen Alta, Ga. 212
Glendale Cemetery (Umatilla, Fla.) 381
Glendale, Ariz. 62
Glenn Curtiss Flying School 53, 195
Glenn L. Martin Aircraft Co. 80
Glenn, Helen Mildred Lewis 413
Glenview Cemetery (East Palestine, Ohio) 142
Gloucester Co., Va. 88
Gloxner, Joseph G. 64
Godman AAF 202, 445, 451
Godman, Louis K. 202
Gold Life Saving Medal 428
Gold Medal (Mexico) 148
Gold Medal (Texas Legislature) 187
Gold Star 367
Goldberg Stagefield 202, 445, 449
Goldberg, Joseph A. 202–203, 204
Golden (Colorado) *Transcript* 243
Golden Gate National Cemetery (San Bruno, Calif.) 271, 372, 400, 429
Golden, Colo. 243
Goldsboro, N.C. 93
Golkrath, Germany 299
Gomez, Maximo 138
Gonsalves, Harold 372
Gonsenheim-Mainz, Germany 300
Good Conduct Medal 195
Goodfellow AFB 40, 443, 454
Goodfellow, John James, Jr. 40
Göppingen, Germany 282
Gordon, John Brown 158
Gordon-Bennett International Balloon Race 76, 123, 203
Gorman Field 83

Goshen Springs, Miss. 7
Gould, Jay 140
Governador, N.Mex. 336
Gowen Field 116, 444, 451
Gowen, Paul R. 116–117
Grace Church (Va.) 251
Grafenwöhr, Germany 279
Grafton, Gilbert Collins 242–243
Grand Army of the Republic 244
Grand Cross of the Order of Leopold (Belgium) 242
Grand Forks, N.Dak. 289
Grand Island, Subic Bay, Philippines 186
Grand Officer of the Order of the Crown of Rumania 233
Grandcourt, France 93
Grandview Cemetery
   (Chillicothe, Ohio) 183
   (Florence, Pa.) 319
Grandview, Mo. 85
Grange movement 261
Grant County International Airport 58
Grant High School (Portland, Ore.) 357
Grant, Ulysses Simpson 9, 140, 143, 147, 173, 178, 182, 240, 250
Graves Barracks 290, 447, 456
Graves, William E. 290
Gravette, Ark. 55
Gray AAF 40, 203, 445, 455
Gray AFB 40
Gray Eagle Award 437
Gray, Hawthorne C. 203–204
Gray, Robert Manning 220
Great Britain 6
Great Falls AFB 64, 65
Great Falls, Mont. 53, 64
Greaves, Clinton 349–350
Greely Fjord 159
Greely Relief Expedition of 1881 408
Greely, Adolphus Washington 159, 408
Green Bay, Wisc. 414
Green Hill Cemetery (Bedford, Ind.) 81
Greene, Nathanael 244
Greenfield, Mass. 154
Greenlawn Cemetery (Columbus, Ohio) 86, 349
Greenlief Training Site 265, 446, 453
Greenlief, Francis Stevens 265

Greenock, Scotland 126
Greenville Cemetery (Miss.) 293
Greenville High School (S.C.) 204
Greenville, Miss. 292, 293
Greenville, S.C. 22, 137
Greenville, Tenn. 377, 378
Greenwich, Conn. 11
Green-Wood Cemetery (Brooklyn, N.Y.) 95
Greenwood, Miss. 52
Greenwood, S.C. 365
Grenada, Miss. 250
Grenier AFB 41, 443, 453
Grenier, Jean Donat 41
Greussen, Germany 283
Griffey Industries 307
Griffiss AFB 41, 219, 443, 453
Griffiss, Townsend E. 41–42
The Grim Reaper 414
Grissom AFB 42, 443, 451
Grissom, Virgil "Gus" Ivan 42–43
Gruber, Edmund Louis "Snitz" 244–245
Grumman
   F-4F Wildcat 118, 430
   F4F-3 Wildcat 93
   F6F Hellcat 430
   F9F Panther 419
   TBF Avenger 422
Grumman Aerospace Corp. 114
Guadalcanal 389, 394, 457
   first American land victory 314
Guam 45, 457
Guantanamo Bay, Cuba 424
Guébling, France 323
Guild, Curtis, Jr. 239
Gulfport, Miss. 204
Gunter, William A. 66–67
Guthrie Stagefield 204, 445, 449
Guthrie, Harold Lee 203, 204

H

Hagerstown, Md. 255
Hagler AAF 204, 445, 452
Hagler, Bill "Jimmie" 204–205
Haiti 396
Haitian Campaign Medal 371
Halberstadt 56
   C 208

Halifax, Nova Scotia 97
Hall of Fame
    Fort Benning Infantry Officers School 241
Hall of Great Westerners. *See* National Cowboy Hall of Fame
Hall, Donna Wild 118
Hall, Ill. 68
Halsey Field 419, 448, 450
Halsey, William Frederick "Bull," Jr. 419–420
Hamborn, Germany 325
Hamilton AFB 26, 43, 79, 90, 443, 450
Hamilton Boy's Catholic High School (Ohio) 330
Hamilton, Lloyd Andrews 43–44
Hamilton, Ohio 330
Hammelburg, Germany 273
Hammond, Ind. 7
Hammonds Barracks 290, 447, 456
Hammonds, Robert M. 290–291
Hammondsport, N.Y. 405
Hampton Roads, Va. 435
Hampton, Va. 57, 156, 174, 201, 223
Hanchey AH 205, 445, 449
Hanchey, Charles Wesley 205
Hancock AAF 205, 445, 450
Hancock AFB 44, 443, 453
Hancock Park 206
Hancock School of Aeronautics 206
Hancock, Clarence Eugene 44
Hancock, George Allan 205–206
Hanover College (Indiana) 64
Hanover, N.H. 254
Hanscom AFB 45, 443, 452
Hanscom, Laurence Gerald 45
Hansen, Dale Merlin 374
Hardee, William Joseph 149
Harmon AFB (Guam) 45
Harmon AFB (Newfoundland) 46, 443, 457
Harmon International Trophy 28, 89, 128
Harmon, Ernest Emery 46–47
Harmon, Millard Fillmore 4, 45–46
Harmony, N.Y. 50
Harris Barracks 291, 447, 456
Harris, James L. 291–292
Harrisburg International Airport 75

Harrisburg, N.C. 123
Harrisburg, Pa. 70
Harrison, Benjamin 146–147
Harrison, George 249
Harrison, Virginia L. 158
Harrison, William Henry 252, 264
Hart, Susannah 256
Hartell, Lee Ross 245–246
Hartford, Conn. 410
Hartland Cemetery (Kearny Co., Kans.) 96
Harvard Law School 11, 154, 168, 174
Harvard Medical School 167
Harvard Observatory 58
Harvard University 11, 43, 77, 126, 154, 156, 239
Harvey Barracks 292, 447, 456
Harvey Field 420, 448, 450
Harvey, James R. 292
Harvey, N.D. 127
Harvey, Warren Wallace 420–421
Haskell Institute (Lawrence, Kans.) 97
Hastings, Neb. 265
Hat in the Ring Squadron 87, 108
Hatch Stagefield 206, 445, 449
Hatch, Steve Eldredge 206
Hatfield, Wisc. 356
Hattiesburg, Miss. 204, 255
Hatton, N.Dak. 28
Havana, Cuba 175, 249
Haverford College (Pa.) 126
Hawaii 451
Hawaii Army National Guard Military Academy 9
Hawaiian Islands
    airmail 19
    aviator 19
    first inter-island flight 19
Hawkins Field 388, 448, 457
Hawkins, Anne Chiffelle 352
Hawkins, William Deane 388
Hayes, Rutherford B. 154
Haywood's Ice Cream Parlor 75
Hazen, Lake 159
Hazleton, Pa. 278
Heidelberg, Germany 277, 315, 330
Heilbronn, Germany 288, 289, 290, 332, 339
Hemman, Harriette 364

Henderson Field 389, 395, 448, 457
Henderson Hall 390, 448, 455
Henderson, Archibald 390
Henderson, Lofton R. 389
Hendersonville, Sumner Co., Tenn. 150
Hendricks Field 15
Hennen, Anna Marie 161
Henri-Chapelle American Cemetery and Memorial (Henri-Chapelle, Belgium) 16, 74, 298, 303, 305, 329
Henri-Chapelle, Belgium 16, 74, 298, 303, 305, 329
Henry Draper Medal 57
Henry J. Reilly AAF 206, 445, 449
Henry Kaserne 292, 447, 456
Henry Post AAF 207, 445, 454
Henry, Frederick F. 350
Henry, Robert T. 292–293
Hensley Field 421, 448, 455
Hensley, William Nicholas 421
Hermitage (Nashville, Tenn.) 163, 164
Hermitage, Tenn. 163
Hero of Fort Sumter 233
heroes 185
Hickam AFB 47, 97, 98, 443, 451
Hickam, Helen 48
Hickam, Horace Meek 38, 47–48
Hicks Field 65
highway centerline 52
Highwood Cemetery (Pittsburgh, Pa.) 262
Hill 376, Quang Tin Province, Republic of Vietnam 210
Hill AFB 48, 443, 455
Hill, Ambrose Powell 145–146
Hill, Daniel Harvey 158
Hill, Ployer Peter 48–49
Hillcrest Cemetery
 (Gravette, Ark.) 55
 (Texarkana, Tex.) 94
Hillsboro, Tex. 291
Hillsboro, Wisc. 425
Hillsborough, Fla. 347
Hilo, Hawaii 403
Hines, Sarah 184
Hinsdale, Mass. 37
Hiryu 389
Hobart College (N.Y.) 175
Hoboken, N.J. 218

Hoengseon, South Korea 354
Hoffman, Emily 173
Hohenwald, Tenn. 168
Hoke, Robert Frederick 149
Holabird, Samuel Beckley 160
Holcomb, Thomas 375–376
Holley, Adele 185
Holloman AFB 49, 443, 453
Holloman, George Vernon 49–50
Hollywood Cemetery (Richmond, Va.) 174, 176
Homelake, Colo. 244
Homer Ramsdell & Co. 126
Hondo Airfield 12
Honiara International Airport 389
Honolulu International Airport 422
Honolulu, Hawaii 47, 69, 76, 85, 97, 187, 200, 208, 295, 388, 389, 427, 430, 436
Honorary Citizen
 Angers 358
 Chartres 358
 Chateau-Thierry 358
 City of Luxembourg 358
 Epernay 358
 Fontainebleau 358
 Mélun 358
 Metz 358
 Reims 358
 Saint Symphorien 358
 Thionville 358
 Verdun 358
Honorary Doctor of Laws 242
 (Temple Univ.) 233
 (Univ. of Pa.) 233
 (Villanova Univ.) 233
 (Yale) 233
Honorary Doctor of Military Science 34
Honorary Doctor of Science 128
Honorary Doctorate 42
Honorary Masters of Arts (Yale) 233
Hood, John Bell 147, 160–161, 187
Hopkinsville, Ky. 150
Horne, Frederick J. 406
Hospital Corps School (San Diego, Calif.) 379
Hot Springs, Ark. 10
Houston, Samuel 180–181
Houston, Tex. 29, 187, 421

Hovey, Howard Cleasby 351–352
Howard, Thomas Benton 376
Howze, Robert Lee 352
Huff-Daland 47
Hughes Aircraft Co. 26
Hughes Tool Co. 26
Hunt AH 207, 449
Hunt County, Tex. 178
Hunt Heliport 445
Hunt, William Patrick, Jr. 207–208
Hunter AAF 50, 208, 445, 451
Hunter AFB 50
Hunter, Frank "Monk" O'Driscoll 208–209
Hunter–Liggett Military Reservation (Calif.) 226
Huntsville, Walker Co., Tex. 180
Hurlburt Field 50, 443, 450
Hurlburt, Donald Wilson 50
Hürtgen Forest, Germany 287
Hürtgenwald, Germany 310
Hyde, Dorothy Gretchen 88
hydrogen bomb 102

I

Iceland 4, 99
ice-making machine
    first commercial 214
Idaho 299, 451
Illesheim, Germany 331
Illinois 376, 451
Illinois Central Railroad 169
Illinois National Guard 289
Independence, Mo. 331, 354
Indian Campaign Medal 200
Indian Wars 168, 182, 184, 186, 257, 349, 352, 390
Indiana 147, 451
Indianapolis, Ind. 146, 304, 307
Indianhead, Md. 405
Indianola, Iowa 347, 348
The Infantry Journal 6
Institute of Aeronautical Sciences 419
International Aerospace Hall of Fame 6, 17, 25, 86, 107, 112, 115, 425, 437
International Air Races 47
International Prime Meridian Conference 89

Interstate Commerce Commission 147
Inyokern, Calif. 420
Iowa 451
Iowa State College 3
Ireland 207
Iruma, Japan 50
Irwin, George LeRoy 163
Isely Field 422, 448, 457
Isely, Robert Henry 422
Ishpeming Cemetery (Michigan) 51
Ishpeming, Mich. 51
Island Cemetery (Newport, R.I.) 251
Italian Order of Saints Maurice and Lazarus 161
Italian War Cross 255
Italy 81
Ithaca, N.Y. 31

J

Jackson, Andrew 163–164
Jackson, Mich. 134, 392
Jacksonville Naval Air Station (Fla.) 437
Jacksonville School of Technology (Fla.) 204
Jacksonville, Fla. 407
Jacksonville, N.C. 370, 376, 377, 378
Jamestown, R.I. 394
Japan 457
Japanese ships
    Hiryu 389
    Mikasa 429
    Ryujo 97
    Shokaku 401
Jaramillo, Maria Josefa 151
Java, Indonesia 59
Jefferson Barracks National Cemetery (St. Louis, Mo.) 438
Jefferson Hills, N.H. 214
Jefferson, Iowa 270, 275, 276
Jefferson, Okla. 346
Jefferson, Tex. 248, 249
Jefferson, Thomas 141, 169
Jenkins, Ky. 353
Jenson Barracks 293, 447, 456
Jenson, Richard N. 293
Joe Foss Field 117, 444, 454
John Rodgers Field 422, 448, 451
John Tarleton College (Stephenville, Tex.)

24
Johns Hopkins University Hospital 153
Johnson AB 50, 443, 457
Johnson Barracks 294, 447, 456
Johnson City Airport 108
Johnson City, Tenn. 204
Johnson, Andrew 182
Johnson, Edward 158
Johnson, Elden Harvey 294
Johnson, Gerald Richard 50–51
Johnson, Gilbert Hubert "Hashmark" 376–377
Johnson, Herbert Thomas 246–247
Johnson, Seymour Anderson 93
Johnston, Gordon 139–140
Johnston, Iowa 240
Johnston, Joseph E. 95
Johnstown, Pa. 78
Joint Air Reserve Base 22, 92, 104
Joint Army-Air National Guard Bureau Advisory Council 241
Joint Forces Maneuver Training Center 232
Jones, Aden 220
Jones, Mary Howard 147
Joseph G. LaPointe AH 210, 446, 451
Joseph, Ferdinand Maximilian, archduke of Austria and emperor of Mexico 182
Josephine Ford 416
Junction City, Kans. 138, 152, 179, 215
Jungle Battery 248

K

K. I. Sawyer AFB 51, 443, 452
Käfertal, Germany 288, 332, 333
Kaiserslautern, Germany 294
Kalamazoo, Mich. 181
Kamiakin, Chief 157
Kamil-ni, S. Korea 353
Kaneohe, Hawaii 436
Kansas 145, 166, 266, 346, 451
Kansas City, Kans. 152, 165, 205, 223, 244
Kansas City, Mo. 85, 354
Kansas National Guard 55, 138
Kansas State College 36
Kapaun Barracks 294, 447, 456
Kapaun, Emil Joseph 294–295
Karlsruhe, Germany 289

Kassel, Germany 334
Kealakekua, Kona, Hawaii 76
Kearny Co., Kans. 96
Keasbey, N.J. 327
Keesler AFB 52, 443, 452
Keesler Field 205
Keesler, Samuel Reeves, Jr. 52
Kegelman AF Auxiliary Field 118, 444, 454
Kegelman, Charles Clark "Sonny" 118–119
Kelley Barracks 296, 447, 456
Kelley, Jonah Edward 296–297
Kelly AFB 12, 53, 443, 454
Kelly Field 12, 21, 25, 28, 30, 34, 38, 39, 41, 48, 54, 55, 57, 66, 67, 68, 72, 80, 83, 90, 97, 99, 101, 106, 112, 116, 201
Kelly, Alice 93
Kelly, Charles E. 262–263
Kelly, Charles L. 195–196
Kelly, George Edward Maurice 53
Kelly, Hugh 30
Kelty, Asher 62
Kemper Co., Miss. 119
Kenilworth, Ill. 50
Kenmore, Ohio 51
Kennedy Space Center 42, 76
Kennedy, John F. 303
Kenner, La. 258
Kenosha, Wisc. 170
Kentish Guards 244, 258
Kentucky 150, 256, 451
    first governor 256
Kentucky Military Institute (Lyndon, Ky.) 245
Kerprich Hemmersdorf, Germany 309
Kesternich, Germany 296
Key Brothers Flying Service 120
Key Field 119, 120, 444, 452
Key, Algene 119
Key, Frederick 119–120
Keyes, Erasmus Darwin 247–248
Keyser, W.Va. 296
Keystone
    XB-1B 99
Kilbourne Barracks 297, 447, 456
Kilbourne, Charles Evans, Jr. 297
Killeen City Cemetery (Tex.) 220

Killeen, Tex. 160, 220
Kimbro Kaserne 298, 447, 456
Kimbro, Truman Carol 298
Kimmel, Husband E. 429
Kincheloe AFB 53, 444, 452
Kincheloe Trophy 54
Kincheloe, Iven Carl, Jr. 53–54
Kindley AFB 54, 444, 456
Kindley, Eugene 54–56
King, Bessie 80
Kingsley Field 120, 444, 454
Kingsley, David Richard 120–121
Kingsport, N.Y. 408
Kingston High School 320
Kingston, N.Y. 320
Kingwood, W.Va. 239
Kinney Co., Tex. 236
Kinser, Elbert Luther 377–378
Kirtland AFB 56, 444, 453
Kirtland Field 120, 275
Kirtland, Roy Carrington 56–57
Kisatchie National Forest 141
Kitty Hawk, N.C. 107
Kitzingen, Germany 292, 299
Klamath Falls, Ore. 120
Knapp, Electa 166
Knight Barracks 299, 447, 456
Knight Grand Cross 288
   (Netherlands) 375
Knight, Jimmie S. 299
Knights Templar 36
Knob Noster, Mo. 105
Know-Nothing riots 390
Knox, Henry 164–165
Knoxall Corp. 307
Knoxville, Tenn. 71
Kobangsan-ni, Korea 246
Kobbe, William August 165
Koblenz, Germany 280
Kokomo, Ind. 42
Kontum, South Vietnam 217
Korea 85, 127, 200, 207, 354, 369, 457
Korean Presidential Unit Citation 381
Korean Service Medal 60, 191, 200, 222, 227, 295, 380
Korean War 54, 102, 195, 213, 227, 241, 246, 277, 336, 346, 347, 348, 350, 351, 353, 354, 355, 357, 358, 359, 369

   first Wisc. pilot killed 127
Korean War Medal 85
Kortright, Elizabeth 174
Kosovo 134, 142, 457
Kulis Field 121, 444, 449
Kulis, Albert 121–122
Kumchon, Korea 346
Kurtz, Frank 38
Kyle, Darwin Keith 353

L

La Brea Tar Pits 206
Labonte, Roland Charles 248
labor strikes 247
Lackland AFB 57, 444, 454
Lackland, Frank Dorwin 57
Ladd Field 103, 150, 201, 211, 446, 449
Ladd, Arthur K. 211
Lafayette Escadrille 124
Lafayette, Ind. 54
Laffite, Jean 235
LaFountain, Charles H. 28, 36
Lagnicourt, France 43
Lahm, Frank Purdy 122–123
Lake Charles, La. 18, 124
Lake Ontario, Canada 252
Lakehurst, N.J. 407, 423
Lakeview Cemetery
   (Burlington, Vt.) 105
   (Cheyenne, Wyo.) 37
Lamar Rifles 249
Lamar School (El Paso, Tex.) 192
Lambert Field 122, 444, 452
Lambert Pharmacal Co. 122
Lambert, Albert Bond 122
Lambert-St. Louis International Airport 122
Lamington, N.J. 252
Lancaster, Ohio 143
Lancaster, Pa. 149
Landstuhl, Germany 342
Langley AFB 14, 57, 421, 444, 455
Langley Field 5, 28, 31, 33, 39, 48, 56, 57, 65, 89, 104, 106, 198, 199, 201, 223, 391
Langley, Samuel Pierpont 57–58, 408
LaPointe, Joseph Guy, Jr. 210–211
Laredo, Tex. 134

Larson AFB 58, 444, 455
Larson Barracks 299, 447, 456
Larson, Donald A. 58–59
Larson, Stanley L. 299–300
Las Vegas, Nev. 74, 241
Laughlin AFB 59, 444, 454
Laughlin, Jack Thomas 59
Laurel Hill Cemetery (Philadelphia, Pa.) 173
Lawrence, Kans. 97
Lawrenceville, Ill. 40
Lawson AAF 59, 212, 446, 451
Lawson AFB 59, 444, 450
Lawson General Hospital (Atlanta, Ga.) 330
Lawson, Ted W. 59–60, 212
Lawson, Walter Rolls 59, 212
Lawton, Alexander R. 158
Lawton, Okla. 163, 183, 207
Leavenworth, Henry 165–166
Leavenworth, Kans. 89
Lebanon, Ky. 67
Lebanon, Tenn. 151
Ledward Barracks 300, 447, 456
Ledward, William J. 300
Lee Barracks 300, 447, 456
Lee, Henry 166
Lee, Robert E. 88, 140, 146, 158, 166–167, 176, 177, 300
Leesburg, Va. 136
Legion of Honor 98, 242, 375
Legion of Merit 4, 13, 16, 20, 24, 25, 30, 32, 51, 70, 82, 101, 112, 123, 128, 194, 197, 208, 241, 253, 295, 302, 306, 315, 325, 331, 358, 380, 391, 392, 393, 414, 427, 432, 437, 440
Leighton Barracks 301, 447, 456
Leighton, John A. 301
Lejeune, John Archer 378–379
Lemoore, Calif. 434
Lepping, Father George 79
Lesser, Clare C. 28, 36
Lester, Fred Faulkner 379–380
Letter of Commendation 407
Letter of Commendation Ribbon 364
Letterkenny Ordnance Depot 280
Lewis and Clark Expedition 169
Lewis, Meriwether 168–169

Lewisburg, W.Va. 78
Lewistown, N.J. 154
Lexington, Mo. 97, 237
Lexington, Va. 166, 251
Libby AAF 213, 353, 446, 449
Libby, George Dalton 213
Liberty Bell 7 43
Liberty Co., Ga. 183, 184
Liberty Loan campaign 202
Liege, Belgium 16
Liggett, Hunter 161–162
Lighter-Than-Air Service 123
Light-Horse Harry. *See also,* Lee, Henry 166
Limestone, Maine 60
Lincoln Co., Ky. 256
Lincoln, Abraham 151, 181, 247
Lincoln, Calif. 27
Lincoln, Neb. 34
Lindbergh, Charles 122
Lindsey, Darrell Robins 275–276
Linkfert, Germany 224
Linwood Cemetery (Columbus, Ga.) 147
Linwood, N.J. 203
Little American (Byrd) 113
Little Big Horn, battle at 263
Little Falls, Minn. 219, 254
Little Rock, Ark. 221
Littlefield, Catharine 244
Livingston, Robert R., Jr. 141
Lloyd Barracks 301, 447, 456
Lloyd, Edgar Harold 301–302
Lockbourne AFB 65
Lockheed
    F-4 Lightning 81
    F-80 Shooting Star 54, 61, 122, 128
    F-104 Starfighter 54, 129
        Mach 3 70
    P-28 Lightning 209
    P-38 Lightning 25, 36, 51, 72, 81, 84, 118
    P-80 Shooting Star 85
    T-33 Shooting Star 65
Lockport, N.Y. 39
Locust Grove Cemetery (St. Feliciana, La.) 254
Logan Co. Neb. 172
Lohne, Germany 307

London Book Store 164
London, England 53
Long Branch, Ill. 260
Long Island National Cemetery (Farmingdale, N.Y.) 286, 321
Long Island, N.Y. 114
The Long Walk 152
Long, Charles R. 354
longitude and latitude device 214
Longmeadow Cemetery (Mass.) 340
Longmeadow, Mass. 340
Longmont High School 13
Longmont, Colo. 13
Longstreet, James 177
Longwood, Mo. 105
Lonoke, Ark. 221
Lorain, Ohio 389
Lorena Cemetery (Texas) 227
Lorena, Tex. 227
Loring AFB 60, 444, 452
Loring, Charles Joseph, Jr. 60–61
Lorraine American Cemetery and Memorial (Saint Avold, France) 274, 278, 281, 284, 309, 311, 320, 323, 329, 335
Los Alamitos, California Reserve Center 325
Los Angeles 38
Los Angeles City College 60
Los Angeles Times 26
Los Angeles, Calif. 202, 206
Louisiana 136, 141, 177, 182, 258, 259, 451
Louisiana Army National Guard 237, 238
Louisiana Commendation Medal 237
Louisiana Distinguished Service Medal 237
Louisiana Longevity Medal 237
Louisiana Longevity Ribbon 237
Louisiana National Guard 399
Louisiana Purchase 141, 253
Louisiana State Normal School (Natchitoches) 18
Louisiana State University 143, 250
Louisiana Territory 169
Loup Cemetery (Logan Co., Neb.) 172
Lovejoy, Harriet 166
Lovelock, Nev. 201
Low Moor, Va. 142

Lowe AAF 213, 446, 449
Lowe, Thaddeus S.C. 213–214
Lowry AFB 61, 444, 450
Lowry Field 62
　first Coloradan flying accident 80
Lowry, Francis Brown 61–62
Loyola University (Chicago) 367
Lubbock, Tex. 84, 337
Lucas AAF 214, 446, 449
Lucas, Andre Cavaro 214–215
Luchem, Germany 293
Lucius D. Clay Kaserne 302, 447, 456
Ludwigsburg, Germany 311
Luke AFB 62, 444, 449
Luke Field (Arizona) 7, 27, 69, 128
Luke Field (Hawaii) 14, 21, 46, 63, 105, 106
Luke, Frank, Jr. 62–63
Luneville, France 320
Luxembourg American Cemetery and Memorial (Luxembourg City, Luxembourg) 274, 304, 315
Luxembourg City, Luxembourg 274, 304, 315
Luzon, Philippines 66, 145, 354
Lyndon, Ky. 245
Lyon, Iowa 234

M

Mabry, Woodford Haywood 248–249
MacArthur, Arthur, Jr. 200–201
MacArthur, Douglas 39, 83, 126, 156, 200
MacDill AFB 64, 70, 444, 450
MacDill Field 275
MacDill, Leslie 64
Macedon, N.Y. 236
Mackall, John Thomas "Tommy" 141–142
Mackay Trophy 6, 22, 25, 34, 49, 53, 86, 128, 198, 201
　first name inscription 6
MacLeod, Arminia Rosengarten 233
MacMillan Expedition to the Arctic 416
Macon 418
Macon, Ga. 88, 196
Madison Co., Ky. 151
Madison Co., Va. 349
Madison, Wisc. 127
Madisonville, Tex. 298

Magee, John Gillespie, Jr. 1
Magee, Walter W. 44
Magnolia Cemetery
  (Charleston, S.C.) 404
  (Meridian, Miss.) 119
Maher, Peter 249
Maidens, Va. 67
Maine 452
Mainz-Gonsenheim, Germany 300
Malcolm Grow Medical Center (Md.) 25
Malmstrom AFB 64, 444, 452
Malmstrom, Einar Axel 64–65
Managua, Nicaragua 363
Manch, Jack 220
Manchester, N.H. 41
Manchester, Tenn. 6
Manila American Cemetery and Memorial
  (Manila, Philippines) 10, 79, 92, 225,
  279, 364, 394, 401
Manila, Philippines 10, 16, 73, 79, 92, 225,
  279, 364, 394, 401
Manitowoc, Wisc. 308
Mannheim, Germany 278, 281, 330, 335
Mansfield Kaserne 303, 447, 456
Mansfield, Clayton J. 303
Mansfield, Ohio 122
Mansfield-Lahm Field 122, 444, 453
Mansfield-Lahm Municipal Airport (Ohio)
  122
*Manual of Signals for the United States
  Army and Navy* (Myer) 175
Maple Grove Cemetery (Fairchance, Pa.)
  342
Marburg an der Lahn, Germany 308
March AFB 65, 444, 450
March Field 6, 26, 39, 41, 46, 57, 77, 90,
  101, 103, 124
March, Peyton C., (Sr.) 65
March, Peyton Conway, Jr. 65
Marcy, Mary Ellen 170
Marengo Co., Ala. 66
Margraten, Netherlands 224, 299, 304,
  318, 325, 341
Mariana Island 457
Marietta, Ga. 22, 302
Marietta, Ohio 258
Marine Corps Aviation 396
Marine Corps Brevet Medal 366

Marine Corps Expeditionary Force 368
Marine Corps Expeditionary Medal 373,
  378
Marine Corps Reserve 394
Marine Corps' official colors 379
Marine Scout Bombing Squadron (VMSB-
  132) 395
Marlow, Okla. 337
Marquette Co., Mich. 52
Marquette University (Milwaukee, Wisc.)
  128
Marquette, Mich. 51
Marshall AAF 215, 446, 451
Marshall Islands 4, 45, 457
Marshall Plan 288
Marshall University 128
Marshall, Francis Cutler 215–216
Marshall, George Catlett 288–289, 315
Marthaville, La. 237
Martin
  B-2 21
  B-4 90
  B-10 49, 68, 90, 117
    round-trip flight 6
  B-12 5, 49
  B-26 Marauder 27, 80, 96, 97
Martin Aircraft Co., Glenn L. 80
Marwitz, Eleanor 33
Maryland 25, 452
Maryland National Guard 153
Marysville, Calif. 8
Mason, Elizabeth Champlin 252
Massachusetts 154, 165, 274, 282, 452
Massachusetts Air National Guard 77
Massachusetts Civil Air Reserve 45
Massachusetts Department of the Ameri-
  can Legion 242
Massachusetts General Hospital (Boston)
  242
Massachusetts Institute of Technology
  381, 406, 427
Mateur, Tunisia 222
Mather AFB 66, 444, 450
Mather Airport 66
Mather Field 31, 66
Mather, Carl Spencer 66
Maxey, Samuel Bell 249–250
Maxfield Field 423, 448, 453

Maxfield, Louis Henry 423
Maximilian. *See* Joseph, Ferdinand Maximilian, archduke of Austria and emperor of Mexico
Maxwell AFB 114
Maxwell Field 18, 28, 34, 39, 42, 46, 50, 67, 73, 101, 103
Maxwell, William C. 66
Maxwell-Gunter AFB 66, 444, 449
Mayflower 258
McCain Field 424, 448, 452
McCain, Henry Pinckney 250–251
McCain, John Sidney, Sr. 424
McCalla Field 424, 448, 456
McCalla, Bowman Henry 424
McChord AFB 58, 67, 220, 444, 455
McChord, William Caldwell 67–68
McClellan AFB 68, 76, 201, 444, 450
McClellan, George Brinton 137, 169–170, 247
McClellan, Hezekia 68
McClung, Kitty Morgan 146
McConnell AFB 69, 444, 451
McConnell, Edwin M. 69
McConnell, Fred J. 69
McConnell, Thomas Laverne 69
McCook Field 7, 12, 35, 99, 212, 216, 446, 454
McCook, Alexander McDowell 216–217
McCoy AFB 69, 444, 450
McCoy, Michael Norman Wright 69–70
McCoy, Robert Bruce 170
McCully Barracks 304, 447, 456
McCully, William C. 304
McCutcheon, Keith Barr 380–381
McDonnell
    F2H Banshee 419
    F-101 Voodoo 54
McDonnell-Douglas
    F-4 Phantom II 49
    F-15 Eagle 129
McDowell, Irwin 171, 231
McEntire AFB 70, 444, 454
McEntire, Barnie B., Jr. 70–71
McGee Barracks 304, 447, 456
McGee, William D. 304–305
McGhee Tyson AFB 71, 444, 454
McGrath, Alaska 103

McGraw Kaserne 305, 447, 456
McGraw, Francis X. 305–306
McGregor, Tex. 20
McGrew, Myrtle 122
McGuire AFB 72, 444, 453
McGuire, Thomas "Tommy" Buchanan, Jr. 72–73
McKee Barracks 306, 447, 456
McKee, John Lloyd, Jr. 306
McKees Rocks, Pa. 319
McKinley Tariff Act 147
McMurdo Sound, Antarctica 442
McMurdo Station 442
McMurray, Dorothy 414
McNair, Lesley James 171–172
McPheeters Barracks 307, 447, 456
McPheeters, John "Jon" W. 307
McPherson, James Birdseye 172–173, 187
McTureous, Robert Miller, Jr. 381–382
Meade, George Gordon 173–174
Mechanics American Bank 122
Mechanics Trading Co. 243
Medaille Militaire 111
Medal of Honor 15, 16, 37, 60, 62, 72, 78, 84, 86, 99, 102, 112, 117, 120, 134, 138, 139, 142, 145, 159, 167, 181, 185, 193, 200, 210, 213, 214, 246, 255, 256, 262, 275, 279, 291, 293, 294, 296, 297, 298, 301, 304, 305, 308, 309, 310, 311, 312, 316, 317, 318, 319, 321, 322, 323, 324, 327, 328, 334, 335, 336, 337, 338, 340, 341, 342, 348, 349, 350, 352, 353, 354, 355, 356, 364, 366, 367, 369, 372, 374, 377, 379, 381, 383, 384, 387, 388, 403, 410, 415, 416, 426, 430, 438
    first American aviator recipient 62
Medal of the Aeronautical Society 408
Medal of the National Geographic Society 416
Medals of Valor (Italy and Britain) 262
Medicine Hat, Alberta, Canada 27
Medina, N.Y. 193
Mediterranean Sea 22
Mediterranean Theater of Operations 14, 280
Memorial High School (Campbell, Ohio) 81
Memorial Park Cemetery

(Sedalia, Mo.) 105
(Tulsa, Okla.) 383
Memories of Two Wars (Funston) 138
Menominee, Mich. 51
Merced, Calif. 16
Mercersburg, Pa. 149
Meridian, Miss. 119, 424
Meritorious Service Citation 373
Meritorious Service Medal 192, 237, 271
Meriwether Lewis Park (Hohenwald, Tenn.) 168
Merrell Barracks 307, 447, 456
Merrell, Joseph Frederick 307–308
Merrimack, N.H. 416
Merritt Field 391, 448, 454
Merritt, Lewis Griffith 391
Merritt, Wesley 238
Messerschmitt
 Me-109 121, 206
Metairie Cemetery (New Orleans, La.) 135, 160, 233
meteorological observations 175
Metz, France 335
Meuse-Argonne American Cemetery and Memorial (Romagne, France) 13, 62, 85, 255
Meuse-Argonne offensive 85
Mexican Border Service Medal 212, 253
Mexican Expedition 315
Mexican Revolution 424, 426
Mexican Service Medal 253, 315, 373, 378, 406, 408, 409, 419
Mexican-American War 140, 146, 148, 149, 151, 157, 169, 171, 173, 176, 177, 179, 390
Mexico 6
Meyer, George 412
Miami University (Ohio) 146
Miami, Fla. 158
Michigan 163, 452
 gas and weight tax laws 52
Michigan Aviation Hall of Fame 53
Michigan National Guard 170
Mid West Soap Co. 307
Middleburg, Fla. 370
Middletown, Conn. 44, 325
Middletown, Pa. 11, 38, 75
Midway Cemetery (Liberty Co., Ga.) 184

Midway Island (Pacific) 439
Mikasa 429
Mile 26 Airfield 29
Military Affairs Committee 94
military aircraft
 first American military aviator to die 53
Military Order Medal of Vietnam 195
military signals 175
Miller Barracks 308, 447, 456
Miller, Andrew 308–310
Miller, Ray Simeon 219
Milling, Thomas 223
Mills Field 66
Milton, Fla. 441
Milwaukee Balloon Race 104
Milwaukee Co., Wisc. 115
Milwaukee, Wisc. 101, 115, 200
Mindanao, Philippines 118
Mineral Wells, Tex. 142, 186, 187, 205
Minick Kaserne 310, 447, 456
Minick, John W. 310
Minneapolis, Minn. 170, 222, 265, 415
Minnesota 335, 452
Minnesota Aeronautics Commission 219
Minnesota Distinguished Service Medal 219
Minnesota Medal for Merit 219
Minnesota Military Museum 254
Minnesota National Guard 219
Minnesota Service Ribbon 219
Miraflores Locks, Panama 19
Miramar, Calif. 425
Mississippi 136, 177, 452
Mississippi National Guard 204
Mississippi State College 8
Missouri 191, 330, 452
Missouri Compromise 174
Missouri National Guard 237
Missouri River
 railroad bridge 17
Missouri, Bates Co. 237
Mitchel Field 14, 33, 47, 49, 50, 89, 112
Mitchell, Ind. 42, 81
Mitchell, William Lendrum "Billy" 6, 21, 115–116, 156, 219
Mitchum, Robert 220
Mitscher Field 425, 448, 450

Mitscher, Marc Andrew "Pete" 425
Mitsubishi
  G4M "Betty" 430
  "Zero" 439
Mobile Bay (Ala.) 185
Mobile, Ala. 11, 148
Moffett Field 56, 426, 448, 450
Moffett, William Adger 426–427
Moffett, William Adger, Jr. (son) 427
Möhringen-Stuttgart, Germany 296
Mojave Desert 53
Moline High School 77
Momyer, William W. 14
Monmouth, Ill. 64
Monroe County Democrat 170
Monroe Doctrine 174
Monroe, James 174, 252
Montana 452
Montargis, France 277
Monteith, Jimmie W., Jr. 142–143
Monterey Bay Peninsula, Calif. 175
Monterey, Calif. 161, 226
Montford Point (N.C.) 377
Montford Point Marine Association 377
Montgomery Regional Airport (Ala.) 113
Montgomery, Ala. 66, 67
Monthan, Oscar 21
Montpelier (estate) 165
Montrebeau Forest, France 255
Moody AFB 73, 444, 451
Moody Field 50
Moody, George Putnam 73
Moog, Hazel 36
Moore AAF 217, 446, 452
Moore, Betty 43
Moore, Douglas Fillebrown 217
Moore, Milton 237
Mooresville, N.C. 98
Moret Field 392, 448, 458
Moret, Paul 392
Morgan, Catherine 155
Mormon Battalion 136
Morocco 6
Moron AB 129
Morris Field 123, 444, 453
Morris, William Colb 123–124
Morrison Field 30
Morrison, Elizabeth Eunice 166

Moses Lake, Wash. 58
Most Excellent Order of the British Empire 194
Mound Cemetery (Marietta, Ohio) 258
Mount Auburn Cemetery
  (Boston, Mass.) 156
  (Cambridge, Mass.) 154, 231
  (St. Joseph, Mo.) 125
Mount Clemens, Mich. 92
Mount Crest Abbey Mausoleum (Salem, Ore.) 261
Mount French Cemetery (France) 124
Mount Hebron, Ala. 377
Mount Hope Cemetery (San Diego, Calif.) 144
Mount McGregor, N.Y. 140
Mount McKinley 29
Mount Olive Cemetery (Troy, Kans.) 316
Mt. Vassilio, Sicily 322
Mount Washington Cemetery (Independence, Mo.) 354
Mountain View Cemetery
  (Altadena, Calif.) 214
  (West Hazleton, Pa.) 278
Mounted Service School (Ft. Riley, Kans.) 152
Muir AAF 217, 446, 454
Muir, Charles Henry 217–218
Mulberry Grove (Bamberg Co., Ga.) 244
Mulheim an der Ruhe, Germany 304
Mullinnix Field 427, 448, 457
Mullinnix, Henry Maston 427–428
Munfordville, Ky. 150
Munich, Germany 292, 293, 305, 318, 338, 341
Munn Field 392, 448, 450
Munn, John Calvin 392–393
Murfreesboro, Tenn. 179
Murnau, Germany 298
Muroc AFB 36
Muroc Dry Lake, Calif. 27, 35
Murphy Barracks 311, 447, 456
Murphy, Frederick C. 311
Murray Junior College (Stillwater, Okla.) 112
Murvaux, France 62
Mustin Field 428, 448, 454
Mustin, Henry Croskey 428–429

Myer, Albert James 175
Myra, W.Va. 128

N

Namur Island, Marshall Islands 387
Nanuk 29
Naples, Italy 416
Narragansett, R.I. 244, 257
NASA Distinguished Service Medals 42
NASA Exceptional Service Medal 42
Nashua, N.H. 248
Nashville, Tenn. 4, 92, 157, 163, 168
Natchez, Miss. 66
Natchitoches, La. 18
National Academy of Sciences
    Henry Draper Medal 57
National Aeronautics and Space Administratio 43
National Air Race (Dayton) 11
National Aviation Hall of Fame 5, 6, 17, 18, 28, 42, 57, 62, 72, 84, 86, 90, 92, 101, 107, 112, 114, 115, 117, 123, 128, 385, 413, 425, 426, 437
National Balloon Race 27, 123
National Cemetery (Fort Leavenworth, Kans.) 223
National Cowboy Hall of Fame
    Hall of Great Westerners 240
National Defense Service Medal 76, 191, 295, 358, 380, 414, 419, 429, 432
National Elimination Balloon Race 33, 203
National Foundation for the March of Dimes 158
National Geographic Society 159
National Guard
    aviation units 219
National Guard Armory (Portland, Ore.) 357
National Guard Association 265, 266
National Guard Association Distinguished Service Medal 253
National Memorial Cemetery of the Pacific (Honolulu, Hawaii) 69, 76, 85, 97, 200, 208, 295, 388, 389, 427, 430, 436
National Museum of Naval Aviation 441
National Naval Medical Center (Bethesda, Md.) 370, 380, 431
National Park Service 416

National Veteran Award 117
Native American Indians 8, 143, 173, 176, 179, 186, 390
    352
    and Custer 263
    and Harrison 264
    Apache 152, 349
    Apaches 216
    Arapahoe 151
    Arikara 166
    Barrock 257
    battle of Fallen Timbers 264
    Cherokee 148, 180
    Cheyenne 151, 182, 257
    Chickamauga 256
    Chief Kamiakin 157
    Comanche 136, 166, 182
    Crazy Horse 263
    Creek 156, 164, 184, 390
    Federal Indian agent 151
    Florida Wars 151
    Geronimo 168, 200
    Hopi 152
    in Oregon 157
    Indian affairs 249
    Kickapoo 236
    Kiowa 182
    Lipan Apaches 236
    The Long Walk 152
    Navajo 152
    Osage Nation (Okla.) 97
    Pawnee 166
    Pueblo 152
    Red River War 236
    Rogue River 176
    Second Seminole War 156
    Seminole 157, 173, 176, 390
    Sioux 253, 257, 263
    Sitting Bull 263
    Spokane 176
    Treaty of Greenville 264
    Ute 152, 216, 244, 257
    war compaigns 168
    Zuni 152
Naval Air Landing Field 417
Naval Air Station
    first at Pensacola, Fla. 437
Naval Air Station Anacostia, D.C. 420

Naval Air Station Joint Reserve Base 14, 399
Naval Air Station Patuxent River, Md. 418
Naval Air Station San Diego, Calif
 establishment of 423
Naval Air Technical Training Center 409
Naval Aircraft Factory 440
 PN-9 407
Naval Proving Ground (Indianhead, Md.) 405
Naval War College 406
Navassa Island (West Indies) 406
Navy and Marine Corps Medal 433
Navy Commendation Medal 393
Navy Cross 26, 112, 355, 363, 369, 370, 375, 382, 385, 389, 394, 401, 402, 404, 410, 413, 414, 417, 418, 419, 422, 424, 425, 430, 431, 434, 435, 436, 437, 439, 441
Navy Occupation Service Medal 191, 380, 393
Navy Unit Commendation 380, 393, 432
NC-4 Medal 435, 437
NCO Academy 238
Nebraska 453
Negley, Ohio 141
Negros Island, Philippines 72
Nellis AFB 54, 74, 444, 453
Nellis, William Harrell 74
Nelson Barracks 311, 447, 456
Nelson, William Lloyd 311–312
Neosho, Mo. 238
Netherlands American Cemetery and Memorial (Margraten, Netherlands) 224, 299, 304, 318, 325, 341
Nettuno, Italy 22, 272, 282
Neupre, Belgium 275, 332
Neu-Ulm, Germany 311
Nevada 277, 453
Nevada Air National Guard 96
Nevada National Guard 241
Nevada, Mo. 236
New Albany, Ind. 232
The New Astronomy (Langley) 58
New Carlisle, Ohio 138
New Castle Co., Del. 224
New Castle, Del. 375
New Deal 221

Federal Credit Union Act 94
New England National Guard 215
New Hampshire 453
New Hampshire National Guard 248
New Haven, Conn. 165
New Hebrides Island 458
New Jersey 141, 218, 285, 331, 426, 453
New Market, Frederick Co., Va. 153
New Mexico 453
New Orleans Cotton Exchange 161
New Orleans, La. 18, 135, 160, 233, 399
New River, N.C. 380
New River, Tenn. 407
New Rumley, Ohio 263
New Saint Peters Cemetery (Danbury, Conn.) 246
New Ulm, Tex. 186
New York 154, 155, 166, 178, 207, 214, 215, 226, 247, 263, 302, 314, 320, 352, 453
New York City, N.Y. 28, 105, 115, 140, 141, 143, 154, 155, 174, 193, 280
New York Department of Docks 170
New York Law School 44
New York National Guard 39, 227
New York State Soldiers' and Sailors' Home 96
Newark Air Service 23
Newburgh, N.Y. 126, 175, 345
Newburyport, Mass. 48, 159
Newfoundland 99, 457
Newport News, Va. 156, 184, 194, 195, 199
Newport, R.I. 251, 252
Nicaragua 458
Nicaraguan Campaign Medal 370
Nicaraguan Medal of Distinction and Diploma 371
Nice, France 115, 247
Nichols Field 33, 49
Nickell Hall 266, 446, 451
Nickell, Joe 266
nighttime landings
 first 56
Nikolski Village, Aleutian Island, Alaska 103
Nimitz Field 429, 448, 450
Nimitz, Chester William 27, 417, 429, 432

Nistelrode, Holland 76
Nobel Peace Prize 288
Nonquitt, Mass. 182
Norbeck, Md. 93
Nord, France 399
Norden bombsight 201, 394
Norfolk Naval Station 408
Norfolk, Va. 176, 369, 408, 409, 413, 425
Normandy American Cemetery and Memorial (Colleville-sur-Mer, France) 142, 171, 322, 331
Normandy, France 171, 193, 292, 322, 339
   landings 142
North African American Cemetery and Memorial (Carthage, Tunisia) 222, 285
North African Theater of Operations 198
North American
   B-25 Mitchell 33, 51, 108, 115, 220
   B-25B Mitchell 60
   BC-1 64
   F-100 Super Sabre 54
   F-86 Sabre 32, 42, 54
   F-86 Sabrejet 102
   FJ Fury 419
   P-51 Mustang 7, 32, 96, 119, 128
North Bend, Ohio 146, 264
North Carolina 453
North Carolina State University 49
North Dakota 453
North Dakota National Guard 29, 243, 265
North Dayton, Ohio 210
North High School (Wichita) 69
North Island Naval Air Station (Calif.) 419
North Korea 200
North Little Rock, Ark. 221, 252
North Pole
   first aviator 29
   first heavier-than-air flight 416
   first to fly over 416
North Sea 71
Northern Formosa 49
Northfield, Mass. 154
Northridge High School (Dayton, Ohio) 210
Northrop
   A-17 28, 68, 104
   YB-49 Flying Wing 28, 36

Northumberland, Pa. 32
Northwest Territory 258
Northwestern University 9
Norton AFB 74, 129, 444, 450
Norton, Leland F. 74–75
Norwich University (Vt.) 240
Norwich, Vt. 157
Notre Dame University 114, 201
Nouméa, New Caledonia (South Pacific) 392
Nürnberg, Germany 307
Nut Cove, Newfoundland 30
Nutley, N.J. 199

O

O'Brien Barracks 312, 447, 456
O'Brien, Thomas F. 312–313
O'Hare Field 430, 448, 457
O'Hare International Airport 431
O'Hare, Edward Henry "Butch" 430–431
Oahu, Hawaii 181, 373
Oak Harbor, Wash. 401
Oak Hill Cemetery
   (Birmingham, Ala.) 179
   (Butler, Mo.) 236
Oakdale, Pa. 262
Oakfield, Maine 23
Oakland Cemetery (Atlanta, Ga.) 158
Oakwood Cemetery
   (Fort Worth, Tex.) 15
   (Huntsville, Tex.) 180
Oceanside, Calif. 382, 392
Ocotal, Nicaragua 395
Octave Chanute Award 418, 419
Odd Fellows Cemetery (Georgetown, Tex.) 36
Office of the Pacific Railroad Surveys 231
Offutt AFB 75, 444, 453
Offutt, Jarvis Jennes 75
Ofstie Field 431, 448, 458
Ofstie, Ralph Andrew 431–432
Ogden, Utah 48
Ohio 453
Ohio & Mississippi Railroad 169
Ohio National Guard 370
Oil City, Pa. 114
Okinawa 150, 365, 366, 367, 369, 372, 374, 377, 379, 381, 383, 384, 458

Okinawa, Ryukyu Islands 367
Oklahoma 166, 454
Oklahoma Aviation and Space Hall of
  Fame 117
Oklahoma City, Okla. 97, 120
Olathe, Kans. 414
Old Gray Cemetery (Knoxville, Tenn.) 71
Old Live Oak Cemetery (Selma, Ala.) 20
Old St. David's Church Cemetery (Radnor,
  Pa.) 233
Oliver Barracks 313, 447, 456
Oliver, Francis M. 313
Olmsted AFB 38, 71, 75, 444, 454
Olmsted, Robert Sanford 75–76
Olney, Ill. 29
Omaha, Neb. 75, 125, 238
Onizuka AS 76, 444, 450
Onizuka, Ellison Shoji 76
Oosterhout, Holland 334
Operation
  Anvil 314
  Bolero 209
  Cobra 172
  Deep Freeze 442
  Dragoon 314
  Flintlock 387
  Husky II 22
  Pegasus 222
  Tidalwave 33
  Torch 142
Oppenheim, Germany 270
Oppenheim, N.Y. 442
Orange, N.J. 169, 199
Orchard Depot Airport. *See,* O'Hare International Airport 431
Ord, Edward Ortho Cresap 175–176
Order of Avis 406
Order of Boyaca of Columbia (Grand Officer) 5
Order of Daedalians 82, 124
Order of DeMolay
  Searcy Chapter 272
Order of Kutuzov (USSR) 16
Order of St. Stanislav 404
Order of the British Empire 108
Order of the Sun of Peru 5
Order of the White Eagle of Serbia 233
Order of Vasco Nunez de Balboa of Panama 5

Oregon 260, 454
Oregon Agricultural College (Corvallis) 261
Oregon's State Police 254
Oregonian (Portland) 260
Orlando Sanford International Airport 433
Orleans, Ind. 69
Orleans, Neb. 80
Orsbon Barracks 313, 447, 456
Orsbon, Herman L. 313
Orwell, Ohio 77
Osage Co., Okla. 97
Osage Nation (Okla.) 97
Oschersleben, Germany 16
Oscoda, Mich. 108
Ostend Manifesto 149
Oswald, Mae B. 170
Oswald, Sarah Susannah 184
Otay Mesa, Calif. 405
Otis AFB 77, 444, 452
Otis, Frank J. 77
Our Lady of the Snows 442
The Outdoorsman—Joe Foss 118
Overbrook Cemetery (Overbrook, Kans.) 35
Overbrook, Kans. 35
Overton, Rush County, Tex. 352
Owen, Frances 151
Owingsville, Ky. 160
Ozark, Ala. 179, 192, 193, 202, 204, 205, 206, 207, 213, 214, 221, 222, 224, 225

P

P.P. & L. Co.
  Hauto Plant 279
Pacific Air Command 98
Pacific Ocean 415
Pacific Theater of Operations 15, 150
Page Field 393, 448, 454
Page, Arthur Hallet, Jr. 393–394
Page, John Upshur Dennis 354–356
Page's School (Va.) 122
Paine AFB 77, 444, 455
Paine, Topliff Olin 77
Paint, Oil & Drug Co. 122
Paju, Gyeonggi-do Province, South Korea 347, 349, 352
Palmer, Susan Bonaparte 257
Palmyra, N.Y. 88

Panama 116, 458
Panama Canal Air Force 5
Panama Canal Department 5
Panama Canal Zone 3, 207
Panama City, Fla. 98
Panama City, Panama 3, 165
Pan-American Conference 238
Pan-American Goodwill Flight 5, 26, 35, 78, 201
Panmunjom, South Korea 345
Paris, France 17, 124
Paris, Tex. 249
Parker, Helen Kansas 57
Parkland, Wash. 168, 203
Parris Island, S.C. 393
Parson 251
Parsons, Kans. 266
Pasadena, Calif. 184, 214, 421
Pascagoula, Miss. 148
Pasco, Wash. 203
Pas-de-Calais, France
    first preoperational "circus" over 89
Paso Robles, Calif. 255
Patch Barracks 314, 447, 456
Patch, Alexander McCarrell, Jr. 314
Patrick AFB 78, 444, 450
Patrick, Mason Matthew 78
Patterson Field 31
Patterson, Frank Stuart 107
Patton Barracks 315, 447, 456
Patton, George Smith, Jr. 255, 293, 315, 351, 359
Patuxent River, Md. 418
Paul W. Litchfield Trophy 26
Paw Paw, Mich. 66
Pawhuska, Okla. 97
Pea Ridge, Ark. 54
Pearl Harbor 106
    first American airmen killed 105
Pearl Harbor, Hawaii 105, 408, 425
Pease AFB 78, 444, 453
Pease, Harl, Jr. 78–79
Peden Barracks 316, 447, 456
Peden, Forrest E. 316
The Pegasus 35
Peking, China 207
Pen Argyl, Pa. 225
Pender, Martha 184

Pendleton Barracks 317, 447, 456
Pendleton, Jack James 317
Pendleton, Joseph Henry 382–383
Pendleton, William Nelson 251
Penn Charter School (Philadelphia) 11
Pennsylvania 232, 257, 284, 331, 428, 454
Pennsylvania Historical Society 174
Pennsylvania National Guard 218
Pennsylvania Railroad 233, 307
Pensacola, Fla. 113, 405, 409, 410, 413, 416, 435
Peoria, Ill. 17, 77
Perrin AFB 54, 80, 444, 454
Perrin Field 197
Perrin, Elmer Daniel 80
Perry, Matthew C. 423
Perry, Oliver Hazard 251
Perry, Sarah 422
Pershing, John J. 37, 47, 55, 78, 88, 105, 155, 158, 161, 162, 198, 232, 253, 260, 289
    punitive expedition 352
Perth Amboy, N.J. 327
Petersburg, Va. 146, 156
Peterson AFB 80, 444, 450
Peterson Kaserne 318, 447, 456
Peterson, Edward Joseph 80–81
Peterson, George 318
Phelps Collins Field 124, 444, 452
Phi Beta Kappa society 75
Phi Gamma Delta fraternity 23
Philadelphia Academy of Natural Sciences 174
Philadelphia, Pa. 22, 169, 173, 174, 186, 198, 246, 305, 365, 428
Philippine and Victory Medals 297
Philippine Campaign Medal 186, 200
Philippine Insurrection 137, 138, 139, 145, 155, 163, 186, 200, 218, 236, 297, 298, 352, 366, 368
Philippine Islands 10, 19, 145, 458
Philippine Liberation Medal 381, 414, 419, 432
Philippines
    Negros Island 72
Phillips AAF 218, 446, 452
Phillips, Anna Tucker 11
Phillips, Wendell Kingsley 218–219

Phoenix, Ariz. 62
Piccolo Field 81, 444, 450
Piccolo, Anthony D. 81
Pickett, George Edward 176–177
Pickett's Charge 177
Pieri, Francis W. 276–277
Pike, Zebulon Montgomery 252–253
Pike's Peak 243
Pikesville, Md. 328
pilot certification
    first 56
Pinder Barracks 319, 447, 456
Pinder, John J., Jr. 319
Pine Camp 155, 226
Pine Mountain, Ga. 177
Pinecastle AAF 69, 70
Pinecastle, Fla. 69, 70
Pineville, Rapides Parish, La. 233
Pioneer Mustang Group 7
Piper
    L-4 Grasshopper 223
    Navaho 331
Pirie Barracks 319, 447, 457
Pirie, James M. 319–320
Pitman Barracks 320, 447, 457
Pitman, James H. 320
Pittsburgh, Pa. 262, 341
Placer College (Auburn, Calif) 27
Plainfield, N.J. 78
Plasterco, Va. 369
Platteville, Wisc. 170
Ploesti, Rumania 120
Pluto 82
Plymouth, N.H. 78
Pohang, Republic of Korea 213
Point Pleasant, Ohio 140
Pointe Coupee, La. 378
Polish Croix des Vaillants 114
Polk Monument 178
Polk, James 149
Polk, Rev. Leonidas 177–178
Polonia Restituta (Poland) 242
Pompey, France 301
Poole, Eleanor 6
Pope AFB 81, 444, 453
Pope, Harley Halbert 81–82
Poplar Cemetery (Poplar, Wisc.) 84
Poplar, Wisc. 84

Poquette, Mae 21
Pork Chop Hill, Sokkagae, South Korea 351
Port Clinton, Ohio 251
Port Huron, Mich. 417
Port of Spain, Trinidad 252
Port Townsend, Wash. 384
Portland, Maine 60, 156
Portland, Ore. 120, 253, 260
Portsmouth, N.H. 78
Portuguese Order of Avis 123
Post, Henry Burnet "Roy" 207
Potowomut, R.I. 244
Prescott, Ark. 392
Presidential Medal of Freedom 128
Presidential Medal of Merit of Nicaragua 5
Presidential Unit Citation 191, 253, 364, 369, 370, 377, 393, 403, 414, 419, 432
Presidio (San Francisco, Calif.) 138
Presque Isle AFB 42
Preston Co., W.Va. 240
Preston County Journal 240
Priest Point, Md. 440
Prince George, Va. 166
Prince, Fred A. 259
Princeton Training School 199
Princeton University 27, 71, 111, 139, 394
Princeton, Ill. 227
private pilot license
    first in St. Louis 122
Progress in Flying Machines (Chanute) 17
Project Delta 272
Prospect Hill Cemetery (Elkhorn, Neb.) 197
Providence, R.I. 409
Prümzurlay, Germany 337
Puerto Cabezas, Nicaragua 365
Puerto Rico 458
Puffendort, Germany 300
Pulitzer Trophy Race 11
Punitive Expedition 88, 172, 198, 232, 257, 352
Punitive War 170
Purdue University 42, 54, 133, 172, 307, 400
Purple Heart 4, 7, 10, 15, 16, 20, 22, 26, 58, 60, 69, 72, 74, 78, 82, 85, 98, 99, 102, 105, 120, 128, 137, 139, 142, 194, 195,

200, 207, 213, 217, 218, 221, 222, 224, 225, 253, 271, 273, 274, 278, 281, 283, 284, 285, 295, 303, 304, 305, 309, 315, 323, 325, 330, 331, 332, 339, 345, 363, 364, 367, 369, 373, 374, 375, 377, 383, 387, 396, 401, 403, 427, 430, 436
Pyoktong, North Korea 295

Q

Quantico, Va. 331, 396
Quebec, Canada 416
Queens Meadow Point Cemetery (Keyser, W.Va.) 296
Queens, N.Y. 437
Queensborough, N.Y. 23
The Quiet Birdmen 45
Quincy, Fla. 410

R

Rabaul, New Britain, New Guinea 78, 102
Racine College (Wisc.) 257
Racine, Wisc. 4
Radcliff, Ky. 164, 202
Radford Field 432, 448, 458
Radford, Arthur William 432–433
radio communication 6
Radnor, Pa. 233
Raids, France 301, 331
railroad bridge 17
railroads 17, 214
Raleigh, N.C. 177
Ramey AFB 82, 444, 458
Ramey Field 433, 448, 450
Ramey, Howard Knox 82–83
Ramey, Robert Winford 433–434
Ramstein Air Base 129
Rancho La Brea 206
Randolph AFB 83, 444, 454
Randolph Field 14, 20, 23, 30, 34, 68, 72, 88, 99, 101, 105, 116, 119, 123, 220
Randolph, William Millican 83
Ransom, Ruth 266
Rantoul, Ill. 17
Rapid City AFB 30
Rapid City, S.D. 30, 103
Ray Barracks 321, 447, 457
Ray S. Miller AAF 219, 446, 452
Ray, Bernard James 321
Reading, Pa. 161

Ready Barracks 322, 447, 457
Ready, John P. 322
"The Rear Guard at Malvern Hill," *Battles and Leaders of the Civil War* (Keyes) 248
Reaume, Mary 156
"Recent Progress in Aviation" (Chanute) 17
Red Cloud, Mitchell, Jr. 356–357
Reese AFB 84, 444, 454
Reese Barracks 322, 447, 457
Reese, Augustus Franklin, Jr. 84
Reese, James William 322–323
Reeves Field 434, 448, 450
Reeves, Joseph Mason "Bull" 434
refrigerated steamer 214
regenerative metallurgical furnace 214
Regensburg, Germany 299
Reilly, Henry Joseph 206–207
Reno, Nev. 96
Republic
    F-84 Thunderjet 85, 102, 421
    F-105 Thunderchief 54
    P-47 Thunderbolt 59, 74
Republic of Korea Order of Military Merit 431
Republic of Texas 181
Republic of Vietnam Campaign Medal 381
Resolution by the Executive Committee of the Fourth Liberty Loan 202
Reynolds Metals 60
Rhode Island 454
Rhode Island College (now Brown Univ.) 258
Rice, Clara 96
Rich Square, Va. 49
Richard Bong AFB 84, 444, 455
Richards, John Francisco 85
Richards-Gebaur AFB 85, 444, 452
Richardson Highway 178
Richardson, Wilds Preston "Dick" 178
Richecourt, France 320
Richmond International Airport (Va.) 112
Richmond, Ind. 395
Richmond, Va. 136, 146, 174, 176, 251, 413
Rickenbacker AFB 86, 444, 453
Rickenbacker/Rickenbacher, Edward "Ed-

die" Vernon 63, 84, 86–87, 114, 118
Ridge Spring, S.C. 391
Ridgewood, N.J. 72
Riege, Lillian 170
Rilea, Thomas E. 253–254
Riley, Bennett C. 179
Riley, Harold W. 52
Rio, Wisc. 260
Ripley, Eleazar Wheelock 254
Rivers Barracks 323, 447, 457
Rivers, Rubin 323–324
Riverside Cemetery (West Milton, Ohio) 210
Riverside Park (New York City) 140
Riverside, Calif. 65, 124
Riverton, Utah 259
Riverview Abby Mausoleum (Portland, Ore.) 253
Riverview Cemetery
    (Portland, Ore.) 260
    (Trenton, N.J.) 169
roadside parks 52
Robert Gray AAF 220, 446, 455
Roberts, Harold W. 255
Roberts, Richard 259
Robins AFB 88, 444, 451
Robins, Augustine Warner 88
Robinson AAF 221, 252, 446, 449
Robinson Barracks 324, 447, 457
Robinson Hall 325
Robinson, James E., Jr. 324–325
Robinson, Joseph Taylor 221
Rocherath, Belgium 298
Rochester, Pa. 382
Rockbridge Co., Va. 180
rocket aircraft
    first research 129
Rockford, Ill. 140
Rockville, Md. 126
Rockwell Field 21, 48, 63, 67, 83, 124, 216
Rockwell International
    Space Shuttles
        STS-51-C Discovery (OV103) 76
        STS-51-L Challenger (OV099) 76
Rockwell, Lewis G. 91
Rocky Mountain Fur Co. 151
Rocky Mountain News 243
Roda, W.Va. 296

Rodd Field 435, 448, 455
Rodd, Herbert Charles 435
Rodes, Robert Emmett 158
Rodgers, John (1773–1838) 422
Rodgers, John (1881-1926) 422–423
Rodgers, Sarah (Perry) 422
Röhrnbach, Germany 277
Roi Island, Kwajalein Atoll, Marshall Islands 387
The Role of Defensive Pursuit (Chennault) 18
Rolla School of Mines (Rolla, Mo.) 105
Romagne, France 13, 62, 255
Rome, Ga. 437
Rome, N.Y. 41
Roosevelt Roads Naval Station (Puerto Rico) 431
Roosevelt, Franklin D. 41, 234, 289
Roosevelt, Theodore 168, 181, 184, 236, 429
Rosamond, Calif. 27
Rose Barracks 325, 447, 457
The Rose Pocket 326
Rose, Maurice 325–326
Rosecrans Field 125, 444, 452
Rosecrans, Guy Wallace 125
Rosedale Cemetery (Orange, N.J.) 199
Roselawn Memorial Park (Little Rock, Ark.) 221
Rosenkrantz, France 336
Roswell AAF 102
Roswell, N.Mex. 102
Rough Rider Award 28
Rough Riders 139, 168, 181
Round-the-rim flight 47
Roxbury, Mass. 57
Royal Air Force Cross 435, 437
Royal Aircraft Factory
    SE-5 55, 75
    S.E.5a 399
Royal Canadian Air Force 74
Royal Flying Corps 199
Royal Society of Northern Antiquaries of Copenhagen, Denmark 148
Rucker, Edmund Winchester 179–180
Rucker, Irene 183
Rufus King High School (Milwaukee, Wisc.) 127

Ruhr Pocket 326
Rules of War Commission of Jurist 223
Rumsford Medal 57
Runkle TS 221, 446, 449
Runkle, Robert Leslie 221–222
runway markers 49
Rushville, Ind. 133
Rüsselsheim, Germany 271
Russian Civil War 404
Russian Revolution 178
Russo-Japanese War 238
Ryder Cemetery (Lebanon, Ky.) 67
Ryujo (Japanese carrier) 97
Ryukyu Islands, Okinawa 383

S

Saarlautern, Germany 311
Sabinal, Tex. 192
Sack, Carl J. 226–227
Sackett's Harbour (Lake Ontario) 252
Sacramento, Calif. 66, 68
Sadowski Barracks 326, 447, 457
Sadowski, Joseph J. 326–327
Sailer Field 394, 448, 457
Sailer, Joseph, Jr. 394–395
Saint Augustine, Fla. 187
Saint Avold, France 274, 278, 281, 284, 309, 311, 320, 323, 329, 335
St. James, France 7
Saint Jean de Monts, France 125
Saint Johns Cemetery (Hatton, N.Dak.) 28
Saint Johns Parish, Ga. 183
St. Louis, Mo. 143
Saint Mary's Cemetery
    (Hamilton, Ohio) 330
    (Medina, N.Y.) 193
Saint Mihiel American Cemetery and Memorial (Thiaucourt, France) 9, 40, 52, 243
Saint Mihiel, France 9
St. Paul, Minn. 243
Saint Paul's Episcopal Church (Tivoli, N.Y.) 141
Saint Peters Cemetery (West New Brighton, N.Y.) 308
St. Petersburg, Fla. 149
Saint Stephens Cemetery (Keasbey, N.J.) 327

Saint-Denis-le-Gast, France 281
Saipan International Airport 422
Saipan, Mariana Islands 422
Salem, Ore. 261
Salina, Kans. 89, 266
Salmson
    2A-2 40, 62
Salt Lake City, Utah 13, 273
Salzburg, Austria 144
Sampson AFB 88, 444, 453
Sampson Medal 378
Sampson State Park 88
Sampson, William Thomas 88–89
San Angelo High School 40
San Angelo, Tex. 40
San Antonio National Cemetery (San Antonio, Tex.) 53, 134, 236
San Antonio, Tex. 12, 53, 54, 57, 83, 84, 90, 112, 123, 134, 138, 180, 185, 191, 195, 198, 220, 235, 236, 256, 324, 391, 403
San Bernardino Valley College 74
San Bernardino, Calif. 74, 75
San Bruno, Calif. 271, 372, 400, 429
San Carlos, Ariz. 197
San Clemente Island, Calif. 417
San Diego Bay, Calif. 20, 207
San Diego, Calif. 29, 124, 144, 215, 293, 368, 373, 375, 376, 382, 392, 393, 402, 406, 418
San Fernando Cathedral (San Antonio, Tex.) 235
San Francisco Bay, Calif. 171
San Francisco National Cemetery 138, 161, 165, 171, 181
San Francisco, Calif. 92, 127, 161, 165, 171, 181, 248, 255
San Gabriel, Calif. 315
San Juan, Puerto Rico 149
San Marcos Airport 38
San Marcos City Cemetery (San Marcos, Tex.) 38
San Marcos, Tex. 38, 222
San Pedro, Calif. 200
San Rafael, Calif. 43
Sanderson, Lucile 95
Sandusky, Ohio 122
Sanford, Fla. 433

Santa Anna, Antonio Lopez de 180, 235
Santa Barbara, Calif. 424
Santa Fe National Cemetery (N.Mex.) 336
Santa Fe, N.Mex. 336
Santa Maria Junior College 206
Santa Maria, Calif. 101, 136, 205
Santa Rita, N.Mex. 74
Sapotilla Ridge, Nicaragua 386, 395
Sarasota, Fla. 385
Sardinia, Italy 84
Saufley Field 435, 448, 450
Saufley, Richard Caswell 435–436
Saugus, Mass. 45
Sault Ste. Marie, Mich. 53, 155
Savannah, Ga. 98, 183, 208, 227
Sawyer, Kenneth Ingalls 51–52
Scabbard and Blade 23
Schelling Award 53
Schenectady, N.Y. 126
Schevenhutte, Germany 305, 321
Schiefbahn, Germany 332
Schilling AFB 89, 444, 451
Schilling, David Carl 89–90
Schlosser, Kathryn Ellen 383
Schofield Barracks 101, 187, 445, 451
Schofield, John McAllister 187–188
School of Application for Cavalry and Infantry 143
School of Military Aeronautics 66
School of the Line 137, 155
Schriever AFB 90, 444, 450
Schriever, Bernard Adolph 90–91
Schwab, Albert Earnest 383–384
Schwabach, Germany 339
Schweinfurt, Germany 300
Schwetzingen, Germany 297, 333
Scientific American Trophy 92
Scituate, Mass. 294
Scott AFB 91, 203, 444, 451
Scott, Frank S. 91
Scott, Winfield 169, 247
Scottsdale, Ariz. 117
Scranton, Pa. 186
Seale, Ala. 373
Searcy, Ark. 271
Sears Hall 357
Sears, Jerome F. 357–358
Seattle, Wash. 103

Seckenheim, Germany 278, 290
Second Bank of the United States 164
Second Nicaraguan Campaign Medal 371, 378, 393
secretary of war
 first 164
Sedalia, Mo. 105
Sedjenane, Tunisia 312
Sehon, Leicester 144
Selected Outstanding Young American 273
Selective Service Act 95
Selfridge AFB 5, 14, 16, 31, 53, 57, 92, 114, 444, 452
Selfridge Field 31
Selfridge, Thomas Etholen 92
Selma, Ala. 20
Seminole Wars 95, 146, 149, 157
 Second 156
Sentinel Butte, N.Dak. 317
Service Medal (Korea) 346
Sewall's Point, Fla. 98
Sewart AFB 444, 454
Sewart, Allan Jackson, Jr. 92–93
Seymour Johnson AFB 93, 129, 444, 453
Seymour, Evelyn 351
Seymour, Ind. 201
Shafter, William Rufus 181–182
Shallowater, Tex. 84
Shaw AFB 93, 114, 444, 454
Shaw, Ervin David 93–94
Shea Field 436, 448, 452
Shea, John Joseph 436
Sheepshead Bay, N.Y.
 airplane race 195
Shelby, Isaac 255–256
Sheldon Village Cemetery (Franklin Co., Vt.) 76
Sheldon, Vt. 76
Shell AH 222, 446, 449
Shell, John R. 222–223
Shemya, Alaska 26
Sheppard AFB 94, 444, 454
Sheppard, Morris 94–95
Sheppard-Towner Act 94
Sheridan Barracks 327, 447, 457
Sheridan, Carl Vernon 327–328
Sheridan, Philip Henry 182–183, 187

Sherman AAF 95, 223, 446, 451
Sherman AFB 95
Sherman Antitrust Act 147
Sherman, Forrest Percival 416–417
Sherman, Frederick Carl "Ted" 417–418
Sherman, Robert 141
Sherman, Tex. 80
Sherman, William Carrington 223–224
Sherman, William Tecumseh 95, 140, 143–144, 173, 176, 188, 217, 241
Sherwood Young Barracks 328, 447, 457
Shields, Marvin Glen 384–385
Shokaku 401
Short Brothers R-38/ZR-2 423
Shreveport, La. 7
Shrines of Colon 36
Siberia 28
Sicily-Rome American Cemetery and Memorial (Nettuno, Italy) 22, 272, 282
Sidamak, Korea 357
Sidney J. Brooks Jr. Memorial Park (San Antonio, Tex.) 12
Siegfried Line (Germany) 340
Sierra Vista, Ariz. 106, 168, 213, 216
Sill, Joshua Woodrow 183
Sille-le-Guillaume, France 313
Silver Life Saving Medal 429
Silver Star 16, 24, 25, 26, 32, 47, 51, 53, 58, 84, 89, 92, 99, 101, 102, 105, 108, 114, 128, 137, 139, 155, 195, 200, 208, 210, 218, 221, 222, 227, 241, 242, 262, 265, 271, 272, 274, 278, 281, 282, 283, 284, 285, 287, 288, 289, 290, 301, 303, 306, 313, 315, 320, 322, 323, 325, 329, 330, 331, 332, 333, 335, 347, 352, 357, 358, 375, 380, 390, 393, 400
Silverbrook Cemetery (Wilmington, Del.) 312
Simmons AAF 224, 446, 453
Simmons, Herbert W., Jr. 224
Sioux Falls, S.Dak. 117
Skelly Stagefield 224, 446, 449
Skelly, Thomas McFarland 224
Sketch of the Resources of the City of New York (Dix) 155
Skyward (Byrd) 113
slavery 149

Slidell, La. 258
Slocum AFB 95, 444, 453
Slocum, Henry Warner 95–96
Smartt Field 436, 448, 452
Smartt, Joseph Gillespie 436–437
Smith Academy 122
Smith Barracks 329, 447, 457
Smith, Harold D. 329
Smith, Holland McTyeire "Howling Mad" 373
Smith, Laura Condit 168
Smith, Tom 94
Smithsonian Institution 58, 59
Smokey Hill AFB 36
Smyrna, Tenn. 92
Sniper Ridge (North Korea) 60
Society of Experimental Test Pilots 54
Sokkagae, South Korea 347, 351
Soldier's Medal 24, 97, 282
Soldiers and Sailors Home (Homelake, Colo.) 244
Soldiers Home National Cemetery 256
Solomon Islands 92, 364, 394, 438
Somme American Cemetery and Memorial (Bony, France) 11
Somme offensive 8
Songnam-dong, S. Korea 348
Sonoma, Calif. 6
Sopwith Camel 43, 52
sound barrier 129
  first man to break the 128
South Carolina 211, 387, 454
South Carolina Air National Guard 70
South Carolina Aviation Association Hall of Fame 70
South Charleston, W.Va. 353
South China Sea 15
South Dakota 200, 454
South Dakota Aviation Hall of Fame 117
South Dakota Sports Hall of Fame 117
South Kingston, R.I. 251
South Pacific 436
South Vietnam 195, 203, 204, 221, 248
South Weymouth, Mass. 436
Southeast Air Corps Training Center 103
Southeastern Oklahoma State University (Durant) 25

Southside Cemetery (Troy, N.C.) 338
Southwest Texas State College 38
Southwestern College 225
SPAD
    VII 125
    XIII 208
Spain 149
Spanish Campaign Medal 200, 378
Spanish-American War 88, 89, 137, 138, 155, 159, 162, 163, 165, 170, 181, 186, 187, 200, 218, 236, 237, 239, 242, 243, 247, 249, 250, 257, 260, 297, 352, 368, 425, 426, 428
Sparks, Nev. 96
Sparta, Wisc. 127, 170, 260, 261
Special Medal of Honor 115
speed of sound 128
Spencer, Ind. 47, 427
Sperry Gyroscope Co. 394
Spinelli Barracks 330, 447, 457
Spinelli, Dominic Vito 330
The Spirit of the Selective Service (Crowder) 239
Spoils System 164
Spokane International Airport 38
Spokane, Wash. 34, 38, 157, 199
Spring Creek, Ky. 235
Spring Grove Cemetery (Cincinnati) 216
Spring Hill, Md. 4
Springdale Cemetery (Peoria, Ill.) 17
Springfield, Mass. 104, 200
St. Albans Naval Hospital (Queens, N.Y.) 437
St. Bernard Parish, La. 233, 258
St. Charles, Mo. 436
St. Johnsbury, Vt. 351
St. Joseph, Mo. 125, 316
St. Louis University 330
St. Louis, Mo. 122, 430
St. Mary's Co., Md. 179
St. Michael's Catholic Church (Portland, Ore.) 120
St. Paul, Minn. 19, 219, 393, 415, 423
Stamford, Conn. 46
Stanford University 90
Stanford, Ky. 390, 435
Stanley, David Sloane 256–257
Starke, Fla. 234

State of Georgia 158
State of Virginia Jeweled Sword presentation 390
Staten Island, N.Y. 307
Stead AFB 96, 444, 453
Stead, Bill 96
Stead, Croston K. 96
Steffes, Eugene Q. 98
Stem Kaserne 330, 447, 457
Stem, David H. 330–331
Stephenville, Newfoundland 46
Stephenville, Tex. 220
Stevens, Mary 141
Stevick, Marajen 25
Stewart Field 126, 444, 453
Stewart International Airport (Newburgh, N.Y.) 126
Stewart, Daniel 183–184
Stewart, Lachlan 126
Stillman College 377
Stillwater, Okla. 112
Stockbridge, Mass. 441
Stockman, R. E. 127
Stockton, Robert 8
Stone's River, Tenn. 183
Stonewall Jackson Memorial Cemetery (Lexington, Va.) 251
Storck Barracks 331, 447, 457
Storck, Louis J. 331–332
"Story of Experiments in Mechanical Flight," *The Annual Aeronautical* (Langley) 58
Story, John Patton 184–185
Stout, Laverne 241
Strategic Air Command 6, 70, 98, 101
Strategic Air Command Bombing Navigation and Reconnaissance Competition 70
Stratford Hall, Westmoreland Co., Va. 166
Stratton Air National Guard Base 126, 444, 453
Stratton, Samuel Studdiford 126–127
Straubing, Germany 303
Strother AAF 225, 446, 451
Strother Field Industrial Park 225
Strother, Donald Root 225
Stuart, J.E.B. 137
Sturgis, S.Dak. 30

Stuttgart, Germany 280, 314, 324, 336, 340
sugar mill
    first steam-powered 235
Sullivan Barracks 332, 447, 457
Sullivan Co., Tenn. 136
Sullivan, George F. 332
Summerall, Charles P. 106
Sumter, S.C. 93
Sunnyvale, Calif. 56, 76, 426
Superior, Wisc. 84
Susquehanna River 71
Sussex Co., Va. 135
Swan, LeRoy Amos 107
Sweden 194
Swift and Co. 125
Swift, Eben 257
Swindell, Edward Lee 28, 36
Symmes, Anna 264
Syracuse University 43, 242
Syracuse, N.Y. 44, 95

T

Tacoma, Wash. 67
Tactical History 224
Taegu, S. Korea. *See also,* (Daegu, S. Korea) 348, 350, 358
Taejon, Korea 213
Taft, William Howard 412
Tahoma Cemetery (Yakima, Wash.) 317
Taiwan 49
Taliaferro, Walter R. 144
Tampa, Fla. 64
Tampico Affair 426
Tampico, Ill. 434
Taos, N.Mex. 151
Tarawa, Gilbert Islands 388, 403, 427
Tarleton College (Stephenville, Tex.) 220
Taukkunen Barracks 332, 447, 457
Taukkunen, Ernest 332–333
Taylor Barracks 333, 447, 457
Taylor, Cecil V. 333
Taylor, Mary Elizabeth 148
Taylor, Zachary 140, 148, 149, 173
Tecumseh, Okla. 323
Teel, Dorothy 133
Tennessee 136, 151, 454
    first congressman from 164
Tennessee Mounted Volunteers 151

Tentative Manual for the Employment of the Air Service, revised as Notes on Recent Operations (Sherman) 224
Tenth Army Cemetery (Okinawa) 150
Teoc Creek, Carroll Co., Miss. 250
Teoc, Miss. 424
Terrapin Creek, Ky. 235
test pilots
    instruction 419
Texarkana, Tex. 94
Texas 181, 182, 211, 249, 454
Texas A&M University 10, 20, 21, 38, 83, 90, 220
Texas Air National Guard Base 421
Texas Cavalry Service Medal 187
Texas Christian University 15
Texas National Guard 187
Texas Volunteer Summer Encampment 249
Thaw, Major 125
Thiaucourt, France 9, 40, 52, 243
"Thinking and Planning for the Future," *The Pegasus* (Fairchild) 35
Thirty Seconds Over Tokyo 60, 220
This Flying Game (Arnold & Eaker) 26
Thomas Field 395, 448, 458
Thomas, Earl Albert 386, 395
Thomaston, Maine 164, 165
Thompson Trophy Race 394
Thompson, Nell 18
Thornbrough AFB 96, 444, 449
Thornbrough, George Wayne 96–97
Three Years of Arctic Service (Greely) 159
Thua Thien-Hue Province, South Vietnam 214
Tibbets, Paul 33
Tinker AFB 97, 444, 454
Tinker, Clarence Leonard 97
Tivoli, N.Y. 141
Tokyo Bay, Japan 51
Toledo, Ohio 324
Tompkins Barracks 333, 447, 457
Tompkins, George S., Jr. 333–334
Tompkinsville, Ky. 249
Tonkin, Lieutenant 19
Topeka, Kans. 35, 266
Torbole, Italy 283
Toronto, Canada 199

Torres Strait, South Pacific 82
Toth Stagefield 225, 446, 449
Toth, Donald Bonney 225
Toul, France 196
Toul-Rosières Air Base (France) 32
Towers Field 437, 448, 450
Towers, John Henry 409, 413, 437–438
Towle Barracks 334, 447, 457
Towle, John Roderick 334–335
transatlantic cable
    first 214
transatlantic flight 402, 406, 435, 437
    first nonstop jet 90
    first USAF jet 90
Transcontinental Air Race 22, 199
Transcontinental Railroad 241
transpacific flight 423
Trapnell, Frederick M. 418–419
Traveller's Rest, Ky. 255
Travis AFB 98, 444, 450
Travis, Robert Falligant 98
Travis, William B. 180
Treasure Island, San Francisco Bay 429
Treaty of Greenville 264
Trebnitz, Germany 306
Tredegar, Wales 259
Trenton, N.J. 72, 169
Trinidad 251
Trinity Cemetery (New York City, N.Y.) 154
Trousdale, William 151
Troy, Kans. 316
Troy, N.C. 338
Troy, N.Y. 43
Truax Field 127, 444, 455
Truax, Thomas Leroy 127
Truman, Harry S. 185
Truscott, Al 144–145
Tucson High School 21
Tucson, Ariz. 21
Tulane University 399
Tullahoma, Tenn. 24
Tulsa High School 383
Tulsa University 383
Tulsa, Okla. 383
Tunisia 286, 293
Turley Barracks 335, 447, 457
Turley, Samuel J. 335

Turner Barracks 335, 447, 457
Turner Field 396, 448, 455
Turner, Charles William 335–336
Turner, Thomas Caldwell 396
Tusi AH 226, 446, 450
Tusi, Ronald L. 226
"Twelve O'clock High" 16
Twelve O'clock High 16
Twin Falls, Idaho 117
Tyndall AFB 98, 444, 450
Tyndall, Frank B. 98–99
Tyson, Charles McGhee 71–72
Tyson, Lawrence Davis 71

U

U.S. Air Force
    founder 6
    missile program
        Atlas 90
        Jupiter 90
        Minuteman 90
        Thor 90
        Titan 90
U.S. Air Force Academy 35
U.S. Air Mail Service 73, 77
U.S. Air Service
    first member to lose his life on a combat mission 124
U.S. Army War College 331
U.S. Constitution 141, 174
U.S. Forest Service 77
U.S. Highway 41
    first highway centerline 52
U.S. Military Aviation Service 11
U.S. Naval Hospital
    (Bethesda, Md.) 414, 422, 432, 434, 441
    (Norfolk, Va.) 409
    (Philadelphia, Pa.) 365
    (San Diego, Calif.) 373
U.S. Naval Postgraduate School 381
U.S. Navy
    catapult 410, 413
    first aircraft carrier 438, 441
    first airplane 408
    first fighter pilot Medal of Honor recipient 430
    first naval aviator 413

U.S. Navy Test Pilot School 419
U.S. Soldiers' and Airmen's Home National Cemetery (Washington, D.C.) 160
U.S. Steel 11
Uckange, France 284
Uelzen, Germany 58
Uijeongbu-si, Gyeonggi-do Province, South Korea 353, 356, 357, 358
Ulm, Germany 287
Umatilla, Fla. 381
unification of the armed services 101
Union Cemetery (Scituate, Mass.) 294
Union Memorial Hospital (Baltimore, Md.) 378
Union Pacific Railroad 240
Union Springs, Ala. 406
Union stockyards 17
Uniontown, Pa. 288
United Air Lines 394
United California Bank 206
United Nations Service Medal 191, 346, 381
United States Army Camel Corps 8
The United States in the Air (Patrick) 78
United States Naval Academy 8, 29, 58, 88, 89, 93, 113, 364, 376, 379, 382, 389, 392, 393, 394, 401, 404, 405, 406, 407, 408, 409, 410, 411, 412, 413, 414, 417, 418, 419, 421, 422, 423, 424, 425, 426, 427, 428, 429, 430, 431, 432, 434, 435, 437, 438, 439, 440, 441
United States Naval Academy Cemetery (Annapolis, Md.) 413, 434
United States Soldiers Home (Washington, D.C.) 250
United States Strategic Institute 26
University Chapel (Lexington, Va.) 166
University of Alabama 113, 373
University of Arizona 21
University of Arkansas 221, 271
University of California at Berkeley 27, 68, 300
University of Cincinnati 330
University of Colorado 76
University of Dayton 330
University of Detroit 108
University of Florida 234
University of Georgia 94, 158, 196

University of Hawaii (Honolulu) 133
University of Idaho 7
University of Illinois 198
    School of Military Aeronautics 55
University of Indiana 64
University of Maine 23, 48
University of Michigan 51, 62
University of Minnesota 103, 217, 367, 415
University of Missouri 238
University of Nebraska 197
University of Nevada 96, 241
University of New Hampshire 41
University of North Carolina 93, 111
University of North Dakota 29
University of Oklahoma 119
University of Omaha 266
University of Pennsylvania 168, 233
University of Pittsburgh 58
University of Rochester 126
University of South Carolina 70
University of South Dakota 117
University of Southern California 206
University of Texas 9, 12, 36, 40, 59, 94
    School of Military Aeronautics 9
University of the State of New York 141
University of Tulsa 383
University of Virginia 221
University of Washington 46, 58, 77
University of Wisconsin 29
    Law School 170
Untergriesheim, Germany 324
Upper Peninsula Road Builders Association 52
Upton City, Ga. 158
Urbach, Germany 206
USNS *General William O. Darby* (T-AP-127) 284
USS *Albany* 407
USS *Albemarle* 427
USS *Alfred A. Cunningham* 386
USS *Arizona* 404
USS *Aroostook* 407, 409, 432
USS *Arthur L. Bristol (DE-281)* 405
USS *Augusta* 429
USS *Ault* 402
USS *Balch* 427
USS *Baltimore* 368

USS *Barry* 417
USS *Belleau Wood* 433
USS *Benham* 419
USS *Biddle* 435
USS *Birmingham* 409
USS *Block Island* 414
USS *Breckinridge* 404
USS *Brooks* 427
USS *California* 29, 407, 425
USS *Charleston* 426
USS *Chattanooga* 431
USS *Chauncey* 419
USS *Chesapeake* 376
USS *Chester* 426
USS *Chicago* 429
USS *Cincinnati* 378, 379, 401
USS *Clarence King Bronson* 405
USS *Colorado* 89, 413, 432
USS *Congress* 8, 89
USS *Connecticut* 366, 412
USS *Constitution* 390
USS *Coral Sea* 419
USS *Cummings* 404
USS *Dale* 419
USS *Delaware* 371
USS *Detroit* 431
USS *Dolphin* 412
USS *DuPont* 419
USS *Dyess* 387
USS *Earle* 412
USS *Enterprise* 418, 420, 430, 431, 433, 438
USS *Essex* 412, 418, 431
USS *Flusser* 419
USS *Forrest Sherman* 417
USS *Frolic* 368
USS *General C. G. Morton* 370
USS *George F. Elliott* 368
USS *Georgia* 408
USS *Gridley* 427
USS *Harding* 407
USS *Henderson* 389, 390
USS *Honolulu* 438
USS *Hornet* 60, 412, 420, 425, 439
USS *Hunter Liggett* 162
USS *Huntington* 425
USS *Idaho* 407
USS *Iowa* 89

USS *Jarvis* 404, 419
USS *Jason* 404
USS *Java* 252
USS *John Adams* 252
USS *John Francis Burnes* 419
USS *Jupiter* 441
USS *Kansas* 410, 419, 434, 435
USS *Kenneth Whiting* 441
USS *Lake Champlain* 414
USS *Lamson* 419
USS *Lancaster* 385
USS *Langley* 389, 393, 434, 438, 441
USS *Lawrence* 252
USS *Lester* 380
USS *Lexington* 26, 393, 401, 402, 406, 414, 417, 418, 422, 430
USS *Liscombe Bay* 427, 428
USS *Lunga Point* 434
USS *MacDonough* 406
USS *Maine* 88, 434
USS *Marblehead* 425
USS *Maryland* 424, 438
USS *Massachusetts* 412
USS *McCalla* 425
USS *McFarland* 365
USS *Mississippi* 411, 426, 429, 436, 438
USS *Missouri* 412, 413, 417, 420, 424, 429
USS *Monadnock* 407
USS *Monongahela* 368
USS *Montana* 407
USS *Monterey* 407, 433
USS *Mullinnix* 428
USS *Murray* 417
USS *Mustin* 429
USS *Nashville* 417
USS *Nebraska* 406
USS *Nevada* 376
USS *New Hampshire* 409
USS *New Jersey* 385
USS *New Mexico* 391, 424
USS *Newark* 425
USS *Niagara* 252
USS *Nitro* 424
USS *Nonsuch* 252
USS *North Carolina* 409, 410, 429, 436
USS *North Dakota* 385, 434
USS *O'Bannon* 431
USS *O'Brien* 419, 420

USS *Ohio* 376
USS *Olympia* 376
USS *Oregon* 434
USS *Osborne* 419
USS *Overton* 404
USS *Palos* 407
USS *Patapsco* 88
USS *Pennsylvania* 410, 413, 432
USS *Pensacola* 383
USS *Philip H. Sheridan* 183
USS *Pittsburgh* 434
USS *Porpoise* 441
USS *Potomac* 88
USS *Rainbow* 413
USS *Ranger* 223, 381, 389, 404, 417, 424, 438
USS *Reid* 417
USS *Relief* 381
USS *Revenge* 252
USS *Richmond* 416
USS *Samar* 428
USS *San Francisco* 364
USS *Saratoga* 389, 393, 406, 407, 417, 418, 420, 427, 430, 431, 432, 438
USS *Saufley* 436
USS *Seal* 413, 441
USS *Seattle* 410, 439
USS *Shark* 413, 441
USS *Shaw* 419, 420
USS *Shawmut* 407
USS *South Carolina* 429, 432
USS *South Dakota* 383
USS *Swatara* 89
USS *Tarantula* 413
USS *Tarpon* 441
USS *Tennessee* 376
USS *Terry* 404, 435
USS *Texas* 413
USS *Utah* 417
USS *Vermont* 368
USS *Waldron* 439
USS *Wasp* 381, 417, 436
USS *West Virginia* 407, 413
USS *Whipple* 431
USS *Wickes* 419
USS *Wisconsin* 371
USS *Wright* 407, 413, 427, 432
USS *Wyoming* 377, 420

USS *Yankee* 383
USS *Yorktown* 381, 401, 420, 431, 432, 438
Utah 41, 77, 259, 455
Utah Agricultural College 14
Utah National Guard 260

V

VA Medical Center 143
Vagney, France 291
Valdez Barracks 336, 447, 457
Valdez, Jose F. 336–337
Valdez-Fairbanks Trail 178
Valdosta, Ga. 73
Valenciennes Cemetery (St. Roch) Communal (Nord, France) 399
Valheureux, France 75
Valhey, France 327
Valley, Neb. 196
Valmontone, Italy 294
Valparaiso, Fla. 24, 28, 34, 50, 81
Van Buren, Martin 264
Van Nuys, Calif. 84
Van Voorhis Field 438, 448, 453
Van Voorhis, Bruce Avery 438–439
Van Wert, Ohio 219
Vance AFB 99, 118, 444, 454
Vance, Leon Robert, Jr. 99–100
Vandenberg AFB 20, 101, 136, 444, 450
Vandenberg, Hoyt Sanford 101–102
Varnum, James Mitchell 257–258
Vaulx, Katherine 424
Velero III 206
Velletri, Italy 272
Veracruz Expedition 172, 358
Veramendi, Ursula de 235
Verdun, France 52
Vermont 455
Vermont National Guard Association 247
Verndale, Minn. 171
Veterans of Foreign Wars 127
Vian, Okla. 350
Victoria, Tex. 36
Victorville, Calif. 39
Victory Medal 370
Vienna, Austria 133
Vietnam 214, 272, 273
Vietnam Cross of Gallantry 217, 226, 381

Vietnam Memorial Wall 204
Vietnam Military Merit Medal 217
Vietnam Service Medal 345, 380
Vietnam War 135, 195, 217, 222, 226, 248, 271, 384
Vietnamese Medal of Honor 381
Vila, New Hebrides Island 364
Villa, Pancho 47, 88, 138, 232
Villere, Jacques Philippe Roi de 258–259
Virgil 163
Virginia 174, 251, 256, 455
Virginia Beach, Va. 184, 251
Virginia Military Institute 103, 249, 289, 297, 379
Virtuti Militari Silver Cross Class V (Poland) 16
Viviers, France 273
Vockrath, Germany 270
Volk Field 260, 444, 455
Volk Field Air National Guard Base 127
Volk, Jerome A. 127–128
Vought
    02U-1 Corsair 394
Voyage of Discovery (Lewis) 169

W

Wachenheim, Germany 304
Waco, Tex. 20
Waegwan, Korea 346
Wahiawa, Oahu, Hawaii 105
Wah-Sha-She News 97
Waimanalo, Hawaii 9
Wainwright, Jonathan Mayhew 185–186
Wakefield, Mass. 239
Walden, Catherine 175
Waldron Field 439, 448, 455
Waldron, John Charles 439
Walker AFB 102, 444, 453
Walker, Kenneth Newton 102
Walker, Walton Harris 358–359
Wall, Pa. 310
Walla Walla, Wash. 185
Wallace Barracks 337, 447, 457
Wallace, George W. 145
Wallace, Herman C. 337–338
Wallrich, Ruth 81
Walnut Hill Cemetery (Council Bluffs, Iowa) 240

Walseth AFB 444, 449
Walseth, Marvin E. 103
Walter Reed Army Medical Center 3, 31, 57, 78, 101, 103, 178, 288, 297
Wana-Dakeshi Ridge, Okinawa 374
War in an Open Cockpit: The Wartime Letters of Captain Alvin Andrew Callender, RAF 399
War of 1812 154, 164, 166, 179, 180, 184, 252, 254, 264, 390
Ward, Artemas 164
Warm Springs, Ga. 195
Warner Barracks 338, 447, 457
Warner Kaserne 338
Warner, Henry F. 338–339
Warren, Francis E., AFB 37
Warren, Francis Emory 37
Warrensburg, N.Y. 416
Warrenton, N.C. 148
Warrenton, Ore. 253
Washburn Law School 266
Washington 293, 455
Washington National Guard 35
Washington State National Guard 65
Washington University 257
Washington, D.C. 3, 8, 10, 11, 37, 44, 78, 88, 90, 94, 159, 160, 171, 214, 221, 238, 250, 256, 257, 368, 376, 383, 390, 408, 422, 455
Washington, George 88, 164, 166
Watertown, N.Y. 155, 226
Watkins, Eleanor 434
Waukesha, Wisc. 184
Waxhaw, S.C. 163
Way of a Fighter: The Memoirs of Claire Lee Chennault (Chennault) 18
Wayne, Anthony 264
Waynesboro, Miss. 82
Waynesville, Mo. 167, 200
Weaver AFB 30, 103, 444, 454
Weaver, Walter Reed 103–104
Weaverville, Calif. 271
Webster Field 440, 448, 452
Webster, Walter Wynne 440
Weiden, Germany 313, 320
Weilburg, Germany 326
Weir, Tex. 36
Weisweiler, Germany 328

Wellsville, Ohio 142
Wendover Field 99
Wentworth Military Academy (Lexington, Mo.) 97, 197, 237
Wertheim, Germany 316
Wesleyan University 44
West Chester, Pa. 365, 366
West Feliciana, La. 254
West Hazleton, Pa. 278
West Milton, Ohio 210
West New Brighton, N.Y. 308
West Point 4, 5, 6, 16, 27, 30, 33, 34, 38, 41, 46, 47, 67, 73, 78, 88, 92, 95, 98, 99, 101, 103, 104, 105, 106, 116, 123, 124, 136, 140, 143, 146, 148, 149, 150, 152, 157, 160, 161, 163, 166, 169, 171, 172, 173, 175, 176, 177, 178, 182, 183, 184, 185, 187, 194, 197, 200, 201, 208, 214, 215, 216, 218, 223, 231, 232, 233, 238, 242, 245, 247, 249, 250, 251, 256, 257, 263, 277, 280, 283, 302, 313, 315, 320, 331, 345, 352, 358
  first flight training class 4
West Point Cemetery (N.Y.) 73, 163, 178, 214, 215, 247, 263, 302, 314, 352
West Virginia University 128
West, George 243
Western Mountaineer 243
Western University of Pennsylvania 58
Westhampton Beach, N.Y. 113
Westminister Cemetery (Carlisle, Pa.) 310
Westmoreland Co., Va. 166, 174
Westover AFB 104, 444, 452
Westover Memorial Park Cemetery (Augusta, Ga.) 387
Westover, Oscar M. 104
Westville Cemetery (Atlanta, Ga.) 22
Wetzlar, Germany 301
Whalen, Dennis D. 277
Wharton Barracks 339, 447, 457
Wharton, James E. 339
Wheatland, Pa. 149
Wheatville, Tex. 94
Wheeler AFB 105, 106, 226, 444, 451
Wheeler Field 31, 105
Wheeler, Curtis 226–227
Wheeler, Sheldon Harley 105
Wheeler-Sack AAF 226, 446, 453

Wheeling, W.Va. 363
Whidbey Island Naval Air Station (Oak Harbor, Wash.) 401
White City, Ore. 260
White Sands, N.M. 196
White, Ared. *See,* White, George Ared
White, Edward 43
White, George Ared 260
Whitehall, N.Y. 148
Whitely, John 5
Whiteman AFB 105, 444, 452
Whiteman, George Allison 105–106
Whiting Field 441, 448, 450
Whiting, Kenneth 441
Whiting, William Henry 161
Whitson Kaserne 339, 447, 457
Whitson, William H. "Red" 339–340
Whitton, Jeanette 427
WIBW radio (Topeka) 266
Wichita Fall, Tex. 94
Wichita University 36
Wichita, Kans. 69, 73, 295
Wickliffe, Ky. 290
Wiesbaden, Germany 275
Wiesbaden-Dotzheim, Germany 276
Wilder, Vt. 247
Wildwood Cemetery (Wilmington, Mass.) 45
Wilkin Barracks 340, 447, 457
Wilkin, Edward G. 340–341
Wilkins, Sir Hubert 29
Wilkinson, Ada 373
Will Kaserne 341, 447, 457
Will Rogers Field 120
Will, Walter J. 341–342
William Henry Harrison Memorial State Park (North Bend, Ohio) 264
Williams AFB 106, 444, 449
Williams Field 442, 448, 456
Williams, Charles Linton 106
Williams, Charles R. 260–261
Williams, Richard Thomas 442
Williams, William Gray 259
Willsbach, Germany 330
Wilmington International Airport (N.C.) 111
Wilmington, Del. 312
Wilmington, Mass. 45

Wilmington, N.C. 111
Wilson Barracks 342, 447, 457
Wilson, Alfred Leonard 342
Wilson, Betty 117
Wilson, Woodrow 234, 239
Wiltwyck Cemetery (Kingston, N.Y.) 320
Winamac High School (Ind.) 201
Winamac, Ind. 201
Winchester, N.H. 167
Winchester, Va. 112, 151
Windsor Locks, Conn. 112, 245
Winfield High School (Kans.) 225
Winfield, Kans. 225
Winged Warfare (Arnold & Eaker) 26
Wint, Theodore Jonathan 186
Winterville, Ga. 199
Wisconsin 257, 455
Wisconsin Air National Guard 127, 128
Wisconsin Aviation Hall of Fame 84
Wisconsin National Guard 170, 261
Wisconsin-Madison High School 127
Wisner Cemetery (Wisner, Neb.) 374
Wisner, Neb. 374
Withers, Josephine 236
Withycombe, James 261
Wolters AFB 107, 186
Wolters, Jacob Franklin 186–187
Wonju, Gangwon (Kangwon) Province, South Korea 354
Wood, Leonard 167–168
Woodfin, Mary A. 180
Woodland Cemetery (Dayton, Ohio) 107
Woodlawn Cemetery
 (Sparta, Wisc.) 170
 (Syracuse, N.Y.) 44
Woodruff, Kans. 364
Woods Cross, Utah 206
Wool Market Review 239
Worcester Polytechnic Institute 412
Worcester Telegram-Gazette 45
Worcester, Mass. 154, 412
World War I 9, 11, 18, 21, 22, 25, 31, 32, 39, 40, 44, 52, 55, 63, 65, 66, 77, 81, 85, 87, 94, 97, 105, 114, 118, 124, 134, 137, 139, 155, 163, 170, 172, 187, 195, 198, 208, 211, 218, 225, 233, 234, 238, 239, 243, 245, 253, 255, 257, 259, 261, 265, 266, 297, 315, 326, 352, 358, 366, 371, 399, 407, 411, 412, 418, 420, 423, 438, 441
 first air casualty 75
 first high-ranking American officer killed 11
 first Longmont, Colo. native killed in 13
 first San Antonian to lose his life in 12
World War I Campaign Medal 219
World War I Victory Medal 25, 57, 104, 212, 253, 315, 358, 373, 375, 378, 401, 406, 407, 408, 409, 411, 413, 419, 427, 429, 432, 440
World War II 4, 6, 10, 14, 15, 16, 18, 20, 22, 35, 46, 58, 70, 72, 74, 79, 84, 89, 90, 96, 98, 100, 101, 102, 108, 117, 118, 120, 121, 133, 142, 150, 155, 157, 185, 191, 193, 195, 197, 205, 206, 208, 224, 227, 254, 262, 265, 266, 274, 276, 278, 279, 280, 283, 288, 291, 293, 294, 296, 298, 300, 301, 303, 304, 305, 308, 309, 310, 311, 312, 313, 314, 315, 316, 317, 318, 319, 320, 321, 322, 323, 324, 325, 326, 327, 328, 329, 331, 332, 333, 334, 335, 336, 337, 338, 340, 341, 342, 347, 351, 356, 358, 364, 367, 370, 371, 372, 373, 374, 377, 378, 379, 381, 383, 387, 388, 389, 391, 394, 401, 403, 404, 414, 415, 417, 418, 422, 424, 427, 429, 430, 432, 437, 438, 439
 first American airman to die in Europe 41
 first American general to die 97
 first combat casualty 59
 first San Marcos resident killed in 38
World War II Campaign Medal 219
World War II Victory Medal 25, 50, 58, 101, 105, 191, 200, 222, 241, 253, 285, 295, 302, 315, 330, 358, 364, 369, 371, 373, 375, 377, 380, 393, 401, 403, 414, 419, 427, 429, 432, 440
Worms, Germany 332
Wright
 C Flyer 30
 Flyer 92
 Military Flyer 91
Wright AAF 227, 446, 451
Wright brothers 6, 17, 423

first students 56
Wright engines
  Cyclone 5
Wright Field 27, 31, 36, 48, 49, 68, 85, 90, 103, 107, 201, 216, 219
Wright, George 157
Wright, Lyle Henry 227
Wright, Orville 92, 107, 122, 123, 441
Wright, Wilbur 107
Wright-Patterson AFB 42, 107, 216, 444, 453
Wurtsmith AFB 108, 444, 452
Wurtsmith, Paul Bernard 108
Würzburg, Germany 285, 301
Wyoming 456
  first Statehood governor 37
  first U.S. senator from 37
  last Territorial governor 37

Y

Yakima Indian War 157
Yakima Morning Herald 58
Yakima, Wash. 58, 317
Yale University 75, 94, 107, 197, 233
Yamamoto, Isoruku 425
Yamashita, Tomoyuki 126
Yeager Field 128, 444, 455
Yeager, Charles Elwood "Chuck" 128–129
Yellow Hill Cemetery (Cherokee, N.C.) 348
Yellowstone National Park 183
Yigo, Guam 4
Yokohama, Japan 20
Yongsan, South Korea 335
Yongsan-gu, Seoul, South Korea 347
Yonkers, Westchester Co. N.Y. 126
York, Ontario, Canada 252
Yoshida, Lorna Leido 76
Young, Ruth 36
Young, Sherwood M., Jr. 328–329
Youngstown College (Ohio) 81
Yugoslavia 6

Z

Zamboanga, Philippine Islands 392, 400
Ziegenberg, Germany 273
Zirndorf, Germany 269, 319
Zurich, Switzerland 86

About the Author

LINDA D. SWINK was a member of the United States Air Force for fifteeen years and an army wife for ten. Her father was a U.S. Marine and served during World War II in the Battle of Peleliu, giving her a deep understanding and respect for military veterans of past wars and the men and women serving our country today.

Ms. Swink holds a degree in journalism from the University of Texas at El Paso and has written for a wide variety of consumer and trade magazines.

She is a professional speaker and her previous publication, *Speak With Power and Grace: A Woman's Guide to Public Speaking* (Citadel Press, 1997), has helped thousands of women overcome their fear of public speaking and become more confident at the lectern.

She lives in Hamilton, Ohio.